On
KNOWING
and the
KNOWN

On
KNOWING
and the
KNOWN

Introductory Readings in Epistemology

Edited by
KENNETH G. LUCEY
State University of New York College at Fredonia

Prometheus Books

59 John Glenn Drive
Amherst, New York 14228-2197

For

Carol Ann

Published 1996 by Prometheus Books

On Knowing and the Known: Introductory Readings in Epistemology. Copyright © 1996 by Kenneth G. Lucey. All rights reserved. No part of this publication may be reproduced, stored in a retrieval system, or transmitted in any form or by any means, electronic, mechanical, photocopying, recording, or otherwise, without prior written permission of the publisher, except in the case of brief quotations embodied in critical articles and reviews. Inquiries should be addressed to Prometheus Books, 59 John Glenn Drive, Amherst, New York 14228–2197, 716–691– 0133. FAX: 716–691–0137.

00 99 98 97 96   5 4 3 2 1

Library of Congress Cataloging-in-Publication Data

On knowing and the known : introductory readings in epistemology / edited by Kenneth G. Lucey.
    p.   cm.
Includes bibliographical references.
ISBN 1–57392–050–9 (pbk.)
    1. Knowledge, Theory of. I. Lucey, Kenneth G., 1942–.
BD143.06   1996
121—dc20   96–12549
                                                  CIP

Printed in the United States of America on acid-free paper

Contents

Introduction   9

PART I. THE PROBLEM OF ANALYZING KNOWLEDGE

1. Knowledge and True Opinion   31
    Roderick M. Chisholm

2. Is Justified True Belief Knowledge?   49
    Edmund L. Gettier

3. Knowledge and Grounds: A Comment on Mr. Gettier's Paper   52
    Michael Clark

4. Mr. Clark's Definition of 'Knowledge'   55
    John Turk Saunders and *Narayan Champawat*

5. Truth and Evidence   57
    Robert Almeder

6. Almeder on Truth and Evidence   62
    William E. Hoffmann

5

6   Contents

7. An Alleged Defect in Gettier Counterexamples   65
   Richard Feldman

8. Knowledge as Justified True Belief   68
   Roderick M. Chisholm

9. The Gettier Problem and the Analysis of Knowledge   75
   Keith Lehrer

10. The Gettier Problem   89
   John L. Pollock

PART II. THE PROBLEM OF THE CRITERION

11. The Problem of the Criterion   105
   Roderick M. Chisholm

12. Roderick Chisholm and the Problem of the Criterion   119
   Robert P. Amico

13. Reply to Amico on the Problem of the Criterion   129
   Roderick M. Chisholm

14. Skepticism and the Problem of the Criterion   132
   Robert P. Amico

15. Reply to Amico on Skepticism and the Problem of the Criterion   142
   Sharon Ryan

PART III. THE FOURTH CONDITION OF KNOWLEDGE

16. Knowledge: Undefeated Justified True Belief   151
   Keith Lehrer and *Thomas Paxson, Jr.*

17. A Proposed Definition of Propositional Knowledge   163
   Peter D. Klein

18. Misleading Defeaters   174
   Steven R. Levy

19. Misleading "Misleading Defeaters"   178
    Peter D. Klein

PART IV. RELIABILITY AND JUSTIFICATION

20. What Is Justified Belief?   185
    Alvin I. Goldman

21. *Contra* Reliabilism   206
    Carl Ginet

22. What's Wrong with Reliabilism?   218
    Richard Foley

PART V. CERTAINTY AND KNOWING THAT ONE KNOWS

23. Philosophical Certainty   233
    Harry G. Frankfurt

24. On Analyzing Knowledge   252
    John Tienson

25. Fallibilism and Knowing that One Knows   257
    Richard Feldman

26. Chisholm on Certainty   271
    Keith Lehrer and *Keith Quillen*

27. Reply to Keith Lehrer and Keith Quillen   281
    Roderick M. Chisholm

PART VI. HOW DOES EPISTEMIC APPRAISAL
YIELD JUSTIFICATION?

28. The Principles of Epistemic Appraisal   287
    Roderick M. Chisholm

29. Scales of Epistemic Appraisal   301
       Kenneth G. Lucey

30. Concepts of Epistemic Justification   310
       William P. Alston

31. Evidentialism   340
       Richard Feldman and *Earl Conee*

32. The Evidence of the Senses   357
       Roderick M. Chisholm

PART VII. KNOWING ONESELF AND OTHERS

33. Knowledge by Acquaintance and Knowledge by Description   377
       Bertrand Russell

34. On the Nature of the Psychological   391
       Roderick M. Chisholm

35. On the Logic of Self-Knowledge   400
       Hector-Neri Castañeda

Bibliography   413

Introduction

What is *knowing*? What kinds of beings have *knowledge*? What sorts of things are *known*? These are some of the questions considered in this collection of readings. For two thousand years philosophers have asked and attempted to answer these questions. This ongoing discussion constitutes the subject matter of the philosophical area called the *theory of knowledge*, or *Epistemology*. By way of introduction, let's observe a fictional incident and treat it as a sort of case study concerning knowledge. Thomas Perry's second novel begins with a scene that is saturated with a variety of kinds of knowledge:

> Chinese Gordon was fully awake. He'd heard the clinking noise again, and now there was no question the cat was listening, too. The cat, Doctor Henry Metzger, had assumed the loaf-of-bread position on Gordon's blanket, his ears straight up like a pair of spoons to catch the sound and lock onto it. Doctor Henry Metzger sat up and licked his paw, then froze as he detected some variation in the sound that Chinese Gordon's ears couldn't hear.
>
> "What is it?" whispered Chinese Gordon. "Somebody trying to break in, isn't it?"
>
> Doctor Henry Metzger turned from the sound, walked up Chinese Gordon's chest, and stepped on his forehead on the way to the spare pillow. He'd identified it as a human sound, which placed it outside Doctor Henry Metzger's sphere of interest.
>
> Damn, thought Chinese Gordon. Burglars. He slipped out of bed, moved quietly to the doorway, and listened. He could hear from downstairs the faint squeaking of the garage door to the shop moving on its rollers. His eyes strained, but he could see nothing below except the familiar dim shapes of the shop machines. Then, as the garage door opened farther, he saw a man silhouetted for a moment. The man entered, followed by another, and another.

Chinese Gordon stayed low, watching from the upper landing without moving. There were three of them. The gun was locked in the bottom of the tool chest in the back room downstairs, which meant it was worse than nothing because if he gave them enough time they'd find it.

He could tell they were just inside the garage door now, probably standing there waiting for their eyes to adjust to the darkness before trying to move into the shop. It was a lousy situation, thought Chinese Gordon. They might be just kids or winos or junkies trying to score a lot of expensive tools and machinery, but that didn't mean they wouldn't kill him if he switched on the light or made a noise.

Beside him he felt Doctor Henry Metzger rubbing against him, purring. When Doctor Henry Metzger stopped purring and stared down into the shop, Chinese Gordon knew the men had begun to move. He watched the cat's face, the intent unblinking eyes focused on the darkness below. Then Doctor Henry Metzger crouched low and peered over the edge of the landing, his ears back so his head would have no silhouette. One of them must be directly below, looking up at the power tools hanging on the pegboard on the wall. Chinese Gordon listened, and he could feel the shape of the man below him, leaning forward over the bench, his face staring up at the tools to assess their value, weight, and bulk. Now he would be reaching up for the electric drill.

Chinese Gordon felt a twinge of guilt about what had to be done. He knew it wasn't fair, and there would be resentment, there might even be consequences he couldn't imagine. He gently placed his hand on Doctor Henry Metzger, feeling the thick, soft fur. Then, without warning, he scooped the cat up and dropped him. Doctor Henry Metzger screamed as he fell, the terror, surprise, and anger howled into the darkness in a high pitched screech.

Chinese Gordon could tell immediately that he'd judged the trajectory correctly. Doctor Henry Metzger could only have dropped five or six feet before the tone of the howling changed and the human scream joined it. The cat had definitely landed on the man's head, scrambling desperately with claws out for a foothold, from the sound of it tearing great gashes, because the man's shouts weren't just terror, they were pain.

There were other sounds now, too. The shouts of both of the man's companions competed with the howling and screaming. "What?" one yelled. "What? What?" Then he ran into the lathe, which rocked slightly although it was bolted to the pavement, and must have injured himself somehow, because then his voice came from the floor in a breathless, inarticulate moan. The other screamed, "Hold still! Freeze, you bastard!" as though he were either contemplating shooting someone or merely advocating keeping calm.

On the landing Chinese Gordon lay flat on his belly and listened. The man on the ground said, "We've got to get out of here."

"What the hell happened?" said the one with the commanding voice. "It sounded like a baby."

"God, I'm bleeding!" said the other.

> Chinese Gordon heard them move away, then peered over the edge to watch them, one by one, escape under the partially opened garage door. A few seconds later he heard car doors slam and an engine start."[1]

Let us consider this incident from the point of view of the many sorts of knowledge involved. Gordon is awake wondering what he has just heard. The behavior of his cat clearly indicates that it has heard something also, and then its further behavior is taken to show that the cat is hearing sounds that Gordon himself cannot perceive. Gordon formulates the hypothesis that someone is attempting to force an entry into his home. This clearly isn't knowledge yet, but when the cat loses interest, Gordon thereby acquires evidence sufficient for him to conclude that it is human agency involved, and he now knows that someone is breaking into his house.

Moments later Gordon has visual evidence that at least three persons have entered the machine shop over which he lives. At the same time, Gordon *knows* where his pistol is located and is further *aware that* (yet another kind of knowledge) the location of the firearm poses a future danger to himself. The first of these is an instance of a kind of knowledge which pervades this vignette, namely, *knowledge where*. Gordon knows where his gun is located and at various times knows where his intruders have positioned themselves. He furthermore knows where the various contents of his shop are located in relation to one another.

Gordon also has formulated a hypothesis about the motive of his intruders and believes that if he reveals his presence to them by sound or action he could easily end up dead. So here we have *knowledge* of possible motives and further *knowledge* of possible consequences of his own actions. Gordon is also able to interpret the behavioral states of his cat so as to *know when* one of the burglars is directly below them.

Gordon has *moral knowledge* as well. Perry tells us "He knew it wasn't fair" the way he was about to use his pet as a tool for getting out of his own difficult position. Gordon knows by touch the location of his cat and how to utilize the feline as a weapon. So we have knowledge how, knowledge that, knowledge who, knowledge why, knowledge whether, knowledge where, knowledge when, plus moral knowledge and practical knowledge about various "what ifs?" Perry has woven for us a rich tapestry that serves as a sampler of the multitude of sorts of knowledge we will be exploring in this volume.

WHY BOTHER?

Any student opening the present book at random and attempting to jump into the middle of the ongoing discussions might find the whole business a little technical, somewhat confusing, fairly unmotivated, and might therefore ask "So What?" or "Why bother?" The philosophical investigation of knowledge has been a central issue of liberal education in general and of philosophy in particular for the last two thousand years and has enjoyed the near unanimous endorsement of traditional philosophers and academics. So a blatant appeal to authority might be one kind of justifying answer. A much better answer to the "So What?" question can be given, and it has three major parts.

In the first place it is a mistake to simply jump into the middle of the discussions offered here. The selections constitute an ongoing discussion that exhibit an organic growth. By understanding the complexities of the discussion as it has historically developed, many of the difficulties become much easier to master. Part One, "The Problem of Analyzing Knowledge," in particular, consists of a series of short selections that develop an ongoing dialogue. For this reason they readily suggest the continuing, ongoing nature of the discussion to which readers from a variety of disciplines and interests could conceivably contribute as a positive result of understanding the dialectic as it has developed.

The second major reason for bothering with these issues is that there is no better area in which to learn the methodology of analyzing concepts. Theory of knowledge (or Epistemology) is a prime example of an arena in which there exists a whole array of concepts exhibiting complex, subtle, and sophisticated interconnections and interrelationships. Most students arriving at their first course in theories of knowledge have had no previous opportunity to work with concepts as entities in themselves whose interconnections are fixed, necessary, and objectively true or false. So, this is where many philosophy students first encounter theoretical definitions, which can be treated as hypotheses, and shown to be mistaken by means of counterexamples, where a counterexample is a logically possible case that establishes the falsity of a proposed definition. Generally, a counterexample shows a definition to be either (1) too broad, (2) too narrow, or (3) simultaneously both too broad and too narrow.

In the same vein many students have only the most tenuous grasp of the interrelationships among the following concepts: definitions, biconditional statements, conditional statements, necessary conditions and sufficient conditions; or of how the notion of a counterexample connects up with all of the foregoing. In a word, the study of the classic articles in Epistemology is where these relationships are most easily mastered.

Finally, the third answer to the question "Why bother?" is that the mastery of the subtle distinctions among these concepts is intrinsically valuable. Students who have mastered the distinctions among the certain, the known, the believed, the justified, the true, etc., thereby acquire a richly textured multidimensional conceptual scheme that could permanently alter their view of the world and their modes of grasping its various truths, both necessary and contingent.

PRACTICAL APPLICATIONS

What students may not realize is that, properly understood, Epistemology is vitally relevant to the broad sweep of views and opinions that are constantly impinging upon their lives. The modern media constantly espouse views about ESP, ghosts, poltergeists, UFOs, Bigfoot, the Bermuda Triangle, channeling, crystal power, and New Age whatever. What should you believe and how should you decide to what you should give your assent? While not the subject matter of this present volume, the relevance of Epistemology to such issues has been documented in great detail in the book *How We Know What Isn't So* by Thomas Gilovich, who makes the point that "people do not willy-nilly believe what they want to believe. Instead, people's preferences generally have their influence through the way they guide their evaluation of the pertinent evidence."[2] In a word, the key to getting a handle on the issue of what we ought to believe lies in our raising our intellect and consciousness about the concepts of evidence and justification. In a very real sense the whole topic of the Theory of Knowledge might more accurately be called the Theory of Justification. And *that* is our subject matter here.

By acquiring sophistication about the nature of evidence in general and of concepts of degrees of justification in particular, students will acquire skills that will be invaluable for wading through the muck of beliefs of everyday life with its occasional perplexity about what they should believe. Herein students shall acquire subtlety in the evaluation of evidence claims. Acquiring this knowledge is a difference that can make a difference in their lives. By learning to make the appropriate distinctions concerning degrees of justification, it comes to be seen that there *really* is a difference between knowing something and merely believing it. Another result of mastering this material is that readers learn when it is appropriate to desire certainty and when the fallible character of the subject matter makes that desire totally inappropriate. And in the latter cases, just because certainty cannot be attained, that does not mean that the floodgates open and all sorts of speculation can be accepted as knowledge.

HOW DO NECESSARY AND SUFFICIENT CONDITIONS WORK?

The concepts of necessary and sufficient condition are required for a full mastery of the discussion of theoretical definitions, which comes next. There is a simple way of understanding the terminology of necessary and sufficient conditions by using conditional statements. The general form of a conditional statement is:

If (the antecedent) then (the consequent).

An example here would be: If (Tom is a brother) then (Tom is a male). The parentheses are used here just to call attention to the distinct units that constitute the antecedent and the consequent, and in more complex examples are used to clarify the grouping of the parts of the conditional. When a conditional statement is true the following holds:

> The antecedent is a sufficient condition for the consequent, and the consequent is a necessary condition for the antecedent.

A simple memory device for remembering this relationship is the acronym SIN, where S = sufficient condition, I = implies, and N = necessary condition. That is, in any true conditional the antecedent is a sufficient condition for the consequent, and the consequent is a necessary condition for the antecedent. Or, to express it differently, the truth of the antecedent holding *implies* the truth of the consequent holding, but not vice versa. So, in the example just given it is the case that Tom being a brother is a sufficient condition for Tom being a male, and Tom being a male is a necessary condition for Tom being a brother. The relationship expressed by any true conditional statement is called the *reciprocity of sufficiency and necessity,* i.e., if A is sufficient for C, then C is necessary for A. But note that in this case the consequent is *not* sufficient for the antecedent, and the antecedent is *not* necessary for the consequent. And this is because there are males who are not brothers.

WHAT IS A THEORETICAL DEFINITION?

A theoretical definition is a kind of equation. This is shown in the general form of any definition which goes as follows:

$$\text{Definiendum} =_{df} \text{definiens}$$

where the 'Definiendum' is that which is being defined, and the 'definiens' is that which is doing the defining. This general form gets abbreviated as 'D =df d', where '=df' is read as 'equals by definition'. So, the whole abbreviation could be read as: Big D equals by definition little d. Theoretical definitions are so called because they represent a kind of theory about their subject matter. The definition is understood to be a hypothesis about the content of the definition, and the philosophical task is that of investigating whether the theoretical definition is true or false. The crucial point about theoretical definitions is that if they are true, they are necessarily true, and if they are false, they are necessarily false. Consider, by way of an example, this definition, which Plato refuted long ago: Knowledge =df perception. If this definition were true, what it would be saying is that it is necessarily the case that every instance of knowledge is an instance of perception, and every instance of perception is a case of knowledge.

The philosophical method of investigating the truth of such a definition is by the method of counterexample. To understand the role of counterexamples in the evaluation of theoretical definitions it is helpful to understand what the logical form of a definition implies. Consider the following sequence:

$$D = df\ d,$$

for example: x is a brother =df x is a male sibling;

implies

Necessarily, x is a D if and only if x is a d,

that is: Necessarily, x is a brother if and only if x is a male sibling;

which implies

Necessarily, if D then d, and if d then D,

i.e.: Necessarily, if x is a brother then x is a male sibling,
and if x is a male sibling then x is a brother; which in turn implies

Necessarily, it is not the case that both (D and not d)
and it is not the case that both (d and not D).

I.e.: Necessarily, it is not the case that both x is a brother and not a male sibling, and it is not the case that both x is a male sibling and not a brother.

'Necessarily' is equivalent to 'It is not possible that not . . .'.

So,

It is not possible that either (D and not d) or (d and not D).

I.e.: It is not possible that either x is a brother and not a male sibling, or x is a male sibling and not a brother. If either of these *is* possible, i.e., if it is possible that (D and not d), or it is possible that (d and not D), then a *counterexample* to the original hypothesis, which claimed that D =df d, has been found.

WHAT KINDS OF COUNTEREXAMPLES ARE THERE?

Refutation by counterexample can occur in any of three ways, which will here be called (with credit to Steven Spielberg's "Close Encounters ..." movie) "Counterexamples of the First Kind," "Counterexamples of the Second Kind," and "Counterexamples of the Third Kind." The logical form of the first two of these can be compared and contrasted as follows:

Counterexamples of the First Kind	*Counterexamples of the Second Kind*
D and not d	d and not D

Illustrated in terms of the faulty definition which asserted that "Knowledge =df perception," a Counterexample of the First Kind would be an instance of knowledge which was not an instance of perception; and a Counterexample of the Second Kind (if such were possible) would be an instance of perception which was not an instance of knowledge.

What do these counterexamples show? If actually produced what they illustrate is that the definition is false because:

(1) *D is* not *a sufficient condition for d.*	(1) *d is* not *a sufficient condition for D.*
(2) *d is* not *a necessary condition for D,*	(2) *D is* not *a necessary condition for d.*
(3) *the definition as a whole is* too narrow, *because the extension of the definiens is smaller than the extension of the Definiendum.*	(3) *the definition as a whole is* too broad, *because the extension of the definiens is larger than the extension of the Definiendum.*

The extension of a term is the set of all the items to which the term refers. So, the extension of the term 'dog' is the set of all the dogs that ever have or will exist.

What I call a Counterexample of the Third Kind is the joint production of a pair of distinct cases (counterexamples); one of which shows that the definition is false in that it is *too broad,* and one that shows it to be *too narrow.* Providing two such counterexamples to a proposed definition is the most devastating sort of critique possible. What such a pair of cases establishes is that the Definiendum is neither necessary nor sufficient for the definiens, and that the definiens is neither necessary nor sufficient for the Definiendum. Such a theoretical definition is very defective indeed, and the successful showing of it constitutes a very elegant refutation of the proposed definition.

COUNTEREXAMPLES: TOO BROAD, TOO NARROW, OR BOTH?

A Counterexample of the First Kind has been represented as having the logical form of: *D & not d*, i.e., as a case where the Definiendum applies, but the definiens does not apply. This counterexample establishes a definition as being too narrow. A convenient way of remembering this is by noticing how if one draws a pair of lines above and below the the schema, connecting the top of the *D* with the circle of the *d*, the lines *narrow* when drawn from left to right:

$$\overline{\text{D \& not-d}}$$

Using circles to represent the extension of D and d, the result is:

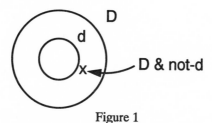

Figure 1

In this case *x* marks the individual of the counterexample which lies within the extension of D and outside the extension of d. Consider the definition: *x* is a brother =df *x* is a married male sibling. The *x* of the counterexample is an individual who is a brother but who isn't a married male sibling. The defect of a definition which is too narrow results from a definiens which is too restrictive or too strong or too complex.

A Counterexample of the Second Kind has the logical form: *d & not D*, which is to say that it represents a case where the definiens holds, but the Definiendum does not hold. This counterexample establishes a definition as being too broad. Once again, a memory device for remembering this consists of drawing a pair of lines connecting the top of the circle of *d* with the top of the *D*, and noticing how the lines *broaden* when drawn from left to right:

$$\overline{\text{d \& not-D}}$$

Again, using circles to represent the extension of D and d, the result is:

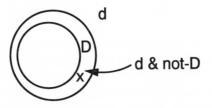

Figure 2

In this instance *x* marks the individual of the counterexample, which lies within the extension of d, but outside the extension of D. As an example, consider the definition: *x* is a brother =df *x* is a male. The *x* of the counterexample is an individual who is a male but who is not a brother. Such a definition is too broad because the extension of the definiens 'male' is larger than the extension of the Definiendum 'brother'. This results from the definiens being too liberal or too weak or too general.

A Counterexample of the Third Kind consists of a pair of cases which together confirm the logical form:

$$(D \text{ \& not } d) \text{ \& } (d \text{ \& not } D).$$

Each case confirms one of the pair of 'and' statements. Such cases are produced to refute a definition that is both too broad and too narrow. In such a situation, the extensions of the two terms get represented as two overlapping circles, as follows:

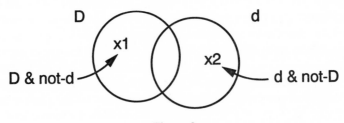

Figure 3

The two *x*s each represent a completely distinct individual. An example of a definition that is doubly false in this way would be: *x* is a brother =df *x* is a married male. In this case *x*1 would be a brother who isn't a married male, and *x*2 would be a married male who isn't a brother. In this sort of example the definiens is simultaneously both too liberal and too restrictive, or at once both too broad and too narrow.

A CLASSIC APPLICATION

The second selection in this volume is Edmund L. Gettier's modern classic, "Is Justified True Belief Knowledge?" Gettier is considering the traditional definition of knowledge, which goes as follows: A subject S knows that p =df (1) p is true, (2) S believes that p, and (3) S is justified in believing that p. Gettier's purpose in this paper is *not* to challenge that truth, belief, and justification are each necessary conditions of knowledge. His purpose is rather, by the use of two distinct ingenious counterexamples, to show that justification, truth, and belief are not *jointly sufficient* for knowledge. In other words, Gettier is constructing two Counterexamples of the Second Kind, namely: d & not D. His cases are possible scenarios in which the subject S has justified true belief, but nevertheless does *not* know that p. The point is to show that the traditional definition is false because it is *too broad*, i.e., the set of cases of justified true belief is larger than the set of all cases of knowledge. We shall return to this case in more detail below.

THE BIG PICTURE

The methodology used by Gettier can be exploited in a systematic way to describe the relationships among any number of concepts. Consider, for example, the question of how the following eight concepts interrelate one with another. The eight are: (1) the understood, (2) the true, (3) the certain, (4) the believed, (5) that about which one feels sure, (6) the known, (7) the justified true beliefs, and (8) the set of that for which one has adequate evidence.

My view of the truth of how these concepts relate to one another is contained in a diagram I call "The Big Picture." As an exercise for the reader, I have constructed in the column on the left a series of false definitions of knowledge using, in turn, each of these concepts in the definiens. The column in the center gives the logical form of the type of counterexample that it is possible to construct. Then the column on the right spells out a moral or derived principle that can be extracted from having shown each definition respectively to be false. The point of the exercise is for the reader to imagine an actual or possible concrete case that fits the counterexample. That is, to show the falsity of each of these definitions, the reader thinks of a case which illustrates each false definition in turn. For example, in the first definition the reader need only think of a proposition, such as that there is intelligent life elsewhere in the universe, which is a proposition we understand the meaning of, but which we currently do not know whether it is true or false.

THE BIG PICTURE

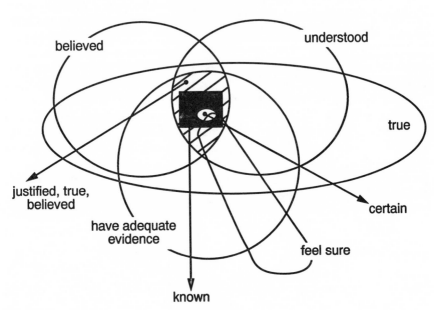

Figure 4

Definition	Counter example	Derived Principle
1. Ksp =df S understands that p ('Ksp' is 'S knows that p')	d & not D	Realm of understood larger than realm of the known.
2. Ksp =df p is true	d & not D	Realm of truth larger than realm of the known.
3. Ksp =df S believes (accepts) that p	d & not D	Being true is a necessary condition of being known; and realm of beliefs is larger than the realm of knowledge.
4. Ksp =df S is certain that p	D & not d	Realm of the certain is smaller than that of the known.

5. Ksp =df *S* has true belief that *p*	d & not D	Adequate evidence (justification) is a necessary condition of knowledge; the realm of true belief is larger than that of knowledge.
6. Ksp =df *S* has adequate evidence that *p*	d & not D	Belief is a necessary condition of knowledge.
7. Ksp =df *S* has justified belief that *p*	d & not D	Justified belief alone is not a sufficient condition for knowledge. Truth is necessary also.
8. Ksp =df *S* feels sure that *p*	d & not D & D & not d	Feeling sure is neither sufficient nor necessary for knowledge.

As an example consider the second of these definitions, namely: *S* knows that *p* =df *p* is true. This is most assuredly a false definition in that it is far too broad. The realm of the true, which in "The Big Picture" gets expressed as a great ellipse, is far more encompassing than the black box representing the realm of the known. But this definition is *not* doubly false; it is definitely not too narrow. Truth is, indeed, a necessary condition of knowledge. This is what I call the First Great Principle of Epistemology, that is: *You can't know what isn't so*. The truth of the matter is: Necessarily, if *S* knows that *p* then *p* is true, but it is not necessary that if *p* is true then *S* knows that *p*.

The counterexample that shows this definition to be false is an example of a Counterexample of the Second Kind, namely: d & not D. That is, there is some proposition *p*, such that *p* is true but *p* isn't known to be true. The production of the counterexample consists in the posing of the possible case. Let the proposition *p* be some genuinely open (i.e., unproven) theorem of mathematics, such as Goldbach's Conjecture (which says that "every even number is the sum of two prime numbers"). Now, assuredly, either proposition *p* is true or its negation, *not p*, is true. Suppose for the moment that the true one is *p*. The counterexample, d & not D, just is the fact that Goldbach's Conjecture is true, but it is not known to be true. If it should turn out that the Conjecture really is false, then the needed counterexample is the case one gets by substituting '*not p*' for '*p*' throughout; i.e., the denial of Goldbach's Conjecture is true, but it is not known to be true.

COUNTEREXAMPLES AND BORDERLINE CASES

Under what conditions will a counterexample serve to refute a philosophical thesis? When must such a counterexample be an actual case? When is it appropriate to identify a proposed case as "borderline," and therefore as unsuitable for providing a successful philosophical refutation? These questions are clearly related in that each involves the posing of a case as a type of refuting evidence to a philosophic thesis or theory.

COUNTEREXAMPLES AGAIN

As already mentioned above, one of the most clear-cut cases, in the recent philosophic literature, of a proposed counterexample offered in refutation of a philosophic thesis is that found in Gettier's justly famous "Is Justified True Belief Knowledge?"—the second selection contained in this anthology. Therein Gettier constructs two cases that he suggests are counterexamples to the thesis that: *Anything is an instance of knowledge that* p *if and only if it is an instance of justified true belief that* p. (To clarify the logical form involved, these propositions shall be expressed symbolically. Readers unfamiliar with the logical notation may ignore it and concentrate on the statement formulations.) Using 'Kxp' for 'x knows that p', 'Jxp' for 'x has justification for p', 'Tp' for 'p is true' and 'Bxp' for 'x believes that p', then the thesis in question could be expressed symbolically as shown in (1). The dash sign is the symbol for negation in this context, and '(x)' is the universal quantifier.

$$(1) \qquad (x)[\text{K}xp \equiv (\text{T}p \ \& \ \text{J}xp \ \& \ \text{B}xp)]$$

where 'p' is an individual constant which is taken to be a name of the proposition p. Since the thesis takes the form of a universally quantified biconditional, it can be transformed into the conjunction of two conditionals, which say: *If anything is an instance of knowledge then it is an instance of justified true belief, and if anything is an instance of justified true belief, then it is an instance of knowledge.*

$$(2) \quad (x)\{[\text{K}xp \supset (\text{T}p \ \& \ \text{J}xp \ \& \ \text{B}xp)] \ \& \ [(\text{T}p \ \& \ \text{J}xp \ \& \ \text{B}xp) \supset \text{K}xp]\}$$

Expressed in this way, the first conditional asserts that justified true belief is a necessary condition for knowledge, and the second conditional says that justified true belief is a sufficient condition of knowledge. Gettier's *goal* is to show that the second conditional is false. Each of the conditionals may in turn be transformed so as to eliminate the conditionals. The results would be: *Nothing is knowledge and not justified true belief, and nothing is justified true belief and not knowledge.*

$$(3)(x)\{ - [Kxp \& - (Tp \& Jxp \& Bxp)] \& - [(Tp \& Jxp \& Bxp) \& - Kxp]\}$$

When the conditionals have been eliminated, the result is a conjunction made up of two compound expressions each of which is negated as a whole. Thus, it can now be seen that if one can construct a case that exemplifies either one of the compounds without its outermost negation, then a counterexample will have been produced to the original thesis. Two possible counterexamples to the original thesis are as follows:

A case of knowledge which is not a case of justified true belief.

(4) $$Kxp \& - (Tp \& Jxp \& Bxp)$$

A case of justified true belief which is not a case of knowledge.

(5) $$(Tp \& Jxp \& Bxp) \& - Kxp$$

Gettier's two examples were instances of counterexample (5), and thus were intended to show that justified true belief is *not* a sufficient condition of knowledge.

An interesting feature of Gettier's examples is that they are just two hypothetical or imagined cases. Reflection upon this might lead one to ask: When may a counterexample be a merely *possible* case? The key to answering this question lies in the *modal status* of the thesis in question; that is, whether the thesis is being asserted as a necessary truth, such as: *It is necessarily the case that anything is an instance of knowledge if and only if it is an instance of justified true belief.* Symbolically, this would be:

(6) $$[] (x) [Kxp \equiv (Tp \& Jxp \& Bxp)],$$

where the box operator, [], is the standard symbol for *necessity*. In such a case all that would be required as a counterexample is a *possible* or imagined case. On the other hand, if the thesis in question is meant simply as an empirical or factual general truth, then one must produce an *actual* case in order to have successfully achieved a counterexample. It is clear that Gettier was construing the analysis of knowledge as justified true belief in terms of an assertion of a necessary truth along the lines of (6).

The conclusion to be drawn from this example is that at least one instance in which counterexamples are appropriate is whenever a philosophic thesis can be expressed as a *universal assertion*, i.e., expressed in the form a universally quantified expression. In the example I have been discussing the thesis was a universally quantified expression, the major connective of which was a biconditional. It may be concluded that *any* universally quantified statement is susceptible to counterexample, except those truly expressing logical truths. To say that any such are susceptible is of course not to say that one can actually produce a counterexample to a universal statement that really is *true*! The moral of (6) above was that an expression being an "alleged" necessary truth doesn't make it immune to counterexample, but rather only shows that all one need do is produce a *possible* counterexample.

BORDERLINE CASES

When is it appropriate to react to a proposed counterexample as follows: "The case you have proposed, unfortunately, is not a genuine counterexample to my thesis, inasmuch as it is merely a borderline case, and thus not a refutation of the thesis"?

A classic example of this type of response would be that found in the H. P. Grice and P.F. Strawson article "In Defense of a Dogma,"[3] written in response to, and in criticism of, W.V.O. Quine's "Two Dogmas of Empiricism."[4] In the latter article, Quine can be seen as attempting to propose several counterexamples to the analytic/synthetic distinction. In offering them, Quine treats this distinction as if it were to be expressed as: *Any proposition is analytic if and only if it is not synthetic.* Taking 'A' as an abbreviation for 'is analytic' and 'S' for 'is synthetic', then Quine's construal of the analytic/synthetic distinction would be expressed symbolically as:

$$(7) \qquad (x) [Ax \equiv -Sx]$$

or equivalently as:

$$(8) \qquad (x) \{[Ax \supset -Sx] \& [-Sx \supset Ax]\}$$

I.e., *Every proposition is such that if it is analytic then it is not synthetic, and if it is not synthetic then it is analytic.* The result of systematically interchanging 'S' and 'A' in the original biconditional would give an equivalent result, i.e.,

$$(9) \qquad (x)[Sx \equiv -Ax]$$

Every proposition is synthetic if and only if it is not analytic.

This would be to construe the categories of being analytic and being synthetic as mutually exclusive, in that nothing could be both analytic and synthetic at the same time. Just as with the case of knowledge and justified true belief, two types of case would constitute a counterexample, i.e.,

$$(10) \qquad Ax \& Sx$$

I.e., *a proposition which is both analytic and synthetic.*

(11) $- Sx \And - Ax$

I.e., *a proposition which is neither analytic nor synthetic.*

That is, in order to show a counterexample to the analytic/synthetic distinction one would have to come up with a clear-cut case of a proposition that is either (a) both analytic and synthetic, or (b) neither analytic nor synthetic. Seemingly, then, this case is exactly the same as the previous case considered.

Where, then, do the *borderline* cases come in? In the case of a philosophical distinction, such as that between the analytic and the synthetic, the philosopher proposing the distinction will provide a criterion or set of rules to be used in applying one (or both) parts of the distinction. In some cases a separate criterion will be provided for each part of the distinction. A *borderline* case would then be an instance in which one simply cannot tell, by the criterion provided, which half of the distinction would apply in that case. It is *undecidable* on the criteria provided which half of the distinction applies. For example, if one were told that a proposition is *analytic* if and only if there is a subject and a predicate such that the concept of the predicate is contained in the concept of the subject, then the corresponding criterion for a proposition's being *synthetic* might be given as that there is a subject and a predicate such that the concept of the predicate was not so contained. On such a set of criteria one might argue that the proposition that $2 + 3 = 5$, constitutes a *borderline case*, inasmuch as it is not grammatically of the subject/predicate form. That is, $2 + 3 = 5$ is taken as a borderline case, since we cannot tell by the criteria provided whether it is analytic or synthetic.

As another example, let us suppose that a sheep farmer introduces a distinction between "wheeps" and "bleeps." The criteria supplied are that: (a) Any animal is a wheep if and only if it is a sheep of a whitish color. (b) Any animal is a bleep if and only if it is a sheep of a blackish color. Further, suppose that our farmer asserted the empirical thesis (S) that: Every sheep is either a wheep, or if not a wheep, a bleep, and vice versa. Imagine then that someone came along with a gray sheep, i.e., one that wasn't really either black or white, but rather some intermediate shade. Suppose then that the question arises whether this creature is a bleep or a wheep, and further whether this sheep constitutes a counterexample to the thesis (S)? In this case we would properly have to say that the sheep was a *borderline case* in that it isn't clear from the criteria given whether or not it was to be classed as one or the other. Is the gray sheep then a counterexample to the thesis (S)? Well, no, since it is a borderline case to the distinction as given, and as such we aren't able to tell whether it was or wasn't a wheep or a bleep.

What then would constitute such a counterexample? Clearly, if someone produced a Kelly green ewe, then, by the criteria given, it would be neither a bleep nor a wheep. Yet since it is certainly a sheep, it would (if actually produced) provide a decisive counterexample to the thesis (S), which was to the effect that every sheep is either a bleep and not a wheep, or a wheep and not a bleep. In this example we have distinguished between a *borderline case* and a *counterexample*. A borderline case is seen to occur when the criteria given for each part of the distinction *do not* completely specify which half of the distinction applies in the given case. The assertion that a counterexample has been successfully constructed presupposes that one has produced an example to which the criteria apply unambiguously, and yet which falsify the thesis under consideration. In this case the empirical nature of the thesis dictates that an *actual* counterexample would have to be produced. If the thesis had instead been " *Necessarily*, every sheep is either a wheep or a bleep, and not both, and not neither," then a merely *possible* Kelly green ewe would have sufficed as a counterexample.

The distinction that comprises any *philosophical dichotomy* (such as that between the analytic and the synthetic) can thus be taken as a philosophical thesis, in the sense of a universal statement, only when *distinct criteria* have been proposed for each part of the dichotomy. That is, it *cannot* be that one criterion is just the negation of the other. For, suppose the criterion of a proposition's being analytic is given as C. If the criterion for a proposition's being synthetic is given as simply "not C," or "non-C," then it obviously follows that there can be *no* counterexamples to the thesis that "*any proposition is analytic if and only if it is not synthetic.*" If the criteria are so constructed as to be contradictories, there can be *borderline cases*, but no *counterexamples*. A counterexample to such a formulation of the analytic/synthetic distinction could only be constructed with regard to some thesis employing one term of the distinction (e.g., All propositions known *a priori* are analytic), but not with regard to the universal statement produced from the distinction itself, i.e., any proposition is analytic if and only if it is not synthetic.

It can be further noted that where the criteria used for applying the terms of the distinction are contradictories, there can be no counterexamples to a conditional thesis, such as that considered above in the case of the wheeps and bleeps, i.e., *If anything is a sheep then it is a bleep if and only if it is not a wheep.* That is, taking 'S' for 'is a sheep', 'B' for 'is a bleep', 'W' for 'is a wheep', the thesis under consideration was:

(12) $(x) [Sx \supset (Bx \equiv - Wx)]$

Thus, if the criterion for being a wheep were the negation of the criterion for being a bleep, then no counterexample could be possible to the thesis that every sheep is a bleep if and only if it is not a wheep. With the criteria formulated as contradictories, everything not a wheep would of necessity be a bleep, or *vice versa*. Likewise, if the criterion for being analytic were the negation of the criterion for being synthetic, then such a thesis as "every scientific truth is analytic if and only if it is not synthetic" would be trivially true due to the fact that the biconditional in the consequent couldn't possibly be false.

The moral to be drawn from these considerations concerns attempts to provide counterexamples to philosophical distinctions. Before looking for a counterexample to a philosophical distinction or dichotomy, one should first look to the criteria proposed in the formulation of that distinction. If the criteria are the contradictories of one another, then there can be no hope of finding true and acceptable counterexamples to the distinction. The very best one could do would be to come up with cases that were *borderline*, wherein one can not tell, i.e., it is undecidable, whether the terms applied or not.

SUMMARY OF SECTION CONTENTS

Part One of this volume, "The Problem of Analyzing Knowledge," focuses upon the development and criticism of the traditional definition of knowledge as justified true belief. In the opening selection, "Knowledge and True Opinion," Roderick M. Chisholm places the whole issue in a broad context both historically and within the context of various areas of philosophy. The rest of this part is an extended debate on the revolution in epistemology caused by Edmund L. Gettier in 1963 when he definitely established that the traditional definition of knowledge was false because it was too broad.

Part Two consists of five papers devoted to "The Problem of the Criterion." This is the ancient problem of "the wheel," which explores the interconnections between the two questions: "What is the *extent* of our knowledge?" and "What are the *criteria* of knowledge?" Chisholm explores the three possible general responses to this problem—what he calls the positions of the methodist, the particularist, and of the skeptic—and himself endorses the second of these. The ensuing discussions of Amico, Chisholm, and Ryan explore further facets of this perplexing traditional problem.

Part Three, "The Fourth Condition of Knowledge," explores some of the most promising attempts to provide clear and illuminating specifications of the missing fourth condition of knowledge. That is, they attempt to say what must be added to justified true belief to complete a definition that would necessarily be sufficient for knowledge.

Part Four explores the development of, and some trenchant criticisms of, the highly influential attempt to explicate the concept of epistemic justification in terms of the reliability of the methods by which one's beliefs are supported.

Part Five investigates several facets of the nature of knowing that one knows. It illuminates the connections between second-order knowledge and the concept of certainty. This section also explores the doctrine of fallibilism, which defends the thesis that it is possible to know a proposition even when it is possible that one might have been mistaken.

Part Six explores the fascinating issue of degrees of epistemic justification. Roderick M. Chisholm has been the most influential philosopher attempting to develop a systematic theory of the hierarchy of levels of epistemic appraisal. The readings present several different models of how these concepts of justification interrelate. The selection by Alston along with that of Feldman and Conee explore further perspectives on the concept of epistemic justification.

Finally, Part Seven examines some of the the profound issues that center upon the the analysis of the concept of knowledge as applied to other persons generally, and to oneself in particular.

NOTES

1. Thomas Perry, *Metzger's Dog* (New York: Charter Books, 1983), pp. 1–3.
2. (New York: Macmillan, Inc., The Free Press, 1991), p. 174.
3. *The Philosophical Review* 65 (1956): 377–88.
4. *The Philosophical Review* 60 (1951): 20–43.

Part I

The Problem of
Analyzing Knowledge

1

Knowledge and True Opinion

Roderick M. Chisholm

In Plato's dialogue, the *Meno,* Socrates remarks: "That there is a difference between right opinion and knowledge is not at all a conjecture with me but something I would particularly assert that I know. There are not many things of which I would say that, but this one, at any rate, I will include among those that I know" [97C]. The distinction would seem to be obvious. If one has knowledge, then one also has right or true opinion. But the converse is not true: one may have right or true opinion without having knowledge. Thus, we may guess correctly today, and therefore, have true opinion, but not know until tomorrow. Or we may have true opinion and never know at all.

In the *Theaetetus,* Plato poses the following question: What is the distinction between knowledge and true, or right, opinion? He then sets out to "bring the many sorts of knowledge under one definition" [148]. It is doubtful that he succeeded and it is certain that we cannot do any better. But we may throw some light upon "the many sorts of knowledge" if we consider the difficulties that are involved in answering Plato's question.

One approach to the question, which Plato himself suggests, is to assume, first, that if one man knows and another man has true opinion but does not know, then the first man has everything that the second man has and something else as well. Then, having made this assumption, we ask: What is that which, when added to true opin-

From *Theory of Knowledge* (Upper Saddle River, N.J.: Prentice-Hall, Inc., © 1966), pp. 5–23. Reprinted by permission of the publisher.

ion, yields knowledge? This approach to Plato's question may be put more schematically. The expression "*S* knows that *h* is true," where "*S*" may be replaced by a name or description of some person and where "*h* is true" may be replaced by a sentence such as "It is raining" or "Anaxagoras was a Greek philosopher," is assumed to tell us three different things:

1. *S* believes that *h*

e.g., the person in question believes that it is raining, or believes that Anaxagoras was a Greek philosopher. It also tells us that

2. *h* is true

e.g., that it is raining, or that Anaxagoras was a Greek philosopher. And finally, it tells us something else:

3. ———.

Thus, we have a blank to fill. What shall we say of 3?

We may begin by approaching our problem in this way, keeping in mind the possibility that we should have begun in some other way.

We will find that most of the expressions that come to mind as possible candidates for 3 will be expressions that seem to leave us with our problem. For when we try to say what *they* mean, we again come back to "know."

ADEQUATE EVIDENCE

It is often said that *adequate evidence* is that which, when added to true opinion, yields knowledge. May we fill in our blank, then, by saying "*S* has adequate evidence for *h*"?

Some have objected to this type of definition by saying: "Consider a man who has adequate evidence (not only has he heard the opinions of all the experts, but he has also had access to all of the evidence that they have had) and who believes what he does not because of the evidence that he has, but for some entirely frivolous reason (he follows what the tea leaves say). However good his evidence may be, such a man surely cannot be said to know, even if what he believes is true, for he hasn't recognized his evidence for what it's worth." But what this objection shows us, one could argue, is not that it is possible for a man with a true belief to have adequate evidence and at the same time not to know; it shows us, rather, that it is possible for such a man to have adequate evidence, and therefore, to know, but without *knowing* that he knows.

There are other reasons, however, for rejecting the definition.

For one thing, it is possible to add adequate evidence to true belief or opinion without obtaining knowledge. Many of those who predicted the election results correctly had adequate evidence—even at an early point in the campaign—for what they believed and predicted, but no one, at that time, knew that the predictions were true.

And for another thing, the expression "adequate evidence," as it is ordinarily interpreted, presupposes the concept of *knowledge*—knowledge, not of that for which we are said to have adequate evidence, but of something else. If a man says, for example, that we have adequate evidence for the hypothesis that no one can live on the planet Mercury, he is likely to mean that on the basis of what we know, there is very good reason to believe that no one can live on the planet Mercury. Or, in slightly more technical language, he is saying that in relation to what is known, it is highly improbable that there can be life on Mercury.

We may say of this type of definition, then, what Socrates said of the attempt to define knowledge in terms of reason or explanation: "If, my boy, the command to add reason or explanation means learning to know and not merely getting an opinion . . . , our splendid definition of knowledge would be a fine affair! For learning to know is acquiring knowledge, is it not?" [*Theaetetus* 209E]

PROBABILITY

The concept of adequate evidence presupposes the concept of knowledge, but the concept of probability need not do so. May we say, then, that *probability* is that which, when added to true opinion, yields knowledge?

The term "probability," as it is ordinarily used, may be taken in a variety of senses. Of these, the most common are the *statistical* sense, the *inductive* sense, and the *absolute* sense. Whichever of these interpretations we adopt, we will find that the concept of probability does not provide us with the solution to Plato's problem.

(1) Taking the term in its statistical sense, we may say with Aristotle that the probable is "that which happens for the most part." Probability statements, when taken in this way, tell us something about the relative frequency with which a given property or event (say, death before the age of 100) occurs within a certain reference class or population (say, the class of men, or of philosophers, or of ancient Greek philosophers). Thus, the statement "It is highly probable that a given ancient Greek philosopher, for example, Anaxagoras, died before he reached 100," when taken in this way, will tell us that Anaxagoras was a member of a certain class of entities (ancient Greek philosophers), the vast majority of which died before they reached 100. Statistical probability statements, which may be arithmetically more complex, are analogous.

But just how are we to go about defining knowledge in terms of statistical probability? Let us allow ourselves to say that if a man believes something, then *what* he believes is a proposition. Then, we shall try to say something of this sort: If a man knows a given proposition to be true, then the proposition is a member of a certain wider class of propositions, the vast majority of which have a certain further property *P.* And we will hope to find a property *P* which is such that if a proposition is a member of a class of propositions, the vast majority of which have that property *P,* then the proposition is one that can be said to be known to be true—but *what* class of propositions, and what additional property *P*? It will not be enough to say that the class of propositions is the class of propositions that *S* believes and that *P* is the property of being true, for in this case we shall not have made any distinction between knowledge and true opinion. And it will be too much to say that the class is the class of true propositions that *S* believes and that the additional property *P* is the property of being *known* to be true, for in this case we will be presupposing the distinction we are trying to define.

(2) The *inductive* sense of "probable" may seem to be more promising. If, once again, we allow ourselves the term "proposition," then we may say that "probable," in its inductive sense, refers to a certain logical relation that holds between propositions.[1] Two propositions, *e* and *h*, may be so related logically that the proposition *h* may be said to be probable—that is, more probable than not—in relation to the proposition *e*. In such a case, *h* may be said to be *probable in relation to e*. If the reader can identify a good inductive argument, then he will have no trouble in identifying this relation. For to say that *h* is probable in relation to *e* is tantamount to saying that an argument having *e* as premise (*e* may be a conjunction of many propositions) and *h* as conclusion, would be a good inductive argument in favor of *h*. Let us say, for example, that "Anaxagoras lived to be 500 years old" is probable in relation to "Anaxagoras was an ancient Greek philosopher, and the vast majority of Greek philosophers lived to be 500 years old." The latter proposition, if we knew it to be true, would provide good inductive support for the former. Unfortunately, however, the question "What is a good inductive argument?" is at least as difficult as the question "What is the distinction between knowledge and true opinion?" And even if this were not so, inductive probability would not provide us with the answer to our question.

If we attempt to draw the distinction between knowledge and true opinion by reference to the inductive sense of "probable," then presumably we will say that our subject *S* knows the proposition *h* to be true, provided that *h* is probable in relation to a certain other proposition *e*. But *what* other proposition *e*? It will not be enough to say that there is a certain true proposition *e* which is such that *h* is probable on the basis of *e*, for in this case we will not be able to draw the distinction between knowledge and true opinion. We must say not only that *e* is true, but also that *e* has some further property as well. And what could this further property be except that of being known by *S* to be true? Hence, the problem of the *Theaetetus* recurs, this time with respect to *e* instead of *h*. How are we to define "*S* knows that *e* is true"?

(3) When the term "probable" is used in the *absolute* sense, and this would seem to be its most frequent use, it is closely related to what is intended by the term "know." The phrase "in all probability" is often used to express the absolute sense of "probable." Thus, if we say "In all probability it will rain tomorrow," we mean that the hypothesis or proposition that it will rain tomorrow is more probable than not, in the inductive sense of "probable" just considered, in relation to those propositions that are *known* to be true or that could, very readily, be known to be true. We may be relating the hypothesis to what it is we happen to know ourselves; or we may be relating it to what it is we believe the experts happen to know (as we would be doing if we said "In all probability, a man will be landed on the moon before the century is over"); or we may be relating the hypothesis to the knowledge of some subclass of experts who are indicated by the context of utterance.

In its most straightforward sense, the concept of absolute probability might be defined in this way: A proposition *h* is probable in the absolute sense for a given subject *S*, provided that *h* is *probable in the inductive sense*, in relation to the conjunction of all those propositions that *S* knows to be true.[2] (Hence, we may equate what is expressed by "*h* is probable in the absolute sense for *S*" with what is expressed by "*S* has adequate evidence for *h*.") Since we must appeal to the concept of knowledge to explicate the concept of absolute probability, we cannot make use of the concept of absolute probability in order to complete our definition of knowledge.[3]

OBSERVATION

In writings on the philosophy of science, it is often assumed (1) that knowledge may be defined in terms of *observation* and (2) that observation, being a concept of physiology and psychology, can be defined in terms of those sciences and without reference to knowledge. In support of the first contention, one might formulate the following definition: To say of someone *S* that *S* knows a certain proposition *h* to be true is to say that *S* has true opinion with respect to *h* and that *h* is an observation proposition for *S*. And in support of the second, one might point out that to say of a man that he observes a cat, for example, is to say that a cat is, for him, a stimulus object, that it has caused him to have a certain sensation, and perhaps also that it has "entered into his field of vision."

This approach to Plato's question will not serve to "bring the many sorts of knowledge under one definition," for as we shall see later in some detail, there are many sorts of knowledge that are not observational—for example, our knowledge of logic and mathematics and our knowledge of some of our own states of mind. But there is another difficulty that is even more serious.

The term "observation" is a member of a certain family of terms (compare "perceive," "see," "hear," "feel") each of which is subject to two quite different types of interpretation. If we interpret any one of these terms in such a way that, on that interpretation, one of the two contentions comprising the present suggestion will be true (and we may do this), then on that interpretation of the term, the other contention will be false.

We may say of a man simply that he observes a cat on the roof. Or we may say of him that he observes *that* a cat is on the roof. In the second case, the verb "observe" takes a "that"-clause, a propositional clause, as its grammatical object. We may distinguish, therefore, between a "propositional" and a "nonpropositional" use of the term "observe," and we may make an analogous distinction for "perceive," "see," "hear," and "feel."

If we take the verb "observe" propositionally, saying of the man that he observes that a cat is on the roof, or that he observes a cat to be on the roof, then we may also say of him that he *knows* that a cat is on the roof; for in the propositional sense of "observe," observation may be said to imply knowledge. But if we take the verb nonpropositionally, saying of the man only that he observes a cat which is on the roof, then what we say will not imply that he knows that there is a cat on the roof. For a man may be said to observe a cat, to see a cat, or hear a cat, in the nonpropositional sense of these terms, without his knowing that a cat is what it is that he is observing, or seeing, or hearing. "It wasn't until the following day that I found out that what I saw was only a cat."

The distinction between these two senses of "observe" and the other related terms may also be illustrated by the following passage in *Robinson Crusoe*: "When, one morning the day broke, and all unexpectedly before their eyes a ship stood, what it was was evident at a glance to Crusoe. . . . But how was it with Friday? As younger and uncivilized, his eyes were presumably better than those of his master. That is, Friday saw the ship really the best of the two; and yet he could hardly be said to see it at all." Using "see" nonpropositionally, we may say that Friday not only saw the ship, but saw it better than Crusoe did; using it propositionally, we may say that Crusoe, but not Friday, saw *that* it was a ship and hence, that Friday hardly saw a ship at all.

We can define the Friday, nonpropositional sense of "observe" by means of the terms of psychology and physiology. But this sense of observation does not imply knowledge, and we cannot use it to complete our definition of knowledge. We must appeal instead to the Crusoe, propositional sense of "observe." What, then, did Crusoe have that Friday did not have?

The obvious answer is that Crusoe had *knowledge*. His senses enabled him to *know*, with the result that "what it was was evident at a glance." This sense of "observation," therefore, must be defined in terms of knowledge, and so we are left, once again, with Plato's problem.

KNOWLEDGE AS AN ETHICAL CONCEPT

If we are to solve the problem, we must find a definition of *knowledge* that is not patently circular. We cannot be content to define knowledge by reference, say, to "that which falls within our cognizance." Nor will it do merely to introduce some technical term and then resolve to use it in the way in which we ordinarily use the word "knowledge." We may say, if we like, that to constitute knowledge, a true opinion must also be one that is "evident," but we must not suppose that the introduction of the technical term is itself sufficient to throw any light upon our problem.

Let us consider, then, the possibility of defining knowledge in ethical terms. To know that *h* is true will be not only to have true opinion with respect to *h,* but also to have a certain right or duty with respect to *h.* Whether such a definition will turn out to be circular will depend upon how we specify the right or duty in question. The terms "right" and "duty" are not technical terms invented merely in order to complete our definition. We may assume that "right" and "duty" are correlative terms: A man has a right to perform a certain act A if, and only if, it is not his duty to refrain from performing A, and he has a duty to perform A if, and only if, he does not have the right to refrain from performing A. Instead of saying "He has a duty to perform A," we may also say "He ought to perform A."

One may object that any such definition would throw no light upon the concept of knowledge, for what it is to have a right or a duty is at least as obscure as what it is to know. The obvious reply is: The philosopher is indeed confronted not only with the difficult concept of knowledge, but also with the difficult concept of a right or a duty; but if he can succeed in defining one of these by reference to the other, then he will have progressed at least to the extent of finding himself with one difficult concept, where formerly he had found himself with two.[4]

What right or duty, then, does the knower have with respect to that which he knows? A simple answer would be: If a man knows that a certain proposition is true, then he has the duty to accept or believe that proposition. More exactly, *S* knows that *h* is true, provided that (1) *S* accepts or believes *h*; (2) *h* is true; and (3) *S* has the duty to accept or believe *h.* Would this be an adequate definition?

The term "duty" must be taken in its ordinary sense if the definition is to be of any significance. But "duty," as we ordinarily understand the term, is used in connection with actions, or possible actions, that are within the agent's power and for which he can be held responsible if he performs them. (" 'Ought' implies 'can.' ") But are beliefs actions, or possible actions, that are within anyone's power?[5] And can a man be held responsible for what he believes, or fails to believe? (We often speak of what a man ought to know, but seldom, if ever, of what a man ought to believe.)

There is a difficulty that is even more serious: If beliefs—more exactly, believings—are actions for which we can be held responsible, then the proposed definition would imply that to turn a man's true opinion into knowledge, it would be sufficient to make the holding of that opinion a duty. But it is at least conceivable that a man may have the duty to accept a true proposition which he does not know to be true. For example, a man may have the duty to believe that the members of his family are honest or faithful without in fact knowing that they are. Or a sick man, who has various unfulfilled obligations, may have the duty to accept certain propositions if, by accepting them, he can make himself well and useful once again. The proposed definition would have the consequence that, if these duties to believe are fulfilled, and if the propositions thus believed happen to be true, then the believer, *ipso facto,* knows that they are true. And this is absurd.[6]

Analogous considerations hold if we define knowing in terms of "the right to believe," instead of "the duty to believe."

Let us consider, then, another type of right or duty, one that is more closely related to the concept of knowing—the right or duty that we have, in certain cases, to take precautions. Taking precautions is a kind of activity. When a man takes precautions, he prepares for the worst, even though he may not expect it to happen. For example, he may not believe that his house will burn, but he takes precautions by buying fire insurance. But if he knows that a given proposition is true, then, it would seem, there is no point in his taking any precautions against the possibility that the proposition is false. If, somehow, he knew that his house would never burn, then, it would seem, there would be no point in his insuring the house against fire or otherwise taking precautions against the possibility that his house might burn. Suppose, then, we say that a man knows h to be true, provided that no matter what he may do, he has the right to rely upon h—that is to say, no matter what he may do, he does not have the duty to take precautions against the possibility that h is false.

This definition has been suggested by a familiar doctrine of scholastic philosophy: If a man *knows,* then he need have no "fear of error," and so far as what is known is concerned, his intellect may be in "a state of repose."[7] A. J. Ayer has suggested a similar definition, saying that the man who knows, as contrasted to the man who merely has true opinion, is the man who has the "right to be sure."[8]

But here, too, there are difficulties. The duty to take precautions in any particular case is a function not only of what is known, but also of what happens to be at stake—if not, indeed, of what is *known* to be at stake. Where the stakes are small, there may be no need to take precautions—whether or not one knows. And where the stakes are large, there may be a duty to take precautions—whether or not one knows. Moreover, the duty to take precautions may arise in still other ways. Even if a captain knows that his ship is seaworthy, he may yet have the obligation to provide lifeboats and to take other precautions against the possibility that it is not. For he may have the obligation to reassure his passengers; or he may have sworn to obey the law and thus have acquired the obligation to take precautions with every sailing.

Again, there are circumstances under which a man may be said to have the duty to rely upon certain propositions about his friends, or upon certain propositions that his friends have assured him are true, even though he does not know these propositions to be true. One of the duties of the Christian, for example, is said to be that of faith—where faith is a matter of trust, a matter of relying upon the several tenets that make up the doctrine of Christianity. The virtue of having faith is thought by some Christians to be in the very fact that the tenets of the faith are propositions which are *not* known to be true and which, indeed, are extremely unreasonable.[9] If it is the duty of the Christian to have faith, and if the tenets of that faith happen to be true, then, according to the proposed definition of knowledge, it will follow from these facts alone that the Christian *knows* these tenets to be true.

It is not enough, then, to define "*S* knows that *h* is true" by reference merely to the right not to take precautions against the possibility that *h* is false. For *S* may know that *h* is true and yet not have this right; or he may have the right (for he may have the duty, and if he has the duty he has the right) and yet not know that *h* is true.

By introducing proper qualifications, we would conceivably formulate an ethical definition of "know" that would not be subject to such difficulties. But no one has yet been able to formulate satisfactorily just what the qualifications are that are needed. At the present time, then, we do not have an ethical definition that will constitute a solution to the problem of the *Theaetetus*.[10]

"PERFORMATIVE UTTERANCES"

It may well be asked, at this point, whether our problem has not been misconceived—whether what we take to be a problem may not actually rest upon a false presupposition. We have been supposing all along that there is something *x* such that, when *x* is added to true opinion, the result is knowledge, and we have sought, so far in vain, for this something *x*. But is it necessary to make any such supposition in order to make the distinction between knowledge and true opinion?

There are those who believe that if we note certain ways in which people use the *word* "know," we will then be able to see that the supposition in question is mistaken. One source of this belief is an influential paper by J. L. Austin, in which he describes what he calls the "performative" function of "I know."[11]

The concept of a "performative" function may be illustrated by referring to the ordinary use of the expression "I promise." Usually, when a man utters the words "I promise," the point of his utterance is not to report anything; the man's concern is to make the promise, not to describe himself as making a promise. To utter the words "I promise," under ordinary conditions, is to promise. "I request" is similar. Thus, if a man uses the word "request" in the third person, saying "He requests," then he is describing or reporting what some other person is doing; or if he uses the word in the first person, but in the past tense, saying "I requested," then he is describing or reporting something that he himself was doing; but if he uses the word in the first person and in the present tense, saying "I request," then his point is not to report or describe himself as requesting—his point is to make a request. The same thing holds for such verbs as "order," "warn," "guarantee," and "baptize." (One indication of a performative use, Austin remarks, is the fact that "the little word 'hereby' actually occurs or might naturally be inserted"—as in "Trespassers are hereby warned that cars will be towed away at owner's expense.")

The expression "I know," Austin points out, performs a function very similar to that of "I promise." When a man utters the words "I promise" he provides a guarantee; he stakes his reputation and binds himself to others—and similarly, for saying "I know." Saying "I know," Austin writes, "is not saying 'I have performed a specially striking feat of cognition, superior, in the same scale as believing and being sure, even to being merely quite sure'; for there is nothing in that scale superior to being quite sure. Just as promising is not something superior, in the same scale as hoping and intending, even to merely fully intending: for there is nothing in that scale superior to fully intending. When I say 'I know,' I *give others my word. I give others my authority* for saying that '*S* is *P.*' "[12] And Austin concludes: "To suppose 'I know' is a descriptive phrase, is only one example of the *descriptive fallacy,* so common in philosophy."[13]

It is in the spirit of these observations also to note that where "I know" performs the function of giving assurance, "I believe" may perform that of taking it away. For to say "I believe," under certain circumstances, is tantamount to saying "Don't take my word for it—I won't be responsible." How, then, could "knowing" ever be thought to imply "believing"—if the function of the one is to give, and that of the other, to take away?

On the basis of such considerations, some philosophers have concluded that the problem of the *Theaetetus* is a pseudo-problem. It is said to be a pseudo-problem because it is thought to be based upon a false assumption, the assumption, namely, that there is a state which may be described or reported by means of the word "know." And it is by committing the "descriptive fallacy" that one is led to make this assumption.

But let us look more carefully at the concept of a "performative utterance."

Almost every utterance may be said to be performative in at least one respect, for almost every utterance is intended to have effects other than those of simply describing or reporting. What, then, is the peculiarity of the particular expressions that Austin calls "performative"? Austin did not provide a clear definition of the concept, but I think that "performative utterances" might be described as follows.

There are certain acts—e.g., requesting, ordering, guaranteeing, baptizing—which have this characteristic: When the circumstances are right, then to perform the act it is enough to make an utterance containing words which the speaker commonly uses to designate such an act. A standard way of making a request, among English-speaking people, is to make an utterance beginning with "I request" (the same thing holds for promising, ordering, guaranteeing, baptizing). Let us say, then, of anyone who performs an act in this way, that his utterance is a "performative utterance"—in what we may call the strict sense of this term.

An utterance beginning with "I want" is not performative in this strict sense, for it cannot be said to be an "act" of wanting. But "I want" is often used to accomplish what one might accomplish by means of the strict performative "I request." Let us say, then, that "I want" may be a "performative utterance" in an extended sense of the latter expression.

In which of these senses may an utterance of "I know" be said to be performative? Clearly, "I know" is not performative in what I have called the strict sense of the term, for knowing is not an "act" that can be performed by saying "I know." To say "I *promise* that p," at least under certain circumstances, *is* to promise that p; but to say "I know that p" is not itself to know that p. (One may say "I hereby promise," but not "I hereby know.") "I know" is related to "I guarantee" and "I give you my word" in the way in which "I want" is related to "I request." For "I know" is often used to accomplish what one may accomplish by the strict performative "I guarantee" or "I give you my word." Hence, "I know" may be performative in an extended sense of the term.

"I want" is not always a substitute for "I request." I may tell you what I want, and thus, describe my psychological state, even when I know there is no possibility of your helping me in getting what I want. And "I know" is not always a substitute for "I guarantee." I may tell you—confess or boast to you—that I know some of the things that you also know, and on an occasion when you neither need nor want my guarantee. ("I believe," similarly, is not always a substitute for "I can't provide you with any guarantees," for I may tell you what I believe on occasion when I *am* prepared to give you guarantees.)

What, then, of Austin's remark "To suppose 'I know' is a descriptive phrase, is only one example of the *descriptive fallacy,* so common in philosophy"? It looks very much as though Austin was assuming mistakenly that "I know" is performative in the strict sense and not merely in the extended sense. Yet, just as an utterance of "I want" may serve both to say something about me and to get you to do something, an utterance of "I know" may serve both to say something about me and to provide you with guarantees. To suppose that the performance of the nondescriptive function is inconsistent with a simultaneous performance of the descriptive function might be called, therefore, an example of the *performative fallacy.*

The expression "I know" is not to be taken lightly, and therefore, if we are philosophers, we may ask what the conditions are that entitle one to say it. Thus,

Austin says: "If you say you *know* something, the most immediate challenge takes the form of asking 'Are you in a position to know?'; that is, you must undertake to show, not merely that you are sure of it, but that it is *within your cognizance.*"[14]

If a man is entitled to say "I know that *h*," it may well be that he has performed no striking feat of cognition, but *h* does "fall within his cognizance." And if *h* does thus fall within his cognizance, then surely, whether or not he *says* "I know," he *does* know. ("He knows but he isn't saying.") Hence, it would seem there is a state, after all, that may be described or reported by means of the word "know."[15] It is by committing the "performative fallacy" that one is led to suppose that there is not.

OTHER EPISTEMIC TERMS

"Know" is one of a family of terms—we might call them terms of epistemic appraisal—which present us with essentially similar problems. We can throw some light upon "know" by noting its relations to other members of the same family.

Just as we may say of a man that he knows a certain hypothesis or proposition to be true, we may also say: a certain hypothesis is evident to him; it is reasonable of him to accept a certain hypothesis; one hypothesis is, for him, more reasonable than another; a certain hypothesis is for him gratuitous, or indifferent, or acceptable, or unacceptable.

If we say that a certain hypothesis or proposition is "unacceptable," where "unacceptable" is to be taken as a term of epistemic appraisal, we mean not that the proposition is incapable of being accepted, but rather, that epistemically it is unworthy of being accepted. The negation of any proposition that a man knows to be true, or of any proposition that is evident to him, could be said to be a proposition that is, for him, unacceptable. Hence, for most of us, "Chicago is not on Lake Michigan" would be unacceptable. Other propositions may be unacceptable even though their negations are not evident or not known to be true. For there are some propositions which are such that both they and their negations are unacceptable. These are the propositions which, in terms of the ancient skeptics, any reasonable man would *withhold*; he would neither believe them nor disbelieve them, neither affirm them nor deny them. Obvious examples of such propositions are those that generate paradox, e.g., Russell's "The class of all classes that are not members of themselves is a member of itself." According to the rigid ethics of belief advocated by W. K. Clifford, every proposition for which there is "insufficient evidence" is also unacceptable.[16] According to positivistic philosophers, some propositions that are unverifiable and all propositions that have a metaphysical subject matter may also be said to be unacceptable.

A "gratuitous" proposition may be described as one which there is no point in accepting. If we could say that an unacceptable proposition is one that ought not to be accepted, then we could say that a gratuitous proposition is one that need not be accepted. Hence, the charge of gratuitousness is less serious than that of unacceptability: Every unacceptable proposition is gratuitous, but some gratuitous propositions (unless Clifford is right) are not unacceptable. The astronomy of Copernicus, according to some, makes that of Ptolemy gratuitous, but it does not make it unacceptable. The Ptolemaic astronomy is not unacceptable, but since it is needlessly complex, it is gratuitous.

Sometimes propositions are said to be epistemically "indifferent," but we must distinguish two quite different uses of this term. (1) Will it rain in Baltimore a year from today? For most of us, the proposition is epistemically "indifferent" in that there is as much, or as little, reason for believing it as there is for disbelieving it. Any proposition that has a probability of .5 in relation to everything that is known could be said to be indifferent in this first sense of the term. (2) An act is said to be morally indifferent if performance of the act is permissible and if nonperformance is also permissible. It is sometimes said analogously that a proposition is epistemically indifferent if the proposition is acceptable and if its negation is also acceptable.

If a proposition is indifferent in the first of these two senses of the term, then it is not indifferent in the second. For if there is no ground for choosing between the proposition and its negation, then suspension of belief would seem to be the reasonable course, in which case neither the proposition nor its negation would be acceptable. It may well be, in fact, that no proposition is indifferent in the second sense of the term.

Some propositions are "beyond reasonable doubt." Or as we may also say, they are such that it is "reasonable" for a man to believe them. These include those propositions for which he has adequate evidence (in the sense of "adequate evidence" discussed earlier). For presumably, it is reasonable for a man to believe any proposition that is more probable than not in relation to the totality of what he knows. (This is the epistemic thesis that is sometimes expressed by saying "induction is justified."[17]) An important epistemological question concerns whether or not there are any other propositions which it is reasonable for a man to accept.

Some propositions are "evident" as well as reasonable. Any proposition that a man knows to be true is one that may be said to be evident for him. But it may be that some propositions that are evident for him are not propositions that he knows to be true. Thus, it has been held that whatever is logically entailed by what is evident, is itself evident. But some of the propositions that are logically entailed by what a man knows may be such that he does not know that they are entailed by what he knows, and they may even be propositions which he does not accept (he may know that all philosophers are men and yet refrain from believing that everything that is not a man is something that is not a philosopher). In this case, he will refrain from accepting or believing certain propositions which are evident for him; and an evident proposition that is not accepted cannot be said to be a proposition that is known. Again, any proposition that is both evident and false would be a proposition that is evident but not known; whether there are any such propositions is an extraordinarily difficult question to which we shall return.

Hence, there are important differences between saying that a certain proposition is "evident" for a man and saying that he has "adequate evidence" for that proposition. We may note three such differences: (1) A man may have adequate evidence for a proposition that is not evident to him. If he happens to know, for example, that there are 1,000 balls in the urn and that 999 of them are red, and if he knows further that one of them will be drawn at random, then he might be said to have adequate evidence for the proposition that the ball to be drawn will be red; but before the ball is drawn it will not be evident for him that it is red. (2) The "logic" of the concept of the evident differs from that of the concept of adequate evidence. Thus, if the balls in the urn are to be taken out one at a time, and none of them returned, perhaps we may say that the man now has adequate evidence, with respect to *each* particular drawing, that the ball drawn on that particular occasion will be red, but he does not have adequate evidence for the proposition that, on every occasion, the ball that is drawn will be red. But if, somehow, it were *evident* for him, with respect to *each* occasion, that on that occasion a red ball would be drawn, then it would also be evident for him that on *every* occasion a red ball would be drawn. (3) There may be propositions that are evident for a man, but which are such that he cannot properly be said to *have* adequate evidence for them. For if we follow ordinary usage, we will say of such propositions as "I seem to remember having been in this place before," that they are propositions which may *be* evident for a man at a given time, but not that they are propositions for which he *has* evidence at that time. Thus, if I *have* evidence for a given proposition, then I will be able to cite certain *other* propositions as being my evidence for that proposition; but even though it is evident for me that I seem to remember having been in this place before, there are no other propositions I could cite as being my *evidence* for the proposition that I seem to remember having been in this place before.[18]

SOME DEFINITIONS

If "know" and the other epistemic terms we have been discussing can all be defined in terms of one epistemic term or locution, then perhaps it can be said that we have provided a partial solution to Plato's problem.

Let us remind ourselves, first, that we may take one of three different attitudes toward any given proposition: we may believe or accept the proposition; we may disbelieve or reject the proposition (and this is the same as believing or accepting the negation of the proposition); or we may "withhold" the proposition—that is, we may refrain from believing it and we may also refrain from disbelieving it. And secondly, let us remind ourselves that for any proposition and any person, some of these attitudes will be *more reasonable,* at any given time, than others. Thus, St. Augustine suggested that even though there might be ground to question the reliability of the senses, it would be more reasonable for most of us most of the time to believe that we could rely upon them than to believe that we could not. Presumably, for most of us at the present time, it is more reasonable to withhold the proposition that there is life on Venus than it is to accept it; but it is more reasonable to accept the proposition that there is life on Venus than it is to accept the proposition that there is life on Mercury. What is suggested when we say of one of these attitudes that it is more reasonable than another, is this: If the person in question were a rational being, if his concerns were purely intellectual, and if he were to choose between the two attitudes, then he would choose the more reasonable in preference to the less reasonable.[19]

By reference to this concept of one epistemic attitude being more reasonable than another for a given subject at a given time, we can define and systematize our various epistemic concepts. A proposition is *reasonable* or "beyond reasonable doubt," if believing it is more reasonable than withholding it; it is *gratuitous* if believing it is not more reasonable than withholding it; it is *unacceptable* if withholding it is more reasonable than believing it; and it is *acceptable* if withholding it is not more reasonable than believing it.[20] And a proposition *h* may be said to be evident for a subject *S* provided (1) that *h* is reasonable for *S* and (2) that there is no proposition *i* such that it is more reasonable for *S* to believe *i* than it is for him to believe *h*. We thus have a hierarchy of epistemic terms: Every proposition that is evident is reasonable, but not conversely; and every proposition that is reasonable is acceptable, but not conversely.[21]

Having defined the evident, we may now return to the problem of the *Theaetetus* and to the definition with which we began.

S knows at *t* that *h* is true, provided: (1) *S* believes *h* at *t*; (2) *h* is true; and (3) *h* is evident at *t* or *S*.[22]

We thus have a partial solution to the problem. We have defined "know" in terms of "evident." And we have defined "evident" in terms of "more reasonable." The definition of "evident" is not completely empty, for we have seen that "more reasonable" is also adequate for the definition of other basic terms of epistemic appraisal. Our definition, therefore, enables us to see the ways in which these various concepts are related. We may leave unanswered the important question of whether it is possible to define "more reasonable" in strictly ethical terms.

What propositions, then, can be said to be evident?

NOTES

1. The term "proposition" is a convenient abbreviatory device which we will use throughout. . . .

2. The following definition would achieve the same end without referring to "the conjunction of all those propositions that S knows to be true." A proposition h is probable in the absolute sense for S provided: there is a conjunction e of propositions that S knows to be true; h is probable in relation to e; and there is no proposition i such that both (1) S knows i to be true and (2) h is not probable in relation to the conjunction of e and i.

3. The distinction between the inductive and statistical senses of "probable" is clearly drawn by Rudolf Carnap in The Logical Foundations of Probability (Chicago: University of Chicago Press, 1950). The expression "absolute probability," interpreted somewhat as here, was used by Bernard Bolzano in his Wissenschaftslehre, III (Leipzig: Felix Meiner, 1930: 267—68; this work was first published in 1837. Still another sense of "probable" is distinguished in note 17 of this chapter.

4. Thus, some moral philosophers have attempted to define "duty" in terms of "know"—e.g., in terms of what an "ideal observer" would approve if only he knew all of the relevant facts. See Francis Hutcheson, An Essay on the Nature and Conduct of the Passions, with Illustrations upon the Moral Sense (1728); see also Roderick Firth, "Ethical Absolutism and the Ideal Observer," Philosophy and Phenomenological Research 12 (1952): 317–45. This way of defining "duty," however, involves difficulties analogous to those encountered in trying to define "know." If the characteristics that would make an observer "ideal" include certain moral qualifications, then an "ideal-observer" definition of "duty" may become circular; and if they do not, then it may be impossible to determine what such an observer would approve, in which case the definition would be inapplicable.

5. Descartes assumed that beliefs are acts which are within our power, and Spinoza, that they are not. This general problem is discussed in: C. S. Peirce, Collected Papers, Charles Hartshorne and Paul Weiss, eds. (Cambridge: Harvard University Press, 1931): 331—34; H. H. Price, "Belief and Will," Aristotelian Society Supplementary Volume XXVIII (1954): 1–26; C. I. Lewis, The Ground and Nature of the Right, "Right Believing and Right Concluding" (New York: Columbia University Press, 1955), chap. 2; and Stuart Hampshire, Thought and Action (New York: The Viking Press, Inc., 1959), chap. 2.

6. See Roderick Firth, "Chisholm and the Ethics of Belief," Philosophical Review 68 (1959): 493–506.

7. See D. J. Mercier, Critériologie générale, ou Théorie générale de la certitude, 8th ed. (Paris: Felix Alcan, 1923), pp. 420—21; P. Coffey, Epistemology, or the Theory of Knowledge, I (London: Longmans, Green & Company, Ltd., 1917): 54–55.

8. The Problem of Knowledge (New York: St. Martin's Press, Inc., 1955), pp. 31–35.

9. Cf. the following passage from Kierkegaard's Concluding Unscientific Postscript: "Suppose a man who wishes to acquire faith; let the comedy begin. He wishes to have faith, but he wishes also to safeguard himself by means of an objective inquiry and its approximation process. What happens? With the help of the approximation process the absurd becomes something different: it becomes probable, it becomes increasingly probable, it becomes extremely and emphatically probable. Now he is ready to believe it, and he ventures to claim for himself that he does not believe as shoemakers and tailors and simple folk believe, but only after long deliberation. Now he is ready to believe it [i.e., to accept it on faith]; and lo, now it has become precisely impossible to believe it. Anything that is almost probable, is something he can almost know, or as good as know, or extremely and emphatically almost know—but it is impossible to believe. For the absurd is the object of faith, and the only object that can be believed." From A Kierkegaard Anthology, Robert Bretall, ed. (Princeton: Princeton University Press, 1947), pp. 220–21.

10. Still other difficulties are noted by Herbert Heidelberger in "On Defining Epistemic Expressions," Journal of Philosophy 60 (1963): 344–48.

11. "Other Minds," *Proceedings of the Aristotelian Society,* Supplementary Volume XX (1946); reprinted in Austin's *Philosophical Papers,* J. O. Urmson and G. J. Warnock, eds. (New York: Oxford University Press, 1961), pp. 44–84.

12. *Philosophical Papers,* p. 67. Cf. C. S. Peirce, *Collected Papers,* V (1932): 383–87.

13. Ibid., p. 71.

14. *Philosophical Papers,* p. 68. I have italicized the final three words.

15. J. O. Urmson proposed an account of the use of "I know" similar to Austin's and then attempted to extend the account to second and third persons and to other tenses in the following way: To say, for example, that Mr. Jones *knew* some proposition to be true is to say that Mr. Jones was "in a position in which he was entitled to say 'I know.' " And what is it to be "in a position in which one is entitled to say 'I know' "? According to Urmson, it is to be in the position of having "all the *evidence* one could need"— which brings us back to the point at which we began our discussion of Plato's problem. See "Parenthetical Verbs," in *Essays in Conceptual Analysis,* A. G. N. Flew, ed. (New York: St. Martin's Press, Inc., 1956), p. 199; the italics are mine.

16. See "The Ethics of Belief," in *Lectures and Essays,* II (London: Macmillan & Co., Ltd., 1879): 163–205.

17. We have been using *"h is probable for S,"* in its *absolute* sense, to mean that *h* is inductively supported by (is more probable than not in relation to) what is known by *S.* But sometimes the expression is used *epistemically* to mean merely that *h* is a proposition which is reasonable for *S* to accept. This ambiguity seems to have misled some philosophers into supposing that they can easily demonstrate the justifiability of induction. Taking "probable" in its epistemic sense, they note that a probable proposition is one that is reasonable; then, taking "probable" in its *absolute* sense, they note that a probable proposition is one that is inductively supported by what is known; and finally, by committing the fallacy of equivocation, they deduce that if a proposition is inductively supported by what is known, then it is one that is reasonable to accept.

18. For further discussion of some of these points, cf. Herbert Heidelberger, "Knowledge, Certainty, and Probability," *Inquiry* 6 (1963): 242–50.

19. The following observation by William James reminds us that such a person—a rational being whose concerns are purely intellectual—would not be motivated merely by the desire to play it safe. "There are two ways of looking at our duty in the matter of opinion,—ways entirely different, and yet ways about whose difference the theory of knowledge seems hitherto to have shown very little concern. We must *know the truth*: and *we must avoid error,*—these are our first and great commandments as would-be knowers; but they are not two ways of stating an identical commandment, they are two separable laws. . . . By choosing between them we may end by coloring differently our whole intellectual life. . . . For my part, I can believe that worse things than being duped may happen to a man." From *The Will to Believe and Other Essays in Popular Philosophy* (New York: David McKay Co. Inc., 1911), pp. 17–19.

20. Of the two senses of "indifferent" distinguished above, a proposition could be said to be *indifferent,* in the first sense, if believing it is not more reasonable than disbelieving it and if disbelieving it is not more reasonable than believing it. It would be indifferent, in the second sense, if both it and its negation were acceptable; but as we have noted, there is ground for questioning whether any proposition is indifferent in this second sense.

21. An "epistemic logic," exhibiting the logical relations among these concepts, could be developed on the basis of these three assumptions: (1) If one attitude is more reasonable than another and the other more reasonable than a third, then the first is more reasonable than the third. (2) If one attitude is more reasonable than another, then the other is not more reasonable than it. (3) If withholding a given proposition is not more reasonable than believing it, then believing it is more reasonable then disbelieving it (e.g., if agnosticism is not more reasonable than theism, then theism is more reasonable than atheism).

22. If we countenance the possibility that some propositions are both evident and false, we must add

a qualification to the definition in order to remove a difficulty pointed out by Edmund L. Gettier in "Is Justified True Belief Knowledge?" *Analysis* 25 (1963): 121–23. Suppose "I see a sheep in the field" is a false proposition *i* that is evident for *S* (he mistakes a dog for a sheep); then "A sheep is in the field" (*h*) will also be evident for *S*. Suppose further that there happens to be a sheep in the field that *S* does not see. This situation, obviously, would not warrant our saying *S knows* that there is a sheep in the field; yet it satisfies the conditions of our definition, for *S* believes *h*, *h* is true, and *h* is evident for *S*. To rule out this type of situation, it would be necessary to add a qualification to our definition of "know."

Let us say that a proposition *e* "justifies" a proposition *h* provided *e* and *h* are such that, for any subject and any time, if *e* is evident to that subject at that time then *h* is evident to that subject at that time; and let us say that a "basic proposition" is an evident proposition such that the only evident propositions that thus justify it are propositions that entail it. To meet the difficulty, we might consider adding the following clause which would make our definition of "know" recursive:

"Either (1) *h* is a basic proposition for *S* at *t*, or (2) *h* is entailed by a set of propositions that are known by *S* at *t*, or (3) a proposition that is known by *S* at *t* and that does not justify any false proposition justifies *h*."

. . . If it is necessary to add such a fourth clause to our definition of "know," then *knowing that one knows*, i.e., being certain, is considerably more difficult than merely knowing. For discussion of this latter question, see Jaakko Hintikka, *Knowledge and Belief* (Ithaca: Cornell University Press, 1962), chap. 5, and Roderick M. Chisholm, "The Logic of Knowing," *Journal of Philosophy* 60 (1963): 775–95.

2

Is Justified True Belief Knowledge?

Edmund L. Gettier

Various attempts have been made in recent years to state necessary and sufficient conditions for someone's knowing a given proposition. The attempts have often been such that they can be stated in a form similar to the following:[1]

(a) *S* knows that *P*   *IFF*   (i) *P* is true,
                                       (ii) *S* believes that *P*, and
                                       (iii) *S* is justified in believing that *P*.

For example, Chisholm has held that the following gives the necessary and sufficient conditions for knowledge:[2]

(b) *S* knows that *P*   *IFF*   (i) *S* accepts *P*,
                                       (ii) *S* has adequate evidence for *P*, and
                                       (iii) *P* is true.

Ayer has stated the necessary and sufficient conditions for knowledge as follows:[3]

(c) *S* knows that *P*   *IFF*   (i) *P* is true,
                                       (ii) *S* is sure that *P* is true, and
                                       (iii) *S* has the right to be sure that P is true.

From *Analysis* 23, no. 6 (June 1963): 121–23, © Edmund L. Gettier. Reprinted by permission of the author.

I shall argue that (a) is false in that the conditions stated therein do not constitute a *sufficient* condition for the truth of the proposition that S knows that P. The same argument will show that (b) and (c) fail if "has adequate evidence for" or "has the right to be sure that" is substituted for "is justified in believing that" throughout.

I shall begin by noting two points. First, in the sense of "justified" in which S's being justified in believing P is a necessary condition of S's knowing that P, it is possible for a person to be justified in believing a proposition that is in fact false. Secondly, for any proposition P, if S is justified in believing P, and P entails Q, and S deduces Q from P and accepts Q as a result of this deduction, then S is justified in believing Q. Keeping these two points in mind, I shall now present two cases in which the conditions stated in (a) are true for some proposition, though it is at the same time false that the person in question knows that proposition.

CASE I:

Suppose that Smith and Jones have applied for a certain job. And suppose that Smith has strong evidence for the following conjunctive proposition:

(d) Jones is the man who will get the job, and Jones has ten coins in his pocket.

Smith's evidence for (d) might be that the president of the company assured him that Jones would in the end be selected, and that he, Smith, had counted the coins in Jones's pocket ten minutes ago. Proposition (d) entails:

(e) The man who will get the job has ten coins in his pocket.

Let us suppose that Smith sees the entailment from (d) to (e), and accepts (e) on the grounds of (d), for which he has strong evidence. In this case, Smith is clearly justified in believing that (e) is true.

But imagine, further, that unknown to Smith, he himself, not Jones, will get the job. And, also, unknown to Smith, he himself has ten coins in his pocket. Proposition (e) is then true, though proposition (d), from which Smith inferred (e), is false. In our example, then, all of the following are true: (*i*) (e) is true, (*ii*) Smith believes that (e) is true, and (*iii*) Smith is justified in believing that (e) is true. But it is equally clear that Smith does not *know* that (e) is true; for (e) is true in virtue of the number of coins in Smith's pocket, while Smith does not know how many coins are in Smith's pocket, and bases his belief in (e) on a count of the coins in Jones's pocket, whom he falsely believes to be the man who will get the job.

CASE II:

Let us suppose that Smith has strong evidence for the following proposition:

(f) Jones owns a Ford.

Smith's evidence might be that Jones has at all times in the past within Smith's memory owned a car, and always a Ford, and that Jones has just offered Smith a ride while driving a Ford. Let us imagine, now, that Smith has another friend, Brown, of whose whereabouts he is totally ignorant. Smith selects three place-names quite at random. and constructs the following three propositions:

(g) Either Jones owns a Ford, or Brown is in Boston;
(h) Either Jones owns a Ford, or Brown is in Barcelona;
(i) Either Jones owns a Ford, or Brown is in Brest-Litovsk.

Each of these propositions is entailed by (f). Imagine that Smith realizes the entailment of each of these propositions he has constructed by (f), and proceeds to accept (g), (h), and (i) on the basis of (f). Smith has correctly inferred (g), (h), and (i) from a proposition for which he has strong evidence. Smith is therefore completely justified in believing each of these three propositions. Smith, of course, has no idea where Brown is.

But imagine now that two further conditions hold. First, Jones does not own a Ford, but is at present driving a rented car. And secondly, by the sheerest coincidence, and entirely unknown to Smith, the place mentioned in proposition (h) happens really to be the place where Brown is. If these two conditions hold then Smith does *not* know that (h) is true, even though (*i*) (h) is true, (*ii*) Smith does believe that (h) is true, and (*iii*) Smith is justified in believing that (h) is true.

These two examples show that definition (a) does not state a *sufficient* condition for someone's knowing a given proposition. The same cases, with appropriate changes, will suffice to show that neither definition (b) nor definition (c) do so either.

NOTES

    1. Plato seems to be considering some such definition at *Theaetetus* 201, and perhaps accepting one at *Meno* 98.
    2. Roderick M. Chisholm, *Perceiving: A Philosophical Study* (Ithaca, N.Y.: Cornell University Press, 1957), p. 16.
    3. A. J. Ayer, *The Problem of Knowledge* (London: Macmillan, 1956), p. 34.

3

Knowledge and Grounds:
A Comment on Mr. Gettier's Paper

Michael Clark

In his paper "Is Justified True Belief Knowledge?"[1] Mr. Gettier provides two counterexamples which show that it need not be. In each case a proposition which is in fact true is believed on grounds which are in fact false. Since the grounding proposition in each case entails the proposition it justifies (the conclusion), and the grounding proposition, although false, is justifiably believed, the conclusion is also justifiably believed.

Gettier's examples are stronger than they need have been to prove his point. Grounds need not of course entail their conclusions in order to be good grounds. Cases can be devised in which true justified belief fails to be knowledge because a *nondeductive* ground is false. To adapt Gettier's second case, take the proposition

(1) Jones owns a Ford.

Smith believes this because his friend Brown, whom he knows to be reliable and honest, has told him that Jones always has owned one, etc. Now as it happens, Brown, despite his general reliability, has made an unusual slip: he has mixed Jones up with someone else. Jones never did have a Ford. However, he just happens to have bought one. So Smith truly believes that he owns one, but he cannot be said to know this since he believes it on false grounds. He is nonetheless justified both in accepting the grounds and in accepting Jones's past ownership, etc., as grounds for the (nondeductive) inference to present ownership.

It is not enough, however, to add the truth of the grounds to a version of the de-

---

From *Analysis* 24, no. 2 (December 1963): 46–48, © Michael Clark. Reprinted by permission of the author.

finitions Gettier criticizes as a further necessary condition of knowing a proposition. The following definition of knowledge still fails to give conditions which are jointly sufficient:

S knows that p *IFF*   (i) p is true,
   (ii) S believes that p,
   (iii) S is justified in believing that p, and
   (iv) it is on true grounds that S believes that p.

For consider this further adaptation of the example. It is true that Jones always owned a Ford and he still does. Brown, who is known by Smith to be generally reliable and honest, tells Smith that Jones has always owned one. But, in fact, Brown knows nothing about Jones or his Ford; he has just invented what he tells Smith (an act quite out of character), and he happens by chance to be right. Now Smith's belief is not only true and justified, but the grounds on which he holds his belief are true. Yet Brown's wild guess can hardly be regarded as providing Smith with knowledge merely because it happens to be right. In this case, then, the grounds on which Smith believes (1) are true, but the grounds on which he accepts these grounds, viz., that Brown knows them, are false; but Brown's general reliability and honesty justify his believing it to be true.

Very often we can go on for quite a long time asking why, asking for the grounds for the grounds, for the grounds for these second-order grounds, and so on, but eventually the question will become logically odd. For example,

(2) "What are your grounds for saying Jones owns a Ford?"
(3) "Brown told me he always has owned one."
(4) "What are your grounds for claiming Brown knows this?"
(5) "He is generally reliable and honest."
(6) "What are your grounds for saying Brown is reliable and honest?"
(7) "I am nearly always with him and I seem to remember no unreliable or dishonest act on his part."

It would clearly be out of order to ask for Smith's grounds for saying he seems to remember. (We might question the reliability of his memory. In this example I assume that we may take his memory to be reliable so that I may avoid having too long a chain of reasons.) If any ground in this chain, that is, either (3) or (5) or (7), is false, we may properly deny that Smith *knows* that Jones owns a Ford. If each ground in this chain is true, then I will say that the belief is "fully grounded." We may now modify the definition under consideration by changing (iv), so that it reads:

(iv)′ S's belief that p is fully grounded,

in which form (i)–(iv)' jointly will give the necessary and sufficient conditions for knowing that *p*.

It might be thought that the addition of (iv)' would enable us to drop (iii). For surely, if *p* is fully grounded in the sense specified, then *S* is justified in believing that *p*. Yet he might believe all the grounds, and they night be good grounds without his seeing that they were *good* grounds; he might be sure of what he believed but not appreciate how the evidence he had for it really justified his belief.[2] In such a case we might want to deny that S was fully justified in his belief, and, if so, we need to retain (iii).

I think that the revised definition illuminates the issue as to whether so-called incorrigible knowledge is to be counted as knowledge at all. If I can't (logically) be wrong, for example, as to whether I am in pain, then, it is claimed, it is not properly a question of knowledge. For knowing entails having found out, and finding out is something which I may fail to do. If I say I am in pain and you ask me how I found out, you have asked an obviously silly question. Now it might be thought that this argument could be met by denying that knowing entails having found out: might I not be born having certain concepts and knowing certain truths? But the need for condition (iv)' in any definition of knowledge shows that where the question "How did you find out?" is inappropriate the term "know" is also inappropriate. For it is usually just as odd to ask, "On what grounds do you say you are in pain?" Where one knows in virtue of having grounds, it seems plausible to say that it is a case of finding out. To talk of knowledge in the cases in question precludes a unitary definition of knowing, for we should have to say that condition (iv)' was inapplicable in these cases.

In particular, the question "If I know that *p*, does it follow that I know that I know that *p*?" is seen to be odd (unless it is a question about my having the concept of knowing). For, among other things, it asks whether my belief that I know that *p* is fully grounded. And, among other things, *this* question asks whether the belief's being fully grounded is itself fully grounded, that is, whether the grounds for saying that the complete chain of grounds for *p* do actually constitute grounds for *p*, are true. Thus, if *p* is "He is running away" and my grounds for believing that *p* are that I am watching him (in this case the chain has only one link), the question is "Why is your watching him a ground for saying what he is doing?" Now this question is very odd; special circumstances might be devised for giving it point, but generally there is no question as to the grounds for this being a good ground which is not silly or of a special, philosophical nature.

NOTES

1. *Analysis* 23, no. 6 (June 1963).
2. Cf. Cohen, "Claims to Knowledge," *Proceedings of the Aristotelian Society, Supplementary Volume* (1962): 35ff.

4

Mr. Clark's Definition of 'Knowledge'

John Turk Saunders and Narayan Champawat

In "Knowledge and Grounds: A Comment on Mr. Gettier's Paper,"[1] Michael Clark claims that

    (i) p is true,
    (ii) S believes that p,
    (iii) S is justified in believing that p, and
    (iv)' S's belief that p is fully grounded

"Jointly will give the necessary and sufficient conditions for knowing that p." He seems to mean by (iv)' that each link in the chain consisting of S's grounds (g_1) for p, S's grounds (g_2) for g_1, etc. is true. Mr. Clark advances this definition of "'knowledge' as the result of his consideration of counterexamples which reveal the inadequacy of the rather traditional definition of 'knowledge' consisting in (i)–(iii). We wish in turn, however, to provide counterexamples to Mr. Clark's definition, using the first (A) to show that Clark's definition is too weak, and the second (B) to show that it is too strong.

A. Suppose that Smith believes

(p) Jones owns a Ford

because his friend Brown, whom he knows to be generally reliable and honest, yesterday told Smith that Jones had always owned a Ford. Brown's information was correct, but

From *Analysis* 25, no. 1 (October 1964): 8–9, © John Turk Saunders and Narayan Champawat. Reprinted by permission of the authors.

today Jones sells his Ford and replaces it with a Volkswagen. An hour later Jones is pleased to find that he is the proud owner of two cars: he has been lucky enough to win a Ford in a raffle. Smith's belief in p is not only justified and true, but it is fully grounded, e.g., we suppose that each link in the following chain of Smith's grounds is true:

(g_1) Up to yesterday, Jones had always owned a Ford.

(g_2) Brown told Smith (g_1) and Brown knows (g_1).

(g_3) Smith ostensibly remembers Brown's telling him, and Brown is generally reliable and honest.

(g_4) Smith is nearly always with Brown and Smith seems to remember no unreliable or dishonest act on his part.

Clearly our example satisfies (i)—(iv)'. Clearly, too, it is not a case of knowledge, for Smith's belief in p just happens to be right owing to a lucky coincidence.

B. Suppose a scientist, Smith, believes

(p) All mixtures of X and Y explode   *Natunecessarily*

because he believes that he has obtained this result 10,000 times. In fact, he has achieved this result on 9,999 times, for in one of the experiments in which Smith thought he was mixing X and Y he was really mixing Z and Y, although even then there was an explosion. We further suppose that p is true and that Smith has performed his work in accordance with rigorous scientific standards. Here, then, it is easy to see that Smith may very well know that p, even though his belief is not fully grounded: it is not fully grounded because his grounds (g_1) for p include the false statement that in all 10,000 experiments X was mixed with Y and an explosion resulted.

Our first counterexample (A) proves that Clark's definition of 'knowledge' is too weak, and our second (B) that it is too strong. We conclude that Clark's definition of 'knowledge' must be rejected as it stands. Rather than offer a surrogate, we would suggest that it is a mistake to believe that there is some essence of knowledge, some set of conditions which are individually necessary and jointly sufficient for knowledge. It is our opinion that the instances of knowledge share at most a family resemblance. Although the search for the essence of knowledge is misguided, since there is no essence, it is surely of value: the dialectic of would-be definition and counterexample enlightens us as it reveals the multifarious nature of knowledge.

NOTE

1. *Analysis* 24, no. 2 (December 1963).

5

Truth and Evidence

Robert Almeder

An alarming number of philosophers think that because the truth condition for knowledge is logically distinct from the evidence condition, the satisfaction of the latter does not entail the satisfaction of the former. Alternatively put, there is a pervasive tendency among philosophers to hold that the evidence a person has can be sufficient for knowledge without thereby entailing the truth of what he professes to know. And it is a view which is implied by every claim to the effect that a person may fail to know what he claims to know because, even though his evidence may be sufficient for knowledge, it is possible that what he claims to know may be false. What is alarming about this view is that it is obviously wrong (which I shall show), and that failure to detect the error has infected well over a decade of intense speculation on the nature of knowledge. Indeed, beginning at least as far back as Gettier's important paper, "Is Justified True Belief Knowledge?"[1] *every* counterexample to the classical definition of knowledge and *every* attempt either to repair the definition (because of the usual counterexamples), or to reject outright the possibility of successfully defining the concept, has rested essentially on the untested assumption that evidence sufficient for knowledge does not entail truth. Proving this assumption false will, I hope, have the effect of redirecting epistemological reflections along more fruitful fines. But let us first show that the assumption is essential to every analysis of knowledge which begins by accepting such counterexamples.

From *The Philosophical Quarterly 24* (October 1974): 365–68. Reprinted by permission of Blackwell Publishers. For a fuller discussion of these and other arguments against Gettier-type counterarguments see Almeder's *Blind Realism: An Essay on Human Knowledge and Natural Science* (Rowman and Littlefield, 1991).

I

There are two kinds of alleged counterexamples to the traditional definition of knowledge. The first kind, initially proposed by Gettier, is as follows: assume that Smith is completely justified in believing the proposition *p* and that the proposition *q* is a logical consequence of the proposition *p*. Seeing that *p* entails *q*, Smith infers that *q* must also be true. Suppose, however, that (unknown to Smith) even though Smith is completely justified in believing that *p*, *p* is false and *q* is true. It would then follow that (i) *q* is true, (ii) Smith believes that *q*, and (iii) Smith is completely justified in believing that *q*.[2] But of course Smith does not know that *q* because, even though he is completely (sufficiently, adequately) justified in believing that *q*, his justification is in some sense defective. In counterexamples of this sort, it is obviously assumed that a person can be completely (sufficiently, adequately) justified in believing a false proposition. In this case it is assumed that Smith is completely justified in believing that *p* although *p* is false. And the counterexamples would not work if Smith's being completely justified in believing that *p* entailed the truth of *p*.

Nor could it be thought that Smith would have known that *q* if only his justification had not involved an inference through the false proposition *p*. That the classical definition of knowledge cannot be saved by our insisting that one's justification must involve only true statements is the line of the second well-known type of counterexample. Consider for example the case recently proposed by M. Swain:

> Suppose that Smith has wired up a detonator box to a charge of TNT and is about to flip the switch. He has checked the wiring carefully, and he knows that the TNT is brand X and the batteries are brand Y. He has used those products many times and they have in the past always worked. On the basis of this and only this evidence he "concludes" (inductively) that the TNT will explode when he flips the switch. When he flips the switch the TNT does explode. However, it explodes because a hunter coincidentally fires a high-powered shell into the charge at the moment the switch is flipped. Had the hunter not done so the charge would not have exploded because in fact the battery in the detonator did not have enough power to cause the explosion. Hence Smith's justification is defective. But, we may suppose, his reasoning did not involve any false premises. Smith *might* have reasoned that the battery was powerful enough and hence the TNT would explode. But he did not reason in that way, and his justification is still sufficiently good to render it evident for him that the TNT would explode. Even so, from the point of view of knowledge his justification is defective.[3]

Here again, this kind of counterexample (like the preceding) cannot achieve its effect without our assuming that Smith can be completely justified in believing what is false, namely, that the battery is powerful enough to cause the TNT to explode. What is important in all this is not that these counterexamples are thought to be different in kind, but rather that every counterexample to the classical definition of knowledge is an instance of one of these two types; and that, in every case, the counterexamples purchase their desired effects only because we can suppose a person completely justified in believing what is false.

Accepting the force of these counterexamples, most philosophers have generally concluded that, in addition to being completely justified in believing what is in fact true, a person's justification must be *non-defective* in order for him to know what he claims to know. For this reason the bulk of recent analyses of knowledge begin by accepting such counterexamples and then seek to characterize the concept of a *non-defective* justification as a further condition of knowledge.[4] And where this is not the case, there has been a strong inclination to believe that what the counterexamples really demonstrate is not that we need to characterize the concept of a *non-defective* justification, but rather that wholesale skepticism is in order.[5] At any rate, it seems clear that every analysis of knowledge which begins by accepting the usual counterexamples to the classical definition of knowledge is a valid analysis only if it is true that a person can be completely (adequately, sufficiently) justified in believing what is false. And this assumption is wrong for no less than two reasons.

II

In the first place, if the satisfaction of the evidence condition does not entail the satisfaction of the truth condition, then how could the truth condition be satisfied at all? In other words, if after determining that a person's evidence is adequate for knowledge, there remains the separate task of determining the truth of what the person professes to know, by what possible means could this be achieved? Barring divine illumination, if the satisfaction of the evidence condition does not entail the satisfaction of the truth condition, then the satisfaction of the truth condition could rest only upon some direct or mystical insight wherein one simply "sees" (quite independently of the evidence provided) that the knowledge claim is true or false. But surely this must be wrong; for if the ascertainment of truth were to rest ultimately and only upon some direct intuitive or mystical insight, then, for obvious reasons, there could be no satisfactory way to adjudicate epistemological differences over the truth of statements when there is some doubt about whether or not a person knows what he claims to know. Accordingly, if we are to avoid such mysticism (a patently desirable feature for any epistemology), we are driven in the end to the view that if one's evidence is deemed sufficient for knowledge, then what one professes to know must be true.

Secondly, and more importantly, to suppose that a person's evidence can be sufficient for knowledge without thereby entailing the truth of what he claims to know involves a flagrant disregard of our usage. In the typical case, doubts about the legitimacy of knowledge claims move immediately and directly to questions about the adequacy of the evidence offered in support of the claims. And it is generally granted by native speakers that if a person's evidence is judged adequate for knowledge, then *ipso facto* what he claims to know is true. For example, if a person claims to know that *p* and there is some doubt about whether he knows what he claims to know, we do not in the first instance ask whether what he professes to know is true. Rather we ask for his evidence ("How do you know?"); and if his evidence is judged adequate, we never say "Well, your evidence is adequate but is there any reason to think that what you claim to know is true?" or "I grant you that your evidence is conclusive, but now is what you claim to know true?" We do not, and cannot, say this sort of thing because (as noted above) there really is no adequate way to answer such a question if it is not to be answered in terms of the adequacy of one's evidence. Moreover, if we were to say such things, the person making the knowledge claim would be at a loss to say anything other than "If the truth of my claim does not follow from the fact that my evidence is sufficient for knowledge, how else is one to ascertain the truth of *any* knowledge claim?" or "But I just showed you by the acknowledged sufficiency of my evidence that what I claim to know is true. What else could be the purpose behind seeking my evidence if it is not to certify the truth of my claim?" And what could we say to this? Certainly we could not say that the point of seeking his evidence is not to ascertain the truth of what he claims to know, but rather simply to determine whether his belief that *p* is true is based on sufficient evidence. For this reply brings us back again to the problem of ascertaining (independently of the evidence offered) the truth of what he is sufficiently justified in believing.

These reflections also indicate that, as a matter of fact, in the practice of assessing knowledge claims the truth condition is superfluous—although it is certainly not *logically* superfluous for any analysis of knowledge.[6] To suggest anything to the contrary, would, I am arguing, commit us to what can at best be called a free-floating truth condition—meaning thereby a condition which, for all its necessity, could not, by any conceivable means short of some mystical intuition, admit of satisfaction at all. Moreover, there is nothing about our usage which would constrain us to such a view. Indeed, our usage supports precisely the view I have taken.

NOTES

1. *Analysis* 23 (1963).
2. Ibid., p. 316.
3. M. Swain, "An Alternative Analysis of Knowing," *Synthese* 24 (1972): 420–30. For another instance of this type, see K. Lehrer, "A Fourth Condition of Knowledge: A Defense," *The Review of Metaphysics* 20 (1970): 125–27.
4. Examples of such analyses are: Peter Klein, "A Proposed Definition of Propositional Knowledge,"

The Journal of Philosophy 68 (1971); Marshall Swain, "Knowledge, Causality, and Justification," *The Journal of Philosophy* 69 (1972), and "An Alternative Analysis of Knowledge," *Synthese* 23 (1972); R. Hilpinon, "Knowledge and Justification," *Ajatus* 33 (1971); Ernest Sosa, "An Analysis of 'Knowledge that *p*,'" *Analysis* 25 (1964), "Propositional Knowledge," *Philosophical Studies* 20 (1969), and "Two Conceptions of Knowledge," *The Journal of Philosophy* 67 (1970); Keith Lehrer, "Knowledge, Truth, and Evidence," *Analysis* 25 (1965), and "The Fourth Condition of Knowledge: A Defense," *The Review of Metaphysics* 23 (1970); Keith Lehrer and Thomas Paxson, "Knowledge: Undefeated Justified True Belief," *The Journal of Philosophy* 66 (1969); Gilbert Harman, "Induction" in M. Swain (ed.), *Induction, Acceptance, and Rational Belief* (Dordrecht, 1970). That every analysis of knowledge (including these "defensibility" analyses) which begins by accepting the usual counterexamples to the classical definition of knowledge will entail skepticism because ultimately they reflect only a partial analysis of the concept of knowledge is argued in my 'Defensibility and Skepticism," *The Australasian Journal of Philosophy* 51 (1973): 238–44.

5. See for example, Keith Lehrer, "Why Not Skepticism?" *Philosophical Forum* (Spring 1971); Peter Unger, "A Defense of Skepticism," *The Philosophical Review* 80 (1971); and W. W. Rozeboom, "Why I Know So Much More Than You Do," *American Philosophical Quarterly* 4 (1967).

6. The truth condition is *logically* superfluous only if we hold that "is true" *means* "is sufficiently (adequately, completely) justified," thereby asserting a strict equivalence between the truth condition and the evidence condition. I have argued only that what a person claims to know is true if (not if and only if) he is completely (adequately, sufficiently) justified in believing it.

6

Almeder on Truth and Evidence

William E. Hoffmann

In his recent paper "Truth and Evidence," Robert Almeder attacks an assumption that is central to the discussions of the classical definition of knowledge that have been precipitated by the Gettier counterexamples.[1] This is the assumption that evidence sufficient for knowledge does not entail truth. Almeder correctly argues that this assumption is essential to every analysis of knowledge which begins by accepting counterexamples such as Gettier's, and then argues that this assumption is false. I shall argue that this assumption is true, that Almeder's arguments attacking it are mistaken, and that the rejection of this assumption leads to highly counterintuitive results.

To see that the rejection of the assumption that evidence sufficient for knowledge does not entail truth leads to counterintuitive results, imagine the following two cases. The first case finds Jones sitting in the lobby of the hotel where he resides and focusing his attention on a point a few feet in front of him on the floor. For no particular reason, Jones begins to wonder if the floor at that point will support him, as it has so many times before, or if he will go crashing through the floor if he walks across that point. Having nothing better to do, Jones attempts to answer his query by watching people, many of whom are obviously heavier than he, tread across this point. After several hours without seeing a plank bow or hearing one creak despite heavy traffic, Jones walks over to the point, cautiously tests it by tapping his foot, then confidently walks across it. The second case is exactly like the first in every relevant detail except that it occurs at a different place and time, our man is named Smith, and that when Smith begins to walk across the observed point, owing to some freak ac-

From *The Philosophical Quarterly* 25 (January 1975): 59–61. Reprinted by permission of Blackwell Publishers.

cident, the floor caves in. Engineers later attempting to find the cause of the accident are unable to explain the structural failure.

Putting aside the difficulty of defining knowledge, in the first case Jones clearly knew that the floor would support him; that is, Jones had knowledge of the following proposition (hereafter referred to as P): "The floor at that point will support me." To deny this is tantamount to denying that we ever have knowledge based on inductive evidence, and any analysis of knowledge that is incompatible with the claim that Jones has knowledge in this case is so counterintuitive that it does not merit serious consideration as an elucidation of our concept of knowledge. Such an analysis flies in the face of ordinary usage, and, as we shall see, one of Almeder's main concerns is to avoid such conflicts. Further, it is clear that the reason Jones knew P was the evidence obtained from his vigil in the lobby (in addition to the type of evidence we all have when we put one foot ahead of the other without thinking about the structural soundness of the surface on which we walk). This evidence is surely sufficient for Jones's knowledge of P. Indeed, we must agree that it is sufficient if Jones knows P, for he has nothing else on which to base this knowledge.

Now what of the unfortunate Smith? He had exactly the same evidence for P as Jones, yet according to the undisputed conventional wisdom, Smith could not have known P since P was false. It follows, then, that Smith had evidence sufficient for knowledge (since this evidence was sufficient for knowledge in Jones's case) yet this evidence does not entail truth since P is false in this case. Thus evidence sufficient for knowledge does not entail truth.

I have argued by means of a counterexample that Almeder is wrong in thinking that evidence sufficient for knowledge entails truth, but it may be worthwhile underscoring my claim that this position leads to highly counterintuitive results. This further claim follows from what I have said so far. If evidence sufficient for knowledge does entail truth, it follows that Jones does not possess sufficient evidence for knowledge of P since the evidence, as illustrated by Smith's case, does not entail P. Of course I do not have to resort to Smith's case to show that this evidence does not entail P, since the fact that many people have not fallen through an apparently solid part of the floor clearly does not entail that the next person to cross that spot will not. It may offer us evidence that he will not, but it does not entail that he will not. So since, given Almeder's position, Jones does not possess sufficient evidence for knowledge, it follows that Jones does not know P. This, of course, assumes that having sufficient evidence for knowledge of P is a necessary condition for knowing P. Now we find the absurdity. Unless Almeder intends to analyze a concept different from our ordinary concept of knowledge, and it is clear that he does not, it is absurd to say that Jones does not know P.

Almeder supports his claim that the adequate-evidence condition in the classical definition of knowledge entails the truth condition with two arguments. His first argument is that there is no possible way to determine if the truth condition required in the classical definition is satisfied apart from determining whether the evidence of the person claiming to know is adequate. In some cases, at least, this is clearly false. In the example I have given, we can determine, after the fact, whether or not the truth condition was satisfied by determining whether or not the floor supports Smith or Jones. As we see Smith disappear through the rubble, we have determined, independently of Smith's evidence, that the truth condition was not satisfied. It might be objected that Almeder's argument still applies to cases where after-the-fact determinations of truth are impossible, the type of case we should have if Jones had never ventured across the point of the floor despite his knowledge that it would support him. To avoid this problem we need only remind ourselves that we do not have to determine that the truth condition is satisfied in order for it to be satisfied. This point is apparently overlooked by Almeder. He asks ". . . if the satisfaction of the evidence criterion does not entail the satisfaction of the truth condition, then how could the truth condition be satisfied at all?"[2] He then goes on to restate his query by saying, "In other words, if, after determining that a person's evidence is adequate for knowledge, there remains the separate task of determining the truth of what the person professes to know, by what possible means could this be achieved?"[3] Here Almeder has not really restated the first quotation "in other words"; rather, he has switched from the satisfaction of the truth condition to our determining that the truth condition is satisfied. The classical definition does not require that we determine or know that the truth condition is satisfied, it only requires that it be satisfied, Perhaps whether it is or not actually satisfied is something we can only know after the fact. For this reason it follows from the classical definition that a person can know without his or anyone else's knowing that he knows.

Almeder's second argument turns on his claim that ". . . to suppose that a person's evidence can be sufficient for knowledge without it thereby entailing the truth of what he claims to know, is a flagrant disregard of our usage."[4] My example shows that this is false. Indeed, to say that Jones does not know *P* or have adequate evidence for knowledge of *P*, despite the fact that the evidence does not entail *P* as shown in Smith's case, constitutes a flagrant disregard of the way we use the word "know."

It would appear, then, that Almeder's arguments do not show that the assumption that adequate evidence for knowledge does not entail truth is "obviously wrong."[5]

NOTES

1. *The Philosophical Quarterly* 24 (October 1974): 365–68. See also Edmund L. Gettier, "Is Justified True Belief Knowledge?" *Analysis* 23 (1963).

2. Almeder, "Truth and Evidence," p. 367.

3. Ibid.

4. Ibid., p. 368.

5. Ibid., p. 365.

7

An Alleged Defect in Gettier Counterexamples

Richard Feldman

A number of philosophers have contended that Gettier counterexamples to the justified true belief analysis of knowledge all rely on a certain false principle. For example, in their recent paper, "Knowledge Without Paradox,"[1] Robert G. Meyers and Kenneth Stern argue that "[c]ounterexamples of the Gettier sort all turn on the principle that someone can be justified in accepting a certain proposition h on evidence p even though p is false."[2] They contend that this principle is false, and hence that the counterexamples fail. Their view is that one proposition, p, can justify another, h, only if p is true. With this in mind, they accept the justified true belief analysis.

D. M. Armstrong defends a similar view in *Belief, Truth, and Knowledge*.[3] He writes:

> This simple consideration seems to make redundant the ingenious argument of . . . Gettier's . . . article . . . Gettier produces counterexamples to the thesis that justified true belief is knowledge by producing true beliefs based on justifiably believed grounds, . . . but where these grounds are in fact *false*. But because possession of such grounds could not constitute possession of *knowledge*, I should have thought it obvious that they are too weak to serve as suitable grounds.[4]

Thus he concludes that Gettier's examples are defective because they rely on the false principle that false propositions can justify one's belief in other propositions. Arm-

From *The Australasian Journal of Philosophy* 52, no. 1 (May 1974): 68–69. Reprinted by permission of the publisher.

strong's view seems to be that one proposition, *p*, can justify another, *h*, only if *p* is known to be true (unlike Meyers and Stern who demand only that *p* in fact be true).[5]

I think, though, that there are examples very much like Gettier's that do not rely on this allegedly false principle. To see this, let us first consider one example in the form in which Meyers and Stern discuss it, and then consider a slight modification of it.

> Suppose Mr. Nogot tells Smith that he owns a Ford and even shows him a certificate to that effect. Suppose, further, that up till now Nogot has always been reliable and honest in his dealings with Smith. Let us call the conjunction of all this evidence *m*. Smith is thus justified in believing that Mr. Nogot who is in his office owns a Ford (*r*) and, consequently, is justified in believing that someone in his office owns a Ford (*h*).[6]

As it turns out, though, *m* and *h* are true but *r* is false. So, the Gettier example runs, Smith has a justified true belief in *h*, but he clearly does not know *h*.

What is supposed to justify *h* in this example is *r*. But since *r* is false, the example runs afoul of the disputed principle. Since *r* is false, it justifies nothing. Hence, if the principle is false, the counterexample fails.

We can alter the example slightly, however, so that what justifies *h* for Smith is true and he knows that it is. Suppose he deduces from *m* its existential generalization:

(*n*) There is someone in the office who told Smith that he owns a Ford and even showed him a certificate to that effect, and who up till now has always been reliable and honest in his dealings with Smith.

(*n*), we should note, is true and Smith knows that it is, since he has correctly deduced it from *m*, which he knows to be true. On the basis of *n* Smith believes *h*—someone in the office owns a Ford. Just as the Nogot evidence, *m*, justified *r*—Nogot owns a Ford—in the original example, *n* justifies *h* in this example. Thus Smith has a justified true belief in *h*, knows his evidence to be true, but still does not know *h*.

I conclude that even if a proposition can be justified for a person only if his evidence is true, or only if he knows it to be true, there are still counterexamples to the justified true belief analysis of knowledge of the Gettier sort. In the above example, Smith reasoned from the proposition *m*, which he knew to be true, to the proposition *n*, which he also knew, to the truth *h*; yet he still did not know *h*. So some examples, similar to Gettier's, do not "turn on the principle that someone can be justified in accepting a certain proposition . . . even though [his evidence] . . . is false."[7]

NOTES

1. *The Journal of Philosophy* 70 (March 22, 1973): 147–60.
2. Ibid., p. 147.
3. (1973).
4. Ibid., p. 152.
5. Armstrong ultimately goes on to defend a rather different analysis.
6. Meyers and Stern, "Knowledge Without Paradox," p. 151.
7. Ibid., p. 147.

8

Knowledge as Justified True Belief

Roderick M. Chisholm

INTRODUCTION

According to one traditional view, knowledge may be defined as follows:

S knows that *p* =Df *p*; *S* believes that *p*; and *S* is justified in believing that *p*.

If in this definition, we take "*S* is justified in believing that *p*," as many of us have done, to mean the same as "It is evident for *S* that *p*," then the definition is not adequate. For E. L. Gettier has shown that, unless we are willing to be skeptics, we must concede that there is evident true belief that isn't knowledge.[1] Hence, if we understand the traditional definition this way, we are faced with the problem of replacing it. But we could also take Gettier's results as showing that "*h* is justified for *S*," as it is to be interpreted in the traditional definition, cannot be taken to mean the same as "*h* is evident for *S*." Then we would be faced with the task of finding another analysis of "*h* is justified for *S*."

Let us view the problem in the second way. For simplicity, we will assume that all justified true belief is propositional.

From *The Foundations of Knowing* (Minneapolis: University of Minnesota Press, 1982), pp. 43–49. © 1982. Reprinted by permission of the publisher.

GETTIER CASES

When might one have a true belief in what is evident without that belief being an instance of knowing? This may happen when a false evident proposition makes evident a proposition that is true. In one of Gettier's examples, we consider a conjunction *e* of propositions ("Jones keeps a Ford in his garage; Jones has been seen driving a Ford; Jones says he owns a Ford and he has always been honest and reliable in the past . . ."). This proposition is said to make evident for a certain subject *S* a false proposition *f* ("Jones owns a Ford").[2] This false proposition *f*, in turn, makes evident for *S* a true proposition *h* ("Jones owns a Ford or Brown is a Barcelona"). The latter proposition has an evident disjunct that is not true ("Jones owns a Ford") and a true disjunct that is not evident ("Brown is in Barcelona"). Moreover, the true disjunct, we may suppose, is not a proposition that *S* accepts. The disjunction, then, could be said to derive its truth from its nonevident disjunct and to derive its evidence from its false disjunct. Suppose now that *S* accepts this disjunctive proposition, *h*, having inferred it from its first disjunct and having no beliefs with respect to the second disjunct. Then he will be accepting a true proposition that is evident to him. But this circumstance hardly warrants our saying that he *knows* the proposition to be true.

But not all "Gettier type" problems thus involve disjunctions. Consider a second example, proposed by Keith Lehrer.[3]

Smith knows something to be true that he expresses as follows: (e) "Nogot is in my office; she told me she owns a Ford; she has always been honest and reliable in the past; I have just seen her stepping out of a Ford. . . ." This *e* makes evident the following proposition: (f) "Nogot is in my office and owns a Ford." And Smith sees that *f* makes evident for him the following proposition: (h) "Someone in my office owns a Ford." We suppose that all three propositions are accepted by Smith.

Now suppose further that Nogot has lied on this occasion—and therefore that *f* is false. Suppose also that, entirely unsuspected by Smith, a third person in his office—Havit—*does* own a Ford. The *e*, *f*, and *h* of this example will be related as are the *e*, *f*, and *h* of the first example: *e* will be a proposition that is known by Smith, but *h*—although it is true, evident, and accepted—will not be a proposition that is known by Smith. In place of the disjunction of the first example, we have in this case an existential generalization, which could be said to derive its truth from an instance of it that is not accepted and to derive its evidence from an instance of it that is accepted but false.

Hence, if we retain the traditional definition of knowledge, we cannot interpret "*h* is justified for *S*" to mean that *h* is evident for *S*.

DIAGNOSIS OF THE DIFFICULTY

We will consider the problem only in reference to the first of the two examples. What we will say holds, *mutatis mutandis,* of the second and of all other "Gettier type" cases.

The difficulty arises in part because, as we have noted, the relation of making evident may be nondeductive. That is to say, it is possible for a proposition *e* to make evident a proposition *f* even though *e* is true and *f* is false. The false *f* may then, in turn, make evident a proposition *h* that happens to be true. And this true proposition *h,* in the Gettier cases, is the one that makes difficulties for the traditional definition of knowing.

Could we deal with Gettier's example, then, by stipulating that one proposition cannot make another proposition evident for a given subject unless the first proposition *entails* the second? This move would rule out the *h* of Gettier's example; we would no longer have to say that *S knows* that either Jones owns a Ford or Brown is in Barcelona. But such a move would also have the consequence that *S* knows very little about the world around him. In fact it would restrict the evident—and therefore what is known—to those Cartesian propositions that are self-presenting and to what can be apprehended a priori.

A more precise diagnosis of the problem would seem to be this: the proposition *h* is based on evidence that nondeductively makes evident a false proposition. So to repair the traditional definition, we may be tempted to say, in effect, that belief in an evident true proposition constitutes knowledge *provided* that the basis for that proposition does *not* make evident any false proposition. But this would have the consequence that the *e* of Gettier's example would not be known. And this is an undesirable consequence. Although the *f* of Gettier's example—Jones owns a Ford—should not be counted as knowledge, we *should* say that the conjunction *e* of propositions constituting *S*'s evidence for *h*—i.e., "Jones keeps a Ford in his garage; Jones has been seen riding in a Ford . . ."—is a proposition that *S* knows to be true. Yet it is based on evidence that makes evident a proposition that is false.

Our definition, then, should have the following consequences in application to Gettier's example:

(1) The *h* of that example ("Jones owns a Ford or Brown is in Barcelona") is *not* known by the subject *S*—even though *h* is evident, true, and accepted by *S*.

(2) The conjunction of propositions *e* ("Jones keeps a Ford in his garage; Jones has been seen riding in a Ford; and . . ."), which Gettier cites as *S*'s evidence for *e,* *is* a proposition that is known by *S.*

(3) The conjunction *b* of directly evident propositions constituting *S*'s ultimate *basis* for *e* is also a proposition that is known by *S.*[4]

We can satisfy these conditions by introducing the concept of that which is *de-*

fectively evident. Roughly speaking, we will say (1) that a proposition is defectively evident for a given subject *S* provided the propositions on which it is based make evident a proposition that is false and (2) that what is known must be evident but not defectively evident. But it will be necessary to characterize the defectively evident somewhat more precisely. To fulfill the desiderata listed above, we shall say that *some* defectively evident propositions—those of a certain sort that we will specify—*can* be known.

PROPOSED SOLUTION

To deal with the Gettier problem we need three definitions: that of a *basic proposition*; that of the *defectively evident*; and that of *justification.*
Elsewhere we defined the concept of a basic proposition as follows:

b is a basic proposition for *S* =Df *b* is evident for *S*; and everything that makes *b* evident for *S* entails *b*.

We next define the defectively evident:

h is defectively evident for *S* =Df (i) there is a basic proposition for *S* that makes *h* evident for *S* and does not logically imply *h*; and (ii) every such basic proposition makes evident a proposition that is false.

Now we are in a position to define the type of justification presupposed by the traditional definition of knowledge:

S is justified in believing that *p* =Df (i) it is evident for *S* that *p*; and (ii) if it is defectively evident for *S* that *p*, then the proposition that *p* is entailed by a conjunction of propositions each of which is evident but not defectively evident for *S*.

And so we retain the traditional definition of knowledge:

S knows that *p* =Df *p*; *S* believes that *p*; and *S* is justified in believing that *p*.

We now return to the three desiderata listed above.
(1) The proposition *h* of Gettier's example ("Jones owns a Ford or Brown is in Barcelona") will not be counted as known. It is defectively evident for *S*—since it is made evident by a basic proposition that makes evident a proposition ("Jones owns

a Ford") that is false. It does not satisfy the second condition of the definition of justification.

(2) The evident proposition e that was cited as S's evidence for h ("Jones keeps a Ford in his garage; and . . .") is defectively evident by our definition. But it is justified for S, since it is entailed by a conjunction of propositions each of which is made evident for S by a basic proposition that does not make evident a proposition that is false.

(3) And that proposition b which is S's directly evident basis for e is not defectively evident, for it fails to satisfy condition (i) of the definition of the defectively evident. There is no basic proposition that nondeductively makes b evident for S.

But the proposed solution has one difficulty: our definitions are not adequate to the possibility that S may *know that he knows*. If we think that this possibility is a real one (I defend this view in another essay), then we must modify our account.

AN ALTERNATIVE SOLUTION

Consider once again the defectively evident e of Gettier's example ("Jones keeps a Ford in his garage; and . . ."). Can S *know that he knows* this proposition? In such a case, the object of his knowledge would be

(1) S knows that e.

This is equivalent to the following conjunction

(2) e; and S believes that e; and S is justified in believing that e.

Now we have noted that, although e is defectively evident, it is entailed by a conjunction of propositions—let us call this conjunction "m & n"—each of which is evident but not defectively evident. Hence (2) is entailed by

(3) m; and n; and S believes that e; and S is justified in believing that e.

The first three conjuncts of (3) are such that they are evident but not defectively evident for S. What of the last conjunct—"S is justified in believing that e"?

If the proposition expressed by "S knows that e" is itself an object of S's knowledge, then the proposition expressed by "S is *justified* in believing that e" must be evident for S. And if the latter proposition is evident for S, then it is made evident at least in part by e and by the basic proposition b that makes e evident. (This point is discussed in further detail in my "Knowing that One Knows.") Therefore "S is justified in believing that *e*" will be defectively evident for *S*. But, since it is not entailed by a conjunction of nondefectively evident propositions, we cannot say—given our definition of justification—that *S* is *justified* in believing it. And therefore we cannot say that *S* knows that he knows that *e*. Hence, if we are to say that *S can* know that he knows that *e*, we must qualify our definitions of justification.

Can we find a special mark that is satisfied just by the final conjunct of (3)—by "*S* is justified in believing that *e*"? I think we can. "*S* is justified in believing that *e*" implies with respect to one of the *other* conjuncts—the first as well as the second— that it is evident for *S*. Hence we may modify our definition of justification this way:

S is justified in believing that *p* =Df (i) it is evident for *S* that *p*; and (ii) if it is defectively evident for *S* that *p*, then the proposition that *p* is entailed by a conjunction of propositions each of which is either (a) evident but not defectively evident for *S* or (b) a proposition implying with respect to one of the other conjuncts that it is evident for *S*.

CONCLUSION

With these definitions, I believe we have adequately dealt with Gettier's example. What we have said may also be applied to the second example, as well as to the other cases of evident true belief that are not cases of knowing. In all such cases, the object of the evident true belief is a proposition that is defectively evident: it is a proposition such that every proposition, which is basic for that subject and which makes *h* evident for him, also makes evident for him a proposition that is false. And, unlike Gettier's *e* and its basis *b*, it is not a proposition that is entailed by a conjunction of evident propositions each of which is nondefectively evident.

In recent philosophical literature, many "Gettier cases" have been formulated— many examples purporting to be cases of evident true belief that are not cases of knowing. If the examples are indeed cases of evident true belief that are not cases of knowing, then our definitions should insure that they are not counted as cases of knowing. But the reader may find that, in application to *some* of the examples that have been offered, application of the definitions will *not* have this result.[5] I recommend that, in such cases, she look to the proposition corresponding to the *e* of the original example—the proposition that is supposed to make *h* evident to the subject in question. She will then find, if I am not mistaken, that *e* does *not* make *h* evident. The relation that *e* bears to *h* will be some weaker epistemic relation—that, say, of making *h* beyond reasonable doubt, or perhaps merely that of making *h* such as to have some presumption in its favor. If this is the case, then the example in question will not be an example of *evident* true belief.

NOTES

1. E. L. Gettier, "Is Justified True Belief Knowledge?" *Analysis* 23 (1963): 121–23. (See reading number 2 of this volume—Ed.)

2. It should be noted that our formulation of *e* contains a blank and is therefore incomplete. The conjunction of propositions that are explicit in our formulation of *e* is *not* sufficient to make *f* evident for the subject of Gettier's example.

3. Keith Lehrer, "Knowledge, Truth, and Evidence," *Analysis* 25 (1965): 168–75.

4. Earl Conee has pointed out to me that my earlier attempts to deal with the Gettier problem do not satisfy the third condition. See his "The Analysis of Knowledge in the Second Edition of *Theory of Knowledge*," *Canadian Journal of Philosophy* 10 (1980): 295–300.

5. Possibly this is true of the example of the pyromaniac proposed by Brian Skyrms in "The Explication of "S knows that P,' " *Journal of Philosophy* 64 (1967): 373–89. Skyrms considers these two propositions, *e* and *h*: (e) "Sure-Fire matches have always and often lit for me when struck except when wet, and this match is a Sure-Fire and is dry"; (h) "This match will light now as I strike it." He assumes—mistakenly, it seems to me—that *e* makes *h* evident. I believe the most we can of *e* in this connection is that it makes *h* such as to be beyond reasonable doubt.

9

The Gettier Problem
and the Analysis of Knowledge

Keith Lehrer

The problem that Edmund Gettier formulated is, I believe, still unsolved.[1] It has been explored and developed to such an extent that it is worthwhile stating just what the problem is. It is, in my opinion, the problem of showing that a falliblistic theory of epistemic justification is possible. For, the problem arises in certain cases in which a person is justified, whether he knows it or not, in believing or accepting some false proposition which transmits justification to some true proposition. Thus, for a Cartesian who held that epistemic justification must proceed from what is certain by certain steps to arrive at what is known, the problem would not arise. For a philosopher who avers, as I do, that epistemic justification is fallible, the problem is to articulate a theory of fallible epistemic justification which allows us to distinguish between those cases in which justification, though fallible, yields knowledge, and those in which some false proposition deprives one of obtaining knowledge from justification. I shall present an analysis of knowledge and theory of justification incorporating a fourth condition to solve the problem Gettier raised.

THE ANALYSIS OF KNOWLEDGE

To formulate my solution to the Gettier problem, I shall introduce some familiar notions which I shall use in a special way. On the analysis of knowledge I wish to de-

From George S. Pappas, ed., *Justification and Knowledge* (Dordrecht, Netherlands: D. Reidel Publishing Company, 1979), pp. 65–78. Copyright © 1979 by D. Reidel Publishing Company. Reprinted by permission of Wolters Kluwer Academic Publishers.

fend, S knows that h if and only if (i) h, (ii) S accepts h, (iii) h is evident for S, and (iv) there is no false proposition f such that if f were doubtful for S, then h would not be evident for S. The terms of this definition are, in the first three conditions, taken from Chisholm, but I intend to use them in my own way.[2]

ACCEPTANCE AND BELIEF

Let us first consider acceptance. A person may accept something he believes, but he may also accept something he does not believe, and he may refuse to accept something he does believe. To accept a proposition in this context means to assent to it when one's only purpose is to assent to what is true and to refuse to assent to what is false. What a person believes is not entirely up to him. One is endowed with certain beliefs, and one may conclude that some of what one believes one should not accept as a truth seeker. One person may find, for example, that he believes that someone is tenderly concerned about his welfare, but, looking at the evidence, conclude that this is probably not true. He wishes it to be so with such fervor that he cannot help but believe it nonetheless. Similarly, there may be something that is so distasteful for a second person to believe that he cannot do so, even though the person becomes aware that it is evidently true. In the quest for truth, the first person might refuse to assent to what he believes, and the second might assent to what he does not believe. In this way, acceptance may differ from belief.

This distinction is of some importance in judging whether a person knows, for philosophers have erroneously held a person who believes something from irrational motives lacks knowledge. This is a mistake. A person may believe something for the wrong reasons, perhaps he cannot help but do so, and, nevertheless, know that it is true because he assents to it for the right reasons. A person may believe something because the stars or the tarot deck tell him it is so, but in the quest for truth, he may assent to it on proper grounds. The man, then, accepts the proposition as well as believing it to be true, and the reasons for which he accepts it may lead us to conclude that the third and fourth conditions of knowledge are satisfied.

This distinction between belief and acceptance also vitiates those causal theories of knowledge that maintain that whether a person knows something to be true depends on the causal relation between a person believing something and the fact that it is so. Belief may arise in particular and sundry ways, but no matter how a person comes to believe something, and no matter how his belief is sustained, he may know that what he believes is true if he accepts the proposition in question on proper grounds.

Drawing upon an analogy suggested by Dennett, one might think of relation between belief and acceptance in a way similar to the way one thinks of the relation between desire and choice.[3] A person finds himself with a natural endowment of desires and beliefs at any given moment which he may not be able to alter immediately. But one may refuse to accept what one cannot help but believe just as one may refuse to choose what one cannot help but desire. To borrow from Descartes, it is as though we find ourselves with a basket of apples, some of which we picked and others of which were given to us, and we face the problem of sorting through the collection to decide which ones are good to eat and which are not. We sort through our collection of desires and beliefs to decide which desires should be acted on and which ones not, and we sort through our beliefs to decide which ones should receive our assent and which ones not.

THE EVIDENT

With these remarks concerning acceptance, let us turn to the question of what is epistemically justified or evident for a person. Whether a proposition is evident for a person depends, I maintain, on how well the proposition fares in conflict with other propositions. Thus, I propose that h is evident for S if and only if, for any proposition c that competes with h for S, either h beats c for S or c is neutralized with respect to h for S. To elucidate this definition, we shall have to explicate what it means to say that a proposition competes with, beats, or neutralizes another. I shall take as primitive for this discussion a comparative notion of epistemic reasonableness. Thus, I shall say that one epistemic state is more reasonable than another, for example, that accepting a proposition is more reasonable than accepting another. This is Chisholm's strategy. However, I do this only for convenience. Epistemic reasonableness is epistemic expected utility, and the latter may be explicated in terms of probability and utility.

COMPETITION

To elucidate the definiens of the definition given above, let us first turn to the notion of a competitor. A proposition need not contradict another to conflict with it. The proposition that I am now undergoing intensive hallucination does not contradict the proposition that I am now seeing a table because one may see objects when one is hallucinating. But the proposition that I am hallucinating in this way competes with the proposition that I am now seeing a table in that the former deprives that latter of epistemic status. If I am now hallucinating, then it is not as reasonable for me to accept that I see a table as it would be if I were not hallucinating. Thus, a competitor of a proposition is one that diminishes the epistemic worth or reasonableness of accepting the proposition. I am certain that I am not now hallucinating, and I am also certain that I see a table before me. Suppose, on the contrary, that I were certain that I was now hallucinating. In that case it would be less reasonable for me to accept that I now see a table. It would be by no means certain that I do.

These reflections suggest the following definition of competition: c competes with h if and only if it would be less reasonable for S to accept h if c were certain for S than if the denial of c were certain for S. We may here define certainty as Chisholm does and say that k is certain for S if and only if it is more reasonable for S to accept k than not to, and there is no proposition that it is more reasonable for S to accept than k. The certain is the maximally reasonable.[4]

BEATING AND NEUTRALIZING

We must say what it is for a proposition to be beaten or neutralized. As definitions, I propose that if c competes with h for S, then h beats c if and only if it is more reasonable for S to accept h than to accept c, and c is neutralized with respect to h for S if and only if there is some proposition n such that the conjunction of n and c does not compete with h for S and it is as reasonable for S to accept the conjunction as it is for him to accept just c.

Let me illustrate the implications of these definitions. For a proposition to be evident for a person, the proposition must meet two kinds of skeptical challenge. The first is one that comes from a skeptic who advances a hypothesis that contradicts what a person claims to know. If a skeptic claims that I am not now seeing but am asleep and dreaming, I shall reply to him that it is more reasonable for me to accept the proposition that I now see a table than to accept the proposition that he avers to be true. That reply would require defense before the skeptic would be satisfied, but the reply is, as stated, perfectly true. This means that a competitor that the skeptic suggests is beaten by the proposition I claim to know.

A more subtle skeptical challenge might have to be neutralized rather than beaten. For a subtle skeptic might remark, when I claim to know that I now see a table, that people sometimes dream such things. That people sometimes dream such things competes with the proposition that I now see a table, and it is by no means obvious that it is more reasonable for me to accept the latter than the former. This skeptic has challenged my claim to know without contradicting the proposition that I now see a table. He has attempted to defeat my claim to know, not by contradicting the proposition that I now see a table, but by diminishing the claim by innuendo, by reminding me of something that I know to be true which seems to diminish the reasonableness of my claim. What he says is perfectly true, and it does compete with what I aver. How should I reply?

This sort of information cannot be beaten, but it may be neutralized. For, the innuendo is that I am now dreaming. If I am not now dreaming, then the fact that people sometimes dream that they see tables loses its competitive force. The conjunction of the propositions that people sometimes dream they see tables and that I am not now dreaming does not compete with the proposition that I now see a table. Moreover, it is as reasonable for me to accept the conjunction as it is for me to accept the skeptic's remark alone. So the remark of the skeptic, though not beaten, is neutralized. Many skeptical challenges must be dealt with by neutralization.

A remark here is necessary about my claim that it is as reasonable for me to accept the conjunction as it is for me to accept just the skeptic's claim that people sometimes dream. The skeptic might reply that his claim is more reasonable because it is less likely to be false than the conjunction of his claim and mine. For a conjunction like this one is less probable than a conjunct within it. My answer is that the probability of error is not the only relevant consideration, and the assumption that it is so gives unnecessary succor to the skeptic. For, as truth seekers, we are interested not only in avoiding error, we are also interested in getting hold of truth. The greater the content of a proposition, the more truth we obtain when it is true. Thus, expected epistemic utility or reasonableness of accepting a proposition is a function of our interest in content and our interest in avoiding error. These two objectives must be balanced one against the other. We want to avoid error in the story we tell, but we want to tell the whole story. A conjunction can be no more reasonable to accept than the least reasonable conjunct, but it may be just as reasonable as the least reasonable conjunct. Since it is so improbable that I am now dreaming, the epistemic utility of accepting that I am not together with the skeptical remark outweighs epistemic utility of accepting just the latter. The conjunction is more informative, surely, and the added risk of error is worth taking.

It might appear that the appeal to content would allow a skeptic to concoct an unbeatable competitor for any hypothesis or a dogmatist to fabricate an artificial neutralizer. For, suppose that a skeptic has a competitor c for h which is beaten by h. The skeptic could conjoin to c a proposition p, which, though irrelevant to h, is virtually immune from error and highly informative. Then the conjunction of c and p would compete with h and more effectively so, one might think, because the conjunction is so much more informative than the c alone. Similarly, a dogmatist trying to find some proposition n to neutralize a competitor c might conjoin some irrelevant information to a neutralizing proposition attempting to bolster the reasonableness of it. The addition of irrelevant information by either the skeptic or the dogmatist is a sort of smokescreen intended to obscure the relevant weakness of a competitor or neutralizer. However, such a ruse will be ineffective. For, as we noted above, a conjunction can be no more reasonable than the least reasonable conjunct of it just as a chain can be no stronger than the weakest link of it. The fight of reason clears the smokescreen when we note that the conjunction of c and p concocted by the skeptic can be no more reasonable than c alone. Hence, if h beats c, then h will also beat the conjunction of c and p in spite of the informativeness of p. Similarly, if the intended neutralizer n fabricated by the dogmatist contains a proposition r that is relevant to the original competitor c but less reasonable than c, and another irrelevant but informative proposition q that is more reasonable than c, the proposition n will be no more reasonable than r, and, therefore, less reasonable than c. A smokescreen of irrelevant information is epistemically impotent.

It is perhaps worth noting that some of the foregoing ideas are relevant to historical epistemological disputes. Thomas Reid claimed that perceptual claims such as that I see that there is a table are certain, indeed, as certain as the more cautious claim that I *think* I see that there is a table.[5] The latter is less likely to be erroneous than the former. So how can the former be as certain as the latter? If we suppose that informativeness is an epistemic virtue, then we may defend Reid by saying that the perceptual claim, that I see that there is a table, though more likely to be in error than the claim that I think that I see that there is a table, is also more informative, and hence equally reasonable in epistemic terms. The greater content balances the greater risk of error, and the result is maximal reasonableness. This claim may be controverted, but it does show how we may defend claims that propositions are certain or evident even though there is some risk of error in accepting them.

THE GETTIER PROBLEM: A FOURTH CONDITION

With this discussion of the notion of evidence before us, let us turn to the Gettier problem. The fourth condition I propose is as follows:

(iv) There is no f such that f is false and such that if f were doubtful for S, then h would not be evident for S.[6]

I use the expression "doubtful" in a technical sense. It is that f is doubtful for S if and only if it is more reasonable for S to decline f than to accept f. To say that S declines f means that he does not accept f but leaves open the question of whether he accepts the denial of f.

A number of philosophers suggest the following sort of condition, though sometimes in other terms, which I think is defective.

(ive) There is no f such that f is false and such that if the falsity of f were evident for S, then h would not be evident for S.[7]

One way of explaining the advantage of the condition I propose is to show how it remedies a defect in (ive). There are two problems with (ive) that are paramount. The first concerns misleading evidence, and the second concerns extraneous information.

MISLEADING EVIDENCE

For an example of misleading evidence, consider the case of Tom Grabit that Paxson and I proposed.[8] The example is one in which I see Tom Grabit, a student in a very small class of six members, take a book off the shelf in a library, conceal it beneath his coat, and walk out of the library. I know that Tom Grabit took a book out of the library. Now suppose that, quite unknown to me, Mr. Grabit, Tom's father, is just now remarking that Tom Grabit is not in Tucson today (where I am) and that his identical twin John is in Tucson, indeed, at the library. With only this much of the story told, some might doubt whether I really do know that Tom Grabit took a book out of the library. However, Mr. Grabit is entirely demented, talking only to an imaginary person in a room in the mental hospital. There is no brother John, and Mr. Grabit has no information whatever concerning the whereabouts of Tom. Since Mr. Grabit's remarks were heard by no one, they are not testimony in the public domain. Moreover, we may imagine that if anyone were to ask Mr. Grabit where Tom is today he would stare blankly in catatonic silence. The mere coincidental remark of Mr. Grabit about Tom surely fails to show that I do not know that I saw Tom Grabit take a book out of the library.

Let us consider how conditions (iv) and (ive) deal with this case. Let m be the proposition that Tom Grabit was not in Tucson today and that his identical twin brother was in town at the library. Mr. Grabit said that m. Each condition asks us to evaluate the statement

(c) It is not evident for me that Tom Grabit took a book from the library,

given a counterfactual assumption. Condition (ive) asks us to consider the assumption equivalent to

(ae) It is evident for me that Mr. Grabit said that m.

While conditions (iv) asks us to consider the condition

(a) It is doubtful for me that Mr. Grabit did not say that m,

where the latter means that declining the proposition that Mr. Grabit did not say that m is more reasonable than accepting that Mr. Grabit did not say that m.

Assumption (a) is one that would already have been fulfilled in the original case. When I see Tom Grabit take the book from the library, I do not know anything about Mr. Grabit, not even that such a person lives. In this circumstance, declining propositions about Mr. Grabit is surely more reasonable than accepting such propositions.

I have no information that would make it reasonable for me to accept any proposition about what Mr. Grabit might or might not say. Thus, assuming that it is evident for me that Tom Grabit took the book, which it is, assumption (a) introduces no epistemic alternation. Therefore, condition (iv) is satisfied. My analysis is, therefore, consistent with the correct conclusion that I know that Tom took a book from the library.

But the situation is different with respect to (ae) and condition (ive). For if it were to become evident to me that Mr. Grabit said that Tom was not in Tucson and that his identical twin John was in Tucson at the library, then it would no longer be evident for me that it was Tom who took the book from the library. For, I have no other information about Mr. Grabit. It is as though some completely dependable person told me that Mr. Grabit said what he did and then the informant left without giving any other information about Mr. Grabit. I have no reason to think Mr. Grabit is lying or ignorant or that his remarks are in any way deceptive. In short, I have no way of neutralizing the proposition that Mr. Grabit said that m which competes with the proposition that Tom Grabit took the book from the library. If we attempt to neutralize it with the proposition that Mr. Grabit is lying or misinformed, we fail. It is by no means evident that this is so and, by assumption, it is evident that Mr. Grabit said that m. Thus (ive) is not satisfied in this case, and the analysis containing it yields the incorrect result that I do not know that Tom took the book.

EXTRANEOUS INFORMATION

Let us now consider the case of extraneous information. Suppose I am sitting in my office and begin to put away some implements in my office. I put my pen in the middle drawer in my desk, knowing that I do this, and then put the manuscript I was working on in the top drawer of the filing cabinet, knowing that I do this. I would claim to know that my pen is in the middle drawer of my desk and the manuscript is in the top drawer of my filing cabinet. Now imagine that, quite unknown to me, a workman came in to repair my desk, leaving a hole in the back of the drawer so that, unknown to me, the pen slipped into the opening and fell out of the drawer. I do not know that the pen is in the middle drawer of my desk because it is not there. I do know that my manuscript is in the top drawer of the filing cabinet, having placed it there.

Condition (ive) yields the incorrect result that I do not know that the manuscript is in the top drawer of my filing cabinet, while condition (iv) yields the correct result that I do know this. Consider the conjunctive proposition, k, that my fountain pen is in the middle drawer of my desk and my manuscript is in the top drawer of the filing cabinet. That conjunction is false because the proposition about the pen is false. Consider the following two assumptions to evaluate (ive) and (iv) respectively:

(ae) It is evident for me that it is false that *k*.

(a) It is doubtful for me that *k*.

The question is whether we would conclude from these assumptions that

(c) It is not evident for me that my manuscript is in the top drawer of my filing cabinet.

Now (ae) amounts to the assumption that it is evident for me that either the pen is not in the middle drawer of the desk or the manuscript is not in the top drawer of the filing cabinet. That proposition competes with the proposition that my manuscript is in the top drawer of my filing cabinet. Can it be neutralized? One way to neutralize it would be with the proposition that my pen is not in the middle drawer of my desk. But I have no way, from the evidence I possess, of deciding whether I am wrong about the whereabouts of the pen or the manuscript. Consequently, I cannot reason from my evidence that my manuscript is in the top drawer of my filing cabinet.

Now consider assumption (a). Here we are required to assume that declining *k* is more reasonable than accepting *k*. We are not required to assume that it is evident that *k* is false. Since the proposition that *k* is false is not evident on this assumption, I may reason that the proposition that my manuscript is in the top drawer of the filing cabinet because I put it there. The assumption that declining *k* is more reasonable than accepting *k* does not render it evident or even reasonable to suppose that *k* is false. Hence, the denial of *k,* which competes with the proposition that my manuscript is in the top drawer of the filing cabinet, is easy enough to neutralize. The proposition that I put my manuscript in the top drawer of the filing cabinet will neutralize the denial of *k*. The conjunction of that proposition and the denial of *k* is surely as reasonable to accept as the denial of *k* alone.

Perhaps a less technical way of representing the difference between (ive) and (iv) would be helpful. To that end, imagine that some completely reliable person tells me after examining the two drawers in question that conjunction *k* is false. That would make it evident for me that I was wrong about the location of either the pen or manuscript. It would not, then, be evident for me that the manuscript is in the top drawer of the filing cabinet. This result corresponds to condition (ive). Imagine now that the man who tells me this often enjoys fooling me on such matters and I cannot ever tell when he is deceiving me. Declining the conjunction is more reasonable than accepting it, but it might remain evident for me that the manuscript is in the top drawer of the filing cabinet. I put it there, after all. This result corresponds to condition (iv).

GETTIER COUNTEREXAMPLES

Having argued that condition (iv) allows us to say that we know when we do know, does it rule out typical Gettier counterexamples? Take the case in which I have strong evidence that Nogot, who is in my class, owns a Ford, no evidence that anyone else does, but Havit, who is also in my class, owns a Ford, quite unknown to me, and Nogot does not. I do not know that someone in my class owns a Ford. Condition (iv) asks us to consider the assumption that declining the proposition that Mr. Nogot owns a Ford is more reasonable than accepting that Mr. Nogot owns a Ford. This has the effect of blocking my reasoning from the evidence for Nogot owning a Ford to the conclusion that someone in my class owns a Ford. We have evidence that seems to make it evident that Mr. Nogot owns a Ford. We have his testimony, seen him drive the car, examined documents, and so forth. But in spite of that we must assume that it is more reasonable to decline the proposition that Nogot owns a Ford than to accept that proposition. This can only mean that evidence is in some way deceptive. Otherwise it would be evident for me that Nogot owns a Ford.

The proposition that evidence we have that Nogot owns a Ford is deceptive competes with the proposition that someone in the room owns a Ford. Moreover, it cannot be neutralized. That Nogot owns a Ford anyway is not as reasonable for me to accept given our assumption as the proposition that my evidence about Nogot owning a Ford is deceptive. Thus, the proposition that Nogot owns a Ford, when taken in conjunction with the proposition that my evidence about Nogot owning a Ford is deceptive, is not as reasonable for me to accept as the simple proposition about the evidence being deceptive. In short, given our assumption, it is very reasonable for me to accept that my evidence is deceptive. Because it is so reasonable to accept that, potential neutralizers of that proposition fail. Condition (iv) is not satisfied and this explains why I do not know that someone in my class owns a Ford.

A slight modification of this counterexample reveals the superiority of condition (iv) to other methods for dealing with the Gettier problem. Other solutions depend on the assumption that the proposition that someone in my class owns a Ford is *inferred* from the proposition that Nogot owns a Ford or that I *believe* that Nogot owns a Ford.[9] These solutions require that justification not be based essentially on any false belief or lemma of inference. However, we can modify the example so that no false lemma or belief is involved. Suppose that in the previous example I am asked whether I know that there is a Ford owner in my class. I claim that I do know this. It is then suggested to me that I claim to know this because I believe that Nogot owns a Ford, or because I inferred my conclusion from that premise. But I demur. I point out that, though I do have excellent evidence that Nogot owns a Ford, I have not been asked whether I know that *he* owns a Ford, and so there is no need for me to take a stand on that issue. For, I note, even though my primary evidence for claiming to know that there is a

Ford owner in my class is the evidence I have concerning Nogot, there are many other members of the class, and, if by some odd quirk it should turn out that Nogot does not own a Ford, someone else in the class might own one. Thus, even if the proposition that Nogot owns a Ford should happen to be false, I might still be correct in claiming that someone in my class owns a Ford. So I choose to decline the proposition that Nogot owns a Ford, in order to guard against the remote chance of being in error there. I need not commit myself on that proposition in order to claim that *someone* in my class owns a Ford. My inference proceeds directly from my evidence, which consists of propositions I know to be true. This is, in fact, the reply that Gettier gave to Harman when the latter claimed that the problem can be solved by requiring that the inference to a conclusion not involve a false lemma.[10]

The method for dealing with the original Nogot example based on condition (iv) works equally well for the modified example. The proposition that Nogot owns a Ford is false whether or not it is believed or is a lemma of inference. Since it is false, we must ask whether the proposition that someone in my class owns a Ford remains evident for me on the assumption that it is doubtful for me that Nogot owns a Ford. If that is doubtful, then, again, my evidence must be deceptive, because the evidence I have for that proposition would, if not deceptive, render it evident and not at all doubtful. Then, as before, the proposition that my evidence is doubtful cannot be beaten or neutralized. Again, (iv) is not satisfied.

It is worth noting in passing that condition (iv) is not so strong that it yields the result that a person lacks knowledge when there is a good inferential chain as well as a defective inferential chain to a conclusion. Thus, if the situation concerning Nogot is as before, I have good evidence he owns a Ford, though he does not, but I also *know* that Havit, who is also in my class, owns a Ford, it will turn out that I know that someone in my class owns a Ford. We shall have to consider the consequences of declining on the proposition that both Nogot and Havit own Fords, for that proposition is false. But that does not block me from reasoning from the evidence that I have that Havit owns a Ford to the conclusion that he owns a Ford and, therefore, to the conclusion that someone in my class owns a Ford. On the assumption that it is doubtful that they both own Fords, I must concede that the evidence that they *both* own Fords is deceptive, but I need not concede that the evidence that I have that Havit owns a Ford is deceptive.

While considering modifications of the original Nogot example, I should also like to make it clear that a very simple modification of that example suffices to defeat attempts to deal with the Gettier problem in causal terms, for example, by requiring the fact that makes a proposition a person believes true be a cause of his believing it. For, it may well have occurred to some readers of the original Nogot example to wonder why Nogot should have gone to so much trouble to deceive me into believing that he owned a Ford when he did not. The answer, we may suppose, is that Nogot knows that Havit owns a Ford and Nogot has a compulsion to try to trick people into believing true propositions by getting them to believe some false propositions. Thus, the fact that someone in my class owned a Ford caused Nogot to cause me to believe that someone in my class owned a Ford. So the fact that someone in my class owned a Ford is, indirectly, the cause of my believing that someone in my class owns a Ford. But this is still not anything I know. Moreover, the deception need not involve a human agent but might arise from some peculiarity in the natural cause of events, like a name fading in a peculiar way on a document.

There are two other cases that might profitably be considered here. One is the Chisholm example in which a man who usually knows a sheep when he sees one, looks out into a field, sees a rock which looks very much like a sheep, and, consequently, takes the rock to be a sheep.[11] Let us suppose that the rock looks so much like a sheep that it is evident for him that there is a sheep in the field. Moreover, let us suppose that there is, in fact, a sheep in the field, though he does not notice this sheep. It is false that what appears to him to be a sheep is a sheep. So, by condition (iv) we consider the assumption that it is doubtful for him that what appears to him to be a sheep is a sheep. If that is doubtful for him, then appearances are misleading. The way the object appears is misleading in some way, and the proposition that it is misleading in some way cannot be beaten or neutralized, Therefore, on the assumption in question, it is not evident for the person that there is a sheep in the field. Hence, by (iv) the person does not know that there is.

Another, rather difficult, example from Skyrms concerns the man who is striking a Sure-Fire match, a kind of match that has always lighted before when struck.[12] However, we are supposed to imagine that the person who has witnessed the perfect regularity with which Sure-Fire matches have lighted when struck has no causal hypothesis about the relation between striking and lighting. He proceeds according to the Newtonian directive of hypotheses *non fingo*. He infers from the past correlation that the present match he is about to strike will light, but without any causal assumption. The match does light, but in fact it is a defective match which only lights because some Q-radiation raises the temperature of the match. Why does he not know the present match will light if struck?

Again, this case can be dealt with in the manner of the modified Nogot case. Our condition does not require that a person believe or infer anything from a false proposition for the falsity of that proposition to be relevant to whether the person knows. In this case, the false proposition is that the present match is in as good a condition for lighting when struck under similar circumstances as the previously observed matches. This proposition is false. Thus we must consider the consequences of assuming that it is doubtful. If it is doubtful that the match is in as good a condition for fighting when struck under similar circumstances as the previously observed Sure-Fire matches, then the evidence of the previous lighting of the other Sure-Fire matches fails to make it evident that the present match will light. Again the reasonableness of declining the proposition blocks the chain of inference from the evidence to the conclusion that the match will light. If it is more reasonable to decline than accept the proposition that this match is in as good a condition for lighting when struck under similar circumstances as the previously observed Sure-Fire matches, then it is very reasonable to accept that the evidence from previous matches may be misleading. There is no way that this proposition can be neutralized, and it competes with the proposition that the present match will light if struck. The proposition is, therefore, not evident for the man. Condition (iv) is not satisfied, and he does not know the proposition is true.

In summary, the fourth condition I have proposed requires that for a person to know something it must remain evident for him when any false proposition is assumed to be doubtful for him. This does not require that he assume that it is evident for him that the proposition is false. Moreover, the condition does not depend on the person believing or inferring anything from the false propositions that deprive him of knowledge. The false propositions, when assumed to be doubtful, block the transmission of justification from false propositions to true ones. In that way our analysis provides a falliblistic theory of epistemic justification.

NOTES

1. Edmund L. Gettier, "Is Justified True Belief Knowledge?" *Analysis* 23, no. 6 (1963): 121–23, Articles on the problem are collected in Roth, Michael D., and Leon Galls, eds., *Knowing: Essays in the Analysis of Knowledge* (New York: Random House, 1970). Also see the bibliography in George S. Pappas and Marshall Swain, eds., *Essays on Knowledge and Justification* (Ithaca, N.Y.: Cornell University Press, 1978), pp. 370–74.

2. Roderick M. Chisholm, *Theory of Knowledge,* 2d ed. (Englewood Cliffs, N.J.: Prentice-Hall, 1977). Note that in the foregoing definitions time references are not made explicit, but all definitions and conditions are assumed to be relativized to some specific time.

3. Daniel Dennett formulated this idea at a Chapel Hill symposium, 1977.

4. Chisholm, *Theory of Knowledge,* p. 10.

5. Reid, Thomas, *Essays on the Intellectual Powers of Man,* 1785, Essay II, chapter 20.

6. The subjunctive conditional "if *f* were doubtful for *S*, then *h* would not be evident for *S*" imbedded in (iv) may be eliminated in terms of current possible worlds analyses of such conditionals provided that consideration of possible worlds is restricted to those in which *f* is doubtful for *S* in a way that is the least unfavorable to *h* being evident for *S*.

7. Cf. Risto Hilpinen, "Knowledge and Justification," *Ajatus* 33, no. 1 (1971): 7–39, and Peter D. Klein, "A Proposed Definition of Propositional Knowledge," *Journal of Philosophy* 68, no. 16 (1971): 471–82.

8. Keith Lehrer and Thomas Paxton, Jr., "Knowledge: Undefeated Justified True Belief," *Journal of Philosophy* 66, no. 8 (1969): 225–37.

9. A solution depending on inference is proposed in Gilbert Harman, *Thought* (Princeton, N.J.: Princeton University Press, 1973), and one depending on belief in Keith Lehrer, *Knowledge* (New York: Oxford University Press, 1974).

10. Gettier was replying to Harman at a symposium of the American Philosophical Association, Eastern Division, 1970.

11. Chisholm, *Theory of Knowledge,* p. 105.

12. Brian Skyrms, "The Explication of '*X* knows that *p*,' " *Journal of Philosophy* 64, no. 12 (1967): 373–89.

10

The Gettier Problem

John L. Pollock

INTRODUCTION

It is rare in philosophy to find a consensus on any substantive issue, but for some time there was almost complete consensus on what is called "the justified true belief analysis of knowing." According to that analysis:

> S knows P if and only if:
> (1) P is true;
> (2) S believes P; and
> (3) S is justified in believing P.

In the period immediately preceding the publication of Gettier's [1963] landmark article "Is Justified True Belief Knowledge?" this analysis was affirmed by virtually every writer in epistemology. Then Gettier published his article and singlehandedly changed the course of epistemology. He did this by presenting two clear and undeniable counterexamples to the justified true belief analysis. Recounting Gettier's example, consider Smith, who believes falsely but with good reason that Jones owns a Ford. Smith has no idea where Brown is, but he arbitrarily picks Barcelona and infers from the putative fact that Jones owns a Ford that either Jones owns a Ford or Brown is in Barcelona. It happens by chance that Brown is in Barcelona, so this dis-

From John L. Pollock, *Contemporary Theories of Knowledge*, appendix (Totowa, N.J.: Rowman and Littlefield Publishers, 1986), pp. 180–93. © 1986 Rowman and Littlefield Publishers. Reprinted by permission of the publisher.

junction is true. Furthermore, as Smith has good reason to believe that Jones owns a Ford, he is justified in believing this disjunction. But as his evidence does not pertain to the true disjunct of the disjunction, we would not regard Smith as *knowing* that either Jones owns a Ford or Brown is in Barcelona.

Gettier's paper was followed by a spate of articles attempting to meet his counterexamples by adding a fourth condition to the analysis of knowing. The first attempts to solve the Gettier problem turned on the observation that in Gettier's examples, the epistemic agent arrives at his justified true belief by reasoning from a false belief. That suggested the addition of a fourth condition something like the following:

> *S*'s grounds for believing *P* do not include any false beliefs.[1]

It soon emerged, however, that further counterexamples could be constructed in which knowledge is lacking despite the believer's not inferring his belief from any false beliefs. Alvin Goldman [1976] constructed the following example. Suppose you are driving through the countryside and see what you take to be a barn. You see it in good light and from not too great a distance, it looks the way barns look, and so on. Furthermore, it is a barn. You then have justified true belief that it is a barn. But in an attempt to appear more opulent than they are, the people around here have taken to constructing very realistic barn facades that cannot readily be distinguished from the real thing when viewed from the highway. There are many more barn facades around than real barns. Under these circumstances we would not agree that you know that what you see is a barn, even though you have justified true belief. Furthermore, your belief that you see a barn is not in any way inferred from a belief about the absence of barn facades. Most likely the possibility of barn facades is something that will not even have occurred to you, much less have played a role in your reasoning.

We can construct an even simpler perceptual example. Suppose *S* sees a ball that looks red to him, and on that basis he correctly judges that it is red. But unbeknownst to *S*, the ball is illuminated by red lights and would look red to him even if it were not red. Then *S* does not know that the ball is red despite his having a justified true belief to that effect. Furthermore, his reason for believing that the ball is red does not involve his believing that the ball is not illuminated by red lights. Illumination by red lights is related to his reasoning only as a defeater, not as a step in his reasoning. These examples, of other related examples,[2] indicate that justified true belief can fail to be knowledge because of the truth values of propositions that do not play a direct role in the reasoning underlying the belief. This observation led to a number of "defeasibility" analyses of knowing.[3] The simplest defeasibility analysis would consist of adding a fourth condition requiring that there be no true defeaters. This might be accomplished as follows:

There is no true proposition Q such that if Q were added to S's beliefs then he would no longer be justified in believing $P.$[4]

But Keith Lehrer and Thomas Paxson [1969] presented the following counterexample to this simple proposal:

> Suppose I see a man walk into the library and remove a book from the library by concealing it beneath his coat. Since I am sure the man is Tom Grabit, whom I have often seen before when he attended my classes, I report that I know that Tom Grabit has removed the book. However, suppose further that Mrs. Grabit, the mother of Tom, has averred that on the day in question Tom was not in the library, indeed, was thousands of miles away, and that Tom's identical twin brother, John Grabit, was in the library. Imagine, moreover, that I am entirely ignorant of the fact that Mrs. Grabit has said these things. The statement that she has said these things would defeat any justification I have for believing that Tom Grabit removed the book, according to our present definition of defeasibility. . . .
>
> The preceding might seem acceptable until we finish the story by adding that Mrs. Grabit is a compulsive and pathological liar, that John Grabit is a fiction of her demented mind, and that Tom Grabit took the book as I believed. Once this is added, it should be apparent that I did know that Tom Grabit removed the book. (p. 228)[5]

A natural proposal for handling the Grabit example is that in addition to there being a true defeater there is a true defeater defeater, and that restores knowledge. For example, in the Grabit case it is true that Mrs. Grabit reported that Tom was not in the library but his twin brother John was there (a defeater), but it is also true that Mrs. Grabit is a compulsive and pathological liar and John Grabit is a fiction of her demented mind (a defeater defeater). It is difficult, however, to construct a precise principle that handles these examples correctly by appealing to true defeaters and true defeater defeaters. It will not do to amend the above proposals as follows:

> If there is a true proposition Q such that if Q were added to S's beliefs then he would no longer be justified in believing P, then there is also a true proposition R such that if Q and R were both added to S's beliefs then he would be justified in believing P.

The simplest difficulty for this proposal is that adding R may add new reasons for believing P rather than restoring the old reasons. It is not trivial to see how to formulate a fourth condition incorporating defeater defeaters. I think that such a fourth condition will ultimately provide the solution to the Gettier problem, but no proposal of this sort has been worked out in the literature.[6] I will pursue this further in the next section.

Objective Epistemic Justification

The Gettier problem has spawned a large number of proposals for the analysis of knowledge. As the literature on the problem has developed, the proposals have become increasingly complex in the attempt to meet more and more complicated counterexamples to simpler analyses. The result is that even if some very complex analysis should turn out to be immune from counterexample, it would seem *ad hoc*. We would be left wondering why we employ any such complicated concept. I will suggest that our concept of knowledge is actually a reasonably simple one. The complexities required by increasingly complicated Gettier-type examples are not complexities in the concept of knowledge, but instead reflect complexities in the structure of our epistemic norms.

In the discussion of externalism I commented on the distinction between subjective and objective senses of "should believe" and how that pertains to epistemology. The subjective sense of "should believe" concerns what we should believe given what we actually do believe (possibly incorrectly). The objective sense of "should believe" concerns what we should believe given what is in fact true. But what we should believe given what is true is just the truths, so the objective sense of "should believe" gets identified with truth. The subjective sense, on the other hand, is ordinary epistemic justification. What I now want to suggest, however, is that there is an intermediate sense of "should believe," that might also be regarded as objective but does not reduce to truth.

It is useful to compare epistemic judgments with moral judgments. Focusing on the latter, let us suppose that a person S subjectively should do A. This will be so *for particular reasons*. There may be relevant facts of which the person is not apprised that bear upon these reasons. It might be the case that even in the face of all the relevant facts, S should still do A. That can happen in either of two ways: (1) among the relevant facts may be new reasons for doing A of which S has no knowledge; or (2) the relevant facts may, on sum, leave the original reasons intact. What I have been calling "the objective sense of 'should' " appeals to both kinds of considerations, but there is also an important kind of moral evaluation that appeals only to considerations of the second kind. This is the notion of the original reasons surviving intact, and it provides us with another variety of objective moral evaluation. We appraise a person and his act simultaneously by saying that he has a moral obligation to perform the act (he subjectively should do it) and his moral obligation derives from what are in fact good reasons (reasons withstanding the test of truth). It seems to me that we are often in the position of making such appraisals, although moral language provides us with no simple way of expressing them. The purely objective sense of "should" pertains more to acts than to agents, and hence does not express moral obligation. Therefore, it should not be confusing if I express appraisals of this third variety artificially by saying that S has an *objective obligation* to do *A* when he has an obligation to do *A* and the obligation derives from what are in fact good reasons (in the face of all the relevant facts).

How might objective obligation be analyzed? It might at first be supposed that *S* has an objective obligation to do *A* if and only if (1) *S* subjectively should do *A*, and (2) there is no set of truths *X* such that if these truths were added to *S*'s beliefs (and their negations removed in those cases in which *S* disbelieves them) then it would not be true that *S* subjectively should do *A* *for the same reason*. This will not quite do, however. It takes account of the fact that moral reasons are defeasible, but it does not take account of the fact that the defeaters are also defeasible. For example, *S* might spy a drowning man and be in a position to save him with no risk to himself. Then he subjectively should do so. But suppose that, unbeknownst to *S*, the man is a terrorist who fell in the lake while he was on his way to blow up a bus station and kill many innocent people. Presumably, if *S* knew that then he would no longer have a subjective obligation to save the man, and so it follows by the proposed analysis that *S* does not have an objective obligation to save the man. But suppose it is also the case that what caused the man to fall in the lake was that he underwent a sudden religious conversion that persuaded him to give up his evil ways and devote the rest of his life to good deeds. If *S* knew this, then he would again have a subjective obligation to save the man, for the same reasons as his original reasons, and so he has an objective obligation to save the man. There is, however, no way to accommodate this on the proposed analysis. On that analysis, if a set of truths defeats an obligation, there is no way to get it undefeated again by appealing to a broader class of truths.

What the analysis of objective obligation should require is that if *S* were apprised of "enough" truths (all the relevant ones) then he would still be subjectively obligated to do *A*. This can be cashed out as requiring that there is a set of truths such that if *S* were apprised of them then he would be subjectively obligated in the same way as he originally was, and those are all the relevant truths in the sense that if he were to become apprised of any further truths that would not make any difference. Precisely:

S has an objective obligation to do *A* if and only if:
(1) S subjectively should do *A*; and
(2) there is a set *X* of truths such that, given any more inclusive set *Y* of truths, necessarily, if the truths in *Y* were added to *S*'s beliefs (and their negations removed in those cases in which *S* disbelieves them) then it would still be true *for the same reason* that *S* subjectively should do *A*.

Now let us return to epistemology. An important difference between moral judgments and epistemic judgments is that basic moral judgments concern obligation whereas basic epistemic judgments concern permissibility. This reflects an important difference in the way moral and epistemic norms function. In morality, reasons are reasons for obligations. Anything is permissible that is not proscribed. In epistemology, on the other hand, epistemic justification concerns what beliefs you are permitted to hold (not "obliged to hold"), and reasons are required for permissibility. Thus the analogy between epistemology and morality is not exact. The analog of objective moral obligation is "objective epistemic permissibility," or as I will say more simply, *objective epistemic justification*. I propose to ignore our earlier concept of objective epistemic justification because it simply reduces to truth. Our new concept of objective epistemic justification can be defined as follows, on analogy to our notion of objective moral obligation:

> S is objectively justified in believing P if and only if:
> (1) S is (subjectively) justified in believing P; and
> (2) there is a set X of truths such that, given any more inclusive set Y of truths, necessarily, if the truths in Y were added to S's beliefs (and their negations removed in those cases in which S disbelieves them) and S believed P *for the same reason* then he would still be (subjectively) justified in believing P.

Despite the complexity of its definition, the concept of objective epistemic justification is a simple and intuitive one. As is so often the case with technical concepts, the concept is easier to grasp than it is to define. It can be roughly glossed as the concept of getting the right answer while doing everything right. I am construing "S is justified in believing P" in such a way that it entails that S does believe P, so objective justification entails justified belief. It also entails truth, because if P were false and we added ~P to Y then S would no longer be justified in believing P. Thus, objective epistemic justification entails justified true belief.

My claim is now that objective epistemic justification is very close to being the same thing as knowledge. We will find in section three that a qualification is required to turn objective justification into knowledge, but in the meantime it can be argued that the Gettier problem can be resolved by taking objective epistemic justification to be a necessary condition for knowledge. This enables us to avoid the familiar Gettier-type examples that create difficulties for other analyses of knowledge. Consider one of Gettier's original examples. Jones believes, correctly, that Brown owns a Ford. He believes this on the grounds that he has frequently seen Brown drive a particular Ford, he has ridden in it, he has seen Brown's auto registration which lists him as owning that Ford, and so forth. But unknown to Jones, Brown sold that Ford yesterday and bought a new one. Under the circumstances, we would not agree that Jones now knows that Brown owns a Ford, despite the fact that he has a justified true belief to that effect. This is explained by noting that Jones is not objectively justified in believing that Brown owns a Ford. This is because there is a truth—namely, that

Brown does not own the Ford Jones thinks he owns—such that if Jones became apprised of it then his original reasons would no longer justify him in believing that Jones owns a Ford, and becoming apprised of further truths would not restore those original reasons.

To take a more complicated case, consider Goldman's barn example. Suppose you are driving through the countryside and see what you take to be a barn. You see it in good light and from not too great a distance, and it looks like a barn. Furthermore, it is a barn. You then have justified true belief that it is a barn. But the countryside here is littered with very realistic barn facades that cannot readily be distinguished from the real thing when viewed from the highway. There are many more barn facades than real barns. Under these circumstances we would not agree that you know that what you see is a barn, even though you have justified true belief. This can be explained by noting that if you were aware of the preponderance of barn facades in the vicinity then you would not be justified in believing you see a barn, and your original justification could not be restored by learning other truths (such as that it is really a barn). Consequently, your belief that you see a barn is not objectively justified.[7]

Finally, consider the Grabit example. Here we want to say that I really do know that Tom Grabit stole the book, despite the fact that Mrs. Grabit alleged that Tom was thousands of miles away and his twin brother John was in the library. That she said this is a true defeater, but there is also a true defeater defeater, viz., that Mrs. Grabit is a compulsive and pathological liar and John Grabit is a fiction of her demented mind. If we include both of these truths in the set X then I remain justified *for my original reason* in believing that Tom stole the book, so in this case my belief is objectively justified despite the existence of a true defeater.

To a certain extent, I think that the claim that knowledge requires objective epistemic justification provides a solution to the Gettier problem. But it might be disqualified as a solution to the Gettier problem on the grounds that the definition of objective justification is vague in one crucial respect. It talks about being justified, *for the same reason,* in believing P. I think that that notion makes pre-theoretic good sense, but to spell out what it involves requires us to construct a complete epistemological theory. That, I think, is why the Gettier problem has proven so intractable. The complexities in the analysis of knowing all have to do with filling out this clause. The important thing to realize, however, is that these complexities have nothing special to do with knowledge per se. What they pertain to is the structure of epistemic justification and the way in which beliefs come to be justified on the basis of other beliefs and nondoxastic states. Thus even if it is deemed that we have not yet solved the Gettier problem, we have at least put the blame where it belongs—not on knowledge but on the structure of epistemic justification and the complexity of our epistemic norms.

Let us turn then to the task of filling in some of the details concerning epistemic justification. Earlier I proposed an analysis of epistemic justification in terms of ultimately undefeated arguments. That analysis proceeded within the context of a subsequently rejected foundationalist theory, but basically the same analysis can be resurrected within direct realism. For this purpose we must take arguments to proceed from internal states (both doxastic and nondoxastic states) to doxastic states, the links between steps being provided by reasons. Within direct realism, reasons are internal states. They are generally doxastic states, but not invariably. At the very least, perceptual and memory states can also be reasons.

Our epistemic norms permit us to begin reasoning from certain internal states without those states being supported by further reasoning. Such states can be called *basic states*. Paramount among these are perceptual and memory states. Arguments must always begin with basic states and proceed from them to nonbasic doxastic states. What we might call *linear arguments* proceed from basic states to their ultimate conclusions through a sequence of steps each consisting of a belief for which the earlier steps provide reasons. It seems likely, however, that we must allow arguments to have more complicated structures than those permitted in linear arguments. Specifically, we must allow "subsidiary arguments" to occur within the main argument. A subsidiary argument can begin with premises that are merely assumed for the sake of the argument rather than because they have already been justified. For instance, in the forms of conditional proof familiar from elementary logic, in establishing a conditional $(P \supset Q)$, we may begin by taking P as a premise (even though it has not previously been established), deriving Q from it, and then "discharging" the assumption of the antecedent to obtain the conditional $(P \supset Q)$. It seems that something similar occurs in epistemological arguments. We can accommodate this by taking *an argument conditional on a set X of propositions* to be an argument beginning not just from basic states but also from doxastic states that consist of believing the members of X. Then an argument that justifies a conclusion for a person may have embedded in it subsidiary arguments that are conditional on propositions the person does not believe. For present purposes we need not pursue all the details of the permissible structures of epistemological arguments, but the general idea of conditional arguments will be useful below.

An argument *supports* a belief if and only if that belief occurs as a step in the argument that does not occur within any subsidiary argument. A person *instantiates* an argument if and only if he is in the basic states from which the argument begins and he believes the conclusion of the argument on the basis of that argument. Typically, in reasoning to a conclusion one will proceed first to some intermediate conclusions from which the final conclusion is obtained. The notion of holding a belief on the basis of an argument is to be understood as requiring that one also believes the intermediate conclusions on the basis of the initial parts of the argument.

Epistemic justification consists of holding a belief on the basis of an ultimately undefeated argument, that is, instantiating an ultimately undefeated argument supporting the belief. To repeat the definition of an ultimately undefeated argument, every argument proceeding from basic states that S is actually in will be *undefeated at level 0* for S. Of course, arguments undefeated at level 0 can embed subsidiary arguments that are conditional on propositions S does not believe. Some arguments will support defeaters for other arguments, so we define an argument to be undefeated at level 1 if and only if it is not defeated by any other arguments undefeated at level 0. Among the arguments defeated at level 0 may be some that supported defeaters for others, so if we take arguments undefeated at level 2 to be arguments undefeated at level 0 that are not defeated by any arguments undefeated at level 1, there may be arguments undefeated at level 2 that were arguments defeated at level 1. In general, we define an argument to be *undefeated at level* n + 1 if and only if it is undefeated at level 0 and is not defeated by any arguments undefeated at level n. An argument is *ultimately undefeated* if and only if there is some point beyond which it remains permanently undefeated; that is, for some N, the argument remains undefeated at level n for every $n > N$.

This gives us a picture of the structure of epistemic justification. Many details remain to be filled in, but we can use this picture without further elaboration to clarify the concept of objective epistemic justification. Roughly, a belief is objectively justified if and only if it is held on the basis of some ultimately undefeated argument A, and either A is not defeated by any argument conditional on true propositions not believed by S, or if it is then there are further true propositions such that the initial defeating arguments will be defeated by arguments conditional on the enlarged set of true propositions. This can be made precise by defining an *argument conditional on Y* to be any argument proceeding from basic states S is actually in together with doxastic states consisting of believing members of Y. We then say that an argument instantiated by S (not an argument conditional on Y) is *undefeated at level* n + 1 *relative to Y* if and only if it is undefeated by any argument undefeated at level n relative to Y. An argument is *ultimately undefeated relative to Y* if and only if there is an N such that it is undefeated at level n relative to Y for every $n > N$. Then the concept of objective epistemic justification can be made more precise as follows:

> S is objectively justified in believing P if and only if S instantiates some argument A supporting P which is ultimately undefeated relative to the set of all truths.

I will take this to be my official definition of objective epistemic justification. I claim, then, that the Gettier-style counterexamples to the traditional definition of knowledge can all be met by taking knowledge to require objective epistemic justification. This makes precise the way in which knowledge requires justification that is either undefeated by true defeaters, or if defeated by true defeaters then those defeaters are defeated by true defeater defeaters, and so on.

A common view has been that the reliability of one's cognitive processes is required for knowledge, and thus reliabilism has a place in the analysis of knowledge quite apart from whether it has a place in the analysis of epistemic justification.[8] The observation that knowledge requires objective epistemic justification explains the appeal of the idea that knowledge requires reliability. Nondefeasible reasons logically entail their conclusions, so they are always perfectly reliable, but defeasible reasons can be more or less reliable under various circumstances. Discovering that the present circumstances are of a type in which a defeasible reason is unreliable constitutes a defeater for the use of that reason. Objective justification requires that if a belief is held on the basis of a defeasible reason then there are no true defeaters (or if there are then there are true defeater defeaters, and so on). Thus knowledge automatically requires that one's reasons be reliable under the present circumstances. Reliabilism has a place in knowledge even if it has none in justification. It is worth emphasizing, however, that considerations of reliability are not central to the concept of knowledge. Rather than having to be imposed on the analysis in an *ad hoc* way, they emerge naturally from the observation that knowledge requires objective epistemic justification.

SOCIAL ASPECTS OF KNOWLEDGE

It is tempting to simply identify knowledge with objective epistemic justification. As I have pointed out, objective justification includes justified true belief, and it is immune from Gettier-style counterexamples. It captures the idea underlying defeasibility analyses. The basic idea is that *believed* defeaters can prevent justification, and defeaters that are true but not believed can prevent knowledge while leaving justification intact. However, there are also some examples that differ in important ways from the Gettier-style examples we have discussed so far, and they are not so easily handled in terms of their being true defeaters. These examples seem to have to do with social aspects of knowing, The philosopher most prominently associated with these examples is Gilbert Harman.[9] One of Harman's examples is as follows:

> Suppose that Tom enters a room in which many people are talking excitedly although he cannot understand what they are saying. He sees a copy of the morning paper on a table. The headlines and main story reveal that a famous civil-rights leader has been assassinated. On reading the story he comes to believe it; it is true. . . .
>   Suppose that the assassination has been denied, even by eyewitnesses, the point of the denial being to avoid a racial explosion. The assassinated leader is reported in good health; the bullets are said, falsely, to have missed him and hit someone else. The denials occurred too late to prevent the original and true story from appearing in the paper that Tom has seen; but everyone else in the room has heard about the denials. None of them know what to believe. They all have information that Tom lacks. Would we judge Tom to be the only one who knows that the assassination has actually occurred? . . . I do not think so.[10]

This example cannot be handled in the same way as the Grabit example. As in the Grabit example there is a true defeater, viz., that the news media have reported that the assassination did not occur. But just as in the Grabit example, there is also a true defeater defeater, viz., that the retraction of the original story was motivated by an attempt to avoid race riots and did not necessarily reflect the actual facts. The appeal to true defeaters and true defeater defeaters should lead us to treat this example just like the Grabit example, but that gives the wrong answer. The Grabit example is one in which the believer has knowledge, whereas the newspaper example is one in which the believer lacks knowledge.

Harman gives a second kind of example in a recent article:

> In case one, Mary comes to know that Norman is in Italy when she calls his office and is told he is spending the summer in Rome. In case two, Norman seeks to give Mary the impression that he is in San Francisco by writing her a letter saying so, a letter he mails to San Francisco where a friend then mails it on to Mary. This letter is in the pile of unopened mail on Mary's desk before her when she calls Norman's office and is told he is spending the summer in Rome. In this case (case two), Mary does not come to know that Norman is in Italy.
>
> It is important in this case that Mary could obtain the misleading evidence. If the evidence is unobtainable, because Norman forgot to mail the letter after he wrote it, or because the letter was delivered to the wrong building where it will remain unopened, then it does not keep Mary from knowing that Norman is in Italy.[11]

Again, there is a true defeater, viz., that the letter reports Norman to be in San Francisco. But there is also a true defeater defeater, viz., that the letter was written with the intention to deceive. So Mary's belief is objectively justified. Nevertheless, we want to deny that Mary knows that Norman is in Italy.

Harman summarizes these examples by writing, "There seem to be two ways in which such misleading evidence can undermine a person's knowledge. The evidence can either be evidence that it would be possible for the person to obtain himself or herself or evidence possessed by others in a relevant social group to which the person in question belongs."[12] We might distinguish between these two examples by saying that in the first example there is a true defeater that is "common knowledge" in Tom's social group, whereas in the second example there is a true defeater that is "readily available" to Mary. I will loosely style these "common knowledge" and "ready availability" defeaters.

It is worth noting that a common knowledge defeater can be defeated by a defeater defeater that is also common knowledge. For example, if it were common knowledge that the news media was disclaiming the assassination, but also common knowledge that the disclaimer was fraudulent, then Tom would retain his knowledge that the assassination occurred even if he were unaware of both the disclaimer and its fraudulence. The same thing is true of ready availability defeaters. If Norman had a change of heart after sending the false letter and sent another letter explaining the trick he played on Mary, and both letters lay unopened on Mary's desk when she called Norman's office, her telephone call would give her knowledge that Norman is in Italy.

What is more surprising is that common knowledge and ready availability defeaters and defeater defeaters can be combined to result in knowledge. For instance, if Norman's trick letter lays unopened on Mary's desk when she makes the call, she will nevertheless acquire knowledge that Norman is in Italy if Norman is an important diplomat and, unbeknownst to her, the news media have been announcing all day that Norman is in Rome but has been trying to fool people about his location by sending out trick letters. This shows that despite the apparent differences between common knowledge and ready availability defeaters, there must be some kind of connection between them.

My suggestion is that these both reflect a more general social aspect of knowledge. We are "socially expected" to be aware of various things. We are expected to know what is announced on television, and we are expected to know what is in our mail. If we fail to know all these things and that makes a difference to whether we are justified in believing some true proposition P, then our objectively justified belief in P does not constitute knowledge. Let us say that a proposition is *socially sensitive for S* if and only if it is of a sort S is expected to believe when true. My claim is that Harman's examples are best handled by taking them to involve cases in which there are true socially sensitive defeaters. This might be doubted on the grounds that not all readily available truths are socially sensitive. For instance, suppose that instead of having his trick letter mailed from San Francisco, Norman had a friend secrete it under Mary's doormat. We are not socially expected to check regularly under our doormats, but nevertheless this is something we can readily do and so information secreted under our doormats counts as readily available. It does not, however, defeat knowledge. If the trick letter were secreted under Mary's doormat, we would regard her as knowing that Norman is in Italy. Suppose, on the other hand, that we lived in a society in which it is common to leave messages under doormats and everyone is expected to check his doormat whenever he comes home. In that case, if the trick letter were under Mary's doormat but she failed to check there before calling Norman's office, we would not regard that call as providing her with knowledge. These examples seem to indicate that it is social sensitivity and not mere ready availability that enables a truth to defeat a knowledge claim.

My suggestion is that we can capture the social aspect of knowledge by requiring a knower to hold his belief on the basis of an argument ultimately undefeated relative not just to the set of all truths, but also to the set of all socially sensitive truths. My proposal is:

S knows *P* if and only if *S* instantiates some argument *A* supporting *P* which is (1) ultimately undefeated relative to the set of all truths, and (2) ultimately undefeated relative to the set of all truths socially sensitive for *S*.

This proposal avoids both the Gettier problem and the social problems discussed by Harman. At this stage in history it would be rash to be very confident of any analysis of knowledge, but I put this forth tentatively as an analysis that seems to handle all of the known problems.

NOTES

1. See, for example, Michael Clark, "Knowledge and Grounds: A Comment on Mr. Gettier's Paper," *Analysis* 24 (1963): 46–48.

2. See, for example, Brian Skyrms, "The Explication of 'X knows that p,' " *Journal of Philosophy* 64 (1967): 373–89.

3. The first defeasibility analysis was that of Keith Lehrer, "Knowledge, Truth, and Evidence," *Analysis* 25 (1965): 168–75.That was followed by Lehrer and Thomas Paxson, Jr., "Knowledge: Undefeated Justified True Belief," *Journal of Philosophy* 66 (1969): 225–37; Peter Klein, "A Proposed Definition of Propositional Knowledge," *Journal of Philosophy* 68 (1971): 471–82, "Knowledge, Causality, and Defeasibility," *Journal of Philosophy* 73 (1976): 792–812, "Misleading 'Misleading Defeaters,' " *Journal of Philosophy* 76 (1979): 382–86, and "Misleading Evidence and the Restoration of Justification," *Philosophical Studies* 37 (1980): 81–89; Lehrer, *Knowledge* (Oxford: Oxford University Press, 1974) and "The Gettier Problem and the Analysis of Knowledge" in George Pappas, ed., *Justification and Knowledge: New Studies in Epistemology* (Dordrecht, Netherlands: D. Reidel Publishing, 1979); Ernest Sosa, "How Do You Know?" *American Philosophical Quarterly* 11 (1974): 113–22, and "Epistemic Presupposition," in George Pappas, ed., *Justification and Knowledge: New Studies in Epistemology* (Dordrecht, Netherlands: D. Reidel Publishing, 1980); and Marshall Swain, *Reasons and Knowledge* (Ithaca, N.Y.: Cornell University Press, 1981).

4. This is basically the analysis proffered by Klein in "A Proposed Definition of Propositional Knowledge," 1971.

5. See Lehrer and Paxson, "Knowledge: Undefeated Justified True Belief," p. 228.

6. A good survey of the literature on the Gettier problem, going into much more detail than space permits here, can be found in Robert K. Shope, *The Analysis of Knowing* (Princeton, N.J.: Princeton University Press, 1983).

7. This can be formulated in terms of defeaters and defeater defeaters. "Most of the things around here that look like barns are not barns" is a true reliability defeater, but there is no true defeater defeater. In particular, "That really is a barn," although true, does not restore your original justification—instead, it constitutes a new reason for believing that what you see is a barn.

8. See, for example, Alvin Goldman, "The Internalist Conception of Justification," *Midwest Studies in Philosophy*, vol. 5 (Minneapolis: University of Minnesota Press, 1981), pp. 27–29.

9. See Gilbert Harman, "Knowledge, Inference, and Explanation," *American Philosophical Quarterly* 5 (1968): 164–73 and "Reasoning and Explanatory Coherence," *American Philosophical Quarterly* 17 (1980): 151–58. Harman credits Ernest Sosa's "The Analysis of 'Knowledge that p' " (1964) with the original observation that social considerations play a role in knowledge.

10. "Knowledge, Inference, and Explanation" (1968), p. 172.

11. "Reasoning and Evidence Ones Does Not Possess," *Midwest Studies in Philosophy*, vol. 5 (Minneapolis: University of Minnesota Press, 1981), p. 164.

12. Ibid.

Part II

The Problem of the Criterion

11

The Problem of the Criterion

Roderick M. Chisholm

1

"The problem of the criterion" seems to me to be one of the most important and one of the most difficult of all the problems of philosophy. I am tempted to say that one has not begun to philosophize until one has faced this problem and has recognized how unappealing, in the end, each of the possible solutions is. I have chosen this problem as my topic for the Aquinas Lecture because what first set me to thinking about it (and I remain obsessed by it) were two treatises of twentieth century scholastic philosophy. I refer first to P. Coffey's two-volume work, *Epistemology or the Theory of Knowledge,* published in 1917.[1] This led me in turn to the treatises of Coffey's great teacher, Cardinal D. J. Mercier: *Critériologie générale ou théorie générale de la certitude.*[2]

Mercier and, following him, Coffey set the problem correctly, I think, and have seen what is necessary for its solution. But I shall not discuss their views in detail. I shall formulate the problem; then note what, according to Mercier, is necessary if we are to solve the problem; then sketch my own solution; and, finally, note the limitations of my approach to the problem.

The Aquinas Lecture, 1973 (Milwaukee, Wisc.: Marquette University Press, 1973). © Marquette University Press. Reprinted by permission of the publisher.

2

What is the problem, then? It is the ancient problem of "the diallelus"—the problem of "the wheel" or "the vicious circle." It was put very neatly by Montaigne in his *Essays*. So let us begin by paraphrasing his formulation of the puzzle. To know whether things really are as they seem to be, we must have a *procedure* for distinguishing appearances that are true from appearances that are false. But to know whether our procedure is a good procedure, we have to know whether it really *succeeds* in distinguishing appearances that are true from appearances that are false. And we cannot know whether it does really succeed unless we already know which appearances are *true* and which ones are *false*. And so we are caught in a circle.[3]

Let us try to see how one gets into a situation of this sort.

The puzzles begin to form when you ask yourself, "What can I really know about the world?" We all are acquainted with people who think they know a lot more than in fact they do know. I'm thinking of fanatics, bigots, mystics, various types of dogmatists. And we have all heard of people who claim at least to know a lot less than what in fact they do know. I'm thinking of those people who call themselves "skeptics" and who like to say that people cannot know what the world is really like. People tend to become skeptics, temporarily, after reading books on popular science: the authors tell us we cannot know what things are like really (but they make use of a vast amount of knowledge, or a vast amount of what is claimed to be knowledge, to support this skeptical conclusion). And as we know, people tend to become dogmatists, temporarily, as a result of the effects of alcohol, or drugs, or religious and emotional experiences. Then they claim to have an inside view of the world and they think they have a deep kind of knowledge giving them a key to the entire workings of the universe.

If you have a healthy common sense, you will feel that something is wrong with both of these extremes and that the truth is somewhere in the middle: we can know far more than the skeptic says we can know and far less than the dogmatist or the mystic says that he can know. But how are we to decide these things?

3

How do we decide, in any particular case, whether we have a genuine item of knowledge? Most of us are ready to confess that our beliefs far transcend what we really know. There are things we believe that we don't in fact know. And we can say of many of these things that we know that we don't know them. I believe that Mrs. Jones is honest, say, but I don't know it, and I know that I don't know it. There are other things that we don't know, but they are such that we don't know that we don't know them. Last week, say, I thought I knew that Mr. Smith was honest, but he turned out to be a thief. I didn't know that he was a thief, and, moreover, I didn't know that I didn't know that he was a thief; I thought I knew that he was honest. And so the problem is: How are we to distinguish the real cases of knowledge from what only seem to be cases of knowledge? Or, as I put it before, how are we to decide in any particular case whether we have genuine items of knowledge?

What would be a satisfactory solution to our problem? Let me quote in detail what Cardinal Mercier says:

> If there is any knowledge which bears the mark of truth, if the intellect does have a way of distinguishing the true and the false, in short, *if* there *is* a criterion of truth, then this criterion should satisfy three conditions: it should be *internal, objective,* and *immediate.*
>
> It should be *internal.* No reason or rule of truth that is provided by an *external authority* can serve as an ultimate criterion. For the reflective doubts that are essential to criteriology can and should be applied to this authority itself. The mind cannot attain to certainty until it has found *within itself* a sufficient reason for adhering to the testimony of such an authority.
>
> The criterion should be *objective.* The ultimate reason for believing cannot be a merely *subjective* state of the thinking subject. A man is aware that he can reflect upon his psychological states in order to control them. Knowing that he has this ability, he does not, so long as he has not made use of it, have the right to be sure. The ultimate ground of certitude cannot consist in a subjective feeling. It can be found only in that which, objectively, produces this feeling and is adequate to reason.
>
> Finally, the criterion must be *immediate.* To be sure, a certain conviction may rest upon many different reasons, some of which are subordinate to others. But if we are to avoid an infinite regress, then we must find a ground of assent that presupposes no other. We must find an *immediate* criterion of certitude.
>
> Is there a criterion of truth that satisfies these three solutions? If so, what is it?[4]

4

To see how perplexing our problem is, let us consider a figure that Descartes had suggested and that Coffey takes up in his dealings with the problem of the criterion.[5] Descartes' figure comes to this.

Let us suppose that you have a pile of apples and you want to sort out the good ones from the bad ones. You want to put the good ones in a pile by themselves and throw the bad ones away. This is a useful thing to do, obviously, because the bad apples tend to infect the good ones and then the good ones become bad, too. Descartes thought our beliefs were like this. The bad ones tend to infect the good ones, so we should look them over very carefully, throw out the bad ones if we can, and then—or so Descartes hoped—we would be left with just a stock of good beliefs on which we could rely completely. But how are we to do the sorting? If we are to sort out the good ones from the bad ones, then, of course, we must have a way of recognizing the good ones. Or at least we must have a way of recognizing the bad ones. And—again, of course—you and I do have a way of recognizing good apples and also of recognizing bad ones. The good ones have their own special feel, look, and taste, and so do the bad ones.

But when we turn from apples to beliefs, the matter is quite different. in the case of the apples, we have a method—a criterion—for distinguishing the good ones from the bad ones. But in the case of the beliefs, we do not have a method or a criterion for distinguishing the good ones from the bad ones. Or, at least, we don't have one yet. The question we started with was: How *are* we to tell the good ones from the bad ones? In other words, we were asking: What is the proper method for deciding which are the good beliefs and which are the bad ones—which beliefs are genuine cases of knowledge and which beliefs are not?

And now, you see, we are on the wheel. First, we want to find out which are the good beliefs and which are the bad ones. To find this out we have to have some way— some method—of deciding which are the good ones and which are the bad ones. But there are good and bad methods—good and bad ways—of sorting out the good beliefs from the bad ones. And so we now have a new problem: How are we to decide which are the good methods and which are the bad ones?

If we could fix on a good method for distinguishing between good and bad methods, we might be all set. But this, of course, just moves the problem to a different level. How are we to distinguish between a good method for choosing good methods? If we continue in this way, of course, we are led to an infinite regress and we will never have the answer to our original question.

What do we do in fact? We do know that there are fairly reliable ways of sorting out good beliefs from bad ones. Most people will tell you, for example, that if you follow the procedures of science and common sense—if you tend carefully to your observations and if you make use of the canons of logic, induction, and the theory of probability—you will be following the best possible procedure for making sure that you will have more good beliefs than bad ones. This is doubtless true. But how do we know that it is? How do we know that the procedures of science, reason, and common sense are the best methods that we have?

If we do know this, it is because we know that these procedures work. It is because we know that these procedures do in fact enable us to distinguish the good beliefs from the bad ones. We say: "See—these methods turn out good beliefs." But *how* do we know that they do? It can only be that we already know how to tell the difference between the good beliefs and the bad ones.

And now you can see where the skeptic comes in. He'll say this: "You said you wanted to sort out the good beliefs from the bad ones. Then to do this, you apply the canons of science, common sense, and reason. And now, in answer to the question,

'How do you know that that's the right way to do it?' you say, 'Why, I can see that the ones it picks out are the good ones and the ones it leaves behind are the bad ones.' But if you can *see* which ones are the good ones and which ones are the bad ones, why do you think you need a general method for sorting them out?"

5

We can formulate some of the philosophical issues that are involved here by distinguishing two pairs of questions. These are:

A) *"What* do we know? What is the *extent* of our knowledge?"

B) "How are we to decide *whether* we know? What are the
   criteria of knowledge?"

If you happen to know the answers to the first of these pairs of questions, you may have some hope of being able to answer the second. Thus, if you happen to know which are the good apples and which are the bad ones, then maybe you could explain to some other person how he could go about deciding whether or not he has a good apple or a bad one. But if you don't know the answer to the first of these pairs of questions—if you don't know what things you know or how far your knowledge extends—it is difficult to see how you could possibly figure out an answer to the second.

On the other hand, *if,* somehow, you already know the answers to the second of these pairs of questions, then you may have some hope of being able to answer the first. Thus, if you happen to have a good set of directions for telling whether apples are good or bad, then maybe you can go about finding a good one—assuming, of course, that there are some good apples to be found. But if you don't know the answer to the second of these pairs of questions—if you don't know how to go about deciding whether or not you know, if you don't know what the criteria of knowing are—it is difficult to see how you could possibly figure out an answer to the first.

And so we can formulate the position of *the skeptic* on these matters. He will say: "You cannot answer question A until you have answered question B. And you cannot answer question B until you have answered question A. Therefore you cannot answer either question. You cannot know what, if anything, you know, and there is no possible way for you to decide in any particular case." Is there any reply to this?

6

Broadly speaking, there are at least two other possible views. So we may choose among three possibilities.

There are people—philosophers—who think that they do have an answer to B and that, given their answer to B, they can then figure out their answer to A. And there are other people—other philosophers—who have it the other way around: they think that they have an answer to A and that, given their answer to A, they can then figure out the answer to B.

There don't seem to be any generally accepted names for these two different philosophical positions. (Perhaps this is just as well. There are more than enough names, as it is, for possible philosophical views.) I suggest, for the moment, we use the expressions "methodists" and "particularists." By "methodists," I mean, not the followers of John Wesley's version of Christianity, but those who think they have an answer to B, and who then, in terms of it, work out their answer to A. By "particularists" I mean those who have it the other way around.

7

Thus John Locke was a methodist—in our present, rather special sense of the term. He was able to arrive—somehow—at an answer to B. He said, in effect: "The way you decide whether or not a belief is a good belief—that is to say, the way you decide whether a belief is likely to be a genuine case of knowledge—is to see whether it is derived from sense experience, to see, for example, whether it bears certain relations to your sensations." Just what these relations to our sensations might be is a matter we may leave open, for present purposes. The point is: Locke felt that if a belief is to be credible, it must bear certain relations to the believer's sensations—but he never told us *how* he happened to arrive at this conclusion. This, of course, is the view that has come to be known as "empiricism." David Hume followed Locke in this empiricism and said that empiricism gives us an effective criterion for distinguishing the good apples from the bad ones. You can take this criterion to the library, he said. Suppose you find a book in which the author makes assertions that do not conform to the empirical criterion. Hume said: "Commit it to the flames: for it can contain nothing but sophistry and illusion."

8

Empiricism, then, was a form of what I have called "methodism." The empiricist—like other types of methodist—begins with a criterion and then he uses it to throw out the bad apples. There are two objections, I would say, to empiricism. The first—which applies to every form of methodism (in our present sense of the word)—is that the criterion is very broad and far-reaching and at the same time completely arbitrary. How can one begin with a broad generalization? It seems especially odd that the empiricist—who wants to proceed cautiously, step by step, from experience—begins with such a generalization. He leaves us completely in the dark so far as concerns what *reasons* he may have for adopting this particular criterion rather than some other. The second objection applies to empiricism in particular. When we apply the empirical criterion—at least, as it was developed by Hume, as well as by many of those in the nineteenth and twentieth centuries who have called themselves "empiricists"— we seem to throw out, not only the bad apples but the good ones as well, and we are left, in effect, with just a few pairings or skins with no meat behind them. Thus Hume virtually conceded that, if you are going to be empiricist, the only matters of fact that you can really know about pertain to the existence of sensations. " 'Tis vain," he said, "To ask whether there be body." He meant you cannot know whether any physical things exist—whether there are trees, or houses, or bodies, much less whether there are atoms or other such microscopic particles. All you can know is that there are and have been certain sensations. You cannot know whether there is any you who experiences those sensations—much less whether any other people exist who experience sensations. And I think, if he had been consistent in his empiricism, he would also have said you cannot really be sure whether there have been any sensations in the past; you can know only that certain sensations exist here and now.

9

The great Scottish philosopher Thomas Reid reflected on all this in the eighteenth century. He was serious about philosophy and man's place in the world. He finds Hume saving things implying that we can know only of the existence of certain sensations here and now. One can imagine him saying: "Good Lord! What kind of nonsense is this?" What he did say, among other things, was this: "A traveller of good judgment may mistake his way, and be unawares led into a wrong track; and while the road is fair before him, he may go on without suspicion, and be followed by others but, when it ends in a coal pit, it requires no great judgment to know that he hath gone wrong, nor perhaps to find out what misled him."[6]

Thus Reid, as I interpret him, was not an empiricist; nor was he, more generally, what I have called a "methodist." He was a "particularist." That is to say, he thought that he had an answer to question A, and in terms of the answer to question A, he then worked out kind of an answer to question B.[7] An even better example of a "particularist" is the great twentieth-century English philosopher G. E. Moore.

Suppose, for a moment, you were tempted to go along with Hume and say: "The only thing about the world I can really know is that there are now sensations of a certain sort. There's a sensation of a man, there's the sound of a voice, and there's a feeling of bewilderment or boredom. But that's all I can really know about." What would Reid say? I can imagine him saying something like this: "Well, you can talk that way if you want to. But you know very well that it isn't true. You know that you are there, that you have a body of such and such a sort and that other people are here, too. And you know about this building and where you were this morning and all kinds of other things as well." G. E. Moore would raise his hand at this point and say: "I know very well this is a hand, and so do you. If you come across some philosophical theory that implies that you and I cannot know that this is a hand, then so much the worse for the theory." I think that Reid and Moore are right, myself, and I'm inclined to think that the "methodists" are wrong.

Going back to our questions A and B, we may summarize the three possible views as follows: there is skepticism (you cannot answer either question without presupposing an answer to the other, and therefore the questions cannot be answered at all); there is "methodism" (you begin with an answer to B); and there is "particularism" (you begin with an answer to A). I suggest that the third possibility is the most reasonable.

10

I would say—and many reputable philosophers would disagree with me—that, to find out whether you know such a thing as that this is a hand, you don't have to apply any test or criterion. Spinoza has it right. "In order to know," he said, "there is no need to know that we know, much less to know that we know that we know."[8]

This is part of the answer, it seems to me, to the puzzle about the diallelus. There are many things that quite obviously, we do know to be true. If I report to you the things I now see and hear and feel—or, if you prefer, the things I now think I see and hear and feel—the chances are that my report will be correct; I will be telling you something I know. And so, too, if you report the things that you think you now see and hear and feel. To be sure, there are hallucinations and illusions. People often think they see or hear or feel things that in fact they do not see or hear or feel. But from this fact—that our senses do sometimes deceive us—it hardly follows that your senses and mine are deceiving you and me right now. One may say similar things about what we remember.

Having these good apples before us, we can look them over and formulate certain criteria of goodness. Consider the senses, for example. One important criterion—one epistemological principle—was formulated by St. Augustine. It is more reasonable, he said, to trust the senses than to distrust them. Even though there have been illusions and hallucinations, the wise thing, when everything seems all right, is to accept the testimony of the senses. I say "when everything seems all right." If on a particular occasion something about *that* particular occasion makes you suspect that particular report of the senses, if, say, you seem to remember having been drugged or hypnotized, or brainwashed, then perhaps you should have some doubts about what you think you see, or hear, or feel, or smell. But if nothing about this particular occasion leads you to suspect what the senses report on this particular occasion, then the wise thing is to take such a report at its face value. In short the senses should be regarded as innocent until there is some positive reason, on some particular occasion, for thinking that they are guilty on that particular occasion.

One might say the same thing of memory. If, on any occasion, you think you remember that such-and-such an event occurred, then the wise thing is to assume that that particular event did occur—unless something special about this particular occasion leads you to suspect your memory.

We have then a kind of answer to the puzzle about the diallelus. We start with particular cases of knowledge and then from these we generalize and formulate criteria of goodness—criteria telling us what it is for a belief to be epistemologically respectable. Let us now try to sketch somewhat more precisely this approach to the problem of the criterion.

11

The theory of evidence, like ethics and the theory of value, presupposes an objective right and wrong. To explicate the requisite senses of "right" and "wrong," we need the concept of *right preference*—or, more exactly, the concept of one state of mind being *preferable*, epistemically, to another. One state of mind may be *better*, epistemically, than another. This concept of epistemic preferability is what Cardinal Mercier called an *objective* concept. It is one thing to say, objectively, that one state of mind is *to be preferred* to another. It is quite another thing to say, subjectively, that one state of mind is in fact preferred to another—that someone or other happens to prefer the one state of mind to the other. If a state of mind A is to be preferred to a state of mind B, if it is, as I would like to say, intrinsically preferable to B, then anyone who prefers B to A is *mistaken* in his preference.

Given this concept of epistemic preferability, we can readily explicate the basic concepts of the theory of evidence. We could say, for example, that a proposition p is *beyond reasonable doubt at time t* provided only that believing p is then epistemically preferable for S to withholding p—where by "withholding p" we mean the state of neither accepting p nor its negation. It is evident to me, for example, that many people are here. This means it is epistemically preferable for me to believe that many people are here than for me neither to believe nor to disbelieve that many are people here.

A proposition is *evident* for a person if it is beyond reasonable doubt for that person and is such that his including it among the propositions upon which he bases his decisions is preferable to his not so including it. A proposition is *acceptable* if withholding it is *not* preferable to believing it. And a proposition is *unacceptable* if withholding it is preferable to believing it.

Again, some propositions are not beyond reasonable doubt but they may be said to have *some presumption in their favor.* I suppose that the proposition that each of us will be alive an hour from now is one that has some presumption in its favor. We could say that a proposition is of this sort provided only that believing the proposition is epistemically preferable to believing its negation.

Moving in the other direction in the epistemic hierarchy, we could say that a proposition is *certain,* absolutely certain, for a given subject at a given time, if that proposition is then evident to that subject and if there is no other proposition that is such that believing that other proposition is then epistemically preferable for him to believing the given proposition. It is certain for me, I would say, that there seem to be many people here and that 7 and 5 are 12. If this is so, then each of the two propositions is evident to me and there are no other propositions that are such that it would be even better, epistemically, if I were to believe those other propositions.

This concept of epistemic preferability can be axiomatized and made the basis of a system of epistemic logic exhibiting the relations among these and other concepts of the theory of evidence.[9] For present purposes, let us simply note how they may be applied in our approach to the problem of the criterion.

12

Let us begin with the most difficult of the concepts to which we have just referred—that of a proposition being *certain* for a man at a given time. Can we formulate *criteria* of such certainty? I think we can.

Leibniz had said that there are two kinds of immediately evident proposition—the "first truths of fact" and the "first truths of reason." Let us consider each of these in turn.

Among the "first truths of fact," for any man at any given time, I would say, are various propositions about his own state of mind at that time—his thinking certain thoughts, his entertaining certain beliefs, his being in a certain sensory or emotional state. These propositions all pertain to certain states of the man that may be said to manifest or present themselves to him at that time. We could use Meinong's term and say that certain states are "self-presenting," where this concept might be marked off in the following way.

A man's being in a certain state is *self-presenting* to him at a given time provided only that (i) he is in that state at that time and (ii) it is necessarily true that if he is in that state at that time then it is evident to him that he is in that state at that time.

The states of mind just referred to are of this character. Wishing, say, that one were on the moon is a state that is such that a man cannot be in that state without it being evident to him that he is in that state. And so, too, for thinking certain thoughts and having certain sensory or emotional experiences. These states present themselves and are, so to speak, marks of their own evidence. They cannot occur unless it is evident that they occur. I think they are properly called the "first truths of fact." Thus St. Thomas could say that "the intellect knows that it possesses the truth by reflecting on itself."[10]

Perceiving external things and remembering are not states that present themselves. But thinking that one perceives (or seeming to perceive) and thinking that one remembers (or seeming to remember) *are* states of mind that present themselves. And in presenting themselves they may, at least under certain favorable conditions, present something else as well.

Coffey quotes Hobbes as saying that "the inn of evidence has no sign-board."[11] I would prefer saying that these self-presenting states are sign-boards—of the inn of indirect evidence. But these sign-boards need no further sign-boards in order to be presented, for they present themselves.

13

What of the first truths of reason? These are the propositions that some philosophers have called "a priori" and that Leibniz, following Locke, referred to as "maxims" or "axioms." These propositions are all necessary and have a further characteristic that Leibniz described in this way: "You will find in a hundred places that the Scholastics have said that these propositions are evident, *ex terminis,* as soon as the terms are understood, so that they were persuaded that the force of conviction was grounded in the nature of the terms, i.e., in the connection of their ideas."[12] Thus St. Thomas referred to propositions that are "manifest through themselves."[13]

An axiom, one might say, is a necessary proposition such that one cannot understand it without thereby knowing that it is true. Since one cannot know a proposition unless it is evident and one believes it, and since one cannot believe a proposition unless one understands it, we might characterize these first truths of reason in the following way:

A proposition is *axiomatic* for a given subject at a given time provided only that (i) the proposition is one that is necessarily true and (ii) it is also necessarily true that if the person then believes that proposition, the proposition is then evident to him.

We might now characterize the *a priori* somewhat more broadly by saying that a proposition is a priori for a given subject at a given time provided that one or the other of these two things is true: either (i) the proposition is one that is axiomatic for that subject at that time, or else (ii) the proposition is one such that it is evident to the man at that time that the proposition is entailed by a set of propositions that are axiomatic for him at that time.

In characterizing the "first truths of fact" and the "first truths of reason," I have used the expression "evident." But I think it is clear that such truths are not only evident but also certain. And they may be said to be *directly,* or *immediately,* evident.

What, then, of the indirectly evident?

14

I have suggested in rather general terms above what we might say about memory and the senses. These ostensible sources of knowledge are to be treated as innocent until there is positive ground for thinking them guilty. I will not attempt to develop a theory of the indirectly evident at this point. But I will note at least the *kind* of principle to which we might appeal in developing such a theory.

We could *begin* by considering the following two principles, **M** and **P**; **M** referring to memory, and **P** referring to perception or the senses.

(M) For any subject S, if it is evident to S that she seems to remember that a was F, then it is beyond reasonable doubt for S that a was F.

(P) For any subject S, if it is evident to S that she thinks she perceives that a is F, then it is evident to S that a is F.

"She seems to remember" and "she thinks she perceives" here refer to certain self-presenting states that, in the figure I used above, could be said to serve as sign-boards for the inn of indirect evidence.

But principles **M** and **P**, as they stand, are much too latitudinarian. We will find that it is necessary to make qualifications and add more and more conditions. Some of these will refer to the subject's sensory state; some will refer to certain of her other beliefs; and some will refer to the relations of confirmation and mutual support. To set them forth in adequate detail would require a complete epistemology.[14]

So far as our problem of the criterion is concerned, the essential thing to note is this. In formulating such principles we will simply proceed as Aristotle did when he formulated his rules for the syllogism. As "particularists" in our approach to the problem of the criterion, we will fit our rules to the cases—to the apples we know to be good and to the apples we know to be bad. Knowing what we do about ourselves and the world, we have at our disposal certain instances that our rules or principles should countenance, and certain other instances that our rules or principles should rule out or forbid. And, as rational beings, we assume that by investigating these instances we can formulate criteria that any instance must satisfy if it is to be countenanced and we can formulate other criteria that any instance must satisfy if it is to be ruled out or forbidden.

If we proceed in this way we will have satisfied Cardinal Mercier's criteria for a theory of evidence or, as he called it, a theory of certitude. He said that any criterion, or any adequate set of criteria, should be internal, objective, and immediate. The type of criteria I have referred to are certainly *internal,* in his sense of the term. We have not appealed to any external authority as constituting the ultimate test of evidence. (Thus we haven't appealed to "science" or to "the scientists of our culture circle" as constituting the touchstone of what we know.) I would say that our criteria are *objective.* We have formulated them in terms of the concept of epistemic preferability—where the location of "p is epistemically preferable to q for S" is taken to refer to an objective relation that obtains independently of the actual preferences of any particular subject. The criteria that we formulate, if they are adequate, will be principles that are necessarily true. And they are also *immediate.* Each of them is such that, if it is applicable at any particular time, then the fact that it is then applicable is capable of being directly evident to that particular subject at that particular time.

15

But in all of this I have presupposed the approach I have called "particularism." The "methodist" and the "skeptic" will tell us that we have started in the wrong place. If now we try to reason with them, then, I am afraid, we will be back on the wheel.

What few philosophers have had the courage to recognize is this: we can deal with the problem only by begging the question. It seems to me that, if we do recognize this fact, as we should, then it is unseemly for us to try to pretend that it isn't so.

One may object: "Doesn't this mean, then, that the skeptic is right after all?" I would answer: "Not at all. His view is only one of the three possibilities and in itself has no more to recommend it than the others do. And in favor of our approach there is the fact that we do know many things, after all."

NOTES

1. Published in London in 1917 by Longmans, Green and Co.

2. The eighth edition of this work was published in 1923 in Louvain by the Instiut Supérieur de Philosophie, and in Paris by Félix Alcan. The first edition was published in 1884. It has been translated into Spanish, Polish, Portuguese, and perhaps still other languages, but unfortunately not yet into English.

3. The quotation is a paraphrase. What Montaigne wrote was: "Pour juger des apparences que nous recevons des subjects, il nous faudroit un instrument judicatoire; pour verifier cet instrument, il nous y faut de la demonstration; pour verifier la demonstration, un instrument; nous voylà au rouet. Puisque les sens ne peuvent arrester notre dispute, éstans pleins eux-mesmes d'incertitude, il faut que se soit la raison; aucune raison s'establira sans une autre raison: nous voylà à reculons jusques à l'infiny." The passage appears in book 2, ch. 12 ("An Apologie of Raymond Sebond"); it may be found on page 544 of the Modern Library edition of *The Essays of Montaigne.*

4. *Critériologie,* op. cit., eighth edition, p. 234.

5. See the reply to the seventh set of Objections and Coffey, vol. 1, p. 127.

6. Thomas Reid, *Inquiry into the Human Mind,* ch. 1, sec. 8.

7. Unfortunately Cardinal Mercier takes Reid to be what I have called a "methodist." He assumes, incorrectly I think, that Reid defends certain principles (principles that Reid calls principles of "common sense") on the ground that these principles happen to be the deliverance of a faculty called "common sense." See Mercier, pp. 179–81.

8. *On Improvement of the Understanding,* in *Chief Works of Benedict de Spinoza,* vol. 2, trans, R. H. M. Elwes, rev. ed. (London: George Bell and Sons, 1898), p. 13.

9. The logic of these concepts, though with a somewhat different vocabulary, is set forth in Roderick M. Chisholm and Robert Keim, "A System of Epistemic Logic," *Ratio* 15 (1973).

10. *The Disputed Questions on Truth,* question 1, article 9;trans. Robert W. Mulligan (Chicago: Henry Regnery Company, 1952).

11. Coffey, vol. 1, p. 146. I have been unable to find this quotation in Hobbes.

12. *New Essays concerning Human Understanding,* book 4, ch. 7, n. 1.

13. *Exposition of the Posterior Analytics of Aristotle,* lectio 4, no. 10; trans. Pierre Conway (Québec: M. Doyon, 1956).

14. I have attempted to do this to some extent in *Theory of Knowledge* (Englewood Cliffs, N.J.: Prentice-Hall, Inc., 1966). Revisions and corrections may be found in my essay "On the Nature of Empirical Evidence" in Roderick M. Chisholm and Robert J. Swartz, eds., *Empirical Knowledge* (Englewood Cliffs, N.J.: Prentice-Hall, Inc., 1973).

12

Roderick Chisholm and the Problem of the Criterion[1]

Robert P. Amico

The current revival of interest in the problem of the criterion can, in great part, be attributed to Roderick Chisholm. As early as 1957 Chisholm addressed the problem in *Perceiving*. A modified treatment can be found later in *Theory of Knowledge,* and a more recent modification can be found in *The Foundations of Knowing.* This characterization first appeared as the Aquinas Lecture of 1973. Chisholm begins his lecture with these words:

> "The problem of the criterion" seems to me to be one of the most important and one of the most difficult of all the problems of philosophy. I am tempted to say that one has not begun to philosophize until one has faced this problem and has recognized how unappealing, in the end, each possible solution is.[2]

In this paper I will evaluate how well Chisholm has "faced" this problem and how satisfactory his "unappealing" solution is. I will be considering only Chisholm's most recent characterization of the problem of the criterion described in *The Foundations of Knowing.* Chisholm begins his discussion with a paraphrase of Montaigne's account of the problem:

> To know whether things really are as they seem to be, we must have a *procedure* for distinguishing appearances that are true from appearances that are false. But to know whether our procedure is a good procedure, we have to know whether it really *suc-*

From *Philosophical Papers* (South Africa) 17, no. 3 (1988): 217–29. © 1988. Reprinted by permission of the publisher.

ceeds in distinguishing appearances that are true from appearances that are false. And we cannot know whether it does really succeed unless we already know which appearances are *true* and which ones are false. And so we are caught in a circle. (p. 62)

Chisholm sets out to illustrate the problem of the criterion with the help of Descartes' reply to the seventh set of objections to his *Meditations*. The following is a paraphrase of this illustration. Suppose you had a basket of apples and you wanted to sort out the good apples from the bad apples. It seems that you would need a criterion by which you could sort them, either a criterion for recognizing good apples or a criterion for recognizing bad apples. But how could you ever tell whether your criterion for sorting apples was a good criterion, one that really selected out only the good ones or only the bad ones? It seems that in order to tell whether or not you have a good criterion, you already need to know which apples are good and which are bad; then you could test proposed criteria by their fidelity to this knowledge.

So, if you don't already know which apples are good and which are bad, how can you ever hope to sort them out correctly? And if you already know which are good and which are bad, by what criteria did you learn this?

Chisholm claims that if one substitutes "beliefs" for "apples" we encounter the epistemological problem of how we decide which beliefs are "good ones," i.e., actual cases of knowledge, and which are "bad ones," i.e., not cases of knowledge. Chisholm summarizes the philosophical issues involved in this problem by two pairs of questions:

(A) *What* do we know? What is the *extent* of our knowledge?

(B) How are we to decide *whether* we know? What are the *criteria* of knowledge?

He suggests that if we had an answer to (A), then we might be able to fashion an answer to (B) on the basis of (A). Also, if we had an answer to (B), then we might be able to fashion an answer to (A) on the basis of (B). He then explains that philosophers' opinions have divided three ways with respect to this problem. One group purports to know the answer to (A), i.e., they purport to know what particular things we do know, and on the basis of this they fashion a criterion in accord with their answer. This group may be called *particularists*. They would include common-sense philosophers like Reid, G. E. Moore, and Chisholm himself. Another group claims to know the answer to (B), i.e., they claim to know what the criterion for knowledge is, and on the basis of their answer to (B), they are able to fashion an answer to (A). That is, by knowing the answer to (B) they are then able to distinguish true cases of knowledge from those that are merely apparent cases of knowledge—not knowledge at all.

This group may be called *methodists*. They would include philosophers like Descartes, and empiricists like Hume and Locke. The third group are those who claim that you cannot answer question (A) until you know the answer to (B), and you cannot answer (B) until you know the answer to (A). Therefore, you cannot answer either question. "You cannot know what, if anything, you know, and there is no possible way for you to decide in any particular case" (p. 66). Thus, for Chisholm there are three basic possible views. We can characterize the problem of the criterion, then, by the following:

> If you cannot answer (A) until you know the answer to (B), and if you cannot answer (B) until you know the answer to (A), then how can you answer either question?

Let us now examine Chisholm's criticisms of methodism and his own arguments for particularism—his "solution" to the problem. Chisholm begins with a criticism of methodism, and of empiricism in particular. He has two objections; the first applies to all forms of methodism, while the second applies only to empiricism:

1st Obj. "The criterion is very broad and far-reaching and at the same time completely arbitrary" (p. 67).

Chisholm explains this objection as follows: "How can one *begin with* a broad generalization? . . . He leaves us completely in the dark so far as concerns what *reasons* he may have for adopting this particular criterion rather than some other" (p. 67).

2nd Obj. "When we apply the empirical criterion . . . we seem to throw out not only the bad apples but the good ones as well, and we are left, in effect, with just a few parings or skins with no meat behind them" (p. 67).

In other words, in this second objection, if we apply the empirical criterion, the only things (matters of fact) that turn out to count as knowledge are certain present sensations: "Thus Hume virtually conceded that . . . the only matters of fact that you can really know about pertain to the existence of sensations" (p. 67). The empirical criterion referred to here is: "whether [a belief] is derived from sense experience . . . whether it bears certain relations to your sensations" (p. 67). And that position, according to Chisholm, sounds like nonsense. Chisholm explains that the commonsense philosophers like Reid and G. E. Moore would contend that any philosophy which implies that we cannot know things like that this is a hand, should be rejected immediately. He states: "I think that Reid and Moore are right, myself, and I'm inclined to think that the methodists are wrong" (p. 69). Let us evaluate Chisholm's criticisms of methodism and empiricism.

In his first objection, which is directed at all forms of methodism, he claims that the criterion is very broad and far-reaching and at the same time completely arbitrary. How do we interpret these two claims? I suggest four possible interpretations:

I. He might be claiming that the *broadness and far-reaching character* of a criterion, in itself, is something to be avoided. But I cannot imagine why. On the contrary, these qualities seem desirable because they suggest that the criterion would be applicable to many cases. Thus we can reject that first interpretation.

II. He might be claiming that we should avoid *arbitrarily* beginning with anything. There must be *reasons* given for adopting this criterion over other possible criteria. Thus, this interpretation of Chisholm's criticism could be avoided if the methodist gives us some reason for adopting his criterion over others. It is the *arbitrariness* that is the issue in this interpretation. Certainly the methodist would be able to afford us *some* reasons for his choice. A methodist would possibly reply that he is not arbitrarily beginning with a broad and far-reaching criterion. This criterion is known a priori. Certainly having a priori knowledge of a particular criterion is a *reason* for adopting such a criterion, but perhaps his reason would strike Chisholm as a bad reason because it is simply false. Nonetheless, this interpretation of Chisholm's objection to methodism claims that if the adoption of a criterion is *completely arbitrary* then the methodists have offered us no reasons for their adoption of this particular criterion as opposed to some other criterion: "He leaves us completely in the dark so far as concerns what *reasons* he may have for adopting this particular criterion rather than some other" (p. 67). Thus, if it is true that the methodists indeed offer *no* reason to adopt their criterion, then they would be susceptible to this criticism.

III. He might be claiming that we should avoid adopting a criterion with these two particular characteristics in combination: a) broad and far-reaching, b) arbitrary. On this interpretation it is somehow the *combination* of "broad and far-reaching" with "arbitrary" that is deadly. But if this is his objection, then he has given us no reason why *this combination* in particular is problematic. If there is some *additional* problem over and above the difficulties mentioned in I and II, which arises from this particular combination of characteristics, then it is incumbent upon Chisholm to tell us what this difficulty is. And Chisholm offers no such explanation. I can see no reason why the *combination* presents an especially vexing problem over and above the sum of the problems involved in each. And without such an explanation from Chisholm, this interpretation comes to no more than I and II. One might argue that a broad arbitrary assumption is more irrational than a narrow arbitrary assumption, but this does not seem necessarily so. The content of what is assumed in each case may be the determining factor in deciding which is more irrational.

IV. He might be claiming that we simply cannot justifiably *begin* with a *criterion*, because it always presupposes some knowledge of particulars to determine whether it succeeds in distinguishing between true and false cases of knowledge. This seems to come to half of the skeptic's claim that in order to answer (B) we already need an answer to (A). This interpretation comes from focusing on Chisholm's stress on the word "begin" in: "How can one *begin* with a broad generalization?" The reason why Chisholm finds this question compelling (so this interpretation argues), is that it is puzzling how the methodist can *begin* with a criterion, when such a criterion always seems to presuppose *some* knowledge of particulars to determine whether it really succeeds in distinguishing between true and false cases of knowledge.

It is not clear from what Chisholm states, just which interpretation he means to express by his objection. He seems to conflate aspects of the second and fourth interpretations as possible criticisms of methodism. Rather than try to defend methodism here, let us wait and see if Chisholm's positive thesis—particularism—avoids the very criticisms he levels against methodism. For if both positions—particularism and methodism—are vulnerable to his criticisms, then, as far as these criticisms are concerned, we would have no reason to favor one over the other. Before reviewing his positive thesis, let us examine his second objection against methodism—one that is aimed more narrowly just at empiricism.

Chisholm claims that by adopting empiricism we not only throw out the bad apples, but the good ones as well. But how can Chisholm claim this without *assuming* that either his particularist position is the correct one, or at least that knowledge extends farther than the empiricist's position allows (which is also an assumption about what in fact we do know)? In other words, Chisholm seems to be assuming an answer to the very question at issue by having already assumed which apples are bad and which are good. He is criticizing empiricism for adopting a criterion which does not agree with his *assumed* position. The very point that we are trying to determine is which apples are bad and which are good, and appeal to such a particularist position (which is, in essence, what his assumption amounts to) simply will not do. Chisholm is *assuming* he already knows the answer to (A) in order to criticize the empiricist's answer to (B). If this kind of faulty reasoning is allowed for Chisholm, then it is also allowed for the empiricist; i.e., the empiricist can then argue that Chisholm's position is unacceptable because it leads one to adopt a "bad criterion"—one that conflicts with our intuitions about methods and rules (thereby assuming to know an answer to [B] in order to criticize Chisholm's answer to [A]). It forces us to accept the bad apples!

Thus, we can reject Chisholm's second objection on the grounds that it assumes an answer to the issue in question, in order to answer the issue in question. Indeed, Chisholm admits that he begs the question, and believes that only by doing so can anyone "deal with the problem." I will return to this question shortly, but for now let us assume that begging the question is good reason to reject Chisholm's second objection.

We can now examine Chisholm's positive thesis and determine whether his position is vulnerable to either interpretation (II or IV) of his first objection to methodism. He says:

> I would say—and many reputable philosophers would disagree with me—that to find out whether you know such a thing as that this is a hand, you don't have to apply any test or criterion. Spinoza has it right. "In order to know," he said, "there is no need to know that we know, much less to know that we know that we know." (p. 67)

Thus, Chisholm adopts the particularist's thesis and denies the skeptic's claim that in order to answer (A) we must first answer (B). As he states: "There are many things that quite obviously we do know to be true." And from this he concludes that "having these good apples before us, we can look them over and formulate certain criteria of goodness" (p. 67). This is the particularist thesis.

Chisholm's positive thesis (cited above), however, seems somewhat garbled. Just exactly what he means by "to find out whether you know" is unclear, but he seems to be equating it with "to know" in his second statement, because his second statement reads like a reiteration of the first: "Spinoza has it right. In order to know," he said, "there is no need to know that we know, much less know that we know that we know." Any other reading of "to find out whether you know" makes this passage completely confusing. However, to add to this confusion, Chisholm also seems to be conflating two different ideas. His first claim is that "to find out whether you know such a thing as that this is a hand, you don't have to apply any test or criterion." His second claim is that in order to know there is no need to know that you know. Even if I am correct in interpreting "to find out whether you know" as simply "to know" (thereby making the subject of his two claims identical, i.e., both claims are about what is necessary or not necessary "to know," and thus making sense of how these two sentences relate to each other), the two claims assert completely different theses. His two claims read:

(1) In order to know, you don't have to apply any test or criterion.

(2) In order to know, there is no need to know that you know.

The first claims that applying a test or criterion is not necessary in order to know something, while the second claims that second-order knowledge (knowledge about knowledge) is not necessary in order to know, i.e., is not necessary for first-order knowledge. Possession of second-order knowledge is quite different from applying a test or criterion. Chisholm makes the two claims as if they asserted the same thesis. Now two criticisms are in order here. One concerns the confused statement of his positive thesis, while the other concerns how his positive thesis relates to his criticisms of methodism. I will discuss his positive thesis first.

If we assume for the moment that by "to find out whether we know" Chisholm simply means "to know," then both statements he makes are concerned with what is necessary to know something. It seems clear that we may be able to know something without knowing that we know it.[3] And so, I am in agreement here with Chisholm and Spinoza. But this brings us no closer to a solution to the problem of the criterion, for the same claim can be made true by the methodist. He need not know that he knows some criterion to be a correct criterion for sorting the true from the false.

Thus it seems that it is quite a different thing to speak about what is required to find out whether we know something. How can we find out whether we know such a thing, unless we have some kind of criterion for distinguishing such things from things that are not such things? And "finding out whether we know" (when *not* understood as simply knowing) is what Chisholm needs to solve the problem. Finding out whether we know something seems to require more than what is required to simply know something. It seems to require some kind of *determination* that is not required for simple knowing, because it is a determining or knowing *about* knowledge. Yet Chisholm has an answer, of sorts, to this. He states: "There are many things that quite obviously we do know to be true" (p. 69). "And in favor of our approach there is the fact that we do know many things after all" (p. 75). "But our view is no more arbitrary than either of the others. And, unlike them, it corresponds with what we do know."[4] Chisholm seems to be saying that in some cases we can find out whether we know something simply by knowing it. In other words, I am interpreting the above quotes as: "There are many things that quite obviously (i.e., *we have found out*) we do know to be true." "And in favor of our approach there is the fact (i.e., *we have found out*) that we do know many things after all." The methodist, however, can use the same strategy to argue that we can find out whether we know some method works simply by knowing it. This line of argumentation, by itself, puts Chisholm's position in no better standing than the position of the methodist. In effect, this strategy involves *presupposing* the approach one is attempting to establish. As Chisholm states:

> But in all of this I have presupposed the approach I have called "particularism." The "methodist" and "skeptic" will tell us that we have started in the wrong place. If now we try to reason with them, I am afraid, we will be back on the wheel.

What is puzzling is that Chisholm thinks that only by doing so, can he "deal with the problem': "What few philosophers have had the courage to recognize is this: we can deal with the problem only by begging the question" (p. 75). This is a rather puzzling statement because it prompts one to wonder what Chisholm might mean by "deal with the problem." Perhaps a passage from *Perceiving* will give us a clue. There he states:

> We cannot "test" every mark of evidence in this way unless we reason in a circle. But even if we do thus reason in a circle, we may take some comfort if by doing so we find that induction does not discredit the marks of evidence of its premises.[5]

I believe that what Chisholm is saying is that by begging the question we "deal with the problem" insofar as we can take some comfort if our theory—particularism—does not conflict with what we ordinarily take ourselves to know. But we could take no comfort in the fact that our circular reasoning did not conflict with what we are trying to establish, because circular reasoning will not allow such conflicts; that is what is wrong with such reasoning—anything can be so "proven." If Chisholm is saying what I have just suggested, then one criticism is in order. The fact that he begs the question is completely independent of the fact that what he sets out to test corresponds with what we ordinarily take ourselves to know. He could "take comfort" that his reasoning does not conflict with what we ordinarily take ourselves to know, even if his reasoning did not beg the question. It just so happens that particularism coincides with common sensism, and that is a fact which is independent of the fact that Chisholm believes that he can only deal with the problem by begging the question.

The only other interpretation of "deal with the problem" that comes to mind is one in which "deal" is not a success word. "Dealing with the problem," then, is not a solution. But the only avenue open to *any* of the three possible respondents—particularists, methodists and skeptics—is to beg the question in favor of their own position. And so, if begging the question is "dealing with the problem," then the methodist has the same recourse open to him. He could claim that his view is no more arbitrary than either of the others, and his view corresponds with what we do know (i.e., what true methods are). Chisholm's position does have the merit of corresponding to what we ordinarily take ourselves to know, but one could certainly question whether this is really a merit. Indeed, throughout history, many of the things we ordinarily took ourselves to know have been shown to be in error. So it is questionable whether this is really a merit of Chisholm's position. Furthermore, this "merit" only sets him apart from the empiricist, not all methodists. There is nothing about methodism that precludes the possibility of it coinciding with our commonsense beliefs.

Thus, we can question Chisholm's positive thesis not only on the grounds given above (i.e., that none of his arguments in favor of particularism are convincing; that his arguments give us no good reason to prefer particularism over methodism or skepticism), but also because if my interpretation IV of his objection to methodism is correct, then his own position is subject to the very same objection, i.e., he is just "beginning" with particularism. We can now see that since Chisholm's position deals with the problem only by begging the question, the methodist can argue, as Chisholm concedes, that we simply cannot begin with a particular, because it always presupposes some knowledge of a method or criterion to determine whether it is a case of true knowledge or merely apparent knowledge (not knowledge at all); i.e., the other half of the skeptic's claim that in order to answer (A) we need an answer to (B).

It seems that Chisholm's last recourse is to appeal to interpretation II of his objection to methodism, for if his position is immune to his criticism of methodism under this interpretation, then at least he can claim that his position has this advantage over methodism. Recall that on this interpretation of his objection it is the *arbitrariness* of methodism that is at issue. And on this point Chisholm himself concedes that his position is no more arbitrary than the others. If *all* he can claim is that his position is no more arbitrary than the others, then he cannot claim that his position is less arbitrary. And if he cannot even make the claim that his position is somewhat *less* arbitrary than the others, then his only remaining objection to methodism (interpretation II) is just as effective against his own position as it is against methodism. In other words, if it is true that we should avoid arbitrarily beginning with anything, and the most that Chisholm can say is that particularism is no more arbitrary than methodism or skepticism, then particularism is also vulnerable to his criticism of methodism. And it seems that Chisholm cannot argue that his position is less arbitrary (as he apparently recognizes) without, as Chisholm says, going right back on the wheel. In effect, all that he is left with is his claim that his position has it right, and alas, each of the other views can claim just as much of their position.

We have discovered, then, that Chisholm's solution to the problem of the criterion is more than "unappealing," it is unsatisfactory because: (1) he has given us no good reason to reject the other positions, (2) he has given us no good argument to favor his position over the others, (3) his position begs the question.

Now, if Chisholm concedes that he has *presupposed* particularism, then it seems that what he means by "start with particular cases" is presuppose the truth of particularism, i.e., presuppose the truth of particular cases. And indeed, the methodist is doing the very same thing with his criterion or method. He is presupposing the truth of the particular distinguishing principles. Both positions seem question begging because they both presuppose the truth of the position they are trying to show solves the problem. Thus, *if* we assume the truth of particularism, then we have a solution to the problem of the criterion and *if* we assume the truth of methodism, then we also have a solution. Chisholm's criticisms of methodism and skepticism are his way of arguing that his question begging and arbitrary solution is preferable to its alternatives, which are also question begging and arbitrary. It is somewhat puzzling, then, why Chisholm then says: "If now we try to reason with them, then, I am afraid, we will be back on the wheel." What is puzzling is the "if." He already admitted that he has presupposed the truth of particularism. Thus, he is already on a wheel. He seems to think that if he does not try to reason with the methodist and skeptic, then he will *not* be back on the wheel. How could this be possible? Only if his proposed solution is not circular. If it is true that he can find out whether he knows such a thing as that this is a hand without applying any test or criterion, then it is true that he *can* answer (A) before or without answering (B). And *answering* (A) does not, by itself, beg the question. I believe that this is what Chisholm is saying when he characterizes his solution as "a kind of answer to the puzzle about the diallelus." By answering (A) he has provided a *kind* of answer to the puzzle without begging the question; but two things can be said about this answer: (1) the methodist can also do the same. If it is true that he can find out whether he knows some criterion without looking to any particulars, then it is true that he *can* answer (B) before or without answering (A). And *answering* (B) does not, by itself, beg the question. This is also a *kind* of answer to the puzzle; and (2) neither kind of answer is a *solution* to the problem of the criterion because a solution must remove the initial rational doubt about which position is rationally preferable. Here I am relying on my understanding of what makes something a problem—an inconsistent set of individually reasonable beliefs (particularism, methodism, skepticism) of which there is rational doubt about which one(s) to reject and accept. If neither answer removes rational doubt, then neither is a solution to the problem. For these reasons we can also claim that there is no good reason to think that begging the question can ever be a rational means of "dealing with the problem." Therefore, Chisholm's position offers an answer to the question: Is a criterion necessary to adjudicate between the true and the false? Chisholm's answer is no. If he could remove rational doubt about his answer (show it to be rationally preferable to the other positions—thereby removing the rational doubt about which answer is correct), then his answer would be a solution to the problem of the criterion. But this has not been established.

NOTES

1. Presented at the Pacific Division Meeting of the American Philosophical Association, Portland, Oregon, March 1988.

2. Roderick Chisholm, *The Foundations of Knowing* (Minneapolis: University of Minnesota Press, 1982), p. 61. All parenthetical page references are to this book.

3. See Richard Feldman, "Fallibilism and Knowing That One Knows," *The Philosophical Review* 90 (1981): 226–82.

4. Roderick Chisholm, *Theory of Knowledge* (Englewood Cliffs, N.J.: Prentice Hall, Inc., 1977), p. 121.

5. Roderick Chisholm, *Perceiving: A Philosophical Study* (Ithaca, N.Y.: Cornell University Press, 1957), p. 38.

13

Reply to Amico on the Problem of the Criterion[1]

Roderick M. Chisholm

It is good to have occasion to reply to Professor Amico's challenging comments. For I am convinced that, so far as the problem of the criterion is concerned, most philosophers—and most epistemologists—prefer to bury their heads in the sand.

I had put the problem this way:

> One may ask "*What* do we know—what is the extent of our knowledge?" One may also ask, "How do we decide in any particular case *whether* we know—what are the *criteria,* if any, of knowing?" The problem of the criterion arises out of the fact that if we do not have the answer to the second pair of questions, then, it would seem, we have no reasonable procedure for finding out the answer to the first; and if we do not have the answer to the first pair of questions, then, it would seem, we have no reasonable procedure for finding out the answer to the second.[2]

Amico quotes my statement: "What few philosophers have had the courage to realize is this: we can deal with the problem [of the criterion] only by begging the question." And then he says that this is a "puzzling statement." What is puzzling about it?

Amico is puzzled because he thinks that, in setting forth my approach to the problem, I was trying to solve the problem. He then criticizes this supposed "solution" and says of it what I had said of any attempt to solve the problem—namely, that it "begs the question."

From *Philosophical Papers* (South Africa) 17, no. 3 (1988): 231–34. © 1988. Reprinted by permission of the publisher.

He does not consider the possibility that what I have said positively about the problem is *not* intended as a solution to the problem. He certainly has a right to ask, therefore: "If you weren't trying to solve the problem, what did you mean when you spoke of providing a 'kind of answer' to the questions that the problem involves?" And so I will try to answer this question.

We raise the most fundamental questions of epistemology when we ask ourselves: "What can I know? How can I distinguish those things I am justified in believing from those things I am not justified in believing? What can I do to replace unjustified beliefs by justified beliefs that pertain to the same subject-matter? What can I do to replace less justified beliefs by more justified beliefs?" And—the most puzzling question of all is this: "How can I reasonably *decide* how to go about doing these things?"

Like many others, I remain puzzled by such questions and cannot prevent myself from trying to answer this—despite the insoluble problem of the criterion. I retain the commonsense conviction that there *are* things that I know—such things as the fact that at this moment I am in a room with other people. There are, as I have said, only three approaches to the problem: (1) there is what I can call "methodism"—one starts out with general principles; (2) there is what I have called "particularism"—one starts out with particular cases; and (3) there is "skepticism"—one doesn't do anything. I have chosen the path of "particularism." And so we have Professor Amico's question: "If you cannot solve the problem of the criterion, what can you say in defense of your particularism?"

My answer involves two things: first, I find that by beginning as a particularist I *can* provide an account of knowledge that seems to me to be reasonably satisfactory; and, secondly, I cannot see how, by taking either of the other two approaches, one can make any progress at all.

To evaluate this contention one must try all three approaches and then compare the results. And, of course, I cannot do this in a brief note. But I will try to say briefly what my own approach has been.

The particularist who is also a "common sensist"—and that is how I would describe myself—will tell us that, in trying to find out what we know and are justified in believing and in trying to improve our general epistemic situation, we should begin with the set of beliefs that we have (where else *could* we begin?) and then try to refine upon those beliefs and make the set one that seems to us to be more respectable, epistemically. The mere fact that we find ourselves inclined to believe one thing rather than another is itself a provisional—or *prima facie*—justification *for* believing the one thing rather than the other. "So far, so good," we tell ourselves.

But, to use C. S. Peirce's phrase, our commonsensism should be a "*critical* commonsensism." Although we start out with a mass of uncritical beliefs, we will refine upon this set of beliefs and improve it. One way of improving it is to sift it down, so to speak, and cast away the things that shouldn't be there.

And how do we do this? All I can offer here is a sketch of an answer.

If we find a pair of beliefs that *contradict* each other, we will reject at least one of them.

If, after removing the contradictions that we find among our system of beliefs, we find that the set of beliefs that remains tends to *disconfirm* some of its members, then we will reject the ones that are disconfirmed.

Of the commonsense beliefs that then remain, some will strike us as being *more* justified than others. These will include beliefs about what we *perceive* and what we *remember.* We could say of the ostensible deliverances of perception and memory that it is reasonable for us to accept them—*unless* we have positive grounds for rejecting them. They should be held to be innocent, epistemically, until there is ground to think them guilty. If you *think* you see familiar objects in front of you, then it is reasonable for you to suppose that there are such objects in front of you—*unless* you have reason for supposing that, on this particular occasion, your senses are deceiving you. And analogously for memory.

Can we improve further upon this refined set of beliefs? There is also the importance of *mutual support,* or *coherence.* When propositions thus mutually support each other, then, it would seem, each of the mutually supporting propositions serves to add to the positive epistemic status of the other.

And there are other things we can do. In each case, starting with particular cases which we hold to be provisionally respectable, we try to arrive at epistemic principles that will then provide what *seems* to us to be satisfactory answers to the questions "What can I know" and "What am I justified in believing?"

In reply to Professor Amico, then, I would make these four points. (1) By proceeding in the way I have just described we can make *some* progress toward answering the traditional questions of epistemology. (2) This procedure seems to me to work out in a much more satisfactory way than anything that has been provided by "methodism" and by "skepticism." But (3) we should be open to the possibility that some day the "methodist" might work out an answer that will take us farther than traditional empiricism has done. And, finally, (4) to say these things is not to *solve* the problem of the criterion—for the problem of the criterion *has* no solution.[3]

NOTES

1. Presented at the Pacific Division Meeting of the American Philosophical Association, Portland, Oregon, March 1988.

2. See *Theory of Knowledge,* 2d ed. (Englewood Cliffs, N.J.: Prentice-Hall, Inc., 1977).

3. The points made here are developed in further detail in *Theory of Knowledge,* 3d ed. (Englewood Cliffs, N.J.: Prentice-Hall, Inc., 1989).

14

Skepticism and the Problem of the Criterion

Robert P. Amico

The problem of the criterion has been characterized by Roderick Chisholm by means of the following two pairs of questions:

(A) What do I know? What is the extent of my knowledge?

(B) How do I decide whether I know? What are the criteria of knowledge?

According to Chisholm the skeptic claims that you cannot answer (A) unless you already know the answer to (B), and you cannot answer (B) unless you already know the answer to (A); so if you do not already know the answer to both, how can you answer either? In *Foundations of Knowing*[1] Chisholm claimed that there were three possible "solutions" to the problem: *skepticism*—denying that one can answer either question; *particularism*—claiming to know an answer to (A), by means of which one then fashions an answer to (B); *methodism*—claiming to know an answer to (B), by means of which one then fashions an answer to (A). Chisholm admits that each possible "solution" begs the question, but he argues that particularism is the best question begging "solution." More recently[2] Chisholm has clarified his position by stating that when he claims to "deal" with the problem of the criterion, "deal" is not being used as a success word—"the problem of the criterion *has* no solution."[3] I have argued briefly elsewhere that the problem of the criterion has a *dissolution* and in this paper I would like to explore the implications of this claim.[4] It should be noted that the skeptic whom Chisholm speaks of is not of the Pyrrhonian sort, but rather one who makes certain dogmatic claims.

Let me begin with a brief synopsis of my argument that there is a dissolution to the problem of the criterion. Many, if not all, philosophical problems are problems because one maintains a set of beliefs, each of which seems quite reasonable on its own, but which together are inconsistent. For example, one might characterize the "problem of free will" with the following propositions:

1. All events, including human actions, are causally determined.
2. Some human actions are done freely.
3. #1 and #2 are incompatible.

In this case, one might argue that each proposition seems quite reasonable on its own, and yet they cannot all be true. Hence, the "problem" arises in trying to determine which one(s) are false and which are true. There is *rational doubt* about which propositions to accept and reject. Rational doubt is the earmark of this kind of philosophical problem. Hence, a solution to such a problem should remove that rational doubt.

In the case of the problem of the criterion, it seems reasonable to accept the proposition that in order to answer (A) one needs to know already the answer to (B) because one could justify a knowledge claim to (A) in terms of a known answer to (B); and it seems reasonable to accept the reverse, that in order to answer (B) one needs to know already the answer to (A), for one could justify a knowledge claim to (B) in terms of a known answer to (A); and it also seems reasonable to accept the claim that one cannot answer each prior to the other, because the relation of "prior to" is asymmetrical. The problem of the criterion can be posed with the following question: If you cannot answer (A) until you know the answer to (B), and you cannot answer (B) until you how the answer to (A), then how can you answer either question?

The term "answer" here has a rather special meaning, certainly more than simply giving a semantically appropriate response or a correct response because this would not eliminate cases of luck or guesswork. And "answer" does not mean a reply which is rationally justified because both particularists and methodists would claim to *be* justified in their knowledge claims, but the skeptic would contest this. To "answer" (A) or (B) to the satisfaction of the skeptic one must *justify* one's answer (knowledge claim) to (A) or (B). And the skeptic claims that the only kind of rational justification for such a claim (to [A] for example) is or relies on an "answer" to (B). And "answer" here implies having an "answer" to (A), If each "answer" requires the prior "answering" of the other, then since both "answers" cannot be prior to each other, neither is "answerable." The conditions for an "answer" are in principle impossible to meet. As I have argued elsewhere,[5] the problem of the criterion is dissolved once one realizes that the conditions set by the skeptic for solving the problem are in principle impossible to meet. This is because rational doubt is the earmark of a philosophical problem, and since there is no longer any rational doubt about how to answer the question, there is no longer any problem. The question has a simple answer—you can't. But it is no wonder that we cannot do the impossible. It is no more of a problem than the question: how do you make a circle square?

But there are now a series of interesting questions that need to be addressed. Why should we accept the skeptic's conditions for an acceptable answer to (A) or (B)? Why does the skeptic accept *only* these conditions? What presuppositions is the skeptic making about the nature of justification? Need we accept these presuppositions? If meeting the skeptic's impossible conditions for an answer to (A) or (B) is sufficient for justifying a knowledge claim, is it also necessary? Might meeting other conditions also be sufficient for justifying a knowledge claim to (A) or (B)? I will argue that there are other sufficient conditions for justifying such knowledge claims and that the skeptic cannot justifiably reject them because they are presupposed by the skeptic in maintaining her skeptical position.

Let us begin with the first question—why should we accept the skeptic's conditions for an acceptable answer to (A) or (B)? The skeptic claims that in order to justify one's claim to know the answer to (A)—e.g., that I have a left hand, I must know the answer to (B)—i.e., I must know some criterion or method by means of which I can identify this as a case of actual knowledge as opposed to merely apparent knowledge. If I knew such a criterion, I could be absolutely guaranteed that this was an instance of knowledge. There would be no possibility of error. The skeptic would argue similarly in the case of a knowledge claim to (B). In order to justify one's claim to know the answer to (B)—e.g., to know the criterion by means of which we can distinguish true knowledge from merely apparent knowledge, I must know the answer to (A)—I must know some actual instances of true knowledge so that I can test the criterion by its fidelity to this knowledge and so ensure absolutely that the criterion is the true criterion of knowledge. Again, the skeptic accepts this condition for the justification of a knowledge claim because if one could meet it, it would absolutely guarantee truth. Hence, even though the skeptic's conditions are in principle impossible to meet, if one could meet them, truth would be guaranteed.

Since we would all embrace an absolute guarantee of truth, we now have a reason why we should accept the skeptic's conditions as an acceptable means of justifying one's knowledge claim to (A) or (B). Why does the skeptic accept only these conditions? Quite simply, because anything less would not constitute a justification of our knowledge claim because we could be mistaken. The skeptic seems to be presupposing that a justification of a knowledge claim must have deductive force—it must be a logically airtight guarantee.[6]

At this point we are entitled to ask the skeptic for some kind of justification for these presuppositions (just as the skeptic has required of the particularist and methodist). It would seem that the skeptic has a certain metaepistemological position concerning what knowledge is and what it is not. As Richard Fumerton claims: "The arguments of the skeptic most often *presuppose* metaepistemological positions but there is often far too little explicit discussion of the nature of knowledge or justified belief."[7]

The discussion of the problem of the criterion with the skeptic is now on the metaepistemological level. It seems that much of the disagreement between skeptic, particularist, and methodist arises because they have "started" with different metaepistemological presuppositions about the nature of knowledge and justification. Many philosophers begin by presupposing that skepticism is false, like Roderick Chisholm and G. E. Moore. On the other hand, many skeptics seem to presuppose that knowledge must be indubitable. How should we evaluate metaepistemological views? How do we determine where to begin in epistemology? This question is at the heart of the problem of the criterion and too little attention has been given to it. If we wish to engage in a dialogue with the skeptic about where to begin in epistemology, one way that we might begin is by determining the common ground. Where do we all agree? It seems to me that we can uncover and understand significant disagreements by uncovering and understanding where disputants agree. Since this involves determining the skeptic's presuppositions and background beliefs, I should begin by saying a few words about presuppositions and background assumptions.

Generally speaking, philosophers mean something different by the term presupposition than logical implication. Both presupposition and contextual implication are weaker notions that may be useful to this analysis. For our purposes we may only need a rough sketch of these concepts to get us going. A completely adequate account of presupposition is, to the best of my knowledge, nonexistent. Strawson's account[8]— S presupposes S' =def. the truth of S', is a necessary condition of the truth or falsity of the statement that S—is the one most well known and it has been shown to be inadequate.[9] Roughly then, a presupposition refers to those "conditions that must be satisfied before an utterance . . . can be either true or false,"[10] whereas a contextual implication, refers to "those conditions that must be satisfied before an utterance can count as 'normal' in the circumstances in which it is made."[11] An example to illustrate these concepts might help. Suppose that I say: "The house on the hill is haunted." There must be a house on the hill for my utterance to be true or false—hence, in uttering the statement, it presupposes that there exists a house on the hill. This means that presupposition bears no relation to the beliefs of the person uttering the statement. But in normal circumstances my utterance of such a statement contextually implies that I believe that there is a house on the hill. Contextual implication bears no relation to whether or not a house actually exists on the hill.

Now let us return to the skeptic's claims. The skeptic claims that if her impossible condition for answering (A) or (B) were met, then one would be able to justify one's knowledge claim (i.e., "answer" [A] or [B]) to her satisfaction. Why? Because meeting such a condition would *deductively guarantee* the truth of such a knowledge claim. Hence, it is at least contextually implied that the skeptic believes in the rules of deductive logic and accepts them as a means to justify a knowledge claim. As it turns out, Strawson's account of presupposition is not useful here, but we may be able to be even more precise about the skeptic's background beliefs by stipulating the following definition of epistemic presupposition as a way of characterizing the idea that one belief is based upon another:

$EP-P'$ is an epistemic presupposition of P for S =def. at least part of S's justification for believing in P relies on believing in or accepting P' (i.e., relies on employing P' in the justification of P).

So, for example, if P = the proposition that the house on the hill is haunted, and I believe P because I saw ghosts there last week, then P' = the proposition that I saw ghosts there last week. P' is an epistemic presupposition of P for me because at least part of my justification for believing that P is that I believe that P'. Whether or not my justification is adequate is not important to this concept. It is enough that I *take* there to be a connection between P and P' such that I believe that accepting P' at least partially justifies me in accepting P.

Now in the case of the skeptic let P' = the skeptic's ultimate canon(s) of deductive logic; P = the claim that if her impossible condition were met, then one would be able to "answer" (A) or (B) because its truth would be deductively guaranteed. Then we can see that P' is an epistemic presupposition of P for the skeptic, for at least part of her justification for believing in P relies on accepting P' (i.e., relies on her employing P' in the justification of P). Hence, this (P') is one of the skeptic's background assumptions. But the very standard which is both contextually implied and epistemically presupposed by her claim that answering (A) or (B) is impossible, cannot itself be justified by satisfying the skeptic's conditions. In other words, the skeptic cannot meet the very condition which she sets up to argue that neither particularism nor methodism can "answer" (A) or (B). Does the skeptic have some other way to justify her reliance on and acceptance of the canons of deductive logic? And of course, if we accept such canons as well, then it is incumbent upon us to examine our justification for accepting them. But here I think we have some advantage over the skeptic.

Let us suppose that we claim to know or be justified in believing that: "If P then Q, and P, therefore Q" is a valid deductive rule. If this is one of our basic, primitive or ultimate rules, then it has been shown that one cannot justify it by means of an argument (either deductively or practically);[12] i.e., it cannot be shown to be valid in a non–question begging way. Does this mean that we cannot justify our claim that we know Modus Ponens (MP) to be a valid rule? I think not. Some think that our intuition of the validity of MP justifies our claim that we know MP is a valid rule. Some might also claim that MP needs no justification.[13]

With MP, it is not that a justification through argument is not needed, but that it cannot be obtained. But our inability to provide such a justification has not led philosophers to be skeptical about MP (including our skeptic). Why not? Perhaps it is because our intuition about MP is so strong that it seems to provide us with a kind of justification for our claims about MP. There is a point of similarity here between our inability to provide a justification by argument for our knowledge claim in answer to either (A) or (B) and in the case of our ultimate canons of logic, e.g., MP. Perhaps there is also a similarity between what it is about MP that justifies us in our claims about it and what it is about an answer to either (A) or (B) that justifies us in our claims about it.

One might argue that what it is about MP that justifies us in our claims that it is a valid rule is our logical intuitions. Where argument fails to give a justification, our logical intuitions justify our claims that MP is a valid rule and, for example, Modus Morons (MM)[14] is not a valid rule.

Is there anything about answers to (A) and (B) which parallels the claims about MP? One might argue that there is a parallel. One could claim that we have certain epistemic intuitions which justify our answer to (A) or (B). For example, Descartes had an answer to (B) by claiming to know anything which he clearly and distinctly perceived. What justifies Descartes in this claim? His intuitions. One might claim along with Descartes that to think contrary to these intuitions would be just as irrational as it would be to think otherwise in logic and accept, for example, MM. I am not endorsing this position here, but simply pointing out that there is an alternative way of justifying an answer to (A) or (B).

This suggestion would be a kind of justification that is different from giving an argument, and in our case one could appeal to intuition to justify an answer to (A) or (B). If someone like the skeptic were to claim that she does not have such intuitions about the answer to (A) or (B), there seems to be no way of rationally convincing her otherwise. The same is true in logic. As Lewis Carroll and Carnap have pointed out,[15] one could never rationally convince someone who was deductively blind of the validity of MP. Thus, one might argue that the epistemic status of one's answer to (A) or (B) is in no more trouble than MP.

The skeptic accepts MP and uses deductive logic to argue against both the methodist and the particularist. She cannot justify her reliance and acceptance of these canons by means of the very standard she sets up to criticize others. The standard is in principle impossible to meet.

Now Chisholm believed that his position was no worse (no less arbitrary) than any of the others; that the skeptic's position has no more to recommend it than the others do.[16] But I believe that Chisholm is wrong here. It seems that we do have good reason to believe that meeting some impossible condition is not the only way to justify our knowledge claims. This is what Chisholm failed to see.

The real question at hand, then, seems to be: What means of justification of some knowledge claim are or count as good/acceptable/rational justifications of such claims? Here the skeptic is claiming that only a justification which is in principle impossible to give is acceptable. Indeed, if this were the only way to justify such a claim, then the skeptic would not be able to justify her claim that answering (A) or (B) is impossible because such a claim relies on certain canons of deductive logic which she cannot so justify.

Now the skeptic may have an answer to our criticism. I have argued that the skeptic must accept that there are other acceptable methods for justifying a knowledge claim (other than her impossible condition) like intuition in the case of logic, because she employs and accepts logical canons to argue her position against opponents. If her criticism rests on propositions which she cannot justify then her argument has no force against her opponents. To the extent that it has force, to that extent she must admit that she is justified in believing them even though she cannot justify them by means of argument. She may reply that she cannot justify her assumptions and that she too is caught on the wheel of her own making. She is not immune to these epistemological dilemmas either.

I think that this response is misleading and incorrect. The point that I have been trying to get at is that the problem of the criterion is only a problem if one accepts all those propositions which are presupposed and contextually implied by the skeptic's way of framing the question. I have tried to show that the problem that the skeptic characterizes, when clearly understood, has a dissolution. Furthermore, this dissolution leads us to question what metaepistemological assumptions underlie the skeptic's position. By trying to enter into a dialog with the skeptic we are then entitled to ask for a justification for her claim that only meeting an impossible condition can justify a knowledge claim to (A) or (B). The skeptic needs to justify her claim before she can convince anyone that there is rational doubt about which propositions to accept and reject. And without this rational doubt there is no problem. The skeptic, then, is not caught on a wheel of her own making until there is a problem. So, if she claims that she is not justified in her assumptions, then we need not have any reason to accept her claim that (A) or (B) are not answerable, and hence, there is no problem—no wheel. If she claims that she is justified in her assumptions, then she must tell us how. If she claims that she *is* justified but cannot justify her position (certainly not in terms of her own condition for acceptable justifications), then two points can be made. First, if the skeptic cannot justify by means of her own impossible condition her claim that only meeting some impossible condition constitutes an acceptable justification of some knowledge claim, then her claim that such a condition is the only acceptable condition is undermined. This puts the skeptic at an epistemological disadvantage when compared to the particularist and methodist. For while both the particularist and methodist also cannot justify their respective knowledge claims in terms of the skeptic's impossible condition, the need to meet such a condition is called into question by the skeptic's inability to meet her own condition. Second, consider the following principle of justification:

JP—If *S is* justified in believing that *P* at least partially on the basis of *Q*, and *S* believes that *S* is justified in believing that *P* at least partially on the basis of *Q*, and *Q* is an epistemic presupposition of *P* for *S*, then *S* accepts *Q* as a means of at least partially justifying *S*'s belief that *P*.

If the skeptic believes that her ultimate canons of deductive logic are at least partially a means of justifying her belief that only meeting some impossible condition can justify an answer to (A) or (B), then not only does she believe that there are other sufficient conditions for justifying a knowledge claim, but she is employing a means of justification other than one which meets her impossible condition. In other words, by relying on the canons of deductive logic to justify her claim about acceptable justifications, she *ipso facto* contradicts her claim about acceptable justifications. This not only undermines her position but it strengthens the position of the particularist and methodist alike. For if there are other sufficient conditions for justifying a knowledge claim, then our position is vindicated and we have some reason for preferring methodism and particularism over skepticism.

One might argue that *if* one *were* to accept the ultimate canons of logic (as we all do), then the skeptic has made her point—nothing short of meeting her impossible condition is acceptable as a justification of a knowledge claim. However, if we accept the ultimate canons of logic as justified, then we *ipso facto* accept that there are claims that do not meet the skeptic's impossible condition that *are justified* and can be used *to justify* other claims. This, in effect, is an admission that there are other sufficient conditions for justifying a knowledge claim and it opens the door on the question of what should count as an acceptable/rational justification and what should not.

If we assume that there are other sufficient conditions for justifying a knowledge claim, then we are faced with the task of determining how to choose between them— a metametaepistemological question. What kinds of metacriteria should we accept and reject? Answering this question is well beyond the scope of this paper. One way to approach a beginning might be to try to achieve some kind of consensus among the disputants, perhaps in terms of our epistemological goals. There may be some fundamental principles that we can all agree upon such as:

1. Metacriteria and criteria should be consistent with the law of non-contradiction and should yield beliefs that are not inconsistent.

2. All other things being equal, criteria and metacriteria with greater explanatory power should be preferred.

3. A metacriterion should apply to itself, i.e., it should be knowable by its own principle.

Even if we had agreement here, however, these principles are not specific enough to rule out various forms of methodism, particularism, and skepticism. Yet more specific principles are likely to spawn disagreement among our disputants. If we find that the skeptic, methodist, and particularist cannot come to an agreement on this third-order question, then we may be at an impasse in our dialog. If this is so, it seems to me to be preferable to be clear that we disagree at some absolutely fundamental level with the skeptic than to mistakenly think that we are caught in a circle of someone else's making or that skepticism is on an equal footing with methodism and particularism.[17]

NOTES

1. Roderick M. Chisholm, *The Foundations of Knowing* (Minneapolis: University of Minnesota Press, 1982), p. 64.

2. Roderick M. Chisholm, "Reply to Amico on the Problem of the Criterion," *Philosophical Papers* 17, no. 3 (November 1988): 231–34.

3. Ibid., p. 234.

4. Robert P. Amico, "Reply to Chisholm on the Problem of the Criterion," *Philosophical Papers* 17, no. 3 (November 1988): 235–36.

5. Ibid

6. She also seems to presuppose that if knowing something like "I have a left hand" entails being able to "answer" (A), then fallibilism is false. Roughly speaking, fallibilism is the view that one can know some proposition *P* and not have deductively conclusive evidence to justify one's belief that *P.* (See Richard Feldman, "Fallibilism and Knowing That One Knows," *The Philosophical Review* 90 (1981): 266–82.]

7. Richard Fumerton, "Metaepistemology and Skepticism," delivered at the University of Rochester 6th Annual Conference—Skepticism, May 5–6, 1989.

8. P. F. Strawson, *Introduction to Logical Theory* (London: Methuen & Co., 1952), p. 175.

9. See *Encyclopedia of Philosophy,* "Presupposing" (New York: Macmillan Publishing Co., Inc., 1972), Vols, 5–6, pp. 447–49.

10. Ibid.

11. Ibid.

12. See Susan Haack, "The Justification of Deduction," *Mind* 85 (1976): 112–19; and Robert P. Amico, "On the Vindication of Deduction and Induction," *Australasian Journal of Philosophy* (September 1986): 322–30,

13. When is a call for justification rationally appropriate? Max Black claimed that: "A demand for justification is normally taken to imply a *discrepancy with some standard.* And a satisfactory justification is one which neutralizes the apparent discrepancy by showing it to be consistent with, or deducible from, the relevant standard." (Max Black, *Language and Philosophy* [Ithaca, N.Y.: Cornell University Press, 1949], p. 63). This claim is so broad that we can understand a call for justification to be appropriate whenever anyone with *any* standard claims discrepancy with their standard. But even this seems too restrictive, for it seems that one could call for a justification of some claim even if one has no "acceptable standard." One may simply be asking for another person's reasons for claiming something without having any standard oneself. Black's characterization seems too narrow and restrictive. Almost any conditions may be rationally appropriate to call for a justification of some claim. So, if what is meant by this claim (that MP needs no justification) is that a call for justification in this case is not rationally appropriate, then some rea-

son would need to be given in support of this claim, because it seems that almost any conditions may be rationally appropriate to call for a justification of some claim. If this is not what is meant, then it is unclear to me just what such a claim means.

14. This is Haack's appellative for the invalid rule: If *P* then *Q,* and *Q,* therefore *P.* Ibid, p. 115.

15. Lewis Carroll, "What the Tortoise Said to Achilles," *Mind* (1895); and Rudolf Carnap, "Inductive Logic and Inductive Intuition," in *The Problem of Inductive Logic,* I. Lakatos, ed. (New York: North-Holland, 1968).

16. Chisholm, *The Foundations of Knowing,* p. 75.

17. My thanks to Mike Chiariello, Doug Davis, and Barry Gan for their comments on an earlier draft of this paper.

15

Reply to Amico on Skepticism and the Problem of the Criterion

Sharon Ryan

In "Skepticism and the Problem of the Criterion," Robert P. Amico claims to have *dissolved* the problem of the criterion and argues that the skeptical position is the least tenable solution to the problem. In this paper, I argue that Amico has not dissolved the problem. I also argue that he has not provided a sound argument against the skeptic.

Let me begin by restating the problem of the criterion and giving a brief summary of Professor Amico's position. The problem is a metaepistemological problem. It stems from trying to decide which of our beliefs are "good" beliefs and which of our beliefs are "bad" beliefs. "Good" means an actual instance of knowledge and "bad" is merely apparent knowledge. So, the problem is *not* a problem concerning whether or not we know anything. It is a problem about justifying our claims *about* knowledge. That is, it is a problem about whether we can have knowledge about what we know and not about whether we can have knowledge. The following two pairs of questions are offered by Professor Chisholm and quoted by Amico to characterize the problem of the criterion:

(A) What do I know? What is the extent of my knowledge?

(B) How do I decide whether I know? What are the criteria of knowledge?

When facing the metaepistemological question of which of our beliefs are actual instances of knowledge and which are not, these two questions become crucial. The question we are faced with in the problem of the criterion is stated in (B). It seems that when trying to justify claims about what one knows, one must consider how to go about deciding how to distinguish the known ones from unknown ones. If there is some criterion that can be applied to one's beliefs, then one could presumably put each belief to the test of the criterion. If it passes the test of the criterion, then it is an instance of knowledge. If it fails the test of the criterion, then it is not an instance of knowledge. However, it also seems that any old criterion won't do. The criterion must itself be accurate and we must have good reasons for using that criterion rather than some other criterion. It must correctly pick out the actual cases of knowledge from the merely apparent cases of knowledge. But, in order to know if the criterion is the right criterion, one must already know which beliefs are knowledge and which are not so that one can tell if the criterion successfully picks out the beliefs that we really know. But to know which beliefs we really know, we need some criterion to decide whether we know. So it seems that we need to know the answer to (A) in order to answer (B) but we must know the answer to (B) before we can answer (A). It also seems that we know we are in big trouble! It looks like we are going to be running around in circles, getting tired and dizzy and never able to know what we really know because we cannot justify such claims.

So, the problem of the criterion is to find a way of giving a justified answer to (B) so that we can distinguish actual cases of knowledge from merely apparent cases of knowledge and know what we know.

Amico and Chisholm present three possible, and mutually incompatible, positions about this problem. They go as follows:

skepticism: We cannot know whether we know the things we think we know because we cannot justify claims about knowledge. In order to justify an answer to (A) we need a justified answer to (B) but we cannot justify an answer to (B) without a justified answer to (A). Hence, we are unable to justify either answer.

particularism: We can know whether we know the things we think we know. We can justify and are justified in our answer to (A) and (B). We can justify our answer to (A) without having to know (B). However, we are justified in our answer to (B) only when we use the answer to (A) to justify (B).

methodism: We can know whether we know the things we think we know. We can justify our answers to both (A) and (B). We can justify our answer to (B) without being justified in (A) and having to use (A) as part of the justification for (B). However (B) is justified only when we use the answer to (B) to justify (A).

Amico, in the first part of his paper, claims to have *dissolved* the problem of the criterion. He asserts, ". . . the problem of the criterion is dissolved once one realizes that the conditions set by the skeptic for solving the problem are impossible to meet. This is because rational doubt is the earmark of a philosophical problem, and since there is no longer any rational doubt about how to answer the question, there is no longer any problem. The question has a simple answer—you can't. But it is no wonder that we cannot do the impossible. It is no more of a problem than the question: how do you make a circle square?"

In the second part of his paper, Amico challenges the skeptic to meet her own conditions for justifying knowledge claims about what one knows. He claims that the skeptical position taken in the problem of the criterion presupposes the truth of the rules of deductive logic. He asks the skeptic what her justification for those rules is? He claims that the skeptic has two routes available to her. Amico thinks the skeptic is headed for trouble either way she turns. Either she is justified in virtue of satisfying her conditions for providing an answer to (A) and (B) or she is justified in accepting the canons of deductive logic in some other way. If she is justified by meeting her own "impossible" conditions, she solves the problem of the criterion. By meeting her own conditions, she demonstrates that there is something that meets the conditions necessary for knowing that one knows. Hence she demonstrates that her own skepticism about the problem of the criterion is false. Amico correctly points out that that is not a happy path for the skeptic to travel.

If her reliance on the rules of logic are not justified by meeting the conditions set for answering (A) and (B), but are justified in some other way, like for example, by our intuitions about logic, then she admits that meeting her conditions is not necessary for justifying knowledge claims. Amico thinks this is also an unhappy path for the skeptic to travel. It looks like the skeptic is in big trouble.

I have a few brief comments about Amico's *dissolution*. First, it is not clear what, according to Amico, *the question* is and what *the problem* is when he claims to dissolve the problem. According to Chisholm, ". . . the problem is: How are we to distinguish the real cases of knowledge from what only seem to be cases of knowledge?"[1] I thought the problem amounted to providing the right answer to *that* question. That's question (B). I'll call this question the old question. The particularist solution has some plausibility, the methodist solution has some plausibility, and the skeptical solution has some plausibility. All seem plausible, yet not all can be true, so we have a problem. Which, if any, of these solutions is the right answer? How can we justify an answer to (B)?

When Amico claims to have *dissolved* the problem of the criterion, he seems to have introduced a slightly different *question* and *problem*. The problem, by page 2 in Amico's paper, has become providing an answer to the following question: "If you cannot answer (A) until you know the answer to (B), and you cannot answer (B) until you know the answer to (A), then how can you answer either question?" I'll call this new question "the new question." It is important to note that the new question is a rhetorical question posed by the skeptic. Remember, Amico's second sentence is, "According to Chisholm the skeptic claims that you cannot answer (A) unless you already know the answer to (B), and you cannot answer (B) unless you already know the answer to (A); so how can you answer either?" So, it seems that Amico has stated the question behind the skeptic's position as the problem. That is, the new question is one way of answering the old question. The *new problem* is how to answer this new question. Amico's *dissolution,* as far as I can tell, amounts to saying that the new question is impossible to answer. It is not clear to me how things progress from there. I have a two possible interpretations.

Here is the first one. Amico thinks that his pointing out the impossibility of answering the question dissolves the problem because it is no longer rational to attempt to give an answer. We can't do the impossible, so why try. Now, an important question comes to my mind. What is the difference between a dissolution and a solution? If the new question is *the question* of the problem of the criterion, then it seems that the skeptic has already given the solution. The skeptic answers the question in the way Amico thinks is the only way to answer the question—you can't. That is exactly why the skeptic about the problem of the criterion thinks that we cannot know whether we know what we think we know. So why not think the problem has been *solved* by the skeptic rather than *dissolved* by Amico?

That first interpretation worries me. Given what follows in the second part of his paper, I think Amico thinks that the problem of the criterion still remains and can be solved by either the methodist or the particularist. If the problem is not really a problem anymore because it began with an impossible question, there would be no obvious reason for Amico to carefully investigate the metaepistemological assumptions of the skeptic about this problem. Why continue to harass them if you know they are right about whether or not the question can be answered? If Amico thinks the problem of the criterion, properly asked, is like asking "how do you square a circle?" it is difficult to see why he continues to take the skeptical position so seriously in the remainder of his paper. He must mean something else. He must think that the skeptically infested, new question cannot be answered, but that is not really *the* question. The *real* question is the old question. Namely, "how are we to distinguish the real cases of knowledge from what only seem to be cases of knowledge?"[2] Let me pursue this line of thought in a second interpretation.

The second interpretation I have for understanding what Amico's dissolution amounts to is that he thinks that the new question is rigged by the skeptic to require conditions that are impossible to meet. Let me just note again that this new question is *not* the question we began with. This question rhetorically states the skeptical solution to the problem. So, to say that the question is rigged is actually to criticize the skeptic's reasons for her answer to the old question. In her answer to the old question, the skeptic argues for the conclusion that we cannot know whether we know. She uses the claim that one cannot know an answer to (A) without already knowing the answer to (B) but one cannot know the answer to (B) without already knowing the answer to (A), as a premise in her argument. She uses that premise to justify her intermediary conclusion that we cannot answer either question. So, Amico's dissolution, on this reading, amounts to rejecting the premise that one cannot answer (A) until we answer (B). . . . His reason for this rejection is simply that if the premise were true then it would follow that we cannot answer the question we began with. On this second interpretation, he is arguing that since the skeptic is claiming that we must meet conditions that are "in principle, impossible to meet" in order to justify our claims about what we know, we can reject the skeptical solution to the problem (or statement of the question). On this interpretation, Amico has not dissolved the problem of the criterion. He has just asserted that the skeptic's argument includes a false premise.

There is a big difference between holding a position that can't possibly be true and holding a position that claims that something or other is impossible. For example if the skeptical position amounted to claiming something of the form (p & ~p), we could, just in virtue of pointing this out about their position, reject it. However, if the skeptic or anyone else holds a position that claims that p is not possible, it is not legitimate to reject her position on that basis alone. Maybe the skeptic is right. Perhaps what she claims is not possible really is not possible. If we are going to justifiably reject her position, we must provide some reasons for thinking that p is possible or at least show why she is not justified in thinking that p is not possible. Amico does spend the second part of his paper addressing the question of whether the "impossible conditions" set by the skeptic are necessary for knowing that we know what we think we know. Until Amico succeeds at this second task, he has not *dissolved* the problem. So, I think his claim to have *dissolved* the problem at the outset of his paper is premature.

Let me now turn to the second part of Amico's paper. In the second part of his paper, Amico asks the skeptic for her justification for presupposing the truth of the rules of deductive logic. I think the skeptic about the problem of the criterion does not have to presuppose anything about logic and need not insist that knowing whether or not one knows requires that there be no possibility of error in order to hold her position. I believe Amico is making this skeptic much more skeptical than she needs to be. However, I am going to grant Amico all of that for the sake of his argument.

Suppose the skeptic does presuppose the rules of deductive logic. If so, a legitimate question for Amico to ask the skeptic is "why do you believe in deduction, what's your *justification* for believing in the canons of deductive logic?" That does seem legitimate but it also seems correct for the skeptic to point out that her position in the problem of the criterion was not to deny that we know things or that we are justified in believing things. She can admit to having first order knowledge and justification. What she denies is that we can know that we know. So it is perfectly consistent for her to say that she is justified in believing that the canons of deductive logic are valid and also claim that she knows they are valid. What she is forced to deny is that she *knows* (which includes justifying the claim) that this is something that she knows.

So, it seems to me that Amico is correct in pointing out that the skeptic's presuppositions about the rules of deductive logic are not able to meet the skeptic's conditions for metaknowledge. I agree, the skeptic agrees, Amico agrees, we all agree, that the skeptic's presuppositions cannot meet the skeptic's conditions for answering (A) and (B). Nothing can. They are impossible to meet. But her presuppositions about logic do not have to meet those conditions in order to be justified. However, by failing to meet her impossible conditions, the skeptic is not forced to admit that she does not know that the canons of deductive logic are valid. She may, when asked what her justification for the first order knowledge claim, give the answer Amico provides for her. She may say that her logical intuitions justify her. But she is not thereby admitting, as Amico charges, that there are other ways to justify our second order knowledge claims. She may hold her ground and say that neither she nor anyone else can justify such second order knowledge claims and consistently claim that there are a lot of justified beliefs around.

Amico seems to think that if she cannot justify her presuppositions, then her argument has no force. The skeptic can respond to Amico by saying "my presuppositions are justified, I just can't justify my claim to know that they are really justified. My intuitions justify my acceptance of deductive logic and so do yours, so unless you have some reason for thinking my first order justification is no good, then I have no reason to worry about my presuppositions. Presuppositions are the things we take for granted and can continue to take for granted until we have some reason to doubt them."

Now, I think Amico would be happy for the skeptic to admit that intuition is an adequate means of justification. He then claims that the methodist and particularist also have intuitions. Amico points to Descartes for an example to demonstrate this fact. ". . . Descartes had an answer to (B) by claiming to know anything which he clearly and distinctly perceived. What justifies Descartes in this claim? His intuitions." It seems to me that Amico's point to the skeptic is if you can use your intuitions, then we can use ours. I think a skeptic can point to a very important difference between these intuitions. Logical intuitions are shared by all sides of the dispute of the problem of the criterion. Methodist intuitions are only shared by methodists and particularist intuitions are shared only by particularists. It seems that the skeptic's intuitions about deduction are innocent, whereas the intuitions of the methodist and particularist are guilty.

Hence, I conclude that the skeptic, by appealing to intuitions as first order justifications about her presuppositions about logic, does not have to satisfy her own requirements for second order justification. That she satisfies the justification condition for first order knowledge with her logical intuitions does not leave the door open for the methodist and particularist to appeal to intuitions for justification of their positions. Their intuitions are in doubt in this problem whereas logical intuitions are not.

I think the second part of Amico's paper has not shown that the skeptical position is any worse than the other two positions. He has not shown that the skeptic is mistaken in thinking that in order to know whether we know one has to meet her conditions. Therefore, I think the problem of the criterion is still a real philosophical problem and the skeptical solution is just as compelling as the other solutions.

NOTES

1. Roderick M. Chisholm, *The Foundations of Knowing* (Minneapolis: University of Minnesota Press, 1982), p. 63.

2. Ibid.

Part III

The Fourth Condition
of Knowledge

16

Knowledge: Undefeated Justified True Belief

Keith Lehrer and Thomas Paxson, Jr.

If a man knows that a statement is true even though there is no other statement that justifies his belief, then his knowledge is basic. Basic knowledge is completely justified true belief. On the other hand, if a man knows that a statement is true because there is some other statement that justifies his belief, then his knowledge is nonbasic. Nonbasic knowledge requires something in addition to completely justified true belief, for, though a statement completely justifies a man in his belief, there may be some true statement that *defeats* his justification. So, we must add the condition that his justification is not defeated. Nonbasic knowledge is undefeated justified true belief. These analyses will be elaborated below and subsequently defended against various alternative analyses.[1]

I

We propose the following analysis of basic knowledge: S has basic knowledge that h if and only if (i) h is true, (ii) S believes that h, (iii) S is completely justified in believing that h, and (iv) the satisfaction of condition (iii) does not depend on any evidence p justifying S in believing that h. The third condition is used in such a way that it entails neither the second condition nor the first. A person can be completely justified in believing that h, even though, irrationally, he does not; and a person can be

From *The Journal of Philosophy* 66, no. 8 (April 24, 1969): 225–37. © 1969. Reprinted by permission of the publisher.

completely justified in believing that h, even though, unfortunately, he is mistaken.[2] Furthermore, the third condition does not entail that there is any statement or belief that justifies S in believing that h. The analysis, then, is in keeping with the characterization of basic knowledge given above. In basic knowledge, S is completely justified in believing that h even if it is not the case that there is any statement or belief that justifies his believing that h.

There are cases in which a person has some, perhaps mysterious, way of being right about matters of a certain sort with such consistency that philosophers and others have said that the person knows whereof he speaks. Consider, for example, the crystal-ball-gazing gypsy who is almost always right in his predictions of specific events. Peter Unger suggests a special case of this.[3] His gypsy is always right, but has no evidence to this effect and, in fact, believes that he is usually wrong. With respect to each specific prediction, however, the gypsy impulsively believes it to be true (as indeed it is). Whether or not the predictive beliefs of the ordinary gypsy and Unger's gypsy are cases of knowledge depends, we contend, on whether they are cases of basic knowledge. This in turn depends on whether the gypsies are completely justified in their beliefs. It is plausible to suggest that these are cases of knowledge, but this is only because it is also plausible to think that the gypsies in question have some way of being right that completely justifies their prognostications. We neither affirm nor deny that these are cases of knowledge, but maintain that, if they are cases of knowledge, then they are cases of *basic* knowledge.

It is consistent with our analysis of knowledge to admit that a man knows something even though no statement constitutes evidence that completely justifies his believing it. Philosophers have suggested that certain memory and perceptual beliefs are completely justified in the absence of such evidential statements. We choose to remain agnostic with respect to any claim of this sort, but such proposals are not excluded by our analysis.

II

Not all knowledge that p is basic knowledge that p, because sometimes justifying evidence is essential. Consider the following analysis of nonbasic knowledge: (i) h is true, (ii) S believes that h, and (iii*) p completely justifies S in believing that h. In this analysis, p is that (statement) which makes S completely justified in believing that h. Note that (iii*), like (iii), does not entail (ii) or (i).

This analysis of nonbasic knowledge is, of course, defective. As Edmund Gettier has shown, there are examples in which some false statement p entails and hence completely justifies S in believing that h, and such that, though S correctly believes that h, his being correct is mostly a matter of luck.[4] Consequently, S lacks knowledge, contrary to the above analysis. Other examples illustrate that the false statement which creates the difficulty need not *entail h*. Consider, for example, the case of the pyromaniac described by Skyrms.[5] The pyromaniac has found that Sure-Fire matches have always ignited when struck. On the basis of this evidence, the pyromaniac is completely justified in believing that the match he now holds will ignite upon his striking it. However, unbeknownst to the pyromaniac, this match happens to contain impurities that raise its combustion temperature above that which can be produced by the friction. Imagine that a burst of Q-radiation ignites the match just as he strikes it. His belief that the match will ignite upon his striking it is true and completely justified by the evidence. But this is not a case of knowledge, because it is not the striking that will cause the match to ignite.

Roderick Chisholm has pointed out that justifications are defeasible.[6] In the examples referred to above, there is some true statement that would defeat any justification of *S* for believing that *h*. In the case of the pyromaniac, his justification is defeated by the true statement that striking the match will not cause it to ignite. This defeats his justification for believing that the match will ignite upon his striking it.

Thus we propose the following analysis of nonbasic knowledge: *S* has nonbasic knowledge that *h* if and only if (i) *h* is true, (ii) *S* believes that *h*, and (iii) there is some statement *p* that completely justifies *S* in believing that *h* and no other statement defeats this justification. The question we must now answer is—what does it mean to say that a statement defeats a justification? Adopting a suggestion of Chisholm's, we might try the following: when *p* completely justifies *S* in believing that *h*, this justification is defeated by *q* if and only if (i) *q* is true, and (ii) the conjunction of *p* and *q* does not completely justify *S* in believing that *h*.[7] This definition is strong enough to rule out the example of the pyromaniac as a case of knowledge. The statement that the striking of a match will *not* cause it to ignite, which is true, is such that when it is conjoined to any statement that completely justifies the pyromaniac in believing that the match will ignite, the resultant conjunction will fail to so justify him in that belief. Given this definition of defeasibility, the analysis of nonbasic knowledge would require that a man who has nonbasic knowledge that *h* must have some justification for his belief that is not defeated by any true statement.

However, this requirement is somewhat unrealistic. To see that the definition of defeasibility under consideration makes the analysis of nonbasic knowledge excessively restrictive, we need only notice that there can be true statements that are misleading. Suppose I see a man walk into the library and remove a book from the library by concealing it beneath his coat. Since I am sure the man is Tom Grabit, whom I have often seen before when he attended my classes, I report that I know that Tom Grabit has removed the book. However, suppose further that Mrs. Grabit, the mother of Tom, has averred that on the day in question Tom was not in the library, indeed, was thousands of miles away, and that Tom's identical twin brother, John Grabit, was in the library. Imagine, moreover, that I am entirely ignorant of the fact that Mrs. Grabit has said these things. The statement that she has said these things would defeat any justification I have for believing that Tom Grabit removed the book, according to our present definition of defeasibility. Thus, I could not be said to have nonbasic knowledge that Tom Grabit removed the book.

The preceding might seem acceptable until we finish the story by adding that Mrs. Grabit is a compulsive and pathological liar, that John Grabit is a fiction of her demented mind, and that Tom Grabit took the book as I believed. Once this is added, it should be apparent that I did know that Tom Grabit removed the book, and, since the knowledge must be nonbasic, I must have nonbasic knowledge of that fact. Consequently, the definition of defeasibility must be amended. The fact that Mrs. Grabit said what she did should not be allowed to defeat any justification I have for believing that Tom Grabit removed the book, because I neither entertained any beliefs concerning Mrs. Grabit nor would I have been justified in doing so. More specifically, my justification does not depend on my being completely justified in believing that Mrs. Grabit did *not* say the things in question.

To understand how the definition of defeasibility must be amended to deal with the preceding example, let us consider an example from the literature in which a justification deserves to be defeated. Suppose that I have excellent evidence that completely justifies my believing that a student in my class, Mr. Nogot, owns a Ford, the evidence consisting in my having seen him driving it, hearing him say he owns it, and so forth. Since Mr. Nogot is a student in my class who owns a Ford, someone in my class owns a Ford, and, consequently, I am completely justified in believing that someone in my class owns a Ford. Imagine that, contrary to the evidence, Mr. Nogot does not own a Ford, that I have been deceived, but that unknown to me Mr. Havit, who is also in my class, does own a Ford. Though I have a completely justified true belief, I do not know that someone in my class owns a Ford. The reason is that my sole justification for believing that someone in my class does own a Ford is and should be defeated by the true statement that Mr. Nogot does not own a Ford.

In the case of Tom Grabit, the true statement that Mrs. Grabit said Tom was not in the library and so forth, should not be allowed to defeat my justification for believing that Tom removed the book, whereas in the case of Mr. Nogot, the true statement that Mr. Nogot does not own a Ford, should defeat my justification for believing that someone in my class owns a Ford. Why should one true statement but not the other be allowed to defeat my justification? The answer is that in one case my justification depends on my being completely justified in believing the true statement to be false while in the other it does not. My justification for believing that Tom removed the book does not depend on my being completely justified in believing it to be false that Mrs. Grabit said Tom was not in the library and so forth. But my justification for believing that someone in my class owns a Ford does depend on my being completely justified in believing it to be false that Mr. Nogot does not own a Ford. Thus, a defeating statement must be one which, though true, is such that the subject is completely justified in believing it to be false.[8]

The following definition of defeasibility incorporates this proposal: when p completely justifies S in believing that h, this justification is defeated by q if and only if (i) q is true, (ii) S is completely justified in believing q to be false, and (iii) the conjunction of p and q does not completely justify S in believing that h.

This definition of defeasibility, though basically correct, requires one last modification to meet a technical problem. Suppose that there is some statement h of which S has nonbasic knowledge. Let us again consider the example in which I know that Tom Grabit removed the book. Now imagine that there is some true statement which is completely irrelevant to this knowledge and which I happen to be completely justified in believing to be false, for example, the statement that I was born in St. Paul. Since I am completely justified in believing it to be false that I was born in St. Paul, I am also completely justified in believing to be false the conjunctive statement that I was born in St. Paul and that q, whatever q is, because I am completely justified in believing any conjunction to be false if I am completely justified in believing a conjunct of it to be false. Therefore, I am completely justified in believing to be false the conjunctive statement that I was born in St. Paul and Mrs. Grabit said that Tom Grabit was not in the library and so forth. Moreover, this conjunctive statement is true, and is such that, when it is conjoined in turn to any evidential statement that justifies me in believing that Tom Grabit removed the book, the resultant extended conjunction will not completely justify me in believing that Tom Grabit removed the book. Hence, any such justification will be defeated.[9] Once again, it turns out that I do not have nonbasic knowledge of the fact that Tom is the culprit.

In a logical nut, the problem is that the current definition of defeasibility reduces to the preceding one. Suppose there is a true statement q such that, for any p that completely justifies S in believing h, the conjunction of p and q does not completely justify me in believing that h. Moreover, suppose that I am not completely justified in believing q to be false, so that, given our current definition of defeasibility, q does not count as defeating. Nevertheless, if there is any true statement r, irrelevant to both p and q, which I am completely justified in believing to be false, then we can indirectly use q to defeat my justification for believing h. For I shall be completely justified in believing the conjunction of r and q to be false, though in fact it is true, because I am completely justified in believing r to be false. If the conjunction of q and p does not completely justify me in believing that h, then, given the irrelevance of r, neither would the conjunction of r, q, and p justify me in believing that h. Hence, my justifications for believing h would be defeated by the conjunction r and q on the current definition of defeasibility as surely as they were by q alone on the preceding definition.

The defect is not difficult to repair. Though S is completely justified in believing the conjunction of r and q to be false, one consequence of the conjunction, q, undermines my justification but is not something I am completely justified in believing to be false, while another consequence, r, is one that I am completely justified in believing to be false but is irrelevant to my justification. To return to our example, I am completely justified in believing to be false the conjunctive statement that I was born in St. Paul and that Mrs. Grabit said that Tom was not in the library and so forth. One consequence of this conjunction, that Mrs. Grabit said that Tom was not in the library and so forth, undermines my justification but is not something I am completely justified in believing to be false, while the other consequence, that I was born in St. Paul, is something I am completely justified in believing to be false but is irrelevant to my justification. The needed restriction is that those consequences of a defeating statement which undermine a justification must themselves be statements that the subject is completely justified in believing to be false.

We propose the following definition of defeasibility: if p completely justifies S in believing that h, then this justification is defeated by q if and only if (i) q is true, (ii) the conjunction of p and q does not completely justify S in believing that h, (iii) S is completely justified in believing q to be false, and (iv) if c is a logical consequence of q such that the conjunction of c and p does not completely justify S in believing that h, then S is completely justified in believing c to be false.

With this definition of defeasibility, we complete our analysis of nonbasic knowledge. We have defined nonbasic knowledge as true belief for which some statement provides a complete and undefeated justification. We previously defined basic knowledge as true belief for which there was complete justification that did not depend on any justifying statement. We define as knowledge anything that is either basic or nonbasic knowledge. Thus, S knows that h if and only if S has either basic or nonbasic knowledge that h. Having completed our analysis, we shall compare it with other goods in the epistemic marketplace to demonstrate the superiority of our ware.

III

The analysis offered above resembles two recent analyses formulated by Brian Skyrms and R. M. Chisholm. Both philosophers distinguish between basic and nonbasic knowledge, and both analyze knowledge in terms of justification. Moreover, these analyses are sufficiently restrictive so as to avoid yielding the result that a person has nonbasic knowledge when his justification is defeated by some false statement. However, we shall argue that both of these analyses are excessively restrictive and consequently lead to skeptical conclusions that are unwarranted.

Skyrms says that a man has nonbasic knowledge that p if and only if he has either derivative or nonderivative knowledge that *p*. He analyzes the latter two kinds of knowledge as follows:

> *Derivative Knowledge:* X has derivative knowledge that *p* if and only if there is a statement '*e*' such that:
> (i) X knows that e
> (ii) X knows that '*e*' entails '*p*'
> (iii) X believes that *p* on the basis of the knowledge referred to in (i) and (ii)

> *Nonderivative Knowledge:* X has nonderivative knowledge that *p* if and only if there is a statement '*e*' such that:
> (i) X knows that *e*
> (ii) X knows that '*e*' is good evidence for '*p*'
> (iii) X believes that *p* on the basis of the knowledge referred to in (i) and (ii)
> (iv) '*p*' is true
> (v) There is no statement '*q*' (other than '*p*') such that:
> (a) X knows that '*e*' is good evidence of '*q*'
> (b) X knows that '*q*' entails '*p*'
> (c) X believes that '*p*' on the basis of the knowledge referred to in (a) and (b)[10]

Later in his paper, Skyrms points out a defect in his analysis of nonderivative knowledge, namely, that the words, "There is a statement '*e*' such that . . ." must be replaced by some such expression as "There is some statement '*e*' consisting of the total evidence of *X* relevant to *p* such that . . ." or else the analysis win lead to trouble.[11]

We shall now show why this analysis is unsatisfactory. According to Skyrms, a man who knows that a disjunction is true without knowing any specific disjunct to be true, has nonderivative knowledge of the disjunction.[12] Indeed, his analysis of nonderivative knowledge is simply a generalization of his analysis of knowledge with respect to such disjunctions. But his analysis is overrestrictive in the case of our knowledge of disjunctions. Suppose I know that a business acquaintance of mine, Mr. Romeo, arrived in Rochester from Atlanta on either one of two flights, either AA 107 or AA 204. My evidence is that these are the only two flights into Rochester from Atlanta, that Mr. Romeo telephoned earlier from Atlanta to say he would be arriving on one of these two flights, that he is now in Rochester, and that no other flight to Rochester or nearby would enable Mr. Romeo to be in Rochester at the present time. On the basis of this evidence, I may on Skyrms's analysis be said to have nonderivative knowledge that Mr. Romeo arrived on either AA 107 or AA 204. So far so good.

However, suppose that we add to my evidence that, when I meet Mr. Romeo at the airport shortly after the arrival of AA 204 (the later flight), he tells me that he just arrived on AA 204. By Skyrms's analysis I now *lack* nonderivative knowledge that Mr. Romeo arrived on either AA 107 or AA 204. The reason is that condition (v) of his analysis of nonderivative knowledge is no longer satisfied with respect to that disjunction. I now have good evidence that Mr. Romeo arrived on AA 204, and I believe that disjunction on the basis of my knowledge that this evidence is good evidence for the statement "Mr. Romeo arrived on AA 204" and this statement entails "Mr. Romeo arrived on either AA 107 or AA 204." Thus, there is a statement 'q' that satisfies condition (a), (b), and (c) under (v) where 'p' is the disjunction.

The consequence that I now lack nonderivative knowledge that Mr. Romeo arrived on either AA 107 or AA 204 would not be fatal if it could be argued that I have derivative knowledge of that disjunction because I know that Mr. Romeo arrived on AA 204. But there is an unmentioned twist of romance in our tale. In fact, Mr. Romeo arrived on the earlier flight, AA 107, and, having entertained his secret love, deceitfully told me he arrived on the later flight. Thus, I do not know that Mr. Romeo arrived on AA 204, because he did not so arrive. By Skyrms's analyses, I have neither derivative nor nonderivative knowledge that Mr. Romeo arrived on either AA 107 or AA 204, and, therefore, I lack nonbasic knowledge of that disjunction. So, as Skyrms would have it, I do not know that Mr. Romeo arrived on either of those flights. However, although there is much of interest that I do not know in this case, I surely do know, on the basis of my original evidence which I may yet brandish with epistemic righteousness, that Mr. Romeo must have arrived on either AA 107 or AA 204. He did so arrive, and my evidence completely justifies me in believing that he did, regardless of the fact that Mr. Romeo spoke with a crooked tongue. Since I do have knowledge of the disjunction, Skyrms's analyses must be rejected.

Chisholm's analysis of knowledge is very similar to ours except for the condition intended to deal with situations in which, though a man has completely justified true belief, his justification is undermined by some false statement. In the sort of cases we have been considering, Chisholm's analysis requires, among other conditions, that if a person knows that h, then there is a proposition p such that p justifies h but p does not justify any false statement.[13] However, it seems reasonable to suppose that every statement, whatever epistemic virtues it might have, completely justifies at least one false statement. This supposition is supported by the fact that justification in Chisholm's system need not be deductive justification. Any nondeductive justification may fail to be truth-preserving; that is, the conclusion may be false though the premise be true. Thus, though our analysis is in a number of ways indebted to Chisholm's proposals, the foregoing argument is our reason for concluding that Chisholm's analysis would lead to some form of skepticism, that is, to the conclusion that people do not know some things they would generally and reasonably be said to know.

IV

Having indicated our reasons for rejecting those analyses which are most similar to our own, we shall now turn to some analyses that differ from ours in more fundamental ways. Peter Unger has analyzed knowledge as follows: For any sentential value of p, (at a time t) a man knows that p if and only if (at t) it is not at all accidental that the man is right about its being the case that p.[14] Unger nowhere rules out the possibility that there are some cases in which it is not at all accidental that a man is right simply because he has justification for believing what he does. So it could be that any case that satisfies our conditions for knowledge would satisfy his as well. But there are cases that satisfy his analysis though they fail to satisfy ours.

Let us consider an example. A hologram, or laser photograph, when illuminated by laser light looks three-dimensional even with respect to parallax effects when the viewer shifts his position. Imagine that holography has been so perfected that a laser-illuminated hologram of an object can, under certain observational conditions, be indistinguishable from the real thing.[15] More particularly, suppose that a man, Mr. Promoter, seeking to demonstrate the remarkable properties of laser photography, constructs a boxlike device which contains a vase, a laser photograph of the vase, and a laser source by which the photograph may be illuminated. The device is so constructed that Mr. Promoter, by turning a knob, may show a viewer the vase or the illuminated laser photograph of the vase, and the visual experience of the viewer, when he sees the vase, will be indistinguishable from his visual experience when confronted with the photograph. Of course, the very purpose of constructing the device is to arrange things so that people will be completely deceived by the photograph. Now suppose I walk up to the viewer, innocent as the fool who stones the water to destroy his twin, and peer in at the illuminated photograph. Blissfully ignorant of the technical finesse being used to dupe me, I take what I see to be a vase. I believe that the box contains a vase. I am right, there is a vase in the box, and it is not at all accidental that I am right. For Mr. Promoter has constructed the device in such a way that, though I do not see the vase, I will believe quite correctly that there is one there. On Unger's analysis, I know that there is a vase in the box when I see the illuminated laser photograph.

However, it is perfectly apparent that I know nothing of the sort. Any justification I have for believing that there is a vase in the box is defeated by the fact that I do not see a vase in the box but merely a photograph of one. On our analysis it would follow that I do *not* know there is a vase in the box, and that result is the correct one.

Unger might object that it is to some extent accidental that I am right in thinking there is a vase in the box, because I might have had the same visual experiences even if there had been no vase in the box. Hence his analysis yields the same result as ours in this case. But this objection, if taken seriously, would lead us to reject Unger as a skeptic. To see why, imagine that, contrary to the preceding example, Mr. Promoter turns off his device for the day, leaving the knob set so that when I enter the room the vase is before my eyes. I could reach out and touch it if I wished, but good manners restrain me. Nevertheless, there is nothing between me and the vase; I see it and know that it is before my eyes in just the way that I see and know that countless other objects sit untouched before me. However, the statement—I might have had the same visual experience even if there had been no vase in the box—is true in this case as in the former one, where I was deceived by the photograph. If this truth shows that my being right in the former case was to some extent accidental, then it would also show that my being right in the present case was to some extent accidental. Therefore, either Unger must agree that the truth of this statement fails to show that my being right in the former case was accidental, in which case his analysis would yield the result that I know when in fact I am ignorant; or he must maintain that its truth shows that my being right in the present case was accidental, in which case his analysis yields the result that I am ignorant when in fact I know. Thus, his analysis is unsatisfactory.

Finally, we wish to consider another kind of theory suggested by Alvin Goldman. His analysis is as follows: S knows that p if and only if the fact that p is causally connected in an "appropriate" way with S's believing that p.[16] We wish to assert, in opposition to Goldman, that the causal etiology of belief may be utterly irrelevant to the question of what a man knows. Consider yet a third round between Mr. Promoter and me. This time I imagine that I enter as in the first example, where the photograph is illuminated, and become completely and thoroughly convinced that there is a vase in the box. Now imagine that Mr. Promoter, amused with his easy success, tells me that I am quite right in thinking there is a vase in the box, but he then goes on to show me how the device is constructed, removing parts and lecturing about lasers from smirk-twisted lips. With respect to the etiology of my belief that there was a vase in the box, it is possible that my belief was fixed from the time I first looked at the photograph and, moreover, was so firmly and unequivocally fixed that the subsequent revelations neither altered nor reinforced it. This belief is to be *causally explained* by my mistakenly believing that I was seeing a vase when I first entered the room and by the facts about the illuminated laser photograph that caused that erroneous belief. There is no "appropriate" causal connection between the fact that there is a vase in the box and my belief that p; so, according to Goldman's analysis, I did not know that there was a vase in the box.

There is something to recommend this result. When I first looked into the device, I did not see the vase, and, consequently, I did not *then* know that there was a vase in the box. However, after Mr. Promoter's revelations, when I do really see the vase, I do then know that there is a vase in the box. This is not due to any change in the causal etiology of my belief that there is a vase in the box. So, according to Goldman,

I still do not know. But Goldman is wrong. I do subsequently know that there is a vase in the box, not because of any change in the causal etiology of the belief, but because I then have some justification for the belief that I formerly lacked. The justification consists of what I learned from Mr. Promoter's demonstration about the box and its contents. In short, there is no reason to suppose that all new evidence that a man could appeal to in order to justify a belief changes the causal etiology of the belief. And such evidence may make the difference between true belief and knowledge.

V

We have contended that our analysis of knowledge in terms of undefeated justified true belief has various advantages over competing analyses. Unlike some of our competitors, we do not presuppose any one theory of justification rather than another. Since current theories of justification are highly controversial, we have employed a notion of justification that is consistent with diverse theories on this subject. By so doing, we hope to have presented a satisfactory analysis of knowledge without waiting for the development of an equally satisfactory theory of justification.

Moreover, the problems that confront a theory of justification can be formulated in terms of the locutions we have introduced in our analysis. For example, Chisholm has maintained that some statements are self-justifying, and, in our terminology, this amounts to answering affirmatively the question whether it is ever the case that some statement h completely justifies a person in believing that h.[17] Some philosophers have affirmed that all justification must be either inductive or deductive; others have denied this and affirmed that there are other forms of justification as well. In our terminology, this question must be formulated as the question whether, when a statement p completely justifies a person in believing h, the justified statement must be deduced or induced from the justifying statement or whether there are other alternatives. Finally, philosophers have disagreed about the kind of statement that may justify a man in believing something: whether those statements must be known, or whether they need not be, whether they must include all of a man's evidence, or whether they might exclude some of this evidence, and so forth. We have avoided dogmatically assuming one or the other of these alternatives.

Nevertheless, it may be found that only one theory of justification is suitable to supplement our analysis. Our claim is that, on any satisfactory theory of justification, some knowledge must be undefeated completely justified true belief, and the rest is basic.

NOTES

1. This analysis of knowledge is a modification of an earlier analysis proposed by Keith Lehrer, "Knowledge, Truth, and Evidence," *Analysis* 25, no. 107 (April 1965): 168–75. It is intended to cope with objections to that article raised by Gilbert H. Harman in "Lehrer on Knowledge," *The Journal of Philosophy* 63, no. 9 (April 28, 1966): 241–47, and by Alvin Goldman, Brian Skyrms, and others. Criticisms of various alternative analyses of knowledge are given in Lehrer's earlier article, and the reader is referred to that article; such discussion will not be repeated here. The distinction between basic and nonbasic knowledge that is elaborated here was suggested by Arthur Danto in "Freedom and Forbearance," in *Freedom and Determinism* (New York: Random House, 1965), pp. 45–63.

2. Harman's criticism of Lehrer's earlier article rested on his interpreting Lehrer as saying that a person can be completely justified in believing something only if he does believe it. This interpretation leads to problems and is repudiated here.

3. "Experience and Factual Knowledge," *The Journal of Philosophy* 64, no. 5 (March 16, 1967): 152–73, esp. pp. 165–67; see also his "An Analysis of Factual Knowledge," *The Journal of Philosophy* 65, no. 6 (March 21, 1968): 157–70, esp. pp. 163–64.

4. "Is Justified True Belief Knowledge?" *Analysis* 33, no. 6, 96 (June 1963): 121–23.

5. "The Explication of 'X knows that p,' " *The Journal of Philosophy* 64, no. 12 (June 22, 1967): 373–89.

6. *Theory of Knowledge* (Englewood Cliffs, N.J.: Prentice-Hall, 1966), p. 48.

7. Chisholm, "The Ethics of Requirement," *American Philosophical Quarterly* 1, no. 2 (April 1964): 147–53. This definition of defeasibility would make our analysis of nonbasic knowledge very similar to one Harman derives from Lehrer's analysis and also one proposed by Marshall Swain in "The Analysis of Non-Basic Knowledge" (unpublished).

8. In Skyrms's example of the pyromaniac cited earlier, the defeating statement is not one which the pyromaniac need believe; Skyrms suggests that the pyromaniac neither believes nor disbelieves that striking the match will cause it to ignite. Nevertheless, the pyromaniac would be completely justified in believing that striking the Sure-Fire match will cause it to ignite. Hence the statement that striking the match will not cause it to light is defeating.

9. A similar objection to Lehrer's earlier analysis is raised by Harman, "Lehrer on Knowledge," p. 243.

10. "The Explication of "X knows that p,' " p. 381.

11. Ibid., p. 387.

12. Ibid., p. 380.

13. Chisholm; see footnote at end of ch. 1, *Theory of Knowledge,* p. 23.

14. "An Analysis of Factual Knowledge," p. 158.

15. Cf. Alvin Goldman, "A Causal Theory of Knowing," *The Journal of Philosophy* 64, no. 12 (June 22, 1967): 357–72; p. 359.

16. Ibid., p. 369.

17. R. M. Chisholm et al., *Philosophy* (Englewood Cliffs, N.J.: Prentice-Hall, 1964), pp. 263–77.

17

A Proposed Definition
of Propositional Knowledge

Peter D. Klein

The development of a satisfactory definition of propositional knowledge is essential if an adequate theory of knowledge is to become possible.* This task becomes all the more urgent because the attempt to develop such a definition of propositional knowledge within the traditional threefold conditions (true, evident or justified, belief) has recently been seriously challenged, and every subsequent attempt to meet this challenge has failed.[1]

I wish to put forth a definition of propositional knowledge and defend it. I think this definition does make a satisfactory epistemology possible because it remains neutral in the conflict between various rival epistemological theories.[2] Neutrality is an essential feature, for if one theory were to claim that a certain type of proposition is not a proper object of knowledge, and another theory were to argue that such a proposition is a proper object of knowledge, both theories must mean the same thing by propositional knowledge if their disagreement is to be genuine.

Although I believe the proposed definition does accomplish what such a definition should, it does not do everything that some may have wished. It cannot encompass all our uses of "S knows that p," simply because that expression functions in so many various ways.

From *The Journal of Philosophy* 68, no. 16 (August 19, 1971): 471–82. © 1971. Reprinted by permission of the publisher.

*This paper was written during a leave of absence financed by a Ford Humanities Grant allocated by the Colgate University Research Council. I had the benefit of discussing parts of this paper with Professor A. J. Ayer and with my colleagues at Colgate (especially John Flynn and Hunt Terrell). In addition, an earlier version was read at Rutgers University.

The relevant use that I am seeking to define occurs in the following paragraph quoted from *Theory of Knowledge* by Chisholm:

> In Plato's dialogue, the *Meno*, Socrates remarks: "That there is a difference between right opinion and knowledge is not at all a conjecture with me but something I would particularly assert that I know. There are not many things of which I would say that, but this one, at any rate, I will include among those that I know." [97C] The distinction would seem to be obvious. If one has knowledge, then one also has right or true opinion. But the converse is not true: one may have right or true opinion without having knowledge. Thus, we may guess correctly today, and therefore, have the opinion, but not know until tomorrow. Or we may have true opinion and never know at all.[3]

Ernest Sosa quotes Russell as saying:

> It is very easy . . . to give examples of true beliefs that are not knowledge. There is the man who looks at a clock which is not going though he thinks it is and who happens to look at it at the moment when it is right; this man acquires a true belief about the time of the day but cannot be said to have knowledge.[4]

I cite these examples not only to illustrate the relevant use of "*S* knows that *p*," but also to underscore the point that propositional knowledge must not be equated with accidentally correct belief.

The traditional analysis of this relevant concept of knowledge is:

S knows that *p*   iff   (1) *p* is true,
                              (2) *S* believes *p*,
                              (3) *p* is evident to *S*.

There are counterexamples to the traditional definition, but before discussing them it is necessary to make a few comments on the third condition of the traditional definition of knowledge. Chisholm says that *p* is evident to *S* if (a) it is more reasonable for *S* to believe *p* than to withhold belief in *p*, and (b) there is no proposition *i* such that it is more reasonable for *S* to believe *i* than it is for him to believe *p*.[5] The second condition is necessary in order to distinguish evident propositions from reasonable ones. It would be a reasonable but not evident belief that the next item I pick from my pocket will be a Lincoln-head penny if I believe the I have only fifty items in my pocket, forty-nine Lincoln-head pennies and one Indian-head penny. Among the evident propositions would be "the probability is .98 that the next coin will be a Lincoln-head penny" and "the next item will be roughly round and copper-colored."[6]

A proposition would be justified or evident for *S* if the standard warranting criteria held and if *S* had no reason to believe that the situation was abnormal. For example, *S* would be justified in believing that it was 5 P.M. if his watch indicated that time, he knew that it had been reliable in the past, and he remembered winding it recently and it appeared to be running. But suppose that it is 5 P.M., but also that the watch had not worked for 24 hours (the second hand moved when *S* turned his wrist to look at the watch); *S* would not know that it was 5 P.M. even though that belief was true and evident.

In order to illuminate the nature of this counterexample, consider a case in which *S* has a true, but not evident, belief. Suppose *S* believes, correctly, that the card which he has not examined and which he just picked at random from a full deck of cards is the six of spades. He believes that because the last time he selected the six of spades. His true belief that it is the six of spades is not certifiable as knowledge because, given his evidence and the way in which he picked the card and the fact that there are fifty-two cards in a deck, it could just as easily have been any other card. The evidence *S* had is not sufficient to "grant entitlement" to knowledge, as Sosa puts it.[7]

For the same reason the example just mentioned is a counterexample to the definition of knowledge as true, evident belief. It is merely a coincidence that *S*'s belief is correct that it is 5 P.M. Of course *normally*, the evidence *S* has would be sufficient to certify his belief as knowledge, and he would be *entitled* to claim that he knew it was 5 P.M. I will return later to the distinction between those times when *S* is entitled to claim that he knows and those times when he does know. What is important here is that in these special circumstances it is merely a felicitous coincidence that his belief is correct. This could be formulated in terms of a general principle which I will call the *felicitous-coincidence principle*: if *S*'s evidence for *p* and a description of some of the particular circumstances in which *S* believes that *p* are such that it would not be reasonable to expect that *p* is true (based upon *S*'s evidence), even if *p* is true, *S* does not know *p*. Consequently, we might tentatively assert that *S*'s evidence for his belief that *p* is not sufficiently strong to certify his belief as knowledge if there is some fact which, were *S* to become aware of it, ought to cause *S* to retract his knowledge claim.

It may be thought that the felicitous-coincidence principle could be satisfied by restricting the set of propositions that renders *p* evident. The accidentally correct, evident beliefs would become uncertifiable as knowledge because of some defect in these propositions. For example, it could be stipulated that the set may neither contain a false proposition nor render evident any false proposition.[8] This surely is an improvement; it would dispose of the counterexample developed above because that set does render evident the false proposition that the watch has been running since it was last wound.

There are, however, additional counterexamples to this strengthened definition which reveal that the restrictions remain too weak. Ernest Sosa[9] develops one which I will modify. Suppose that *S* has been working in an office next to Tom Grabit's office for many years and has often spoken informally with Tom, but does not know anything at all about Tom's personal life. One day he sees what he takes to be Tom stealing a library book. *S* would be justified in believing that Tom did steal the book and he is correct. But, unbeknown to *S*, Tom has an identical twin who was in town in the library on the day in question. Further, Tom has never stolen a book from the library and John, Tom's twin, is a kleptomaniac who steals books quite often. Although *S* has a true and evident belief that Tom stole the book, it can hardly be certified as knowledge, because, given *S*'s evidence and the particular circumstances, it is simply a lucky coincidence that he is correct. The felicitous-coincidence principle is at work here.

This is a counterexample to the improved traditional definition, because in this case there is no false proposition rendered evident to *S*.[10] That is, *S* has no reason to believe anything at all about John. It is not even reasonable for him to believe that Tom does not have a twin brother, although it would be reasonable for him to believe that it is highly probable that Tom does not have a twin brother. But the latter is not false.

The improved definition remains too weak because it is concerned only with the defeat of a knowledge claim by those false propositions rendered evident to *S*; whereas there are occasions when *S*'s true evident belief fails to be knowledge for reasons that *S* had no way of anticipating. To return to the felicitous-coincidence principle, if there is any circumstance such that, given *S*'s evidence for *p*, it is not reasonable to expect that *p* is true (given *S*'s evidence), even if *p* is true, *S* does not know that *p*. The circumstances mentioned in the principle need not be circumstances about which *S* has any evident beliefs. To put the principle in a slightly different manner: If there is any true proposition *d* such that it and *S*'s evidence for *p* would make it unreasonable to expect that *p* is true, *S* does not know *p*.

Based upon these considerations, the definition I propose is as follows:

S knows that *p* at t_1 if and only if
   (i)   *p* is true;
   (ii) *S* believes *p* at t_1;
   (iii) *p* is evident to *S* at t_1;
   (iv) there is no true proposition such that if it became evident to *S* at t_1, *p* would no longer be evident to *S*.

The first three conditions (i)–(iii) have been called the "traditional" conditions, and I will continue so to refer to them. In what follows I will assume that they are necessary conditions of knowledge. For the sake of simplicity I will refer to a true proposition such that if it became evident to *S*, *p* would no longer be evident to *S*, as a *disqualifying proposition.*

Now several points about the proposed definition become immediately obvious.

First, (i) follows from (iv) and is therefore no longer required as a condition. For if *p* were false, there would be a disqualifying proposition, namely ~*p*, and hence, if *S* knows that *p*, *p* must be true. In fact, if one assumes that *S* believes those things which are evident, (ii) and (iii) are implied by (iv), for (iv) asserts that *p* is already evident to *S*, and, if it were, *S* would believe *p*. But for the sake of the argument in this paper, I will continue to use (i), (ii), and (iii) as separate conditions of propositional knowledge because it is condition (iv) that is probably most suspect, and in defending it I cannot assume what follows from it.

A few more comments about the third condition. In spite of its ugliness I will use the expression "the evidence of *p*." A proposition is evident to *S* at t_1 *iff* it is more reasonable for *S* to believe *p* at t_1 (given his evidence for it) than to withhold belief in *p* and there is no more reasonable proposition for *S* to believe at t_1. A proposition may be evident yet false. It may be evident to S_1 but fail to be evident to S_2, because S_1 knows something that S_2 does not know, for example. In that sense evidence is person-relative, but it is person-neutral in the sense that, whatever makes *p* evident to S_1, that and that alone would make *p* evident to S_2. Evidence cannot be defined in a more specific manner because the conventions of evidence will vary depending upon the nature of *p*.

But what of counterexamples? Let us look first at those which attack the definition for being too weak. None of the counterexamples discussed so far work against this definition, for in each case there is a disqualifying proposition: "The watch is not working now" and "Tom, who has never before stolen a book, has an identical twin, kleptomaniac brother, John, who was in the library on the day in question." In other words, what shows that *S* does not have knowledge in each of the previous cases is a true proposition describing the circumstances mentioned in the felicitous-coincidence principle. If the proposed conditions of knowledge are too weak, it must be possible for *S* to fail to know that *p* even though the four conditions are fulfilled. But if *p* is evident to *S* and yet *S* does not know that *p*, there must be some true proposition *d* which shows that in *this* case the evidence *S* has for *p* is insufficient to warrant certification of *S*'s belief as knowledge. The true proposition *d* would disqualify *S*'s belief as knowledge only if it were such as to make *p* no longer evident (given *S*'s evidence alone), and, because of the person-neutral character of evidence, *d* would be such that if it became evident to *S*, *p* would no longer be evident. Hence, there can be no counterexamples to show that the definition is too weak.

A purported counterexample showing that the conditions are too strong would have to show that *S* knows that *p* even though there is a disqualifying proposition. However, as a rough and ready reply it could be pointed out that if there were such a disqualifying proposition, *p* would no longer be evident to the giver of the counterexample, *G*, and hence the giver of the counterexample would find himself in the absurd position of claiming that *S* knows that *p* but he himself does not know that *p*.

I said a moment ago that this was a rough and ready reply, but the situation is more complicated than I just implied. The above response is valid only if the disqualifying proposition d is a disqualifying proposition for both S and G. If it were, then, of course, if d were evident to G, p would no longer be evident to him, and hence he could no longer claim that S knows that p, implying that he knows that p and, therefore that p is evident to him. But suppose that d is not a disqualifying proposition for both S and G, but only for S. Ought we still assert that S knows that p? Consider the following case. Suppose that the gas tank of S's car is one-fourth full and that S sees that his gas gauge reads "¼," remembers that the gauge has been reliable in the past, and consequently believes that the tank is one-fourth full. The three traditional conditions of knowledge are fulfilled. Now let us suppose that the giver of the counterexample, G, knows that the gauge is not working, but that he has sufficiently strong evidence, which S does not have, so that the claim that the tank is one-fourth full remains evident to him. He may have checked the gas in the tank through some other method. Now, since S does not have this additional evidence, the disqualifying proposition d, "the gas gauge is not working properly," would serve as a disqualifying proposition for S but not for G. Now G must maintain in spite of d that S knows that the tank is empty. That is, the giver of the counterexample must believe that there is a disqualifying proposition d, for S, but not for him, which is such that S still knows that the tank is empty. Is G correct?

In some sense of "know," S does know that the tank is one-fourth full. He "knows," but for the wrong reasons. But in the relevant sense, he does not know because he only happens to have a true belief and it is merely an accident (in this case) that his belief is correct. According to the felicitous-coincidence principle, S does not know that the tank was one-fourth full. Of course any given disqualifying proposition d need not disqualify all of S's evidence as it does in this case in order to make p no longer evident to S. Then d would not make accidental the connection between *all* of S's evidence for p and p, but, if the evidence that d does disqualify is essential for the evidency of p to S, then the connection between the remaining evidence and the truth of p becomes insufficiently strong to certify his belief as knowledge. He would no doubt retract p if d were to become evident to him. If d disqualified an essential part of the evidence for p that S has, S would not know that p. On the other hand, if d does not disqualify an essential part of the evidence S has for p, then it would not be a disqualifying proposition as defined.

In spite of what I have just claimed, namely, that if the disqualifying proposition were such that it disqualified something essential, S would not know that p, it may be thought that there might still be some counterexamples lurking here. I would like to deal with one possible counterexample, the strongest that I know of, in order to reinforce the above quite general argument to show that the definition is not too strong.

Consider Mr. Jones, who goes to the house of an acquaintance M for the first time. He sees some flowers on the mantelpiece, and throughout the evening the various guests and M comment on the flowers. Their comments cohere. Later Mr. Jones discovers that M is a magician and delights in fooling his guests by creating some extremely clever devised illusions of flowers on a mantel. Suppose further that on the night in question M was not up to his old tricks. In this example p_1 is "there are flowers on the mantel" and d_1 is "M is a magician."[11]

Now, what about this case? Did Jones know p_1? First, let me point out that our intuitions are likely to diverge here, because this is so artificial and unusual a case.

We might believe that Jones did know that p_1. Our argument would run as follows: proposition d_1 does not disqualify p_1; it does so only in conjunction with d_1', where d_1' equals "M was up to his old tricks last night"; d_1' is made evident by d_1. But d_1' is false; hence the conjunction $d_1' \cdot d_1$ is false, and there is no proposition that is both true and evident and disqualifies p_1. Hence the definition is upheld, and this is not a counterexample, because Jones knew p_1 and there is no disqualifying proposition.

This response is incorrect, however, because d_1 does justify a proposition that is both true and evident and does disqualify p_1, namely, d_1'': "d_1' is highly probable." If it became evident to Jones that it was highly probable that M was up to his old tricks, then it would no longer be evident to him that there were flowers on the mantel. Hence this is not a counterexample, because the fourth condition is not fulfilled and Jones does not know that p_1.

But suppose that someone were to claim that Jones did know that p_1, even though d_1'' is a disqualifying proposition for p_1. Would he be correct? I think not; for what d_1'' asserts is that, in this particular case, even though the standard criteria hold, they are not reliable. Therefore this example is not essentially different from many of the cases presented earlier. In those cases the reason why the subject's belief was not certifiable as knowledge was simply that, although the standard warranting criteria held, in those particular cases the criteria were not reliable. The felicitous-coincidence principle again holds.

If one were to insist that Jones did know p_1, even though there is a disqualifying proposition, one would not only have to reject the felicitous-coincidence principle; one would also be forced to accept the following rather awkward result: Jones did know p_1 before d_1'' became evident, he no longer knew p_1 after it became evident (because p was no longer evident), and then, finally, he knew p_1 again after it became evident that M was not up to his old tricks. A much more plausible rendering of the situation is this: Jones would have been justified in asserting that he knew that p_1 (although he would have been mistaken) before d_1'' became evident to him; after it became evident he would have been justified in asserting that he did not know p_1 (and he would be correct); and finally, after he learned that M was not up to his old tricks, he would be justified in asserting he knew p_1 (and he would be correct). There are many occasions when we are entitled to claim that we know that p_1, although we later find out we were mistaken, for it would seem that we are entitled to claim that we know that p whenever we believe p and are justified in believing that the standard warranting criteria for judgments like p are fulfilled and are justified in believing that the situation is not abnormal. But of course we may be entitled to claim that we know that p and be mistaken in the claim, if either the standard criteria do not hold or the particular situation is not such that the standard criteria are sufficient warranting criteria.[12]

It would seem that those who insist that Jones knew that p_1 before d_1' became evident fail to distinguish between those occasions when S is entitled to claim that he knows that p and those occasions when such a claim is correct. His claim would be correct only when the four necessary conditions of knowledge were fulfilled.

I said earlier that a good definition of propositional knowledge would have to remain neutral with regard to the disputes among rival epistemological theories; and it may be thought that the fourth condition is so strong that it prejudices the issues in favor of one or another form of skepticism. Some may believe that the definition is so strong that:

1. If the definition were accepted, S could never know that p, because S could never know that the fourth condition was fulfilled.

2. If the definition were accepted, S would not be warranted in asserting that he knew that p, because S would never be warranted in asserting that the fourth condition held.

3. If the definition were accepted, it would never be true that S knows that he knows that p because he could never know that the fourth condition held.

Now if any one of these forms of skepticism were implied by the definition, it would lose its neutrality and, hence, would not be acceptable. The definition must allow for the forms of skepticism involved in 1, 2, and 3, but it ought not to imply them.

In reply to 1, let me simply point out that the fourth condition is not "S knows that there is no disqualifying proposition." S can know that p without knowing—or for that matter, without even considering—whether there are any disqualifying propositions. The condition merely asserts that his evidence must be such that there are no disqualifying propositions. A person supporting the skeptical position of 1-type must show that for some reason there is always a disqualifying proposition for any particular type of proposition which he held was not a possible object of knowledge.

In reply to 2, it must be pointed out that S would be warranted in asserting or believing that he knew that p, if it is evident to him that there is no disqualifying proposition for p. Although that is never beyond any conceivable doubt, on many occasions it would be beyond any reasonable doubt. Those are the occasions mentioned earlier when *S* is entitled to claim that he knows that *p*. A skeptic supporting the position involved in 2 would have to show that there never are such occasions.

Finally, the statement "*S* knows that he knows that *p*" would be true whenever the following are true:

1' "*S* knows that *p*" is true; (see reply to 1)
2' *S* believes that he knows that *p*;
3' "*S* knows that *p*" is evident to *S*; (see reply 2)
4' There is no disqualifying proposition for "*S* knows that *p*."

It seems quite clear that these conditions could be fulfilled; or rather, the definition itself does not rule out the possibility that these conditions are fulfilled.

I said earlier that any good definition of knowledge would have to be acceptable to all the rival epistemological theorists, and I have just shown that mine would be acceptable to three forms of skepticism and their rivals. I cannot show that it will be acceptable to all of the other rivals, but I can at least make this claim more plausible if I can show my definition to be acceptable to Descartes and his critics, since the differences there seem to be about as serious as possible.

The Cartesians believe that it is possible to legitimately question what we ordinarily take to be evident claims, for example, that there is now a piece of paper in front of me. These are dubitable, not because we have some evidence against any particular such claim, but because our methods of determining whether such propositions are true or false are themselves in need of confirmation. The anti-Cartesians, on the other hand, argue that the methods are adequate. Now I do not wish to get involved in the particular disputes between Descartes and his critics. Nor do I wish to detail the claims of each rival epistemology. But I do want to show that, given this proposed definition of propositional knowledge, the issue can be joined and perhaps settled.

Cartesian doubt, in its strong form, must grant that a certain proposition *p* is evident, given *all* the standard tests for *p*, but yet it must maintain that it remains possible to doubt that we know *p*. Whereas the anti-Cartesians seem to be maintaining that, if *p* is evident as a result of *all* the standard tests being applied to *p*, then it becomes gratuitous to doubt that we know that *p*.

The issue, then, can be put as follows: Is there a disqualifying proposition for *all* those propositions which we ordinarily take to be beyond doubt true? Will, for example, any of the following serve as a disqualifying proposition?

1. Perhaps I am dreaming now.
2. I have been deceived before, so perhaps I am being deceived now.

3. Something other than material objects may be causing our perceptions, for example, an evil genius.
4. Perhaps I am mad.

Now as I mentioned above, I do not propose to get involved at this time in the dispute over the truth of any of the above propositions. What I wish to point out is that the proposed definition of propositional knowledge does not prejudge the issue at all, in favor of either the Cartesians or the anti-Cartesians. In fact, it clarifies the issues by focusing attention on the considerations surrounding the possibility of the existence of such a disqualifying proposition.[13]

The definition of propositional knowledge that I have proposed seems to meet all the necessary conditions of any such attempt and, in addition, seems to provide a procedure for evaluating various epistemological theories.

NOTES

1. One series of discussions is: Edmund Gettier, "Is Justified True Belief Knowledge?" *Analysis* 23, no. 6 (June 1963): 121–23; Roderick M. Chisholm, *Theory of Knowledge* (Englewood Cliffs, N.J.: Prentice-Hall, 1966), p. 23, n. 22; John Pollock, "Chisholm's Definition of Knowledge," *Philosophical Studies* 19, no. 5 (October 1968): 72–76; another series is Ernest Sosa, "Propositional Knowledge," *Philosophical Studies* 22, no. 3 (April 1969): 33–43; Keith Lehrer and Thomas Paxson, Jr., "Knowledge: Undefeated Justified True Belief," *The Journal of Philosophy* 64, no. 8 (April 24, 1969): 225–37; Sosa, "Two Conceptions of Knowledge," *The Journal of Philosophy* 67, no. 3 (February 12, 1970): 59–68.

2. By "an epistemological theory" I mean a set of beliefs concerning the types of propositions that can (or cannot) be known.

3. Chisholm, *The Theory of Knowledge*, p. 5.

4. Ibid., pp. 30–34.

5. Chisholm, *Theory of Knowledge*, p. 22. Implicit in the concept of *evidency* or *justification* used by Chisholm and the other writers concerned with the adequacy of the traditional definition is the notion of a set of propositions with relative degrees of reasonableness relevant to some evidence. This concept of justification, although sufficient for elucidating the justification of empirical propositions and adequate for the purposes of this essay, must be amended if analytic propositions are to be counted as evident. At some time I intend to explore the evidency of analytic propositions, but it is the class of nonanalytic propositions that has proved troublesome to the traditional definition of knowledge and it is those difficulties with which this essay is concerned.

6. I am indebted to the editors of the *Journal of Philosophy* for pointing out a mistake in an earlier version of this paper; I had failed to note the compatibility of its being more reasonable for *S* to believe *p* than to withhold belief and its being more reasonable to believe *i* than *p*.

7. "Two Conceptions of Knowledge," p. 62.

8. Two such attempts to improve the traditional definition were made by Sosa, "Propositional Knowledge," and Lehrer-Paxson, "Knowledge: Undefeated Justified True Belief."

9. Sosa, "Propositional Knowledge."

10. It may be thought that there is one false proposition rendered evident by the propositions which

render it evident that Tom Grabit stole the book, i.e., S knows that Tom stole the book. If this were the case, not only would it appear to trivialize the improved traditional definition, but also any other proposed fourth condition would fail to explicate the concept of knowledge for the definition would become merely "S knows that p if it is not false that S does not know that p." However, whatever renders p evident to S would not, by itself, render it evident that he knows p, because it would not render it evident to S that he believes p. That is, a proposition may be evident for S without S believing that it is. If it is evident to S, this means that it would be more reasonable for him to believe than withhold belief; but, of course, he may not believe that p.

11. A counterexample similar to this one was suggested to me both by A. J. Ayer and by Marc Cohen.

12. Lehrer-Paxson present and dismiss a definition of knowledge similar to the one developed here. They reject the definition because of a counterexample similar to the Jones case.

> Suppose I see a man walk into the library and remove a book from the library by concealing it beneath his coat. Since I am sure the man is Tom Grabit, whom I have often seen before when he attended my classes, I report that I know that Tom Grabit has removed the book. However, suppose further that Mrs. Grabit, the mother of Tom, has averred that on the day in question Tom was not in the library, indeed, was thousands of miles away, and that Tom's identical twin brother, John Grabit, was in the library. Imagine, moreover, that I am entirely ignorant of the fact that Mrs. Grabit has said these things. The statement that she has said these things would defeat any justification I have for believing that Tom Grabit removed the book, according to our present definition of defeasibility. Thus, I could not be said to have nonbasic knowledge that Tom Grabit removed the book. (228)

But the situation is not quite that simple. I grant that it appears that this is a case of S's knowing, but I do not grant that the claim "Tom's mother said . . ." is, by itself, sufficient to disqualify S's knowledge claim. If we couple what Tom's mother said with the proposition "what mothers say in situations like this is generally reliable," then, if the conjunction of the two propositions is a disqualifying proposition, S would not know that Tom stole the book. That is, if Tom's mother said that John stole the book and mothers' statements are generally reliable, it is only a felicitous coincidence that S's belief is correct. For if mothers' statements are generally reliable in these situations, it is highly probable that John, and not Tom, stole the book and it is merely a lucky coincidence that S's belief is correct because the propositions that render p evident to S are equally compatible with the highly probable denial of p.

13. Let me add that the dispute between the Cartesians and the anti-Cartesians could be viewed as a disagreement over whether the evidence of (iii) to S renders (iv) evident to S.

18

Misleading Defeaters

Steven R. Levy

Defeasibility analyses of knowledge continue to evolve. Peter D. Klein has recently constructed the latest, and by far most powerful such analysis.[1] Klein's analysis handles counterexamples to earlier defeasibility theories of knowledge and does so with remarkable elegance.[2] Nevertheless, I wish to show that it is inadequate. In so doing I wish also to demonstrate that any such attempt to rescue defeasibility analyses of knowledge is self-defeating.

I have argued elsewhere that it is unlikely that any defeasibility theory of knowledge could be successful.[3] The crux of my argument was that such analyses must avoid cases in which a true statement is a defeater only because it is misleading and that to avoid such cases it is necessary to characterize what it is for a defeater to be misleading. Further, to construct such a characterization would be enormously difficult for two reasons. First, true statements can be misleading to varying degrees with respect to each other, and only some should be allowed to defeat a knowledge claim and those only sometimes. Second, sometimes a false statement may be less misleading than a true one. Because of this, I argued, attempts to rule out misleading evidence by an appeal to truth cannot work.

The task here is to show why, in particular, Klein's defeasibility theory (KDT) fails to overcome these difficulties, and why any attempt by a defeasibility theorist to overcome these difficulties by rejecting misleading defeaters must lead to the abandonment of his theory. Klein's analysis is as follows:

From *The Journal of Philosophy* 75, no. 12 (December 1978): 739–42. © 1978. Reprinted by permission of the publisher.

KDT: S knows that h inferentially if and only if:
  (i) h is true.
  (ii) S believes that h.
  (iii) There is some evidence e such that $e\,J_s h$.[4]
  (iv) Every defeater of the justification for S of h by e is a misleading defeater.

d is a misleading defeater of the justification of h by e for S if and only if:
  (i) d is true.
  (ii) $(d \cdot e)\,\bar{J_s}h$.
  (iii) (ii) is true, only because there is some false proposition f such that $d\,J_s f$.

The third condition characterizing a misleading defeater is essentially an appeal to truth—that is, the key reason for rejecting d as a defeater is that it justifies S in believing some other statement that is not the truth. To refute KDT, all that needs to be done is to imagine a situation in which false statements are less misleading than true statements that KDT would nevertheless require to act as genuine defeaters.

Consider this variation of the now celebrated Tom Grabit case.[5] S sees Tom Grabit remove a book from the library by concealing it beneath his coat. S is ultimately going to conclude that Tom stole the book, but first he must rule out other possibilities. To this end we may suppose that S is justified in believing that Tom is not an employee of the library (S inspected the university records the day before and found that Tom was employed by the maintenance division and not the library). Furthermore, S is justified in believing that no employees of the library may remove books (such was printed in the latest bulletin). Given these beliefs, the inference to h, that Tom's removal of the book was unauthorized, is certainly warranted. Since Tom did in fact steal the book, there should be little hesitation in saying that S knows that he did. (For our purposes here we shall also suppose that Tom does not have a twin brother nor did anyone ever assert that he had.) Let us now complicate the case by adding that, on the morning in question, for reasons that only deans and vice-chancellors understand, the names of some maintenance employees, including Tom's, were transferred to the library's budget although there was no change in duties. Technically—Tom became an employee of the library. Also, the rule that no employees may remove books was altered slightly in order to allow the head librarian to examine at home a rare first edition of Rader's anthology. This change was unknown to all but a few. Although the facts stand to the contrary—for all intents and purposes Tom is not an employee of the library, and, even if he were, he would not be one permitted to remove books. S's knowledge that Tom stole the book is not impaired by the bureaucratic shuffling.

What result does KDT yield in analyzing this case? The first three conditions are met. If the fourth is also met, then KDT survives. There is a defeater d to S's justification. It is the proposition that Tom is an employee of the library and some employees of the library may remove books. This, together with *S*'s other beliefs, fails to justify his belief *h* that Tom stole the book. Is this defeater misleading? It certainly is. But is it misleading under Klein's analysis? That is, does it, along with *S*'s other evidence, fail to justify *h* for *S* only because there is some false proposition that *d* justifies *S* is believing? It is hard to imagine what this false proposition might be. It certainly doesn't justify the false proposition that Tom is an employee who is authorized to remove books. It doesn't justify the negation of *h*, that Tom stole the book. In fact, it justifies very little with regard to Tom's removal of the book. All that it serves to do is to defeat *S*'s justification under Klein's and any other presently existing defeasibility analysis of knowledge.

The attempt to characterize a misleading statement by an appeal to truth cannot work. Some true statements are misleading because they justify beliefs in false statements. This can be compared to an act of commission. But others are misleading only because they might wrench other true beliefs away from our corpus of things known. This is the act of omission. KDT adequately rules out defeaters that are misleading in the first sense. It fails to rule out those which are misleading only in the second sense.

Any defeasibility theory that *would* rule out defeaters that are misleading only in the second sense would be self-destructive. The strength of defeasibility theories of knowledge is that they are best able to handle cases in which, although *S* has a justified true belief of *h*, he maintains this belief in virtue of his ignorance of overwhelming evidence to the contrary. Like the drunk who remains totally dry in the rainstorm because he just happens to zig and zag in such a way as to avoid the falling drops—*S* just happens not to stumble across an abundance of evidence that renders *h* unlikely. We wish not to ascribe knowledge to *S* because, if *S* had come across this evidence like the rest of us, he would immediately give up his belief that *h*. Defeasibility theories serve us to deny *S* knowledge by defining defeaters as the kinds of things that would make a reasonable man give up his belief that *h* and by stating that, if such things exist, then *S* does not know that *h*. If we now restrict ourselves only to cases in which *h* is in fact true[6] then we can easily see that all defeaters are going to be misleading in the second sense. They would make us give up true beliefs. But to rule out all defeaters that are misleading in this sense is to rule out all defeaters. It is thus to reject all defeasibility theories.

So the defeasibility theorist wants the existence of some true statements to be a sufficient condition for denying the status of knowledge to some true beliefs. In characterizing the kinds of true statements that may act as defeaters the defeasibility theorist must be very careful to specify that they must not be misleading. But since, as we have seen, all defeaters of true beliefs must be misleading, this approach is futile,

Perhaps the task is now shifted to constructing conditions that discriminate between virtuous misleading statements (those which can serve as defeaters) and vicious misleading statements (those which cannot).[7] Or perhaps we should be content to apply all the valuable lessons that defeasibility theories have taught us (and they are many) to a different approach.

NOTES

1. In "Knowledge, Causality, and Defeasibility," *The Journal of Philosophy* 73, no. 20 (November 18, 1976): 792–812.

2. Some defeasibility theories have extraordinarily long and complicated lists of purported necessary and sufficient conditions of knowledge. See, for example, Ernest Sosa, "The Analysis of 'Knowledge that *p*.' " *Analysis* 25, no. 103 (October 1964): 1–8, and Marshall Swain, "Epistemic Defeasibility," *American Philosophical Quarterly* 11, no. 1 (January 1974): 15–25. Klein's list is short and intuitive.

3. "Defeasibility Theories of Knowledge," *Canadian Journal of Philosophy* 7, no. 1 (March 1977): 115–23.

4. "$e J_s h$" is read "e justifies h for S." "$(d \cdot e) \bar{J_s} h$." is read "d and e fail to justify h for S."

5. Tom Grabit made his philosophical debut in Keith Lehrer and Thomas Paxson, Jr., "Knowledge: Undefeated Justified True Belief," *The Journal of Philosophy* 66, no. 8 (April 24, 1969): 225–37.

6. These are the only interesting cases; for, if *h* is false, then knowledge is denied without resorting to talk of defeaters.

7. The attempt in KDT, as has been shown, is unsuccessful.

19

Misleading "Misleading Defeaters"

Peter D. Klein

In "Misleading Defeaters," Steven R. Levy argues that although the defeasibility approach to the analysis of knowledge has taught us "valuable lessons," a new approach is now required.[1] This overall assessment results from his claim that defeasibility theorists are unable to revise earlier versions of the theory in order to make it immune to a certain class of counterexamples—the so-called misleading-evidence counterexamples.[2]

In particular, he claims that (1) my attempt to characterize misleading defeaters[3] is inadequate because it is subject to further counterexamples; and (2) any "such attempt to rescue the defeasibility analyses of knowledge is self-defeating."[4]

Both claims are incorrect. The second depends upon a terminological confusion; and the purported counterexample, when examined carefully, actually serves to illustrate and, thus, support my characterization of misleading defeaters.

That characterization was introduced to account for the misleading-evidence counterexamples first illustrated in the now famous Grabit case.[5] In that case, although S knows that (h) Tom stole a book from the library, Tom's mother asserts (falsely) that Tom has a twin brother who stole the book. The statement that Mrs. Grabit made that assertion is true and such that its conjunction with S's original evidence for h fails to justify S in believing that h. I called the defeaters present in the misleading-evidence counterexamples "misleading defeaters" and attempted to develop an analysis of knowledge that was immune to these counterexamples. That proposed analysis was:

From *The Journal of Philosophy* 76, no. 7 (July 1979): 382–86. © 1979. Reprinted by permission of the publisher.

KDT: [Klein's defeasibility theory]

  S knows that h inferentially if and only if:
  (i) h is true.
  (ii) S believes that h.
  (iii) There is some evidence e such that $e\,\bar{J}_s h.$[6]
  (iv) Every defeater of the justification for S of h by e is a misleading defeater.
      A defeater d is misleading if and only if:
  D(i) d is true.
  D(ii) $(d \cdot e)\,\bar{J}_s h.$
  D(iii) (ii) is true only because there is some false proposition f such that $d\,J_s f.$

Levy believes that he has discovered a counterexample to this analysis which reveals a difficulty beyond repair. For it shows that there are defeaters that are "misleading" but not identified as such by my proposal; and, further, there is no acceptable way to embellish the theory so as to characterize these defeaters as misleading. The purported counterexample is:

> S sees Tom Grabit remove a book from the library by concealing it beneath his coat. S is ultimately going to conclude that Tom stole the book, but first he must rule out other possibilities. To this end we may suppose that S is justified in believing that Tom is not an employee of the library (S inspected the university records the day before and found that Tom was employed by the maintenance division and not the library). Furthermore, S is justified in believing that no employees of the library may remove books (such was printed in the latest bulletin). Given these beliefs, the inference to h, that Tom's removal of the book was unauthorized, is certainly warranted. Since Tom did in fact steal the book, there should be little hesitation in saying that S knows that he did. (For our purposes here we shall also suppose that Tom does not have a twin brother nor did anyone ever assert that he had.) Let us now complicate the case by adding that, on the morning in question, for reasons that only deans and vice-chancellors understand, the names of some maintenance employees, including Tom's, were transferred to the library's budget although there was no change in duties. Technically—Tom became an employee of the library. Also, the rule that no employees may remove books was altered slightly in order to allow the head librarian to examine at home a rare first edition of Rader's anthology. This change was unknown to all but a few. Although the facts stand to the contrary—for all intents and purposes Tom is not an employee of the library, and, even if he were, he would not be one permitted to remove books. S's knowledge that Tom stole the book is not impaired by the bureaucratic shuffling.[7]

Levy claims that the compound expression (let us call it d^1): "Tom is an employee of the library, and some employees of the library may remove books," is a defeater but not a misleading defeater according to my analysis.

But surely Levy is wrong about that. The purported counterexample depends upon d^1 obscuring the fact that there are two distinct types of library employees—the t-type ("technical" type) whose names *merely appear* on the budget list and the *aip*-type (the "all intents and purposes" type) whose duties and privileges toward the library are determined by the college bulletin and administrative hierarchy. Once the *propositions* expressed by d^1 are delineated, it is clear that either they are not defeaters at all or they are misleading defeaters according to my analysis.

The compound expression d_1 is composed of:

a^1: Tom is an employee
b^1: Some employees of the library may remove books.

Since the meaning of "employee" is ambiguous, a^1 and b^1 express any of the following propositions:

a^1
a_1: Tom is a t-type employee.
a_2: Tom is an *aip*-type employee.
a_3: Tom is either an *aip*- or a t-type employee.

b^1
b_1: Some t-type employees may remove books.
b_2: Some *aip*-type employees may remove books.
b_3: Some *aip*- or t-type employees may remove books.

Thus d^1 expresses any one of nine propositions:

d_1: a_1 & b_1	d_2: a_1 & b_2	d_3: a_1 & b_3	d_4: a_2 & b_1	d_5: a_2 & b_2
d_6: a_2 & b_3	d_7: a_3 & b_1	d_8: a_3 & b_2	d_9: a_3 & b_3	

None of these is a genuine defeater. For d_1 and d_4–d_7 are false; d_2 does not satisfy D (ii): and d_3, d_8, and d_9 could satisfy D (fi) only if they provided some justification for the false d_1, d_5, and (d_3 v d_5), respectively. Thus, although this Grabit example is somewhat more complicated than the original Grabit case, KDT handles it correctly.

Levy's argument for the second claim is summarized in the following:

The attempt to characterize a misleading statement by an appeal to truth cannot work. Some true statements are misleading because they justify beliefs in false statements. . . . But others are misleading only because they might wrench other true beliefs away from our corpus of things known. . . . KDT adequately rules out defeaters that are misleading in the first sense. It fails to rule out those which are misleading only in the second sense.

Any defeasibility theory that *would* rule out defeaters that are misleading only in the second sense would be self-destructive. . . . If we now restrict ourselves only to cases in which *h* is in fact true then we can easily see that all defeaters are going to be misleading in the second sense. They would make us give up true beliefs. But to rule out all defeaters that are misleading in this sense is to rule out all defeaters. It is thus to reject all defeasibility theories.[8]

It is surely correct that if a defeasibility theory characterized a defeater as misleading solely because it robbed *S* of a true proposition, *h*, it would be "self-destructive." I pointed to that very fact in the article Levy is criticizing:

Also, we cannot distinguish misleading from genuine defeaters by requiring that only the misleading lead us away from the truth, since, if *h* is true and justified by *e*, any defeater such that $(d \cdot e) J_s h$ will lead us away from the truth. Genuine defeaters mislead us, in this sense, just as much as misleading defeaters do.[9]

So why does Levy persist in believing that the defeasibility theorists are committed to this self-destructive enterprise? I think there are two explanations. First, as I have already shown, he mistakenly believes that d^1 is a misleading defeater in only the second sense; but, in addition, Levy uses "misleading defeater" in a nontechnical sense to designate any true statement that leads us away from the truth. Thus, *given his use of* "misleading defeater," it is correct, but beside the point, that all defeaters are misleading. Levy has given us no reason to believe that all defeaters will be "misleading" in the sense in which that term was employed by the defeasibility theorists.

This terminological confusion is compounded in his final paragraph:

Perhaps the task is now shifted to constructing conditions that discriminate between virtuous misleading statements (those which can serve as defeaters) and vicious misleading statements (those which cannot). Or perhaps we should be content to apply all the valuable lessons that defeasibility theories have taught us (and they are many) to a different approach.[10]

But since he also says that my attempt to characterize the conditions that discriminate between what he calls "vicious" and "virtuous" misleading statements "has been shown [to be] unsuccessful" (see his final endnote), his new "task" is just the same old task of developing an adequate distinction between misleading and genuine defeaters. Levy has merely renamed the class of propositions which satisfy D(i) and D(ii) but which cannot serve as genuine defeaters. I called them "misleading defeaters"; he calls them "vicious misleading statements."

Thus, not only is a "new" approach to the analysis of knowledge not needed, but, rather, Levy has provided more evidence for my particular "old" analysis.

NOTES

1. *The Journal of Philosophy* 75, no. 12 (December 1978): 739–42.

2. Two earlier versions of the theory were developed by Risto Hilpinen, "Knowledge and Justification," *Ajatus* 33, no. 1 (1971): 7–39, and by me, in "A Proposed Definition of Propositional Knowledge," *The Journal of Philosophy* 68, no. 16 (August 19, 1971): 471–82. The counterexamples were developed by several people, including Marshall Swain, "Epistemic Defeasibility," *American Philosophical Quarterly* 11, no. 1 (January 1974): 15–25; Ernest Sosa, "Two Conceptions of Knowledge," *The Journal of Philosophy* 67, no. 3 (February 12, 1970): 59–66; Bredo Johnson, "Knowledge," *Philosophical Studies* 25, no. 4 (May 1974): 273–82; and Keith Lehrer and Thomas Paxson, Jr., "Knowledge: Undefeated Justified True Belief," *The Journal of Philosophy* 66, no. 8 (April 24, 1969): 225–37.

3. "Knowledge, Causality, and Defeasibility," *The Journal of Philosophy* 73, no. 20 (November 18, 1976): 792–812.

4. Levy, "Misleading Defeaters," p. 739.

5. This case was first suggested by Lehrer and Paxson, "Knowledge: Undefeated Justified True Belief," p. 228.

6. "$e J_s h$" is read "e justifies h for S." "$(d \cdot e)\bar{J}_s h$" is read "d and e fail to justify h for S."

7. Levy, "Misleading Defeaters," pp. 740–41.

8. Ibid., pp. 741–42.

9. "Knowledge, Causality, and Defeasibility," p. 809.

10. Levy, "Misleading Defeaters," p. 742.

Part IV

Reliability and Justification

20

What Is Justified Belief?

Alvin I. Goldman

The aim of this paper is to sketch a theory of justified belief. What I have in mind is an explanatory theory, one that explains in a general way why certain beliefs are counted as justified and others as unjustified. Unlike some traditional approaches, I do not try to prescribe standards for justification that differ from, or improve upon, our ordinary standards. I merely try to explicate the ordinary standards, which are, I believe, quite different from those of many classical, e.g., "Cartesian," accounts.

Many epistemologists have been interested in justification because of its presumed close relationship to knowledge. This relationship is intended to be preserved in the conception of justified belief presented here. In previous papers on knowledge,[1] I have denied that justification is necessary for knowing, but there I had in mind "Cartesian" accounts of justification. On the account of justified belief suggested here, it *is* necessary for knowing, and closely related to it.

The term "justified," I presume, is an evaluative term, a term of appraisal. Any correct definition or synonym of it would also feature evaluative terms. I assume that such definitions or synonyms might be given, but I am not interested in them. I want a set of *substantive* conditions that specify when a belief is justified. Compare the moral term "right." This might be defined in other ethical terms or phrases, a task appropriate to metaethics. The task of normative ethics, by contrast, is to state substantive conditions for the rightness of actions. Normative ethics tries to specify

From George S. Pappas, ed., *Justification and Knowledge* (Dordrecht, Netherlands: D. Reidel Publishing Company, 1979), pp. 1–23. © 1979 by D. Reidel Publishing Company. Reprinted by permission of Wolters Kluwer Academic Publishers.

nonethical conditions that determine when an action is right. A familiar example is act-utilitarianism, which says an action is right if and only if it produces, or would produce, at least as much net happiness as any alternative open to the agent. These necessary and sufficient conditions clearly involve no ethical notions. Analogously, I want a theory of justified belief to specify in nonepistemic terms when a belief is justified. This is not the only kind of theory of justifiedness one might seek, but it is one important kind of theory and the kind sought here.

In order to avoid epistemic terms in our theory, we must know which terms are epistemic. Obviously, an exhaustive list cannot be given, but here are some examples: "justified," "warranted," "has (good) grounds," "has reason (to believe)," "knows that," "sees that," "apprehends that," "is probable" (in an epistemic or inductive sense), "shows that," "establishes that," and "ascertains that." By contrast, here are some sample nonepistemic expressions: "believes that," "is true," "causes," "it is necessary that," "implies," "is deducible from," and "is probable" (either in the frequency sense or the propensity sense). In general, (purely) doxastic, metaphysical, modal, semantic, or syntactic expressions are not epistemic.

There is another constraint I wish to place on a theory of justified belief, in addition to the constraint that it be couched in nonepistemic language. Since I seek an explanatory theory, i.e., one that clarifies the underlying source of justificational status, it is not enough for a theory to state "correct" necessary and sufficient conditions. Its conditions must also be appropriately deep or revelatory. Suppose, for example, that the following sufficient condition of justified belief is offered: "If S senses redly at t and S believes at t that he is sensing redly, then S's belief at t that he is sensing redly is justified." This is not the kind of principle I seek; for, even if it is correct, it leaves unexplained *why* a person who senses redly and believes that he does, believes this justifiably. Not every state is such that if one is in it and believes one is in it, this belief is justified. What is distinctive about the state of sensing redly, or "phenomenal" states in general? A theory of justified belief of the kind I seek must answer this question, and hence it must be couched at a suitably deep, general, or abstract level.

A few introductory words about my *explicandum* are appropriate at this juncture. It is often assumed that whenever a person has a justified belief, he knows that it is justified and knows what the justification is. It is further assumed that the person can state or explain what his justification is. On this view, a justification is an argument, defense, or set of reasons that can be given in support of a belief. Thus, one studies the nature of justified belief by considering what a person might *say* if asked to defend, or justify, his belief. I make none of these sorts of assumptions here. I leave it an open question whether, when a belief *is* justified, the believer *knows* it is justified. I also leave it an open question whether, when a belief is justified, the believer can *state* or *give* a justification for it. I do not even assume that when a belief is justified there is something "possessed" by the believer which can be called a "justification."

I do assume that a justified belief gets its status of being justified from some processes or properties that make it justified. In short, there must be some justification-conferring processes or properties. But this does not imply that there must be an argument, or reason, or anything else, "possessed" at the time of belief by the believer.

I

A theory of justified belief will be a set of principles that specify truth-conditions for the schema [*S*'s belief in *p* at time *t* is justified], i.e., conditions for the satisfaction of this schema in all possible cases. It will be convenient to formulate candidate theories in a recursive or inductive format, which would include (A) one or more base clauses, (B) a set of recursive clauses (possibly null), and (C) a closure clause. In such a format, it is permissible for the predicate "is a justified belief" to appear in recursive clauses. But neither this predicate, nor any other epistemic predicate, may appear in (the antecedent of) any base clause.[2]

Before turning to my own theory, I want to survey some other possible approaches to justified belief. Identification of problems associated with other attempts will provide some motivation for the theory I shall offer. Obviously, I cannot examine all, or even very many, alternative attempts. But a few sample attempts will be instructive.

Let us concentrate on the attempt to formulate one or more adequate base-clause principles.[3] Here is a classical candidate:

(1) If *S* believes *p* at *t*, and *p* is indubitable for *S* (at *t*), then *S*'s belief in *p* at *t* is justified.

To evaluate this principle, we need to know what "indubitable" means. It can be understood in at least two ways. First, "*p* is indubitable for *S*" might mean: "*S* has no *grounds* for doubting *p*." Since "ground" is an epistemic term, however, principle (1) would be inadmissible on this reading, for epistemic terms may not legitimately appear in the antecedent of a base-clause. A second interpretation would avoid this difficulty. One might interpret "*p* is indubitable for *S*" psychologically, i.e., as meaning "*S* is psychologically incapable of doubting *p*." This would make principle (1) admissible, but would it be correct? Surely not. A religious fanatic may be psychologically incapable of doubting the tenets of his faith, but that doesn't make his belief in them justified. Similarly, during the Watergate affair, someone may have been so blinded by the aura of the presidency that even after the most damaging evidence against Nixon had emerged he was still incapable of doubting Nixon's veracity. It doesn't follow that his belief in Nixon's veracity was justified.

A second candidate base-clause principle is this:

(2) If S believes p at t, and p is self-evident, then S's belief in p at t is justified.

To evaluate this principle, we again need an interpretation of its crucial term, in this case "self-evident." On one standard reading, "evident" is a synonym for "justified." "*Self*-evident" would therefore mean something like "directly justified," "intuitively justified," or "nonderivatively justified." On this reading "self-evident" is an epistemic phrase, and principle (2) would be disqualified as a base-clause principle.

However, there are other possible readings of "p is self-evident" on which it isn't an epistemic phrase. One such reading is: "It is impossible to understand p without believing it."[4] According to this interpretation, trivial analytic and logical truths might turn out to be self-evident. Hence, any belief in such a truth would be a justified belief, according to (2).

What does "it is *impossible* to understand p without believing it" mean? Does it mean "*humanly* impossible"? That reading would probably make (2) an unacceptable principle. There may well be propositions which humans have an innate and irrepressible disposition to believe, e.g., "Some events have causes." But it seems unlikely that people's inability to refrain from believing such a proposition makes every belief in it justified.

Should we then understand "impossible" to mean "impossible in principle," or "logically impossible"? If that is the reading given, I suspect that (2) is a vacuous principle. I doubt that even trivial logical or analytic truths will satisfy this definition of "self-evident." Any proposition, we may assume, has two or more components that are somehow organized or juxtaposed. To understand the proposition one must "grasp" the components and their juxtaposition. Now in the case of *complex* logical truths, there are (human) psychological operations that suffice to grasp the components and their juxtaposition but do not suffice to produce a belief that the proposition is true. But can't we at least *conceive* of an analogous set of psychological operations even for simple logical truths, operations which perhaps are not in the repertoire of human cognizers but which might be in the repertoire of some conceivable beings? That is, can't we conceive of psychological operations that would suffice to grasp the components and componential-juxtaposition of these simple propositions but do not suffice to produce *belief* in the propositions? I think we can conceive of such operations. Hence, for any proposition you choose, it will be possible for it to be understood without being believed.

Finally, even if we set these two objections aside, we must note that self-evidence can at best confer justificational status on relatively few beliefs, and the only plausible group are beliefs in necessary truths. Thus, other base-clause principles will be needed to explain the justificational status of beliefs in contingent propositions.

The notion of a base-clause principle is naturally associated with the idea of "direct" justifiedness, and in the realm of contingent propositions first-person-current-mental-state propositions have often been assigned this role. In Chisholm's terminology, this conception is expressed by the notion of a *"self-presenting"* state or proposition. The sentence "I am thinking," for example, expresses a self-presenting proposition. (At least I shall *call* this sort of content a "proposition," though it only has a truth value given some assignment of a subject who utters or entertains the content and a time of entertaining.) When such a proposition is true for person S at time t, S is justified in believing it at t: in Chisholm's terminology, the proposition is "evident" for S at t. This suggests the following base-clause principle.

(3) If p is a self-presenting proposition, and p is true for S at t, and S believes p at t, then S's belief in p at t is justified.

What, exactly, does "self-presenting" mean? In the second edition of *Theory of Knowledge,* Chisholm offers this definition: "h is self-presenting for S at t =df; h is true at t; and necessarily, if h is true at t, then h is evident for S at t."[5] Unfortunately, since "evident" is an epistemic term, "self-presenting" also becomes an epistemic term on this definition, thereby disqualifying (3) as a legitimate base-clause. Some other definition of self-presentingness must be offered if (3) is to be a suitable base-clause principle.

Another definition of self-presentation readily comes to mind. "Self-presentation" is an approximate synonym of "self-intimation," and a proposition may be said to be self-intimating if and only if whenever it is true of a person that person believes it. More precisely, we may give the following definition.

(SP) Proposition p is self-presenting if and only if: necessarily, for any S and any t, if p is true for S at t, then S believes p at t.

On this definition, "self-presenting" is clearly not an epistemic predicate, so (3) would be an admissible principle. Moreover, there is initial plausibility in the suggestion that it is *this* feature of first-person-current-mental-state propositions—viz., their truth guarantees their being believed—that makes beliefs in them justified.

Employing this definition of self-presentation, is principle (3) correct? This cannot be decided until we define self-presentation more precisely. Since the operator "necessarily" can be read in different ways, there are different forms of self-presentation and correspondingly different versions of principle (3). Let us focus on two of these readings: a *"nomological"* reading and a *"logical"* reading. Consider first the nomological reading. On this definition a proposition is self-presenting just in case it is nomologically necessary that if p is true for S at t, then S believes p at t.[6]

Is the nomological version of principle (3)—call it "(3_N)"—correct? Not at all. We can imagine cases in which the antecedent of (3_N) is satisfied but we would not say that the belief is justified. Suppose, for example, that p is the proposition expressed by the sentence "I am in brain-state B," where "B" is shorthand for a certain highly specific neural state description. Further suppose it is a nomological truth that anyone in brain-state B will ipso facto *believe* he is in brain-state B. In other words, imagine that an occurrent belief with the content "I am in brain-state B" is realized whenever one is in brain-state B." According to (3_N), any such belief is justified. But that is clearly false. We can readily imagine circumstances in which a person goes into brain-state B and therefore has the belief in question, though this belief is by no means justified. For example, we can imagine that a brain surgeon operating on S artificially induces brain-state B. This results, phenomenologically, in S's suddenly believing—out of the blue— that he is in brain-state B, without any relevant antecedent beliefs. We would hardly say, in such a case, that S's belief that he is in brain-state B is justified.

Let us turn next to the logical version of (3)—call it "(3_L)"—in which a proposition is defined as self-presenting just in case it is logically necessary that if p is true for S at t, then S believes p at t. This stronger version of principle (3) might seem more promising. In fact, however, it is no more successful than (3_N). Let p be the proposition "I am awake" and assume that it is logically necessary that if this proposition is true for some person S at time t, then S believes p at t. This assumption is consistent with the further assumption that S frequently believes p when it is false, e.g., when he is dreaming. Under these circumstances, we would hardly accept the contention that S's belief in this proposition is always justified. Nor should we accept the contention that the belief is justified when it is *true*. The truth of the proposition logically guarantees that the belief is *held*, but why should it guarantee that the belief is *justified*?

The foregoing criticism suggests that we have things backwards. The idea of self-presentation is that truth guarantees belief. This fails to confer justification because it is compatible with there being belief without truth. So what seems necessary—or at least sufficient—for justification is that belief should guarantee truth. Such a notion has usually gone under the label of "*infallibility*," or "*incorrigibility*." It may be defined as follows.

(INC)   Proposition p is incorrigible if and only if: necessarily, for any S and any t, if S believes p at t, then p is true for S at t.

Using the notion of incorrigibility, we may propose principle (4).

(4)   If p is an incorrigible proposition, and S believes p at t, then S's belief in p at t is justified.

As was true of self-presentation, there are different varieties of incorrigibility, corresponding to different interpretations of "necessarily." Accordingly, we have different versions of principle (4). Once again, let us concentrate on a nomological and a logical version, (4N) and (4L) respectively.

We can easily construct a counterexample to (4N) along the lines of the belief-state/brain-state counterexample that refuted (3N). Suppose it is nomologically necessary that if anyone believes he is in brain-state B then it is true that he is in brain-state B, for the only way this belief-state is realized is through brain-state B itself. It follows that "I am in brain-state B" is a nomologically incorrigible proposition. Therefore, according to (4N), whenever anyone believes this proposition at any time, that belief is justified. But we may again construct a brain-surgeon example in which someone comes to have such a belief but the belief isn't justified.

Apart from this counterexample, the general point is this. Why should the fact that S's believing p guarantees the truth of p imply that S's belief is justified? The nature of the guarantee might be wholly fortuitous, as the belief-state/brain-state example is intended to illustrate. To appreciate the point, consider the following related possibility. A person's mental structure might be such that whenever he believes that p will be true (of him) a split second later, then p is true (of him) a split second later. This is because, we may suppose, his believing it brings it about. But surely we would not be compelled in such a circumstance to say that a belief of this sort is justified. So why should the fact that S's believing p guarantees the truth of p *precisely at the time of belief* imply that the belief is justified? There is no intuitive plausibility in this supposition.

The notion of *logical* incorrigibility has a more honored place in the history of conceptions of justification. But even principle (4L), I believe, suffers from defects similar to those of (4N). The mere fact that belief in p logically guarantees its truth does not confer justificational status on such a belief.

The first difficulty with (4L) arises from logical or mathematical truths. Any true proposition of logic or mathematics is logically necessary. Hence, any such proposition p is logically incorrigible, since it is logically necessary that, for any S and any t, if S believes p at t then p is true (for S at t). Now assume that Nelson believes a certain very complex mathematical truth at time t. Since such a proposition is logically incorrigible, (4L) implies that Nelson's belief in this truth at t is justified. But we may easily suppose that this belief of Nelson is not at all the result of proper mathematical reasoning, or even the result of appeal to trustworthy authority. Perhaps Nelson believes this complex truth because of utterly confused reasoning, or because of hasty and ill-founded conjecture. Then his belief is not justified, contrary to what (4L) implies.

The case of logical or mathematical truths is admittedly peculiar, since the truth of these propositions is assured independently of any beliefs. It might seem, therefore, that we can better capture the idea of "belief logically guaranteeing truth" in cases where the propositions in question are *contingent*. With this in mind, we might restrict (4L) to *contingent* incorrigible propositions. Even this amendment cannot save (4$_L$), however, since there are counterexamples to it involving purely contingent propositions.

Suppose that Humperdink had been studying logic—or, rather, pseudologic—from Elmer Fraud, whom Humperdink has no reason to trust as a logician. Fraud has enunciated the principle that any disjunctive proposition consisting of at least 40 distinct disjuncts is very probably true. Humperdink now encounters the proposition *p*, a contingent proposition with 40 disjuncts, the seventh disjunct being "I exist." Although Humperdink grasps the proposition fully, he doesn't notice that it is entailed by "I exist." Rather, he is struck by the fact that it falls under the disjunction rule Fraud has enunciated (a rule I assume Humperdink is not *justified* in believing). Bearing this rule in mind, Humperdink forms a belief in *p*. Now notice that *p* is logically incorrigible. It is logically necessary that if anyone believes *p*, then *p* is true (of him at that time). This simply follows from the fact that, first, a person's believing anything entails that he exists, and second, "I exist" entails *p*. Since *p* is logically incorrigible, principle (4$_L$) implies that Humperdink's belief in *p* is justified. But surely, given our example, that conclusion is false. Humperdink's belief in *p* is not at all justified.

One thing that goes wrong in this example is that while Humperdink's belief in *p* logically implies its truth, Humperdink doesn't *recognize* that his believing it implies its truth. This might move a theorist to revise (4$_L$) by adding the requirement that *S* "recognize" that *p* is logically incorrigible. But this, of course, won't do. The term "recognize" is obviously an epistemic term, so the suggested revision of (4$_L$) would result in an inadmissible base-clause.

II

Let us try to diagnose what has gone wrong with these attempts to produce an acceptable base-clause principle. Notice that each of the foregoing attempts confers the status of "justified" on a belief without restriction on *why* the belief is held, i.e., on what *causally initiates* the belief or *causally sustains* it. The logical versions of principles (3) and (4), for example, clearly place no restriction on causes of belief. The same is true of the nomological versions of (3) and (4), since nomological requirements can be satisfied by simultaneity or cross-sectional laws, as illustrated by our brain-state/belief-state examples. I suggest that the absence of causal requirements accounts for the failure of the foregoing principles. Many of our counterexamples are ones in which the belief is caused in some strange or unacceptable way, e.g., by the accidental movement of a brain surgeon's hand, by reliance on an illicit, pseudological principle, or by the blinding aura of the presidency. In general, a strategy for defeating a noncausal principle of justifiedness is to find a case in which the principle's antecedent is satisfied but the belief is caused by some faulty belief-forming process.

The faultiness of the belief-forming process will incline us, intuitively, to regard the belief as unjustified. Thus, correct principles of justified belief must be principles that make causal requirements, where "cause" is construed broadly to include sustainers as well as initiators of belief (i.e., processes that determine, or help to overdetermine, a belief's continuing to be held).[8]

The need for causal requirements is not restricted to base-clause principles. Recursive principles will also need a causal component. One might initially suppose that the following is a good recursive principle: "If S justifiably believes q at t, and q entails p, and S believes p at t, then S's belief in p at t is justified." But this principle is unacceptable. S's belief in p doesn't receive justificational status simply from the fact that p is entailed by q and S justifiably believes q. If what causes S to believe p at t is entirely different, S's belief in p may well not be justified. Nor can the situation be remedied by adding to the antecedent the condition that S justifiably believes that q entails p. Even if he believes this, and believes q as well, he might not put these beliefs together. He might believe p as a result of some other, wholly extraneous, considerations. So once again, conditions that fail to require appropriate causes of a belief don't guarantee justifiedness.

Granted that principles of justified belief must make reference to causes of belief, what kinds of causes confer justifiedness? We can gain insight into this problem by reviewing some faulty processes of belief-formation, i.e., processes whose belief-outputs would be classed as unjustified. Here are some examples: confused reasoning, wishful thinking, reliance on emotional attachment, mere hunch or guesswork, and hasty generalization. What do these faulty processes have in common? They share the feature of *unreliability*: they tend to produce *error* a large proportion of the time. By contrast, which species of belief-forming (or belief-sustaining) processes are intuitively justification-conferring? They include standard perceptual processes, remembering, good reasoning, and introspection. What these processes seem to have in common is *reliability*: the beliefs they produce are generally true. My positive proposal, then, is this. The justificational status of a belief is a function of the reliability of the process or processes that cause it, where (as a first approximation) reliability consists in the tendency of a process to produce beliefs that are true rather than false.

To test this thesis further, notice that justifiedness is not a purely categorical concept, although I treat it here as categorical in the interest of simplicity. We can and do regard certain beliefs as more justified than others. Furthermore, our intuitions of comparative justifiedness go along with our beliefs about the comparative reliability of the belief-causing processes.

Consider perceptual beliefs. Suppose Jones believes he has just seen a mountain goat. Our assessment of the belief's justifiedness is determined by whether he caught a brief glimpse of the creature at a great distance, or whether he had a good look at the thing only 30 yards away. His belief in the latter sort of case is (*ceteris paribus*) more justified than in the former sort of case. And, if his belief is true, we are more prepared to say he *knows* in the latter case than in the former. The difference between the two cases seems to be this. Visual beliefs formed from brief and hasty scanning, or where the perceptual object is a long distance off, tend to be wrong more often than visual beliefs formed from detailed and leisurely scanning, or where the object is in reasonable proximity. In short, the visual processes in the former category are less reliable than those in the latter category. A similar point holds for memory beliefs. A belief that results from a hazy and indistinct memory impression is counted as less justified than a belief that arises from a distinct memory impression, and our inclination to classify those beliefs as *"knowledge"* varies in the same way. Again, the reason is associated with the comparative reliability of the processes. Hazy and indistinct memory impressions are generally less reliable indicators of what actually happened; so beliefs formed from such impressions are less likely to be true than beliefs formed from distinct impressions. Further, consider beliefs based on inference from observed samples. A belief about a population that is based on random sampling, or on instances that exhibit great variety, is intuitively more justified than a belief based on biased sampling, or on instances from a narrow sector of the population. Again, the degree of justifiedness seems to be a function of reliability. Inferences based on random or varied samples will tend to produce less error or inaccuracy than inferences based on nonrandom or nonvaried samples.

Returning to a categorical concept of justifiedness, we might ask just *how* reliable a belief-forming process must be in order that its resultant beliefs be justified. A precise answer to this question should not be expected. Our conception of justification is *vague* in this respect. It does seem clear, however, that *perfect* reliability isn't required. Belief-forming processes that *sometimes* produce error still confer justification. It follows that there can be justified beliefs that are false.

I have characterized justification-conferring processes as ones that have a "tendency" to produce beliefs that are true rather than false. The term "tendency" could refer either to *actual* long-run frequency, or to a "propensity," i.e., outcomes that would occur in merely *possible* realizations of the process. Which of these is intended? Unfortunately, I think our ordinary conception of justifiedness is vague on this dimension too. For the most part, we simply assume that the "observed" frequency of truth versus error would be approximately replicated in the actual long run, and also in relevant counterfactual situations, i.e., ones that are highly "realistic," or conform closely to the circumstances of the actual world. Since we ordinarily assume these frequencies to be roughly the same, we make no concerted effort to distinguish them. Since the purpose of my present theorizing is to capture our ordinary conception of justifiedness, and since our ordinary conception is vague on this matter, it is appropriate to leave the theory vague in the same respect.

We need to say more about the notion of a belief-forming *"process."* Let us mean by a "process" a *functional operation* or procedure, i.e., something that generates a *mapping* from certain states—"inputs"—into other states—"outputs." The outputs in the present case are states of believing this or that proposition at a given moment. On this interpretation, a process is a *type* as opposed to a *token*. This is fully appropriate, since it is only types that have statistical properties such as producing truth 80 percent of the time; and it is precisely such statistical properties that determine the reliability of a process. Of course, we also want to speak of a process as *causing* a belief, and it looks as if types are incapable of being causes. But when we say that a belief is caused by a given process, understood as a functional procedure, we may interpret this to mean that it is caused by the particular *inputs* to the process (and by the intervening events "through which" the functional procedure carries the inputs into the output) on the occasion in question.

What are some examples of belief-forming "processes" construed as functional operations? One example is reasoning processes, where the inputs include antecedent beliefs and entertained hypotheses. Another example is functional procedures whose inputs include desires, hopes, or emotional states of various sorts (together with antecedent beliefs). A third example is a memory process, which takes as input beliefs or experiences at an earlier time and generates as output beliefs at a later time. For example, a memory process might take as input a belief *at* t_1 that Lincoln was born in 1809 and generate as output a belief *at* t_n that Lincoln was born in 1809. A fourth example is perceptual processes. Here it isn't clear whether inputs should include states of the environment, such as the distance of the stimulus from the cognizer, or only events within or on the surface of the organism, e.g., receptor stimulations. I shall return to this point in a moment.

A critical problem concerning our analysis is the degree of generality of the process-types in question. Input-output relations can be specified very broadly or very narrowly, and the degree of generality will partly determine the degree of reliability. A process-type might be selected so narrowly that only one instance of it ever occurs, and hence the type is either completely reliable or completely unreliable. (This assumes that reliability is a function of *actual* frequency only.) If such narrow process-types were selected, beliefs that are intuitively unjustified might be said to result from perfectly reliable processes; and beliefs that are intuitively justified might be said to result from perfectly unreliable processes.

It is clear that our ordinary thought about process-types slices them broadly, but I cannot at present give a precise explication of our intuitive principles. One plausible suggestion, though, is that the relevant processes are *content-neutral*. It might be argued, for example, that the process of *inferring* p *whenever the pope asserts* p could pose problems for our theory. If the pope is infallible, this process will be perfectly reliable; yet we would not regard the belief-outputs of this process as justified. The content-neutral restriction would avert this difficulty. If relevant processes are required to admit as input beliefs (or other states) with *any* content, the aforementioned process will not count, for its input beliefs have a restricted propositional content, viz., *"the pope* asserts *p."*

In addition to the problem of "generality" or "abstractness" there is the previously mentioned problem of the *"extent"* of belief-forming processes. Clearly, the causal ancestry of beliefs often includes events outside the organism. Are such events to be included among the "inputs" of belief-forming processes? Or should we restrict the extent of belief-forming processes to *"cognitive"* events, i.e., events within the organism's nervous system? I shall choose the latter course, though with some hesitation. My general grounds for this decision are roughly as follows. Justifiedness seems to be a function of how a cognizer deals with his environmental input, i.e., with the goodness or badness of the operations that register and transform the stimulation that reaches him. ("Deal with," of course, does not mean *purposeful* action; nor is it restricted to *conscious* activity.) A justified belief is, roughly speaking, one that results from cognitive operations that are, generally speaking, good or successful. But *"cognitive"* operations are most plausibly construed as operations of the cognitive faculties, i.e., "information-processing" equipment *internal* to the organism.

With these points in mind, we may now advance the following base-clause principle for justified belief.

(5) If *S*'s believing *p* at *t* results from a reliable cognitive belief-forming process (or set of processes), then *S*'s belief in *p* at *t* is justified.

Since "reliable belief-forming process" has been defined in terms of such notions as belief, truth, statistical frequency, and the like, it is not an epistemic term. Hence, (5) is an admissible base-clause.

It might seem as if (5) promises to be not only a successful base-clause, but the only principle needed whatever, apart from a closure clause. In other words, it might seem as if it is a necessary as well as a sufficient condition of justifiedness that a belief be produced by reliable cognitive belief-forming processes. But this is not quite correct, given our provisional definition of "reliability."

Our provisional definition implies that a reasoning process is reliable only if it generally produces beliefs that are true, and similarly, that a memory process is reliable only if it generally yields beliefs that are true. But these requirements are too strong. A reasoning procedure cannot be expected to produce true belief if it is applied to false premises. And memory cannot be expected to yield a true belief if the original belief it attempts to retain is false. What we need for reasoning and memory, then, is a notion of *"conditional reliability."* A process is conditionally reliable when a sufficient proportion of its output-beliefs are true *given that its input-beliefs are true.*

With this point in mind, let us distinguish *belief-dependent* and *belief-indepen-*

dent cognitive processes. The former are processes some of whose inputs are belief-states.[9] The latter are processes none of whose inputs are belief-states. We may then replace principle (5) with the following two principles, the first a base-clause principle and the second a recursive-clause principle.

(6A) If S's belief in p at t results ("immediately") from a belief-independent process that is (unconditionally) reliable, then S's belief in p at t is justified.

(6B) If S's belief in p at t results ("immediately") from a belief-dependent process that is (at least) conditionally reliable, and if the beliefs (if any) on which this process operates in producing S's belief in p at t are themselves justified, then S's belief in p at t is justified.[10]

If we add to (6A) and (6B) the standard closure clause, we have a complete theory of justified belief. The theory says, in effect, that a belief is justified if and only if it is *"well-formed,"* i.e., it has an ancestry of reliable and/or conditionally reliable cognitive operations. (Since a dated belief may be overdetermined, it may have a number of distinct ancestral trees. These need not all be full of reliable or conditionally reliable processes. But at least one ancestral tree must have reliable or conditionally reliable processes throughout.)

The theory of justified belief proposed here, then, is an *Historical* or *Genetic* theory. It contrasts with the dominant approach to justified belief, an approach that generates what we may call (borrowing a phrase from Robert Nozick) *"Current Time-Slice"* theories. A Current Time-Slice theory makes the justificational status of a belief wholly a function of what is true of the cognizer *at the time* of belief. An Historical theory makes the justificational status of a belief depend on its prior history. Since my Historical theory emphasizes the reliability of the belief-generating processes, it may be called *"Historical Reliabilism."*

The most obvious examples of Current Time-Slice theories are "Cartesian" Foundationalist theories, which trace all justificational status (at least of contingent propositions) to current mental states. The usual varieties of Coherence theories, however, are equally Current Time-Slice views, since they too make the justificational status of a belief wholly a function of *current* states of affairs. For Coherence theories, however, these current states include all other beliefs of the cognizer, which would not be considered relevant by Cartesian Foundationalism. Have there been other Historical theories of justified belief? Among contemporary writers, Quine and Popper have Historical epistemologies, though the notion of "justification" is not their avowed *explicandum.* Among historical writers, it might seem that Locke and Hume had Genetic theories of sorts. But I think that their Genetic theories were only theories of ideas, not of knowledge or justification. Plato's theory of recollection, however, is a good example of a Genetic theory of knowing.[11] And it might be argued that Hegel and Dewey had Genetic epistemologies (if Hegel can be said to have had a clear epistemology at all).

The theory articulated by (6A) and (6B) might be viewed as a kind of "Foundationalism," because of its recursive structure. I have no objection to this label, as long as one keeps in mind how different this "diachronic" form of Foundationalism is from Cartesian, or other "synchronic" varieties of, Foundationalism.

Current Time-Slice theories characteristically assume that the justificational status of a belief is something which the cognizer is able to know or determine at the time of belief. This is made explicit, for example, by Chisholm.[12] The Historical theory I endorse makes no such assumption. There are many facts about a cognizer to which he lacks "privileged access," and I regard the justificational status of his beliefs as one of those things. This is not to say that a cognizer is necessarily ignorant, at any given moment, of the justificational status of his current beliefs. It is only to deny that he necessarily has, or can get, knowledge or true belief about this status. Just as a person can know without knowing that he knows, so he can have justified belief without knowing that it is justified (or believing justifiably that it is justified).

A characteristic case in which a belief is justified though the cognizer doesn't know that it's justified is where the original evidence for the belief has long since been forgotten. If the original evidence was compelling, the cognizer's original belief may have been justified; and this justificational status may have been preserved through memory. But since the cognizer no longer remembers how or why he came to believe, he may not know that the belief *is* justified. If asked now to justify his belief, he may be at a loss. Still, the belief is justified, though the cognizer can't demonstrate or establish this.

The Historical theory of justified belief I advocate is connected in spirit with the causal theory of knowing I have presented elsewhere.[13] I had this in mind when I remarked near the outset of the paper that my theory of justified belief makes justifiedness come out closely related to knowledge. Justified beliefs, like pieces of knowledge, have appropriate histories; but they may fail to be knowledge either because they are false or because they founder on some other requirement for knowing of the kind discussed in the post-Gettier knowledge-trade.

There is a variant of the Historical conception of justified belief that is worth mentioning in this context. It may be introduced as follows. Suppose S has a set B of beliefs at time t_0, and some of these beliefs are *un*justified. Between t_0 and t_1 he reasons from the entire set B to the conclusion p, which he then accepts at t_1. The reasoning procedure he uses is a very sound one, i.e., one that is conditionally reliable. There is a sense or respect in which we are tempted to say that S's belief in p at t_1 is "justified." At any rate, it is tempting to say that the *person* is justified in believing p at t. Relative to his antecedent cognitive state, he did as well as could be expected:

the *transition* from his cognitive state at t_0 to his cognitive state at t_1 was entirely sound. Although we may acknowledge this brand of justifiedness—it might be called *"Terminal-Phase Reliabilism"*—it is not a kind of justifiedness so closely related to knowing. For a person to know proposition *p*, it is not enough that the *final phase* of the process that leads to his belief in *p* be sound. It is also necessary that some entire history of the process be sound (i.e., reliable or conditionally reliable).

Let us return now to the Historical theory. In the next section of the paper, I shall adduce reasons for strengthening it a bit. Before looking at these reasons, however, I wish to review two quite different objections to the theory.

First, a critic might argue that *some* justified beliefs do not derive their justificational status from their causal ancestry. In particular, it might be argued that beliefs about one's current phenomenal states and intuitive beliefs about elementary logical or conceptual relationships do not derive their justificational status in this way. I am not persuaded by either of these examples. Introspection, I believe, should be regarded as a form of retrospection. Thus, a justified belief that I am "now" in pain gets its justificational status from a relevant, though brief, causal history.[14] The apprehension of logical or conceptual relationships is also a cognitive process that occupies time. The psychological process of "seeing" or "intuiting" a simple logical truth is very fast, and we cannot introspectively dissect it into constituent parts. Nonetheless, there are mental operations going on, just as there are mental operations that occur in *idiot savants,* who are unable to report the computational processes they in fact employ.

A second objection to Historical Reliabilism focuses on the reliability element rather than the causal or historical element. Since the theory is intended to cover all possible cases, it seems to imply that for any cognitive process *C,* if *C* is reliable in possible world *W,* then any belief in *W* that results from *C* is justified. But doesn't this permit easy counterexamples? Surely we can imagine a possible world in which wishful thinking is reliable. We can imagine a possible world where a benevolent demon so arranges things that beliefs formed by wishful thinking usually come true. This would make wishful thinking a reliable process in that possible world, but surely we don't want to regard beliefs that result from wishful thinking as justified.

There are several possible ways to respond to this case and I am unsure which response is best, partly because my own intuitions (and those of other people I have consulted) are not entirely clear. One possibility is to say that in the possible world imagined, beliefs that result from wishful thinking *are* justified. In other words we reject the claim that wishful thinking could never, intuitively, confer justifiedness.[15]

However, for those who feel that wishful thinking couldn't confer justifiedness, even in the world imagined, there are two ways out. First, it may be suggested that the proper criterion of justifiedness is the propensity of a process to generate beliefs that are true *in a nonmanipulated environment,* i.e., an environment in which there is no purposeful arrangement of the world either to accord or conflict with the beliefs that are formed. In other words, the suitability of a belief-forming process is only a function of its success in *"natural"* situations, not situations of the sort involving benevolent or malevolent demons, or any other such manipulative creatures. If we reformulate the theory to include this qualification, the counterexample in question will be averted.

Alternatively, we may reformulate our theory, or reinterpret it, as follows. Instead of construing the theory as saying that a belief in possible world W is justified if and only if it results from a cognitive process that is reliable in W, we may construe it as saying that a belief in possible world W is justified if and only if it results from a cognitive process that is reliable *in our world.* In short, our conception of justifiedness is derived as follows. We note certain cognitive processes in the actual world, and form beliefs about which of these are reliable. The ones we believe to be reliable are then regarded as justification-conferring processes. In reflecting on hypothetical beliefs, we deem them justified if and only if they result from processes already picked out as justification-conferring, or processes very similar to those. Since wishful thinking is not among these processes, a belief formed in a possible world W by wishful thinking would not be deemed justified, even if wishful thinking is reliable in W. I am not sure that this is a correct reconstruction of our intuitive conceptual scheme, but it would accommodate the benevolent demon case, at least if the proper thing to say in that case is that the wishful-thinking-caused beliefs are unjustified.

Even if we adopt this strategy, however, a problem still remains. Suppose that wishful thinking turns out to be reliable *in the actual world!*[16] This might be because, unbeknownst to us at present, there is a benevolent demon who, lazy until now, will shortly start arranging things so that our wishes come true. The long-run performance of wishful thinking will be very good, and hence even the new construal of the theory will imply that beliefs resulting from wishful thinking (in *our* world) are justified. Yet this surely contravenes our intuitive judgment on the matter.

Perhaps the moral of the case is that the standard format of a "conceptual analysis" has its shortcomings. Let me depart from that format and try to give a better rendering of our aim and the theory that tries to achieve that aim. What we really want is an *explanation* of why we count, or would count, certain beliefs as justified and others as unjustified. Such an explanation must refer to our *beliefs* about reliability, not to the actual *facts.* The reason we *count* beliefs as justified is that they are formed by what we *believe* to be reliable belief-forming processes. Our beliefs about which belief-forming processes are reliable may be erroneous, but that does not affect the adequacy of the explanation. Since we *believe* that wishful thinking is an unreliable belief-forming process, we regard beliefs formed by wishful thinking as unjustified. What matters, then, is what we *believe* about wishful thinking, not what is *true* (in the long run) about wishful thinking. I am not sure how to express this point in the standard format of conceptual analysis, but it identifies an important point in understanding our theory.

III

Let us return, however, to the standard format of conceptual analysis, and let us consider a new objection that will require some revisions in the theory advanced until now. According to our theory, a belief is justified in case it is caused by a process that is in fact reliable, or by one that we generally believe to be reliable. But suppose that although one of S's beliefs satisfies this condition, S has no reason to believe that it does. Worse yet, suppose S has reason to believe that his belief is caused by an *un*reliable process (although *in fact* its causal ancestry is fully reliable). Wouldn't we deny in such circumstances that S's belief is justified? This seems to show that our analysis, as presently formulated, is mistaken.

Suppose that Jones is told on fully reliable authority that a certain class of his memory beliefs are almost all mistaken. His parents fabricate a wholly false story that Jones suffered from amnesia when he was seven but later developed *pseudo*memories of that period. Though Jones listens to what his parents say and has excellent reason to trust them, he persists in believing the ostensible memories from his seven-year-old past. Are these memory beliefs justified? Intuitively, they are not justified. But since these beliefs result from genuine memory and original perceptions, which are adequately reliable processes, our theory says that these beliefs are justified.

Can the theory be revised to meet this difficulty? One natural suggestion is that the actual reliability of a belief's ancestry is not enough for justifiedness. In addition, the cognizer must be *justified in believing* that the ancestry of his belief is reliable. Thus one might think of replacing (6A), for example, with (7). (For simplicity, I neglect some of the details of the earlier analysis.)

(7) If S's belief in p at t is caused by a reliable cognitive process, and S justifiably believes at t that his p-belief is so caused, then S's belief in p at t is justified.

It is evident, however, that (7) will not do as a base-clause, for it contains the epistemic term "justifiably" in its antecedent.

A slightly weaker revision, without this problematic feature, might next be suggested, viz.,

(8) If S's belief in p at t is caused by a reliable cognitive process, and S believes at t that his p-belief is so caused, then S's belief in p at t is justified.

But this won't do the job. Suppose that Jones believes that his memory beliefs are reliably caused despite all the (trustworthy) contrary testimony of his parents. Principle (8) would be satisfied, yet we wouldn't say that these beliefs are justified,

Next, we might try (9), which is stronger than (8), and, unlike (7), formally admissible as a base clause.

> (9) If S's belief in p at t is caused by a reliable cognitive process, and S believes at t that his p-belief is so caused, and this metabelief is caused by a reliable cognitive process, then S's belief in p at t is justified.

A first objection to (9) is that it wrongly precludes unreflective creatures—creatures like animals or young children, who have no beliefs about the genesis of their beliefs—from having justified beliefs. If one shares my view that justified belief is, at least roughly, *well-formed* belief, surely animals and young children can have justified beliefs.

A second problem with (9) concerns its underlying rationale. Since (9) is proposed as a substitute for (6A), it is implied that the reliability of a belief's own cognitive ancestry does not make it justified. But, the suggestion seems to be, the reliability of a *metabelief*'s ancestry confers justifiedness on the first-order belief. Why should that be so? Perhaps one is attracted by the idea of a "trickle-down" effect; if an n+l–level belief is justified, its justification trickles down to an n-level belief. But even if the trickle-down theory is correct, it doesn't help here. There is no assurance from the satisfaction of (9)'s antecedent that the metabelief itself is *justified.*

To obtain a better revision of our theory, let us reexamine the Jones case. Jones has strong evidence against certain propositions concerning his past. He doesn't *use* this evidence, but if he *were* to use it properly, he would stop believing these propositions. Now the proper use of evidence would be an instance of a (conditionally) reliable process. So what we can say about Jones is that he *fails* to use a certain (conditionally) reliable process that he could and should have used. Admittedly, had he used this process, he would have "worsened" his doxastic states: he would have replaced some true beliefs with suspension of judgment. Still, he couldn't have known this in the case in question. So, he failed to do something which, epistemically, he should have done. This diagnosis suggests a fundamental change in our theory. The justificational status of a belief is not only a function of the cognitive processes *actually* employed in producing it; it is also a function of processes that could and should be employed.

With these points in mind, we may tentatively propose the following revision of our theory, where we again focus on a base-clause principle but omit certain details in the interest of clarity.

(10) If S's belief in p at t results from a reliable cognitive process, and there is no reliable or conditionally reliable process available to S which, had it been used by S in addition to the processes actually used, would have resulted in S's not believing p at t, then S's belief in p at t is justified.

There are several problems with this proposal. First, there is a technical problem. One cannot use an additional belief-forming (or doxastic-state-forming) process as well as the original process if the additional one would result in a different doxastic state. One wouldn't be using the original process at all. So we need a slightly different formulation of the relevant counterfactual. Since the basic idea is reasonably clear, however, I won't try to improve on the formulation here. A second problem concerns the notion of "*available*" belief-forming (or doxastic-state-forming) processes. What is it for a process to be "available" to a cognizer? Were scientific procedures "available" to people who lived in prescientific ages? Furthermore, it seems implausible to say that all "available" processes ought to be used, at least if we include such processes as gathering *new* evidence. Surely a belief can sometimes be justified even if additional evidence-gathering would yield a different doxastic attitude. What I think we should have in mind here are such additional processes as calling previously acquired evidence to mind, assessing the implications of that evidence, etc. This is admittedly somewhat vague, but here again our ordinary notion of justifiedness is vague, so it is appropriate for our analysans to display the same sort of vagueness.

This completes the sketch of my account of justified belief. Before concluding, however, it is essential to point out that there is an important use of "justified" which is not captured by this account but can be captured by a closely related one.

There is a use of "justified" in which it is not implied or presupposed that there is a *belief* that is justified. For example, if S is trying to decide whether to believe p and asks our advice, we may tell him that he is "justified" in believing it. We do not thereby imply that he *has* a justified *belief*, since we know he is still suspending judgment. What we mean, roughly, is that he *would* or *could* be justified if he were to believe p. The justificational status we ascribe here cannot be a function of the causes of S's believing p, for there is no belief by S in p. Thus, the account of justifiedness we have given thus far cannot explicate *this* use of "justified." (It doesn't follow that this use of "justified" has no connection with causal ancestries. Its proper use may depend on the causal ancestry of the cognizer's cognitive state, though not on the causal ancestry of his believing p.)

Let us distinguish two uses of "justified": an *ex post* use and an *ex ante* use. The *ex post* use occurs when there exists a belief, and we say *of that belief* that it is (or isn't) justified. The *ex ante* use occurs when no such belief exists, or when we wish to ignore the question of whether such a belief exists. Here we say of the *person,* independent of his doxastic state vis-à-vis p, that p is (or isn't) suitable for him to believe.[17]

Since we have given an account of *ex post* justifiedness, it will suffice if we can analyze *ex ante* justifiedness in terms of it. Such an analysis, I believe, is ready at hand. *S* is *ex ante* justified in believing *p* at *t* just in case his total cognitive state at *t* is such that from that state he could come to believe *p* in such a way that this belief would be *ex post* justified. More precisely, he is *ex ante* justified in believing *p* at *t* just in case a reliable belief-forming operation is available to him such that the application of that operation to his total cognitive state at *t* would result, more or less immediately, in his believing *p* and this belief would be *ex post* justified. Stated formally, we have the following:

(11) Person *S* is *ex ante* justified in believing *p* at *t* if and only if there is a reliable belief-forming operation available to *S* which is such that if *S* applied that operation to his total cognitive state at *t*, *S* would believe *p* at *t*-plus-delta (for a suitably small delta) and that belief would be *ex post* justified.

For the analysans of (11) to be satisfied, the total cognitive state at *t* must have a suitable causal ancestry. Hence, (11) is implicitly an Historical account of *ex ante* justifiedness.

As indicated, the bulk of this paper was addressed to *ex post* justifiedness. This is the appropriate analysandum if one is interested in the connection between justifiedness and knowledge, since what is crucial to whether a person *knows* a proposition is whether he has an actual *belief* in the proposition that is justified. However, since many epistemologists are interested in *ex ante* justifiedness, it is proper for a general theory of justification to try to provide an account of that concept as well. Our theory does this quite naturally, for the account of *ex ante* justifiedness falls out directly from our account of *ex post* justifiedness.[18]

NOTES

1. "A Causal Theory of Knowing," *The Journal of Philosophy* 64, no. 12 (June 22, 1967): 357–72; "Innate Knowledge," in S. P. Stich, ed., *Innate Ideas* (Berkeley: University of California Press, 1975); and "Discrimination and Perceptual Knowledge," *The Journal of Philosophy* 73, no. 20 (November 18, 1976): 771–91.

2. Notice that the choice of a recursive format does not prejudice the case for or against any particular theory. A recursive format is perfectly general. Specifically, an explicit set of necessary and sufficient conditions is just a special case of a recursive format, i.e., one in which there is no recursive clause.

3. Many of the attempts I shall consider are suggested by material in William P. Alston, "Varieties of Privileged Access," *American Philosophical Quarterly* 8 (1971): 223–41.

4. Such a definition (though without the modal term) is given, for example, by W. V. Quine and J. S. Ullian in *The Web of Belief* (New York: Random House, 1970), p. 21. Statements are said to be self-evident just in case "to understand them is to believe them."

5. *Theory of Knowledge* (Englewood Cliffs, N.J.: Prentice-Hall, Inc., 1977), p. 22.

6. I assume, of course, that "nomologically necessary" is *de re* with respect to "*S*" and "*t*" in this construction. I shall not focus on problems that may arise in this regard, since my primary concerns are with different issues.

7. This assumption violates the thesis that Davidson calls "The Anomalism of the Mental." Compare "Mental Events," in L. Foster and J. W. Swanson, eds., *Experience and Theory* (Amherst: University of Massachusetts Press, 1970). But it is unclear that this thesis is a necessary truth. Thus, it seems fair to assume its falsity in order to produce a counterexample. The example neither entails nor precludes the mental-physical identity theory.

8. Keith Lehrer's example of the gypsy lawyer is intended to show the inappropriateness of a causal requirement. (See *Knowledge* [Oxford: University Press, 1974], pp. 124–25.) But I find this example unconvincing. To the extent that I clearly imagine that the lawyer fixes his belief solely as a result of the cards, it seems intuitively wrong to say that he *knows*—or has a *justified belief*—that his client is innocent.

9. This definition is not exactly what we need for the purposes at hand. As Ernest Sosa points out, introspection will turn out to be a belief-dependent process since sometimes the input into the process will be a belief (when the introspected content is a belief). Intuitively, however, introspection is not the sort of process which may be merely conditionally reliable. I do not know how to refine the definition so as to avoid this difficulty, but it is a small and isolated point.

10. It may be objected that principles (6_A) and (6_B) are jointly open to analogs of the lottery paradox. A series of processes composed of reliable but less-than-perfectly-reliable processes may be extremely unreliable. Yet applications of (6_A) and (6_B) would confer justifiedness on a belief that is caused by such a series. In reply to this objection, we might simply indicate that the theory is intended to capture our ordinary notion of justifiedness, and this ordinary notion has been formed without recognition of this kind of problem. The theory is not wrong *as* a theory of the ordinary (naive) conception of justifiedness. On the other hand, if we want a theory to do more than capture the ordinary conception of justifiedness, it might be possible to strengthen the principles to avoid lottery-paradox analogs.

11. I am indebted to Mark Pastin for this point.

12. Cf. *Theory of Knowledge*, 2d ed., pp. 17, 114–16.

13. Cf. Goldman, "A Causal Theory of Knowing." The reliability aspect of my theory also has its precursors in earlier papers of mine on knowing: "Innate Knowledge" and "Discrimination and Perceptual Knowledge."

14. The view that introspection is retrospection was taken by Ryle, and before him (as Charles Hartshorne points out to me) by Hobbes, Whitehead, and possibly Husserl.

15. Of course, if people in world *W* learn *inductively* that wishful thinking is reliable, and regularly base their beliefs on this inductive inference, it is quite unproblematic and straightforward that their beliefs are justified. The only interesting case is where their beliefs are formed *purely* by wishful thinking, without using inductive inference. The suggestion contemplated in this paragraph of the text is that, in the world imagined, even pure wishful thinking would confer justifiedness.

16. I am indebted here to Mark Kaplan.

17. The distinction between *ex post* and *ex ante* justifiedness is similar to Roderick Firth's distinction between *doxastic* and *propositional* warrant. See his "Are Epistemic Concepts Reducible to Ethical Concepts?" in Alvin I. Goldman and Jaegwon Kim, eds., *Values and Morals, Essays in Honor of William Frankena, Charles Stevenson, and Richard Brandt* (Dordrecht, Netherlands: D. Reidel Publishing Co., 1978).

18. Research on this paper was begun while the author was a fellow of the John Simon Guggenheim Memorial Foundation and of the Center for Advanced Study in the Behavioral Sciences. I am grateful for their support. I have received helpful comments and criticism from Holly S. Goldman, Mark Kaplan, Fred Schmitt, Stephen P. Stich, and many others at several universities where earlier drafts of the paper were read.

21

Contra Reliabilism

Carl Ginet

The reliability of a belief-producing process is a matter of how likely it is that the process will produce beliefs that are true. The term *reliabilism* may be used to refer to any position that makes this idea of reliability central to the explication of some important epistemic concept. I know of three such positions that appeal to some epistemologists: (1) a reliabilist account of what makes a belief justified, (2) a reliabilist account of what makes a true belief knowledge, and (3) a reliabilist answer to the question of the fourth condition, the question of what must be added to justified true belief to make knowledge. Obviously these are alternative positions rather than parts of a single coherent whole. I think of the first as reliabilism's boldest stand, the second as the position to which it may retreat when the first is found untenable, and the third as its last refuge. I will criticize only the first two positions.[1]

RELIABILISM AS AN ACCOUNT OF JUSTIFICATION

Let us elaborate a little on what is meant by the reliability of a belief-producing process. A belief-producing process is a certain *kind* of process that produces beliefs having a certain kind of content. The kind of process is reliable just in case the beliefs of that kind that it produces are true a sufficiently high proportion of the time, or *would* be true a sufficiently high proportion of the time if the process were to occur

From *The Monist* 68, no. 2 (April 1985): 175–87. © 1985 The Monist, LaSalle, IL 61501. Reprinted by permission of the publisher.

frequently: it has a sufficiently strong propensity to produce true rather than false beliefs.

The boldest claim a reliabilist can make about the justification of belief is this: for a belief to be justified is for it to be produced by a reliable process. This simple statement needs some serious refining. For any particular belief, there will be *some* kind to which the producing process belongs and *some* kind to which the content belongs such that it will be of no significance at all that most (or all) or few (or none) of the beliefs of that kind that are (or would be) produced by processes of that kind are true. The kinds can, for example, be specified so narrowly that the production of the particular belief in question will be the only case in point that ever would occur. So the reliabilist must revise the claim to read: for a belief to be justified is for there to be a *relevant* kind to which the belief content belongs and a *relevant* kind of process by which it was produced such that that kind of process reliably produces true beliefs of that kind. It will not be trivial to specify criteria of relevance that are both plausible and informative, but let us assume that it can be done.

However this refinement is worked out, it will be unable to avoid certain clear counterexamples to this boldest of the reliabilist claims, cases where it is clear that what justifies the belief is *not* what causes it (and also, though this is not essential to the counterexample, where it is unlikely that the belief is produced by any relevant kind of reliable process). Suppose, for example, that it is a mild day in Ithaca but the weather forecast I hear on the radio says that a mass of cold air will move into the region tomorrow. As soon as I hear that, I have, we may suppose, good reason to believe that it will be colder in Ithaca tomorrow; and if I were caused to believe it by having that reason then my belief would be produced by a (relevant) reliable process. But let us suppose that I irrationally refuse to believe it until my Aunt Hattie tells me that she feels in her joints that it will be colder tomorrow. She often makes that sort of prediction and I always believe her, even if I have no other supporting evidence. She is right about as often as she is wrong. So the (relevant) process by which my belief is actually caused is not reliable. Nevertheless my belief is justified. I do have justification for it, namely, my justified belief as to what the weather bureau said. Thus I am protected from reproach for holding the belief, though I may deserve reproach for something else, namely, *being moved* to hold it *by* Aunt Hattie's prediction and not by the weather bureau's. I could rebut any reproach for my holding the belief by pointing out that I do have justification for it. My recognizing the evidential value of the weather bureau's forecast is quite compatible with my (irrationally) refusing to be moved to belief by that evidence.

It may help to see the matter right here to consider an analogous situation with respect to the justification of action. Suppose you and I are eating at a restaurant where the chocolate mousse is beyond compare. We both order it. After eating my portion I finish off the major part of your portion while you are away from the table.

This is something I decided to do as soon as you announced your temporary departure. But as you stood up you said to me, "Please finish my mousse: I can't possibly eat any more." So I am perfectly justified in finishing your mousse. You have given me permission and I am aware of this fact and its moral relevance to my action. Still it is not because of this justification I have for it that I perform the action. I would have done it anyway. So there is something here for which I may be censured, namely, what I found to be sufficient reason to act: my gluttonous craving would have led me to eat your mousse even without your permission. But something I should *not* be blamed for is: eating your mousse. Given that I am aware of your permission and its justifying force, that action is above reproach and it would be unjust to inflict on me any of the penalties that should attach to eating someone else's chocolate mousse without their permission.

So the justification of an action or of a belief is not necessarily a matter of how it was actually caused. But the reliabilist can admit this and retreat to the claim that the justification of a belief is a matter either of how it is actually caused or of how it could have been caused in the circumstances actually present. The reliabilist can say that a belief is justified just in case either it is actually caused by a (relevant) reliable process or there are conditions present such that if they had caused the belief then it would have been caused by a reliable process. This is still too crude a formulation of the position but it is refined enough for my purposes.[2] The criticisms I have to make are directed at the basic idea.

Let us note, first, that there are cases that show that the reliabilist condition fails to be *sufficient* for justified belief. A leading reliabilist has himself described such a case. Alvin Goldman, in his paper, "What Is Justified Belief?" says:

> Suppose . . . that p is the proposition expressed by the sentence "I am in brain-state B," where "B" is shorthand for a certain highly specific neural state description. Further suppose it is a nomological truth that anyone in brain-state B will ipso facto *believe* he is in brain-state B.[3]

The reliabilist position would appear to dictate that any such belief is justified, for the process producing it could not be more reliable: it is a causal law about the kind of brain-state that it always produces in its subject a belief that he or she is in a brain state of that kind. But as Goldman himself goes on to say, the claim that any such belief is justified

> is clearly false. We can readily imagine circumstances in which a person goes into brain-state B and therefore has the belief in question, though this belief is by no means justified. For example, we can imagine that a brain-surgeon operating on S artificially induces brain-state B. This results . . . in S's suddenly believing . . . that he is in brain-state B, *without any relevant antecedent beliefs* [my emphasis]. We would hardly say, in such a case, that S's belief that he is in brain-state B is justified.[4]

Consider another example. Suppose some filmmakers have made a film that has a happy ending although things look very bad for the protagonists most of the way through. These same filmmakers had earlier put out a tragic film that had greatly upset many viewers. They want viewers of the new film not to suffer undue anxiety and so they introduce into the film the subliminal message, "Don't worry! Everything turns out all right." That is, this message appears on the screen at frequent intervals but for such a short period each time that it can be perceived only subliminally: the viewers see it but do not know they are seeing it. Their seeing it causes them to have the belief that things will turn out all right, without their knowing how they are caused to have it. It is clear that, in these circumstances, this belief is not justified. Yet the process that produced it may be extremely reliable.

Surprisingly, none of Goldman's refinements on his reliabilist condition for justified belief (in "What Is Justified Belief?") rules out these counterexamples to its sufficiency. The reliabilist might hope that a plausible account of what makes a kind of process relevant, if and when such an account is achieved, will rule that the reliable processes in these examples are not of relevant kinds. But it is hard to see how any non–ad-hoc account could do this without also ruling out kinds that should be ruled in. It would not do, for example, to say that the reliable belief-producing process must be some sort of inference from other beliefs, since there are justified beliefs that are not arrived at by inference. There is, then, reason to suspect that the reliabilist condition cannot be made both plausible and sufficient for justified belief.

As far as being *necessary* is concerned, the reliabilist condition fails no matter how relevance of the kind of process is defined. Consider, for instance, the possibility of a world run by a Cartesian demon who causes its other inhabitants to have sets of perceptual and personal-memory impressions that, though as rich and coherent as yours and mine, are all illusory. The perceptual beliefs and personal-memory beliefs that these hapless subjects are led to have are as justified as any of our current perceptual or memory beliefs. Yet the sort of process by which they are caused has no tendency to cause true beliefs. (It is the case even in this demon-world, however, that the processes producing perceptual and personal-memory beliefs *seem* reliable to the inhabitants of that world, as gauged by the purported beliefs and justified inferences therefrom. The principles of belief-justification should be such that in any possible world the beliefs they justify support the thesis that following the principles generally leads to true beliefs—even in possible worlds where that thesis is false.)

Goldman does not appear to consider just this sort of counterexample but in another connection he makes a move that may seem to help here. He says that the reliability of a kind of belief-producing process is to be gauged in the actual world: if the perceptual and memory processes that cause beliefs in the demon-world are reliable in *our* world then the beliefs they produce in the demon-world are justified even though those same processes are not reliable in that world. Well, let us allow reliabilism to make this ruling in its account of justification: we should assess reliability, and hence justifiedness, by actual-world standards even when considering nonactual worlds. But now, what about the inhabitants of nonactual worlds? How should *they* assess justifiedness of beliefs? By the same lights, their standards cannot be those of any world but their own. If ours must be actual-world standards then theirs must be their-world standards. Yet it seems quite clear that the inhabitants of the demon-world should regard their perceptual and memory beliefs as justified—just as much so as we should—even though they are not produced by processes that are reliable in their world. If *our* world is run by a Cartesian demon, we are still justified in our present perceptual and memory beliefs (or the coherent majority of them, at any rate).

RELIABILISM AS A NONJUSTIFICATIONIST ACCOUNT OF KNOWLEDGE

Here the suggestion is that for a true belief to be knowledge it is not required that the subject have justification for the belief. It is necessary only that the belief be produced by a sufficiently reliable process. I shall not argue directly for my contrary view, that no *un*justified belief can be knowledge however reliable the process by which it was produced. Rather I will rebut the various arguments I know of for the reliabilist position and against the requirement of justification.

It is difficult to find cases in the real world in which a person lacks justification for a belief that has been produced by a reliable process (Why is this?), but it is not hard to imagine them. We described two such cases in the preceding section and here is another. Suppose that *S*, residing in Finland, is frequently caused to have accurate beliefs as to the current temperature in degrees Celsius in Sydney, Australia. But *S* herself does not know how this happens: she just suddenly finds herself with the conviction, for example, that it is now plus five degrees Celsius in Sydney. She knows nothing of the process by which these beliefs are produced and can offer no reasons for holding them, no evidence in favor of them. But, we may suppose, the process actually producing these beliefs is quite reliable. (It is unimportant exactly what this process is, but we might imagine some sort of electronic link between a thermometer in Sydney and *S*'s brain.) My intuition is that, when *S* is caused in this way to have a true belief that the temperature in Sydney is +5° C, *S* does *not know* this if she herself has no good reason for believing it. The reliabilist position says to the contrary that, since *S*'s belief is produced by a process that can be counted on always to produce true beliefs, *S* does know what the temperature is in Sydney.

The reliabilist might be tempted to try to get us to see *S*'s belief as a case of knowledge by suggesting that the case is analogous to ordinary perceptual knowledge of the proximate environment. If we allow that I know that there is a light before me when I am caused via my organs of sight to believe that there is a light before me then, the reliabilist might say, why not allow that *S* knows in an analogous way that the temperature in Sydney is +5° C when *S* is caused, via the Sydney-temperature-detecting-apparatus attached to her brain, to have that belief? Why not see her as having a special sort of perceptual or quasiperceptual knowledge?

Well, in perceptual knowledge—properly so called—there are facts directly accessible to the knower that *justify* the perceptual belief (without entailing its truth or that it was produced by a reliable process): facts about *S*'s sense experience and how the perceptual belief it prompts coheres with those prompted by the rest of *S*'s current and remembered sense experience. (The justification need not be by *inference* from these facts.) *S*'s belief about the temperature in Sydney would need to be made similar in this respect in order to be a candidate for quasiperceptual knowledge. But then, even if it could thereby be made a successful candidate, it would no longer support the reliabilist position now under consideration. For then *S*'s true belief is a candidate for knowledge, not merely because of its being reliably produced, but also because of the directly accessible facts constituting *S*'s quasiperceptual justification for the belief.[5]

An argument that does try to support the position that *S*'s reliably produced beliefs are knowledge even if they lack justification (whether quasiperceptual or other) is the following. Even if *S* does not know that her beliefs have been reliably produced, someone else who does know this can rely on *S*'s beliefs as a guide to the facts about the current temperature in Sydney: she can use *S*'s beliefs as detectors of those facts. *S*'s beliefs convey information to her and that is enough to make those beliefs knowledge. If a person's beliefs reliably convey information, in the way that a properly functioning thermometer conveys information, if they are capable of giving us knowledge, then they should be counted as knowledge.

I cannot see this. I cannot see how the fact that a person's beliefs enable others to have knowledge, through being reliable indicators of something, can make those beliefs themselves knowledge. All sort of things other than true beliefs can be reliable indicators and therefore bases or enablers of knowledge; and being a basis or enabler of knowledge must be distinguished from being knowledge, in true beliefs as in all other things. A certain category of a person's sheer *guesses,* or a certain category of her *false* beliefs, might be reliable indicators of a certain category of facts, but those guesses, or false beliefs, would not *thereby* be knowledge. I do not see why true beliefs should be any different in this respect.

Another argument I have encountered[6] points to the beliefs of animals and very young children, many of which count as knowledge even though none of them is either justified or unjustified (because animals and very young children lack the very notion of justification). If justification is irrelevant to distinguishing *their* true beliefs that are knowledge from those that are not, then, so the argument goes, it is generally irrelevant (and something else is needed, viz., being produced by a reliable process). But this does not follow. It must be admitted that animals and children do counter the claim that *no* belief is knowledge unless it is *justified.* But they do not counter the claim I subscribed to above, that no *un*justified belief can be knowledge, nor the claim that the concept of knowledge does require justification in its primary application, namely to those of us who do have the notion of a belief's being justified or not. In the natural extension of the concept to others who have beliefs this requirement must of course be dropped.

William Alston gives an example that he claims shows the possibility of knowledge without justification.[7] *S* has "friends" who

> convince him that for about half the time his sense experience is a radically unreliable guide to his current situation, and that he cannot tell when this is the case. They produce very impressive evidence. The totality of the evidence available to *S* strongly supports their story. *S* . . . justifiably believes that his senses are not to be trusted.

But there comes an occasion when *S*

> is about to cross a street and seems to see a truck coming down the street. In fact his perceptual belief-forming apparatus is working normally and a truck *is* coming down the street. Forgetting his skepticism for a moment he waits for the truck to pass before venturing into the street. He acquired a momentary perceptual belief that a truck was coming down the street . . . it seems clear that he did acquire knowledge . . . given the fact that his senses were functioning in a perfectly reliable and normal fashion, and given the fact that he thereby felt certain that a truck was coming down the street . . . , is it not clear that *S learned* (*ascertained, found out*) that a truck was coming, that he was *cognizant* of the truck, that he received *information* about the state of affairs in the street?

Perhaps there is a sense in which *S* received the information that a truck was coming down the street (roughly the same sense in which a video-recorder might receive that information), but it seems clear to me that *S* did *not* learn, ascertain, find out, or come to *know* that truth. And this is because *S* did lack adequate justification for believing it. Suppose we make the example clearer in this respect. Suppose that the story *S*'s "friends" tell him is true and that *S* even has memories of many similar sense-experiences that his later experience gave him reason to think were illusory (or at least to mistrust). Now it is quite clear that *S*'s total evidence does not make it likely that his visual experience of the truck is veridical, and it is quite clear to me that *S* therefore does not *know* that it is veridical or that he sees a truck bearing down on him.

Of course, if *S could not help* believing it then he cannot be reproached for doing so and is, in a sense, justified in doing so, though not *rationally* justified. And, whether or not *S* could help believing it, he was rationally justified in not taking any chances, in *acting* as if there were a truck bearing down on him. It may be easy here to fail to distinguish the truth that *S* is justified in the belief because he could not help it or is rationally justified in acting as if it were true from the falsehood that *S knows* what he believes. Consider an example in which such distracting truths are not present. Suppose that what *S* saw was something whose existence had no relevance for *S*'s action (as far as *S* had any reason to believe)—say, a large blinking blue light way down the street—and suppose the sight of this neither justified nor compelled *S*'s belief in its existence (supposing *S* had the same reasons as before for not trusting the general reliability of his senses) but *S* carelessly believed in it anyway. Does *S know* that he sees the blinking light?

How Voluntary Is Belief?

The final argument I will discuss also tries to bolster the reliabilist position we are considering by undermining that of the justificationist. It seeks to discredit the very notion of justification of belief. The argument fastens on the fact that the notion of a belief's being justified or not requires a *voluntaristic* conception of belief and it contends that this conception is inappropriate.[8]

Being justified in believing something is possible only if it is also possible for one to be unjustified in believing something. To be *un*justified in believing something means that one *ought* not to believe it. And this can be true only if one *can* refrain from believing it, only if one has a choice between believing and not believing and makes the wrong choice. But, this argument claims, we never do have any such direct voluntary control over whether or not we believe something. It is conceptually impossible. Believing is just not the sort of thing that involves the will in the direct way that action does. One cannot just decide to believe or not to believe something and forthwith do so, in the way that one can just decide to act or not to act and forthwith do so. Thus, the argument concludes, the notion of a belief's being justified or unjustified is confused and illegitimate, implying that belief is more voluntary than it could conceivably be. Justification should be replaced in the analysis of knowledge with a reliability condition.

It seems to me that, on the contrary, belief is as voluntary as the notion of its being justified or unjustified requires. All that is needed is that direct voluntary control of one's belief should be possible, at least sometimes. If that is so, then we can interpret an ascription of unjustifiedness to a belief that the subject cannot help having as saying that, if the subject were able to help it, she ought not to hold the belief. And we do seem to think that cases of direct voluntary control of belief do actually occur. For we do sometimes reproach people for believing as they do and act as if we think that they should, and could, just stop doing so, and we swallow the voluntaristic implications with equanimity.

Of course we must recognize that many beliefs we have we could not just stop having forthwith and many we do not have we could not just adopt forthwith. I could not, for instance, just for the fun of it simply give up forthwith my belief that the earth has existed for many years past, or that I am married and a father, or that there is a chair in the room where I now sit. I could not simply adopt forthwith a belief in the contradictory of one of these propositions, or a belief that it is at this moment raining (not raining) in Sydney, or that there are (are not) at least thirty-five planets in our galaxy that have life on them. I cannot seriously raise the question of whether or not to do one of these things.

But just the same is true concerning many *intentions* for future action I have and many others I lack. I could not simply give up forthwith my intention to eat tomorrow or to teach my courses next semester or to have clothes on whenever I appear in public. I could not simply adopt forthwith an intention with content contradictory to one of these, or the intention to jump off a tall building tomorrow or to scream loudly the next time I am in a department meeting. And no one (I hope) is going to claim that *intending* future action is not a voluntary matter evaluatable as justified or unjustified.

And no one should have trouble in recognizing that sometimes one does have a choice as to whether or not forthwith to adopt (or give up) a certain intention about one's future action. No one will see any absurdity in supposing that each of the following three alternatives is now in my power to embrace forthwith: decide to take the car to the office this afternoon, decide to walk to the office this afternoon, make no decision either way for the time being. But equally there is no absurdity in supposing that each of the following alternatives is now in my power to embrace forthwith: believe what Sally's confident memory says is the population of Syracuse, believe that her memory must be mistaken (for I seem to remember a much higher figure), believe nothing either way on the matter for the time being. In fact I frequently confront situations where conflicting evidence, or my own uncertain memory, make both my believing something and my not believing it quite *live* options for me and where which I do certainly *seems* to me to be a matter of my simply *deciding* (perhaps after some deliberation) which to do.

I have heard it argued that belief is necessarily not a voluntary matter on the ground that it is impossible to believe something for the sake of an extrinsic reward. If someone were to convince you that he would give you a million dollars if only you start believing within the next ten minutes, and without any investigation, that exactly eight females were born in Tompkins County Hospital in the last 100 hours, you could not do it. But, the argument goes, it should be possible for you to do this if belief could be a voluntary sort of thing.

There are two serious problems with this argument. In the first place, it is far from clear that it is *always* impossible to believe something for the sake of an extrinsic reward. Suppose that, as I am deliberating whether to trust Sally's memory or mine or neither regarding the population of Syracuse, she offers to bring me breakfast in bed if I decide to trust her memory. (She offers this out of an unselfish desire that I not miss out on an opportunity to believe a truth.) Might that not help me to decide to believe the figure she remembers? To be sure, if I did not already have a fairly strong evidential reason to believe it—her sincere testimony as to what she clearly remembers—if she had admittedly just guessed at the figure, then this sort of incentive (even one much greater) could not lead me to believe it. I do not think I could ever believe any such thing without some nonnegligible evidential reason for doing so, and perhaps this is true of most people, but this may, for all I know, be only a contingent fact about us. I have yet to see a convincing argument that it is conceptually impossible that someone should manage to believe such a thing without having any evidence for it for the sake of an extrinsic reward. I think I can imagine observations that would be good evidence that such a thing had happened, at least as far as observations of another person can ever furnish good evidence as to what they believe. It would be amazingly irrational, but, as we all know, people do some amazingly irrational things.[9]

But even if it is a conceptual necessity that we can believe something only when we have evidential reason to do so, this is quite compatible with my deciding to believe for the sake of an extrinsic reward. It means only that a situation in which my decision to believe is motivated in that way must be prepared by my already having some evidential reason which has not yet led me to believe.

Moreover, even if it were true that an extrinsic reward could never be even part of one's motive for believing something, it would not follow that one can never be in a position where one can simply choose which of two or more incompatible alternative options to adopt in one's belief. Compare the following two bits of inner monologue:

> Should I give up my intention to refuse all invitations for the rest of the week, in light of how much I have accomplished in the last two days?

> Should I give up my belief that Rex was lying, in light of Lois's corroboration of his testimony?

In both cases I am deliberating a *decision* as to what my attitude will be toward a certain proposition and I expect my decision to determine my attitude equally directly in both cases.

It does seem clear that no option—whether it is for acting or intending or believing—can be *live* for me unless I have some reason to choose it. And certain sorts of things that can be reasons for adopting the attitude of believing cannot be reasons for adopting the attitude of intending, and vice versa. Possessing evidence that p is reason to believe that p but not reason to intend that p. Possessing evidence that if I act in such-and-such a way then certain results I desire will come about is reason to intend that I so act but not reason to believe that I will so act—except insofar as it is reason for intending it and intending it implies believing it: it is not reason for believing it independently of being reason for intending it. But this difference should not obscure from us the fundamental similarity in their relation to the will that there is between believing and intending: that an unchosen option is live for me only if I have some reason to choose it goes for intending as well as for believing; that conflicting options can all be live for me if I have reason to choose each of them and that when this happens (barring rather special circumstances) I can simply choose which option to adopt and forthwith do so: this goes for believing as well as for intending.

I conclude that belief is as voluntary as it needs to be for the concept of justification to apply (if intention is) and that there is no basis in the consideration of voluntariness for the suggestion that in the analysis of knowledge the notion of a belief's being justified should give way to the notion of its being produced by a reliable process.[10]

NOTES

1. The third position is probably a successful refuge. A reliability account of the fourth condition seems to me as likely to work as any, although I think that an account in terms of a certain notion of undefeated justification is equally adequate. But that is a topic for another paper.

2. In the new second disjunct, something should be said about what it is for the conditions to be present and capable of causing the belief (without actually doing so). Alvin Goldman, in his paper "The Internalist Conception of Justification," in French, Uehling, and Wettstein, eds., *Studies in Epistemology,* Midwest Studies in Philosophy, Vol. 5 (Minneapolis: University of Minnesota Press, 1980), pp. 27–51 (which is the best-developed reliabilist account of justification I know of), allows that the conditions by which a person is justified in changing his or her beliefs should be immediately accessible to the person, a point that seems clearly right to me. He suggests further, however, (and here is the reliabilism) that what makes a complete set of justification principles (which dictate what sorts of immediately accessible facts justify what sorts of beliefs) a *correct* complete set is just the fact that if one always followed those principles in forming one's beliefs then (given the way the world is) one's beliefs would be mostly correct. He argues that there is no other way that the principles of justification can be validated. For an argument in a contrary vein, that some complete set of principles of justification must be such that one needs only to understand them in order to be justified in accepting them (that is, they must be evident a priori), see my "The Justification of Belief: A Primer," in Ginet and Shoemaker eds., *Knowledge and Mind* (Oxford University Press, 1983), p. 36.

3. In Pappas, ed., *Justification and Knowledge* (Dordrecht, Netherlands: D. Reidel Publishing Co., 1979), pp. 1–24.

4. Ibid.

5. I doubt that anything we should count as a perceptual or quasiperceptual justification could be built into the example, given the content of S's belief, which refers to a location specified by proper name rather than in terms of S's point of view and to the Centigrade measure of temperature. A better example of a possible but nonactual kind of perceptual or quasiperceptual justification would be the following: S

is caused by varying intensities of magnetic field around her to have varying intensities of a special sort of sensation and is prompted by that sensation to believe that she feels varying intensities of some sort of force impinging on her. If the content of her sensation-prompted beliefs were, however, that there were variously intense fields of *magnetic* force occurring somewhere in the basement of Goldwin Smith Hall, then her justification for them could not be purely perceptual, any more than my justification for believing that the white grains I see before me are salt obtained from beneath Cayuga Lake can be purely perceptual.

6. In, for example, William Alston's "What's Wrong with Immediate Knowledge?" *Synthese* 55 (April 1983): 73–96.

7. William Alston, "Justification and Knowledge," presented at a Special Session on Knowledge and Justification at the World Congress of Philosophy, Montréal, August 1983.

8. This argument, too, is suggested in Alston, "What's Wrong with Immediate Knowledge?"

9. I would not deny that the very idea of someone's even *offering* a reward for just believing something is strikingly odd, in a way that offering a reward for *acting as if* one believed it would not be so odd. But consider the idea of someone's offering a reward for just *intending* a certain future action (not caring whether or not one carries out the intention when the time comes). That too would be very odd. The oddity in either case can be explained, I think, by two considerations. In the first place, it would be unusual that, and hard to see why, someone would desire one to intend or believe in a particular way without this desire deriving from a desire as to how one should act (a desire whose object at least includes that one should act in the way that the belief and intention would normally lead to). And if it is one's action that is really wanted (or part of what is really wanted), then it would be more sensible to attach the reward to the action (or the whole of which it is part), for then the chances of getting what is really wanted could not be lessened and would most likely be increased. In the second place, there is the difficulty of confirming that one has met the conditions for the reward by really believing or intending as required, rather than merely pretending to do so. The fact that one's motive is the reward makes confirming one's true propositional attitude more difficult than it would ordinarily be, because one might reasonably think that one could gain the reward by acting as if one believed or intended in the required way without actually troubling to believe or intend.

10. An earlier version of this paper was read at a session of the World Congress of Philosophy in Montréal in August 1983. The revision has benefitted from comments made in the discussion on that occasion.

22

What's Wrong with Reliabilism?

Richard Foley

I

An increasing number of epistemologists claim that having beliefs which are reliable is a prerequisite of having epistemically rational beliefs. Alvin Goldman, for instance, defends a view he calls "historical reliabilism." According to Goldman, a person S rationally believes a proposition p only if his belief is caused by a reliable cognitive process. Goldman adds that a proposition p is epistemically rational for S, whether or not it is believed by him, only if there is available to S a reliable cognitive process which if used would result in S's believing p.[1] Likewise, Marshall Swain, Ernest Sosa, and William Alston all claim that reliability is a prerequisite of epistemic rationality. Swain claims that S rationally believes p only if he has reasons for p which are reliable indicators that p is true.[2] Sosa says S rationally believes p only if the belief is the product of an intellectual virtue, where intellectual virtues are stable dispositions to acquire truths.[3] And, Alston says that S rationally believes p only if the belief is acquired or held in such a way that beliefs held in that way are reliable, i.e., mostly true.[4]

Each of these philosophers is suggesting that there is some sort of logical, or conceptual, tie between epistemic rationality and truth. The exact nature of this tie depends on what it means for a cognitive process, or a reason, or an intellectual virtue, to be reliable. But, at least for the moment, let us set aside this question. I will return to it shortly. In particular, let us simply assume that each of the above positions sug-

From *The Monist* 68, no. 2 (April 1985): 188–202. ©1985 The Monist, LaSalle, IL 61301. Reprinted by permission of the publisher.

gests (even if each doesn't strictly imply) the thesis that if one gathered into a set all the propositions it is epistemically rational for a person *S* to believe it would be impossible for the set to contain more falsehoods than truths. Or short of this, let us assume that each suggests the thesis that if one gathered into a set all the propositions which *both are epistemically rational for* S *and are believed by him,* it would be impossible for the set to contain more falsehoods than truths.

Since this amounts to saying that what a person rationally believes, or what it is rational for him to believe, must be a reliable indicator of what is true, any position which implies such a thesis can be regarded as a version of reliabilism.

This is somewhat broader than the usual use of the term "reliabilism." With respect to accounts of rational belief (I will discuss reliabilist accounts of knowledge later), the term often is reserved for accounts which require that a belief be *caused,* or *causally sustained,* by a reliable cognitive process. But, for purposes here I want to distinguish between the causal component of such accounts and the reliability component. The causal component requires a belief to have an appropriate causal ancestry in order to be rational. The reliability component requires a belief to have an appropriate relation to truth in order to be rational; in particular, on the present interpretation of reliability, it requires that more of a person's rational beliefs be true than false.

The advantage of isolating these components is that it makes obvious the possibility of endorsing a reliability requirement for rationality without endorsing a causal requirement, and vice-versa. It is possible, for example, to endorse noncausal versions of reliabilism. Consider a foundationalist position which implies that *S* rationally believes *p* only if either his belief *p* is incorrigible for him or propositions which are incorrigibly believed by him support *p* in a way which guarantees that most propositions so supported are true. A position of this sort is plausibly regarded as a reliabilist position, since it implies that a person's rational beliefs must be mostly true. It implies, in other words, that the set of such beliefs is a reliable indicator of what is true. Yet, it is not a causal position. It does not insist that *S*'s belief *p* be caused or causally sustained in an appropriate way in order to be rational.[5]

So, in my broad sense of "reliabilism" both causal and noncausal accounts of rational belief can be versions of reliabilism. Indeed in my broad sense, Hume and Descartes might be plausibly interpreted as reliabilists. My use of "reliabilism" is weak in one other way. It requires only that there be a very loose connection between epistemic rationality and truth. In order for an account to be a version of reliabilism, it need not guarantee that a huge percentage of the propositions a person *S* rationally believes are true. It need only guarantee that one more such proposition is true than is false.

Unfortunately, even when reliabilism is understood in this very weak way, it is too strong; it is possible for more propositions which *S* rationally believes to be false than true. Consider how this might be so. Consider a world in which *S* believes, seems to remember, experiences, etc., just what he in this world believes, seems to remember, reasonable?

experiences, etc., but in which his beliefs are often false. Suppose further that in this other world the confidence with which he believes, and the clarity with which he seems to remember, and the intensity with which he experiences is identical with the actual world. Suppose even that what he would believe on reflection (about, e.g., what arguments are likely to be truth preserving) is identical with what he would believe on reflection in this world. So, if *S* somehow were to be switched instantaneously from his actual situation to the corresponding situation in this other world, he would not distinguish any difference, regardless of how hard he tried. To use the familiar example, suppose that a demon insures that this is the case. Call such a demon world "*w*" and then consider this question: Could some of the propositions which a person *S* believes in *w* be epistemically rational for him? For example, could some of the propositions which *S* perceptually believes be epistemically rational? The answer is yes. If we are willing to grant that in our world some of the propositions *S* perceptually believes are epistemically rational, then these same propositions would be epistemically rational for *S* in *w* as well. After all, world *w* by hypothesis is one which from *S*'s viewpoint is indistinguishable from this world. So, if given *S*'s situation in this world his perceptual belief *p* is rational, his belief *p* would be rational in *w* as well.

In one sense this is not a particularly surprising result, but in another sense it can seem somewhat surprising. Notice that the possibility of there being such a world *w* follows from the fact that our being in the epistemic situation we are is compatible with our world being *w*. This in no way shows that it is not epistemically rational for us to believe what we do. But, and this is what might seem somewhat surprising, if the mere possibility of our world being a demon world is not sufficient to defeat the epistemic rationality of our believing what we do, then neither should the actuality. Even if, contrary to what we believe, our world is world *w*, it still can be epistemically rational for us to believe many of the propositions we do, since the epistemic situation in world *w* is indistinguishable from the epistemic situation in a world which has the characteristics we take our world to have.

The point here is a simple one. In effect, I am asking you: aren't some of the propositions you believe epistemically rational for you to believe? And wouldn't whatever it is that makes those propositions epistemically rational for you also be present in a world where these propositions are regularly false, but where a demon hid this from you by making the world from your viewpoint indistinguishable from this world (so that what you believed, and what you would believe on reflection, and what you seemed to remember, and what you experienced were identical to this world)?

I think that the answer to each of these questions is yes and I think you do too. But, a yes answer to these questions suggests that the real lesson illustrated by the possibility of demon worlds is not a skeptical lesson as is sometimes thought, but rather an antireliabilist lesson. It suggests, in other words, that the demon by his deceits may cause us to have false beliefs, but he does not thereby automatically cause us to be irrational. And so, the possibility of such demon worlds illustrates that it is possible for more of what we rationally believe to be false than to be true, and it also illustrates that it is possible for more of what it is epistemically rational for us to believe (regardless of what we do in fact believe) to be false than to be true. Correspondingly, it illustrates that any version of reliabilism which implies that these are not genuine possibilities ought to be rejected.

Indeed, in one sense the claim that it is possible for more of what we rationally believe to be false than to be true is not even very controversial. It is but an extension of the claim that it is possible to rationally believe a falsehood. For if we admit that there are situations in which the conditions making a proposition epistemically rational are present but the conditions making it true are not, we will be hard-pressed to avoid the conclusion that it is possible for this to happen frequently. To put the matter metaphorically, if we allow the possibility of a crack developing between epistemic rationality and truth, such that some of what is epistemically rational can be false, we will be hard-pressed to avoid at least the possibility of a chasm developing, such that more of what is epistemically rational can be false than true. This is the lesson of demon examples, brain-in-the-vat examples, etc.

Moreover, examples of this sort also can be used to illustrate the implausibility of variations of what I have defined as reliabilism. Consider a version of reliabilism which implies not that more of S's current rational beliefs must be true than false but rather that more of S's *current and past* rational beliefs must be true than false. Perhaps, for example, one might try arguing for such a version of reliabilism with the help of a causal thesis which implies that S's belief p is rational only if it is the product of a reliable cognitive process, where a reliable cognitive process is one which *is and has* produced mostly true beliefs for S.[6]

It is not difficult to extend the demon example in order to illustrate the inadequacy of this version of reliabilism. Simply imagine a world which both *is and has been* indistinguishable from the actual world given S's viewpoint. Then, imagine that in this world a demon arranges things so that what S believes and has believed is regularly false. In particular, imagine that more of the propositions which he rationally believes in the actual world are false than are true in this demon world. Despite this, what he rationally believes in the actual world he also rationally believes in the demon world, since the two worlds from his viewpoint are indistinguishable in every way.

Consider other variations of reliabilism. Suppose it is claimed that more of S's rational beliefs have to be true than false *in the long run*, or suppose it is claimed that the total set of rational beliefs in the long run—S's as well as everyone else's rational beliefs—must contain more truths than falsehoods. Suppose, for instance, one tried defending this kind of reliabilism with the help of a causal thesis which implies that a person S's belief p is rational only if it is produced by a cognitive process which in the long run will produce more true beliefs than false beliefs.[7]

To illustrate the inadequacy of this version of reliabilism, imagine a world which is and has been from our viewpoint indistinguishable from our world. Imagine even that in this second world the percentage of truths which we have believed up until now or are now believing is about the same as in this world. But then, imagine that in the second world there is a demon who unbeknownst to us insures that our cognitive processes in the long run give rise to more false beliefs than true beliefs.

Or consider counterfactual versions of reliabilism, which imply that more of the rational beliefs S *would have* in appropriate counterfactual situations must be true than false if S's actual belief p is to be rational. One might try to defend this version with the help of the causal thesis which implies that S's belief p is rational only if it is the product of a cognitive process which in close counterfactual situations would produce mostly true beliefs for S.

For this kind of reliabilism, again imagine a world which from S's viewpoint is indistinguishable from the actual world. Only now imagine that in this world there is an antireliabilist demon—one who does not interfere with S but who was and is prepared to do so were things to be even a little different than they in fact are.

The problem with all these versions of reliabilism is essentially the same. They all assume that in the demon worlds described it would be impossible for us to have rational beliefs. The assumption, in other words, is that the deceiving activities of the demon *no matter how cleverly* they are carried out—even if we have no indication that we are (or have been or will be, or would be) so deceived—preclude even the *possibility* of our beliefs being epistemically rational. So, the mere fact that we do have, or have had, or will have, or would have false beliefs, implies that we cannot be epistemically rational.

But, to make such an assumption is counterintuitive. In everyday situations we do not regard deception as precluding rationality. Likewise, we do not regard the fact that we have been deceived, or will be deceived, or would be deceived, as precluding rationality. Suppose I plan an elaborate practical joke on you in order to get you to believe that I have left town. I tell you I am leaving town, I leave my car with you, I have someone send you a postcard signed by me, etc. My deceits may get you to believe the false proposition that I have left town, but from this it does not follow that the proposition is not rational for you to believe. And one way to emphasize this point is to imagine (as I have done with the demon cases) a situation in which you have not been deceived and which in addition from your viewpoint is indistinguishable from the situation in which you have been deceived. In other words, imagine an ordinary situation. If in this ordinary situation it is possible for you to rationally believe that I have left town, it also is possible for you to rationally believe this in the situation in which I have deceived you. Everyone who allows rational beliefs to be false should agree to this. But then, it is natural to wonder why, if relatively modest deceits of this sort need not preclude the possibility of your having rational beliefs, more elaborate deceits of the sort a demon engages in should preclude you from having rational beliefs?

The intuitive answer is that they should not. The demon by his deceits may get you to have mostly false beliefs but this need not indicate that these beliefs also are irrational. This answer, moreover, illustrates something about the way we think of rationality. Namely, we think that what it is rational for a person to believe is a function of what it is appropriate for him to believe given his perspective. More exactly, it is a function of what it is appropriate for him to believe given his perspective *and* insofar as his goal is to believe truths and not to believe falsehoods.[8]

Precisely what makes reliabilist accounts of rational belief unacceptable is that they underemphasize this perspectival element. They imply that it is impossible for our beliefs to be rational if they are not in an appropriate sense reliable indicators of truths. And they imply that this is so regardless of what our perspective might be—even if, for example, it is indistinguishable from current perspective.

Can reliabilist accounts of rational belief be made acceptable by including some such perspectival element in them? Alvin Goldman, for one, hints that he might be willing to include such an element in his account. Goldman's willingness to consider such an element is motivated by his recognizing that it is possible for there to be a benevolent being who, although lazy until now, will shortly start arranging things so that our wishes come true. If there were such a benevolent demon, wishful thinking would be a reliable cognitive process in the long run, and then given Goldman's account it might seem as if the beliefs produced by such wishful thinking would be rational. Goldman, however, rejects this consequence, saying that what matters "is what we *believe* about wishful thinking, not what is true (in the long run) about wishful thinking."[9] What matters if a belief is to be rational, Goldman seems to be suggesting, is not that the belief be produced by a process which in fact is reliable in the long run; what matters is that it be produced by a process which *we take to be reliable* in the long run.

If this suggestion is taken seriously,[10] however, it represents not a way of amending reliabilism but rather a way of abandoning it. Any account of rational belief which incorporates such a suggestion will not be an account which requires that the set of rational beliefs be reliable indicators of what is true. It only will require that we believe this of them.

But if so, so be it; reliabilist accounts of rational belief ought to be abandoned.[11] Reliability is not in any plausible sense a necessary condition of epistemic rationality. In order for S's belief p to be rational, it neither is necessary for most rational beliefs of all people everywhere to be true, nor for most of S's current rational beliefs to be true, nor for most of S's rational beliefs over his lifetime to be true, nor for most of the rational beliefs S would have in close counterfactual situations to be true.

II

I would guess that for many philosophers (but certainly not all) the remarks I have been making about the relationship between rationality and reliability will not seem surprising. The remarks might even strike them as obvious albeit unimportant. For, they would claim that the epistemic significance of reliability has to do not with beliefs which are merely rational but rather with beliefs which are instances of knowledge. So, they would argue that even if reliability is not a prerequisite of rationality, it is a prerequisite of knowledge. Thus, Goldman, Sosa, Alston, Swain, and others with reliabilist sympathies might be willing to agree with me that there is a sense of rationality for which reliability is not a prerequisite. But, they would go on to insist either that rationality is not a prerequisite of knowledge (i.e., it is possible to know p without rationally believing it) or that the kind of rational belief needed for knowledge is more restrictive than the kind with which I have been concerned. Both of these options leave room for the claim that reliability is a prerequisite of knowledge even if it is not a prerequisite of mere rational belief (or of a certain kind of rational belief).

Even so, reliabilist theses about knowledge in the end fare no better than reliabilist theses about rational belief. More exactly, significant, or nontrivial, reliabilist theses about knowledge fare no better. A reliabilist thesis is not significant if it is a thesis which almost any kind of account of knowledge would imply. Thus, suppose it is claimed that reliability is a prerequisite of knowledge in the following sense: Most beliefs which are instances of knowledge have to be true. This thesis about knowledge is true but insignificant; any account of knowledge which requires a belief to be true if it is to be an instance of knowledge implies it.

The problem, then, is to find a *true and significant* reliabilist account of knowledge. I claim it cannot be done; there is no such reliabilist account of knowledge.

To see this, consider how one might try to formulate a reliabilist account of knowledge. The most common approach is by describing a requirement upon knowledge which has both a causal aspect and a reliabilist aspect. In particular, the most common approach is to insist that if S's belief is to be an instance of knowledge, it must be the product of a reliable cognitive process.[12] But as is the case with reliabilist accounts of rational belief, it also is possible to describe noncausal, reliabilist accounts of knowledge. One might insist, for example, that S knows p only if his belief p is supported by evidence to such a degree that most of his beliefs supported to this degree are true. For convenience, however, let us restrict discussion here to causal, reliabilist accounts, since they are the most common. (In any event, the remarks I make about causal accounts will apply *mutatis mutandis* to noncausal accounts as well.)[13]

Given this causal approach, then, the problem facing a proponent of a reliabilist account of knowledge is to explicate the notion of a reliable cognitive process in such a way that it is both true and significant that being the product of such a process is a necessary condition of a belief being an instance of knowledge.

So, suppose that a reliable cognitive process is understood to be one which produces more true beliefs than false beliefs. The claim, then, is that S's belief p is an instance of knowledge only if it is produced (or sustained) by a process which is reliable in this sense. But, the problem with this claim is that S can *know* that the kind of cognitive process (say, a perceptual one) which causes him to believe p generates mostly false beliefs in other people. Indeed, S might be a deceiver who is responsible for this. If so, then S's belief p is produced by a cognitive process which is unreliable. And yet, in this situation it is at least possible for S to know p. To claim otherwise is to claim that by perceptually deceiving other people S inevitably prevents himself from having perceptual knowledge. But, why should this be so?

Suppose, then, that a reliable cognitive process is one which is relativized to persons. Suppose it is understood to be one which *has produced* mostly true beliefs for person S. But then, it is possible for S to *know* that a demon has been deceiving him perceptually but no longer is. And if S does know this, he might very well now know p perceptually even though he also knows that the perceptual process which causes him to believe p is unreliable. The fact that a demon has deceived him perceptually need not make it impossible for him now to have perceptual knowledge. Or, suppose a reliable cognitive process is thought to be one which will in the long run produce mostly true beliefs for S. But, it is possible for S to know that although he is not now under the control of a deceiving demon, he shortly will be. And if he does know this, he might now perceptually know p even though he also knows that the process which causes him to believe p is unreliable in this sense. For, the fact that a demon will deceive him perceptually need not make it impossible for him now to have perceptual knowledge. Or, suppose a reliable cognitive process is one which would produce mostly true beliefs in appropriately close counterfactual situations. But then, S might *know* that there is an antireliabilist demon who is not now deceiving him but is (and was) prepared to do so had the situation been even a little different. And, knowing that there is such a demon who is poised to act but who does not is compatible with now knowing p. The fact that a demon is prepared to deceive him perceptually does not make it impossible for him to have perceptual knowledge.

The same general lesson even applies to a demon who is now deceiving S perceptually. But there is a wrinkle here, since it may be impossible for S to believe (and hence to know) that due to the actions of a deceiving demon more of his current perceptual beliefs are false than are true. This may be impossible because it may be impossible for S to believe a proposition p if he also genuinely believes that p is more likely to be false than true. But even if this is impossible, it nonetheless is possible for S to have adequate evidence for the claim that more of his current perceptual beliefs are false than are true (even if he does not believe it to be true) and yet for him to have perceptual knowledge p. Suppose, for example, he has adequate evidence for the truth that a demon is deceiving him with respect to most objects in his visual field but not those directly in front of him and within two feet of him. If proposition p concerns an object of this latter sort, S might very well know p even though he may have adequate reasons for believing the true proposition that the visual process which causes him to believe p is unreliable—i.e., even though more of S's current visual beliefs are false than true. The fact that a demon is deceiving him perceptually about objects not directly in front of him or not within two feet of him does not make it impossible for him to have perceptual knowledge about objects which are in front of him and within two feet of him.[14]

It may be tempting in this last case to insist that S's belief p *is* the product of a reliable cognitive process—namely, *a process as it operates on objects within two feet of him and directly in front of him.* In other words, it may be tempting to insist that this last case only illustrates that we must allow the notion of a reliable cognitive process to be narrowly specified. In the case here, for example, once we specify the process which causes S to believe p as a visual process as operating on objects directly in front of S and within two feet of him, it by hypothesis is true that his belief p is caused by a reliable process. Indeed, in the case here, perhaps the only beliefs produced by this narrowly specified process are the belief that p and beliefs in other propositions implied by p. And of course, by hypothesis all these propositions are true.

However, any attempt to save a reliabilist account of knowledge by this kind of maneuver is an attempt to save it by destroying it. For any reliabilist account which results from such a rescue maneuver will be an account which is insignificant. Indeed, it will be as insignificant as a reliabilist account which insists that most beliefs which are instances of knowledge must be true, and it will be insignificant for the same reason. Namely, *any* proponent of *any* kind of account of knowledge can endorse a reliabilism of this sort. Or, at least anyone who thinks knowledge requires true belief can endorse a reliabilism of this sort. After all, on any occasion where a person S has a true belief p, there will be *some* narrowly specified cognitive process which causes S to believe p and which in addition is reliable, if only because it is so narrowly specified that it produces only belief p and beliefs in propositions implied by p. So, insofar as a reliabilist resorts to such maneuvers to defend his account, his account will lose whatever distinctive character it was intended to have.

Reliabilist accounts of knowledge, then, face a dilemma. One horn of the dilemma is to allow the notion of a reliable cognitive process to be specified so narrowly that reliabilism is no longer an interesting thesis. It becomes true but trivial, since any true belief can be construed as being the product of a reliable cognitive process. The other horn is not to allow the notion of a reliable cognitive process to be so narrowly specified, in which case it becomes susceptible to demon counterexamples and the like. In other words, it becomes an interesting but false thesis.

III

I have not discussed every possible reliabilist thesis concerning rational belief and knowledge. But, I have discussed a number of representative theses, and neither they nor any other reliabilist thesis I can think of can avoid the difficulties raised for them by demon situations and the like. And so, I conclude that reliability is neither a necessary condition of rational belief (i.e., it is not necessary for more of a person's rational beliefs to be true than false) nor a necessary condition of knowledge (i.e., a belief in order to be an instance of knowledge need not be the product of a reliable cognitive process—provided "reliable" is used in a nontrivial way).

In order to avoid this conclusion, one might be tempted, I suppose, to claim that the counterexamples I have described are not really possible. In arguing against reliabilist theses of knowledge, I have imagined situations in which a person S *knows* that he has been deceived by a demon but no longer is, and situations in which S *knows* that he shortly will be deceived by a demon but is not now, and situations in which S *knows* that in close counterfactual situations he would be deceived by a demon even though he is not being deceived by the demon in the actual situation. Accordingly, in order to save reliabilism, one might try claiming that S cannot know such propositions.

But why not? If such propositions can be true, why might not S be in a position to know that they are true? What is it about knowledge, or about these situations, or about S which is supposed to preclude even the *possibility* of S's knowing such propositions? On the face of it, knowledge of such propositions would seem possible. And if it is possible, is it possible for S's belief p to be an instance of knowledge even though it is not the product of a reliable cognitive process.

But, perhaps the objection here is that it is not possible for such propositions even to be true, and thus *a fortiori* it is not possible for S to know them. In particular, perhaps the objection is that it is not possible for a demon to deceive us so systematically that much of what we believe is false. Several philosophers recently have at least suggested this; they have tried to defend the surprising thesis that it is not possible for most of our beliefs to be false. Both Donald Davidson and Hilary Putnam, for example, recently have defended accounts of belief which imply that this is not possible.[15] Their accounts imply that although it may be possible for there to be evil demons or for us to be brains-in-a-vat, it is not possible for us to be in the grip of an evil demon, or for us to be brains-in-a-vat, *and* for us to believe what we now believe about the external world (assuming that we neither *now* are in the clutches of such a demon nor *now* are in a vat). The reason Davidson claims this (and Putnam claims it for a closely related reason) is because he thinks that the object of a belief at least in a majority of cases is the cause of the belief. So, according to Davidson, if we are brains-in-a-vat hooked up to a machine, it is not ordinary objects in the external world (such as tables, chairs, etc.) which cause our mental states. Rather, it is the inner workings of the machine which cause us to be in the mental states we are. But then, says Davidson, most of our beliefs are about these inner workings of the machine and not about tables, chairs, etc. Moreover, most of these beliefs are true.

I am not inclined to think that an account of belief of this rough sort is very plausible, but for purposes here such qualms can be put aside. For, even if the account is plausible and even if as a result it is impossible for most of a person's beliefs to be false, this does not do the reliabilist any good. To the contrary, it makes reliabilism pointless. At the heart of reliabilist accounts of rational belief is the idea that one crucial difference between rational beliefs and other beliefs is that the former are more intimately related to truth. More of them must be true than false. And, a similar idea lies at the heart of reliabilist accounts of knowledge. Beliefs which are instances of knowledge must be reliably produced, so that most beliefs so produced are true; this supposedly is a crucial element in what distinguishes beliefs which are eligible to be instances of knowledge from those which are not. But if it is impossible for more of a person's beliefs to be false than true, all of this is beside the point. A person's beliefs regardless of what they are—whether or not any of them are instances of knowledge and whether or not any of them are rational—must be mostly true. So, contrary to what is suggested by reliabilist accounts of rational belief and knowledge, reliability is not a significant criterion which can be used to distinguish these epistemically valuable kinds of beliefs from other kinds of beliefs.

All this, however, is not to say that considerations of reliability are altogether unimportant epistemically. As I suggested earlier, epistemic rationality is best understood to be a function of what it is appropriate for a person to believe given his perspective and given the goal of his having true beliefs and not having false beliefs. So, the goal in terms of which epistemic rationality can be understood is the goal of having reliable beliefs—i.e., mostly true beliefs. But, to say that reliability is the goal in terms of which epistemic rationality is to be understood is not to say that achieving that goal is a prerequisite of being epistemically rational. If a person, given his situation, believes what it is appropriate for him to believe with respect to the goal of his having true beliefs and not having false beliefs, then his beliefs can be epistemically rational even if they are mostly false. This is the lesson of demon examples and the like.

Likewise, nothing I have said implies that reliability is not an important consideration in understanding knowledge. Indeed, I think that reliability can be a crucial part of a set of conditions *sufficient* for knowledge. Recall D. H. Lawrence's story of the boy who, when he rides his rocking horse, is able unfailingly to pick the winners at a local race track. It is plausible to think that such a boy *somehow* knows who the winners will be,[16] and it is plausible to suppose this even if we also suppose that the boy has not been told that his picks are always correct. In other words, it is plausible to suppose that the boy somehow knows who the winners will be even if he lacks adequate evidence for his picks. Two lessons are suggested by such cases. First, in order to have knowledge it is not necessary to have a rational belief as has been traditionally claimed. At the very least, this is not necessary in one important sense of rational belief—viz., one which makes rational belief a function of having adequate evidence. Second, having a true belief which is caused by a highly reliable cognitive process can be *sufficient* for knowledge. Or at least, it can be sufficient with the addition of a few other relatively minor conditions.[17] The mistake reliabilists tend to make is to try to draw a third lesson from such cases. Namely, they try to conclude that a necessary condition of a person S's knowing p is that his belief p be reliably produced.

NOTES

1. Alvin Goldman, "What Is Justified Belief?" in *Justification and Knowledge*, G. Pappas, ed. (Dordrecht, Netherlands: D. Reidel Publishing Co., 1979), pp. 1–23.

2. Marshall Swain, "Justification and the Basis of Belief," in *Justification and Knowledge*, pp. 25–49.

3. Ernest Sosa, "The Raft and the Pyramid," in French, Uehling, and Wettstein, eds., *Studies in Epistemology*, Midwest Studies in Philosophy, vol. 5 (Minneapolis: University of Minnesota Press, 1980), pp. 3–25.

4. William Alston, "Self-Warrant; A Neglected Form of Privileged Access," *American Philosophical Quarterly* 13 (1976): 257–72, especially p. 268.

5. I discuss causal, reliabilist accounts of knowledge in section 2. The arguments there also will apply to causal, reliabilist accounts of rational belief. See especially footnote 14.

6. Although this causal thesis does not strictly imply that more of S's current and past rational beliefs are true than are false (since it proposes only a necessary condition of rational belief), the causal thesis might plausibly be used to support this kind of reliabilism. Think of it this way: suppose we gather into a set all of S's current and past beliefs which are the products of a reliable cognitive process and then use the other necessary conditions of rational belief to create a subset, consisting of S's current and past *rational* beliefs. If we assume that in creating this subset we have not lessened the percentage of true beliefs, then the subset, like the original set, will contain more true beliefs than false beliefs. So, although the causal thesis does not imply this version of reliabilism, it can be thought of as being closely related to it—i.e., close enough that the inadequacy of this version of reliabilism will suggest, even if it does not imply, the inadequacy of the causal thesis. (The discussion in section 2 of causal accounts of knowledge will provide additional, and equally telling, reasons to reject *causal,* reliabilist theses about rational belief; see footnote 14.)

7. The causal thesis here supports this version of reliabilism in much the same way that the previous version of reliabilism is supported by the causal thesis mentioned there. See note 6. The remaining versions of reliabilism I discuss in this section can be supported in a corresponding way by corresponding causal theses.

8. This, of course, leaves open the question of what exactly makes it appropriate for a person S to believe a proposition given his perspective and given his goal of believing truths and not believing falsehoods.

9. Goldman, "What Is Justified Belief?" p. 18.

·10. It perhaps is best not to regard even Goldman himself as taking the problem here and his suggestion for how to handle it seriously. His final analysis of rational belief makes reference only to cognitive processes which in fact are reliable (and not to cognitive processes we think to be reliable).

11. This is not to say, however, that there are no problems with the above suggestion that S rationally believes p only if *he believes* of the process which causes his belief that it is reliable. To the contrary, it is no more plausible than causal, reliabilist theses: Just as S's belief p can be rational and yet not be the product of a reliable cognitive process, so, too, S's belief p can be rational and yet not be the product of a process which S *regards* as reliable. See note 14.

12. See Goldman, "What Is Justified Belief?"

13. It is worth noting that it also is possible for there to be causal accounts of knowledge which are not reliabilist accounts. Suppose, for instance, it is claimed that S knows p only if the fact that p causes S to believe p (or only if the fact that p in some appropriate sense is nomologically related to S's believing p). See Alvin Goldman, "A Causal Theory of Knowing," *The Journal of Philosophy* 64 (1967): 355–72. This kind of thesis, as Goldman himself now admits, faces numerous difficulties; it is not a particularly plausible thesis. But, putting aside the question of its plausibility, what is of interest here is that one can endorse this thesis without endorsing any significant reliabilist thesis. (This causal thesis does imply that all beliefs which are instances of knowledge must be true, but this does not indicate that the thesis commits one to a *significant* reliabilist thesis since this is a consequence which almost any account of knowledge implies.)

14. Since in all of the preceding examples S can be assumed to rationally believe p (as well as to know p), the examples also can be used to illustrate the inadequacy of various theses about rational belief. For example, they illustrate that S's believing or having adequate reason to believe that his belief p is caused by a reliable process is not a prerequisite of S's rationally believing p. Likewise, they illustrate that S's belief actually having been caused by a reliable process is not a prerequisite of S's rationally believing p.

15. Hilary Putnam, "Realism and Reason," *Proceedings and Addresses of the American Philosophical Association* 20 (1977): 483–98; Hilary Putnam, *Reason, Truth, and History* (Cambridge: Cambridge University Press, 1981), especially ch. 1; Donald Davidson, "On the Very Idea of a Conceptual Scheme," *Proceedings and Addresses of the American Philosophical Association* 17 (1974): 5–20; Donald Davidson, "A Coherence Theory of Truth and Knowledge," in *Kant oder Hegel?* Dieter Heinrich, ed. (Stuttgart: Klett-Cotta Buchadlung, 1981), pp. 423–33.

16. The story is cited by Roderick Firth, "Are Epistemic Concepts Reducible to Ethical Ones?," in *Values and Morals,* A. Goldman and J. Kim, eds. (Dordrecht, Netherlands: D. Reidel Publishing Co., 1978), pp. 215–29.

17. Perhaps, for example, it would not be plausible to say that the boy on the rocking horse knows who the winners will be if he has adequate evidence for the (false) proposition that the process which causes him to think some horse will win is unreliable. Thus, perhaps something at least roughly resembling the following conditions are sufficient for S's knowing p: S believes p is true, it is caused by a highly reliable process R, and S does not have adequate evidence for believing R is not highly reliable.

Part V

Certainty and Knowing that One Knows

23

Philosophical Certainty

Harry G. Frankfurt

Among the arguments used by philosophers to show that it is never reasonable to regard any empirical statement as altogether certain, one of the most important runs something like this. An empirical statement is tested by checking predictions derived from it, predictions whose falsity would render the statement doubtful in some degree. The relevant predictions are infinite in number, and we can never be certain that the unchecked ones will turn out to confirm the statement. So we can never be altogether certain that the statement is true, for it is always possible that something will happen to make it reasonable for us to doubt the statement. Norman Malcolm calls this "the Verification Argument," and he maintains that it is unsound.* While I am inclined to agree with him about this, I believe that the points he offers against the argument are mistaken. My purpose in this essay is to illuminate the problem of certainty through a discussion of the Verification Argument and of Malcolm's objections to it.

From *The Philosophical Review* 71 (July 1962): 303–27.

*Norman Malcolm, "The Verification Argument," in Max Black, ed., *Philosophical Analysis* (Ithaca, N.Y.: Cornell University Press, 1950), pp. 244–98. Rather than clutter the pages of my essay with numerous footnotes, I have inserted, after quotations in the text, numbers within parentheses; numbers between 244 and 298 refer to pages in "The Verification Argument"; numbers between 18 and 46 refer to another essay by Malcolm entitled "Certainty and Empirical Statements," *Mind* 51 (1942): 18-46.

I

Malcolm provides the following statement of the Verification Argument, in which "*S*"refers to some empirical statement:

    I. *S* has consequences.
    II. The number of consequences of *S* is infinite.
    III. The consequences of *S* *may* fail to occur.
    IV. *If* some of the consequences of *S* *were* to fail to occur, then there would be a reasonable doubt that *S* is true.
    V. If at any time there should be a reasonable doubt that *S* is true then at no previous time did anyone make absolutely certain that *S* is true.

    Conclusion: No one did make absolutely certain that *S* is true [p. 264].

Apparently, Malcolm would accept the conclusion of the argument if he were convinced that its premises are true, for he vindicates the argument of any flaw in its validity. "If all of its premises were true," he says, "the . . . argument would prove the general proposition that *no* empirical statement can be conclusively established" (pp. 265–66). Now Malcolm finds nothing objectionable in the first, second, or fourth premise. But he does object to premises III and V.

Malcolm claims that the fifth premise of the argument is false, and he is clearly correct in this claim. That there is a reasonable doubt about a statement at one time does not entail that no one at any earlier time knew for certain that the statement is true. There is a reasonable doubt about many statements concerning ancient history, for instance, because we have very meager evidence for these statements. But this does not exclude the possibility that, at some point in the past, someone had absolutely conclusive evidence for some of these statements and knew them for certain. As Malcolm puts it, there is no contradiction in supposing "that some person at one time should possess a body of evidence that conclusively established that so-and-so was the case, but that at a later time another person should possess none of that evidence but should possess *other* evidence on the basis of which it was reasonable to doubt that so-and-so was the case" (p. 259).

Although Malcolm does not say so, there is not even a contradiction in supposing that a person at one time should possess evidence conclusively establishing that so-and-so was the case, but that at a later time *that same person* should possess none of that evidence (or only some of it) and should possess *other* evidence which made it reasonable to doubt that so-and-so was the case. Evidence may be forgotten as well as lost, and if the available evidence is weak or even negative at one time it may have been very strong at an earlier time. So it is a mistake, as Malcolm says, to assume "that if something was accepted as a fact at time t_1, but that at time t_2 there arose a reasonable doubt as to whether this something was a fact, then it follows that it was not absolutely verified at t_1 that this something was a fact" (pp. 260–61).

Having established this, Malcolm suggests a way of reformulating the Verification Argument so as to avoid the error contained in V. He proposes to strengthen the fourth step of the original argument by substituting for IV the following statement, IV*a*, which he accepts as true: "If a sufficient number of the consequences of *S* were to fail to occur then it would be absolutely conclusive that *S* is false." He also proposes to replace V by the following statement, V*a*: "If at any time there should be absolutely conclusive grounds that *S* is false then at no previous time did anyone make absolutely certain that *S* is true."

But with IV and V of the original argument replaced by IV*a* and V*a*, Malcolm argues that the argument loses its usefulness. This is because IV*a* "relies on the supposition that a particular statement, the statement '*S* is false,' can be conclusively established as true." Here is what Malcolm says about the revised argument:

> Since one premise assumes that an empirical statement can be conclusively established, it would be wrong to say that the revised argument, if its premises were all true, would prove . . . that *no* empirical statement can be conclusively established. No matter what statement was substituted for *S*, premise IV*a* would assume that the contradictory of that statement can be conclusively established. The revised argument has this peculiar logical character, that if all of its premises were true it would prove, with regard to *any* empirical statement, that the statement cannot be completely verified, but it would not prove that no empirical statement can be completely verified [pp. 265–66].

I shall not discuss the "peculiar logical character" of the revised argument. Instead, I shall show that the original argument need not undergo the revisions that result in its acquiring this peculiar character—that there is a way of reformulating the argument which avoids the error in V, which is not subject to the criticism Malcolm makes of his own reformulation, and which is an accurate expression of what is intended by proponents of the Verification Argument.

To avoid the error in V, it is not necessary to alter IV at all, but only to substitute for V the following statement, V*b*: "If at any time t_2 there should be a reasonable doubt that *S* is true, then at no previous time t_1 did anyone make absolutely certain that *S* is true, *provided that the evidence possessed at t_2 includes all the evidence possessed at t_1.*" Let me clarify the meaning of V*b*.

Suppose that at time t_1 someone who has a body of evidence (E_1) in favor of some empirical statement, claims on the basis of E_1, that the statement is absolutely certain; suppose, in other words, that he regards E_1 as absolutely conclusive evidence for the statement in question. Now suppose that at a later time t_2 someone has another body of evidence (E_2) concerning the same statement, and suppose that (*a*) E_2 includes E_1, and (*b*) it is reasonable, on the basis of E_2, to doubt the truth of the statement. Then the claim of certainty made at t_1 must have been mistaken, and it must also have been a mistake to claim that E_1 constitutes absolutely conclusive evidence for the statement in question. The evidence in favor of a statement cannot be absolutely conclusive if *further* evidence would render the statement subject to a reasonable doubt. To say that evidence is conclusive is to say that it is sufficient to justify the conclusion based on it no matter what further information is obtained.

The original premise V might have been formulated as follows: "If at any time t_2 someone has a body of evidence (E_2) which makes it doubtful that S is true, then at no previous time t_1 did anyone have a body of evidence (E_1) which made S certain." This statement is false, as we have seen, because it does not preclude the possibility that E_1 includes evidence lacking in E_2; it does not preclude the possibility that E_1 is stronger than E_2. But Vb does preclude this possibility, since it specifies that E_2 contains E_1 and that, consequently, E_1 can be no stronger than E_2. It seems evident, then, that Vb is a true statement.

The substitution of Vb for V does not affect the validity of the Verification Argument. It is implied by I, II, and III that E_2 may contain evidence against the truth of S plus all the evidence in E_1 concerning S. Together with IV, this implies that E_2 may provide reasonable grounds for doubting S. Premise Vb says that if E_2 provides reasonable grounds for doubting S, and if the relation between E_1 and E_2 is as the first three premises of the argument imply it may be, then no one ever made absolutely certain that S is true. And the conclusion follows validly as in the original argument.

Moreover, the substitution of Vb for V does not result in the acquisition by the argument of the "peculiar logical character" described by Malcolm as afflicting *his* revision of the original argument. Thus, Malcolm has failed to dispose of the Verification Argument by attacking its fifth premise. For his attack can easily be met by a revision which leaves the force of the argument undiminished.

II

Repelling Malcolm's attack on the Verification Argument's fifth premise does not save the argument from his efforts to impugn its soundness, for he alleges that the argument involves other difficulties as well. Indeed, he offers a criticism of its third premise which he considers to be even more important than his criticism of V. To show what is wrong with the third premise, he says, "is to expose the most important error in the Verification Argument" (p. 292).

Malcolm maintains that "in order for the Verification Argument to be a valid deductive argument . . . III must be understood in such a way that it implies the following proposition, which I will call 'IIIa': 'It is not certain that the consequences of S will occur' " (p. 267). If III does not imply IIIa, he points out, the possibility remains that it is certain that the consequences of S will occur, and as long as this possibility remains the conclusion of the Verification Argument cannot validly be deduced from its premises.

Proponents of the Verification Argument seem to have thought that IIIa is implied by the following statement, which Malcolm calls "III$_2$": "No statement, p, which expresses a consequence of S is entailed by any statement, q, which states the grounds for holding that p is true." For instance, in a passage quoted by Malcolm, C. I. Lewis says this:

> My belief may imply as probable, anything the failure of which I should accept as tending to discredit this belief. . . . Such future contingencies implied by the belief are not such that failure of them can be absolutely precluded in the light of prior empirical corroborations of what is believed. However improbable, it remains thinkable that such later tests could have a negative result. Though truth of the belief itself implies a positive result of such later tests, the evidence to date does not imply this as more than probable. [p. 286]

When Lewis says that the failure of the consequences of his belief to occur is not "absolutely precluded in the light of prior empirical corroboration of what is believed," he seems to be saying that the evidence for thinking these consequences will occur does not entail their occurrence. This interpretation of his position is suggested again by his statement that the evidence that the consequences of his belief will occur "does not imply this as more than probable." Lewis apparently bases his claim that it is not certain that the consequences of his belief will occur on the fact that there is no deductively compelling evidence that they will occur, but only evidence which renders their occurrence probable. In other words, Lewis apparently regards IIIa as established by III$_2$.

Malcolm accepts III$_2$ as a true statement. The soundness of the Verification Argument, then, turns on the question of whether or not III$_2$ entails IIIa. That is, it turns on the question of whether an empirical statement can be certain if it is not entailed by the evidence for it, or whether any evidence can properly be regarded as conclusive which does not entail the conclusion based upon it. Malcolm's opinion is that III$_2$ does not entail IIIa, but his argument in behalf of this opinion is unsatisfactory.

In order to facilitate discussion of these statements and their relationships, Malcolm uses "R" to refer to the statement of the grounds for believing that the consequences of an empirical statement will occur; and he uses "c" to refer to the statement that those consequences will occur. Thus, III$_2$ may be expressed as "R does not entail c"; and IIIa may be expressed as "it is not certain that c." Now he acknowledges that "there is a temptation" to believe that III$_2$ implies IIIa and that "it is easy to be misled" into thinking that it does. However, he asserts that "it does not . . . follow from the fact that R does not entail c either that it is not certain that c is true or that R does not state the grounds on the basis of which it is certain that c is true" (pp. 277–78).

In view of the ease with which he thinks it possible to be misled about the relation between III$_2$ and IIIa, Malcolm offers surprisingly little in the way of support for his view of the relation. Here is the entire passage in which he explains why III$_2$ does not imply IIIa:

> Whether it is certain that c is true depends upon the state of the evidence with regard to c. The statement "R does not entail c" says no more about the state of the evidence with regard to c than does the statement " 'c is false' is not self-contradictory." Both statements are irrelevant to that matter. The statement "The fact that R is true makes it absolutely certain that c is true" is in no way contradicted by the statement "R does not entail c." The two statements are perfectly compatible with one another. One statement describes the evidence concerning c. The other describes a logical relationship between R and c of which one could be aware even though one knew nothing whatever about the state of the evidence concerning c. The fact that R does not entail c provides no ground for doubting that c is true. It is a mistake to suppose that because it is possible that c is false even though R is true, in the sense of III$_2$, that therefore "It is possible that c is false," where these latter words imply that it is not quite certain that c is true [p. 278].

A number of the statements in this passage are merely reformulations of the claim that III$_2$ does not imply IIIa. In fact, Malcolm here offers only one point in support of his claim—the point that the statement "R does not entail c" is irrelevant to any question about "the state of the evidence" with regard to c.

But what can we make of this point? The statement "R does not entail c" is obviously about the evidence for c. It says that the evidence does not entail c, and one question about the state of the evidence for c is the question of the relation between c and the evidence for it. So how can III$_2$ be supposed to be irrelevant to questions about the state of the evidence for c?

Suppose that c were not an empirical statement but a mathematical one, and suppose that R were a statement of the premises in a purported proof of it. Then, as Malcolm would doubtless agree, the statement that R does not entail c would not only be quite relevant to the state of the evidence with regard to c; it would generally be supposed to imply that it is not certain that c. In mathematics, when the evidence for a statement does not entail the statement, this is generally taken to indicate that the statement has not been proven, and that its truth is not certain. It is not only in mathematics that this is the case. Malcolm's own efforts to raise a doubt about the truth of IIIa consist precisely in an attempt to show that IIIa is not entailed by any true statement offered as evidence for it. In his own discussion, Malcolm supposed that the fact that a statement is not entailed by the evidence for it is quite relevant to the question of whether or not the statement is certain.

Of course, Malcolm evidently believes that empirical statements differ from other statements in this respect. He believes not only that an empirical statement may be certain even though there is no deductively compelling evidence for its truth, but also that the lack of such evidence is irrelevant to questions about the state of the evidence with regard to an empirical statement. He may be correct in believing this; nothing I have said demonstrates that he is not. But he cannot establish the correctness of his belief merely by asserting it and without explaining how it is that empirical statements come to differ in this respect from statements of other types.

Although Malcolm does not adduce it, there is an argument which might be thought to support his claim that III_2 is irrelevant to questions about the state of the evidence with regard to c. Since III_2 is true *no matter how much* evidence has been obtained in favor of c, it is useless to know that III_2 is true when one wishes to know how much evidence there is for c. And therefore, it might be argued, the truth of III_2 is irrelevant to questions about the state of the evidence with regard to c. But Malcolm cannot make use of this argument without begging the question of the soundness of the Verification Argument.

The argument might be useful to Malcolm if there were a problem of weighing evidence in order to distinguish cases in which it is certain that c from cases in which it is not certain that c. But the very question at issue in the Verification Argument is whether there is any such problem, and there is no such problem if the Verification Argument is sound. For the Verification Argument purports to establish that no empirical statement can be certain no matter how much evidence for it there may be, and that the evidence for an empirical statement is never conclusive no matter how weighty the evidence is.

Knowing that III_2 is true does not, to be sure, enable one to know whether there is a great deal of evidence for c or only a little. But knowing III_2 may still enable one to know that the evidence for c is inconclusive, if the fact that the evidence is inconclusive does not depend on how much evidence there is. Thus, the argument I have described cannot be used without assuming the falsity of what the Verification Argument seeks to establish, and it would accordingly be fallacious to use it to support the view that III_2 does not entail $IIIa$.

In section V, I shall consider whether any other argument offered by Malcolm provides adequate support of the claim that III_2 does not entail $IIIa$, or for his claim that $IIIa$ is false. But none of his arguments which I have discussed so far succeeds in any way in showing that the Verification Argument is unsound.

III

Another charge that Malcolm levels against proponents of the Verification Argument is that they misuse such expressions as "certain," "absolutely certain," and "theoretically certain." In showing that the arguments with which he supports this charge are inconclusive, I shall at the same time be preparing the way for the next section of my essay, in which I attempt to clarify the meanings of expression such as "certain."

To call attention to what he regards as a misuse of language by proponents of the Verification Argument, Malcolm begins with a question: "What state of affairs, if it could be realized, would they call 'theoretical certainty'?" (p. 297) The answer to this question, he says, is that "it would be 'theoretically certain' that a given statement is true only if an *infinite* number of 'tests' or 'acts of verification' had been performed" (p. 297). But it is logically impossible for an infinite number of tests to have been performed. "Therefore," Malcolm concludes, "these philosophers *misuse* the expression 'theoretically certain.' What they call 'theoretical certainty' cannot be attained even in *theory*" (p. 297).

Malcolm's conclusion that the expression "theoretically certain" is misused by proponents of the Verification Argument is apparently based on the premise that they use the expression in such a way that it is logically impossible for it to be correctly applied to any statement. At any rate, this is the only evidence Malcolm gives for his conclusion. This premise, in turn, is supported by his statement that proponents of the argument use the expression in such a way that it can be correctly applied only when an infinite number of tests has been performed, a circumstance whose occurrence is logically impossible.

Now if they are taken *strictly,* the statements in which Malcolm gives the evidence for his conclusion are false. No proponent of the Verification Argument has held that "it would be 'theoretically certain' that a given statement is true only if an *infinite* number of 'tests' or 'acts of verification' had been performed." What they *have* held is that it would be theoretically certain that a given *empirical* statement is true only if an infinite number of tests had been performed. Lewis and Carnap, as well as other proponents of the Verification Argument, have insisted repeatedly that there are many statements—for instance, statements of logical truths, and "terminating judgments" or "protocol statements"—which may be theoretically certain *without* an infinite number of tests having been performed.

To be sure, proponents of the Verification Argument are committed to the view that it is logically impossible for the expression "theoretically certain" to be applied correctly to any empirical statement. Indeed, it is precisely this view which they seek to establish by their argument. But there is no inevitable misuse of language in arguing that an expression which is applied correctly in some circumstances involves a contradiction when it is applied in other circumstances. Since proponents of the Verification Argument admit the logical possibility of circumstances in which the expression in question would be applied correctly, they do not appear to be open to the charge that they have provided it with no conceivable correct use.

These remarks depend on the supposition that Malcolm intended his statements to be taken strictly, but it is quite likely that he did not. Instead of asserting falsely that proponents of the argument use words in such a way that theoretical certainty cannot be attained even in theory, Malcolm probably intended to assert this: "When proponents of the Verification Argument claim that it is logically impossible for any *empirical* statement to be theoretically certain, they are using the expression 'theoretically certain' in a special sense, and in that sense it is logically impossible for *any* statement to be theoretically certain." Malcolm would doubtless admit that proponents of the Verification Argument sometimes use the expression in *other* senses, in which it *is* logically possible for it to be applied correctly. But he probably wished to suggest that in the *special* sense in which the expression is used in the statement that no empirical statement can be theoretically certain, it is also true that no statement of any kind can be theoretically certain.

Supporting my conjectures is the fact that Malcolm has argued that the meaning of the expression in question (or a similar expression) is not the same when philosophers assert that no empirical statement can be theoretically certain as it is when they apply the expression to statements of logical truths or to protocol statements. In an article published in *Mind* in 1942, Malcolm says that "there are three senses of the expression 'it is certain' which are important" for the problem of whether empirical statements can ever be certain (p. 26). In the same article, he says: "When it is said that a sense-statement [i.e., protocol statement] is certain, what this means is that it does not make sense to doubt or question it. And when it is said that an *a priori* statement is certain, what this means is that the negative of it is self-contradictory" (p. 35). He also observes that "the doctrine that empirical statements are never known with certainty has been held by various philosophers, because these philosophers have been led to attach a self-contradictory meaning to the expression 'it is certain that,' as applied to empirical statements" (p. 46). Apparently, Malcolm believes that when philosophers use the expression "theoretically certain" or similar expressions in the course of the Verification Argument, they use it to mean "confirmed by an infinite number of tests."

If he were correct, the expression would have a self-contradictory meaning on such occasions and this would make plausible the view that it is misused. So the question is whether philosophers who say that no empirical statement can ever be certain do mean by this merely that no empirical statement can ever be confirmed by an infinite number of tests. So far as I can see, Malcolm offers no evidence which establishes that they mean this.

On the other hand, he does offer evidence that they sometimes use the expression "theoretically certain" or similar expressions to mean "has a self-contradictory negative." Since it will be of interest to consider what this evidence is like, I shall quote from the *Mind* article in which it is offered:

> Let us turn for a moment to the philosophers who say that *a priori* statements can be known with certainty, but not empirical statements. They may argue the point by saying that . . . the negative of an *a priori* statement is self-contradictory. Their declaration . . . is a disguised recommendation that the phrase "it is certain that" be applied to a statement if and only if the statement has a self-contradictory negative. . . . So what they are really saying is that no empirical statement has a self-contradictory negative, while every *a priori* statement does. . . . And this is an absolute tautology. For it is the defining characteristic of an *a priori* statement that it has a self-contradictory negative, and it is a defining characteristic of an empirical statement that it does not have a self-contradictory negative [pp. 34–35].

The philosophers in question do not, as Malcolm suggests, declare that "only *a priori* statements can be known with certainty." Generally, they say that protocol statements can also be known with certainty. But deferring this point for the moment, consider the following passage from the same article, in which Malcolm attempts to explain another use of the expression he is examining:

> When the philosopher says that sense-statements can be known with certainty, but that empirical statements cannot, what he is doing is restricting the use of the phrase "known with certainty" in such a way that a statement will be capable of being known with certainty, if and only if it is an incorrigible statement. . . . But then his pronouncement that sense-statements can be known with certainty, but empirical statements cannot, is a plain truism. For it amounts to saying that sense-statements are incorrigible, and empirical statements are corrigible. And incorrigibility is the defining characteristic of sense-statements, while corrigibility is a defining characteristic of empirical statements [pp. 33–34].

In each of these passages, Malcolm describes a philosopher who compares empirical statements with statements of another class, who asserts that empirical statements cannot be certain but statements of the other class can be certain, and who gives as the reason for his assertion the fact that empirical statements lack a characteristic possessed by members of the other class. In each case, the characteristic is one which it is logically impossible for empirical statements to possess but which is the defining characteristic of the other class. And Malcolm asserts that in each case the characteristic mentioned is one which a statement possesses *if and only if* it is certain.

At first glance, it may appear quite plausible for Malcolm to make this last assertion. After all, if a philosopher says that statements of one type are uncertain merely because they lack some characteristic, this suggests strongly that he regards possession of the characteristic as a necessary condition for certainty; and if the philosopher says that statements of another type are certain merely because they have the characteristic, this suggests strongly that he regards possession of the characteristic as a sufficient condition for certainty. If possession of some characteristic is both a necessary and a sufficient condition for certainty, it is not unreasonable to suppose that it is equivalent to certainty, and that its name is a synonym for "certain."

Yet it seems to me quite likely that Malcolm has misrepresented the position of the philosophers he criticizes. In describing those who claim that *a priori* statements can be known with certainty but not empirical statements, he supposes that they offer as the reason for the uncertainty of empirical statements, that such statements do not have self-contradictory negatives. In describing those who claim that protocol statements can be known with certainty but that empirical statements cannot, he supposes that they offer a different reason for the uncertainty of empirical statements, namely, that such statements are not incorrigible. But I doubt that any philosopher ever intended to offer as *the* reason for the uncertainty of empirical statements the fact that they do not have self-contradictory negatives; and I doubt that any philosopher ever intended to offer as *the* reason for the uncertainty of empirical statements the fact that they are not incorrigible. For, to return to the point whose consideration was deferred a little while ago, no philosopher has ever suggested that *a priori* statements are uncertain because they are not incorrigible; and none has ever suggested that protocol statements are uncertain because they do not have self-contradictory negatives. Yet it would be perfectly natural for them to do so if they believed what Malcolm ascribes to them.

Another interpretation of their position is available, and to consider it will prove fruitful. Let us suppose, then, that the philosophers who argue in the way Malcolm describes intend to assert only that having a self-contradictory negative and being incorrigible are two *sufficient* conditions for certainty but that neither of them is *necessary* for it. Then the possibility remains that they use the expression "theoretically certain" consistently and not, as Malcolm suggests, in three different senses. Their position would be that there are various ways in which a statement may attain theoretical certainty: that is, various conditions may satisfy the general criteria of theoretical certainty. Their claim that no empirical statement can ever be theoretically certain would rest on the belief that it is logically impossible for any empirical statement to satisfy these general criteria of theoretical certainty in any way at all. This interpretation seems quite consistent with what the philosophers in question say about the problem of certainty.

It does, however, burden them with a serious failing. That no empirical statement can be certain cannot be established merely by showing that empirical statements do not satisfy the general criteria of theoretical certainty in the same way that these criteria are satisfied by *a priori* statements. Nor can it be established by adding to this the fact that empirical statements do not satisfy these criteria in the way they are satisfied by protocol statements. For it remains open that there are other ways, besides these two, in which the general criteria of theoretical certainty can be satisfied. Clearly, the conclusion can only be established by showing that these general criteria cannot be satisfied by empirical statements in any way at all. But the philosophers in question have never, to my knowledge, stated the general criteria of theoretical certainty which they employ. Until they do so, they cannot hope to show that the criteria cannot be satisfied in any way by any empirical statement.

It is not only the philosophers Malcolm criticizes, however, who are guilty of failing to say what they mean by expressions such as "theoretically certain." Indeed, one of the most striking and curious aspects of the whole philosophical controversy over certainty is that few of the participants in it have ever attempted seriously and precisely to say what certainty is and what its general criteria are. Lewis does not do so, and neither does Carnap. Nor, for all their concern with clarifying the uses of expressions, do Malcolm or Moore. In the next section of my essay, I shall attempt to shed some light on these questions.

IV

Malcolm is anxious to show that empirical statements may be certain, while other philosophers are equally anxious to show that they cannot be. But what precisely is at issue in this controversy? What is the difference between being certain and being uncertain? It is not of much use to answer by saying that a statement is certain if and only if it is supported by conclusive evidence, for this only shifts the focus of attention to another expression whose meaning is equally unclear. Instead of searching for expressions synonymous to or correlative with expressions like "certain," we must make our understanding more concrete.

I suggest that the "cash value" of a claim of certainty lies in the claimant's willingness to take the risks he associates with accepting the statements for which he claims certainty. Whenever someone understands a statement, he supposes that there are some consequences of action which will occur if the statement is true and others which will occur if it is false. If he adopts a belief in the statement, therefore, he stakes something on its truth. An error on his part may result in nothing worse than trivial disappointment, mild embarrassment, or minor inconvenience; or it may have consequences far more grave than these. But there is always *some* penalty associated with a given error, even though a person making an error may escape the penalty and even though an error may also bring rewards.

When a person adopts a belief, he accepts whatever risks he recognizes of being made to suffer the penalty for error. He may, of course, accept these risks even though he believes the statement in question to be probably false. It may even be reasonable for him to do so, if the alternative carries greater risks or if accepting the risk brings closer the attainment of some otherwise unlikely reward. It is often reasonable to make a bet even though there is not much chance of winning it. Thus, a person's willingness to take the risks he associates with some statement does not mean that he regards the statement as certain, or even that he regards it as probably true.

But what about the converse of this? Is regarding a statement as certain compatible with being unwilling to risk what are thought to be the penalties for being mistaken about the statement? Surely, a person who regards some statement as certain can have no expectation of suffering a penalty arising from the statement's falsity. It makes no sense for a person to claim that he knows something for certain and yet at the same time to confess, explicitly or by his actions, that he fears he may be mistaken. Why, then, should he be unwilling to take the risk?

He might be unwilling to take the risk, despite his certainty, because he thinks it immoral, or because there is nothing to be gained by it, or because there is more to be gained in another way. But consider the following hypothetical situation. A person has a number of alternative ways of acting, only one of which is appropriate if he believes that some statement, T, is true. If he chooses any other alternative he suffers P—a penalty. If he acts as if T is true, then the consequences are the same as for the other alternatives except that he suffers no penalty if T is true and suffers a penalty greater than P if T is false. Suppose that the person is aware of all this, that he has no moral compunctions about any of the alternatives as such, and that he is not self-destructive. In such a situation, the person cannot be certain of T if he does not choose the alternative appropriate only if T is true.

If a person regards a statement as certain, he is willing to take the risks associated with the statement if there is nothing to be gained by refusing to do so.* Now it is *reasonable* for a person to regard a statement as certain only if his willingness to take the risks associated with accepting the statement is justified by the evidence he possesses in favor of the statement. And a statement *is* certain only if it would be reasonable for anyone possessing the evidence available for it to regard the statement as certain. It will be noted that none of these remarks constitutes a definition, since none describes sufficient conditions, but only necessary ones.

They do, however, suggest an important relation between certainty and risk taking. That this relation exists is, I believe, implicit in the ordinary usage of terms like "certain," since it is characteristic of that usage that no one can sensibly claim to regard something as certain and at the same time fear that he may be mistaken. As I hope to show, examination of this relation is helpful both in understanding the Verification Argument and in evaluating some of Malcolm's criticisms of that argument. Before proceeding to show this, however, I want to call attention to several facts which, while familiar and relevant, seem to have been overlooked at times in philosophical discussions of certainty.

---

*Instead of repeating this qualification endlessly in what follows, I request the reader to assume it whenever it is appropriate.

Sometimes a person regards a statement as being certain and then discovers evidence against it which compels him to give up as mistaken the claim that he knew it for certain. There is nothing noteworthy in this. But it is also not uncommon for a person to claim at one time that he knows something for certain and then to abandon this claim at another time, even though his knowledge of the relevant evidence is the same at both times. It is noteworthy that apparent inconsistency of this sort need not be unreasonable. When very little is at stake it is only natural to claim all sorts of things, and then to become more cautious as the penalties for error increase. What seems unsusceptible to reasonable doubt under one set of conditions may properly appear to be quite a risky matter when the danger of error has to be taken very seriously because the stakes are high. A doubt that seems fantastic or absurd when the stakes are relatively trivial may be quite natural and appropriate in other circumstances, even though the relevant evidence remains constant.

Another point is this. When a certainty claim is revoked because of new evidence, the original claim of certainty is generally regarded as having been mistaken. This is not always the case, however, when a certainty claim is revoked because of a change in the anticipated penalty for error. Frequently, in such cases, the original claim of certainty is not regarded so much as having been mistaken but as being no longer relevant in the changed circumstances.

The explanation of these facts is, I think, as follows. Certainty is generally thought to be susceptible of variations in degree: people say that statements are "sufficiently certain," "more certain than ever," "quite certain," and so on. If a person regards one statement as being more certain than another he naturally thinks it reasonable to risk more on the truth of the one statement than he thinks it reasonable to risk on the truth of the other. We can imagine bets being made on the truth of various statements. It would make no sense for a person to be willing to bet one amount on a statement he regards as rather uncertain and to be willing to bet only a lesser amount on a statement he regards as certain, assuming that all bets are made at the same odds and that the person is interested only in maximizing the chances of winning his bet. Indeed, a plausible way of testing whether or not a person regards one statement as more certain than another is to determine whether or not he is willing to stake more on the truth of the one than on the truth of the other. If he were not willing to do so, it would be difficult to understand what he meant by claiming that the one is more certain than the other.

People frequently make certainty claims without indicating explicitly the degree of certainty they are claiming; they say that something is certain without saying how certain they think it is. At other times, a degree of certainty may be indicated explicitly, or it may be explicitly indicated that the degree is at least of a particular order of magnitude. For instance, an attorney might say this to a prospective witness: "You say it is certain that Smith was present at the gathering on the evening in question. Do you regard it as being so certain that you are willing to assert it in court under oath, knowing that your testimony may be responsible for sending a man to prison?" Here, the attorney is not attempting to find out precisely how certain the prospective witness thinks his statement to be. He is only trying to discover whether the witness thinks it certain enough to be willing to risk on its truth the penalties indicated—for instance, the penalty of being responsible for sending an innocent man to prison.

Claims that a statement is certain are best understood as being elliptical—as being claims that the statement is *certain enough to justify a willingness to risk such-and-such on the truth of the statement.* Obviously, the evidence may be weighty enough to justify a willingness to take this risk without being sufficiently weighty to justify a willingness to take a greater risk. And the statement that the evidence is not weighty enough to justify a willingness to take the greater risk does not contradict the statement that it is weighty enough to justify a willingness to take the lesser risk.

Let me illustrate some of the points I have been making. There is an object lying before me on my desk, and I believe it to be my notebook. I habitually keep my notebook where the object rests, I remember putting my notebook there not long ago, and I can plainly see, among numerous familiar signs, my own signature near the top of its cover. If my wife Marilyn should ask me where my notebook is, I would assert with no qualms at all that it is here on my desk. If she asked me to make certain, because she suspected that I had left the notebook in the car this afternoon, I would justifiably tell her that I was quite certain of it. It would not occur to me to doubt that I had sufficient evidence for this confident reply.

But suppose that her question had a graver import. Suppose she told me that a great deal depended on my being certain of my answer. Imagine her saying that my notebook had been discovered to possess remarkable properties of some kind, and that she has just learned that our lives and the lives of many others—perhaps even the survival of a free civilization—depend on my answer to her question. Imagine that I accept these statements of hers and do not take them to be part of some silly joke or insane fantasy. Then surely it would reasonable for me to be far more hesitant in my reply, even though I have exactly the same evidence as previously for believing that my notebook is lying in front of me.

Were such horrendous consequences due to follow a mistake on my part, I would begin to consider possibilities that would not even have entered my mind if my wife's question had been only a casual one. What possibilities I considered would depend partly on the richness of my imagination and partly on the circumstances in which the question was asked, insofar as these gave me some clue as to the source from which the danger of error might arise. In certain circumstances, for instance, I might be preoccupied with the techniques of deception available to political enemies. In others, perhaps, I would even consider the possibility that beings from another planet, with an incomprehensibly profound capacity for manipulating the laws of na-

Question isn't can we know, it's
can we have known.

ture, had been active without my knowledge. In any case, I should be extremely re-luctant to risk so much on my answer as long as I could conceive any way at all, how-ever implausible or fantastic, in which I might be mistaken. Indeed, if I could do so without incurring severe penalties, I would decline to answer the question at all.

In this illustration, my first claim of certainty was a reasonable one. Moreover, the subsequent events described do not show that this first claim was mistaken, even though they do result in a reasonable refusal on my part to repeat the claim. To the presumably casual question—"Are you certain of the location of your notebook?"—the correct an-swer was affirmative, and its correctness is not impugned by the fact that the same re-sponse was not reasonable when the question was no longer thought to be such a casual one. For there is a difference in how the two questions were understood, even though both were expressed in the same words. The first question was understood as asking whether I was certain enough to take the minor risks generally associated with being wrong about such things as the locations of inconsequential objects. The second was un-derstood as asking whether I was willing to take far greater risks on the same evidence.

V

This discussion of the relation between certainty and risk taking suggests a way of conceiving the *highest* degree of certainty. A statement enjoys the highest degree of certainty only if it is supported by evidence which justifies a willingness to risk the greatest possible penalty on the truth of the statement. For a person to regard a state-ment as being certain in the highest degree, he must be willing to risk *anything* on its truth. If there is something he is unwilling to risk on the truth of a given statement, it is clearly possible to imagine him regarding some other statement as more certain than the given one—namely, some other statement on which he is willing to risk what he is unwilling to risk on the first.

Now the expression "absolutely certain" is not ordinarily used in such a way that to claim some statement is absolutely certain implies that there is no penalty that the claimant is unwilling to risk on the truth of the statement. Whether consciously or not, one who claims absolute certainty often implies no more than that he is willing to risk on the statement in question all that he would normally expect to have to risk on it. I propose to use the term "philosophical certainty" to refer to the highest degree of certainty. In offering a criterion for this highest degree of certainty, I believe I have preserved the standard for measuring degrees of certainty that is implicit in the ordi-nary usage of terms like "certain."

In my opinion, when proponents of the Verification Argument maintain that no empirical statement can be certain, they mean that none can be philosophically cer-tain; they do not intend to deny that empirical statements may enjoy lesser degrees of certainty. I think they also have philosophical certainty in mind when they discuss the certainty of *a priori* statements or protocol statements. Thus, I believe they use the term "certain" consistently in the sense of "philosophically certain" and not in several different senses. They are concerned with the general question of the conditions in which it is reasonable to regard a statement as philosophically certain, and with the more particular question of whether there is any way in which an empirical statement can satisfy these conditions.

Assuming that this interpretation of the Verification Argument is correct, do any of Malcolm's objections succeed in undermining the argument? In addition to the objections I have already examined, Malcolm observes that if the Verification Argument were sound, it would always be a mistake to claim certainty for an empirical statement, and he points out that such claims are frequently made in the ordinary course of life and frequently accepted as reasonable and correct. This shows, in his opinion, that III$_2$ does not entail IIIa—that is, that an empirical statement may be certain even though it is not entailed by the evidence for it. For if III$_2$ did entail IIIa, the Verification Argument would in his view be sound, and the argument cannot be sound because that would involve the absurdity that people are always wrong when they claim to know some empirical statement for certain.

But the undoubted fact that people frequently claim correctly to know empirical statements for certain does not mean that they ever regard such statements as philosophically certain or that they would ever think it reasonable to do so. It is not obvious that people commonly claim empirical statements to be philosophically certain, and if they do not then the ordinary usage of terms like "certain" is not at all relevant to the position maintained by proponents of the Verification Argument. In fact, it is very likely that people ordinarily claim to be certain of empirical statements without being aware that their claims are elliptical, and that they express by these claims only that they are certain enough of various statements to stake on them the limited penalties they suppose to be associated with them.

On the whole, people do not think in terms of philosophical certainty but in terms of lesser degrees of certainty. When confronted with a question a person may try to estimate the penalties for giving a wrong answer, but he does not normally take into account whether or not he would be willing to risk an answer if the penalties were much greater than these. A person may believe he regards a statement as quite certain without realizing that there is some penalty he would not be willing to risk on his belief in its truth. And when someone thinks there is no reasonable ground for doubting the truth of a statement, he may be correct that no grounds for doubting it are reasonable in the circumstances in which he finds himself. Nonetheless it may be that grounds for doubting the statement would be reasonable in other circumstances, in which a great deal depended on avoiding error.

Indeed, it is not at all easy for someone to know either that he himself or that another regards a statement as philosophically certain. For it is generally very difficult to know what a person would or would not be willing to do when the stakes are very high—as high as can be imagined—and when the alternatives are unlike what is ordinarily encountered in life. There is no reason for supposing that the ordinary man is competent to decide questions of philosophical certainty, since he is altogether without experience in making such decisions.

That the ordinary usage of terms like "certain" is irrelevant to the Verification Argument does not, of course, mean that the Verification Argument is sound. Nor does it mean that Malcolm is wrong in his view that III₂ does not entail IIIa, for his view may be correct even if his attempts to establish it fail. I confess that I cannot see clearly whether Malcolm is right or wrong about this. While admitting that his view may be correct, however, I wish to make a few remarks which suggest that it may be mistaken.

The question is whether a statement can be philosophically certain although it is not entailed by the evidence for it. Now if a statement is not entailed by the evidence for it, it is possible to conceive circumstances in which, even with this evidence, it would be reasonable to regard the statement as false. The force of Malcolm's denial that III₂ entails IIIa derives from the fact that it is often unreasonable to take these conceivable circumstances into account. In the ordinary course of life it is unreasonable to take into account such logical possibilities as that the laws of nature may change or that there are forces operating in the universe with which we are unacquainted and which are capable of producing effects altogether outside our previous experience. To take such possibilities into account would be unreasonable because it would cripple our capacity for action.

But philosophical certainty is not greatly relevant to the practical demands of life, since the necessity to act probably never requires a decision about philosophical certainty. The problem of making such a decision is a philosophical problem, not a practical one. However, it is possible to imagine being faced with the necessity of deciding whether or not a statement is philosophically certain. Suppose I am offered the following bet. If I assert incorrectly that some empirical statement is true (or false), E will occur, where "E" refers to what I regard as the greatest possible evil. If I assert correctly that the statement is true (or false), then E will not occur. In all other respects the consequences of a correct answer and of an incorrect one will be identical.

Obviously the bet is an unfair one, since I have nothing to gain by taking it and everything to lose. But if my opinion of the statement's truth-value is correct, I can take the bet and lose nothing. Now suppose I regard the truth (or falsity) of the statement as philosophically certain. Then I can have no expectation of losing, and if I were to decline the bet it would have to be for reasons altogether extraneous to the likelihood of winning or losing it. If an empirical statement can be philosophically certain, even though it is not entailed by the evidence for it, then there may be situations in which the only reasons for declining a bet such as this would be reasons having nothing to do with the likelihood of winning or losing the bet.

If the evidence that the bet would be won leaves open the logical possibility that it would be lost, would not that alone provide reasonable grounds for declining to take the bet? If Malcolm believes that an empirical statement may be philosophically certain even though it is not entailed by the evidence for it, he must suppose that the answer to this question is negative. While this answer may be correct, it is surely not obviously correct, and none of Malcolm's arguments supports a negative answer to the question. The evidence that the bet would be won might be so strong that only a change in the laws of nature would result in its being lost. But if the stakes were high enough, it would not be implausible to suggest that even this possibility ought to be taken into account and that it would be unreasonable to accept the bet in view of the logical possibility of losing it.

24

On Analyzing Knowledge

John Tienson

Since Gettier showed that knowledge cannot be analyzed as true justified belief,[1] many repairs of this analysis have been proposed. In this work it has almost universally been assumed that the requirement of truth is part of the analysis of knowledge. I believe this assumption is misguided. Of course, I do not mean that one can know what is not true. If John knows that p, then p. It is the *independent* requirement of truth that is objectionable. Whether or not John knows that p depends, I believe, on nothing other than his experiences, dispositions, mental acts, and so forth, that is, on nothing other than facts about John.[2] But whether or not p is true is not, in general, a fact about John.

Suppose there are two people, a and b, who have had, so far as their experiences are concerned, identical life histories, and that there are two propositions p_a and p_b, believed by a and b respectively, and identically related to them. It cannot be the case, I believe, that p_a, is true and a knows that p_a, while b does not know but merely believes p_b because p_b is false. Putting this point another way, there cannot be two possible worlds in which John's experiences, mental acts, disposition, and so forth are exactly alike and which differ in that in one p is true and John knows that p while in the other p is false and John merely believes that p. The difference between knowing and not knowing that p cannot be just the truth or falsity of p.

I cannot prove this to someone who does not share my intuitions, but I will try to make its denial implausible in terms of an example. And I will point out some of the

---

From *Philosophical Studies* 25 (1974): 289–93. © 1974 by D. Reidel Publishing Co., Dordrecht, Netherlands. Reprinted by permission of Wolter Kluwer Academic Publishers.

undesirable consequences of denying it by making the requirement of truth an independent part of the analysis of knowledge. Finally, I will attempt to allay some of the misgivings philosophers may feel at the consequences of rejecting this requirement.

Suppose a famous detective is called upon to investigate a case of embezzling, and that after a lengthy and painstaking investigation he has exactly the same evidence that Black is not the embezzler and that White is not the embezzler. Suppose that Black is in fact the guilty party, and that White is perfectly innocent. Now, given the assumption that his evidence is exactly the same in both cases, it seems to me that *no matter how good that evidence is,* he does not know that White is innocent. He claims to know that Black is innocent on exactly the same grounds, and we cannot accept that claim. If we were to tell the detective that one of the two was guilty, he would no doubt stop believing both that White was innocent and that Black was innocent. But I think that *he* would also agree that he had never known that either was innocent. By filling in details suitably, we will be able to construct a similar example for any analysis of knowledge that makes truth an independent condition. If one is unwilling to say that the detective knows White is innocent in the situation described, he must reject all such analyses.

If one insists that the detective does know that White is innocent, knowledge becomes much less useful than we are inclined to think. Acting on one's knowledge will not lead one astray, but neither will acting on one's true beliefs. And for the same reason, it will not count as knowledge or true belief unless it is true. But it will not be possible for a person to tell what part of his apparent knowledge is knowledge. Consider our poor detective. After he is told that one of the two is guilty, we still must say that a short time ago he knew one of two propositions, but he is not now and never has been in a position to say which. This, I believe, is too much to swallow. At least, it is clear that this is what must be swallowed if truth is an independent requirement.

But now, if the detective does not know that White is innocent in this situation, it cannot be just because of Black's skill at covering his tracks. We do not want to say that the detective does not know that White is innocent, but that he would have known if Black had clumsily given away his guilt (assuming this would not count as more evidence for White's innocence). Knowledge does not disappear just because of the embarrassing parallel.

Having gone this far, I think it is clear, first, that if the detective does not now know that White is innocent, he would not have known even if Black had never existed. Whether or not he knows that *p* certainly does not depend on anything other than *p* and his evidence for *p*. And second, if he does not have knowledge in this situation, he would not have knowledge in any other situation in which his evidence was equally good. But we can allow the evidence to be as good as we like (as long as it does not imply what he is said to know) without altering the situation. Our famous detective knows far less than he is given credit for.

If we take the first step of admitting that the detective does not know that White is innocent, we cannot halt this journey to skepticism, for each subsequent step depends on nothing more than the assumption that if two cases are alike with respect to both the subject and the object, then either both are knowledge or both are not. In the case of Black and White, we assumed that the situations were alike with respect to the subject but not the object. Thus, if we do not allow the requirement of truth to be an independent part of the analysis of knowledge we are led to skepticism. But if we do allow it, we are forced to allow, counterintuitively, that a person can have the same evidence for two propositions, but know only one of them, thereby not being in a position to determine which he knows.

There is another route to skepticism. What one knows is true. Thus, if truth is not an independent part of the analysis of knowledge, it must be implied by the rest of the analysis. If one's knowledge depends only on his experiences, then the analysis of knowledge must be something like: John knows that p if and only if he believes that p and his experiences, mental states, dispositions, and so forth could not be as they are without p being true. There are at least two ways in which this is inadequate. First, if "could" is taken to represent logical possibility, we will know all the necessary truths that we believe. Second, Gettier type examples can easily be constructed using false memory impressions.[3] Thus, a person can have true beliefs which could not be false, given his experiences, but which he now believes for the wrong reason. Thus, we need something more like: John knows that p if and only if John believes that p and John's present mental state guarantees him that p. This is vague, of course, and in particular in need of an account of what it would be for a mental state to guarantee a person in that state that p. But it is not my purpose to attempt an analysis of knowledge, but merely to indicate the kind of analysis required once we abandon truth as an independent requirement.

I believe many philosophers have felt that this kind of analysis could not be correct. Whatever the correct account of the crucial phrase, it will seldom, if ever, be true that one's present mental state guarantees him of the truth of anything. But we claim to know many things, and furthermore, we ought to make these claims. It would, for example, be very misleading to deny knowledge in many situations. But it is the ordinary concept of knowledge that is involved in these claims, and it is this concept that our analysis should aim to capture, not some philosophers' invention.

But these misgivings are based on a misconception, which can be brought out by considering spatial terms like "flat" and "straight." These terms have recently been discussed by Peter Unger in a paper in which he points out their significance for our understanding of skepticism.[4] I will just point out certain features of the use of these terms that are relevant to the considerations of the preceding paragraph. These terms stand for absolutes in the sense that something is flat, for example, only if it is perfectly flat. There are, in fact, no flat physical objects. But we frequently say of a physical object that it is flat. And there are many situations in which it would be misleading or worse to deny that something was flat. Thus, from the fact that we ought to call something flat in certain circumstances, it does not follow that it is flat. Likewise, it does not follow from the fact that we sometimes ought to say that we know things that we do know them.

Whether or not we ought to call an object flat depends not only on the physical characteristics of the object, but also on the circumstances, and in particular, on assumed goals and interests. We might call a certain table flat if we were looking for a place for our picnic, but not if we wanted to mount precision instruments. And you might call a field flat if you wanted to plant corn which you would not call flat if you had in mind playing baseball. Flatness is, in effect, an ideal. In practice, we call things flat if they approach that ideal. How closely they must approach the ideal depends, at least in part, on what uses we have in mind for them. The important point is that what we ought to say varies while the things we talk about remain the same. This is a sure sign that what we ought to say is determined in these instances by something other than truth conditions. Note that if we could infer that the table is flat from the fact that we ought to call it flat, we could also infer that the very same table is not flat from the fact that, the circumstances but not the table being altered, we ought to say that it is not flat.

I believe the same phenomenon emerges with "knows." On a camping trip we might say that John knows that a certain lake is three miles up the valley, but we might not say that he knew if his condition were the same and we were due at the lake in an hour for secret peace talks. And I believe that if Black were not there to perplex matters it would be right to say that the detective knows that White is innocent. But given the equal evidence of Black's innocence, we ought not to say that he knows. It is not implausible to say that knowledge is an ideal—being in a mental state that guarantees the truth of its object—that is seldom realized, but that we ought to say that people have knowledge when their mental state approaches that ideal in various ways depending on the context. It must be admitted, however, that it is more difficult to see what the relationship is between the context and the propriety of knowledge claims. Nor is the ideal obviously imaginable, as it is with spatial concepts.

The important thing shown by the analogy with spatial terms is that nothing is necessarily wrong with an analysis of a concept that makes most of what we say, and ought to say, using that concept false. The analysis is not the philosophical invention of a new concept. It is an analysis of our ordinary concept, which we make use of in ways that are more complicated than we had imagined. The analogy also shows that there is nothing more surprising or philosophically objectionable about the skepticism to which we have been led than there is about the fact that there are no flat physical objects. Perhaps this means that justified belief or something like it is the more interesting concept for epistemology after all. The really significant skepticism (such as Hume's) holds that (rationally) justified belief is impossible, and that is a different matter entirely.

NOTES

1. Edmund Gettier, "Is Justified True Belief Knowledge?" *Analysis* 23 (1963): 121–23.

2. If this is correct, then no doubt so is a stronger condition to the effect that whether or not John knows that p depends only on those of his experiences that are relevant to p, and in fact only on those that John is in a position to realize are relevant.

3. Suppose Jones believes Brown was at a certain party because of his memory impression of seeing Brown there conversing with Green. If Green was not at the party, and has never met Brown, but Jones spent most of the evening in a now forgotten conversation with Brown, then Jones's experiences could not be as they are (have been) without Brown being at the party. But Jones does not know that Brown was at the party.

4. Peter Unger, "A Defense of Skepticism," *Philosophical Review* 80 (1971): 198-219. I am not, however, convinced that "certain" in "John is certain that p" is, in Unger's terminology, an absolute term, like "flat." More likely, I believe, the ideal nature of knowledge is due to the requirement of (completely) *justified* certainty. Compare William W. Rozeboom, "Why I Know So Much More Than You Do," *American Philosophical Quarterly* 4 (1967): 281–91.

25

Fallibilism and Knowing that One Knows

Richard Feldman

Under what conditions do people who know a certain proposition know that they know it? Widely divergent answers to this question have been given. Some philosophers have defended arguments that suggest that people never know that they know. Others have said that whenever people know a proposition, they know that they know it. In this paper I will criticize these extreme views and defend a more moderate position. I am especially interested in discussing the possibility of knowing that one knows if a "fallibilist" account of knowledge is true. In the first part of this paper I will describe fallibilism and in succeeding sections I will discuss the various views on knowing that one knows.

I

A common way to describe fallibilism is as the view that:

(F) S can know that p even if it is possible that S is mistaken in believing that p.

This claim can easily be misunderstood. It does not mean that it is possible for S to know that p even if it is false that p. This amounts to a denial that knowledge requires truth, something not generally intended by fallibilists. (F) also does not mean simply that it is possible for S to know that p even if it is possible that it is false that p. This

From *Philosophical Studies* 90, no. 2 (April 1981): 266–82. © 1981. Reprinted by permission of the publisher.

is equivalent to the assertion that contingent truths can be known, and even nonfallibilists admit that one can know such contingent truths as what one would express by saying "I exist" or "I am in pain."

A better way to understand fallibilism is as the claim that:

(F1) It is possible for S to know that p even if S does not have logically conclusive evidence to justify believing that p.

(F1) itself is in need of clarification, and I will only attempt to give a brief and informal account of it here. What it amounts to is the claim that people can know things on the basis of nondeductive arguments. That is, they can know things on the basis of inductive, perceptual, or testimonial evidence that does not entail what it is evidence for. Many of the things we commonly take ourselves to know are known in this way, so most of what we commonly take ourselves to know can be termed "fallible knowledge." It should be noted that if one proposition, P, is known fallibly, and P entails Q, and Q is believed on the basis of P, then Q is also known fallibly even though the evidence for Q, i.e., P, entails Q.

II

Fallibilism has a slightly counterintuitive consequence that might lead one to think that people never know that they have any fallible knowledge. Suppose that Smith is a detective investigating a murder, and she has uncovered very strong evidence in support of the propositions:

(1) Black is innocent.
(2) White is innocent.

Suppose the evidence is so strong that we are inclined to say that her belief in each proposition is justified. Suppose, moreover, that (1) is true and that (2) is false. On the fallibilist view we seem forced to say that Smith knows (1) but does not know (2).[1] This sort of consequence of fallibilism has seemed unacceptable to some philosophers. John Tienson writes of this example:

> If one insists that the detective does know that Black is innocent, knowledge becomes much less useful than we are inclined to think. Acting on one's knowledge will not lead one astray, but neither will acting on one's true beliefs. And for the same reason: it will not count as knowledge or true belief unless it is true. But it will not be possible for a person to tell what part of his apparent knowledge is knowledge.

Consider our poor detective. After [she] is told that one of the two is guilty, we still must say that a short time ago [she] knew one of two propositions, but [she] is not now and never has been in a position to say which. This, I believe, is too much to swallow.[2]

H. A. Prichard has written:

We must recognize that whenever we know something we either do, or at least can, by reflecting, directly know that we are knowing it. . . .[3]

It is clear that Prichard would find intolerable the conclusion that a person cannot distinguish knowing something from failing to know it. This remark of Prichard's has been quoted with approval by Chisholm and others.[4]

Of course, the view that Prichard and Tienson defend has a counterintuitive consequence of its own. For if knowing must be distinguishable from not knowing in the way they require, then cases that fallibilists would call cases of fallible knowledge are not knowledge at all. Since, as both Tienson and Prichard admit, most of the things we commonly take ourselves to know are things of which we have at best fallible knowledge, they are forced to conclude that we know very little. And this, too, is a counterintuitive consequence that is difficult to swallow.

It is not my purpose in this paper to argue that fallibilism is preferable to skepticism. I will instead assume that fallibilism is true and examine the possibility of knowing that one knows given that assumption.

III

In defending the fallibilist view that in the example described above Smith knows (1) to be true, but does not know (2) to be true, we must admit, as Tienson says, that after Smith learns that one of these two propositions is false she is in no position to say which of the two propositions it is that she knew. In other words, she is unable to tell the difference between the case of actual knowledge and the case of merely apparent knowledge (i.e., the case that seemed like knowledge but wasn't). But if there is no way for Smith to tell whether a given case of apparent knowledge is actual knowledge or not, then, one might argue, surely she does not know that it is actual knowledge. What is true of Smith in this example is true of anyone who has fallible knowledge. From the point of view of a potential knower, there is no apparent difference between actually knowing something and merely seeming to know something. We might put the point by saying that cases of merely apparent knowledge are introspectively indistinguishable from cases of actual knowledge and that, consequently, no one can ever know of a case of apparent knowledge that it is actual knowledge. In short, no one ever knows that he knows anything, except possibly some necessary truths and some infallibly known contingent truths. Let us call this view "metaepistemological skepticism."

A fallibilist could accept metaepistemological skepticism, but it is by no means a consequence to which fallibilists are committed. Let us grant that people cannot tell the difference between actually knowing something and merely apparently knowing it. That is, actual knowledge and merely apparent knowledge are introspectively indistinguishable. The crucial claim in the argument for metaepistemological skepticism is the claim that:

(3) If S cannot tell the difference between knowing that p and merely apparently knowing that p, then S does not know that S knows that p.

(The sentence "S knows that S knows that p" should be interpreted as ascribing to S knowledge of a self-knowledge proposition. By "self-knowledge proposition" I mean a proposition one could express by saying "I know that p." Analogous remarks apply to "S believes that S knows that p" and "S is justified in believing that S knows that p.") The likely reason for asserting (3) is the seemingly plausible claim that:

(4) If S cannot tell the difference between knowing that p and merely apparently knowing that p, then S is not justified in believing that S knows that p.

(3) follows from (4) and the uncontroversial assumption that knowledge requires justification. Given that no one can ever tell the difference between fallibly knowing a proposition and merely apparently knowing it, metaepistemological skepticism follows.

The problem with this argument for metaepistemological skepticism concerns (4). It seems to be an instance of a general principle:

(P) If S cannot tell the difference between S's ϕing and S's ψing, then S is not justified in believing that S ϕs.

But (P) seems to be false, for at least two reasons.

One reason to reject (P) has to do with people who do not believe that there are cases (namely, cases of ψing) that are not cases of ϕing, but nevertheless are indistinguishable from cases of ϕing. For example, consider a novice bird watcher who has been told by some experts that all birds with certain markings are of some given species. When he clearly spots a bird with those markings he becomes justified in believing that he is seeing a bird of that species. The novice is still justified in this belief even if there happens to be another rare species with markings such that he (the novice) cannot tell the difference between seeing a bird of the first species and seeing a bird of the second, or rare, species. The novice is justified in his belief because he is justified in accepting what the experts tell him. We should, therefore, reject (P).

This reason to reject (P) not only removes support for (4), but also provides a reason to reject (4). Anyone who has never realized that there are cases of merely apparent knowledge and that they are indistinguishable from cases of actual knowledge is in a position similar to that of the novice bird watcher. Such a person has every reason to believe that he does know things, and no reason to think that he does not. So such a person seems to be justified in believing that he does know things even though he cannot tell the difference between actual knowledge and merely apparent knowledge. So (4) seems to be false.

(P) could be modified to avoid this objection by limiting it to people who do realize that they are unable to tell the difference between ϕing and ψing. Similarly, (4) could be limited to people who realize that they cannot tell the difference between actually knowing something and merely apparently knowing something. Let us call such people "epistemologists." The conclusion of the metaepistemological argument would now be that no epistemologist is ever justified in believing, and thus no epistemologist ever knows, that he fallibly knows any particular proposition.

There is another objection to (P) and to (4) that applies even when they are modified in the way just suggested. It is that a person can have good reason to believe that he is in one of two states he realizes are indistinguishable. Consider again our detective, Smith, who has equally good evidence for the true proposition (1)—that Black is innocent—and for the false proposition (2)—that White is innocent. Let us assume that Smith is an epistemologist in the special sense just noted. Now, consider the propositions:

(5) Smith knows that Smith knows that Black is innocent.
(6) Smith knows that Smith knows that White is innocent.

It is clear that (6) is false. The reason for this is that White is not innocent, and therefore Smith does not know that White is innocent, and thus Smith does not know that she knows that White is innocent. Note that in order to maintain that (6) is false we need not say that Smith is not justified in believing that Smith knows that White is innocent.

Turning now to (5), we may say that it is true if the conditions for knowledge are satisfied, that is, if each of the following is true:

(5a) It is true that Smith knows that Black is innocent.
(5b) Smith believes that Smith knows that Black is innocent.

(5c) Smith is justified in believing that Smith knows that Black is innocent.

(5d) Smith's justification for believing that Smith knows that Black is innocent is "not defective."[5]

(5a) and (5b) are assumed to be true in the example. Whatever question there is concerning the truth of (5) has to do with (5c) and (5d). Since (5d) has been given no clear meaning it is difficult to argue conclusively for or against it. But I can see no reason to think that it is false in this case or that similar claims are false in typical cases in which a person has a justified true belief that he knows something. That is, such cases do not bear any noticeable similarity to the Gettier-type examples that are supposed to fail the condition of which (5d) is an instance. Smith's justification for the true proposition that she knows that Black is innocent does not seem to depend upon any falsehoods, as is typical of defective justifications. I will therefore assume that (5d) is true and will not discuss it further.

Given that (5a), (5b), and (5d) are all true, we may say that (5) is true if (5c) is true. I believe that it can be agreed that (5c) is true if (but not only if) Smith is justified in believing that she meets all the conditions for knowledge with respect to the proposition that Black is innocent. That is, (5c), and thus (5), will be true if:

(5c-1) Smith is justified in believing that it is true that Black is innocent.

(5c-2) Smith is justified in believing that Smith believes that Black is innocent.

(5c-3) Smith is justified in believing that Smith is justified in believing that Black is innocent.

(5c-4) Smith is justified in believing that Smith's justification for believing that Black is innocent is not defective.

Since it has been assumed that Smith does know that Black is innocent, (5c-1) is clearly true. (5c-2) is also true, given only that Smith knows what she believes. So the only difficult cases are (5c-3) and (5c-4).

It seems clear that a fallibilist should say that (5c-3) is true (or at least that the example can be filled out in a way that makes it true). The reason for this can be seen if we consider for a moment the conditions under which a person is justified in believing that a given belief of another person is justified. If S wants to know whether T's belief that p is justified, S must consider T's reasons for this belief and decide whether the reasons are sufficient reasons. In the case of Smith and her belief that Black is innocent, another person would justifiably believe that Smith's belief is justified if that person determined what Smith's reasons or evidence for her belief is and discovered that Smith's evidence is sufficient. So in thinking about this example, we may easily come to the justified conclusion that Smith is in fact justified in believing that Black is innocent. But if we may justifiably come to this conclusion, then surely Smith can as well. That is, she knows perfectly well what her evidence is and she can evaluate that evidence as well as we can. So she also can be justified in believing that her belief is justified. So we may accept (5c-3).

(5c-4) is the only condition remaining to be considered. Could Smith justifiably believe that her justification is not defective? In effect, this is equivalent to the question, "Could Smith justifiably believe that in believing that Black is innocent she is not the victim of a Gettier-type example?" If we assert that (5c-4) is true, then we are asserting that she is justified in so believing.

There are, I believe, two reasons to think that (5c-4) is true. The first is that, given that Smith is justified in believing that Black is innocent, she is justified in believing that her evidence for the proposition that Black is innocent is true. That is, she is justified in believing that her belief that Black is innocent does not depend upon any false proposition. Since, as Gilbert Harman has argued,[6] this is what usually makes one's justification defective, she is justified in believing that her justification is not defective.

The second reason for thinking that (5c-4) is true is that Smith, if she is like the rest of us, has found that in the past very few of her justified beliefs have been defectively justified. That is, she has very rarely found herself to be the victim of situations somewhat like those in Gettier-examples, in which a person has a justified belief that depends upon some false proposition. She has reason to believe, then, that she is not such a victim in this case. Thus, she is justified in believing that her justification is not defective, and therefore (5c-4) is true.

Conditions (5c-1)–(5c-4) all appear to be true; hence (5) is true, and Smith knows that she knows that Black is innocent. The main point to realize is that once we accept fallibilism we must admit that Smith can be justified in believing that Black is innocent even though she is not able to tell the difference between Black's actually being innocent and Black's merely apparently being innocent. But if we admit this, then we should also admit that Smith can be justified in believing that she knows that Black is innocent even though she cannot tell the difference between actually knowing that Black is innocent and merely apparently knowing that Black is innocent. Thus, the argument for metaepistemological skepticism fails, and fallibilists can hold that people can, and do, know that they know.

The temptation to think otherwise and to accept metaepistemological skepticism stems, I believe, from the failure to realize that one can have fallible knowledge that one knows something. So, when it is argued that one cannot know that one has fallible knowledge that *p*, I suspect that what is behind the argument is the true insight that one cannot have infallible knowledge that one knows that *p*. But that contention is quite innocuous and in no way conflicts with the claim that one can have fallible knowledge that one knows.

IV

Some philosophers have held views quite contrary to the view criticized in section III. One thing such philosophers have pointed out is that it would be an error to require a person who knows that p to acquire more evidence in support of the proposition that p in order to know that he knows that p. No such additional evidence is required. What is required, I shall argue, is evidence that one's belief that p is justified. And while one generally has such evidence, there can be cases in which one does not.

One view, opposed to those discussed in section III, that has found some support is:

(K1) If S knows that p, then S knows that S knows that p.[7]

Various reasons have been given for (K1), but they have been adequately discussed elsewhere, and I will not consider them here.[8]

Against the view that one always knows that one knows, Chisholm argues:

Now it is possible that there is a person who does not yet have the concept of evidence or of knowledge, but for whom, all the same, a certain proposition is known. Such a person, then, would be one for whom it could not be evident that anything is known or evident. Therefore a proposition . . . may be known without it being known that it is known.[9]

Chisholm goes on to defend the principle that:

(K2) If S considers the proposition that S knows that p, and if S does know that p, then S knows that S knows that p.

It seems to me, as it has seemed to others,[10] that (K2) is also too strong. The argument for this is as follows: even if a person does consider, and thus understand, the proposition that he knows that p, the person could conceivably come to the mistaken conclusion that he does not know that p. He might come to this mistaken conclusion because he has a mistaken view about how much evidence is required for knowledge, or a mistaken estimate of the amount of evidence he has in support of p, or because he suffers from a lack of confidence in his own ability to make judgments. If these are possibilities, and a person can mistakenly abandon (or never adopt) the true belief that he does know that p, then a person can know that p, consider the proposition that he knows that p, and not know that he knows that p, since he does not believe that he knows that p. Hence (K2) is false. For those unconvinced by Chisholm's objection to (K1), this can also serve as an objection to (K1).

One possible response to this argument is to retreat to a slightly weaker thesis than Chisholm's, namely:

(K3) If *S* knows that *p* and *S* believes that *S* knows that *p*, then *S* knows that *S* knows that *p*.

This view has been defended by Carl Ginet.[11] It may seem to be supported by the fact that a person who knows that *p* does not need additional evidence supporting the proposition that *p* in order to know that he knows that *p*. In view of this it may seem that nothing more than true belief that one knows is needed to know that one knows.

However, I believe that (K3) is also mistaken. One way to show that (K3) is false is by showing that there are examples in which a person correctly but unjustifiably believes that he or she knows a certain proposition. It is, I believe, beyond dispute that one can correctly but unjustifiably believe that another person knows a certain proposition. I shall argue that a person can correctly but unjustifiably believe a self-knowledge proposition for reasons similar to those for which one can correctly but unjustifiably believe that another person knows a certain proposition.

The belief that a person, *S*, knows that *p* is often based in part on the belief that *S* is justified in believing that *p*. This latter belief often rests on two further beliefs, one about what *S*'s evidence is and one to the effect that this evidence is sufficient to justify *S*'s belief.[12] If either of these last two beliefs is unjustified, then one may fail to be justified in believing that *S*'s belief that *p* is justified, and as a result one will not know that *S* knows that *p* (even if *S* does in fact know that *p*). What I hope to show is that this can happen even when *S* is oneself.

One way in which a person can fail to be justified in his true belief that he knows that *p* is by being mistaken about what his evidence for his belief that *p* actually is. Some conceptions of justification make this more common than others, but nearly any will allow that it is possible. Causal theories of justification make it easiest for a person to be mistaken about his own evidence for a belief. According to some causal theories, a belief is justified if and only if there is an appropriate causal connection between the belief and the state of affairs the belief is about.[13] On other causal theories, a belief is justified if and only if it arises as a result of a reliable belief-forming mechanism.[14] Obviously, these theories need to be filled out in detail before they can be evaluated, but for present purposes it suffices to understand them only in broad outline.

Given some such conception of justification, it is not at all difficult to produce examples in which one correctly believes oneself to have evidence to justify a particular belief, but is not justified in so believing. For example, I might find myself firmly convinced that *The French Connection* won the Academy Award for Best Film in 1971, but fail to be entirely sure what my evidence for this belief is. I think I remember reading about it after the award was announced, but for all I know my belief is based on my reading of some critic's predictions about what film would win, It is not at all implausible to think, as a causal theorist might, that if my belief arose in the former way it is justified, but if it arose in the latter way it is not justified. However, I might unjustifiably but correctly think that it is justified if the cause of my belief that it is justified is my false and unreasonable assumption that I would never believe anything like this on inadequate grounds.

Even if one rejects a causal theory of justification, one may well maintain that a person can be confused or mistaken about what constitutes his evidence for a particular belief. Given that, the person may unjustifiably believe that his evidence is sufficient to yield knowledge. If his evidence is sufficient, then he will have knowledge but not be justified in believing, and thus not know, that he knows.

The second way in which a person can fail to be justified in his true belief that he knows a certain proposition is by being unjustified in his claim that his evidence is sufficient for knowledge (even though he does know what his evidence is). There are many cases in which a person is unsure about whether a given belief is justified. For example, if the day before an election all the generally reliable polls indicate overwhelming support for one candidate, then it is not clear (to me, at least) whether a person who knows all about these polls is justified in believing (and knows) that the leading candidate will win. Other very strongly supported beliefs about the future are similar in this respect, as are some beliefs based on testimony and beliefs based on certain very plausible assumptions. An example of this last sort would be one's belief that one's car is still parked where one left it and locked it a few minutes ago. I believe that such beliefs are generally justified, but some philosophers might disagree. Those who do can find their own examples of beliefs they regard as justified but not obviously so.

Now, suppose S is justified in believing, and does know, a proposition of the sort just described. Suppose further that S was at first unsure about the justificatory status of this belief, but then came to believe that it was justified for entirely unsatisfactory reasons, e.g., because he derives pleasure from thinking that he knows things or because he derives the conclusion that his belief is justified from some confused theory of knowledge he has unreasonably adopted. In such cases as these S correctly believes that he has knowledge, but he is not justified in this belief because it is based on the unjustified (but true) claim that he has evidence sufficient for knowledge.

In order to defend these counterexamples to (K3) and to make more plausible the view that (K3) is false, I will consider two points that might be raised by defenders of (K3). First, it might be thought that denying (K3) requires saying that a person can know that p but "should believe" that he does not know that p. The person should then have the seemingly paradoxical belief. "It is true that p but I don't know that p." However, this is not a consequence of denying (K3). All that is required for the examples to work is that the subject is not justified, in the sense required for knowledge, in believing that he has knowledge. It is consistent with this lack of justification that his belief that he has knowledge is more reasonable than not, and thus that he "should believe" that he has knowledge.

Second, one might reject examples of the second sort described above for the following reason. In these examples a person unjustifiably believes that he knows that *p* because he unjustifiably believes that his evidence, which he has correctly identified, is sufficient to justify believing that *p*. His problem arises from his unjustified acceptance of a true epistemological proposition about the adequacy of this evidence. Defenders of (K3) may argue that such epistemological propositions are "self-evident," and thus always justified for everyone (or everyone who considers them). However, this seems to me to be an implausible claim. Some such propositions seem to be open to real doubt even after careful reflection about them. It is hard to reconcile this fact with the view that such propositions are always justified. Perhaps certain of these epistemological propositions are self-evident. For example, when I seem to see something red in normal circumstances and have no reason to think that I am not seeing anything red, then it may be self-evident to me that I am justified in believing that I do see something red. One might say that this epistemological proposition is evident, come what may. Even if I am unable to refute skeptical arguments against it, I am still justified in believing it. But surely the same cannot be said of more complex epistemological propositions about the justification of beliefs about the future or the other cases mentioned above. Perhaps after further development of epistemological theory we will justifiably conclude that such beliefs are justified, but for now we cannot. So this second defense of (K3) seems unsatisfactory also.

The point here is analogous to a commonly accepted point about mathematical and logical truths. Some elementary truths of logic and mathematics are self-evident, and in no circumstances can one lack justification for them. But more complex mathematical and logical truths are not self-evident, and one can unjustifiably believe them. Similarly, some truths about justification are not self-evident, and one can unjustifiably come to believe them. As a result, one can correctly but unjustifiably believe that one is justified in believing, and knows, that *p*. So (K3) is false.

Principles (K1) and (K3) each assert that in cases in which the proposition that *p* is a self-knowledge proposition, if certain of the conditions for knowing that *p* are satisfied, then so are the others. (K1) implies that if the truth condition is satisfied, then the other conditions are also satisfied. (K3) implies that if the belief condition and the truth condition are satisfied, then so are the others. Given the falsity of (K3), the natural next step is to assert:

(K4) If it is true that *S* knows that *p* and *S* believes that *S* knows that *p* and *S* is justified in believing that *S* knows that *p*, then *S* knows that *S* knows that *p*.

An objection to (K4) would take the form of a Gettier-type example in which the proposition in question is a self-knowledge proposition. Any such example will be artificial, but it does seem to me that such examples are possible. I will first present a general argument for thinking that this is so, and then an example that may be of the desired kind.

In typical Gettier-examples a person justifiably believes a true proposition, but fails to know that proposition because the justification is, in some sense, not connected to the proposition's truth. Usually one's justification depends in some important way upon some false proposition. It is clear from the arguments of section III that in the case of self-knowledge propositions one can be justified in believing one when it is in fact false. The subjects of Gettier's examples are in such a position. But given that one can justifiably believe a false self-knowledge proposition, it seems possible that one could also be justified in believing a self-knowledge proposition that happens to be true when one's justification depends in some important way upon a false proposition. An example of this sort would refute (K4).

Examples to illustrate the falsity of (K4) are contrived but possible. Consider again one of the counterexamples to (K3), the case in which a person justifiably believes that her car is parked where she left it a few minutes previously. I assume that she does know that her car is where she left it, although it is not a clear-cut case of knowledge and she does not know that she knows. (For those who reject this example, any other counterexample to (K3) can be used, in the way this one will be, to construct a counterexample to (K4).) To get a counterexample to (K4), we need only give her defective justification for believing that she does have knowledge in this case. Here is one way that this can be done, Suppose she is an epistemology student and her teacher describes a theory of knowledge that implies that people do have knowledge in cases such as the one under consideration. Since the student is justified in believing that the teacher is an authority and his theory seems correct to her, she becomes justified in believing that she does know that her car is still where she left it. Finally, suppose that the teacher has become senile and his theory is thoroughly confused. Although the student may become justified in believing that she has knowledge on the basis of the teacher's claims, this justification is defective, since it depends upon the false assumption that the teacher is (still) an authority on epistemological matters and that his theory is a plausible one.[15] So she has a defectively justified true belief that she has knowledge. Hence, (K4) is false.

For those who do not find this example convincing, other examples with similar structure can be devised. In any case, it seems reasonably clear that once (K3) is rejected, (K4) ought to be rejected as well. In giving up (K3) one admits that a person can have justification for believing that p without having justification for believing that he has such justification. But if the person acquires additional justification to justify his belief that he is justified in believing (and does know) that p, this additional evidence could be defective. As a result, (K4) is false.

V

If the arguments and examples of the previous section are correct, then it is not the case that everyone knows all his true self-knowledge propositions or all the true ones he believes or even all the true ones he justifiably believes. Instead, one knows a self-knowledge proposition if and only if he has an undefective justified true belief in it. Self-knowledge propositions are not special in the sense that for them, but not for other propositions, the satisfaction of some subset of the conditions for knowledge ensures the satisfaction of the other conditions. There appears to be no true principle along the lines of (K1)–(K4) that specifies the conditions under which one knows that one knows.

This is not to say that there is nothing constructive one can say about the conditions under which one knows that one knows. What would be useful would be determining the conditions under which a person is justified in believing that evidence of a given kind is sufficient for knowledge. Thus, we would learn a great deal about the circumstances in which a person knows that he or she knows something if we determined when a person is justified in believing that perceptual, testimonial, or other kinds of evidence are sufficient for knowledge.[16]

NOTES

1. This example was given by John Tienson in "On Analyzing Knowledge," *Philosophical Studies* 25 (1974): 289–93.

2. Tienson, p. 290.

3. H. A. Prichard, *Knowledge and Perception* (Oxford: The Clarendon Press, 1950), p. 86.

4. Roderick Chisholm, *Theory of Knowledge,* 2d ed. (Englewood Cliffs, N. J.: Prentice-Hall, 1977), p. 116. See also Herbert Heidelberger, "The Self-Presenting," *Grazer Philosophische Studien* 7/8 (1979): 59–76.

5. I do not assume that (5d) is well understood. It is merely a fill-in for whatever the fourth condition for knowledge turns out to be.

6. Gilbert Harman, *Thought* (Princeton, N.J.: Princeton University Press, 1973). See pp. 120f.

7. See, for example, Jaakko Hintikka, *Knowledge and Belief: An Introduction to the Logic of the Two Notions* (Ithaca, N.Y.: Cornell University Press, 1962), ch. 5. See also Risto Hilpinen, "Knowing that One Knows and the Classical Definition of Knowledge," *Synthese* 21 (1970): 109–32.

8. See Carl Ginet, "What Must Be Added to Knowing to Obtain Knowing That One Knows," *Synthese* 21 (1970): 163–86, and Roderick Chisholm, "The Logic of Knowing," *The Journal of Philosophy* 60 (1963): 773–95.

9. *Theory of Knowledge,* 2d ed., p. 114.

10. See Ginet, "What Must Be Added to Knowing," p. 166.

11. See Ginet.

12. I am not claiming that one can be justified in believing that *S* knows that *p* only if one has a justified belief about what *S*'s evidence is and one is justified in believing that this evidence is adequate. There

may be other ways to become justified in believing that S knows that p. My claim is simply that sometimes one's justification is of the sort described here.

13. See, for example, Alvin Goldman, "A Causal Theory of Knowing," reprinted in *Essays on Knowledge and Justification,* George S. Pappas and Marshall Swain, eds. (Ithaca, N.Y.: Cornell University Press, 1978), pp. 67–86. This volume contains several other papers on causal theories.

14. See Alvin Goldman, "Discrimination and Perceptual Knowledge," reprinted in *Essays on Knowledge and Justification,* pp. 120–45. William Alston defends a similar view in an unpublished paper, "Justification and Reliability."

15. Where the proposition in question is not a self-knowledge proposition, examples of this sort work easily. For example, if some recognized authority asserts something, I may justifiably accept that assertion. But if the authority has become senile and no longer understands what he is asserting, then my justification is defective even if his testimony happens to be true.

16. I am grateful to Henry Kyburg, Richard Legum, Peter Markie, Paul Weirich, Edward Wierenga, and the referee for the *Philosophical Review* for helpful comments on earlier drafts of this paper.

26

Chisholm on Certainty

Keith Lehrer and Keith Quillen

Chisholm's writing on the analysis of knowledge has received a great deal of attention in the philosophical literature, and deservedly so, while his writing on the analysis of certainty has received rather less. His contribution to our understanding of certainty is, however, profound and the implications should be noted. To that end, we turn to a discussion of Chisholm's analysis of certainty and to the philosophical implications thereof. We shall first review the definitions of certainty that Chisholm has proposed from time to time, indicate the common elements, and explain why we think it is important. Simply put, the analysis elucidates the nature of skeptical arguments concerning the certainty of empirical matters. We shall then raise an objection we attribute to a skeptic and propose an amendment, one incorporating a modality. Roughly formulated, Chisholm has proposed that something is certain for a person just in case there is nothing that it is more reasonable for the person to accept; and we propose that this should be modified to read that something is certain for a person just in case there could be nothing that it would be more reasonable for the person to accept. Needless to say, the proposal is in the spirit of the original. We end with a question for Chisholm and confess that our objective is to elicit further remarks about certainty with the certainty that illumination will flow therefrom.

In *Perceiving*, Chisholm defined certainty as follows.

From Radu J. Bogdan, ed., *Roderick M. Chisholm* (Dordrecht, Netherlands: D. Reidel Publishing Co., 1986), pp. 157–67. © 1986 D. Reidel Publishing Co. Reprinted by permission of Wolters Kluwer Academic Publishers.

(C1) S is certain that h is true = df (i) S knows that h is true and (ii) there is no
hypothesis i such that i is more worthy of S's belief than h.[1]

In the second edition of *Theory of Knowledge*, Chisholm defined certainty somewhat
differently.

(C2) h is certain for S = df h is beyond reasonable doubt for S (i.e., accepting h
is more reasonable for S than withholding h), and there is no i such that accepting i is more reasonable for S than accepting h.[2]

In more recent work, Chisholm no longer ascribes certainty to propositions, because
the contingent propositions that would turn out to be certain would be first person
propositions, and Chisholm doubts that there are any such propositions. So Chisholm
now defines certainty in terms of the undefined locution, "x directly attributes to y the
property of being F."

(C3) The direct attribution of a property may be said to be objectively *certain*
for a person provided these conditions hold: the direct attribution of that
property is beyond reasonable doubt for that person; and it is at least as reasonable for him as is the direct attribution of any other property.[3]

These definitions differ with respect to both definiens and definiendum, but they all
contain a common element. We shall describe that element as the maximality condition, to wit, the condition that what is certain be at least as reasonable as anything else,
for example, the direct attribution of any other property.

The last definition, (C3), closely resembles the second, (C2), with the modification that it is the direct attribution of a property that is said to be certain in (C3)
rather than a proposition; and, consequently, the comparison articulated in the maximality condition is restricted to direct attributions. The more striking difference is between these two definitions and the earlier definition, (C1), in that the latter required
that the person know that h is true as well as formulating the maximality condition
in terms of a different comparative locution. Of course, the definiendum is not the
same for the various definitions, but we conjecture that the explanation lies elsewhere.
The substitution of "more reasonable" for "more worthy" in the definiens of (C2) and
(C3) is, we conjecture, intended to substitute a more clearly epistemic term of comparative evaluation. The dropping of the knowledge condition we conjecture to be
motivated by a shift in the concept Chisholm intended to define.

Since "S knows that h is true" entails "h is true," the sense of "certain" that (C1)
purports to define is what Roderick Firth has called a "truth-evaluating" sense of that
term.[4] A use of "certain" is truth-evaluating if we can deduce that h is true at t from

the assertion that h is certain for S at t. There may be a purely warrant-evaluating sense of "certain." A use of the term is warrant-evaluating, says Firth, if we can deduce that h is warranted for S at t from the assertion that h is certain for S at t. Perhaps Chisholm's dropping of the knowledge condition then indicates a shift in the sense of "certain" that Chisholm hoped to explicate. With these brief remarks intended to elicit from Chisholm what may have motivated these alterations, we turn to the philosophical implications of the definition.

CERTAINTY AND SKEPTICISM

It has been a philosophical question of some interest whether anything is certain and, if something is, precisely what. Skeptics of both a traditional and modern ilk have rejected various claims to certainty that people ordinarily accept. The skeptic of Descartes's *Meditations* is one such skeptic who argues that perceptual beliefs and, indeed, our arithmetical beliefs fall short of certainty. C. I. Lewis later argued, finding a persistent critic in Norman Malcolm, that no objective statement was certain.[5] Both lines of critical argumentation share the assumption that if we can conceive of conditions under which a statement or belief could turn out to be false, and if the existence of those conditions cannot be totally excluded, then claims of certainty for the statement or belief cannot be upheld. Defenders of common sense, starting from Thomas Reid arguing against Descartes, have argued, to the contrary, that the statements and beliefs in question have the highest level of reasonableness and are, therefore, certain or known for certain.[6]

The great virtue of Chisholm's analysis of certainty is the effect it has of clarifying the nature of the dispute concerning certainty. The disputes are not verbal; rather, they are disputes over the marks of reasonableness or worthiness of acceptance. Philosophers have had and continue to have differing theories about what makes one thing more reasonable to accept than another. Once one notes that the maximality condition is a condition of certainty, the point of the dispute is elucidated. They are disputes about whether, in virtue of some feature or other, some feature of refutability or corrigibility for example, a statement or belief is less reasonable than some other. The skeptic argues that it is less reasonable and concludes that the statement or belief in question falls short of certainty. If the skeptic is right in his claim that the statement or belief has the feature in question and in his claim about the relevance of the feature to comparative reasonableness, then, in terms of Chisholm's definitions, the skeptic's conclusion is validly drawn.

It is thus enlightening to interpret, in terms of the definition, the replies to skepticism offered by G. E. Moore and Thomas Reid.[7] For, both Reid and Moore thought that there were claims about the external world, about the objects we see directly before us, that were as reasonable to accept as any. Reid alleged that such claims about external objects are as reasonable to accept as claims about our thoughts or the most obvious arithmetical truths. Reid concluded that such claims about the external world are certain. To derive that conclusion from his premises, Reid needed another premise, one connecting maximal reasonableness with certainty. Chisholm's definition fills the need. Skeptical detractors, as we have observed, would reply that claims about the external world lack some feature, of incorrigibility or other security from error, and conclude that, therefore, those claims are less reasonable than others. They conclude that the claims about the external world are not certain. To derive their skeptical conclusion from their premises, they also require another premise; and, again, Chisholm's definition would suffice. We propose that most disputes between skeptics and defenders of common sense can be understood in terms of Chisholm's maximality condition on certainty. We turn now, however, to a kind of skeptic that we think cannot be properly understood in terms of Chisholm's conditions.

Consider a skeptic with respect to certainty who affirms Chisholm's definiens with respect to some direct attribution of a property. Our skeptic is one who, having read Descartes, directly attributes the property of thinking to himself, agrees that the attribution is beyond reasonable doubt and at least as reasonable for him as the direct attribution of any other property, but who, being a skeptic with respect to certainty, denies that the attribution is certain for him. What reason could such a skeptic have for denying that a direct attribution that is beyond reasonable doubt and maximally reasonable is certain? Notice that for that attribution to be beyond reasonable doubt in Chisholm's sense, it is only required that it be more reasonable to make the attribution than to withhold. Suppose then that the skeptic accepts that attributing thought to himself is more reasonable than withholding that attribution; but suppose he maintains that it is just barely more reasonable to make the attribution than to withhold. Suppose further that reflection has convinced him that accepting any proposition or making any attribution is at best only barely more reasonable than withholding. We may imagine that the skeptic, having reflected on human ignorance and propensity to err, has concluded that no one ever has any very good reason for accepting any proposition or making any attribution. Although he does think that, in a limited number of cases, it is more reasonable to make a doxastic commitment than to withhold, our skeptic is at once liberal in his estimates of the risk of error and conservative in his epistemic evaluations. He concludes that nothing is certain for anyone. The relevance of this to Chisholm's account of certainty is that, given his definition, it is self-contradictory to affirm that a direct attribution is more reasonable to make than to withhold and also maximally reasonable and yet deny that it is certain. But surely what the skeptic has affirmed is not contradictory.

A MODAL SOLUTION

Our proposal for dealing with this problem is that we regard the notion of certainty as being implicitly modal. Our skeptic has conceded that there are some direct attributions of properties that are at least as reasonable for him as the direct attribution of any other property, though he denies that those attributions are certain. This appears to be logically consistent. Suppose, however, that the skeptic conceded that there are direct attributions of properties, for example, the property of thinking something, that are such that it is not possible that the direct attribution of any other property is more reasonable than the direct attribution of the properties in question. Or, to borrow the locution for *de re* necessity that is used, in other contexts, by Chisholm himself,[8] suppose that the skeptic were to concede that there are direct attributions of properties that are necessarily such that they are maximally reasonable. Would it then be consistent for the skeptic to add that those direct attributions are not certain? In answering this question, we must be sensitive to at least two readings of the modal claim conceded by the skeptic.

For illustrative purposes, we avail ourselves of the fashion these days (though, we should note that it is not followed by Chisholm himself) of explicating modal notions in terms of possible worlds. Put in these terms, one reading of the claim that there is a direct attribution of a property P such that it is not possible for the direct attribution of any other property to be more reasonable than the direct attribution of P, is that the direct attribution of that property is maximally reasonable at all possible worlds. On this reading, the skeptic is conceding that there are some direct attributions of properties for which there is no possible world w such that the direct attribution, in w, of any other property is more reasonable for him than the direct attribution, in w, of the properties in question. Can the skeptic add, without contradiction, that those attributions are not certain? It would appear so. The skeptic might concede that a direct attribution is maximally reasonable in every world in which it is made but deny that the attribution made in actual world conditions is reasonable enough in the actual world to be counted as certain. The level of reasonableness required for maximality might vary across possible worlds, and his claim is that the actual world is a world in which, due to the woeful epistemic conditions that obtain, maximality is inadequate to yield certainty. None of our actual beliefs, he insists, is certain.

One could reply to the skeptic by claiming that it makes no sense to suppose what the skeptic must suppose in order to sustain his objection. There is, however, a second reading of the modal claim that bypasses the problem altogether. On this reading, the claim that there are direct attributions of properties such that it is not possible for the direct attribution of any property to be more reasonable than the direct attribution of the properties in question, is interpreted as affirming that there is no possible world w such that the direct attribution, in w, of some other property is more reasonable than the direct attribution, in the *actual world*, of the properties in question. The relevant comparisons, on this reading, are interworld and not merely intraworld comparisons. This time it does not appear that the skeptic can add, without contradiction, that the attribution in question is not certain. A direct attribution, made in the actual world, that is at least as reasonable as any other made in any logically possible set of epistemic conditions must be certain. For, an attribution made in epistemically ideal circumstances will attain the highest possible level of epistemic evaluation. And any attribution that is as reasonable as one that has attained the highest possible level of epistemic evaluation has itself attained that level of evaluation. For such judgments then, there is no logical space for epistemic improvement. Attainment of the highest logically possible level of epistemic evaluation must suffice for certainty. The skeptic who concedes that this level has been attained and yet denies that certainty results is simply contradicting himself.

To put the matter without the use of Chisholm's special terminology of direct attribution, it seems consistent and not contradictory for one to affirm that, as a matter of fact, it is as reasonable to believe that x is F as to believe anything, but to deny that it is certain on the grounds that, as a matter of fact, nothing is *much* more reasonable to believe than anything else. On the other hand, if one affirms that it is as reasonable to believe that x is F as it possibly could be for one to believe anything, then it is not at all clear that it is consistent and not contradictory to go on to deny that it is certain that x is F. Put another way, modal maximality is a stronger condition than simple maximality, for the latter condition may be satisfied, as the skeptic alleges, by beliefs that are, as a result of our epistemic ineptitude, not really very reasonable. The former condition, of modal maximality, would, by contrast, only be satisfied when nothing could be more reasonable for a person to accept; and, in this case, since the maximality cannot be the result of some factual cognitive incompetence, certainty results. The definition of certainty that emerges from these reflections is as follows:

(Cm) The direct attribution of a property may be said to be objectively *certain* for a person provided these conditions hold: the direct attribution of that property is beyond reasonable doubt for that person; and necessarily, the direct attribution of that property is at least as reasonable as the direct attribution of any other property.

where the modal clause, on a possible worlds analysis, would be interpreted thus:

there is no possible world w in which the direct attribution of any other property is more reasonable for him than the direct attribution of the property in question in the actual world.

This definition has a clear advantage over the original in dealing with the skeptic.

It is a striking consequence of the new definition of certainty that a claim that something is certain will involve the claim that a doxastic attitude has an epistemic, that is, evaluative property necessarily. For reasons to be adduced later on, some philosophers would balk at such a claim. Apparently though, Chisholm would not resist the definition on these grounds. It is characteristic of Chisholm's epistemology to affirm that principles relating doxastic attitudes to epistemic evaluations are *synthetic a priori*.[9] This leads us to conjecture that he would affirm that the epistemic evaluation is a necessary property of the doxastic attitudes in question. Because of this parallel, we expect that Chisholm will find nothing inherently problematic with (Cm).

The new definition of certainty allows us to recast the dispute between defenders of commonsense and their more skeptical detractors. Some philosophers, we have observed, have thought that some perceptual beliefs, for example, beliefs about objects that we see directly before us, are certain. (In Chisholm's terminology, some philosophers would have contended that some direct attributions of properties such as the property of being perceptually stimulated by an object directly before one, are certain.) Others have restricted the domain of the empirically certain in such a way as to exclude such beliefs. They have restricted the empirically certain in this way because they have felt that there is some feature which is possessed by beliefs which are certain, but which is lacking in perceptual beliefs. We mentioned earlier that the feature was often taken to be incorrigibility, irrefutability, or some other security from error. With the insight provided by the new definition of certainty, we can cast the dispute in more general terms. The issue concerns the possibility of epistemic improvement with respect to the belief in question. If epistemic improvement is not possible, then the belief is certain; if, on the other hand, epistemic improvement is possible, then the belief falls short of certainty. Let us then make some comparisons with this standard in hand.

Among the judgments Chisholm takes to be certain for us are those involving the attribution of self-presenting properties. Chisholm has affirmed the following principle concerning the self-presenting:

> If the property of being F is self-presenting, then, for every x, if x has the property of being F and if x considers his having that property, then it is certain for x that he is F.[10]

Chisholm affirms, moreover, that there are properties that are self-presenting in this sense, for example, the property of thinking something, feeling something, or being appeared to in some way. Now, it is at least not obvious that epistemic improvement is possible with respect to direct attributions of self-presenting properties. It is not at all clear, for example, that undergoing *any* cognitive improvement would make it more reasonable for us to believe that we are being appeared to in some way when we are being appeared to in that way, and we consider our having that property.

Perceptual beliefs, however, do not fare nearly as well as beliefs involving self-presenting properties. It seems possible (or, compatible with our nature, to use Chisholm's terminology) that we should be so improved with respect to our perceptual abilities that whenever we form a perceptual belief, it is true. This improvement could be either a result of improvements in perceptual processing or, for those philosophers who suspect that this would violate true principles pertaining to personal identity, a result of different natural laws governing the acquisition of perceptual information by processors with our cognitive structures. Moreover, if such improvement is possible, then it is surely possible that we should come to know that whenever we form perceptual beliefs, they are true. Intuitively, this improvement in our perceptual abilities, and our knowledge of it, would result in epistemic improvement with respect to our perceptual beliefs. It is arguable then that perceptual beliefs in the actual world are not as reasonable as any belief could be; for perceptual beliefs might be more reasonable in some other possible world than they are in actual fact. So, the new definition actually does more than just clarify the dispute; if it is correct, then it vindicates the view of those who are more restrictive in what they count as certain.

We have mentioned that Thomas Reid may be included among those philosophers who have thought that at least some empirical beliefs that take us beyond the self-presenting, some perceptual beliefs, for example, are certain. There is a basis in Chisholm's own writing for him to agree with Reid. The basis may be found in his articulation of our epistemic objectives. Chisholm has noted that our epistemic objectives must go beyond simply that of avoiding error, which we could accomplish by universal withholding, to that of accepting truths.[11] If the second objective is deemed relevant to the determination of what it is reasonable to accept, then it would seem that Chisholm could agree with those who claim that some perceptual beliefs about external objects are certain on the grounds that, though these beliefs run some additional risk of error, they permit us to obtain more truth.[12]

Chisholm apparently does not accept this line of argumentation. However, one accepting it (or some variant of it) would not, of course, wish to accept the modal definition of certainty. The modal clause, as we have suggested, would exclude perceptual beliefs from the domain of the certain. The reason was that there is always some risk of error for perceptual beliefs, and therefore in some possible worlds there might be doxastic improvement with respect to such beliefs. There may be another reason, given the modal definition of certainty, for one to deny that some perceptual beliefs are as reasonable as any beliefs pertaining to the self-presenting. Suppose that some perceptual beliefs in the actual world are as reasonable as those pertaining to the self-presenting. Suppose also that our perceptual beliefs in a world in which our perceptual abilities are significantly more trustworthy than they are in the actual world and known to be such would be more reasonable than our perceptual beliefs in the actual world. If, as we are supposing, some perceptual beliefs are just as reasonable as any beliefs pertaining to the self-presenting, and it is possible for any perceptual belief to be more reasonable than it actually is, then some perceptual beliefs in some possible worlds are more reasonable than any beliefs pertaining to the self-presenting in the actual world. It would follow from the modal definition of certainty that even beliefs pertaining to the self-presenting are not certain. This would appear to be a good reason to agree with Chisholm that no perceptual beliefs are as reasonable as the direct attribution of self-presenting properties.

We conclude with an objection. It might be objected that no direct attribution of a property has any epistemic, that is, evaluative property necessarily. The reason is the level of reasonableness of accepting something depends on our cognitive endowment, and, therefore, there is only a contingent connection between our attributing some property, even directly so, and how reasonable that attribution is. It depends on how trustworthy we are in such attribution and that, presumably, is a contingent matter of fact concerning us. This objection takes us, however, beyond the topic of certainty. In an earlier discussion, we noted that it is characteristic of Chisholm's epistemology to affirm that principles relating doxastic attitudes to epistemic evaluations are *synthetic a priori.* This led us to conjecture that he would affirm that the epistemic evaluation is necessarily a property of the doxastic attitude in question. If, however, the epistemic evaluation depends on the assumption of our trustworthiness in such matters, the epistemic evaluation of how reasonable it would be to make the attribution in question depends on our cognitive endowments.

A possible line of reply to this specific objection would be that, assuming that there must be some first principles, there must be principles that attribute epistemic evaluations to doxastic attitudes which are not themselves justified, and, hence, are *synthetic a priori.* One might also affirm that the assumption of the trustworthiness of some epistemic attitudes is not an empirical hypothesis about the mere frequency of reaching the truth, but a normative assumption about the worthiness of some attribution or belief. If we have correctly anticipated the reply, we continue to wonder whether the first principles are necessary truths or whether the properties of epistemic evaluation are, as a matter of *de re* necessity, properties of some direct attributions and other beliefs.

NOTES

1. Roderick M. Chisholm, *Perceiving: A Philosophical Study* (Ithaca, N.Y.: Cornell University Press, 1957), p. 19.
2. Roderick M. Chisholm, *Theory of Knowledge,* 2d ed. (Englewood Cliffs, N.J.: Prentice-Hall, Inc., 1977), p. 10.

3. Roderick M. Chisholm, *The Foundations of Knowing* (Minneapolis: University of Minnesota Press, 1982), p. 9.

4. Roderick Firth, "The Anatomy of Certainty," in *Empirical Knowledge*, Roderick M. Chisholm and Robert J. Swartz, eds. (Englewood Cliffs, N.J.: Prentice-Hall, Inc., 1973), pp. 207–11.

5. C. I. Lewis, *An Analysis of Knowledge and Valuation* (LaSalle, Ill.: Open Court Publishing Co., 1946), pp. 180–84. Norman Malcolm, *Knowledge and Certainty* (Englewood Cliffs, N.J.: Prentice-Hall, Inc., 1963), pp. 1–57.

6. Thomas Reid, *The Works of Thomas Reid, D.D.* (Edinburgh: James Thin, 1895), pp. 326–30.

7. G. E. Moore, "Proof of an External World," in *Philosophical Papers* (New York: Macmillan, 1959).

8. See, for example, Roderick M. Chisholm, *The First Person* (Brighton: The Harvester Press, Ltd., 1981), pp. 129–31.

9. Chisholm, *Perceiving*, p. 112.

10. Chisholm, *The Foundations of Knowing*, p. 10.

11. See, for example, Chisholm, *Theory of Knowledge*, 2d ed., pp, 14–15.

12. For elaboration on reasonableness as a function of both our interest in content and our interest in avoiding error, see Keith Lehrer, "The Gettier Problem and the Analysis of Knowledge," in George S. Pappas, ed., *Justification and Knowledge* (Dordrecht, Netherlands: D. Reidel Publishing Co., 1979).

27

Reply to Keith Lehrer and Keith Quillen

Roderick M. Chisholm

I read the paper by Lehrer and Quillen with special pleasure. It is gratifying—and surprising—to find that one can be understood so well. They seem to know exactly what it is that I have been trying to do. They have criticized my accounts of certainty and have proposed a revision that makes use of a modal account. I think that their criticism is well-taken and that they have pointed to a distinction of fundamental importance to the theory of knowledge.

They address themselves to the following definition which I had proposed in *The Foundations of Knowing* (p. 9):

> (EC) The direct attribution of a property may be said to be objectively *certain* for a person provided these conditions hold: the direct attribution of that property is beyond reasonable doubt for that person; and it is at least as reasonable for him as is the direct attribution of any other property.

The definition (KD2), proposed in the present book, is substantially the same.

Lehrer and Quillen contend that there is no *contradiction* involved in affirming the above definiens and denying the definiendum. They picture a skeptic who reasons that, in this world, people are so impoverished epistemically that they make attributions which are not certain but which, nevertheless, satisfy the definiens (the attri-

From Radu J. Bogdan, ed., *Roderick M. Chisholm* (Dordrecht, Netherlands: D. Reidel Publishing Co., 1986), pp. 208–12. © 1986 D. Reidel Publishing Co. Reprinted by permission of Wolters Kluwer Academic Publishers.

butions are beyond reasonable doubt and are at least as reasonable as any other that could be made).

To deal with this possibility (if it is one), they propose a modal definition of certainty:

(MC) The direct attribution of a property may be said to be objectively *certain* for a person provided these conditions hold: (1) the direct attribution of that property is beyond reasonable doubt for that person; and (2) necessarily, the direct attribution of that property is at least as reasonable as the direct attribution of any other property.

They also propose a possible worlds analysis of the final clause:

(2) There is no possible world in which the direct attribution of any other property is more reasonable for him than the direct attribution of the property in question in the actual world.

I feel that the final clause needs clarification with respect to two points.

(1) The final clause *could* be taken to presuppose that there are what Stout had called "particular characteristics" and to be saying that these particular characteristics have certain epistemic properties necessarily. In this case, if we say that a given person satisfies the terms of the definition, then it will follow that, in addition to the believer and to the property of believing oneself to be thinking, there is also that particular characteristic of believing oneself to be thinking that the believer happens to have now. (The particular characteristic of believing oneself to be thinking that *you* have would be different from the one that *I* have.) According to this interpretation, the definition would be telling us that that particular characteristic which is had by the believer there referred to is the thing that is necessarily certain. But I have suggested, in the discussion of ontology at the beginning of this book, that there is no good reason for thinking that there *are* such particular characteristics. If this interpretation of the Lehrer-Quillen definition is correct, then I would not be tempted to accept it.

We could, however, take the final clause to pertain, not to a particular characteristic, but to that abstract object which is the property of *taking oneself to be thinking*—an entity which, unlike the supposed particular characteristic, exists "in every possible world." This is the way that I will interpret the proposed definition.

(2) There is a second respect in which the final clause of the definiens needs to be clarified. In the first clause "beyond reasonable doubt" is taken in a *relativized* sense: an attribution is said to be beyond reasonable doubt *for* a particular subject. But in the second clause "at least as reasonable as" may seem to be taken in an *absolute*

sense without reference to any subject, in which case it would constitute an additional epistemic concept. But I will assume that this is an oversight and that we may read the second clause this way: "Being-F is necessarily such that, for every x, directly attributing being-F is at least as reasonable for x as is directly attributing any other property." The definition now becomes:

> (MC') The direct attribution of the property being-F is said to be objectively *certain* for a person provided these conditions hold: (1) the direct attribution of being-F is beyond reasonable doubt for that person; and (2) being-F is necessarily such that, for every x, directly attributing it is at least as reasonable for x as is directly attributing any other property.

I will assume that this is the definition that Lehrer and Quillen intend.

What properties would satisfy the conditions of clause (2)? *Taking oneself to be thinking* is such a property. But there are other properties—say, *feeling sad*—which can also serve as the content of judgments of objective certainty and which do not satisfy the above definiens. The direct attribution of *feeling sad* may be objectively certain for a person S without it being the case that, for every x, the direct attribution of being sad is at least as reasonable as the direct attribution of any other property. For not all people are sad.

My first thought in contemplating the Lehrer-Quillen definition, was that it is not adequate since it makes a distinction between the epistemic status of *taking oneself to be thinking* and *feeling sad*. But my second thought is that, after all, there is this distinction. Lehrer and Quillen, therefore, have made an important contribution in calling it to our attention.

What is the difference, then, between the two types of property? I think we may say that the property of taking oneself to be thinking, unlike the property of being sad, is *epistemically necessary*: necessarily anyone who attributes it to himself is justified in attributing it to himself. We may say more generally:

> (EN) h is epistemically necessary = df Necessarily anyone who accepts h is justified in accepting h.

Other properties that are epistemically necessary are those properties that are included in taking oneself to be thinking—for example, the properties of judging, being conscious, being a person, and being capable of thinking. (I believe that this concept of epistemic necessity would help to settle several recent controversies about the nature of thinking.)

Lehrer and Quillen assume that, if I feel sad, my belief that I am judging (which is epistemically necessary) is even more reasonable than my belief that I am sad (which is epistemically contingent). I am not sure how to decide whether they are right. But I concede that, if they are right, then my proposed definition of objective certainty must be modified. And I think that this can be done.

I would interpret (MC') as defining *maximal certainty* and would now characterize the more general concept of *certainty* this way:

> (EC') The direct attribution of a property P may be said to be objectively certain for a person provided that: either (a) P is epistemically necessary; or (b) P is not epistemically necessary, and the direct attribution of P is beyond reasonable doubt for that person and is at least as reasonable for him as is the direct attribution of any other property that is not epistemically necessary.

I would add this necessary truth: if anyone has a property that is epistemically necessary, then there is a property which is not epistemically necessary and which is such that its direct attribution is objectively certain for that person.

Given the explication of epistemic terms that I have set forth here, we may say that, according to clause (b), whatever is certain is *evident*. For I have said that it is *evident* to a person that he is F, provided only that for him the direct attribution of being-F is more reasonable than is the withholding of any property. If I am thinking, for example, then the direct attribution of the property of thinking is (even) more reasonable than is withholding the direct attribution of, say, being capable of squaring the circle. This presupposes that believing *something* is more reasonable than believing nothing; hence it reflects a rejection of Pyrrhonism.

What of the skeptic with whom Lehrer and Quillen began? If he ventures any opinion at all, even one about his epistemic deprivation, then he will have access to maximal certainty with respect to something that is epistemically necessary. And this implies that he will also have access to objective certainty with respect to something that is epistemically contingent. I would say, therefore, that he doesn't know how well off he is, epistemically.

Part VI

How Does Epistemic Appraisal Yield Justification?

28

The Principles of Epistemic Appraisal

Roderick M. Chisholm

I

Appraisal, according to C. J. Ducasse, constitutes the ultimate subject-matter of philosophy. To appraise a thing is "to judge its merits or worth"; generically, therefore, "appraising is nothing more and nothing less than 'yea-ing' or 'nay-ing.' "[1] Ducasse notes further that there are three fundamental types of appraisal: emotional, as is evidenced in liking and disliking; volitional, as is evidenced in causing and preventing; and epistemic, as is evidenced in believing and disbelieving.[2] The present paper is concerned with epistemic appraisal.

I shall take as my text an important observation that Ducasse has made about such appraisal. For this observation, I think, provides us with a clue that will enable us to understand and answer a number of philosophical questions that have been raised about epistemic appraisal. It suggests, moreover, a way of systematizing the terms of our epistemic vocabulary; for example, "know," "evident," "reasonable," "acceptable," "indifferent," "possible," "doubtful," "gratuitous." And it suggests a way in which we might formulate an epistemic logic, or logic of epistemic appraisal.

From F. C. Dommeyer, ed., *Current Philosophical Issues* (Springfield, Ill.: Charles C. Thomas, Publisher, 1966), pp. 87–104. Reprinted by permission of the publisher.

II

Ducasse's observation is this: "In the large majority of cases, when we declare an opinion to have the status of knowledge, a part at least of what we mean by this is that it is better than—superior to—certain others (which we might appraise more specifically as erroneous, or as possibly sound but unproved, etc.) and better also than absence of opinion, or of opinion having the status of knowledge, on the same subject."[3]

Ducasse speaks here of the relation of being *better than,* or of being *superior to,* which he construes as a relation that holds, not among propositions, but among *opinions,* or, as we may also put it, among *believings*; it may also hold between instances of believing and instances of refraining from believing. Thus, to use an older terminology, it is a relation that holds, not among *objects* of belief, but among *acts* of belief. Believing a given proposition may be, for a particular man at a particular time, better than or superior to believing another; it may also be better than or superior to "mere absence of opinion . . . on the same subject."

The relation in question is an epistemic relation; thus Ducasse uses "superior" as well as "better." If we say that it is better, in this sense, for a man to believe one proposition than to believe another, we may not mean that believing the one is *morally,* or *ethically,* better than believing the other. Hence an alternative to saying that one epistemic attitude is "better than" another would be to say that the one is epistemically "preferable" to the other. Or we might say that the one is "more reasonable" than the other. The latter term is perhaps the most natural and so let us use it in what follows. But let us use it in such a way that we may say that one attitude is *more* reasonable than another without thereby committing ourselves to saying that the attitude *is* reasonable. (In the same way, we allow ourselves to say that the lesser of two evils is the one that is better, without committing ourselves to saying that it is good.)

There are three basic epistemic attitudes that one may take toward a given proposition at any particular time: (1) one may believe or accept the proposition; (2) one may disbelieve the proposition, and this is the same thing as believing its negation; or (3) one may withhold or suspend belief—that is to say, one may refrain from believing and refrain from disbelieving. Philosophical language, as well as ordinary language, frequently obscures the distinction between disbelieving and withholding. If a philosopher tells us that we should "reject" a certain proposition, he may mean that we should disbelieve it—that we should believe its negation. Or he may mean that we should withhold the proposition. And if the man in the street tells us that he "does not believe" a given proposition, he is likely to mean that he believes its negation, but he may mean that he is withholding the proposition.

And so we should emend, in one respect, the observation that "appraising is nothing more and nothing less than 'yea-ing' and 'nay-ing.' " We may vote "Yea" or we may vote "Nay," but we may also abstain from voting. We may abstain in the case of emotional appraisal (there are some things we neither like nor dislike), in the case of volitional appraisal (there are some things we strive neither to cause nor to prevent), and also in the case of epistemic appraisal. And in many cases, epistemic abstinence is more reasonable than believing and more reasonable than disbelieving.

We may ask, then, for any given proposition and any given subject at any given time, which is the more reasonable course: believing the proposition, disbelieving the proposition, or withholding the proposition. In considering such a question, we may refer to any of the following possibilities: (a) believing the proposition is more reasonable than withholding it; (b) believing it is more reasonable than disbelieving it; (c) withholding it is more reasonable than believing it; (d) withholding it is more reasonable than disbelieving it; (e) disbelieving it is more reasonable than believing it; and (f) disbelieving it is more reasonable than withholding it. And then there are the six additional possibilities that we obtain by negating each of these.

III

Let us now consider what is suggested by each of these possibilities.

(a) A proposition falling within our first category is one such that (for a given subject at a given time) believing it is more reasonable than withholding it. Any such proposition could be said to be one that is *reasonable* (for that subject at that time). "Reasonable," in this sense, may be said to be a term of high epistemic praise. If we use it we are "yea"-saying, for of the twelve possibilities that our categories provide, this one puts the proposition in the best possible light.

The propositions that fall within the negation of this first category—those propositions which are such that it is *not* more reasonable to believe them than it is to withhold them—may be said to be epistemically *gratuitous*. They are gratuitous for there is no need, epistemically, to accept them.

(b) The second category comprises those propositions which are such that believing them is more reasonable than disbelieving them. If we say of a proposition that it falls within this category, we are expressing only faint epistemic praise. For believing may be more reasonable than disbelieving only in virtue of the fact that of the two possibilities believing is the lesser evil, epistemically. Consider, for example, the proposition that the pope will be in Rome on the third Tuesday in October, five years from now. Believing it, given the information that we now have, is more reasonable than *disbelieving* it; i.e., it is more reasonable to believe that the pope will be in Rome at that time than it is to believe that he will *not* be there. But *withholding* the proposition, surely, is more reasonable still.

The negation of this second category yields a class of propositions having somewhat questionable epistemic status. The propositions belonging to this class are those which are such that believing them is *not* more reasonable than disbelieving them. Any proposition which is such that withholding it is more reasonable than believing it should fall within this category.

(c) If we say of a proposition that it falls within our third category, we are expressing epistemic dispraise or condemnation, for we are saying of it that withholding is more reasonable than believing. We are saying "Nay"—but in the sense of "Do not believe" and not in the sense of "Believe that not." Let us say that any proposition falling within this category is epistemically *unacceptable*.

Among the propositions that are thus unacceptable are, of course, those propositions such that their negations are reasonable, in the sense defined above. But the class of unacceptable propositions would seem to be considerably wider than the class of propositions that have reasonable negations. Sextus Empiricus tells us that, according to Agrippa, "it is necessary to suspend judgment altogether with regard to *everything* that is brought before us."[4] Other, more moderate skeptics would have us suspend judgment with respect merely to those propositions that refer "beyond the appearances." But according to both types of skeptic, there are unacceptable propositions that have unacceptable negations; for example, the proposition that there are many things "beyond the appearances" is unacceptable and so is its negation. The older positivistic philosophers would say of metaphysical propositions that both they and their negations are unacceptable. Perhaps we can all agree that paradoxical propositions—for example, Russell's "The class of all those classes that are not members of themselves is a member of itself "—fall within this category. And if what we shall say below is correct, there are still other unacceptable propositions that have unacceptable negations. Hence, although we can say that all reasonable propositions have unacceptable negations, we cannot say that all unacceptable propositions have reasonable negations.

If a proposition falls under the negation of this third category, it will be one such that withholding it is not more reasonable than believing it; hence we may say of it that it is epistemically *acceptable*. All propositions that are reasonable will be, of course, acceptable, but there are many acceptable propositions that cannot be said to be reasonable. An adequate theory of memory, for example, might require us to say this: if I have that experience which might naturally be expressed by saying that I "seem to remember" a certain proposition to be true ("I seem to remember having seen that man before") then the proposition that I thus seem to remember (the proposition that I have seen that man before) is one that is, for me, *ipso facto*, acceptable. It may be, however, that although the proposition is acceptable it is not reasonable; i.e., although withholding it is not more reasonable than believing it, believing it cannot be said to be more reasonable than withholding it. "Acceptable," then, expresses less praise than does "reasonable." But it expresses more praise than does the doubtful compliment, "Believing is more reasonable than disbelieving."

(d) Where the third formula says that withholding is more reasonable than believing, the fourth says that withholding is more reasonable than disbelieving. If a proposition falling within the third category is one that is unacceptable, then one falling within the fourth is one that has an unacceptable negation. Hence a proposition falling within the negation of this fourth category—a proposition such that withholding it is *not* more reasonable than disbelieving it—will be a proposition that has an acceptable negation.

(e) If we say of a proposition that disbelieving it is more reasonable than believing it, we are expressing faint praise for the negation of the proposition. This faint praise is also expressed by *one* use of the ambiguous epistemic term "doubtful" (or "dubious"). To say that a proposition is doubtful in this sense of the term is to say that one can make out a better case for the negation of the proposition than one can for the proposition itself. (But in another, and more proper, use of the term, we may call a proposition "doubtful" without in any way expressing praise for the negation of the proposition; in this case we will be saying merely that the proposition is itself unacceptable. And "unacceptable," as we have just seen, though it implies dispraise for the proposition in question, need not imply any praise for the negation of that proposition. Any proposition that is doubtful in the first sense of the term will also be doubtful in the second; but those propositions that ought to be withheld will be doubtful in the second sense of the term but not in the first.[5] When the Pyrrhonist finds us dogmatizing and wishes to show us that a given proposition is doubtful, in the second of these two senses, he will apply the maxim of "opposing every argument with an equal argument," and in so doing he may seem to be concerned with showing us that the proposition is also doubtful in the first. This fact may be one source of the present ambiguity of the term.)

The negation of this fifth category—viz., the class of propositions which are such that disbelieving them is *not* more reasonable than believing them—yields a set of propositions having questionable negations. Any proposition having an unacceptable negation will fall within this class. And so, too, will any proposition that ought to be withheld.

(f) If a proposition falling within our first category is one that is reasonable, then a proposition falling within our fifth category will be one that has a reasonable negation. It will be a proposition such that disbelieving it—i.e., believing its negation—is more reasonable than withholding it. When we say of a proposition that it is unacceptable, we are saying "Nay" only in the sense of "Do not believe." But when we say the proposition has a reasonable negation, we are saying "Nay," not only in the sense of "Do not believe," but also in the sense of "Believe that not."

A proposition falling within the negation of this sixth category will be one that has a gratuitous negation.

IV

We have, then, definitions for at least four epistemic terms. A proposition is *reasonable* or "beyond reasonable doubt" (for a given subject at a given time) if (for that subject at that time) believing it is more reasonable than withholding it; it is *gratuitous* if it is not reasonable; it is *unacceptable* if withholding it is more reasonable than believing it; and it is *acceptable* if it is not unacceptable. Whatever is reasonable is acceptable, but not conversely; and whatever is unacceptable is gratuitous, but not conversely.

Other epistemic terms may be defined merely by combining certain of the categories we have discussed.

Thus, we may say of a proposition that it *ought* to be *withheld* if both it and its negation are unacceptable: withholding the proposition is more reasonable than believing it and also more reasonable than disbelieving it.

Propositions may also be said to be epistemically *indifferent*. But here there is an ambiguity and we will do well to guard against possible confusion. "Indifferent" could be used in analogy with its use in moral philosophy. An act is said to be morally indifferent if it is one such that performance of it is permitted and nonperformance of it is also permitted. Some philosophers have said, similarly, that a proposition is indifferent if it is one such that both it and its negation are acceptable.

But the expression "judgment of indifference" is used in writings on the theory of knowledge and on probability theory in a rather different way. A "judgment of indifference" about a pair of propositions is a judgment to the effect that there is no ground for choice between those propositions—neither proposition is more reasonable than the other. If we follow this use, we may be tempted to say that an indifferent proposition is one such that believing it is not more reasonable than disbelieving it and disbelieving it is not more reasonable than believing it. A proposition that is indifferent in this second sense need not be one that is indifferent in the first sense.

Discussing the second concept of indifference, J. M. Keynes quotes the following conversation:

Absolute.   "Sure, Sir, this is not very reasonable, to summon my affection for a
            lady I know nothing of."
Sir Anthony. "I am sure, Sir, 'tis more unreasonable in you to object to a lady you
            know nothing of."[6]

To be sure, if nothing is known of the lady, then an unfavorable attitude is no more justified than a favorable one. But surely the reasonable thing, moral considerations aside, is to withhold both favor and disfavor until something more is known.

And similarly for our epistemic attitudes: if a proposition is such that believing it is no more nor less reasonable than disbelieving it, then withholding it is more reasonable than either believing it or disbelieving it. Hence a proposition that is indifferent in the second sense, may not—and indeed will not—be one that is indifferent in the first.

V

Let us now consider in more detail the logical properties of *more reasonable than.* I suggest that the following three principles are true and could thus be taken as axioms in an epistemic logic, or logic of epistemic appraisal.

(1) *More reasonable than* is a transitive relation: if one thing is more reasonable than another and the other more reasonable than a third, then the first thing is more reasonable than the third. Thus if for a given subject at a given time believing a certain proposition *h* is more reasonable than disbelieving a certain other proposition *i*, and if disbelieving *i* is more reasonable than withholding still another proposition *j*, then believing *h* is more reasonable than withholding *j*.

(2) *More reasonable than* is also asymmetrical: if one thing is more reasonable than another, then the other is not more reasonable than the one. Thus if withholding a proposition is more reasonable than believing it, then believing it is not more reasonable than withholding it.

(3) And, finally, if withholding is not more reasonable than believing, then believing is more reasonable than disbelieving. Or, more exactly: for any proposition *h*, any subject *S*, and any time *t*, if at *t* it is not more reasonable for *S* to withhold *h* than it is for him to believe *h*, then at *t* it is more reasonable for him to believe *h* than it is for him to disbelieve *h*. An instance of this principle would be: if agnosticism is not more reasonable than theism, then theism is more reasonable than atheism.

Let us now note some of the epistemic principles that are yielded by our three axioms. We may assume that reference to a given subject, time, and proposition is constant throughout.

Three principles follow immediately from the second axiom, according to which *more reasonable than* is asymmetrical.

(4) If believing is more reasonable than withholding, then withholding is not more reasonable than believing.

(5) If believing is more reasonable than disbelieving, then disbelieving is not more reasonable than believing.

(6) If disbelieving is more reasonable than withholding, then withholding is not more reasonable than disbelieving.

Our third axiom tells us that, if withholding is not more reasonable than believing, then believing is more reasonable than disbelieving. Reminding ourselves that believing a proposition is the same thing as disbelieving its negation, and that with-holding a proposition is the same thing as withholding its negation (for to withhold a proposition is to refrain from believing it and to refrain from disbelieving it), we may derive the following consequence from our third axiom.

(7) If withholding is not more reasonable than disbelieving, then disbelieving is more reasonable than believing.

By applying the first axiom, which affirms the transitivity of *more reasonable than*, and contraposing conditionals, we obtain additional results. I shall summarize these by noting, with respect to each of the twelve categories that have been distin-guished, what is implied by saying of a proposition that it falls within that category.

(8) If believing is more reasonable than withholding, then: believing is more rea-sonable than disbelieving; disbelieving is not more reasonable than believing; disbe-lieving is not more reasonable than withholding; withholding is more reasonable than disbelieving; and (as already noted) withholding is not more reasonable than believing.

(9) If believing is more reasonable than disbelieving, then: disbelieving is not more reasonable than withholding; withholding is more reasonable than disbelieving; and (as already noted) disbelieving is not more reasonable than believing.

(10) If withholding is more reasonable than believing, then believing is not more reasonable than withholding.

(11) If withholding is more reasonable than disbelieving, then disbelieving is not more reasonable than withholding.

(12) If disbelieving is more reasonable than believing, then: believing is not more reasonable than disbelieving; believing is not more reasonable than withhold-ing; and withholding is more reasonable than believing.

(13) If disbelieving is more reasonable than withholding, then: disbelieving is more reasonable than believing; believing is not more reasonable than disbelieving; be-lieving is not more reasonable than withholding; withholding is more reasonable than believing; and (as already noted) withholding is not more reasonable than disbelieving.

(14) If believing is not more reasonable than disbelieving, then: withholding is more reasonable than believing; and believing is not more reasonable than with-holding.

(15) If withholding is not more reasonable than believing, then: believing is more reasonable than disbelieving; withholding is more reasonable than disbelieving; disbelieving is not more reasonable than withholding; and disbelieving is not more reasonable than believing.

(16) If withholding is not more reasonable than disbelieving, then: disbelieving is more reasonable than believing; withholding is more reasonable than believing; be-lieving is not more reasonable than withholding; and believing is not more reason-able than disbelieving.

(17) If disbelieving is not more reasonable than believing, then: withholding is

more reasonable than disbelieving; and disbelieving is not more reasonable than withholding.

Our three axioms do not enable us to derive any significant consequences from the hypothesis that a given proposition is such that believing it is not more reasonable than withholding it, or from the hypothesis that a given proposition is such that disbelieving it is not more reasonable than withholding it.

VI

Recalling our epistemic definitions, we may now reformulate some of these results. A proposition is one that is *reasonable,* we said, if believing it is more reasonable than withholding it. A proposition is *gratuitous* if it is not one that is reasonable. A proposition is *unacceptable* if withholding it is more reasonable than believing it; it is *acceptable* if it is not unacceptable. And a proposition is one that *ought to be withheld* if it is itself unacceptable and also has an unacceptable negation.

Thus, principle (8) tells us that if a proposition is one that is reasonable, then it is acceptable and it has a negation that is both gratuitous and unacceptable. Principle (10) tells us that if a proposition is unacceptable, then it is gratuitous. And principle (15) tells us that if a proposition is acceptable, then it has an unacceptable—and therefore gratuitous—negation.

What, then, of *indifference*? In one sense of the term, we said, a proposition may be called "indifferent" if it is itself acceptable and if it also has an acceptable negation. A proposition is indifferent in this sense, therefore, if withholding it is not more reasonable than believing it and if withholding it is not more reasonable than disbelieving it. But principle (15) tells us that if withholding is *not* more reasonable than believing, then withholding *is* more reasonable than disbelieving; and principle (16) tells us that if withholding is not more reasonable than disbelieving, then withholding is more reasonable than believing. Our axioms have the consequence, therefore, that it would be contradictory to say of any proposition that it is epistemically indifferent in the sense defined. Hence no proposition is thus indifferent.

This consequence is as it should be. If we wonder whether it is so, we have only to ask ourselves: What proposition might conceivably be said to be epistemically indifferent? What proposition could be such that withholding it is not more reasonable than believing it and not more reasonable than disbelieving it?

Some moral philosophers affirm a "principle of permission": every possible act is one such that either performance of the act is permitted or nonperformance of the act is permitted.[7] The principle may be widened to say: for every possible state of affairs, either realizing that state of affairs is permitted or realizing the negation of that state of affairs is permitted. A corollary of the principle is that there are some acts that are morally indifferent—some acts which are such that both performance and non-performance are permitted.[8] But in epistemology—in the theory of epistemic appraisal—it would seem that we should have a "principle of nonpermission"; every proposition is such that either it is unacceptable or its negation is unacceptable. Or, in other words, every proposition is such that, either withholding it is more reasonable than believing it or withholding it is more reasonable than disbelieving it. And this is a consequence of our principle (15).

But let us remind ourselves that we have distinguished two senses of "indifference": (1) in the one sense, a proposition is indifferent if it is acceptable and has an acceptable negation; and (2) in the other sense, a proposition is indifferent if it is not more reasonable than its negation and if its negation is not more reasonable than it. According to what we have said, there are no propositions that are indifferent in the first sense of the term. But there are many propositions that are indifferent in the second sense of the term.

If, for example, there is a proposition that has a probability of .5 in relation to the totality of what a given subject knows, then that proposition is, for him, one such that there is no choice between it and its negation: believing it is no more reasonable than disbelieving it, and disbelieving it is no more reasonable than believing it.

But surely any proposition that is indifferent in this second scene is one that ought to be withheld. Indeed, one way of showing that a proposition ought to be withheld is to show that it is indifferent in this sense—that the proposition is no more nor less reasonable than its negation. Thus Sextus tells us that "the main basic principle of the skeptic system is that of opposing to every proposition an equal proposition." The various skeptics sought to apply the maxim "To every argument an equal argument is opposed"; the point in so doing was to establish "equality in respect of probability and improbability," indicating thereby that judgment ought to be suspended.[9] And it is a consequence of our principles that any proposition that is thus indifferent ought to be withheld. According to principle (14), if believing is not more reasonable than disbelieving, then the proposition is unacceptable; according to principle (17), if disbelieving is not more reasonable than believing, then the proposition has an unacceptable negation; and according to our definition, if an unacceptable proposition has an unacceptable negation then it ought to be withheld.[10]

VII

There are, of course, alternative ways of developing a logic of epistemic appraisal. Axiom (3), in particular, might be replaced by one that is more liberal. According to axiom (3), if withholding is not more reasonable than believing, then believing is more reasonable than disbelieving; in other words, if a proposition is acceptable, then it is more reasonable to believe the proposition than to believe its negation. One might consider replacing (3) by this: if believing is more reasonable than withholding, then withholding is more reasonable than disbelieving.

The resulting system would differ from the one that I have expounded in essentially the following respects: (a) we could no longer assert that if believing is more reasonable than disbelieving, then withholding is more reasonable than disbelieving; (b) we could no longer assert that if disbelieving is more reasonable than believing, then withholding is more reasonable than believing; (c) the only significant consequence we could draw from the hypothesis that believing is not more reasonable than disbelieving, and from the hypothesis that withholding is not more reasonable than disbelieving, would be that believing is not more reasonable than withholding; and (d) the only significant consequence we could draw from the hypothesis that disbelieving is not more reasonable than believing, and from the hypothesis that withholding is not more reasonable than believing, would be that disbelieving is not more reasonable than withholding.[11]

These axioms do not allow us to assert that, if withholding is not more reasonable than believing, then withholding is more reasonable than disbelieving. They do not yield the "principle of nonpermission," but allow instead for the possibility that some acceptable propositions have acceptable negations and are therefore "indifferent" in the first of the two senses we have distinguished. In view of what we have said, therefore, such a system would seem to be excessively latitudinarian.

VIII

With these concepts—or, more exactly, with the concept of *more reasonable than* as applied to believing, disbelieving, and withholding—we would seem to have what is essential for our basic vocabulary of epistemic appraisal. "Reasonable" is a term of high epistemic praise; it is the highest praise that is provided by the twelve possibilities we have distinguished. But a proposition may attain to greater heights. A proposition is reasonable, we said, if believing it is more reasonable than withholding it. Consider, then, those propositions that are reasonable and, in addition, are such that there are no propositions that are more reasonable than they are. Let us say that such propositions are *evident*. That is to say, a proposition h is evident to a given subject S at a given time t provided that: it is more reasonable at t for S to believe h than to withhold h, and there is no proposition i which is such that it is more reasonable for S at t to believe i than to believe h. Hence, we can say that whatever is evident is reasonable, but not conversely; just as we can say that whatever is reasonable is acceptable, but not conversely. (And, we may have a solution to one of the problems that troubled Meinong. Put in his terms: does "evident" apply to the *act* or to the *con-*

tent of judgment; does it apply to the *judging* or to that which is *judged?*[12] The answer would seem to be that "evident" applies to the *content* in virtue of what would be the reasonable nature of the *act.*)

We may say that a man *knows* a given proposition to be true, provided that the proposition is one that is believed or accepted by him, is true, and is evident.

Given the logical concept of probability, we can define a weaker sense of "know."[13] Thus a man could be said to *know, for all practical purposes,* that a given proposition *h* is true, provided that *h* is more probable than not in relation to everything that he knows, in the first sense of "know," to be true. (Or, if we wish to eliminate the reference to "everything he knows," we may say instead that *S* knows, for all practical purposes, that *h* is true, provided: there is a conjunction *e* of propositions that *S* knows, in the strict sense, to be true; *h* is more probable than not in relation to *e*; and there is no proposition *i* that such (a) *S* knows *i* to be true and (b) *h* is not more probable than not in relation to the conjunction of *e* and *i*.) As Hume remarked, "One would appear ridiculous who would say that it is only probable that the sun will rise tomorrow, or that all men must die; though it is plain we have no further assurance of these facts than what experience affords us."[14] We *may* say that we know that the sun will rise tomorrow, or that all men must die, despite the fact that these are not propositions that are evident. We can say we know them "for all practical purposes," because they are propositions that are highly probable in relation to what *is* evident. The propositions that we know in this weak sense, then, are propositions that are more probable than not to the totality of what we know in the strong sense.

Given, finally, the concept of logical entailment, we can define various senses of epistemic possibility—various senses of the expression, "It is possible, for all he knows that. . . ." (i) In a basic sense of the term "possible," a proposition *h* may be said to be epistemically possible, for a given subject *S,* provided that not-*h* is not entailed by the set of all of the propositions that *S* knows, in the first sense of "know" just defined.[15] It is possible, for all that I know, that there is life on Venus, for nothing that I know, or no conjunction of things that I know, entails that there is *not* life on Venus. An unacceptable proposition may be epistemically possible, in this sense. And (ii), an even weaker sense of epistemic possibility is obtained if we say this: *h* is possible, for all *S* knows, provided that *S does not know h* to be entailed by any set of things that he knows. In this weak sense of the term, we may say, "It was possible, for all that Thomas Hobbes knew, that someday he would square the circle." Thus, if we say of a proposition only that it is possible, we are not expressing any epistemic praise at all. For, as Sextus observes, the person who restricts himself to saying "Perhaps it is" is "implicitly affirming also the seemingly contradictory phrase 'Perhaps it is not' by his refusal to make the positive assertion that 'It is.' "[16]

NOTES

1. C. J. Ducasse, *Philosophy as a Science* (New York: Oskar Piest, 1941), p. 138.
2. Ibid.
3. Ibid., p. 194.
4. Sextus Empiricus, *Outlines of Pyrrhonism,* book 1, ch. 15, p. 177. Epictetus, however, reminds us that believing is often more reasonable than withholding and says of this type of skeptic: "He has sensation and pretends that he has not; he is worse than dead. One man does not see the battle; he is ill off. The other sees it but stirs not, nor advances; his state is still more wretched. His sense of shame and self-respect is cut out of him, and his reasoning faculty, though not cut away, is brutalized. Am I to call this 'strength'? Heaven forbid, unless I call it 'strength' in those who sin against nature, that makes them do and say in public whatever occurs to their fancy." *Discourses,* book 1, ch. 6 ("Against Followers of the Academy"): quoted from Whitney J. Oates, ed., *The Stoic and Epicurean Philosophers* (New York: Random House, 1940), p. 233.
5. Ducasse notes an analogous ambiguity in the term "doubt." He suggests that when we say "I am in doubt as to whether *S* is *P*" we are expressing the fact that we are withholding the proposition, but when we say "I doubt that *S* is *P*" we are expressing the fact that we are disbelieving it. Taking the term in the first of these two senses, he describes withholding as a state of *dubitancy.* C. J. Ducasse, "Propositions, Opinions, Sentences, and Facts," *Journal of Philosophy* 37, no. 26 (December 19, 1940): 702.
6. J. M. Keynes, *A Treatise of Probability* (London: Macmillan, 1921), p. 41; Keynes says that the passage is quoted somewhere by Bernard Bosanquet. It appears at the heading of Keynes's chapter entitled "The Principle of Indifference," in which the term "indifference" is used in the second of the two senses just distinguished.
7. For example, G. H. von Wright, *An Essay in Modal Logic* (Amsterdam: North-Holland Publishing Co., 1951), p. 38. In ch. 1 of *Perceiving: A Philosophical Study* (Ithaca, N.Y.: Cornell University Press, 1957), I affirmed an analogous principle for epistemology: every proposition is such that either it is acceptable or its negation is acceptable. The principles set forth in my work were excessively latitudinarian; they had the consequence, for example, that if a proposition is unacceptable its negation is evident, and therefore that there is no proposition that ought to be withheld.
8. But compare Kant: "It is, however, of great consequence to ethics in general to avoid admitting, so long as it is possible, of anything morally intermediate, whether in actions (*adiophora*) or in human characters; for with such ambiguity all maxims are in danger of forfeiting their precision and stability. Those who are partial to this strict mode of thinking are usually called *rigorists* (a name which is intended to carry reproach, but which actually praises); their opposites may be called *latitudinarians.* These latter, again, are either latitudinarians of neutrality, whom we may call *indifferentists,* or latitudinarians of coalition, whom we may call *syncretists.*" *Religion within the Limits of Reason Alone,* book 1; quoted from Harper Torchbooks edition (New York: Harper & Brothers, 1960), p. 18.
9. Sextus Empiricus, *Outlines of Pyrrhonism,* book 1, chs. 4, 6, 22, and 24. See the Loeb Library edition of *Sextus Empiricus* (Cambridge: Harvard University Press, 1933), vol. 1, pp. 7, 9, 115.
10. Perhaps we can say that Sextus defined "ought to withhold" in terms of the second sense of "indifference." For he writes in ch. 22 of book 1 of the *Outlines of Pyrrhonism*: "The phrase 'I suspend judgment' we adopt in place of 'I am unable to say which of the objects presented I ought to believe and which I ought to disbelieve,' indicating that the objects appear to us equal as regards credibility and incredibility." Quoted from Loeb Library edition of *Sextus Empiricus,* vol. 1, p. 115.
11. The system could be made even more liberal by adding the axiom: If believing is more reasonable than disbelieving, then withholding is not more reasonable than believing. But such an axiom is not plausible (despite the popular belief that from "Theism is more reasonable than atheism" we may deduce

"Agnosticism is not more reasonable than theism"). Suppose we know that there are 100 balls in the urn, that 51 of them are red and 49 of them are not red, and that a ball is to be drawn at random. It is more reasonable for us to believe that the ball to be drawn is red than to believe that it is not (i.e., to disbelieve). But in this case, clearly withholding is more reasonable than believing.

12. See A. Meinong, *Über Annahmen*, 2d ed. (Leipzig: Johann Ambrosius Barth, 1910), pp. 82ff., and *Über Möglichkeit und Wahrscheinlichkeit* (Leipzig: Johann Ambrosius Barth), pp. 440ff.

13. ". . . to say that inference of a conclusion *C* from premise *P* has probability of degree *D* means that *P* validates degree *D* of *inclination to believe* the proposition which is content of *C*." C. J. Ducasse, "Some Observations Concerning the Nature of Probability," *The Journal of Philosophy* 38, no. 15 (July 17, 1941): 400.

14. David Hume, *Treatise of Human Nature,* book 1, part 3, section 11.

15. On this sense of epistemic possibility, see: C. I. Lewis and C. H. Langford, *Symbolic Logic* (New York: The Century Co., 1932), pp. 161ff.; G. H. von Wright, *An Essay in Modal Logic,* pp. 31–32; Jaakko Hintikka, *Knowledge and Belief* (Ithaca, N.Y.: Cornell University Press, 1962); and Roderick M. Chisholm, "The Logic of Knowing," *The Journal of Philosophy* 60, no. 25 (December 5. 1963): 775–95.

16. *Outlines of Pyrrhonism,* book 1, ch. 21; Loeb Library translation, pp. 113–15. If it is necessary to countenance the possibility that some evident propositions are false, the definition of "know" should be qualified. I have discussed the need for countenancing this possibility and have proposed a qualification in *Theory of Knowledge* (Englewood Cliffs, N.J.: Prentice-Hall, 1966): cf., pp. 23, 48–49, 111–13.

29

Scales of Epistemic Appraisal

Kenneth G. Lucey

People are often surprised to learn that different courtroom situations require that juries use different levels of appraisal in reaching their verdicts. In a civil case (tort law) a jury has only to conclude that there is some presumption in favor of one litigant's case in reaching a verdict. In a criminal case, a jury is required to hold that its verdict is beyond reasonable doubt. Thus, there exists a *scale of appraisals* which contains at least two levels, namely "has some presumption in its favor" and "is beyond reasonable doubt." The exploration of such a scale (or scales) is a primary topic of this paper.

Such scales are those of epistemic appraisal. Epistemic appraisal has previously been systematically discussed by various epistemologists, notably by C. I. Lewis.[1] Three recent writers in this area entitled their article "Reason and Evidence: An Unsolved Problem."[2] Most recently, writings by Roderick M. Chisholm have appeared on numerous occasions expositing, defending and extending a system of the logic of epistemic appraisal. . . . At the heart of this system is the extremely important insight that there exists, with regard to given propositions for a given subject at a given time, a hierarchy of levels of epistemic appraisal in terms of which such propositions may be appraised for that subject at that time.

Professor Chisholm's latest version of his hierarchy of levels of epistemic appraisal is:

From *Philosophical Studies* 29 (1976): 169–79. © 1976 by D. Reidel Publishing Co., Dordrecht, Netherlands. Reprinted by permission of Wolters Kluwer Academic Publishers.

h is certain (absolutely certain)
h is evident
h is beyond reasonable doubt (reasonable)
h has some presumption in its favor
h is counterbalanced
$-h$ has no presumption in its favor
$-h$ is unreasonable (unacceptable)
$-h$ is gratuitous.[3]

This hierarchy is at once generated by and an interpretation of a formal axiomatic system. Each level of the appraisal hierarchy gets defined in terms of a specific well-formed formula of the formal system. For the benefit of readers unfamiliar with Chisholm's system, an appendix has been added to this paper which gives an exposition of some basic features of it.

This paper attempts to offer a new perspective upon the nature of Chisholm's system of epistemic appraisal. It is argued that Chisholm's system is of the "straight steps" variety. My contention is that a "mirrored steps" system of epistemic appraisal is preferable to a "straight steps" system. This preferability is shown through the consideration of Chisholm's own illustrations. Finally, it is argued that Chisholm's hierarchy is actually the result of mixing together several distinct sorts of scales of epistemic appraisal.

I

The first counterintuitive consequence of Chisholm's system to which I would like to call attention is that a relatively weak positive appraisal of a proposition h implies a very strong negative appraisal of the denial of that proposition, i.e., $-h$. That this consequence is counter-intuitive may be seen from the following example.

In "On the Nature of Empirical Evidence"[4] Chisholm offers the following courtroom illustration of the various levels of appraisal in his epistemic hierarchy:

> If the state is justified in bringing you to trial, then the proposition that you did the deed alleged must be one which, for the appropriate officials, has some presumption in its favor. If the jury is justified in finding you guilty, then the proposition should be one which, for it, is beyond reasonable doubt. And its decision should be based upon propositions which, for it, have been made evident during the course of the trial.[5]

I call Chisholm's system a "straight steps" system, because if a given step is true, it follows that all of the appraisals in the hierarchy below that step also are true. Now consider the relationship between the proposition *h* (the defendant committed the crime) and the proposition –*h* (the defendant did not commit the crime). According to Chisholm's "straight steps" system of epistemic appraisal, if the proposition that the defendant committed the crime *has some presumption in its favor,* then it follows as theorems of the system that the appropriate officials are justified in believing that the proposition –*h* (that the defendant didn't commit the crime) has no presumption in its favor, is unreasonable, and is gratuitous.

$$
\begin{array}{llllll}
a & & & & a & = & h \text{ is evident} \\
-c & -c & & & -c & = & h \text{ is beyond reasonable doubt} \\
b & b & b & & b & = & h \text{ has some presumption in its favor}
\end{array}
$$

- - - - - - - - - - - - - *h* is counterbalanced -

$$
\begin{array}{lllllll}
-e & -e & -e & -e & & -e & = & -h \text{ has no presumption in its favor} \\
d & d & d & d & d & d & = & -h \text{ is unreasonable} \\
-f & -f & -f & -f & -f & -f & -f & = & -h \text{ is gratuitous}
\end{array}
$$

Fig. 1.

But surely this is counterintuitive, for one would normally consider that the strongest of these appraisals concerning –*h* would be warranted only after the jury has brought in a verdict of "guilty as charged." Just because there is some presumption in favor of the defendant's guilt, it surely should not follow that it is *unreasonable* to believe that the defendant is innocent. In the absence of other evidence, mere circumstantial evidence would suffice to establish that there is some presumption in favor of the defendant's guilt. But that surely doesn't make *unreasonable* or *gratuitous* the belief that the defendant is nevertheless innocent.

Part of the purpose of this paper is to characterize an alternative to Chisholm's "straight steps" system. My alternative to a "straight steps" system of epistemic appraisal is what I call a "mirrored steps" system of epistemic appraisal. The contrast between these two systems can best be seen in terms of a pair of diagrams. Fig. 1 is a representation of Chisholm's system. The letters used here are the abbreviations Chisholm employs in "On the Nature of Empirical Evidence." The main feature of Fig. 1 is that implications in the "straight steps" system are *only* downward. If the appraisal at any given step is true, then it implies the truth of all the steps below it, and none of the steps above it.

The key notion in my "mirrored steps" system is that an affirmative appraisal of a given level only implies negative appraisals of a comparable level. In the "mirrored steps" system of epistemic appraisal, if the proposition *h* is presumptive or has some presumption in its favor, then the strongest negative appraisal that follows concerning –*h* is that it is nonpresumptive or has no presumption in its favor. In the "mirrored steps" system the defendant's guilt must be established beyond reasonable doubt before $-h$ is shown unreasonable, and h must be established as evident before $-h$ is shown to be gratuitous. Fig. 2 is a representation of the "mirrored steps" system of epistemic appraisal.

X			$X =$ h is evident
Y	Y		$Y =$ h is beyond reasonable doubt
Z	Z	Z	$Z =$ h has some presumption in its favor
- - - - - - - - - - - - - - - - - - -			h is counterbalanced - - - - - - - - - - - - -
Z^*	Z^*	Z^*	$Z^* = -h$ has no presumption in its favor
Y^*	Y^*		$Y^* = -h$ is unreasonable
X^*			$X^* = -h$ is irrational (gratuitous)

Fig. 2.

The conventions are slightly different for interpreting the implications in Fig. 2. Above the counterbalanced the interpretation is the same in that if an appraisal at a given step is true, then it implies all the appraisals below it, respectively concerning h above the counterbalanced, and concerning $-h$ below the counterbalanced. The convention for the levels below the counterbalanced is different in that a negative appraisal implies those other negative appraisals above it up to the counterbalanced, but not above that. Thus X^* implies Y^* and Z^*. Y^* only implies Z^*, and Z^* implies nothing whatsoever. Thus, on the "mirrored steps" system, *irrational* (gratuitous) is the strongest negative appraisal, and *evident* is the strongest level of positive appraisal. On the "straight steps" system there is some ambiguity as to what is the strongest negative appraisal, although perhaps a case can be made for thinking that *has no presumption in its favor* is the strongest negative appraisal. That case would be that, below the counterbalanced, the appraisal "$-h$ has no presumption in its favor" implies all the other negative appraisals, but *none* of them implies it.

Consideration of another example will reinforce my previous claim that Chisholm's "straight steps" system is counterintuitive. In "A System of Epistemic Logic," which was coauthored by Robert G. Keim, we find the following example:

Consider, for example, the proposition expressed by "There are now at least two people in the president's office." For most of us, this is counterbalanced: there is nothing to be said in its favor and there is nothing to be said in favor of its negation. But for one who has read that the president plans to hold a conference there at this time, the proposition may have some presumption in its favor; for one who has heard an official announcement that the conference is now taking place, it may be acceptable; for the guard outside the door, it may be beyond reasonable doubt; and for the president himself, either it or its negation may be evident.[7]

Consider the epistemic situation of the man who has read that the president plans to hold a conference, and thus for whom the proposition h has some presumption in its favor. Chisholm's system implies that for this individual the proposition $-h$, that there are not now at least two people in the president's office, has no presumption in its favor, is unreasonable, and is gratuitous. But surely it would *not* be either unreasonable or gratuitous for this man to believe $-h$, even though h has some presumption in its favor. My claim is that it is counterintuitive to think that $-h$ must be either unreasonable or gratuitous for S at t, just because h has some presumption in its favor. But what support is there for this claim?

What is amiss in Chisholm's system is that *only* a strong positive appraisal of a proposition h ought to imply a strong negative appraisal of the denial of that proposition. It seems to me that a "mirrored steps" system of epistemic appraisal, in which it follows that positive appraisals of a given level only imply negative appraisals of a comparable level, is much to be preferred. The major difference between the "straight steps" and the "mirrored steps" system of epistemic appraisal is that the former assumes that all of the negative appraisals must be true on every occasion that a positive appraisal (no matter how weak) is true. But at least in the examples that I have been examining, it seems wrong or counterintuitive to make that assumption. The problem reduces to the question—Why must "not-h" be unacceptable, unreasonable or gratuitous for the subject, just because h has been seen to have some presumption in its favor?

A distinct critical point would be that it seems to me that Chisholm's appraisal hierarchy contains a serious ambiguity in the appraisal levels below the counterbalanced. The ambiguity concerns what it is that is being measured on the negative half of the scale. When a weak negative judgment is compared with a strong negative judgment, what is the scale upon which the comparison is being made?

There are three scales from which the answer here can be drawn. They are: (1) a scale which measures the strength of one's reasons for withholding $-h$. (2) a scale which measures the strength of one's reasons for refraining from believing $-h$. And (3) a scale which measures the strength of one's reasons for disbelieving $-h$. The first scale mentioned above isn't really a serious option for use in interpreting Chisholm's hierarchy, since a scale of strength of reasons for withholding $-h$ is just as much a scale of strength of reasons for withholding h. If this were the scale at work below the counterbalanced in Chisholm's hierarchy, then positive appraisals of h above the counterbalanced would be implying reasons for withholding h. But clearly that isn't the case!

My contention here is that Chisholm's hierarchy is ambiguous between scales two and three. Chisholm's hierarchy above the counterbalanced is no doubt a scale which measures the strength of one's reasons for believing h in the sense that the higher on the scale an appraisal falls, the more (or better) reason one has for believing h. Scale (3) is quite similar to this in that disbelieving $-h$ is equivalent to believing $-(-h)$. When Chisholm defines "$-h$ is unreasonable" as "withholding $-h$ is epistemically preferable to believing $-h$" he seems to be working with a type (2) scale which would measure strength of one's reasons for refraining from believing $-h$. So, "being unreasonable" would seem to be an appraisal on a "refraining" type of scale. When Chisholm defines "$-h$ has no presumption in its favor" as "it is not the case that believing $-h$ is epistemically preferable to believing h," he seems to be working with a type (3) scale. Thus, "having no presumption" would seem to be an appraisal on a "believing" type of scale. My intuition is less clear as to which of these types of scale the definition of "*gratuitous*" ("believing $-h$ is not epistemically preferable to withholding $-h$") belongs, although perhaps a case could be made for a type (2) scale. In any case, given the way the implications go in Chisholm's hierarchy, *having no presumption in its favor* would seem to be the *strongest* negative appraisal, *being unreasonable* would be a weaker appraisal, and *being gratuitous* would seem to be the *weakest* negative appraisal. Chisholm's choices here are puzzling to say the least, for it seems counterintuitive to say that being *unreasonable* is a weaker negative appraisal than *having no presumption* in its favor.

Yet another feature of Chisholm's system that I would question is the fact that his system implies that every proposition for any individual at any time, will always have either a very strong positive appraisal or a very weak negative appraisal. The feature to which I'm here referring is Chisholm's theorem that every proposition is either *evident* or *gratuitous* (the two poles of the hierarchy). This fact follows directly from the law of the excluded middle and Chisholm's definitions of the levels of appraisal. That is: (1) p or $-p$; (2) $(Bh\ P\ Wh)$ or $-(Bh\ P\ Wh)$; Hence, (3) either h is evident or h is gratuitous. The disjuncts in step 2 are the definiens for the appraisals given in step (3). In a similar way, it follows as a corollary, that every proposition is either beyond reasonable doubt or unreasonable. In all the versions of Chisholm's system prior to [that presented in his 1973 "On the Nature of Empirical Evidence."][8] It was also a theorem that every proposition h is either acceptable or unacceptable.

The fault that I find with these theorems is that they purposefully turn appraisals which one would naturally consider contraries into contradictories. Chisholm's system precludes the possibility of there being a proposition h which is (a) neither evident nor gratuitous, or (b) neither beyond reasonable doubt nor unreasonable, or (c) neither acceptable nor unacceptable. Each of these exclusive disjunctions seems to me to be counter-intuitive.

I conclude that a "mirrored steps" system of epistemic appraisal is preferable to a "straight steps" system. No attempt has been made in this paper to present an axiomatic version of such a system. So, it remains an "open problem" of philosophical logic to construct a simple and elegant version of a "mirrored steps" logic of epistemic appraisal.

II. APPENDIX

This appendix summarizes Chisholm's key definitions, and derives three of his theorems. Chisholm's single primitive is the two place relational predicate ". . . is more reasonable than—" or ". . . is preferable to —." Here "preferable" means epistemically preferable rather than ethically preferable. It relates three basic epistemic attitudes, viz. (1) believing, (2) disbelieving, and (3) withholding or suspending belief. What is being appraised is always a believing, a disbelieving, or a withholding *by a particular subject at a particular time*. And when various attitudes are being ranked it is presupposed that the subject and time are constant throughout. Acts of believing and acts of disbelieving differ only in having contradictory objects. *Withholding* is defined by Chisholm as the compound attitude of refraining from believing and refraining from disbelieving.[9]

There are six ways that these basic attitudes may be related, taking them two at a time. And then if we switch to the relation ". . . is not epistemically preferable to—," there are then six more combinations, making twelve in all. Chisholm defines the basic elements of his vocabulary of epistemic appraisal in terms of these twelve combinations. Here is the latest, 1973, definition of each item of the appraisal vocabulary. (1) h is *evident* for S at t = Df: believing h is epistemically preferable to withholding h (for the subject S at the time t). (2) h is *gratuitous* for S at t = Df: it is not the case that believing h is epistemically preferable to withholding h. (3) h is *unreasonable* for S at t = Df: withholding h is epistemically preferable to believing h. (4) h is *reasonable* (beyond reasonable doubt) for S at t = Df: it is not the case that withholding h is epistemically preferable to believing h. (5) h has some *presumption* in its favor for S at t = Df: believing h is epistemically preferable to disbelieving h (i.e., believing $-h$). (6) h has *no presumption* in its favor for S at t = Df: it is not the case that believing h is epistemically preferable to disbelieving h.

In the system of 1966 Chisholm constructed his system with just three axioms. In later writings, versions of these three axioms remain the core of an expanded set containing seven axioms. The first two spell out logical properties of the primitive predicate ". . . is epistemically preferable to —." The first is an axiom of transitivity. It says that if one act of believing (withholding, etc.) is epistemically preferable to a second such act, and the second epistemically preferable to a third, then the first is epistemically preferable to the third. Again, a strict statement of this axiom would specify a constant subject and a constant time.[10]

Chisholm's second axiom states that ". . . is epistemically preferable to —" is an asymmetric relation. It says that if one epistemic attitude is epistemically preferable to a second, then the second is not epistemically preferable to the first.

A third axiom differs from the first two in that rather than specifying some other logical property of the primitive relation, it specifies an entailment that holds among the basic epistemic attitudes of Chisholm's epistemic vocabulary. It says that if withholding a proposition h is *not* epistemically preferable to believing h, then believing h is epistemically preferable to disbelieving h. That is, if h is beyond reasonable doubt, then h has some presumption in its favor. Chisholm has illustrated this axiom thus: "If agnosticism is not more reasonable than theism, then theism is more reasonable than atheism."[11]

Consider now three of the most controversial results of this system of epistemic appraisal. They are the derivations of the three theorems that follow from the appraisal that h has some presumption in its favor. That is, if h has some presumption in its favor, then: (1) $-h$ has *no* presumption in its favor. (2) $-h$ is unreasonable. (3) $-h$ is gratuitous.

Take "Bh" as "S believing h at t'; "$B-h$" as "S believing $-h$ at t" or "S disbelieving h at t'; "Wh" as "S withholding h at t'; and ". . . P—" as ". . . is epistemically preferable to —." The first theorem is then: If $(Bh \, P \, B-h)$ then $-(B-h \, P \, Bh)$. This theorem is an immediate consequence of Chisholm's second axiom which asserts the asymmetry of ". . . P—." The second theorem is: If $(Bh \, P \, B-h)$ then $(W-h \, P \, B-h)$.

The proof is:

1. If $-(Wh \, P \, Bh)$	then $(Bh \, P \, B-h)$	Axiom #3
2. If $-(W-h \, P \, B-h)$	then $(B-h \, P \, Bh)$	Substitution into 1
3. If $-(B-h \, P \, Bh)$	then $(W-h \, P \, B-h)$	2, Transposition
4. If $(Bh \, P \, B-h)$	then $-(B-h \, P \, Bh)$	Axiom #2 Asymmetry

Thus, 5. If $(Bh \, P \, B-h)$ then $(W-h \, P \, B-h)$ 3,4 Hypothetical Syllogism

The third theorem to be proven is: If $(Bh \, P \, B-h)$ then $- (B-h \, P \, W-h)$.

1. If $(W-h \, P \, B-h)$	then $-(B-h \, P \, W-h)$	Axiom #2 Asymmetry
2. If $(Bh \, P \, B-h)$	then $(W-h \, P \, B-h)$	Previous theorem.

Thus, 3. If $(Bh \, P \, B-h)$ then $-(B-h \, P \, W-h)$ 1,2 Hypothetical Syllogism

These are the theorems which show Chisholm's system a "straight steps" logic of epistemic appraisal, in which a weak positive appraisal of h implies a strong negative appraisal of $-h$.

NOTES

1. C. I. Lewis, *An Analysis of Knowledge and Valuation* (LaSalle, Ill.: Open Court Publishing Co., 1946).

2. Keith Lehrer, Richard Roelff, and Marshall Swain, "Reason and Evidence: An Unsolved Problem" *Ratio* 9 (1967): 38–48.

3. Roderick M. Chisholm, "On the Nature of Empirical Evidence," in *Experience and Theory,* Roderick M. Chisholm and Robert J. Swartz, eds. (Englewood Cliffs, N.J.: Prentice-Hall, Inc., 1973), pp. 226–29.

4. See note 3 and Roderick M. Chisholm, "On the Nature of Empirical Evidence," in *Experience and Theory,* Lawrence Foster and J. W. Swanson, eds. (Amherst: The University of Massachusetts Press, 1970), pp. 103–34.

5. Chisholm, "On the Nature of Empirical Evidence" (1973), p. 227.

6. Ibid., p. 228.

7. Roderick M. Chisholm and Robert G. Keim, "A System of Epistemic Logic," *Ratio* 14 (1972): 99–115.

8. Chisholm, "On the Nature of Empirical Evidence" (1973).

9. Roderick M. Chisholm, "The Principles of Epistemic Appraisal," in F. C. Dommeyer, ed., *Current Philosophical Issues: Essays in Honor of Curt John Ducasse* (Springfield, Ill.: Charles C. Thomas, 1966), pp. 88.

10. Ibid., p. 95.

11. Ibid.

30

Concepts of Epistemic Justification

William P. Alston

I

Justification, or at least "justification," bulks large in recent epistemology. The view that knowledge consists of true-justified-belief (+ . . .) has been prominent in this century, and the justification of belief has attracted considerable attention in its own right. But it is usually not at all clear just what an epistemologist means by "justified," just what concept the term is used to express. An enormous amount of energy has gone into the attempt to specify conditions under which beliefs of one or another sort are justified; but relatively little has been done to explain *what it is* for a belief to be justified, what that is for which conditions are being sought.[1] The most common procedure has been to proceed on the basis of a number of (supposedly) obvious cases of justified belief, without pausing to determine what property it is of which these cases are instances. Now even if there were some single determinate concept that all these theorists have implicitly in mind, this procedure would be less than wholly satisfactory. For in the absence of an explicit account of the concept being applied, we lack the most fundamental basis for deciding between supposed intuitions and for evaluating proposed conditions of justification. And in any event, as philosophers we do not seek merely to speak the truth, but also to gain an explicit, reflective understanding of the matters with which we deal. We want to know not only when our beliefs are justified, but also what it is to enjoy that status. True, not every fundamen-

From *The Monist* 68, no. 1 (1985): 57–89. © 1985 The Monist, LaSalle, IL 61301. Reprinted by permission of the publisher.

tal concept can be explicated, but we shall find that much can be done with this one.

And since, as we shall see in this paper, there are several distinct concepts that are plausibly termed "concepts of epistemic justification," the need for analysis is even greater. By simply using "justified" in an unexamined, intuitive fashion the epistemologist is covering up differences that make important differences to the shape of a theory of justification. We cannot fully understand the stresses and strains in thought about justification until we uncover the most crucial differences between concepts of epistemic justification.

Not all contemporary theorists of justification fall under these strictures. Some have undertaken to give an account of the concept of justification they are using.[2] But none of them provide a map of this entire conceptual territory.

In this paper I am going to elaborate and interrelate several distinct concepts of epistemic justification, bringing out some crucial issues involved in choosing between them. I shall give reasons for disqualifying some of the contenders, and I shall explain my choice of a winner. Finally I shall vouchsafe a glimpse of the enterprise for which this paper is a propadeutic, that of showing how the differences between these concepts make a difference in what it takes for the justification of belief, and other fundamental issues in epistemology.

Before launching this enterprise we must clear out of the way a confusion between one's *being* justified in believing that *p*, and one's *justifying* one's belief that *p*, where the latter involves one's *doing* something to show that *p*, or to show that one's belief was justified, or to exhibit one's justification. The first side of this distinction, on the other hand, is a state or condition one is in, not anything one does or any upshot thereof. I might be justified in believing that there is milk on the table because I see it there, even though I have done nothing to show that there is milk on the table or to show that I am justified in believing there to be. It is amazing how often these matters are confused in the literature. We will be concentrating on the "be justified" side of this distinction, since that is of more fundamental epistemological interest. If epistemic justification were restricted to those cases in which the subject carries out a "justification" it would *obviously* not be a necessary condition of knowledge or even of being in a strong position to acquire knowledge. Most cases of perceptual knowledge, for example, involve no such activity.[3]

II

Let's begin our exploration of this stretch of conceptual territory by listing a few basic features of the concept that would seem to be common ground.

(1) It applies to beliefs, or alternatively to a cognitive subject's having a belief. I shall speak indifferently of *S*'s belief that *p* being justified and of *S*'s being justified in believing that *p*. This is the common philosophical concept of belief, in which *S*'s

believing that p entails neither that S knows that p nor that S does not know that p. It is not restricted to conscious or occurrent beliefs.

(2) It is an evaluative concept, in a broad sense in which this is contrasted with "factual." To say that S is justified in believing that p is to imply that there is something all right, satisfactory, in accord with the way things should be, about the fact that S believes that p. It is to accord S's believing a positive evaluative status.

(3) It has to do with a specifically *epistemic* dimension of evaluation. Beliefs can be evaluated in different ways. One may be more or less prudent, fortunate, or faithful in holding a certain belief. Epistemic justification is different from all that. Epistemic evaluation is undertaken from what we might call the "epistemic point of view." That point of view is defined by the aim at maximizing truth and minimizing falsity in a large body of beliefs. The qualification "in a large body of beliefs" is needed because otherwise one could best achieve the aim by restricting one's belief to those that are obviously true. That is a rough formulation. How large a body of beliefs should we aim at? Is any body of beliefs of a given size, with the same truth-falsity ratio, equally desirable, or is it more important, epistemically, to form beliefs on some matters than others? And what relative weights should be assigned to the two aims at maximizing truth and minimizing falsity? We can't go into all that here; in any event, however these issues are settled it remains true that our central cognitive aim is to amass a large body of beliefs with a favorable truth-falsity ratio. For a belief to be epistemically justified is for it, somehow, to be awarded high marks relative to that aim.

(4) It is a matter of degree. One can be more or less justified in believing that p. If, for example, what justifies one is some evidence one has, one will be more or less justified depending on the amount and strength of the evidence. However, in this paper I shall, for the sake of simplicity, treat justification as absolute. You may, if you like, think of this as the degree of justification required for some standard of acceptability.

III

Since any concept of epistemic justification is a concept of some condition that is desirable or commendable from the standpoint of the aim at maximizing truth and minimizing falsity, in distinguishing different concepts of justification we will be distinguishing different ways in which conditions can be desirable from this standpoint. As I see it, the major divide in this terrain has to do with whether believing, and refraining from believing, are subject to obligation, duty, and the like. If they are, we can think of the favorable evaluative status of a certain belief as consisting in the fact that in holding that belief one has fulfilled one's obligations, or refrained from violating one's obligations, to achieve the fundamental aim in question. If they are not so subject, the favorable status will have to be thought of in some other way.

I shall first explore concepts of the first sort, which I shall term "deontological,"[4] since they have to do with how one stands in believing that *p*, vis-à-vis duties or obligations. Most epistemologists who have attempted to explicate justification have set out a concept of this sort.[5] It is natural to set out a deontological concept on the model of the justification of behavior. Something I *did* was justified just in case it was *not in violation* of any relevant duties, obligations, rules, or regulations, and hence was not something for which I could rightfully be blamed. To say that my expenditures on the trip were justified is not to say that I was obliged to make those expenditures (e.g., for taxis), but only that it was all right for me to do so, that in doing so I was not in violation of any relevant rules or regulations. And to say that I was justified in making that decision on my own, without consulting the executive committee, is not to say that I was required to do it on my own (though that *may* also be true); it is only to say that the departmental bylaws permit the chairman to use his own discretion in matters of this kind. Similarly, to say that a belief was deontologically justified is not to say that the subject was obligated to believe this, but only that he was permitted to do so, that believing this did not involve any violation of relevant obligations. To say that I am justified in believing that salt is composed of sodium and chlorine, since I have been assured of this by an expert, is not to say that I am obligated to believe this, though this might also be true. It is to say that I am permitted to believe it, that believing it would not be a violation of any relevant obligation, e.g., the obligation to refrain from believing that *p* in the absence of adequate reasons for doing so. As Carl Ginet puts it, "One is *justified* in being confident that *p* if and only if it is not the case that one ought not to be confident that *p*; one could not be justly reproached for being confident that *p*."[6]

Since we are concerned specifically with the *epistemic* justification of belief, the concept in which we are interested is not that of *not violating obligations of any sort in believing*, but rather the more specific concept of *not violating "epistemic," "cognitive," or "intellectual" obligations in believing*. Where are such obligations to be found? If we follow out our earlier specification of the "epistemic point of view," we will think of our basic epistemic obligation as that of doing what we can to achieve the aim at maximizing truth and minimizing falsity within a large body of beliefs. There will then be numerous more specific obligations that owe their status to the fact that fulfilling them will tend to the achievement of that central aim. Such obligations might include *to refrain from believing that* p *in the absence of sufficient evidence and to accept whatever one sees to be clearly implied by something one already believes (or, perhaps, is already justified in believing).*[7] Of course other positions might be taken on this point.[8] One might suppose that there are a number of ultimate, irreducible intellectual duties that cannot be derived from any basic goal of our cognitive life. Or alternative versions of the central aim might be proposed. Here we shall think in terms of the basic aim we have specified, with more specific obligations derived from that.

Against this background we can set out our first concept of epistemic justification as follows, using "d" for "deontological":

I. S is J_d in believing that p *iff* in believing that p S is not violating any epistemic obligations.

There are important distinctions between what we may call "modes" of obligation, justification, and other normative statuses. These distinctions are by no means confined to the epistemic realm. Let's introduce them in connection with moral norms for behavior. Begin with a statement of obligation in "objective" terms, a statement of the objective state of affairs I might be said to be obliged to bring about. For example, it is my obligation as a host to make *my guest, G, feel welcome.* Call that underlined state of affairs, "A." We may think of this as an *objective* conception of my obligation as a host. I have fulfilled that obligation *iff* G feels welcome.[9] But suppose I did what I sincerely believed would bring about A? In that case surely no one could blame me for dereliction of duty. That suggests a more *subjective* conception of my obligation as *doing what I believed was likely to bring about A.*[10] But perhaps I should not be let off so easily as that. "You should have realized that what you did was not calculated to make G feel welcome." This retort suggests a somewhat more stringent formulation of my obligation than the very permissive subjective conception just specified. It suggests that I can't fulfill my obligation by doing just anything I happen to believe will bring about A. I am not off the hook unless *I did what the facts available to me indicate will have a good chance of leading to A.* This is still a subjective conception in that what it takes to fulfill my obligation is specified from my point of view; but it takes my point of view to range over not all my beliefs, but only my justified beliefs. This we might call a *cognitive* conception of my obligation.[11] Finally, suppose that I did what I had adequate reason to suppose would produce A, and I did produce A, but I didn't do it for that reason. I was just amusing myself, and I would have done what I did even if I had known it would not make G feel welcome. In that case I might be faulted for moral irresponsibility, however well I rate in the other modes. This suggests what we may call a motivational conception of my obligation as *doing what I believed (or was justified in believing) would bring about A, in order to bring about A.*

We may sum up these distinctions as follows:

II. S has fulfilled his *objective* obligation *iff* S has brought about A.
III. S has fulfilled his *subjective* obligation *iff* S has done what he believed to be most likely to bring about A.
IV. S has fulfilled his *cognitive* obligation *iff* S did what he was justified in believing to be most likely to bring about A.

V. *S* has fulfilled his *motivational* obligation *iff S* has done what he did because he supposed it would be most likely to bring about A.

We can make analogous distinctions with respect to the justification of behavior or belief, construed as the absence of any violation of obligations.[12] Let's indicate how this works out for the justification of belief.

VI. *S* is *objectively* justified in believing that *p iff S* is not violating any objective obligation in believing that *p*.

VII. *S* is *subjectively* justified in believing that *p iff S* is not violating any subjective obligation in believing that *p*.

VIII. *S* is *cognitively* justified in believing that *p iff S* is not violating any cognitive obligation in believing that *p*.

IX. *S* is *motivationally* justified in believing that *p iff S* is not violating any motivational obligation in believing that *p*.

If we assume that only one intellectual obligation is relevant to the belief in question, viz., the obligation to believe that *p* only if one has adequate evidence for *p*, we can be a bit more concrete about this.

X. *S* is objectively justified in believing that *p iff S* has adequate evidence for *p*.[13]

XI. *S* is subjectively justified in believing that *p iff S* believes that he possesses adequate evidence for *p*.

XII. *S* is cognitively justified in believing that *p iff S* is justified in believing that he possesses adequate evidence for *p*.[14]

XIII. *S* is motivationally justified in believing that *p iff S* believes that *p* on the basis of adequate evidence, or, alternatively, on the basis of what he believed, or was justified in believing, was adequate evidence.

I believe that we can safely neglect XI. To explain why I will need to make explicit what it is to have adequate evidence for *p*. First a proposition, *q*, is adequate evidence for *p* provided they are related in such a way that if *q* is true then *p* is at least probably true. But I *have* that evidence only if I believe that *q*. Furthermore I don't "have" it in such a way as to thereby render my belief that *p* justified unless I know or am justified in believing that *q*. An unjustified belief that *q* wouldn't do it. If I believe that [former Israeli Prime Minister] Begin has told the cabinet that he will resign, but only because I credited an unsubstantiated rumor, then even if Begin's having told the cabinet that he would resign is an adequate indication that he will resign, I will not thereby be justified in believing that he will resign.

Now I might very well *believe* that I have adequate evidence for *q* even though one or more of these conditions is not satisfied. This is an especially live possibility with respect to the first and third conditions. I might mistakenly believe that my evidence is adequate support, and I might mistakenly suppose that I am justified in accepting it. But, as we have just seen, if I am not justified in accepting the evidence for p then my believing it cannot render me justified in believing that p, however adequate that evidence. I would also hold, though this is perhaps more controversial, that if the evidence is not in fact adequate my having that evidence cannot justify me in believing that p. Thus, since my believing that I have adequate evidence is compatible with these nonjustifying states of affairs, we cannot take subjective justification, as defined in XI, to constitute epistemic justification.

That leaves us with three contenders. Here I will confine myself to pointing out that there is a strong tendency for J_d to be used in a cognitive rather than a purely objective form. J_d is, most centrally, a concept of freedom from blameworthiness, a concept of being "in the clear" so far as one's intellectual obligations are concerned. But even if I don't have adequate evidence for p, I could hardly be blamed for believing that p (even assuming, as we are in this discussion, that there is something wrong with believing in the absence of adequate evidence), provided I am justified in supposing that I have adequate evidence. So long as that condition holds I have done the right thing, or refrained from doing the wrong thing, so far as I am able to tell; and what more could be required of me? But this means that it is XII, rather than X, that brings out what it takes for freedom from blame, and so brings out what it takes for being J_d.[15]

What about motivational form? We can have J_d in any of the first three forms with or without the motivational form. I can have adequate evidence for p, and believe that p, (XI) whether or not my belief is based on that evidence; and so for the other two. But the motivational mode is parasitic on the other modes, in that the precise form taken by the motivational mode depends on the status of the (supposed) evidence on which the belief is based. This "unsaturated" character of the motivational mode is reflected in the threefold alternative that appears in our formulation of XIII. If S bases his belief that p on actually possessed adequate evidence, then XIII combines with X. If the evidence on which it is based is only believed to be adequate evidence, or only justifiably believed to be adequate evidence, then XIII combines with XI or XII. Of course, it may be based on actually possessed adequate evidence, which is justifiably believed to be such; in which case S is justified in all four modes. Thus the remaining question concerning J_d is whether a "motivational rider" should be put on XII. Is it enough for J_d that S be justified in believing that he has adequate evidence for p, or should it also be required that S's belief that p be based on that evidence? We will address this question in section 5 in the form it assumes for a quite different concept of justification.[16]

IV

We have explained *being* J_d *in believing that* p as *not violating any intellectual obligations in believing that* p. And, in parallel fashion, being J_d in refraining from believing that *p* would consist in not having violated any intellectual obligations in so doing. But if it is possible for me to violate an obligation in refraining from believing that *p*, it must be that I can be obliged, under certain conditions, to believe that *p*. And, by the same token, if I can violate obligations in believing that *p* then I can be obliged to refrain from believing that *p*. And this is the way we have been thinking of it. Our example of an intellectual obligation has been the obligation to refrain from believing that *p* in the absence of adequate evidence. On the other side, we might think of a person as being obliged to believe that *p* if confronted with conclusive evidence that *p* (where that includes the absence of sufficient overriding evidence to the contrary).

Now it certainly looks as if I can be obliged to believe or to refrain from believing, only if this is in my direct voluntary control; only if I can, here and now, believe that *p* or no just by willing (deciding, choosing . . .). And that is the way many epistemologists seem to construe the matter. At least many formulations are most naturally interpreted in this way. Think back, for example, on Chisholm's formulation of our intellectual obligation.[17] Chisholm envisages a person thinking of a certain proposition as a candidate for belief, considering what grounds there might be for belief or refraining from belief, and then effectively choosing belief or abstention on the basis of those considerations.[18] Let's call the version of J_d that presupposes direct voluntary control over belief (and thus thinks of an obligation to believe as an obligation to bring about belief here and now), "J_{dv}" ("v" for "voluntary").

I find this assumption of direct voluntary control over belief quite unrealistic. There are strong reasons for doubting that belief is usually, or perhaps ever, under direct voluntary control. First, think of the beliefs I acquire about myself and the world about me through experience—through perception, self-consciousness, testimony, and simple reasoning based on these data. When I see a car coming down the street I am not capable of believing or disbelieving this at will. In such familiar situations the belief-acquisition mechanism is isolated from the direct influence of the will and under the control of more purely cognitive factors.

Partisans of a voluntary control thesis will counter by calling attention to cases in which things don't appear to be so cut and dried: cases of radical underdetermination by evidence, as when a general has to dispose his forces in the absence of sufficient information about the position of enemy forces; or cases of the acceptance of a religious or philosophical position where there seem to be a number of equally viable alternatives. In such cases it can appear that one makes a decision as to what to believe and what not to believe. My view on these matters is that insofar as something is chosen voluntarily it is something other than a belief or abstention from belief. The general chooses to proceed on the working assumption that the enemy forces are disposed in such-and-such a way. The religious convert to whom it is not clear that the beliefs are correct has chosen to live a certain kind of life, or to selectively subject himself to certain influences. And so on. But even if I am mistaken about these kinds of cases, it is clear that for the vast majority of beliefs nothing like direct voluntary control is involved. And so J_{dv} could not possibly be a generally applicable concept of epistemic justification.

If I am right in rejecting the view that belief is, in general or ever, under direct voluntary control, are we foreclosed from construing epistemic justification as freedom from blameworthiness? Not necessarily. We aren't even prevented from construing epistemic justification as the absence of obligation-violations. We *will* have to avoid thinking of the relevant obligations as obligations to believe or refrain from believing, on the model of obligations to answer a question or to open a door, or to do anything else over which we have immediate voluntary control.[19] If we are to continue to think of intellectual obligations as having to do with believing it will have to be more on the model of the way in which obligations bear on various other conditions over which one lacks direct voluntary control but which one can influence by voluntary actions, such conditions as being overweight, being irritable, being in poor health, or having friends. I can't institute, nullify, or alter any of those conditions here and now just by deciding to do so. But I can do things at will that will influence those conditions; and in that way they may be to some extent under my indirect control. One might speak of my being obliged to be in good health or to have a good disposition, meaning that I am obliged to do what I can (or as much as could reasonably be expected of me) to institute and preserve those states of affairs. However, since I think it less misleading to say exactly what I mean, I will not speak of our being obliged to weigh a certain amount or to have a good disposition, or to believe a proposition; I will speak rather of our having obligations to do what we can, or as much as can reasonably be expected of us, to influence those conditions.[20]

The things we can do to affect our believings can be divided into (1) activities that bring influences to bear, or withhold influences from, a particular situation, and (2) activities that affect our belief-forming habits. (1) includes such activities as checking to see whether I have considered all the relevant evidence, getting a second opinion, searching my memory for analogous cases, and looking into the question of whether there is anything markedly abnormal about my current perceptual situation. (2) includes training myself to be more critical of gossip, talking myself into being either more or less subservient to authority, and practicing greater sensitivity to the condition of other people. Moreover, it is plausible to think of these belief-influencing activities as being subject to intellectual obligations. We might, for example, think of ourselves as being under an obligation to do what we can (or what could reasonably be expected of us) to make our belief-forming processes as reliable as possible.

All this suggests that we might frame a deontological conception of being epistemically justified in believing that *p,* in the sense that one's believing that *p* is not the result of one's failure to fulfill one's intellectual obligations vis-à-vis one's belief-forming and -maintaining activities. It would, again, be like the way in which one is or isn't to blame for other conditions that are not under direct voluntary control but which one can influence by one's voluntary activities. I am to blame for being overweight (being irritable, being in poor health, being without friends) only if that condition is in some way due to my own past failures to do what I should to limit my intake or to exercise or whatever. If I would still be overweight even if I had done everything I could and should have done about it, then I can hardly be blamed for it. Similarly, we may say that I am subject to reproach for believing that *p,* provided that I am to blame for being in that doxastic condition, in the sense that there are things I could and should have done, such that if I had done them I would not now be believing that *p.* If that is the case I am unjustified in that belief. And if it is *not* the case, if there are no unfulfilled obligations the fulfilling of which would have inhibited that belief formation, then I am justified in the belief.

Thus we have arrived at a deontological concept of epistemic justification that does not require belief to be under direct voluntary control. We may label this concept "J_{di}" ("*i*" for "involuntary"). It may be more formally defined as follows:

XIV. *S* is J_{di} in believing that *p* at *t iff* there are no intellectual obligations that (1) have to do with the kind of belief-forming or -sustaining habit the activation of which resulted in *S*'s believing that *p* at *t,* or with the particular process of belief formation or sustenance that was involved in *S*'s believing that *p* at *t,* and (2) which are such that:
A. *S* had those obligations prior to *t.*
B. *S* did not fulfill those obligations.
C. If *S* had fulfilled those obligations, *S* would not have believed that *p* at *t.*[21]

As it stands, this account will brand too many beliefs as unjustified, just because it is too undiscriminating in the counterfactual condition, C. There are ways in which the nonfulfillment of intellectual obligations can contribute to a belief acquisition without rendering the belief unjustified. Suppose that I fail to carry out my obligation to spend a certain period in training myself to observe things more carefully. I use the time thus freed up to take a walk around the neighborhood. In the course of this stroll I see two dogs fighting, thereby acquiring the belief that they are fighting. There was a relevant intellectual obligation I didn't fulfill, which is such that if I had fulfilled it I wouldn't have acquired that belief. But if that is a perfectly normal perceptual belief, it is surely not thereby rendered unjustified.

Here the dereliction of duty contributed to belief-formation simply by facilitating access to the data. That's not the kind of contribution we had in mind. The sorts of cases we were thinking of were those most directly suggested by the two sorts of intellectual obligations we distinguished: (a) cases in which the belief was acquired by the activation of a habit that we would not have possessed had we fulfilled our intellectual obligations; (b) cases in which we acquire, or retain, the belief only because we are sheltered from adverse considerations in a way we wouldn't be if we had done what we should have done. Thus we can avoid counterexamples like the above by reformulating C as follows:

> C. If S had fulfilled those obligations. then S's belief-forming habits would have changed, or S's access to relevant adverse considerations would have changed, in such a way that S would not have believed that p at t.

But even with this refinement J_{di} does not give us what we expect of epistemic justification. The most serious defect is that it does not hook up in the right way with an adequate, truth-conducive ground. I may have done what could reasonably be expected of me in the management and cultivation of my doxastic life, and still hold a belief on outrageously inadequate grounds. There are several possible sources of such a discrepancy. First there is what we might call "cultural isolation." If I have grown up in an isolated community in which everyone unhesitatingly accepts the traditions of the tribe as authoritative, then if I have never encountered anything that seems to cast doubt on the traditions and have never thought to question them, I can hardly be blamed for taking them as authoritative. There is nothing I could reasonably be expected to do that would alter that belief-forming tendency. And there is nothing I could be expected to do that would render me more exposed to counterevidence. (We can suppose that the traditions all have to do with events distant in time and/or space, matters on which I could not be expected to gather evidence on my own.) I am J_{di} in believing these things. And yet the fact that it is the tradition of the tribe that p may be a very poor reason for believing that p.

Then there is deficiency in cognitive powers. Rather than looking at the extremer forms of this, let's consider a college student who just doesn't have what it takes to follow abstract philosophical reasoning, or exposition for that matter, Having read book 4 of Locke's *Essay,* he believes that it is Locke's view that everything is a matter of opinion, that one person's opinion is just as good as another's, and that what is true for me may not be true for you. And it's not just that he didn't work hard enough on this particular point, or on the general abilities involved. There is nothing that he could and should have done such that had he done so, he would have gotten this straight. He is simply incapable of appreciating the distinction between "One's knowledge is restricted to one's own ideas" and "Everything is a matter of opinion." No doubt teachers of philosophy tend to assume too quickly that this description applies to some of their students, but surely there can be such cases; cases in which either no amount of time and effort would enable the student to get straight on the matter, or it would be unreasonable to expect the person to expend that amount of time and effort. And yet we would hardly wish to say that the student is justified in believing what he does about Locke.

Other possible sources of a discrepancy between J_{di} and epistemic justification are poor training that the person lacks the time or resources to overcome. and an incorrigible doxastic incontinence. ("When he talks like that I just can't help believing what he says.") What this spread of cases brings out is that J_{di} is not sufficient for epistemic justification; we may have done the best we can, or at least the best that could reasonably be expected of us, and still be in a very poor epistemic position in believing that p; we could, blamelessly, be believing p for outrageously bad reasons. Even though J_{di} is the closest we can come to a deontological concept of epistemic justification if belief is not under direct voluntary control, it still does not give us what we are looking for.

V

Thus neither version of J_d is satisfactory. Perhaps it was misguided all along to think of epistemic justification as freedom from blameworthiness. Is there any alternative, given the nonnegotiable point that we are looking for a concept of epistemic evaluation? Of course there is. By no means all evaluation, even all evaluation of activities, states, and aspects of human beings, involves the circle of terms that includes "obligation," "permission," "right," "wrong," and "blame." We can evaluate a person's abilities, personal appearance, temperament, or state of health as more or less desirable, favorable, or worthwhile, without taking these to be within the person's direct voluntary control and so subject to obligation in a direct fashion (as with J_{dv}), and without making the evaluation depend on whether the person has done what she should to influence these states (as with J_{di}). Obligation and blame need not come into it at all. This is most obvious when we are dealing with matters that are not even under indirect voluntary control, like one's basic capacities or bodily build. Here when we use positively evaluative terms like "gifted" or "superb," we are clearly not saying that the person has done all she could to foster or encourage the condition in question. But even where the condition is at least partly under indirect voluntary control, as with personal appearance or state of health, we need not be thinking in those terms when we take someone to present a pleasing appearance or to be in splendid health.

Moreover, we can carry out these evaluations from a certain point of view. We can judge that someone has a fine bodily constitution from an athletic or from an esthetic point of view; or that someone's manner is a good one from a professional or from a social point of view.

In like fashion, one can evaluate S's believing that p as a good, favorable, desirable, or appropriate thing, without thinking of it as fulfilling or not violating an obligation, and without making this evaluation depend on whether the person has done what she could to carry out belief-influencing activities. As in the other cases, it could simply be a matter of the possession of certain good-making characteristics. Furthermore, believings can be evaluated from various points of view, including the epistemic, which, as we have noted, is defined by the aim at maximizing truth and minimizing falsity. It may be a good thing that S believes that p for his peace of mind, or from the standpoint of loyalty to the cause, or as an encouragement to the redoubling of his efforts. But none of this would render it a good thing for S to believe that p from the epistemic point of view. To believe that p because it gives peace of mind or because it stimulates effort may not be conducive to the attainment of truth and the avoidance of error.

All of this suggests that we can frame a concept of epistemic justification that is "evaluative," in a narrow sense of that term in which it contrasts with "deontological," with the assessment of conduct in terms of obligation, blame, right, and wrong. Let's specify an "evaluative" sense of epistemic justification as follows:

XV. S is J_e in believing that p iff S's believing that p, as S does, is a good thing from the epistemic point of view.

This is a way of being commendable from the epistemic point of view that is quite different from the subject's not being to blame for any violation of intellectual obligations.[22] The qualification "as S does" is inserted to make it explicit that in order for S to be J_e in believing that p it need not be the case that any believing of p by S would be a good thing epistemically, much less any believing of p by anyone. It is rather that there are aspects of *this* believing of p by S that make it a good thing epistemically. There could conceivably be person-proposition pairs such that any belief in that proposition by that person would be a good thing epistemically; but this would be a limiting case and not typical of our epistemic condition.

Is there anything further to be said about this concept? Of course we should avoid building anything very substantive into the constitution of the concept. After all, it is possible for epistemologists to differ radically as to the conditions under which one or another sort of belief is justified. When this happens they are at least sometimes using the same concept of justification; otherwise they wouldn't be disagreeing over what is required for justification, though they could still disagree over which concept of justification is most fundamental or most useful. Both our versions of J_d are quite neutral in this way. Both leave it completely open as to what intellectual obligations we have, and hence as to what obligations must not be violated if one is to be justified. But while maintaining due regard for the importance of neutrality I believe that we can go beyond XV in fleshing out the concept.

We can get a start on this by considering the following question. If goodness from an epistemic point of view is what we are interested in, why shouldn't we identify justification with truth, at least extensionally? What could be better from that point of view than truth? If the name of the game is the maximization of truth and the minimization of falsity in our beliefs, then plain, unvarnished truth is hard to beat. However, this consideration has not moved epistemologists to identify justification with truth, or even to take truth as a necessary and sufficient condition for justification. The logical independence of truth and justification is a staple of the epistemological literature. But why should this be? It is obvious that a belief might be J_d without being true and vice versa; but what reason is there for taking J_e to be independent of truth?

I think the answer to this has to be in terms of the "internalist" character of justification. When we ask whether S is justified in believing that p, we are, as we have repeatedly been insisting, asking a question from the standpoint of an aim at truth; but we are not asking whether things are in fact as S believes. We are getting at something more "internal" to S's "perspective on the world." This internalist feature of justification made itself felt in our discussion of J_d when we pointed out that to be J_{dv} is to fail to violate any relevant intellectual obligations, *so far as one can tell,* to be J_{dv} in what we call the "cognitive" mode. With respect to J_e the analogous point is that although this is goodness vis-à-vis the aim at truth, it consists not in the beliefs fitting the way the facts actually are, but something more like the beliefs' being true "so far as the subject can tell from what is available to the subject." In asking whether S is J_e in believing that p we are asking whether the truth of p is strongly indicated by what S has to go on; whether, given what S had to go on, it is at least quite likely that p is true. We want to know whether S had *adequate* grounds for believing that p, where *adequate* grounds are those sufficiently indicative to the truth of p.

If we are to make the notion of *adequate grounds* central for J_e we must say more about it. A belief has a certain ground, G, when it is "based on" G. What is it for a belief, B, to be *based* on G? That is a difficult question. So far as I know, there is no fully satisfactory general account in the literature, nor am I able to supply one. But we are not wholly at a loss. We do have a variety of paradigm cases; the difficulty concerns just how to generalize from them and just where to draw the line. When one infers p from q and *thereby* comes to accept p, this is a clear case of basing one belief on another. Again, when I come to believe that there is a tree because this visually appears to me to be the case, that is another paradigm; here my belief that that is a tree is based on my visual experience, or, if you prefer, on certain aspects of that experience. The main difficulties arise with respect to cases in which no conscious inference takes place but in which we are still inclined to say that one belief is based on another. Consider, for example, my forming the belief that you are angry on seeing you look and act in a certain way. I perform no conscious inference from a proposition about your demeanor and behavior to a proposition about your emotional state. Nevertheless it seems plausible to hold that I did learn about your demeanor and behavior through seeing it, and that the beliefs I thereby formed played a crucial role in my coming to believe that you are angry. More specifically, it seems that the former beliefs gave rise to the latter belief; that if I hadn't acquired the former I would not have acquired the latter; and, finally, that if I am asked why I suppose that you are angry I would cite the behavior and demeanor as my reason (perhaps only as "the way he looked and acted"). How can we get this kind of case together with the conscious-inference cases into a general account? We might claim that they are all cases of inference, some of them being unconscious. But there are problems as to when we are justified in imputing unconscious inferences. We might take it that what lets in our problem cases is the subject's disposition to cite the one belief(s) as his reason for the other belief; and then make our general condition a disjunction of conscious inference from q and a tendency to cite q as the reason. But then what about subjects (small children and lower animals) that are too unsophisticated to be able to answer questions as to what their reasons are? Can't their beliefs be based on something when no conscious inference is performed? Moreover, this disjunctive criterion will not include cases in which a belief is based on an experience, rather than on other beliefs. A third suggestion concerns causality. In all the cases mentioned thus far it is plausible to suppose that the belief that q was among the causes of the belief that p. This suggests that we might try to cut the Gordian knot by boldly identifying "based on" with "caused by." But this runs into the usual difficulties of simple causal theories. Many items enter into the causation of a belief, e.g., various neurophysiological happenings, that clearly don't qualify as even part of what the belief is based on. To make a causal account work we would have to beef it up into "caused by q in a certain way." And what way is that? Some way that is paradigmatically exemplified by our paradigms? But how to state this way in such a fashion that it applies equally to the nonparadigmatic cases?[23]

In the face of these perplexities our only recourse is to keep a firm hold on our paradigms, and work with a less than ideally determinate concept of a relationship that holds in cases that are "sufficiently like" the paradigms. That will be sufficient to do the job over most of the territory.[24]

Let's return to "grounds." What a belief is based on we may term the ground of the belief. A ground, in a more dispositional sense of the term, is the sort of item on which a belief can be based. We have already cited beliefs and experiences as possible grounds, and these would seem to exhaust the possibilities. Indeed, some epistemologists would find this too generous already, maintaining that beliefs can be based only on other beliefs. They would treat perceptual cases by holding that the belief that a tree is over there is based on the *belief that* there visually appears to me to be a tree over there, rather than, as we are suggesting, on the visual appearance itself. I can't accept that, largely because I doubt that all perceptual believers have such beliefs about their visual experience,[25] but I can't pause to argue the point. Suffice it to say that since my opponents' position is, to be as generous as possible, controversial, we do not want to build a position on this issue into the *concept* of epistemic justification. We want to leave open at least the *conceptual* possibility of *direct* or *immediate* justification by experience (and perhaps in other ways also), as well as *indirect* or *mediate* justification by relation to other beliefs (inferentially in the most explicit cases). Finally, to say that a subject *has adequate* grounds for her belief that *p* is to say that she has other justified beliefs, or experiences, on which the belief could be based and which are strongly indicative of the truth of the belief. The reason for the restriction to *justified* beliefs is that a ground shouldn't be termed adequate unless it can confer justification on the belief it grounds. But we noted earlier that if I infer my belief that *p*, by even impeccable logic, from an *unjustified* belief that *q*, the former belief is not thereby justified.[26]

To return to the main thread of the discussion, we are thinking of *S*'s being J_e in believing that *p* as involving *S*'s having adequate grounds for that belief. That is, we are thinking of the possession of those adequate grounds as constituting the goodness of the belief from the epistemic point of view. The next thing to note is that the various "modes" of J_d apply here as well.

Let's begin by noting an objective-subjective distinction. To be sure, in thinking of J_e as *having truth-indicative grounds within one's "perspective on the world,"* we are already thinking of it as more subjective than flat-out truth. But within that perspectival conception we can set the requirements as more objective or more subjective. There is more than one respect in which the possession of adequate grounds could be "subjectivized." First, there is the distinction between the existence of the ground and its adequacy. *S* is *objectively* J_e in believing that *p* if *S* does in fact have grounds that are in fact adequate grounds for that belief. A subjective version would require only that *S believe* one or the other part of this, or both; either (a) that there are (possible) grounds that are in fact adequate and he believes of those grounds that he has them; or (b) that he has grounds that he believes to be adequate; or the combination, (c) that he believes himself to have adequate grounds. Moreover, there are two ways in which the possession-of-grounds belief could go wrong. Confining ourselves to beliefs, one could mistakenly suppose oneself to believe that *p*, or one could mistakenly suppose one's belief that *p* to be justified. Lacking time to go into all these variations, I shall confine this discussion to the subjectivization of adequacy. So our first two modes will be:

XVI. Objective—*S* does have adequate grounds for believing that *p*.

XVII. Subjective—*S* has grounds for believing that *p* and he believes them to be adequate.

And here too we have a "justified belief," or "cognitive" variant on the subjective version.

XVIII. Cognitive—*S* has grounds for believing that *p* and he is justified in believing them to be adequate.

We can dismiss XVII by the same arguments we brought against the subjective version of J_d. The mere fact that I believe, however unjustifiably or irresponsibly, that my grounds for believing that *p* are adequate could scarcely render me justified in believing that *p*. If I believe them to be adequate just because I have an egotistical penchant to overestimate my powers, that could hardly make it rational for me to believe that *p*. But here we will not find the same reason to favor XVIII over XVI. With J_d the cognitive version won out because of what it takes for blameworthiness. But whether one is J_e in believing that *p* has nothing to do with whether he is subject to blame. It depends rather on whether his believing that *p* is a *good thing* from the epistemic point of view. And however justifiably *S* believes that his grounds are adequate, if they are not then his believing that *p* on those grounds is not a good move in the truth-seeking game. Even if he isn't to blame for making that move it is a bad move nonetheless. Thus J_e is properly construed in the objective mode.

We are also confronted with the question of whether J_e should be construed "motivationally." Since we have already opted for an objective reading, the motivational version will take the following form:

XIX. Motivational—*S*'s belief that *p* is based on adequate grounds.

So our question is whether it is enough for justification that *S have* adequate grounds for his belief, whether used or not, or whether it is also required that the belief be based on those grounds. We cannot settle this question on the grounds that were available for J_{dv}, since with J_e we are not thinking of the subject as being obliged to take relevant consideration into account in *choosing* whether to believe that *p*.

There is something to be said on both sides of this issue. In support of the first, source-irrelevant position (XVI without XIX), it can be pointed out that *S*'s *having a justification* for believing that *p* is independent of whether *S* does believe that *p*: I can have adequate grounds for believing that *p,* and so *have* a justification, even though I do not in fact believe that *p*. Hence it can hardly be a requirement for having a justification for *p* that my nonexistent belief have a certain kind of basis. Likewise my having adequate grounds for believing that *p* is sufficient for this being *a rational thing for me to believe*. But, says the opponent, suppose that *S* does believe that *p*. If simply having adequate grounds were sufficient for this belief to be justified, then, provided *S* does have the grounds, her belief that *p* would be justified however frivolous the source. But surely a belief that stems from wishful thinking would not be justified, however strong one's (unutilized) grounds for it.[27]

Now the first thing to say about this controversy is that both antagonists win, at least to the extent that each of them is putting forward a viable concept, and one that is actually used in epistemic assessment. There certainly is the concept of *having* adequate grounds for the belief that *p*, whether or not one does believe that *p*, and there equally certainly is the concept of one's belief being based on adequate grounds. Both concepts represent favorable epistemic statuses. *Ceteris paribus,* one is better off believing something for which one has adequate grounds than believing something for which one doesn't. And the same can be said for the contrast between having a belief that is based on adequate grounds and having one that isn't. Hence I will recognize that these are both concepts of epistemic justification, and I will resist the pressure to decide which is *the* concept.

Nevertheless we can seek to determine which concept is more fundamental to epistemology. On this issue it seems clear that the motivational concept is the richer one and thereby embodies a more complete account of a belief's being a good thing from the epistemic point of view. Surely there is something epistemically undesirable about a belief that is generated in an intellectually disreputable way, however adequate the unutilized grounds possessed by the subject. If, possessing excellent reasons for supposing that you are trying to discredit me professionally, I nevertheless believe this, not for those reasons but out of paranoia, in such a way that even if I didn't have those reasons I would have believed this just as firmly, it was undesirable from the point of view of the aim at truth for me to form that belief as I did. So if we are seeking the most inclusive concept of what makes a belief a good thing epistemically, we will want to include a consideration of what the belief is based on. Hence I will take XIX as the favored formulation of what makes a belief a good thing from the epistemic point of view.

I may add that XVI can be seen as derivative from XIX. To simply *have* adequate grounds is to be in such a position that *if* I make use of that position as a basis for believing that *p* I will thereby be justified in that belief. Thus XVI gives us a concept of a potential for XIX; it is a concept of having resources that are sufficient for believing justifiably, leaving open the question of whether those resources are used.

The next point to be noted is that XIX guarantees only *prima facie* justification. As often noted, it is quite possible for my belief that *p* to have been formed on the basis of evidence that in itself adequately supports *p*, even though the totality of the evidence at my disposal does not. Thus the evidence on which I came to believe that the butler committed the murder might strongly support that hypothesis, but when arriving at that belief I was ignoring other things I know or justifiably believe that tend to exculpate the butler; the total evidence at my disposal is not sufficient support for my belief. In that case we will not want to count my belief as justified all things considered, even though the grounds *on the basis of which* it was formed were themselves adequate. Their adequacy is, so to say, *overridden* by the larger perspectival context in which they are set. Thus XIX gives us *prima facie* justification, what will be justification provided it is not cancelled by further relevant factors. Unqualified justification requires an additional condition to the effect that S does not also have reasons that suffice to override the justification provided by the grounds on which the belief is based. Building that into XIX we get:

> XX. Motivational—S's belief that p is based on adequate grounds, and S lacks overriding reason to the contrary.

Even though XX requires us to bring in the unused portions of the perspective, we cannot simplify the condition by ignoring the distinction between what provides the basis and what doesn't, and make the crucial condition something like "The totality of S's perspective provides adequate support." For then we would run up against the considerations that lead us to prefer XIX to XVI.

We have distinguished two aspects of our evaluative concept of justification, the strictly evaluative portion—goodness from the epistemic point of view—and the very general statement of the relevant good making characteristic, *based on adequate grounds in the absence of overriding reasons to the contrary.* In taking the concept to include this second component we are opting for the view that this concept, though unmistakably evaluative rather than "purely factual" in character, is not so purely evaluative as to leave completely open the basis on which this evaluative status supervenes. I do not see how to justify this judgment by reference to any more fundamental considerations. It is just that in reflecting on epistemic justification, thought of in evaluative (as contrasted with deontological) terms, it seems clear to me that the range of possible bases for epistemic goodness is not left completely open by the concept, that it is part of what we mean in terming a belief justified, that the belief was based on adequate grounds (or, at least, that the subject had adequate grounds for it).[28] Though this means that J_e is not maximally neutral on the question of what it takes for justification, it is still quite close to that. It still leaves open whether there is immediate justification and if so on the basis of what, how strong a ground is needed for justification, what dimensions of strength there are for various kinds of grounds, and so on.

Let's codify our evaluative concept of justification as follows:

> XXI. S is J_{eg} in believing that p *iff* S's believing that p, as S did, was a good thing from the epistemic point of view, in that S's belief that p was based on adequate grounds and S lacked sufficient overriding reasons to the contrary.

In the subscript "g" stands for "grounds."

My supposition that all justification of belief involves adequate grounds may be contested. This does seem incontrovertible for beliefs based on other beliefs and for perceptual beliefs based on experience. But what about beliefs in self-evident propositions where the self-evidence is what justifies me in the belief.[29] On considering the proposition that two quantities equal to the same quantity are equal to each other, this seems obviously true to me; and I shall suppose, though this is hardly uncontroversial, that in those circumstances I am justified in believing it. But where are the adequate grounds on which my belief is based? It is not that there are grounds here about whose adequacy we might well have doubts; it is rather that there seems to be nothing identifiable as grounds. There is nothing here that is distinguishable from my belief and the proposition believed, in the way evidence or reasons are distinct from that for which they are evidence or reasons, or in the way my sensory experience is distinct from the beliefs about the physical world that are based on it. Here I simply consider the proposition and straightaway accept it. A similar problem can be raised for normal beliefs about one's own conscious states. What is the ground for a typical belief that one feels sleepy?[30] If one replies "One's conscious of one's feeling of sleepiness," then it may be insisted, with some show of plausibility, that where one is consciously feeling sleepy there is no difference between one's feeling sleepy and one's being conscious that one is feeling sleepy.

This is a very large issue that I will not have time to consider properly. Suffice it to say that one may treat these as limiting cases in which the ground, though real enough, is minimally distinguishable either from the belief it is grounding or from the fact that makes the belief true. In the first person belief about one's own conscious state the ground coincides with the fact that makes the belief true. Since the fact believed is itself an experience of the subject, there need be nothing "between" the subject and the fact that serves as an indication of the latter's presence. The fact "reveals itself" directly. Self-evident propositions require separate treatment. Here I think that we can take the *way* the proposition appears to one, variously described as "obviously true," "self-evident," and "clear and distinct," as the ground on which the belief is based. I accept the proposition because it *seems* to me so obviously true. This is less distinct from the belief than an inferential or sensory experiential ground, since it has to do with how I am aware of the proposition. Nevertheless there is at least a minimal distinctness. I can form an intelligible conception of someone's failing to believe that p, where p seems obviously true. Perhaps this person has been rendered unduly skeptical by overexposure to the logical paradoxes.

VI

Let's go back to the idea that the "based on adequate grounds" part of J_{eg} is there because of the "internalist" character of justification. Contrasts between internalism and externalism have been popular in epistemology lately, but the contrast is not always drawn in the same way. There are two popular ways, both of which are distinct from what I have in mind. First there is the idea that justification is internal in that it depends on what support is available for the belief from "within the subject's perspective," in the sense of what the subject knows or justifiably believes about the world.[31] This kind of internalism restricts justification to mediate or discursive justification, justification by reasons. Another version takes "the subject's perspective" to include whatever is "directly accessible" to the subject, accessible just on the basis of reflection; internalism on this version restricts justifiers to what is directly accessible to the subject.[32] This, unlike the first version, does not limit us to mediate justification, since experience can be taken to be at least as directly accessible as beliefs and knowledge.

In contrast to both these ways of drawing the distinction, what I take to be internal about justification is that whether a belief is justified depends on what it is based on (grounds); and grounds must be other psychological state(s) of the same subject. I am not absolutely certain that grounds are confined to beliefs and experiences, even if experiences are not confined to sensations and feelings but also include, for example, the way a proposition seems obvious to one, and religious and aesthetic experiences; but these are the prime candidates, and any other examples must belong to some kind of which these are the paradigms. So in taking it to be conceptually true that one is justified in believing that p iff one's belief that p is based on an adequate ground, I take justification to be "internal" in that it depends on the way in which the belief stems from the believer's psychological states, which are "internal" to the subject in an obvious sense. What would be an externalist contrast with this kind of internalism? We shall see one such contrast in a moment, in discussing the relation of J_{eg} to reliabilism. Moreover, it contrasts with the idea that one can be justified in a certain belief just because of the status of the proposition believed (necessary, infallible). My sort of internalism is different from the first one mentioned above, in that experiences as well as beliefs can figure as grounds. And it is different from the second if, as I believe, what a belief is based on may not be directly accessible. This will be the case if, as seems plausible, much belief formation goes on below the conscious level. It would seem, for example, that, as we move about the environment, we are constantly forming short-term, perceptual beliefs without any conscious monitoring of this activity.

The most prominent exponents of an explicitly nondeontological conception of epistemic justification have been reliabilists, who have either identified justification with reliability[33] or have taken reliability to be an adequate criterion of justification.[34] The reliability that is in question here is the reliability of belief formation and sustenance.[35] To say that a belief was formed in a reliable way is, roughly, to say that it was formed in a way that can be depended on generally to form true rather than false beliefs, at least from inputs like the present one, and at least in the sorts of circumstances in which we normally find ourselves.[36] Thus if my visual system, when functioning as it is at present in yielding my belief that there is a tree in front of me, generally yields true beliefs about objects that are fairly close to me and directly in front of me, then my present belief that there is a tree in front of me was formed in a reliable manner.

Now it may be supposed that J_{eg}, as we have explained it, is just reliability of belief formation with an evaluative frosting. For where a belief is based on adequate grounds that belief has been formed in a reliable fashion. In fact, it is plausible to take reliability as a *criterion* for adequacy of grounds. If my grounds for believing that *p* are not such that it is generally true that beliefs like that formed on grounds like that are true, they cannot be termed "adequate." Why do we think that wanting State to win the game is not an adequate reason for supposing that it has won, whereas the fact that a victory has been reported by several newspapers is an adequate reason? Surely it has something to do with the fact that beliefs like that when formed on the first sort of grounds are not *generally* true, while they are *generally* true when formed on grounds of the second sort. Considerations like this may lead us to suppose that J_{eg}, in effect, identifies justification with reliability.[37]

Nevertheless the internalist character of justification prevents it from being identified with reliability, and even blocks an extensional equivalence. Unlike justification, reliability of belief formation is not limited to cases in which a belief is based on adequate grounds within the subject's psychological states. A reliable mode of belief formation *may* work through the subject's own knowledge and experience. Indeed, it is plausible to suppose that all of the reliable modes of belief formation available to human beings are of this sort. But it is quite conceivable that there should be others. I might be so constituted that beliefs about the weather tomorrow which apparently just "pop into my mind" out of nowhere are in fact reliably produced by a mechanism of which we know nothing, and which does not involve the belief being based on anything. Here we would have reliably formed beliefs that are not based on adequate grounds from within my perspective, and so are not J_{eg}.

Moreover, even within the sphere of beliefs based on grounds, reliability and justification do not necessarily go together. The possibility of divergence here stems from another feature of justification embodied in our account, the way in which unqualified justification requires not only an adequate ground but also the absence of sufficient overriding reasons. This opens up the possibility of a case in which a belief is formed on the basis of grounds in a way that is in fact highly reliable, even though the subject has strong reasons for supposing the way to be unreliable. These reasons will (or may) override the *prima facie* justification provided by the grounds on which the belief was based. And so *S* will not be justified in the belief, even though it was reliably generated.

Consider, in this connection, a case presented by Alvin Goldman.

Suppose that Jones is told on fully reliable authority that a certain class of his memory beliefs are almost all mistaken. His parents fabricate a wholly false story that Jones suffered from amnesia when he was seven but later developed *pseudo*memories of that period. Though Jones listens to what his parents say and has excellent reasons to trust them, he persists in believing the ostensible memories from his seven-year-old past.[38]

Suppose that Jones, upon recalling his fifth birthday party, believes that he was given an electric train for his fifth birthday because, as it seems to him, he remembers being given it.[39] By hypothesis, his memory mechanism is highly reliable, and so his belief about his fifth birthday was reliably formed. But this belief is not adequately supported by the *totality* of what he justifiably believes. His justifiable belief that he has no real memory of his first seven years overrides the support from his ostensible memory. Thus Jones is not J_{eg} in his memory belief, because the "lack of overriding reasons to the contrary" requirement is not satisfied. But reliability is subject to no such constraint. Just as reliable mechanisms are not restricted to those that work through the subject's perspective, so it is not a requirement on the reliability of belief-formation that the belief be adequately supported by the totality of the subject's perspective. However many and however strong the reasons Jones has for distrusting his memory, the fact remains that his memory beliefs are still reliably formed. Here is another way in which the class of beliefs that are J_{eg} and the class of reliably formed beliefs can fail to coincide.[40]

I would suggest that, of our candidates, J_{eg} most fully embodies what we are looking for under the heading of "epistemic justification." (1) Like its deontological competitors it is an evaluative concept, in a broad sense, a concept of a favorable status from an epistemic point of view. (2) Unlike J_{dv} it does not presuppose that belief is under direct voluntary control. (3) Unlike J_{di}, it implies that the believer is in a strong epistemic position in believing that *p*, i.e., that there is something about the way in which he believes that *p* that renders it at least likely that the belief is true. Thus it renders it intelligible that justification is something we should prize from an epistemic point of view. (4) Unlike the concept of a reliable mode of belief formation it represents this "truth conductivity" as a matter of the belief's being based on an adequate ground within the subject's own cognitive states. Thus it recognizes the "internalist" character of justification; it recognizes that in asking whether a belief is justified we are interested in the prospects for the truth of the belief, given what the subject "has to go on." (5) Thus the concept provides broad guidelines for the specification of conditions of justification, but within those guidelines there is ample room for disagreement over the precise conditions for one or another type of belief. The concept does not leave us totally at a loss as to what to look for. But in adopting J_{eg} we are not building answers to substantive epistemological questions into the concept. As the only candidate to exhibit all these desiderata, J_{eg} is clearly the winner.

VII

It may be useful to bring together the lessons we have learned from this conceptual exploration.

1. Justifying, an activity of showing or establishing something, is much less central for epistemology than is "being justified," as a state or condition.

2. It is central to epistemic justification that *what justifies* is restricted to the subject's "perspective," to the subject's knowledge, justified belief, or experience.

3. Deontological concepts of justification are either saddled with an indefensible assumption of the voluntariness of belief (J_{dv}) or allow for cases in which one believes that p without having any adequate ground for the belief (J_{di}).

4. The notion of one's belief being based on adequate grounds incorporates more of what we are looking for in a concept of epistemic justification than the weaker notion of having adequate grounds for belief.

5. Justification is closely related to reliability, but because of the perspectival character noted in 2, they do not completely coincide; much less can they be identified.

6. The notion of believing that p in a way that is good from an epistemic point of view in that the belief is based on adequate grounds (J_{eg}) satisfies the chief desiderata for a concept of epistemic justification.

VIII

The ultimate payoff of this conceptual exploration is the increased sophistication it gives us in dealing with substantive epistemological issues. Putting our scheme to work is a very large enterprise, spanning a large part of epistemology. In conclusion I will give one illustration of the ways in which our distinctions can be of help in the trenches. For this purpose I will restrict myself to the broad contrast between J_{dv} and J_{eg}.

First, consider what we might term "higher-level requirements" for S's being justified in believing that p. I include under that heading all requirements that S know or justifiably believe something *about* the epistemic status of p, or about the strength of S's grounds for p. This would include requirements that S be justified in believing that:

1. R is an adequate reason for p (where R is alleged to justify S's belief that p).[41]
2. Experience e is an adequate indication that p (where e is alleged to justify S's belief that p).[42]

On J_{eg} there is no temptation to impose such requirements. If R *is* an adequate reason (e *is* an adequate indication), then if one believes that p on that basis, one is *thereby* in a strong position, epistemically; and the further knowledge, or justified belief, that the reason is adequate (the experience is an adequate indication), though no doubt quite important and valuable for other purposes, will do nothing to improve the truth-conduciveness of one's believing that p. But on J_{dv} we get a different story. If it's a question of being blameless in believing that p, it can be persuasively argued that this requires not only forming the belief on what is in fact an adequate ground, but doing so in the light of the realization that the ground is an adequate one. If I decide to believe that p without knowing whether the ground is adequate, am I not subject to blame for proceeding irresponsibly in my doxastic behavior, whatever the actual strength of the ground? If the higher-level requirements are plausible only if we are using J_{dv}, then the dubiousness of that concept will extend to those requirements.[43]

In the above paragraph we were considering whether S's being justified in believing that his ground is adequate is a *necessary* condition of justification. We can also consider whether it is sufficient. Provided that S is justified in believing that his belief that p is based on an adequate ground, G, does it make any difference, for his being justified in believing that p, whether the ground *is* adequate? Our two contenders will line up here as they did on the previous issue. For J_{eg} the mere fact that S is justified is supposing that G is adequate will cut no ice. What J_{eg} requires is that S *actually be* in an epistemically favorable position; and although S's being justified in supposing G to be adequate is certainly good evidence for that, it doesn't *constitute* being in such a position. Hence J_{eg} requires that the ground of the belief actually be an adequate one. As for J_{dv}, where it is a question of whether S is blameworthy in believing that p, what is decisive is how S's epistemic position appears with S's perspective on the world. If, so far as S could tell, G is an adequate ground, then S is blameless, i.e., J_{dv}, in believing that p on G. Nothing else could be required for justification in that sense. If S has chosen his doxastic state by applying the appropriate principles in the light of all his relevant knowledge and justified belief, then he is totally in the clear. Again the superior viability of J_{eg}, as over against J_{dv}, should tip the scales in favor of the more objective requirement of adequacy.[44]

NOTES

1. Of late a number of theorists have been driving a wedge between what it is to *be* P or what *property* P is, on the one hand, and what belongs to the *concept* of P or what is the meaning of "P" on the other. Thus it has been claimed (Kripke, 1972) that *what heat is* is determined by the physical investigation into the nature of heat, whether or not the results of that investigation are embodied in our *concept* of heat or in the meaning of "heat." I shall take it that no such distinction is applicable to epistemic justification, that here the only reasonable interpretation to be given to "what it is" is "what is involved in the concept" or "what the term means." If someone disagrees with this, that need not be a problem. Such a person can simply read "what concept of justification is being employed" for "what justification is taken to be."

2. I think especially of R. M. Chisholm, *Theory of Knowledge* 2d ed. (Englewood Cliffs, N.J.: Prentice-Hall, 1977), ch, 1; C. Ginet, *Knowledge, Perception, and Memory* (Dordrecht, Netherlands: D. Reidel Publishing Co., 1975), ch. 3; A. I. Goldman, "What Is Justified Belief?" in *Justification and Knowledge*, G. S. Pappas, ed. (Dordrecht, Netherlands: D. Reidel Publishing Co., 1979), and "The Internalist Conception of Justification," *Midwest Studies in Philosophy* 5 (1980): 27–51; and N. Wolterstorff, "Can Belief in God Be Rational If It Has No Foundations?" in *Faith and Rationality*, A. Plantinga and N. Wolterstorff, eds. (Notre Dame, Ind.: Notre Dame University Press, 1983).

3. It may be claimed that the activity concept is fundamental in another way, viz., by virtue of the fact that one is justified in believing that *p* only if one is *capable* of carrying out a justification of the belief. But if that were so we would be justified in far fewer beliefs than we suppose. Most human subjects are quite incapable of carrying out a justification of any perceptual or introspective beliefs.

4. I am indebted to Alvin Plantinga for helping me to see that this term is more suitable than the term "normative" that I had been using in earlier versions of this paper. The reader should be cautioned that "deontological" as used here does not carry the contrast with "teleological" that is common in ethical theory. According to that distinction a deontological ethical theory, like that of Kant's, does not regard principles of duty or obligation as owing their status to the fact that acting in the way they prescribe tends to realize certain desirable states of affairs. Whereas a teleological theory, like utilitarianism, holds that this is what renders a principle of obligation acceptable. The fact that we are not using "deontological" with this force is shown by the fact that we are thinking of epistemic obligations as owing their validity to the fact that fulfilling them would tend to lead to the realization of a desirable state of affairs, viz., a large body of beliefs with a favorable truth-falsity ratio.

5. See Chisholm, *Theory of Knowledge*, ch. 1; Ginet, *Knowledge, Perception, and Memory*, ch. 3; and Wolterstorff, "Can Belief in God Be Rational If It Has No Foundations?" An extended development of a deontological concept of epistemic justification is to be found in M. B. Naylor, "Epistemic Justification," unpublished manuscript, 1978. In my development of deontological concepts in this paper I have profited from the writing of all these people and from discussions with them.

6. Ginet, *Knowledge, Perception, and Memory*, p. 28. See also A. J. Ayer, *The Problem of Knowledge* (London: Macmillan, 1956), pp. 31–34; Chisholm, *Theory of Knowledge*, p. 14; and Naylor, "Epistemic Justification," p. 8.

7. These examples are meant to be illustrative only; they do not necessarily carry the endorsement of the management.

8. Here I am indebted to Alvin Plantinga.

9. A weaker objective conception would be this. My obligation is to do what in fact is *likely* to bring out A. On this weaker conception I could be said to have fulfilled my obligation in (some) cases in which A is not forthcoming.

10. We could also subjectivize the aimed at result, instead of or in addition to subjectivizing what it takes to arrive at that result. In this way one would have subjectively fulfilled one's obligation if one had done what one believed to be one's obligation. Or, to combine the two moves to the subjective, one would have subjectively fulfilled one's obligation if one had done what one believed would lead to the fulfillment of what one believed to be one's obligation. But sufficient unto the day is the distinction thereof.

11. I would call this "epistemic obligation," except that I want to make these same distinctions with respect to epistemic justification, and so I don't want to repeat the generic term for one of the species.

12. Since we are tacitly restricting this to epistemic justification, we will also be, tacitly, restricting ourselves to intellectual obligations.

13. Since this is all on the assumption that *S* does not believe that *p*, we need not add that to the right hand side in order to get a sufficient condition.

14. Note that XI, XII, and some forms of XIII are in terms of higher-level beliefs about one's epistemic status vis-à-vis *p*. There are less sophisticated sorts of subjectives. For example:

S is subjectively justified in believing that p iff S believes that q, and q is evidence for p.

(For the reason this does not count as having adequate evidence see the next paragraph in the text.)

Or even more subjectively:

S is subjectively justified in believing that p iff S believes that q and bases his belief that p on his belief that q.

The definitions presented in the text do not dictate what we should say in the case in which S does not have the higher-level belief specified in XI and XII, but satisfies either of the above conditions. A thorough treatment of modes of normative status would have to go into all of this.

15. We have been taking it that to be, for example, subjectively or cognitively justified in believing that p is not to be violating any subjective or cognitive obligations in believing that p. That means that if we opt for cognitive justification we are committed to giving a correspondingly cognitive formulation of what intellectual obligations one has. But that isn't the only way to do it. We could leave all the obligations in a purely objective form, and vary the function that goes from obligation to justification. That is, we could say that one is subjectively justified if one believes that one has not violated an (objective) obligation (or, perhaps believes something that is such that, given one's objective obligations, it implies that none of those obligations have been violated). And a similar move could be made for the other modes.

16. Here are a couple of examples of the attraction of XII for J_d. Chisholm, *Theory of Knowledge*, presents an informal explanation of his basic term of epistemic evaluation, "more reasonable than" in terms of an "intellectual requirement." The explanation runs as follows:

> One way, then, of reexpressing the locution "*p* is more reasonable than *q* for *S* at *t*" is to say this: *S* is so situated at *t* that his intellectual requirement, his responsibility as an intellectual being, is better fulfilled by *p* than by *q*. (p. 14)

The point that is relevant to our present discussion is that Chisholm states our basic intellectual requirement in what I have called "cognitive" rather than "objective" terms; and with a motivational rider.

> We may assume that every person is subject to a purely intellectual requirement—that of trying his best to bring it about that, for every proposition *h* that he considers, he accepts *h* if and only if *h* is true. (p. 14)

The "requirement" is that one *try one's best* to bring this about, rather than that one do bring it about. I take it that to try my best to bring about a result, *R*, is to do what, so far as I can tell, will bring about *R*, insofar as that is within my power. (It might be claimed that so long as I do what I believe will bring about *R* I am trying my best, however irresponsible the belief. But it seems to me that so long as I am not acting on the best of the indications available to me I am not "trying my best.") The motivational rider comes in too, since unless I do what I do *because* I am taking it to (have a good chance to) lead to *R*, I am not trying at all to bring about R.

Of course, Chisholm is speaking in terms of fulfilling an intellectual obligation rather than, as we have been doing, in terms of not violating intellectual obligations. But we are faced with the same choice between our "modes" in either case.

For a second example I turn to Wolterstorff, "Can Belief in God Be Rational If It Has No Foundations?" Wolterstorff's initial formulation of a necessary and sufficient condition of justification (or, as he says, "rationality") for an "eluctable" belief of S that p is: S *lacks adequate reasons for ceasing from believing that* p. (p. 164). But then by considerations similar to those we have just adduced, he recognizes that even if S does not in fact have adequate reason for ceasing to believe that p he would still be unjustified in continuing to hold the belief if he were "rationally obliged" to believe that he does have adequate reason to cease to believe that *p*. Moreover Wolterstorff recognizes that *S* would be justified in believing that *p*, if, even though he does have adequate reason to cease from believing that *p* he is rationally justified in supposing that he doesn't. Both these qualifications amount to recognizing that what is crucial is not what reasons *S* has in fact, but what reasons *S* is justifying in supposing himself to have. The final formulation, embodying these and other qualifications, runs as follows:

> A person *S* is rational in his eluctable and innocently produced belief *p* if and only if *S* does believe *p* and either:
>
> (i) *S* neither has nor ought to have adequate reason to cease from believing *p*, and is not rationally obliged to believe that he *does* have adequate reason to cease; or
>
> (ii) *S* does have adequate reason to cease from believing *p* but does not realize that he does, and is rationally justified in that. (p. 168)

17. Chisholm, *Theory of Knowledge*, p. 14.

18. See also Ginet, *Knowledge, Perception, and Memory*, p. 36.

19. Note that I am not restricting the category of what is within my immediate voluntary control to "basic actions." Neither of the actions just mentioned would qualify for that title. The category includes both basic actions and actions that involve other conditions, where I can satisfy those other conditions, when I choose, just at the moment of choice. Thus my point about believing is not just that it is not a basic action, but that it is not even a nonbasic action that is under my effective immediate control. Whatever is required for my believing that there will never be a nuclear war, it is not something that I can bring about immediately by choosing to do so; though, as I am about to point out, I can affect my believings and abstentions in a more long-range fashion.

20. For other accounts of the indirect voluntary control of beliefs see Naylor, "Epistemic Justification," pp. 19–20, and Wolterstorff, "Can Belief in God Be Rational If It Has No Foundations?" pp. 153–55.

21. Our four "modes" can also be applied to J_{di}. Indeed, the possibilities for variation are even more numerous. For example, with respect to the *subjective* mode we can switch from the objective fact to the subject's belief with respect to (a) the circumstances of a putative violation, (b) whether there was a violation, and (c) whether the violation was causally related to the belief formation in question. We will leave all this as an exercise for the reader.

22. I must confess that I do not find "justified" an apt term for a favorable or desirable state or condition, when what makes it desirable is cut loose from considerations of obligation and blame. Nevertheless, since the term is firmly ensconced in the literature as the term to use for any concept that satisfies the four conditions set out in section 2, I will stifle my linguistic scruples and employ it for a nondeontological concept.

23. There are also problems as to where to draw the line. What about the unconscious "use" of perceptual cues for the depth of an object in the visual field or for "size constancy"? And however we answer that particular question, just where do we draw the line as we move farther and farther from our initial paradigms?

24. For some recent discussion of "based on" see M. Swain, *Reasons and Knowledge* (Ithaca, N.Y.: Cornell University Press, 1981), ch. 3, and G. S. Pappas, "Basing Relations," in G. S. Pappas, ed., *Justification and Knowledge*. One additional point I do need to make explicit is this. I mean "based on" to range over both what initially gave rise to the belief, and what sustains it while it continues to be held. To be precise one should speak of *what the belief is based on at time* t. If *t* is the time of acquisition, one is speaking of what gave rise to the belief; if *t* is later than that, one is speaking of what sustains it.

25. For an interesting discussion of this point see A. Quinton, *The Nature of Things* (London: Rout-

ledge and Kegan Paul, 1973), ch. 7. My opponent will be even more hard pressed to make out that beliefs about one's own conscious experience are based on other beliefs. His best move here would be either to deny that there are such beliefs or to deny that they are based on anything.

26. No such restriction would be required just for having grounds (of some sort). Though even here the word "ground" by itself carries a strong suggestion that what is grounded is, to some extent, supported. We need a term for anything a belief might be based on, however vainly. "Ground" carries too much positive evaluative force to be ideally suitable for this role.

27. For some recent discussion of this issue see G. Harman, *Thought* (Princeton, N.J.: Princeton University Press, 1973), ch. 2; K. Lehrer, *Knowledge* (New York: Oxford University Press, 1974), ch. 6; R. Firth, "Are Epistemic Concepts Reducible to Ethical Concepts?" in *Values and Morals,* A. I. Goldman and J. Kims, eds. (Dordrecht, Netherlands: D. Reidel Publishing Co., 1978); M. Swain, *Reasons and Knowledge,* ch. 3; and R. Foley, "Epistemic Luck and the Purely Epistemic," *American Philosophical Quarterly* (1984).

28. Even though we have opted for the "based on" formulation as giving us the more fundamental concept of epistemic justification, we have also recognized the "has adequate grounds" formulation as giving us a concept of epistemic justification. Either of these will introduce a "basis of evaluative status" component into the concept.

29. This latter qualification is needed, because I might accept a self-evident proposition on authority. In that case I was not, so to say, taking advantage of its self-evidence.

30. We are not speaking here of a belief that one *is* sleepy. There a ground is readily identifiable—one's feeling of sleepiness.

31. See L. Bonjour, "Can Empirical Knowledge Have a Foundation?" *American Philosophical Quarterly* 15 (1978): 1–13; H. Kornblith, "Ever Since Descartes," *The Monist* 68, no. 2 (April 1985); and K. Bach, "A Rationale for Reliabilism," *The Monist* 68, no. 2 (1985).

32. See A. I. Goldman, "The Internalist Conception of Justification"; Chisholm, *Theory of Knowledge,* ch. 4, pp, 63–64; and Ginet, *Knowledge, Perception, and Memory,* pp. 34–37.

33. Swain, *Reasons and Knowledge,* ch. 4.

34. Goldman, "What Is Justified Belief?"

35. For simplicity I shall couch the ensuing formulations solely in terms of belief formation, but the qualification "or sustenance" is to be understood throughout.

36. These two qualifications testify to the difficulty of getting the concept of reliability in satisfactory shape; and there are other problems to be dealt with, e.g., how to identify the general procedure of which the present belief formation is an instance.

37. An alternative to explicating "adequate" in terms of reliability would be to use the notion of conditional probability. G is an adequate ground for a belief that p just in case the probability of p on G is high. And since adequacy is closely related both to reliability and to conditional probability, they are presumably closely related to each other. Swain, *Reasons and Knowledge,* ch. 4, exploits this connection to explicate reliability in terms of conditional probability, though in a more complex fashion than is indicated by these brief remarks.

38. Goldman, "What Is Justified Belief?" p. 18.

39. If you have trouble envisaging his trusting his memory in the face of his parents' story, you may imagine that he is not thinking of that story at the moment he forms the memory belief.

40. In the article in which he introduces this example Goldman modifies the "reliability is a criterion of justification" view so that it will accommodate the example. The modified formulation runs as follows:

If S's belief in p at t results from a reliable cognitive process, and there is no reliable or conditionally reliable process available to S which, had it been used by S in addition to the process actually used, would have resulted in *S*'s not believing *p* at *t*, then *S*'s belief in *p* at *t* is justified. (p. 20)

On this revised formulation, being formed by a reliable process is sufficient for justification only if there is no other reliable process that the subject could have used and such that if he had used it he would not have come to believe that *p*. In the case cited there is such a reliable process, viz., taking account of the strong reasons for believing one's memory of pre-seven-year-old events to be unreliable, The revised reliability criterion yields the correct result in this case. However, this move leaves unshaken the point that in this case Jones's belief *is* reliably formed but unjustified. That remains true, whatever is to be said about the revised criterion.

41. See, for example, D. M. Armstrong, *Belief, Truth and Knowledge* (London: Cambridge University Press, 1973), p. 151, and B. Skyrms, "The Explication of '*S* knows that *p*,' " *The Journal of Philosophy* 64 (1967): 374.

42. See, for example, W. Sellars, *Science, Perception, and Reality* (London: Routledge and Kegan Paul, 1973), pp. 168–69; Bonjour, "Can Empirical Knowledge Have a Foundation?" pp. 5–6; and Lehrer *Knowledge,* pp. 103–105.

43. In my paper, "What's Wrong with Immediate Knowledge?" *Synthese* 5, no. 2 (May 1983): 73–95, I develop at much greater length this kind of diagnosis of Bonjour's deployment of a higher-level requirement in his argument against immediate knowledge (Bonjour, "Can Empirical Knowledge Have a Foundation?").

44. Ancestors of this paper were presented at SUNY at Albany, SUNY at Buffalo, Calvin College, Cornell University, University of California at Irvine, Lehigh University, University of Michigan, University of Nebraska, Syracuse University, and the University of Western Ontario. I wish to thank members of the audience in all these institutions for their helpful comments. I would like to express special appreciation to Robert Audi, Carl Ginet, George Mavrodes, Alvin Plantinga, Fred Schmitt, and Nicholas Wolterstorff for their penetrating comments on earlier versions.

31

Evidentialism

Richard Feldman and Earl Conee

I

We advocate evidentialism in epistemology. What we call evidentialism is the view that the epistemic justification of a belief is determined by the quality of the believer's evidence for the belief. Disbelief and suspension of judgment also can be epistemically justified. The doxastic attitude that a person is justified in having is the one that fits the person's evidence. More precisely:

> EJ   Doxastic attitude D toward proposition p is epistemically justified for S at t if and only if having D toward p fits the evidence S has at t.[1]

We do not offer EJ as an analysis. Rather it serves to indicate the kind of notion of justification that we take to be characteristically epistemic—a notion that makes justification turn entirely on evidence. Here are three examples that illustrate the application of this notion of justification. First, when a physiologically normal person under ordinary circumstances looks at a plush green lawn that is directly in front of him in broad daylight, believing that there is something green before him is the attitude toward this proposition that fits his evidence. That is why the belief is epistemically justified. Second, suspension of judgment is the fitting attitude for each of us toward the proposition that an even number of ducks exists, since our evidence

From *Philosophical Studies* 48 (1985): 15–34. © 1985 by D. Reidel Publishing Co., Dordrecht, Netherlands. Reprinted by permission of Wolters Kluwer Academic Publishers.

makes it equally likely that the number is odd. Neither belief nor disbelief is epistemically justified when our evidence is equally balanced. And third, when it comes to the proposition that sugar is sour, our gustatory experience makes disbelief the fitting attitude. Such experiential evidence epistemically justifies disbelief.[2]

EJ is not intended to be surprising or innovative. We take it to be the view about the nature of epistemic justification with the most initial plausibility. A defense of EJ is now appropriate because several theses about justification that seem to cast doubt on it have been prominent in recent literature on epistemology. Broadly speaking, these theses imply that epistemic justification depends upon the cognitive capacities of people, or upon the cognitive processes or information-gathering practices that led to the attitude. In contrast, EJ asserts that the epistemic justification of an attitude depends only on evidence.

We believe that EJ identifies the basic concept of epistemic justification. We find no adequate grounds for accepting the recently discussed theses about justification that seem to cast doubt on EJ. In the remainder of this paper we defend evidentialism. Our purpose is to show that it continues to be the best view of epistemic justification.

II

In this section we consider two objections to EJ. Each is based on a claim about human limits and a claim about the conditions under which an attitude can be justified. One objection depends on the claim that an attitude can be justified only if it is voluntarily adopted, the other depends on the claim that an attitude toward a proposition or propositions can be justified for a person only if the ability to have that attitude toward the proposition or those propositions is within normal human limits.

Doxastic Voluntarism

EJ says that a doxastic attitude is justified for a person when that attitude fits the person's evidence. It is clear that there are cases in which a certain attitude toward a proposition fits a person's evidence, yet the person has no control over whether he forms that attitude toward that proposition. So some involuntarily adopted attitudes are justified according to EJ. John Heil finds this feature of the evidentialist position questionable. He says that the fact that we "speak of a person's beliefs as being warranted, justified, or rational . . . makes it appear that . . . believing something can, at least sometimes, be under the voluntary control of the believer."[3] Hilary Kornblith claims that it seems "unfair" to evaluate beliefs if they "are not subject" to direct voluntary control."[4] Both Heil and Kornblith conclude that although beliefs are not under *direct* voluntary control, it is still appropriate to evaluate them because "they are not entirely out of our control either."[5] "One does have a say in the procedures one undertakes that lead to" the formation of beliefs.[6]

Doxastic attitudes need not be under any sort of voluntary control for them to be suitable for epistemic evaluation. Examples confirm that beliefs may be both involuntary and subject to epistemic evaluation. Suppose that a person spontaneously and involuntarily believes that the lights are on in the room, as a result of the familiar sort of completely convincing perceptual evidence. This belief is clearly justified, whether or not the person cannot voluntarily acquire, lose, or modify the cognitive process that led to the belief. Unjustified beliefs can also be involuntary. A paranoid man might believe without any supporting evidence that he is being spied on. This belief might be a result of an uncontrollable desire to be a recipient of special attention. In such a case the belief is clearly epistemically unjustified even if the belief is involuntary and the person cannot alter the process leading to it.

The contrary view that only voluntary beliefs are justified or unjustified may seem plausible if one confuses the topic of EJ with an assessment of the *person*.[7] A person deserves praise or blame for being in a doxastic state only if that state is under the person's control.[8] The person who involuntarily believes in the presence of overwhelming evidence that the lights are on does not deserve praise for this belief. The belief is nevertheless justified. The person who believes that he is being spied on as a result of an uncontrollable desire does not deserve to be blamed for that belief. But there is a fact about the belief's epistemic merit. It is epistemically defective—it is held in the presence of insufficient evidence and is therefore unjustified.

Doxastic Limits

Apart from the questions about doxastic voluntarism, it is sometimes claimed that it is inappropriate to set epistemic standards that are beyond normal human limits. Alvin Goldman recommends that epistemologists seek epistemic principles that can serve as practical guides to belief formation. Such principles, he contends, must take into account the limited cognitive capacities of people. Thus, he is led to deny a principle instructing people to believe all the logical consequences of their beliefs, since they are unable to have the infinite number of beliefs that following such a principle would require.[9] Goldman's view does not conflict with EJ, since EJ does not instruct anyone to believe anything. It simply states a necessary and sufficient condition for epistemic justification. Nor does Goldman think this view conflicts with EJ, since he makes it clear that the principles he is discussing are guides to action and not principles that apply the traditional concept of epistemic justification.

Although Goldman does not use facts about normal cognitive limits to argue against EJ, such an argument has been suggested by Kornblith and by Paul Thagard. Kornblith cites Goldman's work as an inspiration for his view that "having justified beliefs is simply doing the best one can in the light of the innate endowment one starts from. . . ."[10] Thagard contends that rational or justified principles of inference "should not demand of a reasoner inferential performance which exceeds the general psychological abilities of human beings."[11] Neither Thagard nor Kornblith argues against EJ, but it is easy to see how such an argument would go: A doxastic attitude toward a proposition is justified for a person only if having that attitude toward that proposition is within the normal doxastic capabilities of people. Some doxastic attitudes that fit a person's evidence are not within those capabilities. Yet EJ classifies them as justified. Hence, EJ is false.

We see no good reason here to deny EJ. The argument has as a premise the claim that some attitudes beyond normal limits do fit someone's evidence. The fact that we are limited to a finite number of beliefs is used to support this claim. But this fact does not establish the premise. There is no reason to think that an infinite number of beliefs fit any body of evidence that anyone ever has. The evidence that people have under ordinary circumstances never makes it evident, concerning every one of an infinite number of logical consequences of that evidence, that it is a consequence. Thus, believing each consequence will not fit any ordinary evidence. Furthermore, even if there are circumstances in which more beliefs fit a person's evidence than he is able to have, all that follows is that he cannot have at one time all the beliefs that fit. It does not follow that there is any particular fitting belief which is unattainable. Hence, the premise of the argument that says that EJ classifies as justified some normally unattainable beliefs is not established by means of this example. There does not seem to be any sort of plausible evidence that would establish this premise. While some empirical evidence may show that people typically do not form fitting attitudes in certain contexts, or that some fitting attitudes are beyond some individual's abilities, such evidence fails to show that any fitting attitudes are beyond normal limits.

There is a more fundamental objection to this argument against EJ. There is no basis for the premise that what is epistemically justified must be restricted to feasible doxastic alternatives. It can be a worthwhile thing to help people to choose among the epistemic alternatives open to them. But suppose that there were occasions when forming the attitude that best fits a person's evidence was beyond normal cognitive limits. This would still be the attitude *justified* by the person's evidence. If the person had normal abilities, then he would be in the unfortunate position of being unable to do what is justified according to the standard for justification asserted by EJ. This is not a flaw in the account of justification. Some standards are met only by going beyond normal human limits. Standards that some teachers set for an "A" in a course are unattainable for most students. There are standards of artistic excellence that no one can meet, or at least standards that normal people cannot meet in any available circumstance. Similarly, epistemic justification might have been normally unattainable.

We conclude that neither considerations of doxastic voluntarism nor of doxastic limits provide any good reason to abandon EJ as an account of epistemic justification.

III

EJ sets an epistemic standard for evaluating doxastic conduct. In any case of a standard for conduct, whether it is voluntary or not, it is appropriate to speak of "requirements" or "obligations" that the standard imposes. The person who has overwhelming perceptual evidence for the proposition that the lights are on, epistemically ought to believe that proposition. The paranoid person epistemically ought not believe that he is being spied upon when he has no evidence supporting this belief. We hold the general view that one epistemically ought to have the doxastic attitudes that fit one's evidence. We think that being epistemically obligatory is equivalent to being epistemically justified.

There are in the literature two other sorts of view about epistemic obligations. What is epistemically obligatory, according to these other views, does not always fit one's evidence. Thus, each of these views of epistemic obligation, when combined with our further thesis that being epistemically obligatory is equivalent to being epistemically justified, yields results incompatible with evidentialism. We shall now consider how these proposals affect EJ.

Justification and the Obligation to Believe Truths

Roderick Chisholm holds that one has an "intellectual requirement" to try one's best to bring it about that, of the propositions one considers, one believes all and only the truths.[13] This theory of what our epistemic obligations are, in conjunction with our view that the justified attitudes are the ones we have an epistemic obligation to hold, implies the following principle:

> CJ Doxastic attitude D toward proposition p is justified for person S at time t if and only if S considers p at t and S's having D toward p at t would result from S's trying his best to bring it about that S believe p at t iff p is true.

Evaluation of CJ is complicated by an ambiguity in "trying one's best." It might mean "trying in that way which will in fact have the best results." Since the goal is to believe all and only the truths one considers, the best results would be obtained by believing each truth one considers and disbelieving each falsehood one considers. On this interpretation, CJ implies that believing each truth and disbelieving each falsehood one considers is justified whenever believing and disbelieving in these ways would result from something one could try to do.

On this interpretation CJ is plainly false. We are not justified in believing every proposition we consider that happens to be true and which we could believe by trying for the truth. It is possible to believe some unsubstantiated proposition in a reckless endeavor to believe a truth, and happen to be right. This would not be an epistemically justified belief."[14]

It might be contended that trying one's best to believe truths and disbelieve falsehoods really amounts to trying to believe and disbelieve in accordance with one's evidence. We agree that gaining the doxastic attitudes that fit one's evidence is the epistemically best way to use one's evidence in trying to believe all and only the truths one considers. This interpretation of CJ makes it nearly equivalent to EJ. There are two relevant differences. First, CJ implies that one can have justified attitudes only toward propositions one actually considers. EJ does not have this implication. CJ is also unlike EJ in implying that an attitude is justified if it would result from the *trying* to form the attitude that fits one's evidence. The attitude that is justified according to EJ is the one that as a matter of fact does fit one's evidence. This seems more plausible. What would happen if one tried to have a fitting attitude seems irrelevant—one might try but fail to form the fitting attitude.

We conclude that the doxastic attitudes that would result from carrying out the intellectual requirement that Chisholm identifies are not the epistemically justified attitudes.

Justification and Epistemically Responsible Action

Another view about epistemic obligations, proposed by Hilary Kornblith, is that we are obligated to seek the truth and gather evidence in a responsible way. Kornblith also maintains that the justification of a belief depends on how responsibly one carried out the inquiry that led to the belief.[15] We shall now examine how the considerations leading to this view affect EJ.

Kornblith describes a case of what he regards as "epistemically culpable ignorance." It is an example in which a person's belief seems to fit his evidence, and thus it seems to be justified according to evidentialism. Kornblith contends that the belief is unjustified because it results from epistemically irresponsible behavior. His example concerns a headstrong young physicist who is unable to tolerate criticism. After presenting a paper to his colleagues, the physicist pays no attention to the devastating objection of a senior colleague. The physicist, obsessed with his own success, fails even to hear the objection, which consequently has no impact on his beliefs. Kornblith says that after this, the physicist's belief in his own theory is unjustified. He suggests that evidentialist theories cannot account for this fact.

Crucial details of this example are left unspecified, but in no case does it provide a refutation of evidentialism. If the young physicist is aware of the fact that his senior colleague is making an objection, then this fact is evidence he has against his theory, although it is unclear from just this much detail how decisive it would be. So, believing his theory may no longer be justified for him according to a purely evidentialist view. On the other hand, perhaps he remains entirely ignorant of the fact that a senior colleague is objecting to his theory. He might be "lost in thought"—privately engrossed in proud admiration of the paper he has just given—and fail to understand what is going on in the audience. If this happens, and his evidence supporting his theory is just as it was prior to his presentation of the paper, then believing the theory does remain justified for him (assuming that it was justified previously). There is no reason to doubt EJ in the light of this example. It may be true that the young physicist is an unpleasant fellow, and that he lacks intellectual integrity. This is an evaluation of the character of the physicist. It is supported by the fact that in this case he is not engaged in an impartial quest for the truth. But the physicist's character has nothing to do with the epistemic status of his belief in his theory.

Responsible evidence-gathering obviously has some epistemic significance. One serious epistemological question is that of how to engage in a thoroughgoing rational pursuit of the truth. Such a pursuit may require gathering evidence in responsible ways. It may also be necessary to be open to new ideas, to think about a variety of important issues, and to consider a variety of opinions about such issues. Perhaps it requires, as Bonjour suggests, that one "reflect critically upon one's beliefs."[16] But everyone has some justified beliefs, even though virtually no one is fully engaged in a rational pursuit of the truth. EJ has no implication about the actions one must take in a rational pursuit of the truth. It is about the epistemic evaluation of attitudes given the evidence one does have, however one came to possess that evidence.

Examples like that of the headstrong physicist show no defect in the evidentialist view. Justified beliefs can result from epistemically irresponsible actions.

Other Sorts of Obligations

Having acknowledged at the beginning of this section that justified attitudes are in a sense obligatory, we wish to forestall confusions involving other notions of obligations. It is not the case that there is always a *moral* obligation to believe in accordance with one's evidence. Having a fitting attitude can bring about disastrous personal or social consequences. Vicious beliefs that lead to vicious acts can be epistemically justified. This rules out any moral obligation to have the epistemically justified attitude.[17]

It is also false that there is always a *prudential* obligation to have each epistemically justified attitude. John Heil discusses the following example.[18] Sally has fairly good evidence that her husband Burt has been seeing another woman. Their marriage is in a precarious condition. It would be best for Sally if their marriage were preserved. Sally foresees that, were she to believe that Burt has been seeing another woman, her resulting behavior would lead to their divorce. Given these assumptions, EJ counts as justified at least some measure of belief by Sally in the proposition that Burt has been seeing another woman. But Sally would be better off if she did not have this belief, in light of the fact that she would be best served by their continued marriage. Heil raises the question of what Sally's prudential duty is in this case. Sally's *epistemic* obligation is to believe that her husband is unfaithful. But that gives no reason to deny what seems obvious here. Sally *prudentially* ought to refrain from believing her husband to be unfaithful. It can be prudent not to have a doxastic attitude that is correctly said by EJ to be justified, just as it can be moral not to have such an attitude.

More generally, the causal consequences of having an unjustified attitude can be more beneficial in *any* sort of way than the consequences of having its justified alternative. We have seen that it can be morally and prudentially best not to have attitudes justified according to EJ. Failing to have these attitudes can also have the best results for the sake of *epistemic* goals such as the acquisition of knowledge. Roderick Firth points out that a scientist's believing against his evidence that he will recover from an illness may help to effect a recovery and so contribute to the growth of knowledge by enabling the scientist to continue his research.[19] William James's case for exercising "the will to believe" suggests that some evidence concerning the existence of God is available only after one believes in God in the absence of justifying evidence. EJ does not counsel against adopting such beliefs for the sake of these epistemic ends. EJ implies that the beliefs would be unjustified when adopted. This is not to say that the believing would do no epistemic good.

We acknowledge that it is appropriate to speak of epistemic obligations. But it is a mistake to think that what is epistemically obligatory, i.e., epistemically justified, is also morally or prudentially obligatory, or that it has the overall best epistemic consequences.

IV

Another argument that is intended to refute the evidentialist approach to justification concerns the ways in which a person can come to have an attitude that fits his evidence. Both Kornblith and Goldman propose examples designed to show that merely *having* good evidence for a proposition is not sufficient to make believing that proposition justified.[20] We shall work from Kornblith's formulation of the argument, since it is more detailed. Suppose Alfred is justified in believing p, and justified in believing if p then q. Alfred also believes q. EJ seems to imply that believing q is justified for Alfred, since that belief does seem to fit this evidence. Kornblith argues that Alfred's belief in q may still not be justified. It is not justified, according to Kornblith, if Alfred has a strong distrust of *modus ponens* and believes q because he likes the sound of the sentence expressing it rather than on the basis of the *modus ponens* argument. Similarly, Goldman says that a person's belief in q is not justified unless the belief is caused in some appropriate way.

Whether EJ implies that Alfred's belief in q is justified depends in part on an unspecified detail—Alfred's evidence concerning *modus ponens*. It is possible that Alfred has evidence against *modus ponens*. Perhaps he has just seen a version of the Liar paradox that seems to render *modus ponens* as suspect as the other rules and premises in the derivation. In the unlikely event that Alfred has such evidence, EJ implies that believing q is not justified for him. If rather, as we shall assume, his overall evidence supports *modus ponens* and q, then EJ does imply that believing q is justified for him.

When Alfred has strong evidence for q, his believing q is epistemically justified. This is the sense of "justified" captured by EJ. However, if Alfred's basis for believing q is not his evidence for it, but rather the sound of the sentence expressing q, then it seems equally clear that there is some sense in which this state of believing is epistemically "defective"—he did not arrive at the belief in the right way. The term "well-founded" is sometimes used to characterize an attitude that is epistemically both well-supported and properly arrived at. Well-foundedness is a second evidentialist notion used to evaluate doxastic states. It is an evidentialist notion because its application depends on two matters of evidence—the evidence one *has*, and the evidence one *uses* in forming the attitude. More precisely:

WF S's doxastic attitude D at t toward proposition p is well-founded if and only if
    (i) having D toward p is justified for S at t; and
    (ii) S has D toward p on the basis of some body of evidence e, such that
        (a) S has e as evidence at t;
        (b) having D toward p fits e; and
        (c) there is no more inclusive body of evidence e' had by S at t such that having D toward p does not fit e'.[21]

Since the evidentialist can appeal to this notion of well-foundedness, cases in which a person has but does not use justifying evidence do not refute evidentialism. Kornblith and Goldman's intuitions about such cases can be accommodated. A person in Alfred's position *is* in an epistemically defective state—his belief in q is not well-founded. Having said this, it is reasonable also to affirm the other evidentialist judgment that Alfred's belief in q is in another sense epistemically right—it is justified.[22]

V

The theory of epistemic justification that has received the most attention recently is reliabilism. Roughly speaking, this is the view that epistemically justified beliefs are the ones that result from belief-forming processes that reliably lead to true beliefs.[23] In this section we consider whether reliabilism casts doubt on evidentialism.

Although reliabilists generally formulate their view as an account of epistemic justification, it is clear that in its simplest forms it is better regarded as an account of well-foundedness. In order for a belief to be favorably evaluated by the simple sort of reliabilism sketched above, the belief must actually be held, as is the case with WF. And just as with WF, the belief must be "grounded" in the proper way. Where reliabilism appears to differ from WF is over the conditions under which a belief is properly grounded. According to WF, this occurs when the belief is based on fitting evidence. According to reliabilism, a belief is properly grounded if it results from a belief-forming process that reliably leads to true beliefs. These certainly are *conceptually* different accounts of the grounds of well-founded beliefs.

In spite of this conceptual difference, reliabilism and WF may be extensionally equivalent. The question of equivalence depends on the resolution of two unclarities in reliabilism. One pertains to the notion of a belief-forming process and the other to the notion of reliability.

An unclarity about belief-forming processes arises because every belief is caused by a sequence of particular events which is an instance of many types of causal processes. Suppose that one evening Jones looks out of his window and sees a bright, shining, disk-shaped object. The object is in fact a luminous frisbee, and Jones clearly remembers having given one of these to his daughter. But Jones is attracted to the idea that extraterrestrials are visiting the earth. He manages to believe that he is seeing a flying saucer. Is the process that caused his belief reliable? Since the sequence of events leading to his belief is an instance of many types of process, the answer depends upon which of these many types is the relevant one. The sequence falls into highly general categories such as perceptually based belief formation and visually based belief formation. It seems that if these are the relevant categories, then his belief is indeed reliably formed, since these are naturally regarded as "generally reliable" sorts of belief-forming processes. The sequence of events leading to Jones's belief also falls into many relatively specific categories such as night-vision-of-a-nearby-object and vision-in-Jones's-precise-environmental-circumstances. These are not clearly reliable types. The sequence is also an instance of this contrived kind: process-leading-from-obviously-defeated-evidence-to-the-belief-that-one-sees-a-flying-saucer. This, presumably, is an unreliable kind of process. Finally, there is the maximally specific process that occurs only when physiological events occur that are exactly like those that led to Jones's belief that he saw a flying saucer. In all likelihood this kind of process occurred only once. Processes of these types are of differing degrees of reliability, no matter how reliability is determined. The implications of reliabilism for the case are rendered definite only when the kind of process whose reliability is relevant is specified. Reliabilists have given little attention to this matter, and those that have specified relevant kinds have not done so in a way that gives their theory an intuitively acceptable extension.[24]

The second unclarity in reliabilism concerns the notion of reliability itself. Reliability is fundamentally a property of kinds of belief-forming processes, not of sequences of particular events. But we can say that a sequence is reliable provided its relevant type is reliable. The problem raised above concerns the specification of relevant types. The current problem is that of specifying the conditions under which a kind of process is *reliable*. Among possible accounts is one according to which a kind of process is reliable provided most instances of that kind until now have led to true beliefs. Alternative accounts measure the reliability of a kind of process by the frequency with which instances of it produce true beliefs in the future as well as the past, or by the frequency with which its instances produce true beliefs in possible worlds that are similar to the world of evaluation in some designated respect, or by the frequency with which its instances produce true beliefs in all possible worlds.[25]

Because there are such drastically different ways of filling in the details of reliabilism the application of the theory is far from clear. The possible versions of reliabilism seem to include one that is extensionally equivalent to WF. It might be held that all beliefs are formed by one of two relevant kinds of belief-forming process. One kind has as instances all and only those sequences of events leading to a belief that is based on fitting evidence; the other is a kind of process that has as instances all and only those sequences leading to a belief that is not based on fitting evidence. If a notion of reliability can be found on which the former sort of process is reliable and the latter is not, the resulting version of reliabilism would be very nearly equivalent to WF.[26] We do not claim that reliabilists would favor this version of reliabilism. Rather, our point is that the fact that this *is* a version shows that reliabilism may not even be a rival to WF.[27]

Evaluation of reliabilism is further complicated by the fact that reliabilists seem to differ about whether they *want* their theory to have approximately the same extension as WF in fact has. The credibility of reliabilism and its relevance to WF depend in part on the concept reliabilists are really attempting to analyze. An example first described by Lawrence Bonjour helps to bring out two alternatives.[28] Bonjour's example is of a person who is clairvoyant. As a result of his clairvoyance he comes to believe that the president is in New York City. The person has no evidence showing that he is clairvoyant and no other evidence supporting his belief about the president. Bonjour claims that the example is a counterexample to reliabilism, since the clairvoyant's belief is not justified (we would add: and therefore ill-founded), although the process that caused it is reliable—the person really is clairvoyant.

The general sort of response to this example that seems to be most commonly adopted by reliabilists is in effect to agree that such beliefs are not well-founded. They interpret or revise reliabilism with the aim of avoiding the counterexample.[29] An alternative response would be to argue that the reliability of clairvoyance shows that the belief *is* well-founded, and thus that the example does not refute reliabilism.[30]

We are tempted to respond to the second alternative—beliefs such as that of the clairvoyant in Bonjour's example really are well-founded—that this is so clear an instance of an ill-founded belief that any proponent of that view must have in mind a different concept from the one we are discussing. The clairvoyant has no reason for holding his belief about the president. The fact that the belief was caused by a process of a reliable kind—clairvoyance—is a significant fact about it. Such a belief may merit some favorable term of epistemic appraisal, e.g., "objectively probable." But the belief is not well-founded.

There are, however, two lines of reasoning that could lead philosophers to think that we must reconcile ourselves to the clairvoyant's belief turning out to be well-founded. According to one of these arguments, examples such as that of Alfred (discussed in section 4 above) show that the evidentialist account of epistemic merit is unsatisfactory and that epistemic merit must be understood in terms of the reliability of belief-forming processes.[31] Since the clairvoyant's belief is reliably formed, our initial inclination to regard it as ill-founded must be mistaken.

This argument is unsound. The most that the example about Alfred shows is that there is a concept of favorable epistemic appraisal other than justification, and that this other concept involves the notion of the *basis* of a belief. We believe that WF satisfactorily captures this other concept. There is no need to move to a reliabilist account, according to which some sort of causal reliability is *sufficient* for epistemic justification. The Alfred example does not establish that some version of reliabilism is correct. It does not establish that the clairvoyant's belief is well-founded.

The second argument for the conclusion that the clairvoyant's belief is well-founded makes use of the strong similarity between clairvoyance in Bonjour's example and normal perception. We claim that Bonjour's clairvoyant is not justified in his belief about the president because that belief does not fit his evidence. Simply having a spontaneous uninferred belief about the whereabouts of the president does not provide evidence for its truth. But, it might be asked, what better evidence is there for any ordinary perceptual belief, say, that one sees a book? If there is no relevant epistemological difference between ordinary perceptual beliefs and the clairvoyant's belief, then they should be evaluated similarly. The argument continues with the point that reliabilism provides an explanation of the crucial similarity between ordinary perceptual beliefs and the clairvoyant's belief—both perception and clairvoyance *work,* in the sense that both are reliable. So beliefs caused by each process are well-founded on a reliabilist account. The fact that reliabilism satisfactorily explains this is to the theory's credit. On the other hand, in advocating evidentialism we have claimed that perceptual beliefs are well-founded and that the clairvoyant's belief is not. But there appears to be no relevant evidential difference between these beliefs. Thus, if the evidentialist view of the matter cannot be defended, then reliabilism is the superior theory and we should accept its consequence—the clairvoyant's belief is well-founded.

One problem with this argument is that reliabilism has no satisfactory explanation of *anything* until the unclarities discussed above are removed in an acceptable way: What shows that perception and clairvoyance are relevant and reliable types of processes? In any event, there is an adequate evidentialist explanation of the difference between ordinary perceptual beliefs and the clairvoyant's belief. On one interpretation of clairvoyance, it is a process whereby one is caused to have beliefs about objects hidden from ordinary view without any conscious state having a role in the causal process. The clairvoyant does not have the conscious experience of, say, seeming to see the president in some characteristic New York City setting, and on that basis form the belief that he is in New York. In this respect, the current version of clairvoyance is unlike ordinary perception, which does include conscious perceptual states. Because of this difference, ordinary perceptual beliefs are based on evidence—the evidence of these sensory states—whereas the clairvoyant beliefs are not based on evidence. Since WF requires that well-founded beliefs be based on fitting evidence, and typical clairvoyant beliefs on the current interpretation are not based on any evidence at all, the clairvoyant beliefs do not satisfy WF.

Suppose instead that clairvoyance does include visual experiences, though of remote objects that cannot stimulate the visual system in any normal way. Even if there are such visual experiences that could serve as a basis for a clairvoyant's beliefs, still there is a relevant epistemological difference between beliefs based on normal perceptual experience and the clairvoyant's belief in Bonjour's example. We have collateral evidence to the effect that when we have perceptual experience of certain kinds, external conditions of the corresponding kinds normally obtain. For example, we have evidence supporting the proposition that when we have the usual sort of experience of seeming to see a book, we usually do in fact see a book. This includes evidence from the coherence of these beliefs with beliefs arising from other perceptual sources, and it also includes testimonial evidence. This latter point is easily overlooked. One reason that the belief that one sees a book fits even a child's evidence when she has a perceptual experience of seeing a book is that children are taught, when they have the normal sort of visual experiences, that they are seeing a physical object of the relevant kind. This testimony, typically from people whom the child has reason to trust, provides evidence for the child. And of course testimony from others during adult life also gives evidence for the veridicality of normal visual experience. On the other hand, as Bonjour describes his example, the clairvoyant has no confirmation at all of his clairvoyant beliefs. Indeed, he has evidence against these beliefs, since the clairvoyant perceptual experiences do not cohere with his other experiences. We conclude, therefore, that evidentialists can satisfactorily explain why ordinary perceptual beliefs are typically well-founded and unconfirmed clairvoyant beliefs, even if reliably caused, are not. There is no good reason to abandon our initial intuition that the beliefs such as those of the clairvoyant in Bonjour's example are not well-founded.

Again, reliabilists could respond to Bonjour's example either by claiming that the clairvoyant's belief is in fact well-founded or by arguing that reliabilism does not imply that it is well-founded. We turn now to the second of these alternatives, the one most commonly adopted by reliabilists. This view can be defended by arguing either that reliabilism can be reformulated so that it lacks this implication, or that as currently formulated it lacks this implication. We pointed out above that as a general approach reliabilism is sufficiently indefinite to allow interpretations under which it does lack the implication in question. The only way to achieve this result that we know of that is otherwise satisfactory requires the introduction of evidentialist concepts. The technique is to specify the relevant types of belief-forming processes in evidentialist terms. It is possible to hold that the relevant types of belief-forming process are believing something on the basis of fitting evidence and believing not as a result of fitting evidence. This sort of "reliabilism" is a roundabout approximation of the straightforward evidentialist thesis, WF. We see no reason to couch the approximated evidentialist theory in reliabilist terms. Moreover, the reliabilist approximation is not exactly equivalent to WF, and where it differs it appears to go wrong. The difference is this: it seems possible for the process of believing on the basis of fitting evidence to be unreliable. Finding a suitable sort of reliability makes all the difference here. In various possible worlds where our evidence is mostly misleading, the frequency with which fitting evidence causes true belief is low. Thus, this type of belief-forming process is not "reliable" in such worlds in any straightforward way that depends on actual frequencies. Perhaps a notion of reliability that avoids this result can be found. We know of no such notion which does not create trouble elsewhere for the theory. So, the reliabilist view under consideration has the consequence that in such worlds beliefs based on fitting evidence are not well-founded. This is counterintuitive.[32]

In this section we have compared reliabilism and evidentialism. The vagueness of reliabilism makes it difficult to determine what implications the theory has and it is not entirely clear what implications reliabilists want their theory to have. If reliabilists want their theory to have approximately the same extension as WF, we see no better way to accomplish this than one which makes the theory an unnecessarily complex and relatively implausible approximation to evidentialism. If, on the other hand, reliabilists want their theory to have an extension which is substantially different from that of WF, and yet some familiar notion of "a reliable kind of process" is to be decisive for their notion of well-foundedness, then it becomes clear that the concept they are attempting to analyze is not one evidentialists seek to characterize. This follows from the fact that on this alternative they count as well-founded attitudes that plainly do not exemplify the concept evidentialists are discussing. In neither case, then, does reliabilism pose a threat to evidentialism.

VI

Summary and Conclusion

We have defended evidentialism. Some opposition to evidentialism rests on the view that a doxastic attitude can be justified for a person only if forming the attitude is an action under the person's voluntary control. EJ is incompatible with the conjunction of this sort of doxastic voluntarism and the plain fact that some doxastic states that fit a person's evidence are out of that person's control. We have argued that no good reason has been given for thinking that an attitude is epistemically justified only if having it is under voluntary control.

A second thesis contrary to EJ is that a doxastic attitude can be justified only if having that attitude is within the normal doxastic limits of humans. We have held that the attitudes that are epistemically justified according to EJ are within these limits, and that even if they were not, that fact would not suffice to refute EJ.

Some philosophers have contended that believing a proposition, *p*, is justified for *S* only when *S* has gone about gathering evidence about *p* in a responsible way, or has come to believe *p* as a result of seeking a meritorious epistemic goal such as the discovery of truth. This thesis conflicts with EJ, since believing *p* may fit one's evidence no matter how irresponsible one may have been in seeking evidence about *p* and no matter what were the goals that led to the belief. We agree that there is some epistemic merit in responsibly gathering evidence and in seeking the truth. But we see no reason to think that epistemic justification turns on such matters.

Another thesis conflicting with EJ is that merely having evidence is not sufficient to justify belief, since the believer might not make proper use of the evidence in forming the belief. Consideration of this claim led us to make use of a second evidentialist notion, well-roundedness. It does not, however, provide any good reason to think that EJ is false. Nor do we find reason to abandon evidentialism in favor of reliabilism. Evidentialism remains the most plausible view of epistemic justification.

NOTES

1. EJ is compatible with the existence of varying strengths of belief and disbelief. If there is such variation, then the greater the preponderance of evidence, the stronger the doxastic attitude that fits the evidence.

2. There are difficult questions about the concept of fit, as well as about what it is for someone to *have* something as evidence, and of what kind of thing constitutes evidence. As a result, there are some cases in which it is difficult to apply EJ. For example, it is unclear whether a person has as evidence propositions he is not currently thinking of, but could recall with some prompting. As to what constitutes evidence, it seems clear that this includes both beliefs and sensory states such as feeling very warm and having the visual experience of seeing blue. Some philosophers seem to think that only beliefs can justify beliefs. See, for example, Keith Lehrer, *Knowledge* (Oxford: Oxford University Press, 1974), pp. 187–88. The application of EJ is clear enough to do the work that we intend here—a defense of the evidentialist position.

3. John Heil, "Doxastic Agency," *Philosophical Studies* 43 (1983): 355–64. The quotation is from p. 355.

4. Hilary Kornblith, "The Psychological Turn," *Australasian Journal of Philosophy* 60 (1982): 238–53. The quotation is from p. 252.

5. Ibid., p. 253.

6. Heil, "Doxastic Agency," p. 363.

7. Kornblith may be guilty of this confusion. He writes, "If a person has an unjustified belief, that person is epistemically culpable." "The Psychological Turn," p. 243.

8. Nothing we say here should be taken to imply that any doxastic states are in fact voluntarily entered.

9. Alvin Goldman, "Epistemics: The Regulative Theory of Cognition," *The Journal of Philosophy* 75 (1978): 509–23, esp. pp. 510 and 514.

10. Hilary Kornblith, "Justified Belief and Epistemically Responsible Action," *The Philosophical Review* 92 (1983): 33–48. The quotation is from p. 46.

11. Paul Thagard, "From the Descriptive to the Normative in Psychology and Logic," *Philosophy of Science* 49 (1982): 24–42. The quotation is from p. 34.

12. Another version of this argument is that EJ is false because it classifies as justified for a person attitudes that are beyond *that person's* limits. This version is subject to similar criticism.

13. Roderick Chisholm, *Theory of Knowledge,* 2d ed. (Englewood Cliffs, N.J.: Prentice-Hall, 1977), especially pp. 12-15.

14. Roderick Firth makes a similar point against a similar view in "Are Epistemic Concepts Reducible to Ethical Concepts," in *Values and Morals,* A. I. Goldman and J. Kim, eds. (Dordrecht, Netherlands: D. Reidel Publishing Co., 1978), pp. 215–29.

15. Kornblith defends this view in "Justified Belief and Epistemically Responsible Action." Some passages suggest that he intends to introduce a new notion of justification, one to be understood in terms of epistemically responsible action. But some passages, especially in section 2, suggest that the traditional analysis of justification is being found to be objectionable and inferior to the one he proposes.

16. Bonjour, op. cit., p. 63.

17. This is contrary to the view of Richard Gale, defended in "William James and the Ethics of Belief," *American Philosophical Quarterly* 17 (1980): 1–14, and of W. K. Clifford, who said, "It is wrong always, everywhere, and for everyone, to believe anything upon insufficient evidence," quoted by William James in "The Will to Believe," reprinted in *Reason and Responsibility,* J. Feinberg, ed. (Belmont, Calif.: Wadsworth Publishing Co., 1981), p. 100.

18. See John Heil, "Believing What One Ought," pp. 752ff.

19. See "Epistemic Merit, Intrinsic and Instrumental," *Proceedings and Addresses of the American Philosophical Association* 55 (1981): 5–6.

20. See Kornblith's "Beyond Foundationalism and the Coherence Theory," *The Journal of Philosophy* 77 (1980): 597–612, esp. pp. 601f., and Goldman's "What Is Justified Belief?" in *Justification and Knowledge,* George S. Pappas, ed. (Dordrecht, Netherlands: D. Reidel Publishing Co., 1979), pp. 1–24.

21. Clause (ii) of WF is intended to accommodate the fact that a well-founded attitude need not be based on a person's whole body of evidence. What seems required is that the person base a well-founded attitude on a justifying part of the person's evidence, and that he not ignore any evidence he has that defeats the justifying power of the evidence he does base his attitude on. It might be that his defeating evidence is itself defeated by a still wider body of his evidence. In such a case, the person's attitude is well-founded only if he takes the wider body into account.

WF uses our last main primitive concept—that of *basing* an attitude on a body of evidence. This notion is reasonably clear, though an analysis would be useful. See note 22 below for one difficult question about what is entailed.

22. Goldman uses this sort of example only to show that there is a causal element in the concept of justification. We acknowledge that there is an epistemic concept—well-foundedness—that appeals to the notion of basing an attitude on evidence, and this may be a causal notion. What seems to confer epistemic merit on basing one's belief on the evidence is that in doing so one *appreciates* the evidence. It is unclear whether one can appreciate the evidence without being caused to have the belief by the evidence. But in any event we see no such causal requirement in the case of justification.

23. The clearest and most influential discussion of reliabilism is in Goldman's "What Is Justified Be-

lief?" One of the first statements of the theory appears in David Armstrong's *Belief, Truth and Knowledge* (London: Cambridge University Press, 1973). For extensive bibliographies on reliabilism, see Frederick Schmitt's "Reliability, Objectivity, and the Background of Justification," *Australasian Journal of Philosophy* 62 (1984): 1–15, and Richard Feldman's "Reliability and Justification," *The Monist* 68, no. 2 (April 1985): 159–74.

24. For discussion of the problem of determining relevant kinds of belief-forming processes, see Goldman, "What Is Justified Belief?"; Schmitt, "Reliability, Objectivity, and the Background of Justification"; Feldman, "Reliability and Justification"; and Feldman, "Schmitt on Reliability, Objectivity, and Justification," *Australasian Journal of Philosophy*.

25. In "Reliability and Justified Belief," *Canadian Journal of Philosophy* 14 (1984): 103–15, John Pollock argues that there is no account of reliability suitable for reliabilists.

26. This version of reliabilism will not be exactly equivalent to WF because it ignores the factors introduced by clause (ii) of WF.

27. It is also possible that versions of reliabilism making use only of natural psychological kinds of belief-forming processes are extensionally equivalent to WF. Goldman seeks to avoid evaluative epistemic concepts in his theory of epistemic justification, so he would not find an account of justification satisfactory unless it appealed only to such natural kinds. See "What Is Justified Belief?" p. 6.

28. See Lawrence Bonjour, "Externalist Theories of Empirical Justification," p. 62.

29. See Goldman, "What Is Justified Belief?" pp. 18–20; Kornblith, "Beyond Foundationalism and the Coherence Theory," pp. 609–11; and Schmitt, "Reliability, Objectivity, and the Background of Justification."

30. We know of one who has explicitly taken this approach. It seems to fit most closely with the view defended by David Armstrong in *Belief, Truth and Knowledge*.

31. We know of no one who explicitly defends this inference. In "The Psychological Turn," pp. 241f., Kornblith argues that these examples show that justification depends upon "psychological connections" and "the workings of the appropriate belief-forming process." But he clearly denies there that reliabilism is directly implied.

32. Stewart Cohen has made this point in "Justification and Truth," *Philosophical Studies* 46 (1984): 279–95. Cohen makes the point in the course of developing a dilemma. He argues that reliabilism has the sort of flaw that we describe above when we appeal to worlds where evidence is mostly misleading. Cohen also contends that reliabilism has the virtue of providing a clear explanation of how the epistemic notion of justification is connected with the notion of truth. A theory that renders this truth connection inexplicable is caught on the second horn of Cohen's dilemma.

Although Cohen does not take up evidentialism as we characterize it, the second horn of his dilemma affects EJ and WF. They do not explain how having an epistemically justified or well-founded belief is connected to the truth of that belief. Evidentialists can safely say this much about the truth connection: evidence that makes believing *p* justified is evidence on which it is *epistemically* probable that *p* is true. Although there is this connection between justification and truth, we acknowledge that there may be no analysis of epistemic probability that makes the connection to truth as close, or as clear, as might have been hoped.

Cohen argues that there must be a truth connection. This shows no flaw in EJ or WF unless they are incompatible with there being such a connection. Cohen does not argue for this incompatibility and we know of no reason to believe that it exists. So at most Cohen's dilemma shows that evidentialists have work left to do.

32

The Evidence of the Senses

Roderick M. Chisholm

I return to an ancient philosophical question: What kind of evidence is provided by the senses? Many will feel, I'm sure, that there is nothing new to be said about this question. And perhaps they are right. But, given the present state of philosophy, something, even if it is nothing new, needs to be said about it. For there is still a great deal of confusion about the nature of perceptual evidence. The most unfortunate confusion, I think, gives rise to the belief that there are no serious problems about perceptual evidence and that, once one sees that this is so, the other problems of traditional theory of knowledge will disappear.

A typical attitude was that of the members of the Vienna Circle. Carnap, for example, saw the need of referring to one's *total evidence* when speaking of the practical application of inductive logic and the theory of probability.[1] But so far as the concept of evidence itself is concerned, he felt that it was sufficient to say that the evidence that a person possesses is "his total knowledge of the results of his observations." One is led to ask, then, what Carnap meant by "the results of one's observations." In his writings on probability, he gives us no answer to this question. And if we look back to his earlier writings on verification, we seem to have traveled in a circle. For he there says, not that the application of probability presupposes the concept of observational knowledge, but that the concept of observational knowledge presupposes the application of probability. He writes, for example: "A predicate '*P*' of a language *L* is called *observable* for an organism (e.g., a person) *N*, if, for suitable arguments, e.g., '*b*,' *N* is able under suitable circumstances to come to a decision with the help of a few observations about a full sentence, say '*P(b)*', i.e., to a *confirmation* of either '*P(b)*' or '*~P(b)*' of such a high degree that he will either accept or reject '*P(b)*.' "[2]

The attitude reflects an earlier view developed by Leonard Nelson in a book on "the so-called epistemological problem." Nelson suggests that the epistemological problems will disappear if we are content to recognize that our knowledge arises out of perception.[3]

My own belief, which I will try to defend here, is that it is only by investigating the nature of perceptual evidence that we can be made to see the difficulties of the epistemological problem and how to deal with them.

The problem of the evidence of the senses involves questions of three different types: (I) *descriptive* or "phenomenological" questions about those aspects of our experience that make it a source of evidence about the external world: (II) *normative* questions about what it is that those aspects of our experience justify us in believing; and (III) *epistemic* questions about the nature of these grounding relations.

This paper, accordingly, is divided into three sections.

I: DESCRIBING THE OBJECTS OF PERCEPTION

The Objects of Perceptual Verbs

We may approach our subject somewhat indirectly by considering the grammatical objects of perceptual verbs—such verbs as "see," "hear," and "perceive." These grammatical objects may be of three different kinds.

(1) Sometimes perceptual verbs take a very simple object, as in "He sees a cat" and "She hears a dog." This first use has no implications about what the perceiver *believes* and it has no implications about the *knowledge* or *evidence* that he or she has. For we may consistently say "He sees a dog but he doesn't think that it is a dog that he sees"; and similarly for "She hears a cat."

(2) Sometimes the grammatical object of a perception verb is a "that"-clause, as in "He sees that a cat is on the roof" and "She hears that the dog is scratching at the door." This use, unlike the first, does have implications with respect to belief and also with respect to knowledge. If she hears that the dog is at the door, then she knows that the dog is there and thus also believes it.

(3) Sometimes the grammatical object is a "semi-complex" one that seems to fall between the simple grammatical object ("a cat," "a dog") and the propositional object ("that a cat is on the roof," "that the dog is scratching at the door"). Examples of such semi-complex objects are provided by "He sees a cat sitting on the roof " and

"She hears the dog scratching at the door." This third use can be misleading, especially in writings on the philosophy of perception.

Such a statement as "He sees a cat on the roof" is relatively simple and straightforward. One philosopher seems to suggest that such statements provide us with no ground for philosophical puzzlement. According to him, they simply refer to the kind of causal process "that standardly takes place when we say that so-and-so sees such-and-such" and the nature of this process is of no special concern to the philosopher: "to a large extent the description of this process must be regarded as a problem for the special sciences, not for philosophy."[4] But a mere description of the causal process has no implications about the perceiver's immediate experience or about what he is justified in believing. And for precisely this reason it does not provide us with what we are looking for.

To get at the nature of perceptual evidence, we must look further at those statements in which the perceptual verb has a complex grammatical object, such statements as "He perceives that a cat is on the roof" and "She hears that the dog is scratching at the door." Ordinarily, when we use our perception words in these ways, our statements commit us to what is affirmed in their subordinate "that"-clauses. "He perceives that a cat is on the roof" implies that there *is* a cat on the roof. And "She hears a dog that is scratching at the door" implies that there *is* a dog that is scratching at the door. *Sometimes,* to be sure we do not take our perception sentences to have such implications, we may say: "Well, *he* perceives that a cat is there, but obviously he is hallucinating once again; he is always seeing some cat or other that isn't really there." But I suggest that, to avoid ambiguity, we renounce this type of use.

If this suggestion is followed, then, "He perceives that a cat is on the roof" will imply, in our use, that there is a cat that is on the roof. And "She hears that the dog is scratching at the door" will imply that there is a dog that is scratching at the door. And when we talk this way, then we may, so to speak, take the subject-term out of the "that"-clause and put it out in front. In other words, we may move from the *de dicto* locution

He perceives that there is a cat on the roof

to the *de re* locution

A cat on the roof is perceived by him to be a cat on the roof.

This is a move we cannot make in the case "He believes that there is a cat on the roof" and "He takes there to be a cat on the roof."

How, then, are we to describe the state of the person who is hallucinating—the person of whom one may be tempted to say, "He perceives that a cat is there, but obviously he is hallucinating once again"? The simplest procedure might be to say, "He *thinks* he perceives that a cat is there" or "He *believes* that he perceives that a cat is there." An alternative would be: "He *takes* something to be a cat."

Being Appeared To

The principal source of our philosophical problem lies in the fact that perception is inextricably bound up with *appearing*—with being appeared to in some way. The person who perceives that there is a tree before him *takes* there to be a tree. And when one takes there to be a tree (when one thinks that one perceives a tree), then one is appeared to in a certain way and one believes that *what* it is that is appearing in that way is a tree. In the case of the person who is hallucinating, we may say that, although he is *appeared to* in a certain way, there is nothing that is *appearing* to him in that way.

Let us, then, define "perceives that" in this way:

> S perceives that there is an F =Df (1) There is an F that is appearing in a certain way to S; (2) S takes there to be an F that is appearing to him in that way; and (3) it is evident to S that an F is appearing to him in that way.

"*S* perceives that there is an *F*," so defined, will imply "*S* knows that there is an *F*."

If you perceive that there is a tree before you, then you believe that your perceptual experience is an experience of a tree—or, in our terminology, you think you are appeared to by a tree. It would be misleading to call the appearance the "*object*" of perception. But it would be accurate to say that, it is *by means of* what you know about the appearance, that you apprehend the object of perception. The philosophical problem of perceptual evidence turns on this question: How is it possible for appearances to provide us with information about the things of which they *are* appearances?

The difficulty, as we know, has to do with what is sometimes called "perceptual relativity." The appearances that we sense are a function, not only of the nature of the things we perceive, but also of the conditions under which we perceive these things. To see that sense-appearances are a function of the conditions of observation, we have only to remind ourselves of this fact: Whenever an external thing appears to us, then, merely by varying the conditions of observation and letting the external thing remain constant, we can vary the appearances that the thing presents.[5]

Sextus Empiricus had cited these examples:

> The same water which feels very hot when poured on inflamed spots seems lukewarm to us. And the same air seems chilly to the old but mild to those in their prime, and similarly the same sound seems to the former faint, but to the latter clearly audible. The same wine which seems sour to those who have previously eaten dates or figs seems sweet to those who have just consumed nuts or chickpeas; and the

vestibule of the bathhouse which warms those entering from the outside chills those coming out.[6]

This completes our discussion of the *descriptive* questions involved in explicating the evidence of the senses. We may now turn to the normative questions.

II: THE NORMATIVE QUESTIONS

If appearances are so variable, and if we perceive the things around us by means of the appearances that they present to us, then how can such perception provide us with any evidence about the external world?

The third clause in our definition of perceiving ("It is evident to S that he is appeared to in that way") is a *normative* expression, for it contains the epistemic locution "It is evident to S that . . ."

The Problem

The normative epistemological problem is analogous to the problem we encounter in ethics or moral philosophy when we attempt to analyze such expressions as "It is right that . . ." and "It is intrinsically good that. . . ." We want to find a *criterion* stating a nonnormative situation that warrants the assertion of a normative statement—a nonnormative situation upon which, as it is sometimes said, a normative situation "supervenes."

Our criterion should be of the form:

So-and-so tends to make it evident to S that he is appeared to by an F.

A criterion might also be formed if we replace "evident" by some epistemic expression, say "probable" or "beyond reasonable doubt." But the expression replacing "So-and-so" should contain no epistemic terms. (We will consider such expressions as "tends to make it evident that" in the final section of the paper.)

Three Types of Perceptual Theory

One way to understand the normative questions about perceptual evidence is to consider three theories that we find in ancient Greek philosophy. These are: (1) the *dogmatic* theory; (2) the *inductive* theory; and (3) the *critical* theory.[7] The first was "the theory of the evident perception" set forth by the Stoic, Chrysippus (279–206 B.C.); the second was the so-called commemorative theory developed by Sextus Empiricus

(c. 150–250); and the third was the theory of the Academic skeptic, Carneades (c. 213–129 B.C.). The first two theories have some initial plausibility, but it is the theory of Carneades, I think, that is closest to the truth.

(1) The Dogmatic Theory

According to "the theory of the evident perception," the appearance presents us with *two* things—the appearance itself and the external thing that appears: there is a way of appearing that presents *itself* to the subject and also presents *another* thing to the subject—a thing that *appears* in a certain way to the subject. It was held that, whenever we have an evident perception, we can tell from the nature of the perceptual experience itself that the perception is veridical. The experience was said to be irresistible. "The perception, being plainly evident and striking, lays hold of us, almost by the very hair, as they say, and drags us off to assent, needing nothing else to help it to be thus impressive."[8] But, more important, it was said that the experience gives us a kind of guarantee.

Just what, then, is supposed to justify what? What is there about the *appearance* that presents the external object to us? And what is it about the *object* that the appearance makes evident to us?

Chrysippus suggested that the nature of the external thing can be "read off" from the nature of the appearances. When I have an evident perception, he said, the external thing "appears so true that it could not appear to me in the same way if it were false."[9]

Hence the "dogmatic" criterion might be put in some way as this:

Being appeared to in such a way that, if one is appeared to in that way then one cannot resist believing that an F is appearing to one in that way, makes it evident that one is appeared to in that way by an F.

What makes this view "dogmatic" is the fact that the criterion contains the guarantee "makes it evident that" rather than the more tentative "tends to make it evident that."

The criterion seems to imply that the appearance that is yielded by a veridical perception could not be duplicated in an unveridical perception or in an hallucination. And this is contrary to what we know. For what the facts of perceptual relativity tell us is that there is no *logical* connection between the nature of any appearance, or way of being appeared to, and the nature of the object that serves to call up that appearance.

The theory is excessively dogmatic. We must go further if we are to have a satisfactory account of the evidence of the senses.

(2) The Inductive Theory

The theory of "the commemorative perception" that was set forth by Sextus was an "inductive" theory.

Sextus agrees with Chrysippus that our perceptual experience provides us with a *sign* of the independently existing external thing. But he rejects the dogmatism of Chrysippus; the nature of the appearance provides no *logical* guarantee of the nature of the object. Sextus points out that normally we do not "read off" the nature of the object from the nature of the appearance—any more than we "read off" the nature of fire from the nature of smoke. Smoke signifies fire for us because we have made an induction that correlates smoke with fire: We have found in the past that smoke is generally accompanied by fire.[10] This much is quite obvious. But now Sextus goes on to take a further step. Many have failed to see just how doubtful this further step is.

He says that the inductive correlation that we have made between smoke and fire give us the clue to the relation between appearances and the external things that the appearances make known to us. He seems to suggest that we have made an inductive correlation between tree-appearances and external trees: We have found that tree-appearances are generally accompanied by an existence of external, physical trees. The nature of an appearance, then, may *make probable* some hypothesis about the nature of the external object. This is what was suggested by our quotation from Carnap above: The content of the observation sentence is *confirmed* by perception. C. I. Lewis, addressing the same problem, says that "the given appearance is a valid *probability-index* of the objective property"; there are, according to him, various "degrees of reliability" that appearances may have with respect to hypotheses about external objects.[11]

We may put one version of the "inductive" criterion this way:

If, for a certain way in which *S* is being appeared to, *S* is such that, more often than not, when he has been appeared to in that way, an *F* has appeared to him in that way, then it is probable for *S* that an *F* is appearing to him in that way.

To see that there is something wrong with this account of perception, we have only to ask: What was the nature of those *earlier* experiences wherein we found that a tree-like appearance was accompanied by the apprehension of an external, physical tree? How was it made known to us *then* that there was a tree there? We are given no clear answers to this question.[12] I would say, therefore, that the "inductive" theory does not provide us with what we are looking for.

An inductive argument need not, of course, be enumerative. That is to say, it need not be of the form: "Most *A*'s are *B*'s and *x* is an *A*; therefore it is probable that *x* is a *B.*" But if any inductive argument tends to make it probable that one is appeared to by something that is *F*, then, presumably, the premises of the argument should include *some* evidence about external things. But where would *S* get *that* evidence? Once we try to answer this question, we see that we are left with our original problem. We had wanted to know just how it comes about that we have evidence about the nature of external things. We had assumed that, in the first instance, such evidence must arise out of perception. But the type of inductive theory now being considered tells us only how it is that, once we already have certain *prior evidence* about external things, perception can then go on to supply us with additional evidence about such things. How, then, did we get the prior evidence?

Yet perception *does* tell us something about the external world. Therefore there must be an alternative account of perceptual evidence.

(3) The Critical Theory

Carneades' critical theory was set forth by Sextus Empiricus in his *Outlines of Pyrrhonism* and in his treatise, *Against the Logicians.*[13]

Carneades says, in effect, that if a person has a perception of something being a tree, then, for that person, the proposition that there is a tree is *probable.* What Carneades here means by "perception," I am convinced, is what we have called "perceptual taking." Carneades begins, then, in the same way that Sextus does. Where, then, does it differ from the view of Sextus?

We have seen that, according to Sextus' inductive theory, the probability of a perceptual taking is derived from an inductive correlation or frequency. But Carneades appeals to no such correlation. When he says that the object of the taking is probable, he does *not* say that this probability derives from any induction. And the reason for not saying this is clear: Carneades knows that we cannot make any inductive inferences about external things until we have some *perceptual data* about such things. And it follows from this that, if we are to have any positive justification for what we believe about the external world, our experience must provide us with a probability that is not derived from an induction.

It would miss the point to object: "But probability is, by definition, a matter involving inductive frequencies. You contradict yourself if you say that there is a kind of probable belief that has nothing to do with such frequencies." The sense of "probable" that we have used to express Carneades' view is quite different: It expresses a *normative* concept. To say that a proposition is probable for a given person, in this normative sense, is to say that the person has a certain positive justification for accepting that proposition. A proposition is *probable,* in this sense, for a given person *S,* if and only if, *S* is more justified in accepting that proposition than he is in accepting its negation.

One of the things Carneades was saying seems to have been this:

Taking something to be *F* tends to make it probable that there is something one is taking to be *F*.

Here, then, we have the beginnings of an answer to our question about perceptual evidence: "What aspect of our experience justifies what kind of belief about physical things?" The fact that the perceiver *takes* there to be a tree is a fact that "presents itself" to the perceiver: If he takes there to be a tree, then it is probable for him that he takes there to be a tree. And this intentional attitude, this taking, tends to make it probable that the taking has an actual object; it tends to make probable that there *is* in fact an external object upon which the taking is directed.

It should be noted that we have brought the quantifier from the inside to the outside of the intentional object of the "taking"-verb. What is probable to the perceiver is that there *is* something that he takes to be a tree.

We may go beyond this claim in two respects. We may say (1) that, under certain conditions, the perceptual taking yields, not only *probability,* but also *evidence* and (2) that *what* it tends to make evident is its own intentional object. In other words:

Taking something to be *F* tends to insure the evidence of there being something that is *F*.

This view was suggested by Meinong in 1906. He said, using a slightly different terminology from that used here, that perceptual judgments may have *presumptive evidence* (*Vermutungsevidenz*): When one takes there to be a tree then the judgment that there *is* a tree that one is perceiving may have presumptive evidence. The qualification "presumptive" was intended to suggest that the judgment may have such evidence without thereby being *true.* Meinong added that there are *degrees* of such justification.[14] This view was subsequently developed further by H. H. Price. He made the following suggestion in his book, *Perception* (1933):

[T]he fact that a material thing is perceptually presented to the mind is *prima facie evidence* of the thing's existence and of its really having that sort of surface which it ostensibly has; . . . there is *some presumption in favor of* this, not merely in the sense that we do as a matter of fact presume it (which of course we do) but in the sense that we are entitled to do so.[15]

Price adds: "Clearly the principle is *a priori*: It is not the sort of thing we could learn by empirical generalization based upon observation of the material world."[16]

The assumption is that, occasionally at least, the senses provide us with evidence pertaining to the existence of such things as trees, ships and houses. And in answer to the question, "What is the nature of this evidence?" Prices's suggestion is the following. The fact that we *take* there to be a tree is itself sufficient to make it *prima facie* evident for us that there *is* a tree that we perceive. And the fact that we are *appeared to* in certain ways is itself sufficient to make it *prima facie* evident to us that there *is* an external thing that is appearing to us in those ways.

This account of perceptual evidence requires further analysis and explication. We should try to describe more accurately the conditions under which our perceptual takings and the ways in which we are appeared to may inform us about the things around us. But the general view of perception that it represents seems to me to be the only coherent alternative to skepticism.

The view implies that the evidence about external things that is yielded by perception is *indirect* and not direct. What we know about such things is made evident to us by our takings and by the ways in which we are appeared to. It is made evident, therefore, by certain psychological facts that present themselves to us directly.

This use of "indirect" may give pause to some. For one may say: "Ordinarily, we perceive such things as trees, ships and house *directly*. If you were standing here before me, I would perceive you directly. I would perceive you *indirectly* if I were to see your shadow on the floor—in which case I would perceive the floor *directly*." But these facts are consistent with saying that, when I *do* perceive you directly, I do so by becoming aware of *other* things that serve to make it evident for me that you are the object of my perception.

Let us now look more carefully at the epistemic concepts suggested by relational epistemic expressions as "*e* tends to insure the evidence of *h*" and "*h* derives its status as being evident for *S* from the fact that *e* is evident for *S*."

III: THE EPISTEMIC QUESTIONS

The Epistemic Hierarchy

I make use of these abbreviations: "—A . . ." for the undefined concept "*S* is at least as justified in—as in . . ."; "—P . . ." for "*S* is more justified in—than in . . ."; "—S . . ." for "*S*'s justification for—is equal to his justification for . . ."; "B*p*" for "Believing *p*"; "W*p*" for "Withholding *p*"; "~*p*" for "not-*p*"; "(*p*)" for "for every proposition *p*"; and "(∃*p*)" for "there is a proposition *p* such that."

I now set forth a hierarchy of absolute epistemic categories.[17] What I will say presupposes the following definitions:

D1 xPy = Df ~(yAx)
D2 xSy = Df xAy & yAx
D3 Wp = Df ~Bp & ~B ~p

It should be noted that withholding a proposition *p* is identical with withholding the negation of *p*.

There are thirteen epistemic steps or levels, each of which is such that, for every conscious subject *S*, some proposition *p* occupies that set or level for *S*. These are the following:

6.	(q) [(Bp P Wq) & (Bp A Bq)]	Certain
5.	(q) (Bp P Wq)	Obvious
4.	(q) ~(Wq P Bp)	Evident
3.	(Bp P Wp)	Reasonable
2.	~(Wp P Bp)	In the Clear
1.	(Bp P B ~p)	Probable
	. . . .	
0.	(B ~pABp) & (BpAB ~p)	Counterbalanced
	. . . .	
−1.	(B ~p P Bp)	Probably False
−2.	~(Wp P B ~p)	In the Clear to Disbelieve
−3.	(B ~p P Wp)	Reasonable to Disbelieve
−4.	(q) ~(Wq P B ~p)	Evidently False
−5.	(q) (B ~p P Wq)	Obviously False
−6.	(q) [(B ~p P Wq) & (B ~p A Bq)]	Certainly False

Making use of the abbreviations here introduced, we next formulate the axioms for our primitive concept:

(A1) xPy ⊃ ~(yPx)
(A2) [(xPy & yPz] ⊃ (xPz)
(A3) (Bp A Wp) ⊃ (Bp P B ~p)
(A4) [(q)(Bp A Wq)] ⊃ (Bp P Wp)
(A5) [(Bp P Wp) & (Bq P Wq)] ⊃ [B(p & q) P (Bp & Wq)]
(A6) [(∃p)(Bp P B ~p)] ⊃ [(∃r)(q)(Br P Wq)]

The Relational Epistemic Concepts

Now we may turn to the difficult task of saying what it is for a proposition to *derive* its evidence from another proposition. I have said that the fact that *something appears* to me in a certain way may be evident to me and derive its evidence from the fact that it is evident to me that I am *sensing* in a certain way. And I have said that the fact that I *perceive* there to be a tree may be evident for me and derive its evidence from the fact that it is evident to me that I *take* there to be a tree. What is it, then, for certain facts thus to present things *other* than themselves?

Our concern is to explicate what might be expressed by saying this: "*h* derives its status as being evident for *S* from the fact that *e* is evident for *S*." I believe that it is possible to explicate this concept in terms of those epistemic concepts just set forth.

I begin by considering those properties that may be said to "present themselves" to the person who has them.

Whatever presents itself also presents whatever it entails (whatever it both implies and conceptually involves). Arriving at the belief, say, that some dogs are brown serves to make known not only that one *does* arrive at that belief, but also that one believes that there are dogs, that one believes that there are things that are brown, and more generally, that one has arrived at *a* belief.

Some things that present themselves *also* present things that they neither imply nor involve. Let us call such things *other-presenting*.[18] Perception provides us with the clearest examples of other-presentation.

Consider once again the experience we have called "taking there to be a tree." From the fact that a person takes there to be a tree we may infer a number of things about what is evident for that person. We may infer that it is evident for the person that he does take there to be a tree. And we may also infer certain further things about the evidence he happens to have. For example, we may affirm this disjunctive proposition: *Either* his *perceiving thereto be a tree* is evident to him or some further fact about his *taking there to be a tree* is evident for him. No matter how small his body of evidence may be, either it will include the proposition that he perceives there to be a tree (and hence also the proposition that there is a tree) or it will include some proposition about the conditions under which he takes there to be a tree.

Another example of other-presentation is provided by the experience one might express by saying "I seem to remember just having heard a bell ring." (I here use "seeming to remember so-and-so" in such way that, in that use, it does not imply "remember so-and-so.") If we know of a person that he seems to remember just having heard a bell ring, then we can also know that *either* his just *remembering* having heard a bell ring is evident for him or something about the *conditions under which he seems to remember* having heard a bell is evident for him. That he seems to remember having heard a bell, therefore, indicates something further about the other things that are evident to him.

It is in virtue of such other-presenting experiences that some of the things that are evident for a given person can be said to *derive their evidence* from other things that are evident for that person.

Let us now try to put these points somewhat more precisely and in the context of the various epistemic concepts we have been using.

We will say that taking there to be a tree tends to insure the evidence of perceiving there to be a tree, and that seeming to remember just having heard a bell *tends to insure the evidence* of remembering having just heard a bell. The relation of tending-to-insure-the-evidence-of is a logical relation between propositions; in other words, it is a relation which is such that, if it holds between two propositions, then it holds *necessarily* between those two propositions. And the relation of *deriving its evidence from* is an *application* of this logical relation—the tending-to-insure relation—to the evidence of a particular person.

I have referred to one's "*body of evidence,*" saying that, no matter how small a person's body of evidence may be, if it is evident for that person that he takes there to be a tree, then something further—either about the tree or about his taking there to be a tree—will also be evident for him. This concept of one's "body of evidence"—one's "total evidence"—will give us the clue to understanding the logical relation, tending-to-insure-the-evidence-of.

Let us say what it is, then, for a proposition to be one's *total evidence*:

D4   *e* is the total evidence of *S* =Df *e* is evident for *S*; and every proposition that is evident for *S* is implied by *e*.

Your total evidence may thus be thought of as a single proposition—a conjunction of propositions each of which is evident for you.

Suppose now that, under quite ordinary circumstances, you were to look out the train window and take something to be a tree. Then—since taking there to be a tree tends to insure the evidence of perceiving there to be a tree—your total evidence may include *both* "I take there to be a tree" and "I perceive there to be a tree." Let us assume that your total evidence does include both of these propositions. Consider now that proposition *w* which results from *subtracting* "I perceive there to be a tree" from your total evidence. This proposition could *not* be anyone's total evidence. Anyone for whom *that* much is evident will also have additional evidence not included in *w*—either evidence to the effect that he perceives a tree and therefore that there is a tree, or evidence about the circumstances under which he takes there to be a tree. Let us, then, define the logical relation expressed by "*e tends to insure* the evidence of *h*" this way:

D5   *e* tends to insure the evidence of *h* =Df *e* is necessarily such that, for every *x*, if *e* is evident for *x*, then there is a *w* such that (i) *w* is evident for x, (ii) *w&e&h* is possibly such that it is someone's total evidence, and (iii) *w&e* is not possibly such that it is anyone's total evidence.

(We could also express the second and third conditions by saying that *w&e* is *evidentially incomplete* and that it is *evidentially fulfilled* by *h*.) Our definition allows for the possibility that a proposition *e* may tend to insure the evidence of a proposition *h* even though *e* does not logically imply *h*. The tending-to-insure relation, therefore, is *inducive*, or *nondemonstrative*.

What if a person *S* takes there to be a tree but does so under conditions which are such that, under those conditions, he does *not* then perceive there to be a tree? Then his total evidence will include, in addition to *w* and *e*, a further proposition *d* about the conditions under which he takes there to be a tree. An example of such a proposition *d* would be: "I seem to recall that I have a perceptual disorder which leads me to take there to be trees when no trees are there." This proposition *d* could be said, in the following sense, to *defeat* the tendency of *e* to insure the evidence of *h*:

> D6 *d* defeats *e*'s tendency to insure the evidence of *h* =Df *e* tends to insure the evidence of *h*; and *d&e* does not tend to insure the evidence of *h*.

Now we may consider the application of this logical relation to the evidence of a particular subject S. We will assume that *S* is a person for whom his perceiving there to be a tree derives its evidence from the fact that he takes there to be a tree. In other words, S's taking there to be a tree *confers* evidence upon—or *lends* evidence to—his perceiving there to be a tree. There are four things to note about this:

(1) It is evident for *S* that he takes there to be a tree.
(2) Taking there to be a tree tends to insure the evidence of perceiving there to be a tree.
(3) Nothing that is evident for *S* *defeats* the tendency of taking there to be a tree to insure the evidence of perceiving there to be a tree.
(4) Taking there to be a tree does not logically entail (does not imply and conceptually involve) perceiving there to be a tree.

Why the fourth condition? The first three conditions together imply that it is evident for *S* that he perceives there to be a tree. But these three propositions do not yield all that is required if we are to define what it is for one proposition that is evident for *S* to derive its evidence *from* another proposition that is evident for *S*. For no proposition can derive its evidence *from itself*—any more than a person can lend money to himself.[19] Therefore I add a fourth condition to our definition—a condition which, as we can see, is fulfilled by the relation between "I take there to be a tree" and "I perceive there to be a tree." (Why not use the concept of logical implication instead of the stronger concept of logical entailment? The answer lies in two facts—first, that every *necessary* proposition is logically implied by every proposition and, secondly, that not every necessary proposition that is evident for a person S derives its evidence from every proposition that is evident for S.)

Our definition, then, is this:

> D7 h derives its status of being evident for S from e =Df (1) e is evident for S; (2) e tends to insure the evidence of h; (3) nothing that is evident for S defeats e's tendency to insure the evidence of h; and (4) e does not logically entail h.

And so we have the desired definition.

Our consideration of perceptual evidence, then, has enabled us to say what it is for one proposition that is evident for a person to derive its evidence from another proposition that is evident for that person. There are other epistemic relations that are similar to this. I suggest that we now have the clue to understanding these concepts.

We may say, for example, that a proposition h which is *probable* for a given subject S *derives* its status of being probable for S from some other proposition e that is evident for S. Here, too, we have the application of a logical relation to the evidence of a particular subject. The logical relation is this:

> D8 e tends to make h probable (e confirms h) =Df e is necessarily such that, for every x, if e is evident for x, then there is a w such that (i) w is evident for x, (ii) w&e could be someone's total evidence, and (iii) h is probable for anyone for whom w&e is the total evidence.

This logical probability relation, like that of tending-to-insure-the-evidence-of, admits of *defeat*:

> D9 d defeats e's tendency to make h probable =Df e tends to make h probable; and e&d does not tend to make h probable.

And the *application* of the logical relation to the evidence of a particular subject S may now be defined this way:

> D10 e makes h probable for S =Df (1) e is evident for S; (2) e tends to make h probable; (3) there is no d such that d is evident for S and d defeats e's tendency to make h probable; and (4) e does not entail h.

Other epistemic relations may be explicated similarly. For example, to get the corresponding explications for "making h such that it is *beyond reasonable doubt* for S," we have only to replace "probable" in the three foregoing formulae by "such as to be beyond reasonable doubt." And analogously for being such as to be *epistemically in the clear.*

Perhaps there are simpler theories which will do justice to the evidence of the senses and which also avoid commitment to skepticism. But I do not know what these theories are.[20]

NOTES

1. See Rudolf Carnap, *Logical Foundations of Probability* (Chicago: University of Chicago Press, 1950), pp. 211ff.

2. The quotation is from pages 454–55 of Carnap's article, "Testability and Meaning," *Philosophy of Science* 3 (1936): 420–71; my emphasis.

3. Compare Leonard Nelson, *Socratic Method and Critical Philosophy* (New Haven, Conn.: Yale University Press, 1949), pp. 191–92. Nelson felt that, by appeal to such considerations, he could show that all theory of knowledge rested upon a mistake. See his *Über das sogenannte Erkenntnisproblem* (Göttingen: Verlag Öffentliches Leben, 1930).

4. Quoted from Alvin Goldman's article, "A Causal Theory of Knowing," reprinted in George S. Pappas and Marshall Swain, eds., *Essays on Knowledge and Justification* (Ithaca, N.Y.: Cornell University Press, 1978), pp. 61–86; the quotation is on p. 69.

5. There had been a tendency in recent Anglo-Saxon philosophy to deny that any such variable sense-content is to be found, but this move, of course, is manifestly absurd. Compare J. L. Austin, *Sense and Sensibilia* (Oxford: The Clarendon Press, 1962).

6. *Outlines of Pyrrhonism,* book 1, ch. 14, abridged from vol. 1 of *Sextus Empiricus,* Loeb Classical Library, pp. 55, 63, 65. Compare K. Lykos, "Aristotle and Plato on 'Appearing,' " *Mind* 73 (1964): 496–514.

7. I discussed these theories in the second edition of my book *Theory of Knowledge* (Englewood Cliffs, N.J.: Prentice Hall, Inc., 1977), but I was not then fully aware of the importance of the theories or of the fact that they seem to cover almost all the possibilities. I first took note of their significance for contemporary philosophy in "Sextus Empiricus and Modem Empiricism," *Philosophy of Science* 8 (1941): 371–84.

8. Quoted by Sextus Empiricus, "Against the Logician," 1, 257–58; vol. 2, pp. 137–39.

9. Cicero uses these words in his *De Academics* 2, 9, 34; Cicero, *De Natura Deorum; Academica,* Loeb Classical Library (New York: G. P. Putnam's Sons, 1933), p. 511.

10. Thus Sextus distinguished between (1) the "indicative" signs of Chrysippus, where one reads off the nature of the signified from the nature of the sign, and (2) the "commemorative signs" of the "empirical" physicians: a certain symptom signifies a certain disorder in virtue of the fact that we have experienced symptom and disorder together. See "Outlines of Pyrrhonism," book 2, ch. 10 ("Concerning Sign") and ch. 11 ("Does Indicative Sign Exist?"); Loeb Library edition, vol. 1, pp. 213–37.

11. C. I. Lewis, "Professor Chisholm and Empiricism," *The Journal of Philosophy* 45 (1948): 517–24; the quotations appear on p. 520. This article is reprinted in C. I. Lewis, *Collected Papers of C. I. Lewis* (Stanford: Stanford University Press, 1970), pp. 317–25.

12. Lewis writes: "In my account, objective statements of fact are said to *entail* such probability consequences because it is consequences of this sort which are *contained in what it means*—in one sense of meaning—to assert the objective statements from which they are derivative" (p. 524). Unfortunately Lewis seems never to have worked out the details of this suggestion.

13. See the Loeb classical library edition of *Sextus Empiricus,* vol. I (London: William Heinemann Ltd., 1933), pp. 139-43, and vol. 2 (London: William Heinemann Ltd., 1935), pp. 87–103. Compare Charlotte I. Stough, *Greek Skepticism: A Study in Epistemology* (Berkeley: University of California Press, 1969), esp. pp. 50–64.

14. A. Meinong, *Über die Erfahrungsgrundlagen unseres Wissens* (1910); see *Meinong Gesamt Ausgabe,* vol. 5 (Graz: Akademische Druck-und Verlagsanstalt, 1973), pp. 458–59, 438. Compare his "Toward an Epistemological Assessment of Memory" (1886), reprinted in Roderick M. Chisholm and Robert J. Swartz, eds., *Empirical Knowledge: Readings from Contemporary Sources* (Englewood Cliffs, N.J.: Prentice-Hall, Inc., 1973), pp. 253–69.

15. H. H. Price, *Perception* (New York: Robert M. McBride and Co., 1933), p. 185.

16. Ibid., p. 186.

17. The construction of this hierarchy accords with a suggestion made by Kenneth G. Lucey in "Scales of Epistemic Appraisal," *Philosophical Studies* 29 (1976): 169–79. Lucey there contrasted the "straight steps" hierarchy I had proposed in earlier writings with what he called "a 'mirrored steps' system of epistemic appraisal" (170). The present hierarchy exemplifies the "mirrored steps" approach.

18. A. Meinong introduced the expressions "self-presenting" and "other presenting" in 1917. See ch. 1 of his *On Emotional Presentation* (Evanston, Ill.: Northwestern University Press, 1972). It should be added for the record, however, that Meinong did not use "other-presenting" in the way that I use it here.

19. "For how could anything transmit evidence to itself? The prospect sounds circular at best (like a witness testifying on behalf of his own credibility), impossible at worst (like a man trying to improve his own net worth by borrowing money from himself." James Van Cleve, "Epistemic Supervenience and the Circle of Belief," *The Monist* 58 (1984): 90–101; the quotation appears on p. 100.

20. I am indebted to Richard Feldman, Richard Foley, and Ernest Sosa for criticisms of earlier portions of this manuscript.

Part VII

Knowing Oneself and Others

33

Knowledge by Acquaintance and Knowledge by Description

Bertrand Russell

The object of the following paper is to consider what it is that we know in cases where we know propositions about "the so-and-so" without knowing who or what the so-and-so is. For example, I know that the candidate who gets most votes will be elected, though I do not know who is the candidate who will get most votes. The problem I wish to consider is: What do we know in these cases, where the subject is merely described? I have considered this problem elsewhere from a purely logical point of view; but in what follows I wish to consider the question in relation to theory of knowledge as well as in relation to logic, and in view of the above-mentioned logical discussions, I shall in this paper make the logical portion as brief as possible.

In order to make clear the antithesis between "acquaintance" and "description," I shall first of all try to explain what I mean by "acquaintance." I say that I am *acquainted* with an object when I have a direct cognitive relation to that object, i.e., when I am directly aware of the object itself. When I speak of a cognitive relation here, I do not mean the sort of relation which constitutes judgment, but the sort which constitutes presentation. In fact, I think the relation of subject and object which I call acquaintance is simply the converse of the relation of object and subject which constitutes presentation. That is, to say that *S* has acquaintance with *O* is essentially the same thing as to say that *O* is presented to *S*. But the associations and natural extensions of the word *acquaintance* are different from those of the word *presentation*. To begin with, as in most cognitive words, it is natural to say that I am ac-

From Bertrand Russell, *Mysticism and Logic* (New York: Doubleday & Co., 1957), pp. 202–24. Originally published 1917. The paper first appeared in *The Proceedings of the Aristotelian Society* for 1910–11.

quainted with an object even at moments when it is not actually before my mind, provided it has been before my mind, and will be again whenever occasion arises. This is the same sense in which I am said to know that 2 + 2 = 4 even when I am thinking of something else. In the second place, the word *acquaintance* is designed to emphasize, more than the word *presentation,* the relational character of the fact with which we are concerned. There is, to my mind, a danger that, in speaking of presentation, we may so emphasize the object as to lose sight of the subject. The result of this is either to lead to the view that there is no subject, whence we arrive at materialism; or to lead to the view that what is presented is part of the subject, whence we arrive at idealism, and should arrive at solipsism but for the most desperate contortions. Now I wish to preserve the dualism of subject and object in my terminology, because this dualism seems to me a fundamental fact concerning cognition. Hence I prefer the word *acquaintance,* because it emphasizes the need of a subject which is acquainted.

When we ask what are the kinds of objects with which we are acquainted, the first and most obvious example is *sense data.* When I see a color or hear a noise, I have direct acquaintance with the color or the noise. The sense datum with which I am acquainted in these cases is generally, if not always, complex. This is particularly obvious in the case of sight. I do not mean, of course, merely that the supposed physical object is complex, but that the direct sensible object is complex and contains parts with spatial relations. Whether it is possible to be aware of a complex without being aware of its constituents is not an easy question, but on the whole it would seem that there is no reason why it should not be possible. This question arises in an acute form in connection with self-consciousness, which we must now briefly consider.

In introspection, we seem to be immediately aware of varying complexes, consisting of objects in various cognitive and conative relations to ourselves. When I see the sun, it often happens that I am aware of my seeing the sun, in addition to being aware of the sun; and when I desire food, it often happens that I am aware of my desire for food. But it is hard to discover any state of mind in which I am aware of myself alone, as opposed to a complex of which I am a constituent. The question of the nature of self-consciousness is too large, and too slightly connected with our subject, to be argued at length here. It is difficult, but probably not impossible, to account for plain facts if we assume that we do not have acquaintance with ourselves. It is plain that we are not only *acquainted* with the complex "Self-acquainted-with-A," but we also *know* the proposition "I am acquainted with A." Now here the complex has been analyzed, and if "I" does not stand for something which is a direct object of acquaintance, we shall have to suppose that "I" is something known by description. If we wished to maintain the view that there is no acquaintance with Self, we might argue as follows: We are acquainted with *acquaintance,* and we know that it is a relation. Also we are acquainted with a complex in which we perceive that acquaintance is the relating relation. Hence we know that this complex must have a constituent which is that which is acquainted, i.e., must have a subject-term as well as an object-term. This subject-term we define as "I." Thus "I" means "the subject-term in awareness of which *I* am aware." But as a definition this cannot be regarded as a happy effort. It would seem necessary, therefore, either to suppose that I am acquainted with myself, and that "I," therefore, requires no definition, being merely the proper name of a certain object, or to find some other analysis of self-consciousness. Thus self-consciousness cannot be regarded as throwing light on the question whether we can know a complex without knowing its constituents. This question, however, is not important for our present purposes, and I shall therefore not discuss it further.

The awarenesses we have considered so far have all been awarenesses of particular existents, and might all in a large sense be called sense data. For, from the point of view of theory of knowledge, introspective knowledge is exactly on a level with knowledge derived from sight or hearing. But, in addition to awareness of the above kind of objects, which may be called awareness of *particulars,* we have also (though not quite in the same sense) what may be called awareness of *universals.* Awareness of universals is called conceiving, and a universal of which we are aware is called a *concept.* Not only are we aware of particular yellows, but if we have seen a sufficient number of yellows and have sufficient intelligence, we are aware of the universal *yellow;* this universal is the subject in such judgments as "yellow differs from blue" or "yellow resembles blue less than green does." And the universal yellow is the predicate in such judgments as "this is yellow," where "this" is a particular sense datum. And universal relations, too, are objects of awarenesses; up and down, before and after, resemblance, desire, awareness itself, and so on, would seem to be all of them objects of which we can be aware.

In regard to relations, it might be urged that we are never aware of the universal relation itself, but only of complexes in which it is a constituent. For example, it may be said that we do not know directly such a relation as *before,* though we understand such a proposition as "this is before that," and may be directly aware of such a complex as "this being before that." This view, however, is difficult to reconcile with the fact that we often know propositions in which the relation is the subject, or in which the relata are not definite given objects, but "anything." For example, we know that if one thing is before another, and the other before a third, then the first is before the third; and here the things concerned are not definite things, but "anything." It is hard to see how we could know such a fact about "before" unless we were acquainted with "before," and not merely with actual particular cases of one given object being before another given object. And more directly: A judgment such as "this is before that," where this judgment is derived from awareness of a complex, constitutes an analysis, and we should not understand the analysis if we were not acquainted with the meaning of the terms employed. Thus we must suppose that we are acquainted with the meaning of "before," and not merely with instances of it.

There are thus at least two sorts of objects of which we are aware, namely, particulars and universals. Among particulars I include all existents, and all complexes of which one or more constituents are existents, such as this-before-that, this-above-that, the yellowness-of-this. Among universals I include all objects of which no particular is a constituent. Thus the disjunction "universal-particular" includes all objects. We might also call it the disjunction of "abstract-concrete." It is not quite parallel with the opposition "concept-percept," because things remembered or imagined belong with particulars, but can hardly be called percepts. (On the other hand, universals with which we are acquainted may be identified with concepts.)

It will be seen that among the objects with which we are acquainted are not included physical objects (as opposed to sense data), nor other people's minds. These things are known to us by what I call "knowledge by description," which we must now consider.

By a "description" I mean any phrase of the form "a so-and-so" or "the so-and-so." A phrase of the form "a so-and-so" I shall call an "ambiguous" description; a phrase of the form "the so-and-so" (in the singular) I shall call a "definite" description. Thus "a man" is an ambiguous description, and "the man with the iron mask" is a definite description. There are various problems connected with ambiguous descriptions, but I pass them by, since they do not directly concern the matter I wish to discuss. What I wish to discuss is the nature of our knowledge concerning objects in cases where we know that there is an object answering to a definite description, though we are not *acquainted* with any such object. This is a matter which is concerned exclusively with *definite* descriptions. I shall, therefore, in the sequel, speak simply of "descriptions" when I mean "definite descriptions." Thus a description will mean any phrase of the form "the so-and-so" in the singular.

I shall say that an object is "known by description" when we know that it is "*the* so-and-so," i.e., when we know that there is one object, and no more, having a certain property; and it will generally be implied that we do not have knowledge of the same object by acquaintance. We know that the man with the iron mask existed, and many propositions are known about him; but we do not know who he was. We know that the candidate who gets the most votes will be elected, and in this case we are very likely also acquainted (in the only sense in which one can be acquainted with someone else) with the man who is, in fact, the candidate who will get most votes, but we do not know which of the candidates he is, i.e., we do not know any proposition of the form "*A* is the candidate who will get most votes" where *A* is one of the candidates by name. We shall say that we have "*merely* descriptive knowledge" of the so-and-so when, although we know that the so-and-so exists, and although we may possibly be acquainted with the object which is, in fact, the so-and-so, yet we do not know any proposition "*a* is the so-and-so," where *a* is something with which we are acquainted.

When we say "the so-and-so exists," we mean that there is just one object which is the so-and-so. The proposition "*a* is the so-and-so" means that *a* has the property so-and-so, and nothing else has. "Sir Joseph Larmor is the Unionist candidate" means "Sir Joseph Larmor is a Unionist candidate, and no one else is." "The Unionist candidate exists" means "some one is a Unionist candidate, and no one else is." Thus, when we are acquainted with an object which we know to be the so-and-so, we know that the so-and-so exists, but we may know that the so-and-so exists when we are not acquainted with any object which we know to be the so-and-so, and even when we are not acquainted with any object which, in fact, is the so-and-so.

Common words, even proper names, are usually really descriptions. That is to say, the thought in the mind of a person using a proper name correctly can generally only be expressed explicitly if we replace the proper name by a description. Moreover, the description required to express the thought will vary for different people, or for the same person at different times. The only thing constant (so long as the name is rightly used) is the object to which the name applies. But so long as this remains constant, the particular description involved usually makes no difference to the truth or falsehood of the proposition in which the name appears.

Let us take some illustrations. Suppose some statement is made about Bismarck. Assuming that there is such a thing as direct acquaintance with oneself, Bismarck himself might have used his name directly to designate the particular person with whom he was acquainted. In this case, if he made a judgment about himself, he himself might be a constituent of the judgment. Here the proper name has the direct use which it always wishes to have, as simply standing for a certain object, and not for a description of the object. But if a person who knew Bismarck made a judgment about him, the case is different. What this person was acquainted with were certain sense data which he connected (rightly, we will suppose) with Bismarck's body. His body as a physical object, and still more his mind, were only known as the body and the mind connected with these sense data. That is, they were known by description, It is, of course, very much a matter of chance which characteristics of a man's appearance will come into a friend's mind when he thinks of him; thus the description actually in the friend's mind is accidental. The essential point is that he knows that the various descriptions all apply to the same entity, in spite of not being acquainted with the entity in question.

When we, who did not know Bismarck, make a judgment about him, the description in our minds will probably be some more or less vague mass of historical knowledge—far more, in most cases, than is required to identify him. But, for the sake of illustration, let us assume that we think of him as "the first chancellor of the German Empire." Here all the words are abstract except "German." The word "German" will again have different meanings for different people. To some it will recall travels in Germany, to some the look of Germany on the map, and so on. But if we are to obtain a description which we know to be applicable, we shall be compelled, at some point, to bring in a reference to a particular with which we are acquainted. Such reference is involved in any mention of past, present, and future (as opposed to definite dates) or of here and there, or of what others have told us. Thus it would seem that, in some way or other, a description known to be applicable to a particular must involve some reference to a particular with which we are acquainted, if our knowledge about the thing described is not to be merely what follows logically from the description. For example, "the most long-lived of men" is a description which must apply to some man, but we can make no judgments concerning this man which involve knowledge about him beyond what the description gives. If, however, we say, "the first chancellor of the German Empire was an astute diplomatist," we can only be assured of the truth of our judgment in virtue of something with which we are acquainted—usually a testimony heard or read. Considered psychologically, apart from the information we convey to others, apart from the fact about the actual Bismarck, which gives importance to our judgment, the thought we really have contains the one or more particulars involved, and otherwise consists wholly of concepts. All names of places—London, England, Europe, the earth, the solar system—similarly involve, when used, descriptions which start from some one or more particulars with which we are acquainted. I suspect that even the Universe, as considered by metaphysics, involves such a connection with particulars. In logic, on the contrary, where we are concerned not merely with what does exist, but with whatever might or could exist or be, no reference to actual particulars is involved.

It would seem that, when we make a statement about something only known by description, we often *intend* to make our statement, not in the form involving the description, but about the actual thing described. That is to say, when we say anything about Bismarck, we should like, if we could, to make the judgment which Bismarck alone can make, namely, the judgment of which he himself is a constituent. In this we are necessarily defeated, since the actual Bismarck is unknown to us. But we know that there is an object B called Bismarck, and that B was an astute diplomatist. We can thus *describe* the proposition we should like to affirm, namely, "B was an astute diplomatist," where B is the object which was Bismarck. What enables us to communicate in spite of the varying descriptions we employ is that we know there is a true proposition concerning the actual Bismarck, and that, however we may vary the description (so long as the description is correct), the proposition described is still the same. This proposition, which is described and is known to be true, is what interests us; but we are not acquainted with the proposition itself, and do not know *it*, though we know it is true.

It will be seen that there are various stages in the removal from acquaintance with particulars: there is Bismarck to people who knew him, Bismarck to those who only know of him through history, the man with the iron mask, the longest-lived of men. These are progressively further removed from acquaintance with particulars, and there is a similar hierarchy in the region of universals. Many universals, like many particulars, are only known to us by description. But here, as in the case of particulars, knowledge concerning what is known by description is ultimately reducible to knowledge concerning what is known by acquaintance.

The fundamental epistemological principle in the analysis of propositions containing descriptions is this: *Every proposition which we can understand must be composed wholly of constituents with which we are acquainted.* From what has been said already, it will be plain why I advocate this principle, and how I propose to meet the case of propositions which at first sight contravene it. Let us begin with the reasons for supposing the principle true.

The chief reason for supposing the principle true is that it seems scarcely possible to believe that we can make a judgment or entertain a supposition without knowing what it is that we are judging or supposing about. If we make a judgment about (say) Julius Caesar, it is plain that the actual person who was Julius Caesar is not a constituent of the judgment. But before going further, it may be well to explain what I mean when I say that this or that is a constituent of a judgment, or of a proposition which we understand. To begin with judgments: a judgment, as an occurrence, I take to be a relation of a mind to several entities, namely, the entities which compose what is judged. If, e.g., I judge that *A* loves *B*, the judgment as an event consists in the existence, at a certain moment, of a specific four-term relation, called *judging*, between me and *A* and love and *B*. That is to say, at the time when I judge, there is a certain complex whose terms are myself and *A* and love and *B*, and whose relating relation is *judging*. My reasons for this view have been set forth elsewhere,[1] and I shall not repeat them here. Assuming this view of judgment, the constituents of the judgment are simply the constituents of the complex which is the judgment. Thus, in the above case, the constituents are myself and *A* and love and *B* and judging. But myself and judging are constituents shared by all my judgments; thus the *distinctive* constituents of the particular judgment in question are *A* and love and *B*. Coming now to what is meant by "understanding a proposition," I should say that there is another relation possible between me and *A* and love and *B*, which is called my *supposing* that *A* loves *B*.[2] When we can *suppose* that *A* loves *B*, we "understand the proposition" *A loves* B. Thus we often understand a proposition in cases where we have not enough knowledge to make a judgment. Supposing, like judging, is a many-term relation, of which a mind is one term. The other terms of the relation are called the constituents of the proposition supposed. Thus the principle which I enunciated may be restated as follows: *Whenever a relation of supposing or judging occurs, the terms to which the supposing or judging mind is related by the relation of supposing or judging must be terms with which the mind in question is acquainted.* This is merely to say that we cannot make a judgment or a supposition without knowing what it is that we are making our judgment or supposition about. It seems to me that the truth of this principle is evident as soon as the principle is understood; I shall, therefore, in what follows, assume the principle, and use it as a guide in analyzing judgments that contain descriptions.

Returning now to Julius Caesar, I assume that it will be admitted that he himself is not a constituent of any judgment which I can make. But at this point it is necessary to examine the view that judgments are composed of something called "ideas," and that it is the "idea" of Julius Caesar that is a constituent of my judgment. I believe the plausibility of this view rests upon a failure to form a right theory of descriptions. We may mean by my "idea" of Julius Caesar the things that I know about him, e.g., that he conquered Gaul, was assassinated on the Ides of March, and is a plague to schoolboys. Now I am admitting, and indeed contending, that in order to discover what is actually in my mind when I judge about Julius Caesar, we must substitute for the proper name a description made up of some of the things I know about him. (A description which will often serve to express my thought is "the man whose name was *Julius Caesar.*" For whatever else I may have forgotten about him, it is plain that when I mention him I have not forgotten that that was his name.) But although I think the theory that judgments consist of ideas may have been suggested in some such way, yet I think the theory itself is fundamentally mistaken. The view seems to be that there is some mental existent which may be called the "idea" of something outside the mind of the person who has the idea, and that, since judgment is a mental event, its constituents must be constituents of the mind of the person judging. But in this view ideas become a veil between us and outside things—we never really, in knowledge, attain to the things we are supposed to be knowing about, but only to the idea of those things. The relation of mind, idea, and object, on this view, is utterly obscure, and, so far as I can see, nothing discoverable by inspection warrants the intrusion of the idea between the mind and the object. I suspect that the view is fostered by the dislike of relations, and that it is felt the mind could not know objects unless there were something "in" the mind which could be called the state of knowing the object. Such a view, however, leads at once to a vicious endless regress, since the relation of idea to object will have to be explained by supposing that the idea itself has an idea of the object, and so on *ad infinitum.* I therefore see no reason to believe that, when we are acquainted with an object, there is in us something which can be called the "idea" of the object. On the contrary, I hold that acquaintance is wholly a relation, not demanding any such constituent of the mind as is supposed by advocates of "ideas." This is, of course, a large question, and one which would take us far from our subject if it were adequately discussed. I therefore content myself with the above indications, and with the corollary that, in judging, the actual objects concerning which we judge, rather than any supposed purely mental entities, are constituents of the complex which is the judgment.

When, therefore, I say that we must substitute for "Julius Caesar" some description of Julius Caesar, in order to discover the meaning of a judgment nominally about him, I am not saying that we must substitute an idea. Suppose our description is "the man whose name was *Julius Caesar.*" Let our judgment be "Julius Caesar was assassinated." Then it becomes "the man whose name was *Julius Caesar* was assassinated." Here *Julius Caesar* is a noise or shape with which we are acquainted, and all the other constituents of the judgment (neglecting the tense in "was") are *concepts* with which we are acquainted. Thus our judgment is wholly reduced to constituents with which we are acquainted, but Julius Caesar himself has ceased to be a constituent of our judgment. This however, requires a proviso, to be further explained shortly, namely, that "the man whose name was *Julius Caesar*" must not, as a whole, be a constituent of our judgment, that is to say, this phrase must not, as a whole, have a meaning which enters into the judgment. Any right analysis of the judgment, therefore, must break up this phrase, and not treat it as a subordinate complex which is part of the judgment. The judgment "the man whose name was *Julius Caesar* was assassinated" may be interpreted as meaning "one and only one man was called *Julius Caesar,* and that one was assassinated." Here it is plain that there is no constituent corresponding to the phrase "the man whose name was *Julius Caesar.*" Thus there is no reason to regard this phrase as expressing a constituent of the judgment, and we have seen that this phrase must be broken up if we are to be acquainted with all the constituents of the judgment. This conclusion, which we have reached from considerations concerned with the theory of knowledge, is also forced upon us by logical considerations, which must now be briefly reviewed.

It is common to distinguish two aspects, *meaning* and *denotation,* in such phrases as "the author of *Waverley.*" The meaning will be a certain complex, consisting (at least) of authorship and *Waverley* with some relation; the denotation will be Scott. Similarly "featherless bipeds" will have a complex meaning, containing as constituents the presence of two feet and the absence of feathers, while its denotation will be the class of men. Thus when we say "Scott is the author of *Waverley*" or "men are the same as featherless bipeds," we are asserting an identity of denotation, and this assertion is worth making because of the diversity of meaning.[3] I believe that the duality of meaning and denotation, though capable of a true interpretation, is misleading if taken as fundamental. The denotation, I believe, is not a constituent of the proposition, except in the case of proper names, i.e., of words which do not assign a property to an object, but merely and solely name it. And I should hold further that, in this sense, there are only two words which are strictly proper names of particulars, namely, "I" and "this."[4]

One reason for not believing the denotation to be a constituent of the proposition is that we may know the proposition even when we are not acquainted with the denotation. The proposition "the author of *Waverley* is a novelist" was known to people who did not know that "the author of *Waverley*" denoted Scott. This reason has been already sufficiently emphasized.

A second reason is that propositions concerning "the so-and-so" are possible even when "the so-and-so" has no denotation. Take, e.g., "the golden mountain does not exist" or "the round square is self-contradictory." If we are to preserve the duality of meaning and denotation, we have to say, with Meinong, that there are such objects as the golden mountain and the round square, although these objects do not have being. We even have to admit that the existent round square is existent, but does not exist.[5] Meinong does not regard this as a contradiction, but I fail to see that it is not one. Indeed, it seems to me evident that the judgment "there is no such object as the round square" does not presuppose that there is such an object. If this is admitted, however, we are led to the conclusion that, by parity of form, no judgment concerning "the so-and-so" actually involves the so-and-so as a constituent.

Miss Jones[6] contends that there is no difficulty in admitting contradictory predicates concerning such an object as "the present king of France," on the ground that this object is in itself contradictory. Now it might, of course, be argued that this object, unlike the round square, is not self-contradictory, but merely nonexistent. This, however, would not go to the root of the matter. The real objection to such an argument is that the law of contradiction ought not to be stated in the traditional form "*A* is not both *B* and not *B*," but in the form "no proposition is both true and false." The traditional form only applies to certain propositions, namely, to those which attribute a predicate to a subject. When the law is stated of propositions, instead of being stated concerning subjects and predicates, it is at once evident that propositions about the present king of France or the round square can form no exception, but are just as incapable of being both true and false as other propositions.

Miss Jones[7] argues that "Scott is the author of *Waverley*" asserts identity of denotation between *Scott* and the *author of* Waverley. But there is some difficulty in choosing among alternative meanings of this contention. In the first place, it should be observed that the *author of* Waverley is not a *mere* name, like *Scott. Scott* is merely a noise or shape conventionally used to designate a certain person; it gives us no information about that person, and has nothing that can be called meaning as opposed to denotation. (I neglect the fact, considered above, that even proper names, as a rule, really stand for descriptions.) But the *author of* Waverley is not merely conventionally a name for Scott; the element of mere convention belongs here to the separate words, *the* and *author* and *of* and *Waverley*. Given what these words stand for, *the author of Waverley* is no longer arbitrary. When it is said that Scott is the author of *Waverley,* we are not stating that these are two *names* for one man, as we should be if we said "Scott is Sir Walter." A man's name is what he is called, but however much Scott had been called the author of *Waverley,* that would not have made him be the author; it was necessary for him actually to write *Waverley,* which was a fact having nothing to do with names.

If, then, we are asserting identity of denotation, we must not mean by *denotation* the mere relation of a name to the thing named. In fact, it would be nearer to the truth to say that the *meaning* of "Scott" is the *denotation* of "the author of *Waverley*." The relation of "Scott" to Scott is that "Scott" means Scott, just as the relation of "author" to the concept which is so called is that "author" means this concept. Thus if we distinguish meaning and denotation in "the author of *Waverley*," we shall have to say that "Scott" has meaning but not denotation. Also when we say "Scott is the author of *Waverley*," the *meaning* of "the author of *Waverley*" is relevant to our assertion. For if the denotation alone were relevant, any other phrase with the same denotation would give the same proposition. Thus "Scott is the author of *Marmion*" would be the same proposition as "Scott is the author of *Waverley*." But this is plainly not the case, since from the first we learn that Scott wrote *Marmion* and from the second we learn that he wrote *Waverley*, but the first tells us nothing about *Waverley* and the second nothing about *Marmion*. Hence the meaning of "the author of *Waverley*," as opposed to the denotation, is certainly relevant to "Scott is the author of *Waverley*."

We have thus agreed that "the author of *Waverley*" is not a mere name, and that its meaning is relevant in propositions in which it occurs. Thus if we are to say, as Miss Jones does, that "Scott is the author of *Waverley*" asserts an identity of denotation, we must regard the denotation of "the author of *Waverley*" as the denotation of what is *meant* by "the author of *Waverley*." Let us call the meaning of "the author of *Waverley*" *M*. Thus *M* is what "the author of *Waverley*" means. Then we are to suppose that "Scott is the author of *Waverley*" means "Scott is the denotation of *M*." But here we are explaining our proposition by another of the same form, and thus we have made no progress towards a real explanation. "The denotation of *M*," like "the author of *Waverley*," has both meaning and denotation, on the theory we are examining. If we call its meaning *M'*, our proposition becomes "Scott is the denotation of M'." But this leads at once to an endless regress. Thus the attempt to regard our proposition as asserting identity of denotation breaks down, and it becomes imperative to find some other analysis. When this analysis has been completed, we shall be able to reinterpret the phrase "identity of denotation," which remains obscure so long as it is taken as fundamental.

The first point to observe is that, in any proposition about "the author of *Waverley*," provided Scott is not explicitly mentioned, the denotation itself, i.e., Scott, does not occur, but only the concept of denotation, which will be represented by a variable. Suppose we say "the author of *Waverley* was the author of *Marmion*," we are certainly not saying that both were Scott—we may have forgotten that there was such a person as Scott. We are saying that there is some man who was the author of *Waverley* and the author of *Marmion*. That is to say, there is someone who wrote *Waverley* and *Marmion*, and no one else wrote them. Thus the identity is that of a variable, i.e., of an indefinite subject, "someone." This is why we can understand propositions about "the author of *Waverley*," without knowing who he was. When we say "the author of

Waverley was a poet," we mean "one and only one man wrote *Waverley*, and he was a poet"; when we say "the author of *Waverley* was Scott" we mean "one and only one man wrote *Waverley*, and he was Scott." Here the identity is between a variable, i.e., an indeterminate subject ("he") and Scott; "the author of *Waverley*" has been analyzed away, and no longer appears as a constituent of the proposition.[8]

The reason why it is imperative to analyze away the phrase "the author of *Waverley*" may be stated as follows. It is plain that when we say "the author of *Waverley* is the author of *Marmion*," the *is* expresses identity. We have seen also that the common *denotation*, namely Scott, is not a constituent of this proposition, while the *meanings* (if any) of "the author of *Waverley*" and "the author of *Marmion*" are not identical. We have seen also that, in any sense in which the meaning of a word is a constituent of a proposition in whose verbal expression the word occurs, "Scott" means the actual man Scott, in the same sense (so far as concerns our present discussion) in which "author" means a certain universal. Thus, if "the author of *Waverley*" were a subordinate complex in the above proposition, its *meaning* would have to be what was said to be identical with the *meaning* of "the author of *Marmion*." This is plainly not the case; and the only escape is to say that "the author of *Waverley*" does not, by itself, have a meaning, though phrases of which it is part do have a meaning. That is, in a right analysis of the above proposition, "the author of *Waverley*" must disappear. This is effected when the above proposition is analyzed as meaning: "Someone wrote *Waverley* and no one else did, and that someone also wrote *Marmion* and no one else did." This may be more simply expressed by saying that the propositional function "*x* wrote *Waverley* and *Marmion*, and no one else did" is capable of truth, i.e., some value of *x* makes it true, but no other value does. Thus the true subject of our judgment is a propositional function, i.e., a complex containing an undetermined constituent, and becoming a proposition as soon as this constituent is determined.

We may now define the denotation of a phrase. If we know that the proposition "*a* is a so-and-so" is true, i.e., that *a* is so-and-so and nothing else is, we call *a* the denotation of the phrase "the so-and-so." A very great many of the propositions we naturally make about "the so-and-so" will remain true or remain false if we substitute *a* for "the so-and-so," where *a* is the denotation of "the so-and-so." Such propositions will also remain true or remain false if we substitute for "the so-and-so" any other phrase having the same denotation. Hence, as practical men, we become interested in the denotation more than in the description, since the denotation decides as to the truth or falsehood of so many statements in which the description occurs. Moreover, as we saw earlier in considering the relations of description and acquaintance, we often wish to reach the denotation, and are only hindered by lack of acquaintance: in such cases the description is merely the means we employ to get as near as possible to the denotation. Hence it naturally comes to be supposed that the denotation is part of the proposition in which the description occurs. But we have seen, both on logical and on epistemological grounds, that this is an error. The actual object (if any) which is the denotation is not (unless it is explicitly mentioned) a constituent of propositions in which descriptions occur; and this is the reason why, in order to understand such propositions, we need acquaintance with the constituents of the description, but do not need acquaintance with its denotation. The first result of analysis, when applied to propositions whose grammatical subject is "the so-and-so," is to substitute a variable as subject; i.e., we obtain a proposition of the form: "There is *something* which alone is so-and-so, and that *something* is such-and-such." The further analysis of propositions concerning "the so-and-so" is thus merged in the problem of the nature of the variable, i.e., of the meanings of *some, any,* and *all.* This is a difficult problem, concerning which I do not intend to say anything at present.

To sum up our whole discussion: We began by distinguishing two sorts of knowledge of objects, namely, knowledge by *acquaintance* and knowledge by *description.* Of these it is only the former that brings the object itself before the mind. We have acquaintance with sense data, with many universals, and possibly with ourselves, but not with physical objects or other minds. We have *descriptive* knowledge of an object when we know that it is *the* object having some property or properties with which we are acquainted; that is to say, when we know that the property or properties in question belong to one object and no more, we are said to have knowledge of that one object by description, whether or not we are acquainted with the object. Our knowledge of physical objects and of other minds is only knowledge by description, the descriptions involved being usually such as involve sense data. All propositions intelligible to us, whether or not they primarily concern things only known to us by description, are composed wholly of constituents with which we are acquainted, for a constituent with which we are not acquainted is unintelligible to us. A judgment, we found, is not composed of mental constituents called "ideas," but consists of an occurrence whose constituents are a mind[9] and certain objects, particulars or universals. (One at least must be a universal.) When a judgment is rightly analyzed, the objects which are constituents of it must all be objects with which the mind which is a constituent of it is acquainted. This conclusion forces us to analyze descriptive phrases occurring in propositions, and to say that the objects denoted by such phrases are not constituents of judgments in which such phrases occur (unless these objects are explicitly mentioned). This leads us to the view (recommended also on purely logical grounds) that when we say "the author of *Marmion* was the author of *Waverley*," Scott himself is not a constituent of our judgment, and that the judgment cannot be explained by saying that it affirms identity of denotation with diversity of meaning. It also, plainly, does not assert identity of meaning. Such judgments, therefore, can only be analyzed by breaking up the descriptive phrases, introducing a variable, and making propositional functions the ultimate subjects. In fact, "The so-and-so is such-and-such" will mean that "*x* is so-and-so and nothing else is, and *x* is such-and-such" is capable of truth. The analysis of such judgments involves many fresh problems, but the discussion of these problems is not undertaken in the present paper.

NOTES

1. *Philosophical Essays*, "The Nature of Truth." I have been persuaded by Mr. Wittgenstein that this theory is somewhat unduly simple, but the modification which I believe it to require does not affect the above argument [1917].

2. Compare Meinong. *Über Annahmen,* passim. I formerly supposed, contrary to Meinong's view, that the relationship of supposing might be merely that of presentation. In this view I now think I was mistaken, and Meinong is right. But my present view depends upon the theory that both in judgment and in assumption there is no single Objective, but the several constituents of the judgment or assumption are in a many-term relation to the mind.

3. This view has been recently advocated by Miss E. E. C. Jones. "A New Law of Thought and Its Implications," *Mind* (January 1911).

4. I should now exclude "I" from proper names in the strict sense, and retain only "this" [1917].

5. Meinong, *Über Annahmen,* 2d ed., Leipzig, 1910, p. 141.

6. *Mind* (July 1910): 380.

7. Ibid., p. 379.

8. The theory which I am advocating is set forth fully, with the logical grounds in its favor, in *Principia Mathematica,* vol. 1, Introduction, ch. 3; also, less fully, in *Mind* (October 1905).

9. I use this phrase merely to denote the something psychological which enters into judgment, without intending to prejudge the question as to what this something is.

34

On the Nature of the Psychological

Roderick M. Chisholm

INTRODUCTION

I shall here formulate a definition of a *psychological attribute*. What I will say pre-supposes the commonsense distinction between the psychological, or mental, and the nonpsychological.

The following may be taken as being paradigmatic cases of psychological at-tributes: judging; being sad about something; being pleased about something; won-dering about something; feeling depressed; seeming to oneself to have a headache; and being appeared to redly. And the following will be paradigmatic cases of nonpsy-chological attributes: being extended; wearing a hat; being green; weighing seven pounds; being the successor of nine; being such that all men are mortal.

There is a simple formula that tells us what the psychological attributes we have listed have in common and what distinguishes them from everything that is nonpsy-chological. It is this:

> Any property which is possibly such that it is exemplified by just one thing and which includes every property it implies or involves is psychological.

This formula provides us with an interpretation of one traditional thesis—namely, that whatever is "purely qualitative" is psychological. We will *define* the psychological

From *Philosophical Studies* 43 (1983): 155–64. © 1983 by D. Reidel Publishing Co., Dordrecht, Nether-lands. Reprinted by permission of Wolters Kluwer Academic Publisher.

by reference to that which is purely qualitative. But we will not define the psychological *as* that which is purely qualitative, since certain psychological attributes—for example, thinking about one's brother—are not purely qualitative.

I will make the following metaphysical presuppositions. (1) It is necessarily the case that there are entities that are not individual things; examples are such abstract objects as propositions, attributes, and numbers. (2) The ontological thesis of materialism ("Every individual thing is a material thing"), even if it is true, is not *necessarily* true. And (3) whatever is a proper part has a proper part.

These presuppositions seem to me to be clearly true, but it is not the point of the present paper to defend them. It is enough to note that, without them, our analysis of the psychological would have to be considerably more complex.

Our first task is to explicate the four expressions we have used in the formula above: "property," "implies," "includes," and "involves." In doing this, I shall make use of four philosophical concepts. These are: (1) the concept of an *individual thing*; (2) the concept of *exemplification* at a time (as in "x exemplifies v at t" or "x has v at t"); (3) the concept of *de re modality* (as in "x is necessarily such that it is F"); and, finally, (4) the intentional concept of *conceiving* (as in "x conceives the property being red").

PROPERTIES

Let us think of an *attribute* as being anything that is capable of being exemplified:

> D1 P is an attribute =Df. P is possibly such that there is something that exemplifies it.

I assume that there are attributes and that some of them are exemplified and others not. I also assume that every attribute is capable of being conceived—i.e., that every attribute is possibly such that there is someone who conceives it.

I will next single out a certain subspecies of attribute I will call a "property." This use of "property" is entirely arbitrary; it is introduced only to avoid circumlocution. The definition of property will be so formulated that each of the psychological attributes on our list above will count as properties. The definition is this:

> D2 P is a property =Df. P is an attribute which is such that: (a) only individual things can have it; (b) anything that can have it can have it, or fail to have it, at any time it exists; and (c) it can be such that some individuals have it and some do not.

Condition (a) tells us that if an attribute may be exemplified by a nonindividual (say, by an attribute or by a number), then that attribute is not a property. Hence being an even number and being exemplified are not properties. And no attribute that is capable of being universal is a property.

Condition (b) tells us that if *P* is a property, then whatever can have it can have it, or fail to have it, at any period of its existence—that is to say, at the time at which the thing comes into being and at any time thereafter up to and including the time it passes away. Hence coming into being and passing away will not themselves be properties. And what we might call "past-tensed attributes'(for example, *being such that it did walk*) and "future-tensed attributes" (for example, *being such that it will walk*) will not be properties.

All the psychological attributes on our list above, as I have said, are *properties,* in the present sense of the term.

IMPLICATION AND INCLUSION

We have now explicated one of the four terms that appear in our general formula. We turn to *implication* and *inclusion.*

D3 *P* implies *Q* =Df. *P* is necessarily such that if anything has it then something has *Q*.

The attribute of being a man implies the attribute of being rational. And the attribute of being a person who owns a boat implies the attribute of being a boat.

Inclusion is a subspecies of implication:

D4 *P* includes *Q* =Df. *P* is necessarily such that whatever has it has *Q*.

If *P* includes *Q*, then *P* also implies *Q*. But *P* may imply *Q* without including *Q*. The attribute of being a person who owns a boat implies but does not include the attribute of being a boat. And the attribute of being populated implies but does not include the attribute of being a living thing.

NONRELATIONAL PROPERTIES

There is one noteworthy feature that has been traditionally associated with psychological or mental properties. It is that of being *internal* or *nonrelational.*

We are now in a position to specify one sense in which certain psychological properties may thus be said to be "nonrelational." For one mark of a *relational* property is this: a relational property implies a property it does not include. (Note I have said "implies a *property* it does not include.") The property of being a biped will be relational according to this account, since it implies but does not include the property of being a foot. But the property of being angry will be nonrelational; it includes every property that it implies. So, too, for the psychological properties with which we began: judging; being sad about something; being pleased about something; wondering about something; feeling depressed; seeming to oneself to have a headache; and being appeared to redly.

To be sure, judging implies but does not include the attribute of *being judged about* or that of *being an object of judgment*; and wondering implies but does not include the attribute of *being wondered about* or that of *being an object of wonder*. But being judged about and being wondered about are not *properties,* in our restricted sense of this term. They may be exemplified by such entities as propositions, attributes, and numbers; hence they are not such that only individual things can have them. ("What, then, of *being an individual that is judged about*? No abstract object can have *that* attribute." This is true; but that attribute, unlike our psychological attributes, implies a property that it does not include—namely, that of judging.)

Psychological properties, however, are not the only properties that are nonrelational by our definition. The properties on the following list are both nonpsychological and nonrelational:

> being either angry or two-legged;
> being intoxicating;
> being potentially dangerous;
> being an individual thing that is nongreen.

But these attributes, unlike our paradigmatic psychological attributes, are all such that they *involve* properties they do not imply.

INVOLVEMENT

What, then, is the requisite sense of involvement? Consider these four attributes: (i) *being either red or round*, (ii) *being nonred*, (iii) *being possibly red*, and (iv) *wanting something that is red*. These attributes all *involve* the property red, yet they do not include or imply it.

Using the intentional expression "conceives," we can say exactly what the requisite sense of "involvement" is. Each of the attributes may be said in the following sense to *involve* the property red: the attribute is such that one cannot *conceive* it without conceiving the property red.

So let us define involvement this way:

D5 *P* involves *Q* =Df. *P* is necessarily such that whoever conceives it conceives *Q*.

We may note, incidentally, that these concepts of inclusion and involvement yield an
identity condition for attributes:

An attribute *P* is identical with an attribute *Q*, if and only if: *P* includes *Q*, *Q* includes *P*, *P* involves *Q*, and *Q* involves *P*.

In other words: an attribute *P* is identical with an attribute *Q*, if and only if, they are
necessarily such that (i) whatever has the one has the other and (ii) whoever conceives
the one conceives the other. Hence attributes that imply and include each other need
not be identical. *Being an equilateral triangle* and *being an equiangular triangle* are
distinct attributes, since neither involves the other. And *being sad* is not identical with
being sad and such that seven and five are twelve, since, although the latter attribute
involves the former, the former does not involve the latter. *Killing* and *being killed*
are distinct attributes, since, although they involve each other, they do not *include*
each other.

A MARK OF THE PSYCHOLOGICAL

We have now defined the terms that occur in our formula:

Any property which is possibly such that it is exemplified by just one thing and
which includes every property it implies or involves is psychological.

It is clear that the nonrelational nonpsychological properties we have listed above do
not satisfy this formula. Thus the disjunctive property of being either angry or two-
legged involves but does not include the property of being angry. One can't *conceive*
the disjunctive property without conceiving the property of being angry; but one can
have the disjunctive property without having the property of being angry. Again, a
thing can have the property of being intoxicating without having the property of being
intoxicated; but one can't conceive the property of being intoxicating without conceiving the property of being intoxicated. Thus we can say of dispositional properties generally that they involve but do not include the property or properties toward
which they dispose their bearers.

But our paradigmatic psychological properties are all such that they include every property that they imply or involve. And, it would seem, only psychological properties satisfy this condition. Hence the formula gives us a *sufficient condition* of the psychological.

SOME TEST CASES

We now consider certain *nonpsychological* attributes which, at first consideration, may seem to satisfy our formula; that is to say, each of them may seem to be a property which is such that it includes every attribute it implies or involves. But a closer examination will show that these attributes do not satisfy our formula. And in most such cases, we will find that the attribute in question does not satisfy our definition of *property*.

Being a proper part of an individual thing does not satisfy our formula, for it is not possibly such that there is just one thing that has it. So, too, for *having a proper part, being extended,* and *being green.* Anything having any one of these properties has a proper part that also has that property. Therefore these properties are not possibly such that they are exemplified by just one thing.

What of such semantical attributes as *referring to something, designating oneself,* and *being heterological*? These attributes involve but do not include such properties as *using a language* and *interpreting a language.*

What of *moving*? The attribute of moving may be defined as follows: being one of several things that are changing their spatial relations to each other. Hence moving does not satisfy our formula, for it cannot be exemplified by just one individual.

The attribute *undergoing change* is not a property. It is necessarily the case that if anything undergoes change then everything undergoes change. Suppose, for example, that a certain individual thing changes from being red to being green. Then each thing changes in the following way: certain relations it had formerly born just to something red become relations that it now bears to something green. Hence *undergoing change* is capable of being universal. But no property—in our present sense of the term—is capable of being universal.

"What of *changing internally*? If eternal objects change (say, from being such that there are dinosaurs to being such that there are no dinosaurs), this change is only external and is a function of internal changes in individual things. Eternal objects would not change at all if there were no individual things. Therefore the attribute of *changing internally* would seem to be a property that includes every property it implies or involves. But it is not a psychological attribute."

What would be an example of an "internal change"? I can think only of four types of such change. (i) There are psychological changes—say, the change from being happy to being sad. But these are not counter to our thesis. (ii) Possibly we can say that *coming into being* and *passing away* are internal changes. But, even if we can say this, we cannot say that they are *properties,* for they are not attributes a thing can have at any period of its existence. (iii) There is the attribute of *undergoing rearrangement of parts.* We could say that a material thing changes internally if it has this attribute—i.e., if its proper parts are changing their spatial relations to each other. Thus a watch, if it is running, is undergoing internal change. But this attribute—*having proper parts that are changing their relations to each other*—implies but does not include *being a proper part.* (iv) There is *undergoing a change of causal properties.* But this is not an attribute that can be exemplified by just one individual. For, if an individual undergoes a change of its causal properties, then it is a member of a set of individuals that are changing their relations to each other. Hence this attribute includes the attribute of *being an individual thing which is such that there is an individual discrete from it.* (Two individual things may be said to be *discrete* from each other if they have no parts in common.) But this attribute cannot be exemplified by just one individual. And therefore *undergoing a change of causal attributes* is not a property.

What of *going, functioning, working*? If these are not purely dispositional, or if they are not to be thought of as species of moving, then they imply the property of *being expected to accomplish certain things* or that of *being designed for a certain purpose.* Therefore they involve but do not include the properties of *expecting* or of *designing* or *intending* something.

Useful and *harmful,* if they are not purely dispositional, involve but do not include such properties as *benefiting from something* and *being harmed by something.*

Good and *bad,* if taken as species of intrinsic value, are attributes that are necessary to the things that have them and are therefore not properties. But if they are taken as species of instrumental value, then they are analogous to useful and harmful.

Beautiful and *ugly,* if they are not merely dispositional, involve but do not include such properties as taking pleasure in perceiving something and taking displeasure in perceiving something.

What of *being alive*? It would seem that the word may be taken in two ways. In one sense, "being alive" connotes a physiological property. And therefore, in this sense, it implies but does not include the property of being a physiological organ. And, in another sense, it is essentially dispositional and thus involves certain properties (physiological or psychological) that it does not imply.

What of *being a person*? It may be plausibly maintained that being a person is necessary to whatever has it and is therefore not a property.

What of *sick* and *healthy*? The words may be taken in one or the other of three different ways—but on no interpretation do they provide us with a counterexample to our thesis. (i) They may refer to certain *physiological* properties; in this case the properties will imply but not include the property of being a physiological organ. (ii) They may be used, psychologically, to mean the same, respectively, as "feeling ill" and "feeling well"; in this case, the properties that they connote will satisfy our thesis. Or (iii) the words may be used in a way that is tantamount to a disjunction of the first two uses—to connote the attribute of either being in such and such a physiological state or feeling in such and such a way. In this case, the attribute in question would involve certain attributes it does not include.

We have been unable to find any nonpsychological attribute that satisfies our formula. I conclude, therefore, that the formula gives us a *sufficient condition* of the psychological.

The Definition

We will now propose a definition which will give a *necessary* as well as a sufficient condition of the psychological.

We could say that any attribute satisfying our formula is "purely qualitative."

> D6 *P* is a purely qualitative attribute =Df. *P* is a property which (a) is possibly such that it is exemplified by just one thing and (b) includes every property it implies or involves.

We will now introduce a somewhat broader concept of *qualitative* which will enable us to say that any disjunction of purely qualitative attributes is a qualitative attribute.[1]

> D7 *P* is a qualitative attribute =Df. Either (a) *P* is a purely qualitative attribute or (b) *P* is equivalent to a disjunction of attributes each of which is purely qualitative.

Judging and *wanting* will be qualitative by this definition. But *judging that there are unicorns* and *wanting a sloop* will not be qualitative, for each involves a property it does not include. Hence, the above concept is not identical with that of the psychological, since *judging that there are unicorns* and *wanting a sloop* are both psychological attributes.

We can now define a broad sense of the psychological:

> D8 *P* is a psychological attribute =Df. *P* includes an attribute that is qualitative.

Some attributes that are thus psychological are not *purely* psychological—e.g., believing truly that it is raining and wishing in vain for a sloop. What, then, would a purely psychological attribute be? I suggest this:

D9 *P* is purely psychological =Df. *P* is psychological and every property it implies involves something qualitative.

Our definition applies only to those psychological attributes that are nondispositional. But one may wish to say of certain dispositions—being irascible, for example—that they, too, are psychological. Given the concept of a disposition, we could readily extend our definition to such cases. We could say that, in an extended sense of "psychological attribute," a disposition to have a psychological attribute is itself a psychological attribute.

Concerning those attributes that are purely psychological, we may affirm the following material epistemic principle:

If the attribute of being *F* is a purely psychological attribute, then, for every *x*, if *x* has the attribute of being *F*, then it is certain for *x* that he is *F*.

This principle could be said to tell us that every purely psychological attribute is "self-presenting." But the principle does not hold of those attributes that are only "partly psychological." A person may have the attribute of thinking while wearing a hat or that of thinking about his brother without thereby being *certain* that he is thinking while wearing a hat or that he is thinking about his brother.[2]

NOTES

1. An attribute *D* may be said to be a disjunction of two attributes, *P* and *Q*, provided only *D* involves *P* and *D* involves *Q*, and *D* is necessarily such that, for every *x*, *x* has *D* if and only if either *x* has *P* or *x* has *Q*.

2. I am indebted to Fred Feldman, Richard Foley, Richard Potter, Philip Quinn, Allen Renear, Bruno Schuwey, Robert Shope, Ernest Sosa, and Michael Zimmerman.

35

On the Logic of Self-Knowledge

Hector-Neri Castañeda

In *Knowledge and Belief* Jaakko Hintikka has made the most important contribution, so far, to the problem of formalizing the logic of the concept *knowledge*.[1] He has construed a semantical system with a primitive modal operator "K" governed by the rule of formation: "K_aP" is a well-formed formula of the system, if *a* is a personal individual constant or a variable ranging over persons and p is a well-formed formula of the system. If *a* is a constant, "K_aP" is to be interpreted as the object-language statement to the effect that the person designated by *a* knows that what p formulates is true. In the *Journal of Symbolic Logic* I pointed out that Hintikka's system suffers from two serious inadequacies as a formalization of the concept *knowledge*.[2]

The first serious inadequacy comes about as follows. In order to meet Quine's challenges[3] about the interpretation of free (but bindable) variables in referentially opaque contexts, Hintikka makes his free variables in contexts of the form "$K_a (\ldots)$" range over objects or persons known to the person referred to by *a*. This is an ingenious device that does meet some of Quine's challenges, but it prevents Hintikka's calculus from allowing consistent formalizations of some consistent statements, e.g., "There is a person such that Jones does not know that he [the person in question] exists." The calculus does allow the natural symbolization of statements like "Jones does not know that Smith is self-identical": introduce the dictionary

Jones: j;   Smith: s;

From *Noûs* 1, no. 1 (March 1967): 9–21. Reprinted by permission of Blackwell Publishers.

and we can symbolize the statement with the formula "~K_j(s = s)." But the calculus does not allow the formalization of the perfectly consistent statement

(P) Everybody identical with Smith is not known by Jones to be self-identical.

The natural candidate "(x) (x = s • ⊃ • ~K_j[x = x])" expresses the quite different statement "Everybody known to Jones who is identical with Smith is not known by Jones to be self-identical," restricting ourselves to a universe of discourse of persons. This is so because the (bindable) variable "x" appears free in "K_j (x = x)" and must, therefore, range over persons known to Jones. Another natural candidate is the formula "(x) (y) (x = y & y = s • ⊃ • ~K_j[x = x])," where the variable "y" does range over all the persons in the universe of discourse, whether known to Jones or not. But the last formula still has "x" ranging over persons known to Jones, so that it only expresses the weaker statement

(Q) Everybody known to Jones who is identical with a person identical with Smith is not known by Jones to be self-identical.

Statements P and Q are not only clearly different, but are particularly different on Hintikka's proposed interpretation for his calculus. Hintikka allows a person to know singular statements to be true, even though the individuals the statements are about do not exist. Thus, Q for Hintikka does not entail R: "Jones does not know that Smith is self-identical," because Jones may very well believe that Smith does not exist and so believing he must know that Smith is self-identical. On the other hand, P does entail R.

The second serious difficulty of Hintikka's calculus consists in that statements formulating self-knowledge cannot be formalized in it. For instance, statements like "Jones knows that he himself is a millionaire" cannot be formalized in his calculus, since the latter has no expression that on the proposed interpretation of the calculus can be adequately interpreted as the "he himself" in this example.

My purpose here is threefold: (a) to formulate some fundamental principles of the logic of self-knowledge, (b) to show that the second inadequacy in Hintikka's calculus is very serious, even more than it was indicated in my review of Hintikka's book, and (c) to suggest some amendments to Hintikka's system that will make it adequate as far as the logic of self-knowledge is concerned. These amendments involve interpreting free variables in the context "K_a (. . .)" just as Hintikka does in his system. Thus, here is a reduction of the second major difficulty to the first one.

Since Hintikka's calculus for "know" attempts to formalize no other psychological (or linguistic) concept, it will save circumlocution to limit our discussion to that part of English which is extensional except for having expressions for the concept of knowledge, but has no expressions for other referentially opaque concepts.

1. *The "he" of self-knowledge.* Hintikka is aware that a statement like "Jones knows that he (himself) is Jones" raises a serious problem of formalization.[4] Obviously, "$K_j(j = j)$" won't do, where "j" stands for "Jones." Hintikka's ingenious interpretation of free variables in contexts of the form "$K_a(\ldots)$" allows him to propose a symbolization that at first sight seems adequate, namely, "$(Ey)(y = j \;\&\; K_j[y = j])$," which is equivalent to "$(Ey) K_j(y = j)$." By his rules of interpretation the latter is to be read as "There exists a person known to Jones such that Jones knows that he [the person in question] is Jones," or as "There exists a person whom Jones knows and knows to be identical with Jones."[5] Since the person in question is Jones himself, it is natural to think that if Jones knows that person he can identify him, in particular, point to him, and surely in such a case he would be pointing to himself; it seems then that for Jones to know that such a person is Jones is for him to know that he himself is Jones.

Yet, on a closer inspection things are not so clear. As Hintikka himself claims:

> The criteria as to when one may be said to know who this or that man is are highly variable. Sometimes knowing the name of the person in question suffices; . . . our discussion is independent of this difficulty, however. We have decided to study sets of statements only when all their members are logically comparable with each other. This presupposes that *one and the same set of criteria is used to decide their truth or falsity.*[6]

Now, on customary criteria that we apply when we claim to know who a certain historical figure is, a man, say, X, can know who a certain person Y is, without knowing that Y is he himself. For example, suppose that X is brought unconscious to a certain military tent; that on gaining consciousness X suffers from amnesia and during the next months becomes a war hero that gets lost in combat and forgets the military chapter of his life, and that later X studies all the accounts of the war hero and discovers that the hero was, e.g., the only one in the war wounded 100 times. For many normal situations, e.g., passing a history examination, X knows who the hero was. In many such situations "There exists a man known to the war hero wounded 100 times such that the war hero wounded 100 times knows that such a man is identical with the war hero wounded 100 times" is true. Yet in all such situations X may fail to know that he himself is the war hero wounded 100 times, that is "The war hero wounded 100 times knows that he himself is the war hero wounded 100 times" may still be false.

The crucial point is this: whereas there are criteria that a man's third-person references to objects or persons must meet to be successful, there are no criteria of success for his first-person references. For any strictly third-person description, or name, D of a person one can come to know whom D applies to by satisfying purely third-person criteria, without in the least being required to take the additional step "and I am the one D refers to." The use of the third-person pronoun at issue here is precisely one that consists of serving to attribute to someone first-person references. To say "X knows that he himself is φ" is to attribute to X knowledge that he can and *must* put by saying "I am φ."[7] Thus, if we are to abide by Hintikka's semantical rule that every interpretation of a set of his formulas presupposes the *same* set of criteria for the truth of "knows who," then: either (i) first-person self-knowledge is left out, in case provision is not made for first-personal reference that involves no criteria, or (ii) some third-person knowledge of oneself is left out in case all contexts of the form "(Ey) (y = a & K$_a$[. . . y . . .])" are interpreted as formulating self-knowledge that involves criterionless first-person reference, or (iii) ambiguities arise by allowing both interpretations.

The difficulties of the "he" of self-knowledge are compounded by the fact that sometimes it is a constant, and sometimes it is a variable of quantification. It is a variable in "A thinking being who knows that he exists is a person."

In my *Journal of Symbolic Logic* review[8] I suggested that a special operator that forms individual signs be employed to represent the "he himself" of self-knowledge. Let "s" be this special operator. Then "s(a)" was to be an individual sign whenever a is an individual sign having no "s." A statement like "Jones does not know that he himself is Jones" was to be symbolized as "~K$_j$(s [j] = j)." Clearly, "~K$_j$ ~(s[j]) = j)" is false, even though Jones can believe" that ~(s[j] = j). On the other hand, for every person x, K$_x$ (s[x] s[x]): this is a fact about himself that every person knows without criterion.

The above suggestion is good as far as the examples go. But it is wholly inadequate to handle certain complexities of the pronoun "he" used to express self-knowledge. To begin with, consider

(1) The tallest man knows that the tallest man knows that he himself is fat.

This sentence is ambiguous in a very interesting way, that can be brought out by considering the first-person counterparts of (1) that the tallest man can formulate:

(2) I know that the tallest man knows that he himself is fat,
(3) I know that the tallest man knows that I am fat.

The statements formulated by (2) and (3) are quite different inasmuch as the tallest man may fail to know that he himself is the tallest man. Syntactically, the ambiguity of (1) lies in that the grammatical and logical antecedent of "he himself" in (1) may be either of the two occurrences of "the tallest man" in (1). Thus, if in accordance with my review, we symbolize "he himself" in (1) as "s(the tallest man)" we produce an ambiguous symbolization.

Fortunately, ordinary language suggests here a solution. The two senses of (1), as clarified by (2) and (3), are naturally formulated by

(4) The tallest man knows that the tallest man knows that the latter is fat,

and (5) The tallest man knows that the tallest man knows that the former is fat,

where the phrases "the former" and "the latter" are certainly not descriptions whose use is attributed to the tallest man. They are simply indices employed by the person using (4) or (5) to indicate the pattern of cross-reference in his own statement: the reference attributed to the tallest man is still first-personal, either directly as in (2), or indirectly as in (3). Taking this cue, I suggest that "he himself" in (1) be symbolized either as "(the tallest man)$_1$" or as "(the tallest man)$_2$," depending on whether (4) or (5) is meant, respectively.

Consider now:

(6) The tallest man knows that *he himself* knows that Mary knows that *he himself* is fat.

The first occurrence of "he himself" refers back to "the tallest man'; and so does the second occurrence of "he himself, except that this pronoun is used to attribute also first-person references to the person referred to as "he himself" in the first occurrence. This may be described by saying that the second occurrence of "he himself" has "the tallest man" as its *remote antecedent* and the first occurrence of "he himself" as its *immediate antecedent*. As in this case, there may be an expression of the form ". . . knows that" between an occurrence of "he himself" and its immediate antecedent.

Let us say that the *distance* between "he himself" and its immediate antecedent is the number of expressions of the form ". . . knows that" in whose scope the occurrence of "he himself" in question lies and in whose scope the immediate antecedent does not lie. I propose to symbolize a given occurrence O of "he himself" that formulates self-knowledge, by means of an expression of the form "$(a)_n$," where "a" stands for the remote antecedent of O and "n" is a numeral expressing the distance between O and its immediate antecedent. Thus, if we let "a" abbreviate "the tallest man" and "m" abbreviate "Mary," we can partially symbolize (6) as "$K_{(a)} K_{(a)1} K_m ([a]_2$ is fat)."

From the above it is apparent that occurrences of "he himself " that express self-knowledge involve indices, and that they can only appear in contexts of the form "X knows that (. . .)" (or of similar contexts of propositional attitudes). To nail this down, consider the inference

(7) Jones knows that he [himself] is wise, hence he is wise.

The occurrence of the pronoun "he" in the conclusion is not of the same logical type as the "he [himself]" in the premise. On the one hand, "he [himself]" attributes first-person references to Jones, while the conclusion's "he" does not do so, but merely formulates a third-person reference by the one who draws the inference to Jones. On the other hand, "he is wise" does not formulate the conclusion by itself: it is merely an abbreviation in the context of the inference of the conclusion "Jones is wise," while the premise including its "he [himself]" is complete as it is (aside from the indeterminacy of "Jones").

Doubtless, the clause "he [himself] is wise" is by itself incomplete. Since "he [himself]" is not here a demonstrative pronoun, it must have an antecedent. But as it is used in the premise of (7), it cannot be replaced by its antecedent, nor by any other description or name of Jones, *salva propositione*: its special sense as a means of attributing first-person references to Jones requires that the whole clause "he [himself] is wise" be subordinated to the verb "know (that)," (or of course, to some other verb that expresses a propositional attitude or act, as "believe," "conjecture," or "assert"). Not only the pronoun "he [himself]" in this special sense, but also the whole clause "he [himself] is wise," is, then, a syncategorematic expression. And this feature is very nicely brought out by our subscript notation. While the name "Jones" and the description "the war hero wounded 100 times" may be said to have an independent or categorematic sense, the expressions "(Jones)$_n$" and "(the war hero wounded 100 times)$_n$," for n = a positive integer, bear on their faces their need for n prefixes of the form "X knows (that)."

To return to inference (7). In the light of the above, and with obvious abbreviations, (7) is really the inference:

(7a) K_j (j_1 is wise), hence j is wise.

This must be carefully distinguished from:

(8) K_j (j is wise), hence j is wise.

Clearly, K_j (j_1 is wise)" may be true while "K_j (j is wise)" is false, and vice versa. Now, (8) is perfectly innocent. It is an illustration of two rules which are widely accepted:

(R1) From "X knows that p" infer that p;

(R2) From a premise of the form "X knows that" detach the clause ". . ." and use it with the same meaning and references to formulate a valid conclusion.

These rules are customarily taken to be grounded in the principle, which is of course true that

> (P) if X knows that (. . .) then the proposition formulated by the clause filling ". . ." is true.

Inference (7), or (7a), on the other hand is interesting in that it is not validated by (R1) or by (R2). It is not validated by (R1) since the proposition (or statement) "Jones is wise," which appears as the conclusion of (7), is not the same proposition that, according to the premise of (7), Jones knows to be true: the latter is constituted by a first-person reference by Jones, while the former is merely a third-person statement by the one who draws the inference. Inference (7) is not validated by (R2), given that the clause "he is wise" in the conclusion of (7) has a different meaning or sense from the one "he [himself] is wise" has in the premise. This is more transparent in the perspicuous version (7a), where detaching "j_1 is wise" produces nonsense. From here on, to avoid circumlocution we shall make our discussion in terms of subscripted nouns or phrases, rather than in terms of the "he" of self-knowledge. This involves no loss of generality.

The fact that (7), or (7a), is not validated by either (R1) or (R2) creates a vexing problem. On the one hand, we must give up the idea of a simple rule of detachment like (R2) if we are to have a formal calculus in which no expression is ambiguous. On the other hand, since (7), or (7a), is clearly valid, we must find the general rule, to replace for the invalid or inapplicable (R1), under which general rule (7) falls as a very simple instance. That the rule to substitute for (R1) is hard to formulate is shown by the following example:

> (9) The war hero wounded 100 times knows that Smith knows that he [= (the war hero wounded 100 times)$_2$] is tall.

How is the proposition that the war hero wounded 100 times knows, to be stated by itself, in direct speech? No doubt, the hero could state it by saying "Smith knows that I am tall." This formulation does raise, however, problems of its own, e.g.: (i) in order for the hero to derive it from (9) he needs another premise, namely, "I am the war hero wounded 100 times," so that his valid inference would not be an instance of (R1); (ii) the hero's statement "Smith knows that I am tall" seems to attribute to Smith a first-person reference, which is out of the question since the word "I" refers here to the hero.[9]

Here let us worry only about how can another person than the hero state the proposition which by (P) one could infer from (9). The problem lies in that the clause

> (10) Smith knows that he [= (the war hero wounded 100 times)$_2$] is tall

is syncategorematic, as the index "2" perspicuously signals. The occurrence of "he" in it stands in need of a grammatical and logical antecedent. If the English clause were to be used as a (complete) sentence by itself, it would be either senseless or would have to be construed as having "Smith" as the antecedent of "he." But in either case, the sentence would fail to formulate what by (9) the hero knows, for it would then formulate the statement "Smith knows that he [=(Smith)$_1$] is tall." The only solution in practical life is to use the clause (10) in dependence of an antecedent especially provided in each occasion. For instance, Brown may say something about the war hero wounded 100 times and then say "Smith knows that he, namely the hero (or Jones, or . . .), is tall," where Brown's "namely the hero (or Jones, or . . .)" is his own device for making cross-references for the benefit of his audience.

In short, there seems to be no fixed sentence for formulating precisely and unambiguously in *oratio recta* the proposition that by (9) our war hero knows to be true. I am inclined to think that the difficulty is due to the fact that the proposition in question involves quantification over properties. I am inclined to hold that (9) should be analyzed as

(9A) The war hero wounded 100 times knows that: there is a property φ-ness such that both he [=(the war hero wounded 100 times)$_1$] is the only one who is φ, and Smith knows that the only one who is φ is tall.

But this view has certain complications. At any rate, it is illuminating to consider other alternatives. One alternative, which can be formalized (up to a point) in Hintikka's calculus, is this. Inasmuch as by (9) the occurrence of "he" ascribes a first-person reference to our war hero, such a reference is not the one that Smith makes to the war hero. Thus, we construe that occurrence of "he" as ascribing to Smith some unspecified reference to the hero, and we construe this unspecified reference, not in terms of quantification over properties, but in terms of quantification over persons. In short, we analyze (9) as

(9B) The war hero wounded 100 times knows that: there is a person, say y, such that both he [=(the war hero wounded 100 times)$_1$] is y and Smith knows that y is tall.

Inasmuch as Hintikka interprets his free variables in "K_a"-contexts as ranging over persons (or objects) known to the person *a*, his analysis of (9) in the framework of our discussion of the "he" of self-knowledge would have to be

(9C) The war hero wounded 100 times knows that: there is a person, say y, known to Smith such that both he [=(the war hero wounded 100 times)$_1$] is y and Smith knows that y is tall.

This last would be symbolizable in Hintikka's calculus extended with the above subscript notation as "K_a (Ey) (y = $[a]_1$ & K_b (Ty)," with an obvious dictionary.

There is no room here for an examination of the merits of each of the analyses (9A)–(9C). Note, however, that there is neither a standard formulation of, nor a settled view on, what exactly is the proposition that by (9) our war hero knows to be true. As a result, there is no simple formulation of the rule which is to replace (R1) and which has inference (7), or (7a), as an instance of its simplest type.

Here I want to develop the point of view of (9B). To start with, note that since we are eliminating the ambiguities of the third-person pronoun when used to attribute self-knowledge by means of the subscript notation, the rule which is to replace (R1) can be taken to be a rule which also replaces (R2).

Suppose that we have a premise of the form "X knows that φ," where φ contains just one occurrence o of just one expression of the form "$(X)_n$" whose immediate antecedent is the very first occurrence of X from the left. By the discussion of inference (7) and sentence (9) we know that we cannot simply detach φ and produce a valid conclusion from our premise: o is nonsensical since it does not have its antecedent in φ. Let n=1. Then, as in the case of (7a), from "X knows that φ" we can derive the statement expressed by φ', where φ' is exactly like φ except for having an occurrence of X instead of o. If n-2, as (9) shows, we cannot validly derive the statement expressed by the corresponding φ'. Then we must analyze "X knows that φ" in the way we analyzed (9) as (9B). This analysis eliminates the occurrence o of "$(X)_2$" in favor of both quantification and an occurrence o' of "$(X)_1$." Now we are back to the case n=1, and can proceed as we did in (7a). Suppose that n=3,4, ... Then the present view can be developed in different ways, for instance: (i) by applying the type of analysis illustrated by (9) and (9B) piecemeal so as to eliminate the occurrence o of "$(X)_n$" in favor of an occurrence of "$(X)_{n-1}$"; (ii) by applying that type of analysis wholesale so as to eliminate o directly in favor of an occurrence of "$(X)_2$." We shall adopt (i) here.

Consider now a case in which there are two occurrences of expressions of the form "$(X)_n$":

(11) A knows that B knows that he [=$(A)_2$] knows that he [=$(A)_1$] is tall.

In (11) the immediate antecedent of "$(A)_2$" is the leftmost occurrence of A, while the immediate antecedent of "$(A)_1$" is "$(A)_2$." In this case we want to apply the type of analysis that we applied to (9), so as to find:

(11B) A knows that: there is a person, say y, such that both y = $(A)_1$ and B knows that y knows that he [= $(y)_1$] is tall.

The interesting things here are that "$(A)_1$" is eliminated, even though its immediate antecedent is not A, and that it yields to a subscripted variable of quantification.

With this background we can now offer the rule which is to replace (R1) and (R2). It is

(R*) From statement expressed with a sentence of the form "X knows that φ," infer the statement expressed with a sentence φ', where φ' is obtained from φ by eliminating every occurrence of "$(X)_n$" whose immediate antecedent is the initial occurrence of X, by the procedure illustrated by (9B) and (11B) if n=2, 3, . . . , and by the procedure illustrated by (7a) if n=1.

2. *Revision of Hintikka's calculus.* The above analysis of statements formulating self-knowledge involves quantification into referentially opaque contexts. Thus, it has to be grounded on some valid approach to the queries raised by Quine.[10] [5], 141–56. We cannot discuss this matter here. But, even though Hintikka's interpretation of such quantification is not wholly adequate, it is at least adequate for some kinds of inferences involving the concept of knowledge. At any rate, the choice between analyses (9B) and (9A) will undoubtedly depend on the final view of the role of free variables in referentially opaque contexts. Thus, it is worthwhile to reduce the question of the analysis of "$(X)_n$" for n=2,3, . . . to the question of free variables in opaque contexts. In the case of Hintikka's calculus, by revising it to include individual signs of the form "$(X)_n$" we at least reduce one of its two major difficulties to the other. This revision is useful also in that it provides an opportunity for stating rule (R*) in a precise way.

The first change that can be made in Hintikka's calculus to make it adequate to handle self-knowledge is to introduce a primitive notation for the numerals. But this can be avoided by making "$(X)_n$" a mere abbreviation of "(X) (X) . . . (X)," n times. Then the first revision should consist of the following *formulation rule*: Expressions of the form "(X) (X) . . . (X)," n times, are well-formed expressions and are individual signs, if X is an individual personal sign, variable or constant.

The second change in Hintikka's calculus consists of dropping his principles that correspond to rules (R1) and (R2). They are his principles (C.K*) and (C.k*).

The third revision consists in dropping Hintikka's principle that involves his inadequate formalization of "X knows that he is X." That principle is (CKK*, qualified form), which amounts to: "$K_a(p)$ & $(Ex) K_a (x=a)$" entails "$K_a K_a(p)$."

The fourth revision consists of introducing to the rest of Hintikka's calculus the principle of the analysis of "$(X)_n$," which in the present case yields analyses of the kind illustrated in (9C). For this we need some machinery. Let μ be a wff of the calculus of the form "$K_a . . . K_b(φ)$" where in φ there are occurrences $o_1, . . . , o_k$, for k > 0, of "$(a)_n$" which occurrences have as immediate antecedent the initial occurrence of a in μ, where n > 1. Let y be a personal variable not occurring at all in μ. Let φ' result from φ by the following operations: each occurrence $o_1, . . . , o_k$, of "$(a)_n$" is replaced by one occurrence of y, and each occurrence of "$(a)_m$" in φ having one of the occurrences $o_1, \ldots,$ o_k as immediate antecedent is replaced by one occurrence of "$(y)_m$." Then:

(P*) μ is equivalent to "$K_a \ldots (Ey) (y = [a]_{n-1} \,\&\, K_b [\varphi'])$"

The fifth revision consists of introducing in Hintikka's calculus a precise formulation of rule (R*). Consider $K_a (\varphi)$." Either φ has no occurrences of "$(a)_n$," for $n=1, 2, \ldots,$ whose immediate antecedent is the initial occurrence o of a in "$K_a (\varphi)$," or φ does have some occurrences. In the former case, let "φ^*" be the same as φ. In the latter case, eliminate each of the occurrences of "$(a)_n$" in question by means of (P*) for $n=2, 3, \ldots,$ and eliminate the new occurrences of "$(a)_n$" until there are only occurrences of "$(a)_1$"; then replace each occurrence of "$(a)_1$" whose immediate antecedent is o by an occurrence of a, and let the final result be "φ^*." Then:

(R*)   From "$K_a (\varphi)$" you may derive "φ^*."

This rule can be easily put in the way Hintikka phrases his rules.

3. *Remarks:* A. What has been said here about "know" applies equally well to all other verbs expressing propositional attitudes like "believe," "think," "imagine that," "conjecture," "say," and "assert."

B. What has been said about the third-person pronoun used to attribute self-knowledge applies also to all other ways of attributing to a person demonstrative reference. For example, in "At time t Gaskon thought that he was to die then" the word "then" has "at time t" as its antecedent, but if it attributes to Gaskon a demonstrative reference to time t, it is syncategorematic and must be construed as "(at time t)₁." Expressions which in *oratio oblique* attribute to someone demonstrative reference, like "he," "then," "there," "it," are called *quasi-indicators* in my work on "Indicators and Quasi-indicators."

NOTES

1. Ithaca, N.Y.: Cornell University Press, 1962.

2. Review of Jakko Hintikka's *Knowledge and Belief* in *The Journal of Symbolic Logic* 29 (1964): 132–34.

3. For example, in W. V. O. Quine, *Word and Object* (New York: The Massachusetts Institute of Technology Press and John Wiley & Sons, 1969), pp. 141–56.

4. Hintikka's *Knowledge and Belief,* p. 159.

5. Ibid., pp. 132, 155, 159.

6. Ibid., p. 149 note 9 (my italics).

7. For a detailed discussion of this use of "he" see Hector-Heri Castañeda " 'He': The Logic of Self-Consciousness," *Ratio* 8, no. 2 (December 1966), section 4.

8. Review, *The Journal of Symbolic Logic,* p. 134.

9. But for these and other questions see " 'He': The Logic of Self-Consciousness," section 3, and my "Indicators and Quasi-indicators," *The American Philosophical Quarterly* 4, no. 2 (April 1967), section 4.

10. Quine, *Word and Object,* pp. 141–56.

Bibliography

Aaron, Richard I. *Knowing and the Function of Reason.* London: Oxford University Press, 1971.

Achinstein, Peter. *The Concept of Evidence: Oxford Readings in Philosophy.* London: Oxford University Press, 1983.

Ackermann, Robert J. *Belief and Knowledge.* New York: Doubleday & Co. Anchor Books, 1972.

Adler, Mortimer J. *Intellect: Mind Over Matter.* New York: Collier Books, 1990.

Agassi, Joseph, and Ian Charles Jarvie, eds. *Rationality: The Critical View.* Dordrecht, Netherlands: Martinus Nijhoff Publishers, 1987.

Almeder, Robert. *Blind Realism: An Essay on Human Knowledge and Natural Science.* Lanham, Md.: Rowman and Littlefield Publishers, Inc. 1992.

Alston, William P. *Epistemic Justification: Essays in the Theory of Knowledge.* Ithaca, N.Y.: Cornell University Press, 1989.

———. *The Reliability of Sense Perception.* Ithaca, N.Y.: Cornell University Press, 1993.

Amico, Robert P. *The Problem of the Criterion.* Lanham, Md., Rowman & Littlefield, Inc., 1993.

Ammerman, Robert R., and Marcus G. Singer, eds. *Belief, Knowledge, and Truth Readings in the Theory of Knowledge.* New York: Charles Scribner's Sons, 1970.

Anderson, Richard C., and David P. Ausubel, eds. *Readings in the Psychology of Cognition.* New York: Holt, Rinehart and Winston, Inc., 1965.

Aquinas, Thomas. *Treatise On Law, On Truth and Falsity, On Human Knowledge.* Los Angeles: Gateway Editions, Inc., 1949.

Archmbault, Reginald D., ed. *Philosophical Analysis and Education.* London: Routledge & Kegan Paul, 1965.

Armstrong, D. M. *Belief, Truth, and Knowledge.* London: Cambridge University Press, 1973.

———. *Bodily Sensations.* London: Routledge & Kegan Paul, 1962.

———. *Perception and the Physical World.* London: Routledge & Kegan Paul, 1961.

Arner, Douglas G., ed. *Perception, Reason, & Knowledge: An Introduction to Epistemology.* Glenview, Ill.: Scott, Foresman & Co., 1972.

Asher, Harry. *Experiments in Seeing.* Greenwich, Conn.: Fawcett Premier, 1961.

Atkinson, R. F. *Knowledge and Explanation in History: An Introduction to the Philosophy of History.* London, Macmillan Education Ltd., 1978.

Audi, Robert. *Belief, Justification, and Knowledge.* Belmont, Calif.: Wadsworth, 1988.

———. *The Structure of Justification.* London: Cambridge University Press, 1993.

Aune, Bruce. *Knowledge, Mind and Nature: An Introduction to Theory of Knowledge and the Philosophy of Mind.* New York: Random House, Inc., 1967.

———. *Rationalism, Empiricism, and Pragmatism: An Introduction.* New York: Random House, Inc., 1970.

Austin, J. L. *Philosophical Papers.* London: Oxford University Press, 1961.

———. *Sense and Sensibilia.* London: Oxford University Press, 1962.

Ayer, Alfred Jules (A. J.). *The Foundations of Empirical Knowledge.* London and New York: Macmillan & Co., 1962. [Original edition 1940.]

———. *Language, Truth, and Logic,* 2d ed. New York: Dover Publications, Inc., 1946. [1st ed. 1936.]

———. *Philosophical Essays.* London and New York, Macmillan & Co., Ltd., 1954.

———. *Probability and Evidence.* New York: Columbia University Press, 1972.

———. *The Problem of Knowledge.* Baltimore, Md.: Penguin Books, 1956.

Ayers, Michael. *Locke: Epistemology and Ontology.* London and New York: Rutledge, 1991.

Baergen, Ralph. *Contemporary Epistemology.* Fort Worth, Tex.: Harcourt, 1995.

Baille, John. *Our Knowledge of God.* New York: Charles Scribner's Sons, 1939.

Bartlett, F.C. *Remembering: A Study in Experimental and Social Psychology.* London: Cambridge University Press, 1932.

Bennett, Jonathan. *Locke, Berkeley, Hume: Central Themes.* London: Oxford University Press, 1971.

———. *Rationality: An Essay Toward Analysis.* London and New York: Routledge & Kegan Paul, 1964.

Bergson, Henri. *Matter and Memory.* Garden City, N.Y.: Doubleday Anchor Book, 1911.

Berkeley, George. *A Treatise Concerning the Principles of Human Knowledge with Critical Essays.* Indianapolis, Ind.: The Bobbs-Merrill Company, Inc., 1957.

Berkson, William, and John Wettersten. *Learning from Error: Karl Popper's Psychology of Learning.* LaSalle, Ill.: Open Court Publishing Company, 1984.

Bigge, Morris L. *Learning Theories for Teachers.* New York: Harper & Row, Publishers, 1964.

Bird, Graham. *Kant's Theory of Knowledge.* London, Routledge & Kegan Paul, 1962.

Blackstone, William T. *The Problem of Religious Knowledge: The Impact of Philosophical Analysis on the Question of Religious Knowledge.* Englewood Cliffs, N.J.: Prentice-Hall, 1963.

Blanshard, Brand. *The Nature of Thought, Volumes One & Two.* New York: The Humanities Press, 1964.

———. *Reason and Analysis.* LaSalle, Ill.: Open Court Publishing Co., 1964.

Boër, Stephen E., and William G. Lycan. *Knowing Who.* Cambridge, Mass.: MIT Press, 1986.

Bogdan, Radu J. *Keith Lehrer.* Dordrecht, Netherlands: D. Reidel Publishing Company, 1981.

———. *Roderick M. Chisholm.* Dordrecht, Netherlands: D. Reidel Publishing Co., 1986.

Bonjour, Laurence. *The Structure of Empirical Knowledge.* Cambridge, Mass.: Harvard University Press, 1985.

Brandl, Johannes, Wolfgang L. Gombocz, and Christian Piller, eds. *Metamind, Knowledge and Coherence: Essays on the Philosophy of Keith Lehrer.* Amsterdam, Netherlands, Rodopi, 1991.

Brentano, Franz. *The Origins of Our Knowledge of Right and Wrong.* New York: Routledge & Kegan Paul, 1969.

———. *The True and the Evident.* London: The Humanities Press, 1966.

Bronowski, Jacob. *The Origins of Knowledge and Imagination.* New Haven, Conn.: Yale University Press, 1978.

Brown, Harold I. *Observation and Objectivity.* New York and Oxford: Oxford University Press, 1987.

———. *Perception, Theory, and Commitment: The New Philosophy of Science.* Chicago and London: The University of Chicago Press, 1977.

Brumbaugh, Robert S. *Philosophers on Education: Six Essays on the Foundations of Western Thought.* Boston: Houghton Mifflin Company, 1963.

Bruner, Jerome. *On Knowing: Essays for the Left Hand.* New York: Atheneum, 1962

———. *The Process of Education.* New York: Random House Vintage Books, 1960.

———. *Toward a Theory of Instruction.* New York: W. W. Norton & Company, 1966.

Buber, Martin. *The Knowledge of Man: A Philosophy of the Interhuman.* New York-Harper Torchbooks, 1965.

Burnyeat, Myles., ed. *The Sceptical Tradition.* Berkeley: University of California Press, 1983.

Butchvarov, Panayot. *The Concept of Knowledge.* Evanston, Ill.: Northwestern University Press, 1970.

Butler, R. J., ed. *Cartesian Studies.* Oxford: Basil Blackwell, 1972.

Canfield, John V., and Franklin H. Donnell, Jr., eds. *Readings in the Theory of Knowledge.* New York: Appleton-Century-Crofts, 1964.

Capaldi, Nicholas. *Human Knowledge: A Philosophical Analysis of Its Meaning and Scope.* New York: Western Publishing Company, Inc., 1969.

Care, Norman S., and Robert H. Grimm, eds. *Perception and Personal Identity.* Cleveland, Ohio: The Case Western Reserve University, 1969.

Carruthers, Peter. *Human Knowledge and Human Nature.* London: Oxford University Press, 1992.

Cassam, Quassim, ed. *Self-Knowledge: Oxford Readings in Philosophy.* London: Oxford University Press, 1994.

Cassirer, Ernst. *The Philosophy of Symbolic Forms, Volume 3: The Phenomenology of Knowledge.* New Haven, Conn.: Yale University Press, 1965.

Castañeda, Hector-Neri, ed. *Action, Knowledge, and Reality: Critical Studies in Honor of Wilfrid Sellars.* Indianapolis, Ind.: Bobbs-Merrill Company, 1975.

Castañeda, Hector-Neri, ed. *Intentionality, Minds, and Perception.* Detroit, Mich.: Wayne State University Press, 1966.

Chappell, V .C., ed. *Hume: A Collection of Critical Essays.* Garden City, N.Y.: Doubleday & Company Anchor Books, 1966.

Chatalian, George. *Epistemology and Skepticism: An Enquiry into the Nature of Epistemology.* Carbondale: Southern Illinois University Press, 1991.

Cherniak, Christopher. *Minimal Rationality.* Cambridge, Mass.: MIT Press, 1986.

Chisholm, Roderick M. *The Foundations of Knowing.* Minneapolis: University of Minnesota Press, 1982.

———. *Perceiving: A Philosophical Study.* Ithaca, N.Y.: Cornell University Press, 1957.

———. *Person and Object: A Metaphysical Study.* LaSalle, Ill.: Open Court Publishing Company, 1976.

———. *The Problem of the Criterion: The Aquinas Lecture.* Milwaukee, Wisc.: Marquette University Press, 1973.

———. *Theory of Knowledge,* 3rd ed. Englewood Cliffs, N.J., Prentice-Hall, Inc., 1989. [2d ed., 1977.] [1st ed., 1966.]

Chisholm, Roderick M., ed. *Realism and the Background of Phenomenology.* Glencoe, Ill.: The Free Press, 1960.

Chisholm, Roderick M., et al. *Philosophy.* Englewood Cliffs, N.J., Prentice-Hall, Inc., 1964.

Chisholm, Roderick M., and Robert J. Swartz, eds. *Empirical Knowledge: Readings from Contemporary Sources.* Englewood Cliffs, N.J.: Prentice-Hall, Inc., 1973.

Chomsky, Noam. *Problems of Knowledge and Freedom: The Russell Lectures.* New York: Random House, Inc., 1971.

Church, Joseph. *Language and the Discovery of Reality: A Developmental Psychology of Cognition.* New York, Random House Vintage Books, 1961.

Clavell, Stanley. *The Claim of Reason: Wittgenstein, Skepticism, Morality, and Tragedy.* London, Oxford University Press, 1979.

Clay, Marjorie, and Keith Lehrer, eds. *Knowledge and Scepticism.* Boulder, Colo., Westview Press, Inc. 1989.

Coady, C. A. J. *Testimony: A Philosophical Study.* London, Oxford University Press, 1992.

Code, Lorraine. *Epistemic Responsibility.* Hanover, N.H.: Brown University Press, 1987.

Cofer, Charles N., ed. *The Structure of Human Memory.* San Francisco, Calif.: W. H. Freeman, 1976.

Coffey, P. *Epistemology: Or the Theory of Knowledge, Volume 1: An Introduction to General Metaphysics.* Bombay and New York: Longman, Green and Company, 1917.

Cohen, L. Jonathan. *The Dialogue of Reason: An Analysis of Analytic Philosophy.* London.: Oxford University Press,1986-

———. *The Probable and the Provable.* London: Oxford University Press, 1977.

Colodny, Robert G., ed. *Beyond the Edge of Certainty: Essays in Contemporary Science and Philosophy.* Englewood Cliffs, N.J.: Prentice-Hall, Inc., 1965.

Cornford, Frances M. *Plato's Theory of Knowledge: The Theaetetus and the Sophist of Plato, Translated with a Running Commentary.* New York, Library of Liberal Arts, 1957.

Cornforth, Maurice. *The Theory of Knowledge, Volume 3 of Dialectical Materialism: An Introduction.* New York: International Publishers, 1954.

Cornman, James W. *Materialism and Sensations.* New Haven, Conn.: Yale University Press, 1971.

———. *Perception, Common Sense, and Science.* New Haven, Conn.: Yale University Press, 1975.

———. *Skepticism, Justification, and Explanation.* Dordrecht, Netherlands: D. Reidel Publishing Company, 1980.

Cornman, James W., and Keith Lehrer. *Philosophical Problems and Arguments: An Introduction,* 2d ed. New York: Macmillan Publishing Co., Inc. 1974, 1st ed., 1968.

Cottingham, John. *Rationalism.* London: Paladin Books Granada Publishing, 1984.

Cournot, Antoine Augustin. *An Essay on the Foundations of Our Knowledge.* New York: The Liberal Arts Press, 1956.

Crombie, I. M. *An Examination of Plato's Doctrines, Volume II: Plato on Knowledge and Reality.* London and New York: Routledge and Kegan Paul, 1966.

Curley, Edwin M. *Descartes Against the Sceptics.* Oxford: Basil Blackwell, 1978.

Dancy, Jonathan. *Introduction to Contemporary Epistemology.* Oxford: Basil Blackwell, 1985.

Dancy, Jonathan, ed. *Perceptual Knowledge: Oxford Readings in Philosophy.* London: Oxford University Press, 1988.

Dancy, Jonathan, and Ernest Sosa, eds. *A Companion to Epistemology.* Oxford: Basil Blackwell, 1992.

Danto, Arthur C. *Analytical Philosophy of Knowledge.* London: Cambridge University Press, 1968.

Day, John Patrick. *Inductive Probability.* New York: The Humanities Press, 1961.

Dearden, R. F., and P. H. Hirst, and R. S. Peters, eds. *Reason: Part 2 of the Education and the Development of Reason.* London: Routledge & Kegan Paul, 1975.

De Condillac, Etienne Bonnot. *An Essay on the Origins of Human Knowledge.* Gainesville, Fla.: Scholars' Facsimiles & Reprints, 1971.

de Sousa, Ronald. *The Rationality of Emotion.* Cambridge, Mass.: MIT Press, 1987.

Detlefsen, Michael, ed. *Proof and Knowledge in Mathematics.* London and New York- Routledge, 1992.

de Vries, Willem A. *Reality, Knowledge, and the Good Life: A Historical Introduction to Philosophy.* New York: St. Martin's Press, 1991.

Dewey, John. *Experience and Education.* New York: Collier Books, 1938.

———. *Experience and Nature.* New York: Dover Publications, Inc., 1929.

———. *Knowing and the Known.* Boston: The Beacon Press, 1949.

———. *Philosophy of Education.* Totowa, N.J.: Littlefield, Adams & Co., 1946.

———. *The Quest for Certainty: Gifford Lectures 1929.* New York: Capricorn Books, 1929.

Dicker, Georges. *Descartes: An Analytical and Historical Introduction.* New York and Oxford: Oxford University Press, 1993.

———. *Perceptual Knowledge: An Analytical and Historical Study.* Dordrecht, Netherlands, D. Reidel Publishing Company, 1980.

Dommeyer, Frederick C., ed. *Current Philosophical Issues Essays in Honor of Curt John Ducasse.* Springfield, Ill.: Charles C. Thomas, Publisher, 1966.

Doney, Willis, ed. *Descartes: A Collection of Critical Essays.* Garden City, N.Y.: Doubleday & Company Anchor Books, 1967.

Doyle, James F., ed. *Educational Judgments: Papers in the Philosophy of Education.* London and Boston: Routledge & Kegan Paul, 1973.

Dretske, Fred I. *Knowledge and the Flow of Information.* Cambridge, Mass.: MIT Press, 1981.

Dretske, Fred I. *Seeing and Knowing.* London: Routledge & Kegan Paul, 1969.

Ducasse, Curt John. *Truth, Knowledge, and Causation.* New York: The Humanities Press, 1969.

Duncan, Ronald, and Miranda Weston-Smith, eds. *The Encyclopedia of Ignorance: Everything You Ever Wanted to Know About the Unknown.* New York: Simon & Schuster, 1977.

Eames, Elizabeth Ramsden. *Bertrand Russell's Theory of Knowledge.* London: George Allen & Unwin Ltd., 1969.

Eaton, Ralph Monroe. *Symbolism and Truth: An Introduction to the Theory of Knowledge.* Cambridge, Mass.: Harvard University Press, 1925.

Edwards, Paul, and Arthur Pap, eds. *A Modern Introduction to Philosophy: Readings from Classical and Contemporary Sources,* rev. ed. New York: The Free Press, 1965.

Eliot, T.S. *Knowledge and Experience in the Philosophy of F. H. Bradley.* New York: Columbia University Press, 1964.

Ellis, Brian. *Rational Belief Systems.* Totowa, N.J.: Rowman and Littlefield, Publishers, 1979.

Ellis, Richard B. *Statistical Inference: Basic Concepts.* Englewood, Cliffs, N.J.: Prentice-Hall, Inc., 1975.

Empiricus, Sextus. *Outlines of Pyrrhonism.* Trans. by R.G. Bury. Amherst, N.Y.: Prometheus Books, 1990.

———. *Outlines of Pyrrhonism, Volume 1.* Cambridge, Mass.: Harvard University Press, 1933.

Engle, Gale W., and Gabriele Taylor, eds. *Berkeley's Principles of Human Knowledge Critical Studies.* Belmont, Calif., Wadsworth Publishing Company, 1968.

Evans, C. O. *The Subject of Consciousness.* London and New York, George Allen & Unwin, 1970.

Evans, J. L. *Knowledge and Infallibility.* London: The Macmillan Press Ltd., 1978.

Ewing, A. C. *The Fundamental Questions of Philosophy.* New York: Collier Books, 1951.

———. *A Short Commentary on Kant's Critique of Pure Reason.* Chicago: University of Chicago Press, 1938.

Feldman, Fred. *A Cartesian Introduction to Philosophy.* New York: McGraw-Hill Book Company, 1986.

Ferrier, J. F. *Institutes of Metaphysic: The Theory of Knowing and Being,* 3rd ed. Edinburgh and London: William Blackwood and Sons, 1875.

Feyerabend, Paul K. *Against Method: Outline of an Anarchist Theory of Knowledge.* Atlantic Highlands and London: Humanities Press, 1975.

Feyerabend, Paul K. *Farewell to Reason.* London: Verso New Left Books, 1987.

———. *Problems of Empiricism: Philosophical Papers, Volume 2.* London: Cambridge University Press, 1981.

Fichte, J. G. *The Science of Knowledge.* Cambridge, U.K.: Cambridge University Press, 1982.

Fireman, Peter. *Perceptualist Theory of Knowledge.* New York: Philosophical Library, 1954.

Flew, Antony. *Hume's Philosophy of Belief: A Study of His First "Inquiry."* New York, The Humanities Press, 1961.

Fogelin, Robert J. *Evidence and Meaning: Studies in Analytic Philosophy.* New York, Humanities Press, 1967.

———. *Hume's Scepticism in the Treatise of Human Nature.* London: Routledge & Kegal Paul, 1985.

———. *Philosophical Interpretations.* London: Oxford University Press, 1992.

———. *Pyrrhonian Reflections on Knowledge and Justification.* London: Oxford University Press, 1994.

Foley, Richard. *The Theory of Epistemic Rationality.* Cambridge, Mass.: Harvard University Press, 1987.

———. *Working Without a Net: A Study of Egocentric Epistemology.* London: Oxford University Press, 1993.

Foster, Lawrence, and J.W. Swanson, eds. *Experience and Theory.* Amherst, Mass.: University of Massachusetts Press, 1970.

Foster, Marguerite H., and Michael L. Martin, eds. *Probability, Confirmation, and Simplicity: Readings in the Philosophy of Inductive Logic.* New York: Odyssey Press, 1966.

Fowler, Harold North. ed. and trans. *Plato's Theaetetus & Sophist.* Cambridge, Mass.: Harvard University Press, 1921.

Frankena, William K. *Three Historical Philosophies of Education: Aristotle, Kant, Dewey.* Glenview, Ill.: Scott, Foresman and Company, 1965,

French, Peter, Theodore E. Uehling, Jr., and Howard K. Wettstein, eds. *Studies in Epistemology, Midwest Studies in Philosophy,* Volume V. Minneapolis: University of Minnesota Press, 1980.

Frye, Albert Morton, and Albert William Levi. *Rational Belief: An Introduction to Logic.* New York: Harcourt, Brace and Company, 1941.

Fumerton, Richard A. *Metaphysical and Epistemological Problems of Perception.* Lincoln: University of Nebraska Press, 1985.

Gallagher, Kenneth T. *The Philosophy of Knowledge.* New York: Sheed and Ward, 1964.

Garnett, A. Campbell. *The Perceptual Process.* Madison: The University of Wisconsin Press, 1965.

Geach, Peter. *Reason and Argument.* Berkeley: University of California Press, 1976.

Geivett, R. Douglas, ed. *Contemporary Perspectives on Religious Epistemology.* New York and Oxford: Oxford University Press, 1992.

Gibson, J. Locke's *Theory of Knowledge and Its Historical Relations.* London and New York: Cambridge University Press, 1917.

Gifford, N. L. *When in Rome: An Introduction to Relativism and Knowledge.* Albany: State University of New York Press, 1983.

Gilovich, Thomas. *How We Know What Isn't So: The Fallibility of Human Reason in Everyday Life.* New York, The Free Press, 1991.

Gilson, Etienne. *Reason and Revelation in the Middle Ages.* New York: Charles Scribner's Sons, 1938.

Ginet, Carl, ed. *Knowledge and Mind: Philosophical Essays.* London: Oxford University Press, 1983.

————. *Knowledge, Perception, and Memory.* Dordrecht, Netherlands: D. Reidel Publishing Co., 1975.

Glenn, Paul J. *Criteriology: A Class Manual in Major Logic.* St. Louis, Mo.: B. Herder Book Co., 1933.

Glouberman, M. *Descartes: The Probable and the Certain.* Amsterdam, Netherlands- Rodopi, 1986.

Glymour, Clark N. *Theory and Evidence.* Princeton, N.J..: Princeton University Press, 1980.

Goheen, John D, and John L. Mothershead, eds. *Collected Papers of Clarence Irving Lewis.* Stanford, Calif.: Stanford University Press, 1970.

Goldman, Alvin I. *Epistemology and Cognition.* Cambridge, Mass.: Harvard University Press, 1986.

Goldstein, Leon J. *Historical Knowing.* Austin: University of Texas Press, 1976.

Goldstein, Martin, and Inge F. Goldstein. *How We Know: An Exploration of the Scientific Process.* New York: Da Capo Press Inc., 1978.

Goodman, Michael F., and Robert A. Snyder, eds. *Contemporary Readings in Epistemolgy.* Englewood Cliffs, N.J.: Prentice-Hall, 1993.

Goodman, Nelson. *The Structure of Appearance,* 2d ed. Indianapolis, Ind.: Bobbs-Merrill, 1966, 1st ed., 1951.

Gregory, R. L. *Eye and Brain: The Psychology of Seeing.* New York and Toronto, Mc-Graw-Hill Book Co., 1966.

Grene, Marjorie. *The Knower and the Known.* Berkeley: University of California Press, 1974.

Grene, Marjorie, ed. *Anatomy of Knowledge.* London: Routledge & Kegan Paul, 1969.

Griffiths, A. Phillips, ed. *Knowledge and Belief.* London: Oxford University Press, 1967.

Gulley, Rev. Anthony D. *The Educational Philosophy of Saint Thomas Aquinas.* New York: Pagent Press, Inc., 1964.

Gunderson, Keith, ed. *Language, Mind, and Knowledge. Minnesota Studies in the Philosophy of Science,* Volume 7. Minneapolis: University of Minnesota Press, 1975.

Guyer, Paul. *Kant and the Claims of Knowledge.* Cambridge and New York: Cambridge University Press, 1987.

Haack, Susan. *Evidence and Inquiry: Towards Reconstruction in Epistemology.* Oxford: Blackwells, 1993.

Hacking, Ian. *The Emergence of Probability: A Philosophical Study of Early Ideas About Probability, Induction, and Statistical Inference.* Cambridge: Cambridge University Press, 1975.

Haldane, E. S. *James Frederick Ferrier.* Edinburgh and London: Oliphant, Anderson & Ferrier, 1899.

Hall, Everett W. *Our Knowledge of Fact and Value.* Chapel Hill: University of North Carolina Press, 1961.

Haller, Rudolf, and Ernest Sosa, eds. *Essays on the Philosophy of Roderick M. Chisholm.* Grazer Philosophische Studien, Amsterdam, Netherlands: Rodopi, 1979.

Hamlyn, D. W. *In and Out of the Black Box: On the Philosophy of Cognition.* Oxford: Basil Blackwell, 1990.

———. *Sensations and Perception: A History of the Philosophy of Perception.* London and New York: Routledge & Kegan Paul, 1961.

———. *The Theory of Knowledge.* Garden City, N.Y.: Doubleday & Company Anchor Books, 1970.

Hampshire, Stuart, ed. *The Age of Reason: The 17th Century Philosophers.* New York, New American Library, 1956.

Hare, Peter H., and Edward H. Madden. *Causing, Perceiving, and Believing.* Dordrecht, Netherlands: D. Reidel Publishing Company, 1975.

Harmon, Gilbert. *Change in View: Principles of Reasoning.* Cambridge, Mass.: MIT Press, 1986.

———. *Thought.* Princeton, N.J.: Princeton University Press, 1973.

Harris, R. Baine, ed. *Authority: A Philosophical Analysis.* University: University of Alabama Press, 1976.

Hartland-Swann, John. *An Analysis of Knowing.* London: George Allen & Unwin Ltd., 1958.

Hartnack, Justus. *Kant's Theory of Knowledge.* New York: Harcourt, Brace & World, 1967.

Hassett, Joseph D., Robert A. Mitchell, and J. Donald Monan, S.J. *The Philosophy of Human Knowing: A Text for College Students.* Westminster, Md.: The Newman Press, 1953.

Hayden, Alice H., ed. *The Body of Knowledge Unique to the Profession of Education.* Washington, D.C.: Pi Lambda Theta, 1966.

Haymes, Brian. *The Concept of the Knowledge of God.* New York: St. Martin's Press, 1988.

Hick, John. *Faith and Knowledge,* 2d ed. Glasgow, Scotland: William Collins Sons, 1966.

Highet, Gilbert. *The Art of Teaching.* New York: Random House Vintage Books, 1950.

Hintikka, Jaakko. *Knowledge and Belief: An Introduction to the Logic of the Two Notions.* Ithaca, N.Y..: Cornell University Press, 1962.

Hirst, R.J. *The Problems of Perception.* London: George Allen and Unwin Ltd., 1959.

Hirst, R.J., ed. *Perception and the External World.* New York: The Macmillan Company, 1965.

Hochberg, Julian E. *Perception.* Englewood Cliffs, N.J.: Prentice-Hall, Inc., 1964.

Hookway, Christopher. *Scepticism.* London and New York: Routledge, 1990.

Horwich, Paul. *Probability and Evidence.* Cambridge, U.K.: Cambridge University Press, 1982.

Houde, Roland, and Joseph P. Mullally, eds. *Philosophy of Knowledge: Selected Readings.* Chicago: J. P. Lippincott Company, 1960.

Hume, David. *A Treatise of Human Nature.* Ed. by L. A. Selby-Bigge. London: Oxford University Press, 1888.

Hunter, Ian M. L. *Memory Facts and Fallacies.* Baltimore, Md., Penguin Books, 1957, 1964.

Huxley, Julian. *Knowledge, Morality, and Destiny.* New York: New American Library, 1957.

Jackson, Frank. *Perception: A Representative Theory.* Cambridge, U.K.: Cambridge University Press, 1977.

James, William. *Essays in Radical Empiricism and a Pluralistic Universe.* Ed. by Ralph Barton Perry. New York: E. P. Dutton & Company, Inc., 1971.

——. *The Principles of Psychology, Volumes One and Two.* New York: Dover Publications, Inc., 1890.

Joad, C. E. M. *Guide to Philosophy.* New York: Dover Publications, Inc., 1957. [Original 1936.]

Johnson, A. H. *Experiential Realism.* London: George Allen & Unwin Ltd. 1973.

Jonas, Doris, and David Jonas. *Other Senses, Other Worlds.* New York: Stein and Day, 1976.

Kant, Immanuel. *The Critique of Judgement.* London: Oxford University Press, 1928.

——. *Critique of Pure Reason.* New York: St. Martin's Press, 1965.

Kant, Immanuel. *Education.* Ann Arbor: The University of Michigan Press, 1960.

Kasher, Asa, ed. *Papers on the Philosophy of Roderick M. Chisholm. Philosophia.* Volume 7, Numbers 3–4, 1978.

Katz, Jerrold J. *Cogitations: A Study of the Cogito in Relation to the Philosophy of Logic and Language and a Study of Them in Relation to the Cogito.* London: Oxford University Press, 1988.

Kelley, David. *The Evidence of the Senses: A Realistic Theory of Perception.* Baton Rouge: Lousiana State University Press, 1986.

Kenny, Anthony, ed. *Rationalism Empiricism, and Idealism: British Academy Lectures on the History of Philosophy.* London: Oxford University Press, 1986.

Kimble, D. P., ed. *The Anatomy of Memory.* Palo Alto, Calif.: Science and Behavior Books,1965.

King-Farlow, John. *Self-Knowledge and Social Relations: Groundwork of Universal Community.* New York: Science History Publications, 1978.

Kitcher, Philip. *The Nature of Mathematical Knowledge.* New York: Oxford University Press, 1984.

Klein, Peter K. *Certainty: A Refutation of Scepticism.* Minneapolis: University of Minnesota Press, 1981.

Klein, Roberta Cutler, ed. *Papers on Epistemology: Philosophical Topics,* Volume 14 Number 1, Fayetteville: The University of Arkansas, 1986.

Klemke, E. D. *The Epistemology of G. E. Moore.* Evanston, Ill.: Northwestern University Press, 1969.

Klemke, E. D., ed. *Studies in the Philosophy of G. E. Moore.* Chicago: Quadrangle Books, 1969.

Kline, Morris. *Mathematics and the Search for Knowledge.* London: Oxford University Press, 1985.

Kneale, William. *Probability and Induction.* London: Oxford University Press, 1949.

Kneller, George F. *Logic and Language of Education.* New York: John Wiley & Sons, 1966.

Kornblith, Hilary, ed. *Naturalizing Epistemology,* 2d ed. Cambridge, Mass., MIT Press, 1994. [1st ed., 1985.]

Körner, S. *Kant.* Baltimore, Md.: Penguin Books, 1955.

Kupperman, Joel J. *Ethical Knowledge.* London: George Allen & Unwin Ltd., 1970.

Kvanvig, Jonathan L. *The Intellectual Virtues and the Life of the Mind: On the Place of the Virtues in Epistemology.* Savage, Md.: Rowman & Littlefield Publishers, Inc., 1992.

Kyburg, Jr., Henry E. *Probability and Inductive Logic.* London: The Macmillan Company, 1970.

———. *Probability and the Logic of Rational Belief.* Middletown, Conn.: Wesleyan University Press, 1961.

Kyburg, Jr., Henry E., and Howard E. Smokler, eds. *Studies in Subjective Probability.* New York: John Wiley & Sons, Inc., 1980.

Lakatos, Imre. *Mathematics, Science, and Epistemology: Philosophical Papers,* Volume 2. Cambridge, U.K.: Cambridge University Press, 1978.

Lakatos, Imre, and Alan Musgrave, eds. *Criticism and the Growth of Knowledge.* London, U.K.: Cambridge University Press, 1970.

Lamprecht, Sterling P., ed. *Knowledge and Society: A Philosophical Approach to Modern Civilization.* New York and London: D. Appleton-Century Company, 1938.

Lange, John. *The Cognitivity Paradox: An Inquiry Concerning the Claims of Philosophy.* Princeton, N.J.: Princeton University Press, 1970.

Larrabee, Harold A. *Reliable Knowledge: Scientific Methods in the Social Studies,* rev. ed. Boston: Houghton Miff lin Company, 1964.

Lehrer, Keith. *Knowledge.* London: Oxford University Press, 1974.

——. *Metamind.* Oxford and New York: Oxford University Press, 1990.

——. *Theory of Knowledge.* Boulder, Colo.: Westview Press, 1990.

Lehrer, Keith, ed. *Analysis and Metaphysics: Essays in Honor of R. M. Chisholm.* Dordrecht, Netherlands: D. Reidel Publishing Company, 1975.

Leibniz, Gottfried Wilhelm von. *New Essays Concerning Human Understanding.* LaSalle, Ill.: The Open Court Publishing Company, 1949.

Leibowitz, Herschel W. *Visual Perception.* New York: The Macmillan Company, 1965.

Levi, Isaac. *The Enterprise of Knowledge: An Essay on Knowledge, Credal Probability, and Chance.* Cambridge, Mass.: MIT Press, 1980.

——. *Gambling with Truth: An Essay on Induction and the Aims of Science.* New York: Alfred A. Knopf, 1967.

Levinsky, Mark, ed. *Human Factual Knowledge.* Englewood Cliffs, N.J.: Prentice-Hall, Inc., 1971.

Lewis, C. I. *An Analysis of Knowledge and Valuation.* LaSalle, Ill.: Open Court Publishing Co., 1946

——. *Mind and the World Order: Outline of a Theory of Knowledge.* New York: Dover Publishing Company Inc., 1929.

Locke, Don. *Memory.* Garden City, N.Y.: Doubleday & Company, Anchor Books, 1971.

——. *Myself and Others: A Study in Our Knowledge of Minds.* London: Oxford University Press, 1968.

——. *Perception and Our Knowledge of the External World.* London: Allen & Unwin, 1967.

Locke, John. *An Essay Concerning Human Understanding.* Ed. by Peter H. Nidditch. London: Oxford University Press, 1979.

Lucey, Kenneth G., and Tibor R. Machan, eds. *Recent Work in Philosophy.* Totowa, N.J.: Rowman and Allanheld, 1983.

Lonergan, Bernard J. F. *Insight: A Study of Human Understanding.* San Francisco: Harper & Row, Publishers, 1958.

Luper-Foy, Steven, ed. *The Possibility of Knowledge: Nozick and His Critics.* Totowa, N.J.: Rowman and Littlefield Publishers, 1987.

Luria, A. R. *The Mind of a Mnemonist.* New York: The Hearst Corp. Avon Books, 1968.

Lycan, William G. *Consciousness.* Cambridge, Mass.: MIT Press, 1987.

———. *Judgement and Justification.* Cambridge, U.K.: Cambridge University Press, 1988.

Lycan, William G., ed. *Mind and Cognition: A Reader.* Oxford: Blackwell, 1990.

Lyons, William. *Gilbert Ryle: An Introduction to His Philosophy.* Sussex, U.K., and Atlantic Highlands, N.J.: Harvester Press, 1980.

Mach, Ernst. *The Analysis of Sensations and the Relation of the Physical to the Psychical.* New York: Dover Publications, Inc., 1959.

———. *Knowledge and Error: Sketches on the Psychology of Inquiry.* Dordrecht, Netherlands: D. Reidel Publishing Co., 1976.

Machamer, Peter K., and Robert G. Turnbull, eds. *Studies in Perception: Interrelations in the History of Philosophy and Science.* Columbus: Ohio State University Press, 1978.

Macmurray, John. *Reason and Emotion.* New York: Barnes & Noble, Inc., 1962.

Malcolm, Norman. *Knowledge and Certainty: Essays and Lectures.* Englewood Cliffs, N.J.: Prentice-Hall,1963.

———. *Memory and Mind.* Ithaca, N.Y.: Cornell University Press, 1977.

———. *Thought and Knowledge: Essays.* Ithaca, N.Y.: Cornell University Press, 1977.

Mandelbaum, Maurice. *The Anatomy of Historical Knowledge.* Baltimore, Md.: The Johns Hopkins University Press, 1977.

———. *Philosophy, Science, and Sense Perception.* Baltimore, Md.: The Johns Hopkins Press, 1964.

———. *The Problem of Historical Knowledge: An Answer to Relativism.* London and New York: Harper & Row, Publishers, 1967.

Margolis, Joseph. *Knowledge and Existence: An Introduction to Philosophical Problems.* New York: Oxford University Press, 1973.

Markie, Peter J. *Descartes' Gambit.* Ithaca, N.Y.: Cornell University Press, 1986.

Marrou, H. I. *A History of Education in Antiquity.* New York: The New American Library, 1956.

Martin, Michael. *Concepts of Science Education: A Philosophical Analysis.* Glenview, Ill., and London: Scott, Foresman and Company, 1972.

Matson, Wallace. *Sentience.* Berkeley: University of California Press, 1976.

Matthews, Gwynneth. *Plato's Epistemology and Related Problems.* London: Faber & Faber, 1972.

Maturana, Humberto R., and Francisco J. Varela. *The Tree of Knowledge: The Biological Roots of Human Understanding.* Boston and London: Shambhala New Science Library, 1987.

Mavrodes, George I. *Belief in God: A Study in the Epistemology of Religion.* New York: Random House, 1970.

McGraw, John E. *Justification.* Kansas City, Mo.: Beacon Hill Press of Kansas City, 1968.

McKinnon, Alistair. *Falsification and Belief.* The Hague and Paris: Mouton, 1970.

Meiland, Jack W. *Scepticism and Historical Knowledge.* New York: Random House, 1965.

Mercier, Cardinal, et al. *A Manual of Modern Scholastic Philosophy, Volume I: Epistemology (Criteriology).* London, Kegan Paul, Truber & Co., 1917.

Merleau-Ponty, Maurice. *Phenomenology of Perception.* London: Routledge & Kegan Paul, 1962.

———. *The Primacy of Perception and Other Essays.* Evanston, Ill., Northwestern University Press, 1964.

Milmed, Bella K. *Kant and Current Philosophical Issues: Some Modern Developments of His Theory of Knowledge.* New York: New York University Press, 1961.

Milne, Lorus, and Margery Milne. *The Senses of Animals and Men.* New York: Atheneum, 1962.

Mischel, Theodore, ed. *Cognitive Development and Epistemology.* New York and London: Academic Press, 1971.

Modrak, Deborah K. W. *Aristotle: The Power of Perception.* Chicago and London: The University of Chicago Press, 1987.

Montague, William Pepperall. *The Ways of Knowing: Or the Methods of Philosophy.* New York: The Macmillan Company, 1925.

Moore, G. E. *The Commonplace Book of G. E. Moore: 1919–1953.* London: George Allen & Unwin, 1962.

———. *Lectures on Philosophy.* London: George Allen & Unwin, 1966.

———. *Philosophical Papers.* New York: Collier Books, 1959.

———. *Philosophical Studies.* London: Routledge & Kegan Paul Ltd., 1922.

———. *Some Main Problems of Philosophy.* New York: Collier Books, 1953.

Morawetz, Thomas. *Wittgenstein and Knowledge: The Importance of On Certainty,* Amherst: University of Massachusetts Press, 1978.

Morick, Harold, ed. *Challenges to Empiricism.* Belmont, Calif.: Wadsworth Publishing Company, 1972.

Morton, Adam. *A Guide Through the Theory of Knowledge*. Encino, Calif.: Dickenson Publishing Company, 1977.

Moser, Paul K. *Knowledge and Evidence*. Cambridge, U.K.: Cambridge University Press, 1989.

Moser, Paul K., ed. *A Priori Knowledge: Oxford Reading in Philosophy*. New York and Oxford: Oxford University Press, 1987.

Moser, Paul K., ed. *Empirical Knowledge: Readings in Contemporary Epistemology*. Totowa, N.J.: Rowman and Littlefield Publishers, 1986.

Moser, Paul K., and Arnold vander Nat, eds. *Human Knowledge: Classical and Contemporary Approaches*, 2d. ed. New York: Oxford University Press, 1995. [1st ed., 1987.]

Muirhead, J. H., ed. *Contemporary British Philosophy: Personal Statements (First Series)*. New York: The Macmillan Company, 1924.

Mundle, C. W. K. *Perception: Facts, and Theories*. London: Oxford University Press, 1971.

Munevar, Gonzalo. *Radical Knowledge: A Philosophical Inquiry into the Nature and Limits of Science*. Indianapolis, Ind.: Hackett Publishing Co., 1981.

Munsat, Stanley, *The Concept of Memory*. New York: Random House, 1967.

Murphy, Murray G. *Our Knowledge of the Historical Past*. Indianapolis, Ind., and New York: The Bobbs-Merrill Company, 1973.

Musgrave, Alan. *Common Sense, Science, and Scepticism: A Historical Introduction to the Theory of Knowledge*. Cambridge, U.K.: Cambridge University Press, 1993.

Naess, Arne. *Scepticism*. New York: Humanities Press, 1969.

Nagel, Ernest. *The Principles of the Theory of Probability*. Chicago and London: University of Chicago Press, 1939.

Nagel, Ernest, and Richard B. Brandt, eds. *Meaning and Knowledge: Systematic Readings in Epistemology*. New York: Harcourt, Brace, World, Inc., 1965.

Nakhnikian, George. *An Introduction to Philosophy*. New York, Alfred A. Knopf, 1967.

Nathan, N. M. L. *Evidence and Assurance*. Cambridge, U.K.: Cambridge University Press, 1980.

Nelson, Leonard. *Socratic Method and Critical Philosophy: Selected Essays*. New York: Dover Publications, Inc. 1965.

Newman, John Henry. *An Essay in Aid of a Grammar of Assent*. Garden City, N.Y.: Doubleday Image Book, 1955.

Nordenstam, Tore. *Empiricism and the Analytic-Synthetic Distinction*. Oslo, Norway: Scandanavian University Books, 1972.

Nozick, Robert. *The Nature of Rationality*. Princeton, N.J.: Princeton University Press, 1993.

Nozick, Robert. *Philosophical Explanations.* Cambridge, Mass.: Harvard University Press, 1981.

O'Connor, D. J. *An Introduction to the Philosophy of Education.* London: Routledge & Kegan Paul, 1957.

O'Connor, D. J., and Brian Carr. *Introduction to the Theory of Knowledge.* Minneapolis: University of Minnesota Press, 1982.

Odegard, Douglas. *Knowledge and Scepticism.* Totowa, N.J.: Rowan and Littlefield, Publishers, 1982.

Oldroyd, David. *The Arch of Knowledge: An Introductory Study of the History of the Philosophy and Methodology of Science.* New York: Methuen, 1986.

O'Neil, Brian E. *Epistemological Direct Realism in Descartes' Philosophy.* Albuquerque: University of New Mexico Press, 1974.

O'Neill, S.J., Reginald F. *Theories of Knowledge.* Englewood Cliffs, N.J..: Prentice-Hall, Inc., 1960.

Owen, John. *Evenings with the Skeptics, Volume One: Or Free Discussion on Free Thinkers.* London: Longmans, Green and Company, 1881.

Owens, Joseph, C.Ss.R. *Cognition: An Epistemological Inquiry.* Houston, Tex.: Center for Thomistic Studies, 1992.

Pap, Arthur. *Elements of Analytic Philosophy.* New York: The Macmillan Company, 1949.

Pappas, George, ed. *Justification and Knowledge: New Studies in Epistemology.* Dordrecht, Netherlands: D. Reidel Publishing Company, 1979.

Pappas, George, and Marshall Swain, eds. *Essays on Knowledge and Justification.* Ithaca, N.Y.: Cornell University Press, 1978.

Passmore, John. *The Philosophy of Teaching.* London: Gerald Duckworth & Co. Ltd., 1980.

Patton, H. J. *Kant's Metaphysics of Experience, Volumes One & Two.* New York: Humanities Press, 1936.

Pears, David. *What Is Knowledge?* New York: Harper & Row, Publishers, 1971.

Pennycuick, John. *In Contact with the Physical World.* New York: Humanities Press, 1971.

Perkins, Moreland. *Seeing the World.* Indianapolis, Ind.: Hackett Publishing Company, 1983.

Peters, R.S. ed. *The Concept of Education.* New York, The Humanities Press, 1967.

Peters, R.S. ed. *The Philosophy of Education.* London: Oxford University Press, 1973.

Piper, Raymond F., and Paul W. Ward. *The Fields and Methods of Knowledge.* New York: F. S. Crofts & Co., 1929.

Pitcher, George. *A Theory of Perception.* Princeton, N.J.: Princeton University Press, 1971.

Plantinga, Alvin. *God and Other Minds: A Study of the Rational Justification of Belief in God.* Ithaca, N.Y.:. Cornell University Press, 1967.

———. *Warrent and Proper Function.* Oxford: Oxford University Press, 1993.

———. *Warrent: The Current Debate.* Oxford: Oxford University Press, 1993.

Plato. *Plato's Theaetetus Part I of the Being of the Beautiful.* Trans. by Jose Benardette. Chicago and London: The University of Chicago Press, 1986.

———. *Theaetetus.* Trans. by John McDowell. London: Oxford University Press, 1973.

———. *Theaetetus.* Trans. by Robin A. H. Waterfield. Harmondsworth, Middlesex, U.K.: Penguin Books, 1987.

Pojman, Louis P. *What Can We Know?: An Introduction to the Theory of Knowledge.* Belmont, Calif.: Wadsworth Publishing Company, 1995.

Polanyi, Michael. *Personal Knowledge: Towards a Post-Critical Philosophy.* New York: Harper & Row, Publishers, 1964.

Pollock, John L. *Contemporary Theories of Knowledge.* Totowa, N.J. : Rowman & Littlefield, Publishers, Inc., 1986.

———. *Knowledge and Justification.* Princeton, N.J.: Princeton University Press, 1974.

Pols, Edward. *Radical Realism: Direct Knowing in Science and Philosophy.* Ithaca, N.Y.: Cornell University Press, 1992.

Popkin, Richard H. *The High Road to Pyrrhonism.* San Diego, Calif.: Austin Hill Press, Inc., 1980.

———. *The History of Scepticism from Erasmus to Descartes.* New York: Harper & Row, Publishers, 1964.

Popper, Karl R. *Conjectures and Refutations: The Growth of Scientific Knowledge.* New York: Basic Books, Inc., 1965.

———. *Knowledge and the Mind-Body Problem: In Defence of Interaction.* London and New York: Routledge, 1994.

———. *Objective Knowledge: An Evolutionary Approach.* Oxford: Oxford University Press, 1972.

Powell, Betty. *Knowledge of Actions.* New York: Humanities Press, 1967.

Price, H. H. *Belief.* London and New York: Humanities Press, 1969.

———. *Perception.* London: Methuen & Co. Ltd., 1954.

———. *Thinking and Experience.* Cambridge, Mass.: Harvard University Press, 1953.

Prichard, H. A. *Knowledge and Perception: Essays and Lectures.* London: Oxford University Press, 1950.

Pryce-Jones, Alan. *The New Outline of Modern Knowledge.* New York: Simon & Schuster, 1956.

Quine, W.V., and J. S. Ullian. *The Web of Belief.* New York: Random House, 1978. [1st ed., 1970.]

Radnitzky, Gerald, and W. W. Bartley, II, eds. *Evolutionary Epistemology, Theory of Rationality, and the Sociology of Knowledge.* LaSalle, Ill.: Open Court Publishing Co., 1987.

Ramsey, F. P. *The Foundations of Mathematics and Other Logical Essays.* Paterson, N.J., Littlefield, Adams Co., 1931.

Rand, Ayn. *Introduction to Objectivist Epistemology.* Ed. by Harry Binswanger and Leonard Peikoff. New York: Meridian Penguin Group, 1990.

Rapaport, Anatol. *Operational Philosophy: Integrating Knowledge and Action.* New York: Harper & Brothers Publishers, 1953.

Rapaport, David. *Emotion and Memory.* New York: Science Editions, Inc., 1942.

Reichenbach, Hans. *Experience and Prediction: An Analysis of the Foundations and the Structure of Knowledge.* Chicago: University of Chicago Press, 1938.

Reid, Louis Arnaud. *Knowledge and Truth: An Epistemological Essay.* London: Macmillan and Co., 1923.

Reid, Thomas. *Essays on the Intellectual Powers of Man.* Cambridge, Mass.: MIT Press, 1969.

Rescher, Nicholas. *American Philosophy Today and Other Philosophical Studies.* Lanham, Md., and London: Rowman and Littlefield, Inc. 1994.

———. *Cognitive Systematization: A Systems-Theoretic Approach to a Coherentist Theory of Knowledge.* Totowa, N.J.: Rowman & Littlefield Publishers, 1979.

———. *Conceptual Idealism.* Oxford: Basil Blackwell, 1973.

———. *Methodological Pragmatism: A Systems-Theoretic Approach to the Theory of Knowledge.* Oxford: Basil Blackwell, 1977.

———. *The Primacy of Practice: Essays Towards a Pragmatically Kantian Theory of Empirical Knowledge.* Oxford: Basil Blackwell, 1973.

Rescher, Nicholas, ed. *Studies in Epistemology,* A.P.Q. Monograph No. 9, Oxford: Basil Blackwell Ltd., 1975.

Rescher, Nicholas, ed. *Studies in the Theory of Knowledge.* Oxford: Basil Blackwell, 1970.

Rickaby, S.J., John. *The First Principles of Knowledge: Manuals of Catholic Philosophy.* New York.: Benziger Brothers, 1920.

Rivlin, Robert, and Karen Gravelle. *Deciphering the Senses: The Expanding World of Human Perception.* New York: Simon and Schuster, 1984.

Rollins, C. D., ed. *Knowledge and Experience.* Liverpool and London: University of Pittsburgh Press, 1963.

Ross, Joshua. *The Appeal to the Given.* London: George Allen & Unwin Ltd. 1970.

Roth, Michael D., and Leon Galis, eds. *Knowing: Essays in the Analysis of Knowl-*

edge, 2d. ed. Lanham, Md.: University Press of America, 1984. [1st ed., Random House, 1970.]

Royal Institute of Philosophy Lectures. *Knowledge and Necessity,* Volume 3. London: Macmillan and Company, 1970.

————. *Reason and Reality,* Volume 5, London: Macmillan and Company, 1972.

Russell, Bertrand. *Education and the Good Life.* New York: The Hearst Corporation Avon Books, 1926.

————. *Education of Character.* New York: Philosophical Library, 1926.

————. *Essays in Scepticism.* New York: Philosophical Library, 1962.

————. *A History of Western Philosophy.* New York: Simon & Schuster, 1945.

————. *Human Knowledge: Its Scope and Limits.* New York: Simon & Schuster, 1948.

————. *Logic and Knowledge: Essays 1901–1950.* London: George Allen & Unwin, 1956.

————. *Our Knowledge of the External World.* New York: The New American Library Mentor Book, 1928.

————. *The Problems of Philosophy.* London: Oxford University Press, 1912.

————. *Sceptical Essays.* London: George Allen & Unwin Ltd., 1928.

————. *Selected Papers of Bertrand Russell.* New York: The Modern Library, 1927.

————. *Theory of Knowledge: The 1913 Manuscript.* London and New York: Routledge, 1984.

————. *The Will to Doubt.* New York: Philosophical Library, 1958.

Ryle, Gilbert. *The Concept of Mind.* New York: Barnes & Noble, Inc., 1949.

————. *Dilemmas: The Tarner Lectures.* London: Cambridge University Press, 1954.

Samuel, Viscount. *Belief and Action: An Everyday Philosophy.* Harmondsworth, Middlesex, U.K.: Penguin Books, 1937.

Santoni, Ronald E., ed. *Religious Language and the Problem of Religious Knowledge.* Bloomington, Ind., and London: Indiana University Press, 1968.

Savage, C. Wade, ed. *Perception and Cognition: Studies in the Foundations of Psychology, Minnesota Studies in the Philosophy of Science.* Minneapolis: University of Minnesota Press, 1978.

Scheffler, Israel. *Conditions of Knowledge.* Chicago: Scott, Foresman and Company, 1965.

————. *The Language of Education.* Springfield, Ill., Charles C. Thomas, 1960.

————. *Reason and Teaching.* Indianapolis, Ind., and New York: The Bobbs-Merrill Company, 1973.

————. *Science and Subjectivity.* Indianapolis, Ind., and New York, The Bobbs-Merrill Company, 1967.

Scheffler, Israel, ed. *Philosophy and Education: Modern Readings.* Boston: Allyn and Bacon, 1966.

Schiller, Ferdinand Canning Scott. *Problems of Belief.* New York: George H. Doran Company, 1924.

Schilpp, Paul Arthur, ed. *The Philosophy of Bertrand Russell,* 3rd. ed. New York: Tudor Publishing Company, 1951.

Schilpp, Paul Arthur, ed. *The Philosophy of C. D. Broad.* New York, Tudor Publishing co., 1959.

Schilpp, Paul Arthur, ed. *The Philosophy of C. I. Lewis.* LaSalle, Ill.: Open Court Publishing Company, 1968.

Schilpp, Paul Arthur, ed. *The Philosophy of G. E. Moore,* 3rd. ed. La Salle, Ill.: Open Court Publishing Company, 1968.

Schilpp, Paul Arthur, ed. *The Philosophy of Karl Popper,* Volumes I & II. LaSalle, Ill.: Open Court Publishing Company, 1974.

Schlesinger, G. *Confirmation and Confirmability.* London: Oxford University Press, 1974.

Schlesinger, George N. *The Range of Epistemic Logic.* Aberdeen, Scotland: Aberdeen University Press, 1985.

Schlick, Moritz. *General Theory of Knowledge.* LaSalle, Ill.: Open Court Publishing Co., 1985.

Schmidt, Paul F. *Religious Knowledge.* Glencoe, Ill.: The Free Press, 1961.

Schmitt, Frederick F. *Knowledge and Belief.* London: Routledge, 1992.

Schmitt, Frederick F., ed. *Socializing Epistemology: The Social Dimensions of Knowledge.* Lanham, Md.: Rowman and Littlefield, 1994.

Schofield, Malcolm, Myles Burnyeat, and Jonathan Barnes, eds. *Doubt and Dogmatism: Studies in Hellenistic Epistemology.* Oxford: Oxford University Press, 1980.

Sellars, Wilfrid. *The Metaphysics of Epistemology.* Atascadero, Calif.: Ridgeview Publishing Company, 1989.

———. *Science, Perception, and Reality.* London and New York: Routledge & Kegan Paul, 1963.

Sesonske, Alexander, and Noel Fleming, eds. *Human Understanding: Studies in the Philosophy of David Hume.* Belmont, Calif.: Wadsworth Publishing Co., 1965.

Shafto, Michael, ed. *How We Know.* San Francisco: Harper & Row, Publishers, 1985.

Shallo, S.J, Michael W. *Lessons in Scholastic Philosophy.* Philadelphia: Peter Reilly, Publisher, 1 905

Shoemaker, Sydney. *Self-Knowledge and Self-Identity.* Ithaca, N.Y.: Cornell University Press, 1963.

Shope, Robert K. *The Analysis of Knowing: A Decade of Research.* Princeton, N.J., Princeton University Press, 1983.

Smith, B. Othanel, and Robert H. Ennis, eds. *Language and Concepts in Education.* Chicago: Rand McNally & Company, 1961.

Smith, Norman Kemp. *A Commentary to Kant's "Critique of Pure Reason,"* 2d. ed. New York: Humanities Press, 1923.

Soltis, J. F. *Seeing, Knowing, and Believing: A Study in the Language of Visual Perception.* London: George Allen & Unwin Ltd., 1966.

Sosa, Ernest. *Knowledge in Perspective: Selected Essays in Epistemology.* Cambridge, U.K., and New York: Cambridge University Press, 1991,

Stalnaker, Robert. *Inquiry.* Cambridge, Mass.: MIT Press, 1984.

Steiner, Mark. *Mathematical Knowledge.* Ithaca, N.Y.: Cornell University Press, 1975.

Stephen, Leslie. *An Agnostic's Apology and Other Essays.* New York: G. P. Putnam's Sons, 1893.

Stevenson, Leslie. *The Metaphysics of Experience.* Oxford: Oxford University Press, 1982.

Stich, Stephen P. *The Fragmentation of Reason: Preface to a Pragmatic Theory of Cognitive Evaluation.* Cambridge, Mass.: MIT Press, 1990.

Stough, Charlotte L. *Greek Skepticism.* Berkeley: University of California Press, 1969.

Strawson, Peter F. *The Bounds of Sense: An Essay on Kant's Critique of Pure Reason.* London: Methuen & Co. Ltd., 1966.

———. *Skepticism and Naturalism: Some Varieties.* New York, Columbia University Press, 1985.

Stroll, Avrum, ed. *Epistemology: New Essays in the Theory of Knowledge.* New York: Harper & Row, Publishers, 1967.

Stroud, Barry. *The Significance of Philosophical Scepticism.* Oxford: Oxford University Press, 1984.

Swain, Marshall. *Reasons and Knowledge.* Ithaca, N.Y.: Cornell University Press, 1981.

Swain, Marshall, ed. *Induction, Acceptance, and Rational Belief.* Dordrecht, Netherlands, D. Reidel Publishing Company, 1970.

Swartz, Robert J., ed. *Perceiving, Sensing, and Knowing: A Book of Readings from Twentieth Century Sources in the Philosophy of Perception.* Garden City, N.Y.: Doubleday & Company Anchor Books, 1965.

Thalberg, Irving. *Perception, Emotion, and Action: A Component Approach.* New Haven, Conn.: Yale University Press, 1977.

Tibbetts, Paul, ed. *Perception: Selected Readings in Science and Phenomenology.* Chicago: Quadrangle Books, 1969.

Tomberlin, James E., ed. *Epistemology: Philosophical Perspectives,* Volume 2 Atascadero, Calif.: Ridgeview Publishing Company, 1988.

Toulmin, Stephen. *Knowing and Acting: An Invitation to Philosophy.* New York: Macmillan Publishing Co, 1976.

Toulmin, Stephen. *Human Understanding: The Collective Use and Evolution of Concepts.* Princeton, N.J.: Princeton University Press, 1972.

Trethowan, Ilityd. *The Basis of Belief.* New York: Hawthorn Books, Publishers, 1961.

Trusted, Jennifer. *An Introduction to the Philosophy of Knowledge.* London: The Macmillan Press Ltd., 1981.

Unger, Peter. *Ignorance: A Case for Scepticism.* London: Oxford University Press, 1975.

Varisco, Bernardino. *Know Thyself.* London: George Allen and Unwin, Ltd., 1915.

Vendler, Zeno. *Res Cogitans: An Essay in Rational Psychology.* Ithaca, N.Y.: Cornell University Press, 1972.

Vernon, M. D. *The Psychology of Perception.* Baltimore, Md.: Penguin Books, 1962.

Vesey, Godrey. *Perception.* Garden City, N.Y.: Doubleday & Company Anchor Books, 1971.

Vesey, Godfrey, ed. *Impressions of Empiricism.* London: The Macmillan Press, 1976.

Vickers, John M. *Belief and Probability.* Dordrecht, Netherlands: D. Reidel Publishing Company, 1976.

Villanueva, Enrique, ed. *Rationality in Epistemology.* Atascadero, Calif.: Ridgeview Publishing Co., 1992.

Villanueva, Enrique, ed. *Information, Semantics, and Epistemology.* Cambridge, Mass., and Oxford: Basil Blackwell, 1990.

Vlastos, Gregory, ed. *Plato I: Metaphysics and Epistemology.* Garden City, N.Y.: Doubleday & Company Anchor Books, 1970.

von Leyden, W. *Remembering: A Philosophical Problem.* London,: Gerald Duckworth & Co., 1961.

von Mises, Richard. *Positivism: A Study in Human Understanding.* New York: Dover Publications, Inc., 1968.

von Wright, G. H. *Explanation and Undersanding.* London: Routledge & Kegan Paul, 1971.

———. *A Treatise on Induction and Probability.* Paterson, N.J.: Littlefield, Adams & Co, 1951.

———. *Truth, Knowledge, and Modality: Philosophical Papers,* Volume 3. Oxford, UK: Basil Blackwell, 1984.

von Wright, G.H. ed. *Problems in the Theory of Knowledge.* The Hague: Martinus Mijhoff, 1972.

Wang, Hao. *Beyond Analytic Philosophy: Doing Justice to What We Know.* Cambridge, Mass.: MIT Press, 1986.

Warnock, G. J. *Berkeley.* Baltimore, Md.: Penguin Books, 1953.

Warnock, G. J., ed. *Essays on J. L. Austin.* London: Oxford University Press, 1973.

Warnock, G. J., ed. *The Philosophy of Perception.* London: Oxford University Press, 1967.

Warnock, Mary. *Memory.* London and Boston: Faber and Faber, 1987.

Watkins, John. *Science and Scepticism.* Princeton, N.J.: Princeton University Press, 1984.

Watts, Alan. *The Book: On the Taboo Against Knowing Who You Are.* New York: Random House Vintage Books, 1966.

Weatherford, Roy. *Philosophical Foundations of Probability Theory.* London and Boston: Routledge & Kegan Paul, 1982.

Weigel, Gustave, S. J., and Madden, Arthur G. *Religion and the Knowledge of God.* Englewood Cliffs, N.J.: Prentice-Hall, Inc., 1961,

Weinberg, Harry L. *Levels of Knowing and Existence: Studies in General Semantics.* New York., Harper & Row, Publishers, 1959.

Weintraub, Daniel J., and Edward L. Walker. *Perception.* Belmont, Calif.: Brooks/Cole Publishing Co., 1966.

Weldon, T. D. *Kant's Critique of Pure Reason,* 2d. ed. London: Oxford University Press, 1958.

Welsh, Paul, ed. *Fact, Value, and Perception: Essays in Honor of Charles A. Baylis.* Durham, N.C.: Duke University Press, 1975.

White, Alan R. *G. E. Moore: A Critical Exposition.* Oxford: Basil Blackwell, 1969.

———. *The Nature of Knowledge.* Totowa, N.J.: Rowman and Littlefield, Publishers, 1982.

White, Morton. *Foundations of Historical Knowledge.* New York and London: Harper & Row, Publishers, 1965.

———. *Toward Reunion in Philosophy.* New York: Atheneum, 1956, 1963.

White, Morton, ed. *The Age of Analysis: 20th Century Philosophers.* New York: The New American Library Mentor Book, 1955.

White, Nicholas P. *Plato on Knowledge and Reality.* Indianapolis, Ind.: Hackett Publishing Company, 1976.

Whitehead, Alfred North. *The Aims of Education and Other Essays.* New York: The New American Library Mentor Book,1929.

———. *The Function of Reason.* Boston: Beacon Press, 1929.

Wild, John. *The Radical Empiricism of William James.* Garden City, N.Y.: Doubleday & Company Anchor Books, 1969.

Wild, John, ed. *The Return to Reason: Essays in Realistic Philosophy.* Chicago: Henry Regnery Company, 1953.

Will, Frederick L. *Induction and Justification: An Investigation of Cartesian Procedure in the Philosophy of Knowledge.* Ithaca, N.Y.: Cornell University Press, 1974.

Williams, Donald Cary. *Principles of Empirical Realism.* Springfield, Ill.: Charles C. Thomas Publishers, 1966.

Williams, Michael. *Groundless Belief: An Essay on the Possibility of Epistemology.* Oxford: Basil Blackwell, 1977.

Wilson, Bryan R., ed. *Rationality.* New York: Harper & Row, Publishers, 1970.

Wittgenstein, Ludwig. *On Certainty.* New York.: J. & J. Harper Editions, 1969.

———. *Philosophical Investigations.* New York: Macmillan Company, 1953.

Wolfe, David L. *Epistemology: The Justification of Belief.* Downers Grove, Ill.: InterVarsity Press, 1982.

Wolff, Robert Paul, ed. *Kant: A Collection of Critical Essays.* Garden City, N.Y.: Doubleday & Company, Anchor Books, 1967.

Wolgast, Elizabeth Hankins. *Paradoxes of Knowledge.* Ithaca, N.Y.: Cornell University Press, 1977.

Wood, Oscar P., and George Pitcher, eds. *Ryle: A Collection of Critical Essays.* Garden City, N.Y.: Doubleday & Company Anchor Books, 1970.

Woozley, A. D. *Theory of Knowledge: An Introduction.* New York, Barnes & Noble, Inc., 1966.

Yolton, John W. *Perceptual Acquaintance from Descartes to Reid.* Minneapolis: University of Minnesota Press, 1984.

———. *Thinking and Perceiving: A Study in the Philosophy of Mind.* LaSalle, Ill.: Open Court, 1962.

Yolton, John W., ed. *Theory of Knowledge.* New York: The Macmillan Company, 1965.

Ziman, John M. *The Force of Knowledge: The Scientific Dimensions of Society.* Cambridge, U.K.: Cambridge University Press, 1976.